*Planting the Province:*
*The Economic History of Upper Canada*
*1784–1870*

# THE ONTARIO HISTORICAL STUDIES SERIES

Peter Oliver, G. *Howard Ferguson: Ontario Tory* (1977)

J.M.S. Careless, ed., *The Pre-Confederation Premiers: Ontario Government Leaders, 1841–1867* (1980)

Charles W. Humphries, *'Honest Enough to Be Bold': The Life and Times of Sir James Pliny Whitney* (1985)

Charles M. Johnston, *E.C. Drury: Agrarian Idealist* (1986)

A.K. McDougall, *John P. Robarts: His Life and Government* (1986)

Roger Graham, *Old Man Ontario: Leslie M. Frost* (1990)

John T. Saywell, *'Just call me Mitch': The Life of Mitchell F. Hepburn* (1991)

A. Margaret Evans, *Sir Oliver Mowat* (1992)

Joseph Schull, *Ontario since 1867* (McClelland and Stewart 1978)

Joseph Schull, *L'Ontario depuis 1867* (McClelland and Stewart 1987)

Olga B. Bishop, Barbara I. Irwin, Clara G. Miller, eds., *Bibliography of Ontario History, 1867–1976: Cultural, Economic, Political, Social* 2 volumes (1980)

Christopher Armstrong, *The Politics of Federalism: Ontario's Relations with the Federal Government, 1867–1942* (1981)

David Gagan, *Hopeful Travellers: Families, Land and Social Change in Mid-Victorian Peel County, Canada West* (1981)

Robert M. Stamp, *The Schools of Ontario, 1876–1976* (1982)

R. Louis Gentilcore and C. Grant Head, *Ontario's History in Maps* (1984)

K.J. Rea, *The Prosperous Years: The Economic History of Ontario, 1939–1975* (1985)

Ian M. Drummond, *Progress without Planning: The Economic History of Ontario from Confederation to the Second World War* (1987)

John Webster Grant, *A Profusion of Spires: Religion in Nineteenth-Century Ontario* (1988)

Susan E. Houston and Alison Prentice, *Schooling and Scholars in Nineteenth-Century Ontario* (1988)

Ann Saddlemyer, ed., *Early Stages: Theatre in Ontario, 1800–1914* (1990)

W.J. Keith, *Literary Images of Ontario* (1992)

Douglas McCalla *Planting the Province: The Economic History of Upper Canada, 1784–1870* (1993)

DOUGLAS McCALLA

# Planting the Province: The Economic History of Upper Canada 1784–1870

A publication of the
Ontario Historical Studies Series
for the Government of Ontario
Published by the University of Toronto Press
Toronto Buffalo London

ISBN 0-8020-3407-1 (cloth)
ISBN 0-8020-3411-X (paper)

Printed on acid-free paper

**Canadian Cataloguing in Publication Data**

McCalla, Douglas, 1942–
  Planting the province

  (Ontario historical studies series)
  ISBN 0-8020-3407-1 (bound). – ISBN 0-8020-3411-X (pbk.)

  1. Ontario – Economic conditions – To 1867.*
  I. Title.   II. Series.

HC117.05M23 1993      330.9713'02      C92-095558-4

This book has been published with the assistance of funds provided by the Government of Ontario through the Ministry of Culture, Tourism and Recreation.

# Contents

# The Ontario Historical Studies Series

For many years the principal theme in English-Canadian historical writing has been the emergence and the consolidation of the Canadian nation. This theme has been developed in uneasy awareness of the persistence and importance of regional interests and identities, but because of the central role of Ontario in the growth of Canada, Ontario has not been seen as a region. Almost unconsciously, historians have equated the history of the province with that of the nation and have often depicted the interests of other regions as obstacles to the unity and welfare of Canada.

The creation of the province of Ontario in 1867 was the visible embodiment of a formidable reality, the existence at the core of the new nation of a powerful if disjointed society whose traditions and characteristics differed in many respects from those of the other British North American colonies. The intervening century has not witnessed the assimilation of Ontario to the other regions in Canada; on the contrary it has become a more clearly articulated entity. Within the formal geographical and institutional framework defined so assiduously by Ontario's political leaders, an increasingly intricate web of economic and social interests has been woven and shaped by the dynamic interplay between Toronto and its hinterland. The character of this regional community has been formed in the tension between a rapid adaptation to the processes of modernization and industrialization in modern Western society and a reluctance to modify or discard traditional attitudes and values. Not surprisingly, the Ontario outlook has been, and in some measure still is, a compound of aggressiveness, conservatism, and the conviction that its values should be the model for the rest of Canada.

From the outset the objective of the Board of Trustees of the series has been to describe and analyse the historical development of Ontario as a distinct region within Canada. When completed, the series will include thirty-one volumes covering many aspects of the life and work of the province from its foundation in 1791 to our own time. Among these will be biographies of several premiers, and thematic works on the growth of the provincial economy, educational institutions, labour, welfare, the Franco-Ontarians, the Native Peoples, and the arts.

In planning this project, the editors and the board have endeavoured to maintain a reasonable balance between different kinds and areas of historical research, and to appoint authors ready to ask new questions about the past and to answer them in accordance with the canons of contemporary scholarship. *Planting the Province* is the tenth theme study to be published and volume one of a three-volume economic history of Ontario. It is a comprehensive and detailed account of the development of the Upper Canadian economy from 1784 to 1870, a period in which a steadily growing population transformed a forested frontier region into a settled and relatively prosperous economy. This process of growth was not driven by one or two primary exports such as wheat and timber, but was 'a case of balanced, relatively self-sustaining development within the context of the dynamic economy of the North Atlantic and North America.'

Douglas McCalla has given us an original and thoughtful analysis of the complex ways in which Upper Canadians constructed an economy with the capacity to flourish in the framework of the North Atlantic world. We hope that others will be sufficiently stimulated by it to undertake new and critical research on this crucial phase in the economic history of Ontario.

The editors and the Board of Trustees are grateful to Douglas McCalla for undertaking this task.

GOLDWIN FRENCH
PETER OLIVER
JEANNE BECK
MAURICE CARELESS, Chairman of the Board of Trustees

Toronto
14 October 1992

# General Preface

The present volume is one of a series of three that treat the economic development of Ontario from the late eighteenth century until the middle of the 1970s. It covers the period that ends with Confederation. The second and third volumes were published some years ago. The second, *Progress without Planning*, by Ian Drummond and several collaborators, deals with the years from Confederation to World War Two. The third volume, *The Prosperous Years*, by K.J. Rea, surveys what most readers will see as the 'modern period,' ending in the mid-seventies. Taken together, the three volumes are meant to provide a general narrative account of economic developments, as well as an interpretative and analytical comment on them. Because the three authors naturally have chosen to emphasize different elements in their stories, because different sorts of questions properly and naturally emerge as decade follows decade, and partly because there is a parallel evolution in the documentary evidence, the three volumes could not conform to a single mould. Thus, for instance, because McCalla must concern himself with settlement and with the role of subsistence production in early Ontario agriculture, he has had to consider the significance of such 'staple products' as wheat and timber, while Rea had to give extensive attention to questions of economic policy, which in earlier decades arose in very different forms or not at all. Similarly, the economic history of pre-Confederation Ontario can and must be written on the basis of the archival materials, but no one could treat the modern period on such a basis; for the period since 1940 there is little archival documentation, and much of it has not been fully explored, while government statistics and government reports exist in great profusion. Inevitably, the character of the evidence affects the texture of the narrative. In principle and to some extent in practice, the existing literature has the same effect. But on most topics in Ontario economic history the scholarly literature is not voluminous, and the popular literature is uneven in quality and coverage. Thus none of the three authors could proceed by summarizing and synthesizing what others have written about Ontario's economic development. For all three authors, but especially for McCalla, the project therefore required a great deal of primary research.

The present volume, like the other two, is written for a wide audience. It tries to supply most of the information which one might expect to find in a work of reference and to avoid, or to underemphasize, certain topics about which only other historians and economists would care. In the space and time that were available, no one could hope to be comprehensive. The authors have conferred about coverage and the distribution of emphasis, but as each author has, in the end, made his own choices, the final products must reflect separate decisions about importance and relevance. Although the three books form part of a single project, and although they provide a single survey with a considerable unity of content, it is not to be expected that they will be homogeneous.

IAN M. DRUMMOND

# Acknowledgments

This book has been a long time in the making, and I have accumulated many more obligations than it is possible to acknowledge fully here. Virtually everyone with whom I have discussed my research offered encouragement, shared ideas, and sustained my sense of participating in a genuine community of scholarship. As I have tried to show by extensive annotation, I have benefited greatly from cognate volumes in the Ontario Historical Studies Series and, more generally, from the work of other historians of Upper Canada. At the risk of omitting some whose names I should have included, I wish to thank a number of those who helped to make the book possible.

The editors of the Ontario Historical Studies Series, Goldwin French, Peter Oliver, and Jeanne Beck, drew me into this venture and have been remarkably patient as I was sidetracked over the years by assorted editorial and administrative duties. Without their understanding, and that of the OHSS Board of Trustees, and without continuing research support provided by the government of Ontario, this book would never have been undertaken or completed.

Ian Drummond, author of the successor volume in the series, coordinated the planning of its three economic history volumes and has been a source of inspiration in many ways. Marvin McInnis has offered more ideas and challenges, both conceptual and empirical, than I could ever address, and he has been truly generous in sharing his own research. Keith Johnson has given the benefit of his comprehensive grasp of the history of Upper Canada. All three encouraged me in seeing this project as worth doing; they have been essential to it throughout.

My research was facilitated by the Social Sciences and Humanities Research Council of Canada, through a leave fellowship and research grant in 1986–7. Trent University subsequently restored intensity and momentum to this project when both were flagging by providing partial relief from regular teaching duties for a year through a Trent Research Fellowship. My departmental colleagues at Trent University have been wonderfully tolerant when I offered obscure papers at colloquia and when I was inattentive to departmental duties. Special thanks are due to Alan Wilson, whose wise advice as I first undertook this project was fundamental to its scope and character, and to Elwood Jones and Dale Standen, with whom I have taught particularly closely, and from whose insights and knowledge I continue to learn.

Nancy Christie, Linda McIntyre Putz, and Jennifer Mueller worked at different times as research assistants. I am grateful to them for all the notes they gathered and for their ideas about the material, offered in discussions and in their written reports. Carol Burrill and Carol Wood were my secretaries for much of the period of research and writing; they assisted at times in manuscript preparation and presentation and were indispensable as creators of time for research and writing. The capable editing of the manuscript by Diane Mew, Beverly Johnston, and Lorraine Ourom has added substantially to the quality of the final version. The graphs and maps were prepared by McGraphics Desktop Publishing Inc.

Economic history is very much on the frontier of two disciplines. As is evident in the way issues are formulated and arguments developed, my own background is in history, not economics. Even though my approach does not involve formal and explicit use of economic theory, I hope the influence of economists will be evident. I thank many of the economists who study Canada's economic history for their tolerance, interest, and consistent helpfulness. In particular, Michael Huberman and Kris Inwood have each contributed in a variety of ways, and I benefited greatly from the regular series of conferences on the Use of Quantitative Methods in Canadian Economic History.

While editing the Champlain Society's Ontario Series, I worked with Colin Read, Ron Stagg, Peter Baskerville, and Richard Reid as volume editors; the many references to their volumes indicate only a small part of what I learned from them about Upper Canadian history. For permission to reprint material previously published, I am grateful to *Agricultural History, Histoire sociale/Social History*, Acadiensis Press, Dundurn Press, and the University of Toronto Press; detailed references are given in chapters 2, 4, 5, 8, and 11. My debt to the many archivists in Ontario who have searched out, organized, and preserved records of routine economic life before there was much demand for them is evident throughout.

Anna McCalla has lived with this project for more than half of our marriage (so far). She has travelled with it, accepted its intrusions in summer vacations, and in a host of ways been essential to it. She has saved the pleasure of actually reading it, however, as a post-retirement project. The book is dedicated to her, in appreciation and with love.

DOUGLAS McCALLA
Dodworth Island, Stony Lake
20 August 1992

# Tables, Figures, and Maps

*Figures*

*Maps*

*Planting the Province:*
*The Economic History of Upper Canada*
*1784–1870*

# 1 Introduction

This is a study of the growth of a new settlement economy on the North American frontier, in the territory that in 1791 became Upper Canada and in 1867 Ontario.[1] Although the fur trade, war, and Indian policy made the region part of a wider economic system even in 1784, its development as a permanent agricultural settlement began when some thousands of Loyalists arrived after the American Revolutionary War. Ninety years later, the province's arable south was largely settled, and the economy was industrializing. Along with the Montreal region, it was the economic heart of the new Dominion of Canada. How did this transition from an economy at the extreme periphery of the European economic system to one at the core of a new national economy occur? This book aims to answer that question, or rather to begin to answer it, for one of its themes is that defining and considering the questions posed by the province's economic development have scarcely begun.

For the first seventy years the story is dominated by extensive growth, in which output grew mainly as a result of the bringing together of new population and new resources.[2] During extensive growth, gross national product can rise rapidly, while the rate of increase in gross national product per capita, the economist's preferred measure, is much slower. Extensive growth can nevertheless deliver large gains in real standards of living to individuals and households; however, their gains are masked in aggregate data by the inclusion of the young and those newly entering the settlement process. All being well, the latter in turn could experience similar gains during their lifetimes. Although it is, in one sense, a simple process, extensive growth has many complexities, as the abundant literature on the economics of prairie settlement in Canada shows.[3]

In Upper Canada, until shortly after 1850, a high birth rate and continuing immigration combined to produce rapid population growth of about 7 per cent per year, a rate at which the population doubled every ten years.[4] The acreage of land under culture grew at virtually the same rate (table 1.1).[5] After 1851 the rate of population increase dropped sharply, and from 1861 until the end of the century Ontario's population growth slowed to the point where there was substantial net emigration. During the second half of the century the dominant process of development was intensive, characterized by urbanization, industrialization, and rising output per capita.[6] There is a full account of these processes in the subsequent period in Ian Drummond's volume in this series, *Progress without Planning*.[7]

Not all the development before 1850 was extensive, nor was all subsequent development purely intensive, but it is clear that a profound transition had begun by the mid-century. The boom of the 1850s, with its unprecedented wheat exports and massive investment in railways; the political transition of the era, as Britain adopted free trade, Canada acquired responsible government, and the processes leading to Confederation took place; and the beginnings of industrialization – all have attracted historians to the study of this transition. Social and economic historians have also been drawn to the period because census manuscripts were available for it.[8] But research focused on the mid-century may not explain the economic processes that preceded the period. Implicitly or explicitly, it may also encourage the anachronism of viewing the long period of economic expansion before the 1840s not in its own terms but in relation to its eventual sequel, the mid-century boom. For example, accounts of the period before 1850 have often stressed things that were lacking in the colonial economy, such as 'impediments' to development and 'obstacles to economic progress.'[9] Such approaches highlight what had not happened rather than what had, and tend to explain events by reference to standards set in a future that immigrants and farmers did not yet know.

Canadians have usually understood their country's economic development, in virtually any region or period, as a process led by the successive exploitation of a number of staples, which are resource-based commodities, typically subject to relatively limited processing and destined primarily for export markets. From a staples perspective, economic growth in a region is a process of unbalanced growth, in which one or two sectors lead or propel the entire regional economy forward. This is the interpretation favoured by McCusker and Menard in their authoritative survey of colonial American development, *The Economy of British America, 1607–1789*.[10] It was also the approach of authors such as Guy Callender and Douglass North to American development in the subsequent period, between 1790 and 1860, which they saw as deriving from interregional specialization and trade, notably among the three major nineteenth-century regions, the east, the west (or northwest), and the south. But subsequent research has shown that American patterns, in the latter period at least, do not support a staples-based argument. The issues posed by critics relate to logic, magnitudes, sequences, and causation. Logically, as Charles Tiebout noted in a critique of North, 'There is no reason to assume that exports are the sole or even the most important autonomous variable determining regional income.'[11] In terms of evidence, Stanley Engerman summarizes the main problem clearly.

[E]mpirical tests leave us in a quandary – it would seem that the foreign and external [i.e. extra-regional] demand sources must have been important to the explanation of what happened, yet the quantitative magnitudes always seem too small to make them necessary conditions for the growth that did occur ... Growth is a rather pervasive process once certain preconditions are met, and ... any one sector is only a relatively small part of the economy.[12]

Kenneth Buckley long ago made a similar argument for Canada in the years after about 1820.[13]

For Upper Canada, the staples perspective leads to study of two principal exports, wheat and pine timber, though government policies have also been seen as important. This book argues that focusing on staples alone yields an oversimplified and fundamentally inaccurate view of the process of economic development in Upper Canada. Exports were just one of the ways the province was connected with and influenced by the wider economic universe. Other external influences included population movements, trends and fluctuations in prices and in rates of exchange, flows of ideas and information (including technology), short- and long-term flows of credit and capital, and the policies of outside governments, including those of Britain, Lower Canada, the United States, and even individual states. None of these was necessarily or simply related to staple production as dependent variables of it, as a concentration on staples implies.

Moreover, if Lower and Upper Canada together constituted a single 'Laurentian' economy, much of the wheat and other farm produce shipped downriver from Upper Canada was not an export, but just a component of the internal trade of that larger economy.[14] The same point can be made for cross-border trades along the rivers marking the border between Canada and the United States. Later, as official data were developed, they showed shipments to Detroit and Buffalo as exports from Upper Canada, though often they were essentially local trades. If by exports we mean long-distance trades, principally across the Atlantic, then only timber, potash, and some other wood products, furs, and sometimes wheat and flour can genuinely be called exports before 1850. For convenience, however, shipments out of Upper Canada, even to nearer markets, are generally termed exports in this book. In part, this is necessitated by the character of the documentation involved.

From early in its history, distinctive internal regions took shape within Upper Canada. They grew despite differing degrees of involvement in staples production and even though trade from those areas more involved in production of staples to those less so appears to have been modest.[15] Similarly, rather than being tied narrowly to harvests and prices of its principal export commodities, the booms and depressions of the province's economy were essentially those of the emerging general pattern of economic fluctuations in the western economy. The economy was resilient in the face of periodic unfavourable shifts in the fortunes of one or other of its principal exports and was sometimes depressed at times of relatively high prices for these commodities.

Production for household consumption and for local markets was at least as vital to the economy's survival and expansion as these external dimensions of the economy. A majority of households farmed for all or a part of their living and supplied many of their needs from their own resources. They also produced for nearby markets, where there was demand for a much wider range of products and services than was the case from export markets. That demand came from farm households themselves, for few were self-sufficient in all locally produced commodities. It also came from the considerable minority of households that were not primarily farmers, which included artisans, labourers, and merchants and professionals. As David Gagan found for Peel County, the countryside 'supported a large and diverse range of economic activities associated with its principal focus, agricultural production.'[16] There were limits on how much of any one commodity or service the local market could absorb, and there were many potential producers of standard farm outputs. But the local market gave Upper Canadians choices of what to produce and meant they were not dependent on a single export commodity. A farm provided much more than wheat, and the forests provided many other products besides the familiar staple, squared white pine timber.

Choice is important to understanding economic behaviour in this setting. The argument below depends in part on inferences from the choices people made, including the choice to continue to do what they were doing already. Throughout the period under consideration this was an open economy, with much movement of people in and out, and with one of the world's most dynamic economies immediately adjacent. That people chose to come and to advise others to follow suggests that, to them, the provincial economy offered a level of well-being and opportunity preferable to what they thought possible for themselves at home, whether in the eastern states or in Britain. That people chose to stay suggests that they considered themselves to be in a satisfactory situation, by comparison with the nearby American states. This is not to argue that the average standard of living, to the extent we can calculate it, was identical on either side of the border. It is rather an argument that there must have been some consistency in the relationship between them. Of course, from the individual's or the household's point of view, the decision to stay or move was a function not of some abstract average, but of that person or family's predicted gains and losses. Thus the decision was related to their understanding of present and future prospects for security, wealth, and income in a specific occupation or sector of the economy, and even on a specific piece of land.

The border between the province and the United States was a constraint on population movements, to the extent that migrants took diverging political philosophies into account, and especially after Upper Canada passed its alien laws. And it was also a barrier to trade, to the extent that governments on either side of the lakes could enforce policies that at times sought to tax or inhibit some trades. But people, goods, and information moved both ways, and people in Upper Canada could always move south and west in search of higher living standards. The continental character of the development process is suggested by relative rates of population growth north and south of the lower Great Lakes. The timing and rate of Upper Canada's expansion were in essential accord with adjacent states, in particular Ohio, Michigan, and western New York (figure I.I).

A sense of the overall scale of the economy is required if we are to assess the relative importance of its components at various times. Hence this study presents cross-sectional data and time series on population, commodity prices, and aspects of production and exchange. Sometimes these are partial or include hypothetical reconstitution of parts of the economy, created by extrapolating from limited evidence where more comprehensive data are not available, with a view to estimating orders of magnitude. In general, such statistics are descriptive and presented in a form that does not obscure the underlying evidence and its provenance or the assumptions used. Estimates are normally biased so as not to underestimate the significance of familiar staples and the export sector. More analytic statistical procedures are frequently inappropriate because of the inadequacy, inconsistency, or ambiguity of documentation, and because our lack of knowledge about the era can lead to erroneous aggregation and specification of variables and relationships. For ex-

FIGURE 1.1
Rates of Population Growth, Selected Areas, 1784–1871

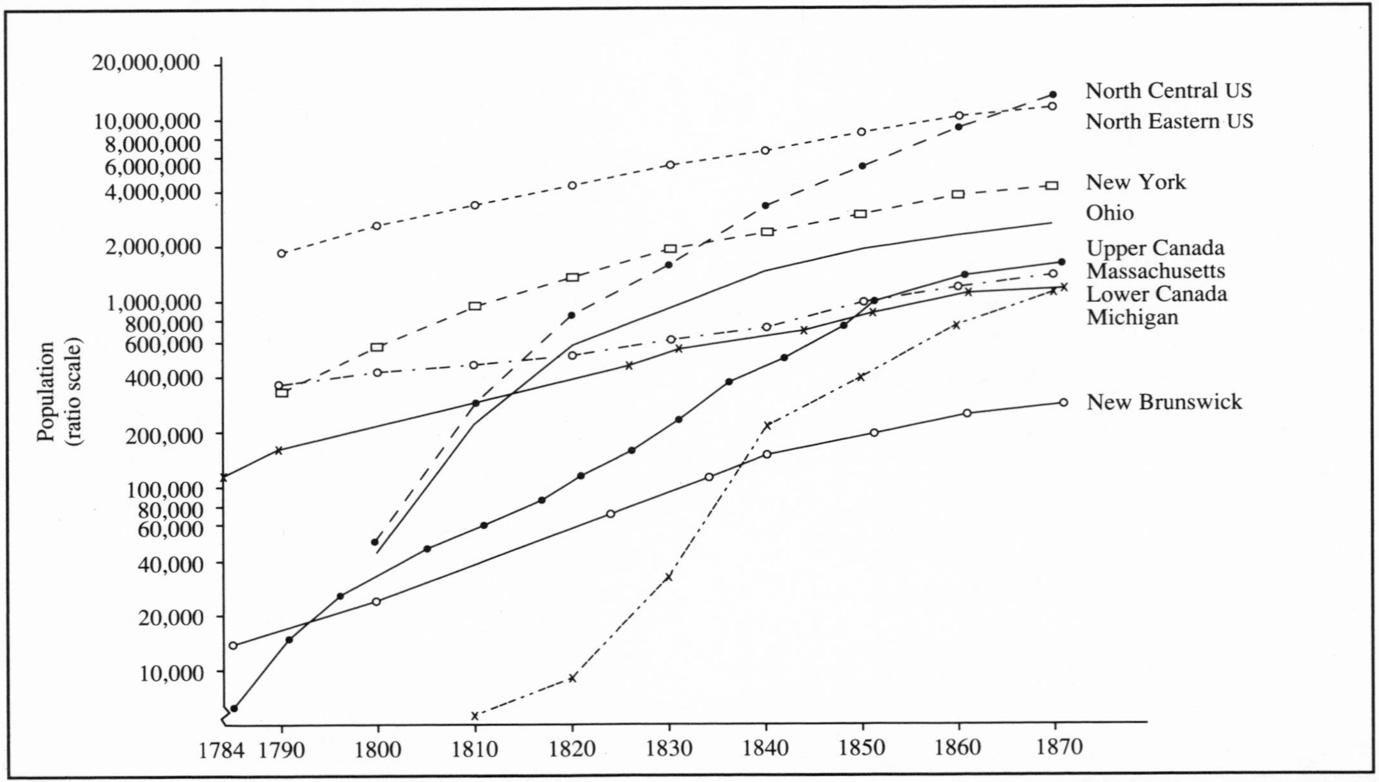

ample, because it is difficult to know what weights to assign individual commodities, prices are not combined here into more general indexes.

While this study emphasizes expansion, it is important also to consider why the economy was not larger and more developed; that is, what were the constraints on its scale and complexity? By comparison with rural Lower Canada, Upper Canadian agriculture marketed more produce per farm. Yet even in 1860, the 'typical' successful farm in the province produced only enough to feed its occupants and two other equivalent households, and techniques of production used would have been familiar to generations of farmers.[17] In the staple model, demand for the staple is essentially exogenous (that is, external) to the specific economy. But in a local exchange economy, local supply and demand were endogenous to the system (that is, functions of one another). The levels of economic activity and exchange that prevailed at a particular time were functions not only of such factors as prior investment and the technology of transport and farming but also of social structure, community values, and institutions. In a rural society that included many relatively equal and autonomous households which aimed at independence, farmers may have been slow to raise their costs by hiring additional labour and making capital investments that would quickly and substantially increase their output, because they did not expect that such additional produce could be sold at a remunerative price. Such a reluctance to hire more labour and to buy more local goods and services could itself constrain local market development.

The values and expectations of such pioneer farmers have been the subject of considerable debate by historians. The argument here is compatible with the position of those who have seen the farm household as essentially a pre-capitalist social unit seeking autonomy. But it stresses that market relationships involving buying and selling, borrowing and lending, and creating and disposing of capital were an integral part of the universe and the strategies of even the most isolated pioneer household. Farmers' engagements in the marketplace were seldom on the scale that they would be a century or more later. Their tools were relatively simple and, if not always identical to those used in Britain, at least familiar. Yet from the beginning of the economy, farmers were directly involved in the marketplace and responsive to its demands and signals.[18] Making and sustaining a farm was an investment occurring over many years, and the farm household, whether setting out to clear a farm or buying one already begun, needed to take a long view of the enterprise. Moreover, households were engaged not just in making their own farms but in making an entire local economy. The relationship of external demand to that local process of growth still needs fuller exploration and analysis. Those who assert the primacy of the former are effectively assuming a causal relationship between external trade and local growth, rather than demonstrating it.[19]

From what we know of wheat prices, yields, and fluctuations, most farmers had other essential sources of income. Yet literary sources such as emigrant guides stressed wheat's importance, and peaks in immigration sometimes followed peaks in wheat prices. We may therefore wish to see wheat as having a strategic, or at least talismanic, role in inducing and sustaining settlement and the investment process it entailed. To anticipate the argument that follows, it was surely important to many immigrants, whether or not they would eventually be wheat growers themselves, that wheat could be produced in Upper Canada in sufficient quantities to yield a surplus for sale, in a market that would take it at some price. But although wheat and pine were important as sources of income and reassurance, they were nothing like the full story of this economy. Upper Canada does not represent a case of development driven by one or two primary exports, which dictated its pace and without which it would have died, but rather a case of balanced, relatively self-sustaining development within the context of the dynamic economy of the North Atlantic and North America, from which it derived many other stimuli to expansion.

*Part One:*
*Establishing a New Economy*

# 2 The Loyalist Economy, 1784–1805

Upper Canada's growth as a settlement economy began when about six thousand Loyalists of European background arrived in the province during 1784–5.[1] The country they entered had already been penetrated, if hardly occupied, by Europeans, as the St Lawrence and Great Lakes were the route for a far-ranging fur trade and, during the American Revolution especially, the site of important British army operations. Neither the fur trade nor the military offered much basis for substantial permanent settlement, but they provided the settler economy with access to a communications system that linked it to the wider world.[2] Two of the main posts, Kingston and Niagara, were focal points for Loyalist settlements, and on the relatively remote Detroit River frontier, where there had long been an agricultural and commercial community, continuing growth of a settlement economy relied initially on the western fur trade and garrison activities.[3]

As it planned for settlement, the British government with 'legal fastidiousness' began acquiring title to land in the south from the established native peoples, of whom various groups of Ojibwa were the principal.[4] In 1784, for example, a large tract was purchased from the Mississauga to provide lands along the Grand River for the Six Nations. By 1787, when the Mississauga sold a considerable area in what became York County, most of the lake and river front between there and Lower Canada had been obtained. Other purchases in prime settlement zones followed, although the Mississauga withheld the key stretch of land along Lake Ontario between York and Burlington Bay until 1805–6. After 1815, power relationships between native peoples and the British authorities shifted in the latter's favour, and the government was able

This chapter is a revision of my 'The "Loyalist" Economy of Upper Canada, 1784–1806,' HS/SH 16 (1983), 279–304, and is reprinted by kind permission of Histoire sociale / Social History.

systematically to acquire remaining Indian lands all the way from the Ottawa River to the St Clair, in exchange for reserves, annuities, and other considerations. Within a decade, most of the desired territory had been ceded by the Indians.[5]

It is not possible here to retell the history of policy on land grants (to Loyalists, soldiers, officials, and would-be colonizers), crown and clergy reserves, land taxation, and the system of land surveying. But it is important to note that the government, once it had formally acquired the land, turned immediately to alienating it again.[6] Even before Loyalist settlement began, the British government had established the basic survey pattern, which divided the landscape into townships, whose characteristic grid of concession lines every one or two miles still marks much of rural Ontario. In this system, lots were normally two hundred acres in size, and the usual size of a farm in the province was one or two hundred acres.[7]

The land system was criticized then and later. In particular, land policies were said to have retarded development and to have fostered an unequal, hierarchical class structure, and eventually 'a large landless labouring class.'[8] Officials clearly intended the latter, if not the former, but in neither case is the relationship between policy and outcome so direct and so clear. Certainly large land grants and special bargains on crown land were avidly sought; however, most recipients of grants hoped, or had, to resell lands so obtained.[9] Although tenancy had a place in the provincial system, most settlers wanted to own land. Whether they obtained it 'free' or purchased it in the market, the initial cost of uncleared, unfenced land represented a small fraction of the total investment required to make a successful farm; and payments for land could be spread over time rather than having to be made in a lump sum.[10]

The character of property rights is a fundamental element in any economy, and developing the institutional structure by which title could be reliably established and land could be bought, sold, and used as security for debts was an extended process.[11] On the other hand, people found ways to buy and sell land virtually from the beginning of settlement, even before land was actually patented. From the viewpoint of an intending settler, there was always land available, even if much of it was already settled by people who did not wish to sell, or was held out of the market by governments, by land dealers and speculators, and by ordinary individuals who had purchased it with the intention of eventually farming it. As critics charged, undeveloped lands within settlements and between them did not facilitate road construction and community development. But to the individual farm household, undeveloped lands can be seen much as if they were part of the environment, like swamps, rivers, drumlins, and moraines, to be taken into account, if possible, when deciding which land to buy and to be accommodated in the course of everyday life. Land and policies related to it were doubtless significant, yet from the perspective of this study the more striking features of the story of land are the relatively continuous addition of land under culture to the provincial total, the consistency of the ratio of improved land to population throughout the settlement era, and the parallel growth of population on both sides of the border despite policy differences between the jurisdictions.

## I. *The Beginning of Settlement*

About two-thirds of the first Loyalists distributed themselves, with the assistance of British policy, in a relatively dispersed pattern along the St Lawrence from west of its junction with the Ottawa River to the Bay of Quinte. Although some went as far as the Detroit River, most of the remaining Loyalists settled in the Niagara region and westward along Lakes Erie and Ontario. Both the eastern and what would in the new province be central Loyalist settlements became the basis for substantial continuing growth. Despite the barrier posed by the Niagara Escarpment to water access to the rest of the province, settlement was already under way above it.[12]

The Loyalists faced problems that would have arisen anywhere on the North American frontier. They faced greater privations and uncertainties than in more established areas, and also the necessity to acquire knowledge specific to the new area, such as concerning local climate and soils, and the demand for hard physical labour. Their forced migration imposed psychological stress and economic hardship, deriving from having had to leave behind much of whatever wealth they possessed. To overcome such difficulties, they were initially granted government rations, and eventually the British government paid at least partial compensation for losses. It is significant, however, that by 1786, well before Loyalist claims were paid, the new economy was able to survive without direct provision of rations to settlers.

Indeed, the first arrivals were soon followed by others – Loyalists, 'late-Loyalists,' and ordinary pioneers – all of them likely to have been attracted as much by information from those who had gone ahead as by proclamations of free land. By 1791 the province's population of European origin had more than doubled; by 1796 it was about four times its level of 1785; by 1805, twenty years after the Loyalists' arrival, it was probably over 45,000. By comparison, New Brunswick, another new colony, to which about twice as many Loyalists came, had attained a population of about 25,000 at the turn of the century (figure 1.1). In the first twenty years, Upper Canada's non-native population grew at an average rate of over 10 per cent a year, almost four times the rate at which even a young, fast-growing rural economy could grow by natural increase. While some immigrants came to the province from Britain, a large majority (which included some whose original birthplace was in Britain or Europe) came from the United States. Wherever they came from, few were helpless; they had at least some choice of destination, and they were not uninformed.[13] Their selection of Upper Canada suggests that the development of the province in its early years gave some settlers cause to predict success for themselves and for those with whom they were in contact, especially in the United States. Glenn Lockwood has described the settlement of Montague Township in such terms.

[N]one of Montague's first families arrived penniless. These were not frightened exiles, scurrying north of the St. Lawrence at a time of year when circumstances were least accommodating for the clearing of land, sowing of crops and building of houses ... They were the inheritors of a tradition of pioneering, capable of ascertaining the most appropriate time of year at which to commence preparations in all aspects of promoting the early exploitation of the virgin forest.[14]

Not all who came intended to be permanent settlers, nor was success guaranteed. Emigration and transiency were important to provincial demography from the beginning. In the best-studied township, Adolphustown, on the Bay of Quinte, one-quarter of all household heads changed status in their households, died, or left the township in any two-year period between 1793 and 1822.[15] This was one of the first townships to reach its limits in terms of the number of independent farming households it could support;[16] still, some continuing immigration was needed to maintain the overall household structure. We do not know where those who left Adolphustown went,[17] but their departure shows that a decision to immigrate to a specific place was not immutable. In fact, if a location proved unfortunate, departure might be unavoidable. As departures remind us, those who remained were themselves making a decision to stay. Even Loyalists, after the earliest years, were not barred from returning to the United States.

Almost all this population was rural, though not all rural dwellers were farmers. Upper Canada's establishment as a distinct colony in 1791 did not alter Montreal's status as its principal urban entrepôt. Neither of Upper Canada's own leading urban centres, Kingston and York, had attained a population of 1,000 by 1805–6.[18] Adding other incipient urban centres to their populations still leaves the province's population over 90 per cent rural. Despite the province's inland remoteness, its rural nature, and the apparent isolation of the pioneer farmer, there was already a seasonal and short-term labour market.[19] Throughout the settlement era, there were about 1.2 adult males for every adult female in the province (see also table 12.1).[20]

Of the 45,000 Upper Canadian settlers in 1805–6, fully half were located in areas that were less favourably located than the St Lawrence settlements for access to downriver sources of imports and markets for exports. Almost 20 per cent lived above Niagara Falls, in the Western and London districts; over 20 per cent lived in the Niagara District; and almost 10 per cent lived in the Home District, around York, which became the provincial capital in 1796 (table 2.1).

Upper Canada's foundation resulted directly from the Revolutionary War, but its expansion was part of much larger changes occurring in the continental economy in these years, as the United States expanded westward and as the Napoleonic Wars increasingly affected the European economic system. To the south, settlement was pressing into western New York and southern Ohio. To the east, more settled regions were undergoing a process of 'deep change' as American industrialization began, and as the rural economy of New England reoriented itself in terms of markets, demography, and other factors. Downriver, the economy of Lower Canada grew rapidly between 1785 and 1802.[21]

II. *British Expenditures and Colonial Development*

Although the province's growth was paralleled by, and has been seen as part of, the extension of the American frontier, it has also been common to see Upper Canada's early development as a result of British government actions. Particularly important were the substantial and continuing British expenditures made in the province. Thus, Bruce Wilson, the leading modern authority, has argued that 'the most obvious reason for the rapid development of settlement ... was the massive aid the settlers had received from the British government.'[22] Or, as Richard Cartwright Jr put it, 'So long as the British Government shall think proper to hire people to come over and eat our flour, we shall go on very well and continue to make a figure.'[23] Looking back on the province's early years in 1812, Lieutenant-Governor Francis Gore argued that 'the Parent State['s] ... fostering care [was] the first cause, under Providence, of the uninterrupted happiness you have so long enjoyed.'[24]

After rations had been stopped and direct subsidies to most settlers were ended in the middle 1780s, such care took a number of forms. The largest single British expenditure was for Loyalist claims for compensation on account of losses from the revolution. Some hundreds of Upper Canadian residents were awarded a total of between £100,000 and £160,000 sterling, paid out between 1789 and 1795, though recipients, if they wished, could obtain their entire award, at a discount, in 1789.[25] The impact of such payments is difficult to estimate. They might, for example, already have been anticipated by claimants who had incurred debts on the basis of their expectations, or they might have been dissipated in higher than necessary imports from Britain. Still, even if all they did was pay debts, recipients must have been assisted to continue farm-making and mill development.

In the longer term, regular and quite predictable British expenditures were likely more important to the economy's operations. Such payments fell into a number of categories (table 2.2). Retired military officers, of whom there were 110 in the province in 1807, received half pay that amounted to around £6,000 stg in the latter year, and more earlier.[26] The British government provided an annual parliamentary grant in aid of civil administration,[27] paid salaries in the Indian Department, and covered a variety of other expenses of the colonial government on a more ad hoc basis.[28] In total, such payments on civil account annually amounted to more than £10,000 stg (see Appendix A for a general discussion of money and exchange rates). They gave the provincial government a stability in its operations that reliance on local taxes was unlikely to have afforded.

Britain's military expenditures were even larger. The army commissariat purchased pork and flour to a value of £5,000 to £8,000 stg per year. Initially, as a means of inducing local supply, it paid the Montreal price plus an allowance for upriver freight costs for these products. In 1795–6 John McGill was appointed agent of purchases for the province. After an uncertain beginning, his system became one in which annual contracts were issued on the basis of tenders from local suppliers.[29]

Of all the British expenditures, the largest, and the most difficult to calculate precisely, consisted of routine expenditures on the garrison in Upper Canada. These costs included soldiers' and officers' pay and allowances (to the extent that these were actually spent by the recipients) and the purchase of a wide array of goods and services in the local economy. The garrison in Upper Canada by the late 1790s consisted of about one thousand soldiers, and represented about one-third of the British force in the two Canadas. As headquarters were in Lower Canada, rather less than one-third of total expenditures were likely made in the upper province.[30]

Writing in 1809, Lord Castlereagh, the British secretary of war, complained of 'the very great increase of Expences' in the previous eighteen months, during which total expenditures were some £372,000 stg. Such expenditures, he noted, exceeded 'the proportionate Expence in any former year to such an Amount that I am unavoidably obliged to desire ... a detailed explanation.'[31] In 1808–9 the army was thus spending at a rate of £250,000 stg a year in Upper and Lower Canada. Earlier, we might estimate a yearly figure of half this sum, £125,000 stg, of which no more than one-third, about £40,000 stg, would ordinarily have been spent in Upper Canada.[32] After the military provisions already noted are deducted, for a garrison of one thousand, the total represented about £35 stg per man. This is taken as the high estimate for purposes of preparing table 2.2; the lower estimate, £25 per man, is likely a minimum, given pay scales and other costs of operations.[33] At any realistic rate of calculation, ordinary army expenditure represented at least half of total British government outlay in Upper Canada.

Thus, total routine British expenditures were between £54,000 and £77,000 cy per year, at official rates of exchange (see table 2.2). Even the minimum total almost certainly exceeded the value of provincial exports until at least 1803. Because Britain rapidly built up forces in the province after 1808, it is clear that total sterling exchange derived from British expenditures in the province exceeded earnings on export account until after the War of 1812. Such data offer considerable evidence to support the arguments of Bruce Wilson, Cartwright, and Gore.

These expenditures profoundly affected provincial imports, however. Salaried officials and serving or half-pay officers, for example, were likely to demand many more goods from Britain than did ordinary provincial farmers. Similarly, the British army imported rum for its soldiers rather than risk plying them with local whisky. Not all British expenditures were net increments to the province's exchange earnings or stimuli to local development, and we should not assume that their withdrawal would necessarily have crippled the economy. Moreover, in the decade after the mid-1790s, the population was growing rapidly, while British expenditures in the province were stable or shrinking and actually fell sharply on a per capita basis. The minimum total of £54,000 was equivalent to over £2 per person in 1795 (£13 per six-person household) but just over £1 per person (£7 per six-person household) in 1805. Nevertheless, the economy must have derived extra breadth, depth, and resiliency from such considerable outlay by the mother country.

III. *Fluctuations in Wheat Prices*

Agriculture was the principal activity of the new economy. The principal crop, and the one for which markets beyond Upper Canada first

FIGURE 2.1
Wheat Prices in Upper and Lower Canada, 1786–1836

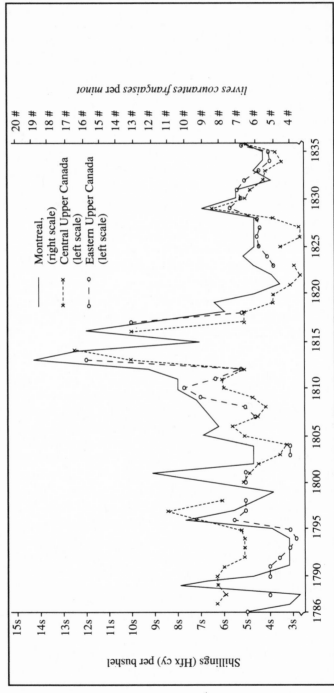

SOURCE: For Upper Canada, table C.1; for Montreal, Fernand Ouellet, Jean Hamelin, and Richard Chabot, 'Les prix agricoles dans les villes et les campagnes du Québec d'avant 1850: aperçus quantitatifs,' *HS/SH* 15 (1982), 95–6.
Note: 1 minot = 1.1 Winchester bushels. This is an approximate rate; see Régis Thibeault, 'Les Unités de mesure dans les documents officiels du dix-neuvième siècle au Bas-Canada et au Québec,' *RHAF* 43 (1989–90), 228.

developed, was wheat. Because for this early period data on prices in Upper Canada are fragmentary and sometimes ambiguous, it is not possible to analyse price differentials and time lags in fine detail. Still, there was an emphatic cyclical pattern to the price of wheat (figure 2.1; see also table C.1). During Upper Canada's first two decades there were three sharp peaks in wheat prices in Britain and in Lower Canada – in 1789, 1796, and 1801.[34] The middle of these peaks is evident in both series of prices for Upper Canada; the earlier and later cycles are marked more by the subsequent troughs. In Upper Canada 1789 was a 'hungry year.'[35] The implication usually drawn from the year's privations is that the province remained very near the margin of subsistence. But the coincidence of such a year with wider market fluctuations suggests a more complex explanation, in which local harvests and conditions were only one factor. For example, high prices outside the province might have deterred importers and/or raised the prices asked by local sellers beyond the reach of many buyers in the province.

By the mid-1790s the price along the St Lawrence and around Kingston was generally lower than in Montreal, the gap between the two markets reflecting both direct downriver shipping costs and the costs of market uncertainties, such as those arising from the time required for information to reach Upper Canada. Wheat was first sent downriver from Lake Ontario in 1793.[36] Given such exports, it is surprising that no 1801 peak appears in provincial series. A major bottleneck in shipping capacity sharply raised shipping costs in the spring of 1801 and may have deprived the province's farmers and merchants of the benefit of the extraordinarily high prices that were reached early in the year in Britain and Montreal.[37]

Salaried officials often complained that Upper Canada was a high-cost, high-wage economy.[38] Farmers and wage-earners may not have entirely shared that perspective, of course. At least during 1796–8, produce prices, notably in the centre of the province, were high by later standards (table C.3). On the other hand, it is striking that in the eastern half of the province, the price of wheat was never very high. Its local price reflected the costs of transport to final markets, in or beyond Lower Canada. Between 1793 and 1795 and again in 1803–4, wheat there earned 3s (60¢) a bushel or less; and from 1786 to 1808 its average annual price in the east exceeded 5s ($1) only once, in 1796 (table C.1).

Farther west, around the head of Lake Ontario and at Niagara, wheat prices were higher than in the east until about 1800 (figure 2.1), and trade data show that the first substantial downriver exports of flour and wheat from the western half of the province occurred in 1801. It was assumed at the time that earlier local price levels resulted from demand from new immigrants and cross-lakes trade, but the more-or-less simultaneous peaks in other price series suggest that local price levels were not solely a function of local supply and demand for each individual commodity. The peak in 1796–7, over 8s a bushel, rewarded established wheat producers. Such brief peaks probably stimulated an enduring increase in provincial wheat output, as farmers responded by increasing production and new settlers were attracted to the economy. Intervening periods of low prices do not appear to have stopped immigration, however, or the continued expansion of the rural economy.

## IV. *The Growth of Exports*

Many of the data that survive on the trade of early Upper Canada, especially in regard to imports, are difficult to interpret. Not only were there inconsistencies and gaps in the records of the customs house at Coteau-du-Lac, at the border between Upper and Lower Canada, but the settlement economy of Upper Canada was initially a kind of appendage to the larger continental trade system of the St Lawrence valley. Imports destined for the fur trade, the military forces, the Indians, and the United States cannot be distinguished from those for the settler population of Upper Canada; in any case, most imports were recorded on an undifferentiated basis by bulk.[39] On the export side, American produce cannot always be clearly distinguished, though this was not an especially large problem in the earliest years. Nor is it always possible to distinguish furs by point of origin.

The most useful early data pertaining specifically to the province's external trade are those of Richard Cartwright Jr of Kingston, one of the two leading merchants in the province. From his estimates of province-wide trade and his records of trade passing Kingston, it is possible to ascertain volumes and/or values for domestically produced downriver shipments at intervals from 1794 to 1803 (table 2.3). Because the eastern regions of the province, which are largely excluded from table 2.3, were the main sources of such shipments, the data do not fully reveal exports of wood products. Their extent is, indicated, however, by the difference in value, almost £20,000, between the two 1801 totals for values. Most of the difference can be accounted for by lumber, principally barrel staves, and most of the £15,600 in exports of them were from east of Kingston.

The other principal component of the province's trade in wood products was potash, exports of which were an early and continuing feature of the economy along the St Lawrence. It was produced more intermittently west of Kingston, in part because of transport costs, and because merchants and farmers there often had better ways of using their time and resources.[40] Total volumes, when worked out on a per capita basis, and merchants' accounts of individual ash deliveries both suggest that few farmers earned as much as £1 per year from the trade. At standard prices, it would have required about 60 bushels of field ashes or 40 of house ashes to earn that amount. The low per-farm value of such exports supports the view that the ash trade was mainly a by-product of land-clearing and household heating. But the long persistence of the trade in the east and its limited extent farther west show that it was less an automatic by-product of clearing and heating than a purposeful trade. Thus, as wheat prices plummeted after 1801, merchants and millers farther west, for example around York, began to find the trade attractive as a means to collect from debtors and make at least some payments to creditors.[41] Similar efforts may account for pork's addition to the list of provincial exports in 1802–3, but pork remained more significant as a product for domestic sale and consumption.

Furs continued to be an important export; in 1801, indeed, the value of furs from east of Detroit represented almost as much as all other provincial exports combined. Furs supplied by Indians and any special-ist trappers in exchange for imported trade goods were not an output of the new settler economy but a persistence of an older economic system. For some settlers, trapping and hunting must have been an important source of income; certainly early store accounts show occasional pay-ments in furs by customers. But the extension of settlement was closely linked to a decline in such trade. As Alexander Wood of York told one correspondent in 1806, 'my business is altogether with the settlers and chance alone throws peltries in my way.'[42]

The fur trade's greatest significance was the overall commercial sys-tem it sustained, which served the farm economy as well. The supply system from Montreal, lake shipping, and the province's credit all originated in the continental fur trade. The leading fur merchants of London and New York were unlikely to be much interested in the risks inherent in lending to a new and marginal farm economy, but they were already involved in supplying merchants such as Hamilton and Cartwright. Although both men derived their incomes from a number of sources, outfitting and transporting furs and their role in military supply were essential foundations of their credit.[43] Similarly, Quetton St George, who became the most prominent merchant in the town of York, began his commercial career by trading for furs with the Mississauga around Lake Simcoe. Furs gradually lost their place as a component in his remittances and, a Montreal correspondent suggested, he lost his skills in the trade.[44] But as his business shifted more and more to supplying townspeople and farmers, he could still deal with his old fur-trade sup-pliers in New York and Montreal.

Furs apart, wheat was the province's leading export in the years just after 1800. Farmers, millers, and merchants responded quickly to the high prices of early 1801, and the volume of shipments to Lower Canada almost tripled from 1800 to 1801. To assess the significance of such exports, it is appropriate to look at them on a per-household basis. In 1803 Upper Canada from the Midland District westward exported over 16,000 barrels of flour, equivalent to 81,000 bushels of wheat. That year's trade, which included 6,400 barrels from Niagara and westward, derived from the entire province west of Kingston. Excluding the two districts along the St Lawrence, the province's population in 1803 was about 29,000 (equivalent to 4,800 households of six people).[45] On this basis, 1803 exports were about 2.8 bushels per capita, or 16.8 per household. At the high end of the price range for wheat in the era, 5s per bushel, that would have yielded an income of £4 4s ($16.80) per household; at the prevalent 1803 price, 3s to 3s 6d per bushel, it would have earned the farm household between £2 10s and £3 at a lakeshore port. However these figures are regarded, and even if only half of all households were engaged in agriculture, they do not seem to represent a large income for a farm family.[46]

In addition to downriver shipments, Upper Canadians earned export-generated income by providing services and supplies to the extra-provincial fur trade; it is difficult to estimate how much was earned in this way.[47] Portaging at Niagara and transshipment at Kingston on both upward and downward cargoes were the main points of contact between the continental fur trade and the local economy of the province; but while rewarding to those involved, they did not in total generate incomes on a scale to match, say, revenues from external shipments of wheat and flour after 1801. There was also cross-lake trade of some significance. For purposes of analysis, the latter is best seen as equivalent in character to the internal trade of Upper Canada itself, for in this period the province and adjacent areas of New York and Ohio were equally distant from the seacoast, their economies were parallel, and the border was open.

## V. *The Local Economy*

The most difficult dimension of the provincial economy to document in this early period is its local, domestic economy. Yet it is important to include it in the analysis if we are to understand the development process. A study that focuses solely on external linkages of the economy cannot represent the whole story. The centrality of agriculture and specifically of wheat make it appropriate to begin with further analysis of the wheat economy. In light of the overall argument of this study, it is best to choose assumptions that tend to maximize rather than minimize wheat's role.

Exports represented only one aspect of the wheat economy. In addition, as we have seen, the British army purchased wheat within the economy. A considerable amount of wheat – in 1803 as much as was exported – was distilled within the province, as millers and merchants sought other sources of income from wheat in the face of sharply falling prices.[48] But the main use for the provincial wheat crop was to feed Upper Canadians and to provide seed for the next crop. When these uses are combined, it is evident that the provincial crop in 1803 was about 500,000 bushels, plus or minus 10 per cent, according to assumptions regarding yields and consumption (see table 2.4). Thus, exports of wheat in 1803 represented less than 20 per cent of provincial output.

The significance of the estimated 1803 output can be suggested in various ways. For example, this estimate of total output was equivalent to 13 bushels per capita, which fell well within longer-term norms for output. The same figure was recorded for Upper Canada in the census of 1851, and per capita output was considerably higher in both years than in, say, 1848 (see table 5.3).[49] If Upper Canada had about 6,700 households in 1803 and if we assume that only half these households were significantly engaged in farming, then 511,000 bushels of output represented 153 bushels per farm. At the lowest average yield per acre suggested for pioneer conditions, 15 bushels per acre, such a crop could have been produced on about ten acres.[50] On the apparently standard rotation, wheat-fallow-wheat, some twenty acres of cleared land per farm could have provided all the wheat grown. In addition, the farm would have needed at least two acres for a garden. At four acres a year, a commonly met figure for rates of land clearing, such a farm could have been created in five or six years.[51] By 1803 Upper Canada had many farms that had existed for a decade or more.

These figures can also be looked at in terms of land use. At a yield of 15 bushels per acre, 511,000 bushels would have required 34,000 acres to grow, or 68,000 over two years. Assessment data show that in six districts in 1805–6 almost 140,000 acres were taxed as 'under culture'; if 40,000 more acres are added to account for the Eastern and London districts, the province had about 180,000 acres of land under culture. Even if much clearing went on between 1803 and 1806, there must have been at least 150,000 acres under culture in 1803. Thus, on upwardly biased assumptions, at most 45 per cent of improved land would have been required to produce the 1803 wheat crop, and only half of that land in any one year (see also table 3.3). The export proportion of the crop and the seed to grow it would have taken less than 7,000 acres a year (that is, less than 5 per cent of the province's land under culture). More than half of the improved land in the province was not required for wheat-growing. But if the farm household had gone to the trouble of clearing the land (or the expense of buying cleared land) and was incurring the higher tax charged on such land, the land was obviously intended for production that was perceived as valuable. We cannot afford to ignore the question of what that further land was for.

Remaining land was kept mainly in fodder crops and pasture. As assessment rolls confirm, animals were an important part of provincial agriculture and of the economy's capital stock. In the six districts for which 1805–6 data are available, over 6,000 horses, 5,000 oxen, 20,000 cattle, and 6,000 swine are recorded. At the standard assessment valuations (£9 per horse, £4 per ox, £3 per cow, £1 per young cow, and 10s per pig), these animals would have been worth, in total, about £125,000; that total was approximately equivalent to the assessed value (at £1 per improved acre) of the land itself.[52] It is often said that animals were 'small, relatively unproductive,'[53] and left largely to fend for themselves, but that criticism is inappropriate. Animals kept over the winter needed fodder for at least the coldest months, and animals for slaughter were typically fattened for several weeks. If the animals were inferior by the standards of later years or of critics familiar with the best practice at the time, this does not mean they were valueless or unimportant in terms of the farm's time and resources devoted to husbandry, or in terms of the food, work, hides, wool, and income to be derived from the farm's livestock.

While there clearly were local markets for animals and their products, pork was the animal product most commonly marketed beyond the immediate locality (see also table 2.3).[54] Following an unsuccessful try at using Upper Canadian pork in the 1790s, the British army began to buy the local product again after 1800.[55] From 1804 on, pork invariably represented more than half of the army's Upper Canadian provisions purchases in terms of value. Because Robert Hamilton and Richard Cartwright Jr were important suppliers of pork to the military, their accounts may be unrepresentative. It is noteworthy, however, that between 1791 and 1796 in Cartwright's case and 1806 and 1812 in Hamilton's, each took pork from customers in payment of accounts to a value equal to half of the wheat taken in during the same period (see table 5.5). And each also supplied the army with wheat. Clearly, pork was a second source of income for a number of provincial farmers.

Beyond wheat and pork, a wide range of other farm-produced goods and services found local markets of varying sizes. In 1802, over three hundred Glengarry residents petitioned the provincial Assembly for the right to hold fairs in May or June and October:

[A] Fair ... would be of essential service to the community, as in a growing country emigrants and others may there be supplied with many necessaries which the vicinity can furnish and the old inhabitants may find it a sort of convenient exchange for bartering with one another cattle, horses, sheep, leather, wool, yarn, butter, sugar, homespun cloth, linen and such other articles as they can spare .... [Y]our Petitioners ... flatter themselves that in a short time they can furnish a surplus of most of the necessaries of life within themselves, and that the establishment of an internal market would be a spur to industry.[56]

Although the petition spoke of barter, in many cases such transactions were valued in money. They frequently entailed extension of credit, because transactions were not simultaneous. And they often involved exchanges more complex than direct swaps between two producers. Notwithstanding the petition, formal fairs were not a prerequisite to such exchanges. Thus, accounts and anecdotal evidence show sales of all the products mentioned and of others such as firewood, hides, and hay. Services such as teaming are also recorded. Another indicator of commercialization in the economy is the number of shops and taverns in the province that were licensed to sell alcohol (over two hundred by 1801–2).[57]

Thus, the buying and selling of goods and services was an essential part of the rural as well as the embryonic urban economy of Upper Canada. Even the classic farmer's bee, Norman Ball has shown, involved a complex and well-understood pattern of exchanges rather than simple neighbourliness.[58] It is difficult to estimate the scale of this local market activity by comparison with production for household consumption and for export, but we cannot ignore the significance of the sector. That families established early in an area were most likely to persist there[59] suggests that earlier settlers benefited from the opportunity to sell to new arrivals as well as from their priority in selecting land. As has been argued for the adjacent area of New York State, 'contemporary observers and historians have focused their attention on the export trades and related industries, to the exclusion of other markets ... [whereas] the less glamorous local market ... surpassed foreign trade in importance.'[60]

## VI. *Native Peoples and the Settlement Process*

To the Loyalists of European background must be added the many Indian Loyalists. The most numerous were about 1,800 members and allies of the Six Nations who settled along the Grand River. Several hundred more Mohawks chose instead to establish a community on the Bay of Quinte. In the 1790s a reserve of 50,000 acres was set aside along the Thames in Orford and Zone Townships, Kent County, for several hundred Delawares who had converted to the Moravian faith.[61] Another settlement, consisting of Munceys and Chippewas, was established a few years later in Caradoc Township, farther up the Thames. Because of the Indians' importance to the British military position, they were the object of considerable attention by Lieutenant-Governor Simcoe and his successors and by the Indian Department.

As protection for their future, the Six Nations sought and received large tracts of land, far more than they could currently use. Like a number of others in the colony's early years, they became, in effect, land speculators. Or at least that is how some, including their principal leader, Joseph Brant, treated this vast territory. Initially, the Grand River Indian lands amounted to almost 700,000 acres, stretching the entire length of the river, from Nichol Township (around present-day Fergus) to Lake Erie; and the Quinte Mohawks received almost 100,000 acres of their own.[62] Very much in the line of advancing settlement, these lands could be a source of conflict with the new settler society that was taking shape. On the other hand, their traditions of organization and of agriculture gave the Six Nations considerable autonomy and capacity for resistance.

The international boundary notwithstanding, groups of Indians continued to move quite freely between Canada and the United States, notably across the St Clair and Detroit rivers. There was also considerable movement among reserves.[63] Although there is some uncertainty about the total, perhaps 7,000 Indians lived in the southern part of the province (south of the French River) in 1800, and seasonal migrations might bring 3,000 to 4,000 more into the area at times.[64] Even by the early 1790s, that is, the Indian population was exceeded by the European population. In military terms, however, the Indians had power beyond their numbers. It is clear that annuities, land sales, and treaty payments could not have sufficed to support any of the native groups or provided their main food supply.[65] As the persistence of the fur trade and the character of the presents given to the Indians also suggest, a relatively traditional woodland native economy continued in much of the province.[66] While native populations had in various ways to come to terms with the new settler society, they were by no means dependent, and they retained considerable autonomy.

## VII. *Conclusion*

By 1805 the provincial economy was well launched on a process of capital creation, of which cleared land probably represented the largest single element. Farm buildings, and those in the villages and towns, represented a further important element in the province's capital. And the value of livestock has already been noted. Neither land nor buildings can easily be valued, except on quite notional terms. Further indication of the economy's ability to create capital is to be found in the rapid establishment of grist and saw mills throughout the settled areas of the province. In the six districts for which data survive, there were 185 such mills in 1805; there must have been at least thirty or forty more in the other two (Eastern and London districts). At their assessed value of £100 per saw mill, £150 per grist mill, and a supplement for each additional run of stones, such mills represented over £30,000 in capital. Except for a few well-documented exceptions, furnished by the British or the provincial government, virtually all were built by private investors. Most were oriented to the local market, were small by later standards, and often had trouble maintaining what critics saw as sufficiently high quality, but it is more significant that they existed at all.[67] Similarly, private investment produced a growing fleet of sailing vessels on the Great Lakes, totalling 500 to 800 tons by 1812, with a capital value of £10,000 or more.[68] A pioneer economy is typically seen as short of capital, but that does not mean that Upper Canada was unable to sustain a process of capital creation from its very beginning.

By about 1800 Upper Canada's economy had many structural elements that would mark it for the next fifty years. Included were its rate of population growth (7 per cent per year), its ratio of improved land to population (some 3.9 acres per capita), its per capita levels of wheat output and exports, the beginnings of some regional economic specialization (such as the Eastern District's role in producing wood exports), and the appearance of economic fluctuations that reflected outside market conditions. This was not, properly speaking, a subsistence economy, given its dynamic growth, its net immigration, its ability to survive harvest and market downturns, its capacity to build up and hold appropriate stocks of relevant commodities, and its apparent responsiveness to changing market conditions.

The components of this economy were part of an overall system, in which external commercial credit, immigrant investment, British government expenditures, and export earnings were the financial links to the outside world. These, with domestic exchange and investment and household production, were all parts of the process that gave momentum to provincial development. It is clear that the development was produced by those who actually came to Upper Canada, invested their time and resources there, and gradually built an economy where none had been before. Given their apparently modest incomes from sale of produce, there is much to be said for the view that their key objective must have been less to earn income than to build wealth, most commonly in the form of a productive, long-term income-earning farm whose capital value could be expected to grow as the economy did.[69]

# 3 The War Economy and After, 1806–22

During the next fifteen years, the Upper Canadian economy was again deeply affected by war, both in Europe, where hostilities between Britain and France had been renewed in 1803, and, in 1812–15, at home. After the war, and especially after 1817, the inflationary pressures of wartime finance in Europe and at home were reversed with a vengeance, and the economy, like those throughout the Atlantic world, underwent severe deflation. Only in 1822 did the slide in prices stop. Deflation did not deter immigration to Upper Canada, and indeed was a factor prompting some in Britain and Ireland to emigrate. Thus began a thirty-year period during which the United Kingdom was the main source of the immigrants who sustained the province's rate of population growth.

Although provincial policy, affected by the issue of wartime disloyalty, now sought to exclude American immigrants, the border remained permeable to both population movements and trade.[1] South of the lakes, people continued to move rapidly into the 'Old Northwest,' the lands west of the Appalachians. Both as a stimulus to intra-state communications and in an effort to secure the trade of that larger territory, New York State in 1817 began construction of the Erie Canal. Opened in 1825, it consolidated the state's leadership, and especially New York City's, in the American economy. Even before then, Upper Canadians and immigrants must have begun to anticipate the canal's impact.[2]

## I. The War of 1812

After touching near record lows in Upper Canada, wheat prices turned upward after 1804. In central areas, wheat was at or above 5s ($1.00) per

Earlier versions of parts of the material in this chapter were presented to seminars at the University of Ottawa and York University; the advice and criticism of both audiences were most appreciated.

bushel in 1805–6 and again from 1810 onward. Prices in the eastern part of the province, where almost half the provincial population lived, were higher (table C.1 and figure 2.1). High potash prices attracted farmers and merchants into the trade from the entire Lake Ontario region.[3] The worsening of the tensions between the United States and Britain, marked by the former's trade embargo (December 1807) and Non-Intercourse Act (1809), led to rapidly rising British military expenditures in the two Canadian colonies. Prompted by Napoleon's blockade of Baltic timber exports, Britain radically revised its timber duties in 1808 to foster colonial production. Except for disruption in trans-border trade, which could be partially overcome by smuggling,[4] all of these were positive factors for producers in Upper Canada.

By the beginning of 1811 Upper Canada's population totalled about 60,000 people. That figure derives from a contemporary estimate of the number of households in the province, multiplied by an average of six persons per household.[5] Thus, the rate of provincial population growth from 1805 to 1811 was, at a minimum, 4.5 per cent per annum (5.5 per cent if 60,000 was reached in 1810). Either rate suggests some slowing of the population growth rate, but continuing net immigration. Because prices for provincial produce were increasing, the slowing of population growth is as likely to be attributable to the political and military insecurity of the period as to purely economic factors.[6]

The uncertainty climaxed in the summer and fall of 1812, when war broke out between Britain and the United States and the latter invaded Upper Canada. British troops, initially numbering less than two thousand, aided by Indian warriors and local militia, successfully defended the province, which was at various times invaded across the Niagara, Detroit, and St Lawrence frontiers, as well as across Lakes Erie and Ontario. Areas occupied by American invaders and those where there was military action suffered considerable destruction.[7] Nevertheless it has been usual to see the war as essentially a period of prosperity for the province. One recent immigrant, Isaac Wilson, wrote late in 1813: 'I do not think there ever was a place equal to this for making money if a person be in any kind of trade or business whatever.'[8] A century later Adam Shortt provided what remains the standard scholarly analysis of the issue:

The War of 1812, instead of being the occasion of loss and suffering to Upper Canada as a whole, was the occasion of the greatest era of prosperity which it had heretofore enjoyed, or which it was yet to experience before the Crimean War and the American Civil War again occasioned quite abnormal demands for its produce at exceptionally high prices.[9]

Actually, the vigour of Shortt's conclusion belied the complexity of his analysis of the war's multiple and ambiguous impacts. Among its dimensions were massive British military spending in the province, the financial system by which those purchases were paid for, the disruption of normal external trade (both imports and exports), the sharply inflationary impact of war finance, and the losses from war operations by both sides.

The war effort in the Canadas was financed largely by the British government. Its spending requirements dramatically affected exchange rates for bills drawn on London from Montreal and Quebec. In 1809 the rate was at par (£1.111 Halifax cy = £1 stg); by 1812 less than £0.87 cy would buy £1 stg.[10] The impact of the swing in rates shows in the price of an export commodity such as wheat, which at the then-prevalent rate of exchange cost more in Upper Canada than in Britain by 1814.[11] Although the colony's propensity to import was checked by the disruptions in trade caused by the war, such exchange rates tended to encourage imports from Britain.[12] In 1813 the total value at Quebec of the wide range of imports subject to ad valorem duty was very low, less than £200,000; but in the next two years for which there are data, 1814 and 1816, such imports were vastly larger, well over £1 million in each case (table 3.5).

The impossibility of using specie for military expenditures in wartime caused the army to develop a new domestic exchange system in the Canadas. The British governor at Quebec, Sir George Prevost, proposed the creation of a paper currency in Lower Canada, for which 'the good faith and the resources of the British Government [would] constitute the foundation.'[13] Known as army bills, the notes were issued by authority of an act of the Lower Canadian legislature. When the system began in July 1812, army bills were limited to a total of £250,000. In small denominations (£1, or $4), they were redeemable in cash at Quebec. Larger denominations ($25 and up) paid interest at 6 per cent and were redeemable at Quebec in sterling exchange on London. By 1814 the total authorized limit for such bills had risen to £1.5 million; during the life of the scheme, over £3.4 million in notes were issued. As the war neared its end in the winter of 1814–15, the system began to be wound down. By the beginning of 1816 only about £325,000 remained in circulation. A year later, bills not yet redeemed totalled less than £90,000. At the end of 1817, when the system was essentially terminated, over £20,000 in army bills were still unaccounted for.[14]

The army bill system evidently worked well for its purposes, and the notes circulated freely in Upper as well as Lower Canada. They brought a liquidity to the provincial economy that had never before existed.

Merchants' correspondence and account books for the period indicate a general shift to payment in cash rather than kind.[15] Army bills were, however, part of an inflationary process. In the Canadas as elsewhere in the period, prices rose rapidly, to what would, for many commodities, prove to be the highest levels of the century (see tables C.3 and C.4). Liquidity and inflation rewarded debtors, who could more readily secure the means to pay debts and who were able to pay in a depreciated currency. Because Upper Canadian creditors, such as merchants, were in turn generally debtors to creditors in Lower Canada and Britain, they could free themselves from debt with the paper they received, rather than having to absorb the costs of inflation themselves. The favourable sterling exchange rate further assisted them in paying external debts.

In its first stages the war posed few unanticipated supply problems. A commissariat officer at Niagara noted in September 1812, 'In present Circumstances People are happy to get rid of their Flour on any terms.' By March 1813, however, a commissariat officer at Prescott was worried: 'I am fully satisfied that the grain sown last Autumn in this District, will prove utterly inadequate for the consumption of the Troops stationed in it.'[16] As the year went on, such problems became more acute. Fresh beef for the army, for example, came increasingly from Vermont and New Hampshire. In an effort to maximize grain supplies, the government actually prohibited exports and the distilling of grains, and, to control costs and speculation, it began, under martial law, to try to fix prices.[17]

The growing supply crisis in 1813 undoubtedly demonstrated the limitations on the economy's productive capacity. But knowledgeable observers considered that the crisis was only partially one of real output; inflation and the payments system also had a part to play. Early in 1814 an official noted 'a disposition on the part of most of the Inhabitants to withold their Grain until the necessities of the Troops should oblige the Commissariat to offer an extravagant premium in Specie.'[18] When farmers pleaded labour scarcity for their inability to thresh and deliver grain, commissariat officers by 1814 were prepared to send troops to bring the grain to market.[19] Alexander Wood reported to his Montreal correspondents in December 1814: 'I fear it will not be possible to procure either Flour or Pork in this neighbourhood for Mr Ermatinger the Comm[issar]y buys not only all that comes for sale but sends his people into the Country to examine what the inhabitants can spare and lays his hand upon it either manufactured or in Grain.' Three months later, Wood considered the supply problem largely over: 'Since the peace has opened the peoples eyes & the Commy not purchasing any more provisions, Flour and other articles have become more plenty & will no doubt soon be reduced in price.'[20]

There were constraints on the economy's ability to respond quickly to unprecedented and clearly short-term demands. Although the war offered Upper Canadians new choices, the net consequences of those choices, especially in the longer term, are not so clear. The wider availability of paid work, for example in teaming, could slow farm-making. Even if such work or the pay and allowances for serving in the militia fully compensated the individual for his loss of output, shifting a person's efforts from one use to another, in this context, was not economic growth, or even a contribution to growth. It was argued, for example, that the militia call-up of 1814 sharply reduced wheat planting for 1815.[21] And Britain's outlay of £630,000 between 1812 and 1815 on freight costs to ship supplies from Quebec to Upper Canada suggests that much of the British expenditure in Upper Canada actually flowed quickly out of the province.[22]

Not for the only time in their history, Canadians (and some subsequent historians) tended to mistake inflation for prosperity. It did little good to receive higher wages if one's costs increased equally or more; and it did equally little good to receive higher prices if one could not compete for hired labour or had to serve in the militia so that one's output diminished. Moreover, some suffered war losses that need to be set against others' gains from the war. Under provisions established after the war, approved claims for war losses in Upper Canada at British hands totalled around £250,000 cy when payment at last began in 1824.[23] If people avoided paying out all their increased incomes in higher costs, and especially if they paid off debts, they could come out of the war ahead. It was important for such a debtor society to pay off accumulated debts and, in effect, to begin the postwar era with a fresh start. But the war proved to be just an interlude. By 1822 the economy had returned in many respects to older patterns of exchange, credit, work, and output.

## II. *Adjusting to Peace, 1815–22*

As the high values of imports in 1814 and 1816 indicate (table 3.5), merchants anticipated substantial sales following the war. But the army bills were speedily being withdrawn from circulation. By 1816, as Dr W.W. Baldwin wrote, 'money [was] disappearing from the Province very fast.' Indeed, even in the spring of 1815, as peace and the initial pressures of deflation began to be felt, merchants began to talk of excessive and overvalued inventory.[24] The exchange rate between local currency and sterling swung quickly back to prewar levels, par (£1.111

cy to £1 stg) being reached again in 1816. After fluctuating around that level until 1820, the rate swung still further. In 1822 it reached £1.245 cy to the pound sterling, the second lowest level for Canadian currency in the entire century. This rate was near what eventually came to be recognized as a new par, £1.217 cy ($4.8667) to the pound sterling (see Appendix A). Thus, a new long-term currency/sterling exchange rate was established. Under it, debts contracted by Canadians in England in the immediate postwar period – for example for imports – had to be repaid in money that was more valuable than had been borrowed. Not surprisingly, debts began to accumulate again, and the long-credit system swiftly re-established itself in Upper Canada.

Following the war, immigration to the province resumed, now primarily from the British Isles. Between 1815 and 1822, approximately 100,000 people left Britain for the British North American colonies, and another 60,000 emigrants said their destination was the United States (table 3.6). Many of the former were en route, immediately or ultimately, to the United States, and some of the latter were destined for the Canadas. Between 1817 and 1820 James Buchanan, British consul at New York, assisted some 7,000 persons to move on to Upper Canada. Included in those to whom he issued passes were many whose occupations suggest their direct exposure to the pressures of enclosure and industrialization, such as farmers and weavers, as well as skilled tradesmen with occupations likely to be of service in Upper Canada, such as blacksmiths, shoemakers, carpenters, masons, and millwrights (see table 6.9).[25]

The majority of emigrants moved independently, though some, including about 10,000 destined for the Glengarry and Lanark regions of Upper Canada, travelled on government and privately sponsored schemes of assisted emigration.[26] Both assisted and independent migration were expressions of the disruptions attending postwar reorientations of the British economy. Social unrest and class tension were high in Britain, and many people faced or feared loss of income and independence in a world of rising population, rural reorganization, and industrialization. The postwar emigrants represented only a small fraction of Britain's population, but their impact in Upper Canada was large. They began a wave that would sustain Upper Canada's exponential rate of population growth to the mid-century (figure 1.1). In addition to the emigrants, a number of British soldiers were demobilized in Canada and at least some took up incentives offered to them to stay.

It was once common to picture such emigrants as poor people, even refugees, evicted from lands and deprived of their crafts by the ruthless capitalism of landlords and industrialists, and desperately risking their lives by journeying across the Atlantic in the squalor of timber ships.

There is some truth in that image, but it is far from adequate to explain the population movement that was getting under way. Even the assisted emigration schemes need to be understood in terms of migrants' own investment decisions as much as of public policy. Emigration was a selective process and frequently part of a family's strategy of investment in the new world. Moreover, because emigrants were often in touch with kin or neighbours who had gone ahead, they could form an idea of what faced them. As Bruce Elliott writes of one early group,

> to a remarkable degree the first shipload of North Tipperary Protestants set the pattern for the chain migration that was to continue for over thirty years. Like the passengers of the *Brunswick,* the later arrivals would be mostly farmers facing declining fortunes. They would travel in family groups and would come out to join relatives already in Canada. Both their places of origin and their destinations were foreshadowed in the pattern established by Richard Talbot's emigrants in 1818.[27]

Immigrants were not obliged to stay where they first landed or origi-nally expected to settle. If things did not work out, they moved – home again, within the colony, to another colony, or to the United States. For some, as the destitution in North American ports of arrival, especially in times of depression, reveals, payment of the costs of transportation used up all their immediate resources. Others had more resources to draw on, either as capital to be moved permanently to the new world or in the form of loans from family at home that were intended to be repaid.[28]

In the postwar era the British and Upper Canadian governments, alarmed by what the war had shown of local disaffection and neutrality, pushed strongly to exclude American settlement from Upper Canada. In this they were opposed by important elements in the provincial élite, especially in the Niagara area. Many had staked their futures on sales of land in the west, for which Americans were the anticipated buyers. After 1815 naturalization and land ownership were made much more difficult for American immigrants.[29] Such restrictions did not entirely check the flow of American movement to and investment in Upper Canada, however, as many individual cases attest. Nor could such laws prevent people in Upper Canada from moving to the United States. Indeed, reference to relative rates of progress in the United States and Upper Canada was a staple of public debate in the colony.[30] Thus, the process of frontier expansion in the province after 1815 continued to parallel and be linked to that of the adjoining states.

These were, in part, longer-term considerations. In the near term, the Upper Canadian economy experienced deflation from the end of the war onward, and acute depression by the early 1820s. Prices for provincial exports declined especially; wheat around Lake Ontario by 1822 was worth just one-quarter of its 1814 level, and half that of 1817. Potash at Montreal in 1820 and 1821 was priced at 23s to 28s per hundredweight, or about half its 1816 price.[31] Produce that was not ordinarily shipped out of Upper Canada fell by varying amounts and in a less linear fashion. On the York market, hay and oats fell quickly in price after the war and by 1817 were at or near the lows of 1822. Beef and pork prices showed a similar pattern. Prices for these commodities all actually rose in 1818–19, and some were again on the rise in 1821. Nevertheless, for every commodity recorded in table C.1 except hay, the price at York in the spring of 1822 was the lowest since early in the century and often the lowest ever (table C.3). Elsewhere, including Lower Canada and the United Kingdom, 1822–3 marked one of the lowest points of the half-century for many commodity prices. At Cincinnati the index of the prices of products of northern agriculture reached its lowest point of the half-century in 1821, and was only slightly higher in 1822–3 (table C.4).

Upper Canada's population grew particularly rapidly after 1815, with a rate of increase between 1817 and 1821 of 9 per cent a year (table 3.1). As the population distribution shows, the frontier of Upper Canadian settlement moved outward from several nodes. In the east, the Johnstown District was the fastest growing, principally because of the settlement of Lanark and Carleton counties, which caused the new Bathurst District to be established in 1822. In the centre, particularly at the western end of Lake Ontario, where settlement earlier had been inhibited by the Mississauga's retention of much prime land, the new Gore District and the Home District grew much faster than the provincial average. In the west, above Niagara Falls, the London District was likewise growing faster than the average.

Land-clearing and farm-making proceeded almost apace, though the ratio of acres cleared to population declined slightly between 1817 and 1821, to 3.7 acres per capita (table 3.2). The Midland, Niagara, Newcastle, and Gore districts all had four or more acres improved per inhabitant in 1821; indeed, the first two, which included some of the longest-settled areas in the province, well located on its communications system, and having significant local urban and military markets, had reached this level in 1805. For the province as a whole, a rate of over four acres per inhabitant would not be reached until the 1850s, when the rate of population increase began to slow.

Wheat continued to be a staple in provincial agriculture, but even on assumptions designed to maximize its significance, it is clear that its cultivation probably took a declining share of the province's improved land (tables 3.3 and 5.1). In 1817 about 20 per cent of improved land could have produced the estimated crop of wheat (or 39 per cent over two years). At yields of 15 bushels per acre, some 16,000 acres would have sufficed to produce the export portion of that crop and seed for it. That was less than 5 per cent of total improved land, and 1817 was a year of relatively high exports, as flour equivalent to 195,000 bushels of wheat was shipped downriver (table 3.4). That equalled 2.3 bushels per Upper Canadian (or 3.3 for those living in or west of the Midland District; see table 5.2).

In a year like 1817, when prices were falling sharply, annual data make it more difficult to value wheat shipments accurately. At one extreme, if wheat is valued at the 10s per bushel recorded for 1817 in eastern Upper Canada (a figure supported also by Ouellet's series for Montreal; see figure 2.1), 195,000 bushels would have earned almost £100,000, or about £1 3s per Upper Canadian (equal to about £7 per six-person household). If we assume that exports came only from the Midland District and west, then they generated earnings in that region equal to £1 13s per person (£10 per household). At the other extreme, if the average price at York for the year (5s per bushel) applied, earnings would have been only half as much. At the higher level, the earnings would rank the year with the best in the province's history (table 5.2).[32] The relative success of wheat exports from Upper Canada in the immediate postwar years, as exemplified by the higher of the 1817 estimates of wheat income, could have contributed to the sharp increase in British emigration to the colonies between 1816 and 1819 (table 3.6).

Although the volume of wheat shipped downriver in 1817 was typical of the postwar years, prices were tending downward. The 153,000 bushels recorded in 1821 would have been valued at less than £25,000 at the price in York that year. On a per capita basis, that was less than one-sixth of the amount in 1817, about 5s ($1) per person in the main producing region of Upper Canada. It is not surprising that Upper Canada was in a deep economic depression in 1821–2.

Imports to the St Lawrence fell sharply in 1817 from their immediate postwar levels, rebounded by 1819, then slid again to a low in 1821 that, in nominal value, was about one-third the total for 1816 (table 3.5). Merchandise paying ad valorem duties does not represent all imports, but the category is the one most comprehensive and representative of trends and fluctuations in overall import levels. In 1815 Upper Canada imported £387,000 in such merchandise, according to records of the customs station at Coteau-du-Lac.[33] From 1817 to 1824 Upper Canada's share of customs revenues from Lower Canada, except when nothing at all was paid, was equal to 20 per cent of receipts at Quebec. Using that proportion, it is possible to estimate Upper Canada's imports of goods paying ad valorem duties on the basis of totals at Quebec. Thus, Upper Canada's merchandise imports would have exceeded £300,000 in 1816, £130,000 in 1817, £190,000 in 1819, and £105,000 in 1821. These are minimum figures: they do not include imports of groceries and merchandise subject to duties different from the standard ad valorem rate (or subject to no duty), the cost of shipment from Quebec to Upper Canada, and imports from the United States. Upper Canadians contended too that they imported more per capita than Lower Canadians, and the province's share of total St Lawrence population was rising. When data on Upper Canadian imports as recorded at Coteau-du-Lac are again available in 1824–5, the province's imports of goods bearing ad valorem duties totalled £193,000 and £282,000 respectively (24 and 28 per cent of Quebec totals for the two years).[34]

At the higher of the prices used here to estimate their value, the province's 1817 wheat exports were nearly sufficient to pay for this minimum estimate of the cost of 1817 'merchandise' imports. But they look much less substantial when set against 1816 imports, for which, under usual credit terms, the province would have had to pay in 1817. And between 1817 and 1822 the value of wheat exports fell faster and farther than the total value of imports. In 1819 the imbalance was particularly evident. Imports increased, while wheat exports that year were exceptionally low; the equivalent of just 60,000 bushels, valued at about £20,000, went down to Montreal. Clearly external sales of Upper Canadian wheat were far from sufficient to pay for the province's imports.

There were other ways for the province to pay for its imports and debts. Potash, for example, continued to be a substantial contributor to the province's total export earnings (table 3.4). At prevalent prices, the 1817 exports of 5,000 barrels would, at 4.5 hundredweight to a barrel, have earned almost £50,000; the same volume in 1820 would have earned less than £30,000.[35] In years such as 1819–20 the value of Upper Canada's potash exports rivalled or exceeded that of wheat. Though data are lacking, it is evident that other forest products, particularly staves and timber, also made an important contribution to export earnings. And some pork was exported (table 3.4); its value would, however, have been much less than that of wheat or potash. Foreign exchange was earned through immigrants' capital and British government expenditures as well as by exports. Nevertheless, it is unlikely that other external earnings covered both annual imports and the legacy of occasional years when imports and exports were especially mismatched, notably 1816 and 1819.[36]

Before 1819, trends in import and export volumes and values, immigration, and commodity prices were sufficiently diverse and ambiguous that they could hardly be read by Upper Canadians as signs of the economic difficulties ahead. Not surprisingly, entrepreneurs and the provincial government – and doubtless many farmers – took on commitments that they would have increasing difficulty in carrying, especially when the economic crisis deepened in 1820. Anyone who assumed debts between 1815 and 1819 would have had problems in paying them off, or even in carrying them, at the exchange rates and the level of produce prices of 1821–2. One well-known case is that of William Hamilton Merritt, whose inability to pay his debts forced him to compromise with his Montreal creditors, who agreed to accept ten shillings to the pound – and was one factor in his subsequent promotion of the idea of a Welland Canal.[37] A major timber firm, the Hamilton Brothers of Hawkesbury, Quebec, and Liverpool, was similarly insolvent. Indeed, so was the government of Upper Canada. It could not sustain payment of militia pensions that the province's politicians had pledged in the aftermath of the war. Unable to force Lower Canada to pay it any customs revenue in 1820 and 1821, it began to interest itself in proposals to establish a chartered bank in Upper Canada. Seeking a way to meet his administration's routine payments and to protect public credit, Sir Peregrine Maitland decided to support the York-based group vying for control of a new Bank of Upper Canada, by having the government subscribe for 25 per cent of its shares.[38]

Wage rates and real wages are difficult to document fully. Rates of pay could be quoted by the day, month, or year; it is not always possible to be sure whether board and accommodation were part of a particular wage; there were seasonal variations in wages; and the intensity and security of work, and the opportunity also to work on their own account, could influence workers' willingness to accept a particular nominal wage. It was common, however, to speak of the wage for ordinary summer day labour in Upper Canada in 1817 as 5s ($1) a day; by 1822–3, 2s 6d per day was common.[39] In the ports of British North America there was much evidence in the early 1820s of extreme poverty, often of newly arrived immigrants who had used much or all of their capital simply to get to the new world. Only public charity kept some alive.[40] On the other hand, immigrants with capital or incomes paid in sterling, as in the case of half-pay military officers, could buy much more in Upper Canada for the same sterling amount in 1821–2 than just a few years earlier. In addition, the British economy was itself descending into depression, and there was much pressure on farmers, craftsmen, and labourers there. As a result, though emigration to the British North

American colonies fell substantially from the 1819 peak of 24,000, thousands continued to leave Britain even in the colonial economy's worst years (table 3.6).

British conditions were also important to the policy regimes that affected trade in two principal colonial exports. Under the 1815 Corn Law, when prices dropped below 67s per quarter (8s 5d stg per bushel), as was the case from 1821 onward, the British market was closed entirely; when it was above 80s, as in 1817–18, the preference for colonial wheat was not operative. In June 1822 the British government attempted to solve a number of Canadian problems, including Upper Canada's lack of public revenue and the obstruction in the Lower Canadian Assembly by nationalist politicians, by introducing an act to unite the two Canadas. Even before the extent of Canadian hostility to this bill could be felt in London, parliamentary opposition prevented its passage. But the British parliament did approve a portion of what had been proposed, in the form of the Canada Trade Act, which provided for determining and paying to Upper Canada a share of most duties at Quebec and set out regulations governing trade with the United States.[41]

The Corn Laws were also revised, and a new scale of preferential duties was established on colonial wheat and flour. Even under these duties, when wheat was under 59s per imperial quarter in Britain, as it was in 1821–3, colonial wheat was barred. In all these revisions to the Corn Laws, domestic and to a degree European conditions shaped British public debate and political choices; colonial preferences were subordinate to such larger considerations and had little impact on the main decisions. Thus, although wheat has usually been seen as a staple exported from Upper Canada to the United Kingdom, the reality is that under the Corn Laws colonial producers could not count on their wheat being admissible there, at least until revisions to the Corn Laws in 1827 and 1828 removed the provision of a minimum price below which imports of all kinds were essentially prohibited.[42] Furthermore, except in years of high British prices, transport costs were a barrier to transatlantic shipment of wheat. Fortunately for Upper Canada, there were at least markets in Lower Canada.[43] Preferential duties favouring colonial timber likewise came under pressure during this period of sharp deflation. There were parliamentary inquiries into the duties in 1820 and 1821, and the preference on square timber was lowered to 45s per load–enough, it soon was clear, to sustain the colonial operators' trades.[44]

By 1822 the basic imperial policies that would govern until the 1840s were in place. As prices fell and Upper Canada returned to indebtedness, the characteristic economic structures of the pre-war years were likewise restored. It is for this reason that the apparent prosperity of the war years should be seen essentially as an interlude. As wheat exports fell to the lower end of the longer-term range in price and income generated per capita, the provincial economy could still sustain a rapidly growing population and the investment process of extensive rural development. Other exports and capital imports helped in the process, as did farmers' sales in local markets. The establishment of a new financial institution, the Bank of Upper Canada, and the first stages in the promotion of a major new transportation facility, the Welland Canal, were other creative responses to adversity. For the next thirty years the provincial economy would develop along the lines already established, at rates of population growth and land clearing already indicated, and with economic fluctuations that reflected the province's links with a wider world. Commodity exports, to which we now turn, were among those links, but by no means the whole story.

*Part Two:*
*Extensive Growth, 1822–51*

# 4 Forest Products and Upper Canadian Development, 1822–46

One legacy of the war years that survived the adjustments of the early 1820s was the British system of preferential duties on colonial timber. Indeed, one of the best-known stories in Canadian economic history is how Napoleon, by successfully if briefly imposing the continental system, called into being the British North American timber staple.[1] By causing Britain to increase tariff preferences to foster the colonial timber trade, he created an 'artificial' new industry, which nevertheless stimulated the development of the North American colonies. Timber became the leading export from Upper and Lower Canada and New Brunswick, and it is argued that its demand for eastbound shipping left excess westbound freight capacity and thereby permitted the massive migration from Britain and Ireland that peopled the colonies. First developed seventy years ago by A.R.M. Lower, this story has gone largely unchallenged, though it has been deepened and modified in detail, particularly by local and regional studies.[2] Its essential implication is that wars and policy decisions far from Canada created 'the great staple of Canadian trade for much of the 19th century' and thus caused a major part of nineteenth-century Canadian economic development.[3]

Paradoxically, the belief that such a stimulus was essential to Canadian economic growth has not affected the widely held Canadian belief that Canada had a comparative advantage in natural products. But if the latter was true, imperial policy, while possibly helpful, was not the key to resource development in Canada. Lower was ambivalent on the point.

An earlier version of this chapter was published as 'Forest Products and Upper Canadian Development, 1815–46,' *CHR* 68 (1987), 159–98. I am grateful to the University of Toronto Press for permission to reprint material here. Minor variations from the quantitative data published there result from a comprehensive recalculation of the various estimates.

Although he emphasized the trade's legislative history, he contended that by the early 1820s the Canadian timber trade did not really need all the protection that it began with, whatever the interests involved contended. The trade survived both the tariff reductions made then and subsequent cuts, including the entire removal of the duties after the 1840s.[4]

Another central theme in Canadian economic history has been the divergence in types of development associated with different staple products. For timber, Lower stressed British metropolitan power: 'a staple trade such as the timber trade is essentially an exploitative trade and in it the dice are loaded in favour of the metropolis.' Graeme Wynn has likewise seen the trade as fostering a type of 'dependent' development in New Brunswick.[5] Along the upper Ottawa River, in northern Quebec and Ontario, and in hinterland British Columbia as well, wood has been associated less with stable long-term local economic progress than with subordination to extra-regional urban centres, continued dependence on the forest, and vulnerability to volatile or declining external demand and the local exhaustion of the resource.

These considerations frame our analysis of the timber economy of southern Upper Canada, which avoided such dependency and was, with the Montreal region, becoming Canada's economic heartland. Usually this area's growth has been explained as a function of wheat rather than wood,[6] but prior to at least 1840, and even excluding the Ottawa valley, the value of Upper Canada's exports of forest products was probably at least as great as its exports of wheat and flour. In addition, well over half of the Ottawa valley's output came from the Upper Canadian side, and Bytown, the region's principal urban centre, was in Upper Canada. To understand the economic development of the province and its evolution from periphery to core, therefore, it is necessary to take account of forest products.

Even in the 1790s, long before the war-era timber duties were imposed, we have seen that Upper Canada was exporting barrel staves and potash. Moreover, before the timber duties were imposed, Upper Canada's population and rate of land-clearing were growing at the same rate as they would in the forty years that followed imposition of the duties. Only on the Ottawa River was there a close correlation between the duties and the beginning of significant forest exploitation. But if the duties were perhaps essential to the Ottawa trade, it is important in understanding their impact to assess how growth there fostered development elsewhere in Upper Canada.

To analyse the role of wood products in nineteenth-century Upper Canadian development, it is necessary to review the evidence on volumes and values of principal wood products, and the links from them to the wider economy. We cannot simply assume, for example, that in years when timber constituted up to 80 per cent of provincial exports, it was central to the income of 80 per cent of Canadians or Upper Canadians, directly or indirectly. Suitable quantitative information on the industry in Upper Canada first becomes available early in the 1820s; 1845–6 was the peak of the trade to that time. Thereafter, substantial sawn lumber exports to the United States began to develop; the story after 1846 is, however, left to chapter 12.

## I. *Forest Products Prices*

To develop consistent data for output and exports is no easy task, even for an industry that generated much public information. Data on exports from Quebec cannot be related specifically to Upper Canada. Within Upper Canada, data do not always permit distinguishing Upper Canadian from American timber on the St Lawrence.[7] For the Ottawa, it would be artificial to attempt to separate Upper from Lower Canadian data, but it is essential to know what territory is referred to by particular data. Some are available only for one side of the river, some only for the river above Bytown, many only for timber produced on crown land, and some for the entire river valley. The largest gap is for the Ottawa valley below Bytown.

Forest products were exported in so wide a variety of sizes and forms that we may question whether they were a single staple at all. Besides square timber, on which the story has tended to focus, exports from the province's forests included deals (thick planks), barrel staves of different sizes (for example, West Indies, standard, and pipe), boards, and pot and pearl ashes. The terminology for volumes included cubic (length x width x thickness) and board (length x width only) measure; a 'load' was 50 cubic feet, and a 'ton' was 40 cubic feet. A 'piece' of timber might be anywhere from 34 (in the case of oak in the early years) to 60, 70, or more cubic feet (in the case of white pine and oak in later years).[8] The designation M in reference to cubic or board feet meant 1,000, but a *mille* of staves was equivalent to 1,200 pieces of standard dimensions. The 'St Petersburgh standard' for deals was 120 deals equivalent to 12 feet long x 11 inches wide x 1¹/₂ inches thick, while the 'Quebec standard' was 100 deals of similar length and breadth, but 2¹/₂ inches thick, so that there was almost 40 per cent more wood in a 'standard hundred' of Quebec deals.[9] Potash was shipped in barrels which usually weighed from over 4 to about 6 hundredweight;[10] the somewhat more refined pearl ash was shipped in slightly smaller barrels, about 3.3 hundredweight.

Many published data, including those for exports at Quebec, do not distinguish between white and red pine, but a piece of the former was typically almost twice as large as one of the latter. Red carried a much higher price per cubic foot than the more celebrated white pine until at least 1850. Oak and barrel staves made of oak were major products which are often underestimated in secondary sources. In some areas, elm was an important output.

To bring all these products to a common base, it is necessary to have appropriate price series. Although graphs of prices have been published for some commodities, they do not permit extraction of prices for particular products in particular years, and sources are not listed.[11] Close reading of any timber merchant's correspondence can bring one to wonder whether quality variations were so substantial that tight and consistent price series cannot be created.[12] To accept that conclusion would, however, render it impossible to arrive at the larger assessment of the timber economy that is needed. Hence the first task is to assemble as consistent a series as possible for the leading items in Upper Canada's timber economy (table 4.1). If no Quebec price was found, a Montreal price has been used when available; the ash trade, in fact, focused at Montreal, not Quebec. Disappointing gaps remain, but the table permits approximation of values where data on volumes exist. Given all these considerations, the data should be read essentially as orders of magnitude for the various dimensions of the industry.

## II. Exports

Although the Ottawa River trade is now more celebrated, the majority of the province's forest product exports passed down the St Lawrence in every year before the early 1840s (table 4.2). Indeed, even in the peak years of the mid-forties, the St Lawrence carried virtually as much timber by value as came from the Ottawa above Bytown. The leading item by value in the St Lawrence trade was typically pot and pearl ashes, made by boiling hardwood house and field ashes to a salt. Their volume rose through the 1820s and, except for 1834 and 1836, remained relatively steady throughout the 1830s. Squared oak timber was the leading product by value in 1825 and 1839, but except in these years and 1846, more oak was exported in the form of barrel staves, principally 'standard' (conventional dimensions 5½ feet long by 1½ inches wide) or 'West Indies' (shorter staves of less than 2½ feet long).[13] Also important was white pine, exported chiefly as timber and to some extent as deals.

The data on volumes, if 1845 and 1846 are excluded, do not show marked growth across the entire period. Volumes of all items except ashes reached substantial peaks at some point in the early or middle 1820s. For square oak and pine the 1820s peak was higher than for any year in the 1830s save the peak year (1839 for the former, 1836 for the latter). The 1830s saw considerable fluctuation in volumes and a lack of close correlation in the patterns of the various products. In 1845 or 1846 all products but deals reached new peaks in response to high British demand and perhaps the impending reduction of timber preferences.[14]

To estimate their collective scale, these volumes need to be brought to a common base by estimating their value (table 4.3). By combined value, there was a marked peak in exports of wood products in 1825, a return to this level in 1830, then a decline until 1834. Of all the data in table 4.2, those for 1835 seem most likely to be exaggerated,[15] but it is clear that values in the 1835–9 period recovered to a level at or above that of 1830. Although data are lacking, values fell back in the early 1840s, but attained new heights in 1845–6.

When the value of all such exports from the St Lawrence–Great Lakes area of Upper Canada is compared to that of wheat and flour, the other leading export in the period, it is evident that in most years forests generated at least as much income as wheat, despite the common image of the province as one dependent on a wheat staple. Over the twelve years from 1828 to 1839 there was a rough equality in the value of each, and wheat clearly exceeded wood products by value only in 1831, 1834, and 1836.[16] The data in table 4.3 also make clear how much more of the province's wood exports came down the St Lawrence than the Ottawa. When exports along the latter are added, the case for forest products' relative pre-eminence as a provincial export is strengthened.

It is tempting to see the St Lawrence timber industry as essentially a by-product of land-clearing. But the high total value of such products; the fact that volumes fluctuated in a period when assessment data indicate a relatively steady rate of land-clearing, and evidence of localization and specialized production and marketing all suggest that these were products in their own right, produced in response to perceived relative costs and opportunities. Nor can we assume that equivalent forest cover in different areas was exploited in identical fashion.

The ash trade, often seen as the classic settlement by-product, remained important in eastern regions of the province long after that area's initial period of settlement. Although there was an ash trade of some consequence from the west in the 1820s, ash exports fell sharply in the 1830s, as settlement and clearing went rapidly forward (see table 4.4 for ash shipments through the Welland Canal).[17] Even sixty years after land-clearing in the region began, elm timber came largely from the St

Lawrence and Lake Ontario area. So did white pine, produced in shanties along the various large and small streams that mark that region.[18] The first peak in oak timber and stave exports, in the 1820s, likewise came from the Lake Ontario and St Lawrence region.

After the opening of the Welland Canal, oak was increasingly likely to come from above Niagara Falls. In 1839 at least one-third of the oak and one-fifth of the staves came from the western peninsula (tables 4.2 and 4.4). In 1844–6, over 80 per cent of the oak sent down the St Lawrence from Upper Canadian sources came from there, as did three-quarters of the West Indies staves and over 90 per cent of the standard staves. As wheat exports expanded rapidly in the late 1830s, over one-third of the value of exports from the relatively remote and apparently wheat-oriented western peninsula consisted of wood and its products (table 4.4C).

Production in the upper Ottawa valley focused heavily on red pine. The data do not all derive from identical territory, but patterns are suggested by the series that make up table 4.5 and by revenue data from the Bytown timber agency (table 4.6). As along the St Lawrence, there was a sharp peak in output in 1830–1. A new plateau for red pine was reached from 1835 to 1838. Total volumes from the upper Ottawa reached a further peak in 1840–1, fell back, then rose dramatically until the mid-1840s. By then, as a result of the extraordinarily rapid rise in production of white pine, which only now became the characteristic Ottawa valley timber, output was about three times the 1838–9 level. A severe setback ensued, but although red pine production tended to decline, output of white pine surpassed 1845–6 levels as early as 1852. Over the entire period, helped by the rise of the white pine trade, there was a more definite rising trend to output than along the St Lawrence. Data are unfortunately too limited to permit assessment of the early years of the lower Ottawa trade in elm, oak, and ashes; all were produced (see table 4.5D for elm and oak), but not in volumes to rival those from the more extensive hardwood forests along the St Lawrence system.[19]

III. *Forests and Development: The St Lawrence*

The implications for regional development of export earnings depended not only on their amount but on where and how that income was spent.[20] If, for example, most inputs needed to produce the export had to be imported, and the income did not develop local assets that could be used later for other purposes, the impact of export-generated income was less than if the local economy both supplied inputs and built its long-term productive powers by so doing. It is important, therefore, to consider how local forest product economies functioned and how funds generated by exports flowed through the provincial system. Here it is convenient to consider the two main regions, the St Lawrence and the Ottawa, separately. Because prices used in valuations in the tables are from the export ports, data on values tend to overstate the Upper Canadian income directly produced by forest product exports.

Evidence on the forest economy is most readily found in documents created by the campaigns to defend the timber duties and to promote public investment in timber slides and other river improvements. Unfortunately, those who testified had every incentive to exaggerate the significance of their industry. Throughout this chapter, accordingly, private accounts and extrapolations from them are used. Even on generous assumptions, the evidence of actual purchases, sales, and output seldom supports numbers as high as those usually cited in the public documents.

Because timber's bulk in relation to its value gave it a high freight factor (that is, a high proportion of final cost was attributable to transportation costs), transportation costs were one determinant of locational patterns. Those delivering staves somewhere on Lake Ontario could in the mid-1840s expect to receive no more than half to two-thirds of the price in Quebec. In 1848, not a year of unusually high rates, the lake shipping rate on square oak from Chatham to Garden Island, at the head of the St Lawrence, was 6d per cubic foot, at a time when the Quebec price was around 15d.[21] Clearly a substantial proportion, probably at least half in the case of oak, of the wood-generated income recorded in table 4.3 went initially to a small segment of the provincial economy – those who moved rather than made the timber. The other half sustained oak production as far west as Chatham. The timber industry was in fact the largest single user of the Upper Canadian schooner fleet.[22] If it is assumed that half the 120 Upper Canadian sailing vessels in 1844 were required for timber movements[23] and that average crews were four men, then some two to three hundred sailors owed their incomes to wood shipments. To them must be added the men handling loading and transshipment in ports, the shipbuilders, and the raftsmen on the St Lawrence. Some of the crews, labourers, and facilities were available for other purposes, of course, and the oak trade also helped meet the overhead costs of facilities such as the Welland Canal.

The stave business, despite its large total scale, could be conducted by farmers on a part-time basis. Between February and April 1847, for example, the Napanee agent for the Calvin firm of Garden Island took delivery of 142 lots of staves with a total value of about £200, delivered by sixty-eight individuals. Of these, only eleven earned more than £5 from staves and only one earned more than £10. The mean value per individual over the season was £2 16s.[24] Stave-making here was a winter occupation, part of the seasonal cycle in which farmers and labourers earned their year's income. In years of peak stave volumes, however, it is impossible to account for all the staves exported in terms of modest deliveries by farmers; staves could also be produced on rather larger scale in shanties operated by contractors and subcontractors.[25]

A similar story can be told for potash. Making it could be organized as a winter activity by a merchant who owned or rented the necessary kettles. By buying the house and field ashes of neighbouring farmers, he could obtain a supply of raw material to keep a man occupied for some months in ash-boiling.[26] The average farmer was unlikely to earn more than a few dollars per year by ash sales, but those who delivered ashes obviously valued the income.[27] Later it became common for farmers either to boil their own ashes or to have them done on commission. One Perth area firm, for example, handled up to 450 barrels of potash per year in the 1840s, principally consigned in lots of one or two barrels by hundreds of men, most with country addresses. The 146 barrels of potash received between November 1843 and June 1844 came from 109 different consigners, including one, apparently a merchant, who alone consigned 17 barrels. For all but a handful, their ashes in this season earned them in the order of £5 or £6, the net price of 5 or 6 hundredweight of potash sold in Montreal.[28]

These sectors of the forest economy were thus integrated into the rural economy where they were appropriate in terms of forest cover, alternative local opportunities, and transportation costs. Whether staves and ashes were mainly produced by farmers themselves or by contractors and labourers, local agriculture and local wood production could reinforce one another.[29] This must also have been true for oak timber-making, for oak came from forests on or near farms and potential farmland. Before 1850, even pine shanties in this region were not far from farms.[30] For the St Lawrence forest economy, it is reasonable to assign the large majority of income from forest products to inputs that could be supplied from within the economy. For all but ashes, about half the income was likely paid for transportation. As we shall see in chapter 5, the proximity of forest and farm (indeed most farms included much forest) sustained a local economy of some complexity, offering numerous choices, to those with and without land, and helping local economies to make fullest use of their land and labour.

IV. *Forests and Development: The Ottawa Valley*

Unlike the St Lawrence, the Ottawa valley had no other exports besides forest products, and here the growth of settlement and the rise of the timber economy were closely linked. On the other hand, because one test of dependence on a staple export is what happens when it ceases, it is important to recall that farmers in fertile areas in the valley would later adapt as timber declined. In parts of the lower valley there would have been mixed forest and farm development such as occurred in Upper Canada's Eastern District even if the larger-scale upper Ottawa timber economy had not come into being.[31] Farther up the valley and back from the river, a different and more dependent pine economy took shape. It is this economy that is best documented by data here (table 4.5). Without timber production, much of this region would simply not have been exploited. But how its growth affected the entire valley and the rest of Upper Canada needs fuller analysis.

The Upper Canadian side of the valley consisted essentially of the counties that made up the Ottawa and Bathurst districts (and, from 1842, the Dalhousie District). Over the twenty-six years from 1825 to 1851 this region's population grew at somewhat over 7 per cent a year, almost exactly the annual rate of population growth for Upper Canada as a whole in the same quarter-century. That is, during the rapid rise of the valley timber economy, the valley maintained its share of provincial population, but did not grow faster. The valley's experience contrasted with that of the longer-established Eastern and Johnstown districts along the St Lawrence, which saw their share of provincial population fall between 1825 and 1841 from 20 to 15 per cent.[32]

As on the St Lawrence, a significant proportion of the delivered price of Ottawa timber was for freight, though that was less apparent in that the timber was typically brought downriver by men who had made it. Because timber was sometimes bought and sold at Bytown, it is possible to indicate the freight factor. In 1824–6, for example, Philemon Wright purchased red and white pine, oak, elm, and staves at Bytown; in no case was the price higher than 75 per cent of known or probable Quebec prices, and often, for hardwood especially, it was closer to half. Thus staves were purchased for £24 when the Quebec price was almost £48 and oak at 7d to 10d per foot in 1825 when the quoted Quebec price was 19d, and the Wrights were actually getting 15d to 18d on sales.[33]

One of the central claims for the timber duties was their large direct impact on employment. In 1835, for example, seven to eight thousand raftsmen were said to be employed on the Ottawa.[34] To assess that claim, it is necessary to estimate the industry's labour requirements. As we have seen, where production was closely integrated with other dimensions of the rural economy – where it was carried on in or near established agricultural settlements, as in parts of the lower Ottawa valley and in areas of the St Lawrence–Great Lakes – it could supply some of a man's yearly work and income. But where larger-scale production was entailed and in remoter areas, timber-making actually required relatively long-term employment for winter production and summer transportation. It is thus convenient to estimate labour demand in 'full-time' equivalents.

One way to assess the demand for labour is by its output. A wide variety of figures is offered on typical output per man per winter season. A commonly reported annual output is 3,000 cubic feet of square timber per man, though figures ranging from 1,200 to 4,000 or more are met.[35] The higher figures may well apply only to actual physical output by timber-makers and neglect many others whose work was essential to the timber firm. A figure in the middle of this range is least likely to lend an extreme bias to conclusions. Output per man of 2,500 feet is also indicated by a calculation in the Wright Papers that thirty barrels of pork (and fifty of flour) were needed to produce 60,000 feet of red pine near Mattawa, high up the Ottawa, and deliver it to Quebec.[36] At standard rations (one pound of meat per person a day),[37] and if it is assumed that it would require the equivalent of nine months of steady work (for example, from 1 November to 31 July) for a crew to make and deliver such timber, then about one and one-third barrels of pork would be needed per man, and something like twenty-three or twenty-four men could be fed with these rations. That Wrights' rafts often measured around 60,000 feet, and had crews of between twenty and twenty-five, tends to confirm that a reasonable output figure is 2,500 feet per man.[38]

At this rate, to produce an annual average of 3.8 million feet of timber on both sides of the upper Ottawa in 1835–9 (table 4.5) would have required about 1,500 men, not 7,000 or 8,000. To be able to estimate an Ottawa force of raftsmen of the latter size, we need to go ahead a decade to the industry's peak and to include, as the estimate noted above did, the whole valley. To produce about 20 million feet as in 1845–6 (table 4.5C) would have taken over 8,000 workers. Before the 1840s it is doubtful if the valley needed even half that number in its shanties and on its rafts in a single year. Along the St Lawrence 52,000 pieces of white pine were sent down in 1836, by far the peak year before the mid-1840s; they would have equalled about 3.6 million feet and might likewise have required the equivalent in full-time work of about 1,500 men to produce. That is, all the square pine produced on both sides of the upper Ottawa and along the St Lawrence in 1836 could have been produced by about 3,000 workers.[39] This was equivalent to less than 3 per cent of the men over sixteen years of age in the province that year; the Ottawa segment was equivalent to about one-sixth of the men over sixteen on the Upper Canadian side of the valley in the mid-1830s.

Another way to consider the scale of the timber workforce is to examine labour costs and wage rates. Worker accounts present a complex picture. Some men worked for years for the same employer, while others worked only casually or briefly. Some served both as employees and suppliers or contractors. A single firm might have as many as fifteen distinct wage rates, and the same worker might be paid at different rates in different seasons. Some drew advances on pay, while others with continuing associations with a firm drew only a part of what was due them. Even so, some conclusions can be drawn. Wages made up one-quarter of the direct operating costs (interest and profits were not recorded in this statement) of one firm in 1859, although the manner in which expenses were recorded suggests this to be a lower bounded figure.[40] On this basis, we might estimate a range for total wages paid in the industry by reckoning them as between one-quarter and one-third of total revenue generated. For square timber on the upper Ottawa in 1835–8, when revenue averaged £113,000 per year, the estimated wage bill would fall between £28,000 and £38,000. For most workers, monthly wages in the shanties and on the rafts in the 1820s and 1830s were between £2 and £3;[41] the lower figure, £28,000, would support payments of £2 10s per month to 1,250 men for nine months, and the higher figure, £38,000, would allow such payments to 1,700 men. Earlier we estimated that no more than 1,500 men were working in the upper Ottawa industry in 1835–8; at £2 to £3 per month for nine months per man, they would have earned £27,000 to £41,000 in total wages in a year.

Such data can be manipulated in many ways, but none lead to a figure of over 7,000 raftsmen on the river in 1835. It is best to see this figure as largely exaggerated, aimed at justifying government investment in river improvements and preservation of the timber duties. For present purposes it is sufficient to conclude that between one-quarter and one-half of the total revenues generated by the square timber trade along the Ottawa went into wages, including the wages of the raftsmen on the Ottawa taking the timber to Quebec.

The winter focus of work in the woods (if not transport) made it apparently complementary to agriculture, and we have seen that only a small proportion of the adult men in Upper Canada would have been needed for the shanties. Nevertheless, Lower Canadian labour was essential to Upper Canadian production. The valley's links by water to Lower Canada and its need for summer labour on the rafts to Quebec made Lower Canada the principal source of migrant workers.[42] Names of French origin made up almost 90 per cent of the more than 230 worker accounts recorded over eight years in one Philemon Wright account book and almost 60 per cent of the 187 in another.[43] That the Wright operations were conducted on the Lower Canada side of the river is unlikely to have made them unrepresentative of the valley as a whole.

For example, in another firm's records, from the Upper Canadian side, twenty of thirty-nine names were French. Probably not all were seasonal migrants, but most undoubtedly were.[44] Even along the St Lawrence, many shanty and river workers were migrant Lower Canadian workers.[45] It is difficult to calculate precisely the role of French Canadians in the entire Upper Canadian pine economy, but it was large. And there may also have been seasonal Irish labourers from Lower Canada involved on the Ottawa. It is reasonable to estimate that at least half the workers in pine shanties and on the rivers came from Lower Canada.

Such men spent part of their wages in Upper Canada, but worker accounts indicate that most took money home when they finished work for the year. Even men who finished work with nothing due them had sometimes had money remitted earlier to families at home. Of 269 accounts in one Wright employee ledger that can conveniently be analysed (for work of varying durations from a few weeks to some cases of a year or more in the 1832–40 period), thirty-four men finished with a debit balance or with nothing due them; 114 had credit balances of less than £10; eighty were owed £10 to £20; and forty-one had credit balances exceeding £20.[46] For the entire group, the mean credit was £12; the mean falls to £8 if we eliminate the extremes (that is, the five with debit balances and the thirty with credits exceeding £25). Almost identical proportions are indicated by similar accounts from 1825. In years such as 1835–9, when there were at least 750 Lower Canadian workers on the upper Ottawa, a minimum of £7,500 in earnings would have been paid and spent not in Upper but in Lower Canada, mainly outside the valley.

Along with wages, the timber industry's expenses included the equiping and provisioning of shanties. In one case from 1859, one-third of total timber production costs was required for these purposes.[47] If this proportion was standard, we could conclude that for the upper Ottawa in 1835–9 a maximum of under £40,000 was required for shanty and raft provisioning and equipment.

The components of shanty diets were universal: basic weekly rations in the Hamilton Brothers operations were seven pounds each of pork and flour, a pound each of butter and sugar, and one-sixth of a pound of tea; sometimes codfish (2$^1$/2 pounds) and potatoes ($^1$/4 bushel) were also included.[48] This ration was valued in 1820 at 10s per man a week. Large-scale operations are often said to have imported many of their provisions from outside the province,[49] thus reducing the local impact of timber-earned income. There was no reason to import potatoes or wheat from outside the province, and Upper Canada usually had a surplus of pork in these years. Accounts often show locally produced as well as imported pork being purchased for shanties.[50] Tea, sugar, and cod aside, most of the food consumed in the shanties in Upper Canada came from within the province. By the Hamiltons' figures, 80 per cent of provisions costs were for items available within Canada.

Such costs can be estimated in greater detail and from another angle by again using the Wrights' estimate of thirty barrels of pork and fifty of flour for 60,000 feet of timber. At this rate (assuming white pine required equivalent labour input per foot), the average of 3.8 million feet of timber produced per year on the upper Ottawa in 1835–9, would have required 1,900 barrels of pork and 3,200 barrels of flour. To this direct shanty and raft demand needs to be added that from Bytown itself and from the lower Ottawa timber industry.[51] That such figures are realistic is indicated by William Stewart, a leading figure in the Bytown supply business, who sold almost 1,700 barrels of pork during the winter of 1835–6.[52] By comparison with 1835–9 average annual pork and flour exports from Upper Canada down the St Lawrence (table 4.2), the volume of pork and flour directly required by timber provisioning equalled no more than one-fifth of the former and 3 per cent of the latter. Moreover, some of the pork may have been American and some of both commodities came from near or within the valley.[53] Clearly the timber business was so small a source of demand for the flour that Upper Canadians produced for sale outside the immediate region of production as not to be of major importance in the wheat economy.[54] Timber-based demand was perhaps more significant to the province-wide pork trade.

At prevalent prices in 1836–7, which were at the high end of the range for the decade, the pork would have been valued as high as £5 per barrel and the flour at £2 10s at Bytown.[55] Thus the maximum value of estimated annual direct requirements for the upper Ottawa before 1840 would have been £9,500 for pork and £8,000 for flour at Bytown. Even if all this pork came from Upper Canada outside the valley, such figures, which represent almost the only items that the rest of the province could supply to the Ottawa, seem modest in relation to average annual provincial exports along the St Lawrence of more than £400,000 in 1835–9.[56]

Shanties also needed draught animals, 'the ox team being the main spring of the business' as one participant put it.[57] If some of the draught animals were imported, a majority probably were Canadian bred, although not necessarily in the immediate region of production.[58] In 1833 the Wright shanties on the Gatineau had eleven yoke of oxen, valued at £220. A Calvin shanty in 1847 spent about £100 on the purchase of eight horses, including five at Coteau-du-Lac for £45 and three nearer the shanty for £18 to £20 each. Hamilton and Low anticipated needing fifteen ox teams in 1835–6 plus six span of horses for their five shanties on the Rouge River, a tributary of the lower Ottawa. Their horses were to move supplies, while the oxen, with some occasional assistance from the horses, were expected to haul a total of 17,500 logs of 12¹/₂ feet during the winter season. Those logs, destined for deal production, represented a minimum of 200,000 cubic feet.[59] To produce some 3.8 million cubic feet per year, as in 1835–9 on the upper Ottawa, might thus have required up to twenty times this number of animals, that is about 300 ox teams and 240 horses. At £20 per yoke and, say, £20 per horse, they would have had a total value of at most £11,000. Because such animals were capital, not all of this would have been required to be paid in one year. Tucker and Laflamme in 1859 hired two yoke of oxen for four and a half months at £1 5s each per month, during the peak months of industry demand for oxen. Even if the same rate had to be paid all year, the annual cost of 300 ox teams would then have been £4,500, much of it paid in the valley. Nor were such numbers large in proportion to local stocks of animals.[60]

To feed these animals during the winter, oats and hay were purchased or produced as close to shanties as possible. Little if any moved from one region of the province to another. Fodder represented a much smaller item in shanty budgets than did the men's food, as a variety of examples suggest. In 1833 the Wrights had 40 tons of hay worth £60 in one shanty. When the Hamilton partners reviewed stock on the Rouge River in the spring of 1834, they valued it at £808, of which oats and provender (500 bushels), clover, and hay (6 tons) represented the principal fodder on hand, with a total value of £135. One Calvin shanty in 1847 purchased about 750 bushels of oats (for £47) and 8¹/₂ tons of hay (£16) over a winter. The McLachlin timber firm ordered 1,000 bushels of oats (£200 delivered on the Madawaska) in January and February 1853. A shanty of the Boyd timber business in 1854–5 purchased 630 bushels of oats (£65) and about 8¹/₂ tons of hay (£31). Tucker and Laflamme in 1859 recorded the purchase of £55 worth of oats among shanty supplies totalling almost £700.[61] While none of these sources is comprehensive, each suggests that a shanty might require about £100 per winter in fodder.[62]

Of other requirements, ironware, rope, blankets, and some saddlery and textile items had to be imported; inputs such as wagons and sleighs could be supplied from within the province. Most were durable items, used over several years, and not a major cost in any one year. For example, only £18 of over £400 of Boyd shanty purchases in 1854–5 were for iron and hardware that likely originated beyond the province. Saddlery and blacksmiths' work represented £37 of the £375 recorded for the Calvin shanty in 1847, while another £53 was spent on sleighs, wagons, and repair.[63] Room, board, travel, and other expenses for partners and senior employees need also to be kept in mind in considering costs. They represented over £60 of the Calvin shanty expenses in 1847 and fully one-quarter of Tucker and Laflamme's 1859 expenses, for example. In all these ways, income generated by timber operations flowed on to others, largely located, in the case of the Ottawa, within the valley, in Lower Canada, and perhaps in adjacent counties along the St Lawrence.

Saw mill investment was claimed as another major consequence of the timber duties. Indeed, one of Canada's largest and most impressive industrial establishments was the Hamilton deal mill at Hawkesbury, on the lower Ottawa. Built shortly after the Napoleonic Wars at a cost of over £15,000, it was said in the mid-1830s to be worth £20,000, and capable of producing 300,000 deals per year. At current prices, these could have earned over £20,000. The logs the firm expected to harvest in 1835–6 would have yielded no more than 150,000 deals, but the firm often bought logs as well. If it produced at capacity, its output alone would have equalled as much as one-sixth of total Quebec deal exports in the 1830s.[64] In the 1840s, when prices for deals of highest quality reached new heights, valley output increased sharply, reaching almost one million pieces in 1845 (table 4.5D). If all that production were of top quality (an unlikely condition, as deals were floated to Quebec), this output would have earned a maximum of £114,000 in Quebec in 1845 (table 4.1), a figure equal to the value of one-quarter of upper Ottawa pine exports in that year. By 1847 the valley had twelve deal mills, with twenty-four gangs of saws, capable of producing 2.5 million deals per year (or four times actual 1846 output); by then, the Hamilton mill alone claimed a capacity of 600,000 deals per year. Had such outputs been achieved, the Ottawa by itself could have supplied virtually all the exports from Quebec in the mid-1840s.[65] Thus capacity figures almost certainly much overstated normal outputs. Capital figures were also inflated: in 1854, for example, George Hamilton Jr claimed that the Hawkesbury establishment was worth £75,000, whereas his accounts show that he currently valued it at £35,000.[66]

During the 1820s and 1830s the St Lawrence region of the province also exported deals, which in total may not have equalled the value of production at Hawkesbury alone. Such exports came from fifty or more relatively small mills, with an average value of not much over £1,000 each and found as far west as the Trent River.[67] Here, whatever we make of the suspect data for 1835, there was no real growth trend in exports. Overall, even with the exceptionally large Hamilton mill included, deal production represented a relatively small part of the total forest industry in Upper Canada, and in terms of the total scale of the forest economy or of the entire provincial economy, its fixed capital investments, made over many years, were likewise relatively modest.

The final input to the industry consisted of the trees themselves. There seems no evident way to value those taken from private land. A royalty was applicable on crown lands after the mid-1820s, at the rate of ¹/₂d per foot of white pine, 1d for red, and 1¹/₂d for oak, payable on a bond due at Quebec when the timber arrived there. Thus dues represented about one-eighth of the typical sale price of pine and somewhat less for oak. With the exception of 1831 and 1832, when gross revenues at the Belleville timber agency exceeded £1,000, the sums derived by government from timber coming down the St Lawrence were modest before 1840. For the upper Ottawa, however, the duties were much larger, amounting to almost £8,000 in 1831 and more than that from 1836 onward (table 4.6). Net of administrative costs of between £500 and £800 per year, these royalties passed eventually to the credit of the provincial government at Toronto. Together with the net value of pork and flour purchased from elsewhere in Upper Canada, they represented the only substantial direct linkages from the valley timber economy to the economy of that part of Upper Canada west of Kingston, where the province's development focused by the 1830s. In total, the three items equalled at most £25,000 per year in 1835–9, and less before then.[68]

## V. Wood in the Local Economy

An often neglected aspect of the forest economy is the domestic lumber and wood trade. Saw mills were actually more numerous in Upper Canada than grist mills. A leading foundry in 1827 estimated that 'the castings for a circular saw ... would cost something like $300,' and an entire 'country' mill could be built (or an existing one adapted) for as little as £100 to £200.[69] Such mills sawed timber into boards of many kinds for local building.

It is necessary to estimate the scale of this sector of the forest economy. The local saw mill of Philemon Wright produced from 14,000 to 25,000 board feet of lumber per month in the spring and summer of 1827. That of Alexander McNeilledge, in Norfolk County, was producing about 20,000 feet per month in the spring of 1828, and had annual output in 1830–2 of 130,000 to 160,000 feet.[70] Prices of lumber varied according to shapes, sizes, and types of boards and lumber. If we credit an average local saw mill with output worth £100 per year (that is, 48,000 board feet at 1/2d per foot),[71] the 425 mills in the province in 1826 would have produced £42,000 in lumber, and the 672 in 1832 would have produced £67,000. The comparisons are notional, but the former figure was equal to the value of wheat exports in 1825 and the latter to the value of upper

Ottawa pine exports in 1831 (table 4.3). Their collective value and output would have exceeded those of the province's deal mills, including the large Hamilton Brothers mill, in the same period. Such calculations are hypothetical, and meant to indicate that country mills, while individually modest, added up collectively to a significant component of the provincial economy.

The other major commercial product of the domestic wood economy was firewood.[72] By 1840 over thirty steamships plied Upper Canadian waters, including the Ottawa-Rideau system, and their demand for wood serves to illustrate that firewood was frequently traded in commercial volumes in local markets. One wharfinger in Hamilton required 1,000 cords of 'Good Steam Boat Wood' (worth £325) for the 1843 season. The steamer *Albion* averaged 50 to 60 cords per month (worth £18 to £20) in wood requirements at Picton, only one of its ports of call. If it took on equal amounts of wood at just one other port, it would have required £250 per year over a seven-month season. The steamer *Queenston*, on the Toronto-Hamilton run in 1834, spent £210 on wood.[73] If we allow for thirty to forty such ships, spending £200 to £250 per year, the market in steamboat wood would have totalled £6,000 to £10,000 per year.[74]

Given the rise of towns and cities, especially from the 1830s, the urban market needs also to be kept in mind. It has been estimated that American consumption of firewood in the years before 1860 was over four cords per person a year.[75] If we apply that estimate to Upper Canada, a colder and coal-less province, we may estimate total consumption of firewood as some one million cords in 1831, and double that a decade later. Much of this wood did not pass through the marketplace, being cut by country-dwellers for burning at home. But even if only 20 per cent of such consumption passed through the market, its value in 1831 would have been around £60,000. Such a figure is only an estimate, but it indicates that this sector of the wood economy involved total sales that rivalled those of local saw mills. As we have seen, up to half the value of provincial wood exports (as recorded in table 4.3) was attributable to transport costs; if the roughly £170,000 a year in wood exports along the St Lawrence in the early 1830s are discounted to make them reflect values near the point of production, their value and that of the two main domestic wood products sectors would not have been far apart. Certainly we would take note of export commodities that generated earnings equivalent to those attributable to sawmilling and cordwood.[76]

## VI. *Indirect Linkages*

It remains to consider indirect linkages between timber and the provincial economy as a whole. Perhaps the most important such connection is the trade's business structure. Some of the large British-based Quebec firms were relatively specialized in timber, while others were directly involved in other sectors of the economy. In either case, there were links through banking, steamshipping, etc. from timber to the wider business system, which was stronger and more complex for its forest dimensions. Timber exports undoubtedly helped sustain the credit and exchange by which the province's economic system was linked to the international economy. On the other hand, Montreal and Toronto, both much less directly involved in the trade than Quebec and Bytown, were the emerging metropolitan centres of the province.

A second indirect link from forests to the Upper Canadian economy was that the wages and profits earned from the Upper Canadian trade by those resident in Lower Canada might have helped Lower Canada to buy more from Upper Canada. But because Lower Canada actually did not buy much from Upper Canada for local consumption except wheat and some pork, whisky, and butter, only a small part of the wages and profits earned there from the trade would have flowed directly and immediately back to Upper Canada. Once spent by their initial recipients, Upper Canada–generated profits and wages merge into the general economic history of Canada and become difficult to distinguish specifically.

The most stressed indirect linkage, joining Napoleon to the forests and thence to provincial development, is timber's impact on immigration. But when timber interests argued that the unused westbound shipping capacity created by timber's bulk fostered emigration through very low westbound fares, they were appealing to an English audience that was presumed to be interested in encouraging pauper emigration. Despite their assertions, satisfactory empirical demonstration of the relationship has never been offered.[77]

The westward movement of emigrants actually correlated only quite imperfectly with eastbound timber shipping volumes, suggesting a weak relationship at best between migration and the physical movement of timber. The patterns are best shown in a comparison of the volume of British imports of timber from all of British North America (both square timber and the total of square timber and deals) with the number of British emigrants bound for British North America (figure 4.1). From 1815 to 1845 the trend in timber imports was generally rising, punctuated by downturns from 1825 to 1827, 1841 to 1842, and 1845 to 1847. From 1847 to 1850 British imports levelled off at volumes that remained higher than before 1845. The trend in British emigration figures was also upward, with extreme fluctuations around the trend. There were sharp peaks in 1819, 1831–2, 1842, and 1847, and deep troughs in 1824–5, 1835, and 1838. From 1820 to 1827 the two series moved in opposite

FIGURE 4.1
British Timber Imports from, and Emigration to, British North America, 1815–50

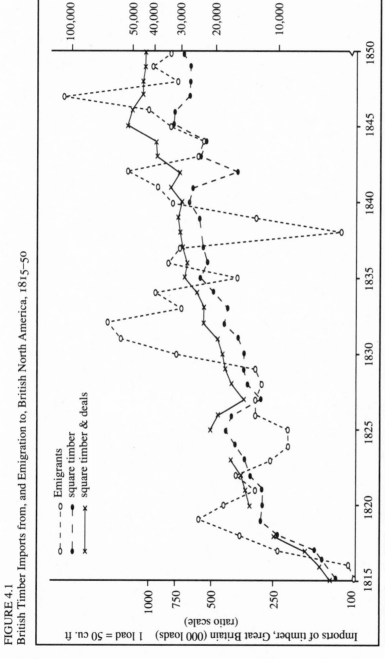

SOURCES: Sandra Gillis, 'The Timber Trade in the Ottawa Valley, 1805–54,' Parks Canada Manuscript Report Series 153, 305–7 (I have assumed a 'great hundred' of deals equalled 4.5 loads in converting data prior to 1842, but other rates do not alter the trends shown); Helen I. Cowan, *British Emigration to British North America: The First Hundred Years*, rev. ed. (Toronto 1961), 288

directions, the peak year for timber being the trough year for emigration. In the 1830s numbers of emigrants varied far more widely from year to year than did timber volumes. The peak years for emigration in the 1840s were 1842 and 1847, years in which timber volumes fell from the previous year.

United States timber did not benefit from the preferential duties. But after 1832, fluctuations in British emigration destined to British North America paralleled those for emigration to the United States; and absolute numbers destined to the latter continued to rise. The trend in British timber imports from Quebec once more moved upward in the 1850s, but emigration to the colonies did not; until 1854 the number of emigrants remained in the range established in 1848–50, then slid sharply to levels not seen since the late 1830s.[78] Meanwhile, British emigration to the United States was reaching unprecedented levels.

The most that low passage rates could do was bring migrants to a timber port; it took much more to keep them in a particular region. New Brunswick must have benefited equally from westbound excess capacity, but the population of that timber-oriented colony grew at only about half the rate of Upper Canada in the first half of the nineteenth century (see figure 1.1).[79] Costs of passage by various types of vessels must have been only a small factor in any migration decision. Thus, cheap freight rates to Quebec were no more than a necessary, not a sufficient, condition for provincial development. They were probably not even necessary for Upper Canadian development to be achieved by Loyalists and their descendants, by subsequent American immigrants, and by that portion of emigrants who travelled on ships other than timber vessels. Timber surely contributed to British North America's image as a place of opportunity, but the physical movement of it was just one, and hardly the most crucial, variable in the process.

## VII. *Conclusion*

When closely examined, the forest economy of Upper Canada cannot be summarized as a story of a single pre-eminent staple, squared pine timber. In the years before 1846 the province's forests yielded red and white pine, square oak and elm, sawn pine deals, pot and pearl ashes, oak staves, boards and building supplies, firewood, and assorted other wood products. Forest products probably accounted for at least half of all the province's export earnings between 1815 and 1840. Despite the scale of the forest economy, the claims for its significance made by those involved in the trade so consistently exaggerated its demand for capital, labour, and provisions that they are simply not to be trusted.

Instead, it is necessary to begin with known volumes and prices, then build a sense of that economy's proportions from micro-level evidence. In doing so, it is essential to include the domestic wood economy which, even at the minimum levels considered here, bears comparison with important components of the export sector.

For the upper Ottawa before 1840, we find from this perspective an industry that purchased provisions, labour, and animals from, and paid duties to, Lower and Upper Canada, but in amounts that were modest by comparison with overall outputs of either province.[80] Even at maximum possible levels, expenditures on duties and provisions, while important costs to those in the industry, seem too limited to have made the Ottawa valley timber industry a strong leading sector for development elsewhere in Upper Canada. This conclusion fully confirms the views of those who have seen the Ottawa as a separate kingdom. And nothing here suggests that the timber industry was not central to its economy.

Up the St Lawrence and as far west as Lake St Clair there was another Upper Canadian forest economy, based much more on hardwood than was that of the Ottawa, and exporting a variety of products. In considering the significance of the export income generated by St Lawrence wood products, it is important to recall that as much as half of it (as shown in tables 4.3 and 4.4C) went initially to the small segment of the population involved in moving the products to market. Had the industry suddenly contracted, this group would have felt the pinch most fully and immediately. In terms of the typically small marketable surpluses produced by most farmers,[81] the data might seem to suggest that, whether paid directly or indirectly, forest income represented the indispensable margin between success and failure for the provincial economy. But while forest-generated income was essential for some farmers, the evidence can be read differently, as indicating that the rural economy was broadly based and could have allocated scarce time and resources in other ways had markets made that more appropriate. From some areas, after all, little wood was exported, despite rapid ongoing clearing. And in the Ottawa valley and up the St Lawrence, migrant French-Canadian labour was essential to Upper Canadian production.

All the products exported down the St Lawrence were protected under the Napoleonic era duties, and the duties may thus appear very important in the development of the province. There is, however, reason not to overstate the claims for these duties as causal factors in provincial development. Most important is that ash and stave exports began under the tariff regime prevailing before 1800.[82] As well, Upper Canada's oak and white pine trades developed (or redeveloped, in the case of oak) very rapidly in the last years of the timber duties, and as we shall see in chapter 12, grew further in volume after the duties ended. White pine prices were actually higher in the 1850s than before. And the domestic markets for building supplies and firewood were affected by the timber duties only indirectly (that is, by their effects on the overall development of the economy).

These points suggest that, however important forest products were in the province's development, the preferential timber duties were not as indispensable as has often been assumed. They did not play an absolute role in creating a pioneer economy where none had or could have existed. We cannot know what an economy without the Napoleonic era timber preferences might have looked like.[83] But we can speculate that because of them, the Upper Canadian timber economy perhaps expanded sooner and in a different product mix than would otherwise have been the case. The upper Ottawa pinery in particular might have had a different history in a world without the timber duties, but even if no development had happened there, it is difficult to make a case that the want of some thousands of pounds per year in pork and flour sales and a similar amount in government revenues could have slowed the momentum of provincial development around Lake Ontario and in the western peninsula. Neither was timber on the Ottawa as essential as it has often been portrayed as a direct employer of men and generator of fixed capital. Particularly along the St Lawrence, it is highly likely that provincial forests would have contributed to growth whatever the course of the duties. There the close proximity of forest and farm made the production of wood and wood products an important element in the mix of activities that sustained a dynamic, balanced process of extensive rural development.

# 5 The Structure of Agriculture, 1821–51

Although forest products were significant sources of income to rural householders in many parts of the province, the majority of Upper Canadians depended on agriculture for their livelihood. The characteristic economic institution throughout the province was the individual family-owned and -operated farm.[1] Wheat was a major element in the income of such farms, and wheat exports have often been assumed to represent the most essential dimension of the Upper Canadian economy. But their peak in the mid-century decades coincided with the end of the province's most rapid population growth, and represented only a phase in the establishment of the rural economy. Until the 1840s the majority of wheat grown in the province was consumed there. And downriver wheat shipments in a number of years were destined mainly for consumption in Lower Canada; in the perspective of the larger Canadian economy, they were not really exports at all. From the farmer's viewpoint, wheat may always have been a staple crop, but prior to the 1840s it was not always a staple Canadian export.

By 1821 there were many well-established farms in areas of early settlement. Nevertheless, for thirty years the agricultural system continued to be dominated by extensive growth, made up of a combination of added acreage cultivated on older farms and the continuing establishment of new farms. Although much development was occurring, measures of per farm and per capita land use and output show little growth until the 1850s. Prior to that time, when the census first permits a sys-

Portions of the data and analysis of this chapter were first developed in my paper 'The Internal Economy of Upper Canada: New Evidence on Agricultural Marketing before 1850,' *Agricultural History* 59 (1985), 397–416, and reprinted in J.K. Johnson and Bruce Wilson, eds., *Historical Essays on Upper Canada: New Perspectives* (Ottawa 1989), 237–60. I am grateful to *Agricultural History* for permission to reprint such material.

tematic overview of the agricultural system, we have few comprehensive indicators of the farm economy. Fortunately, it is possible to extrapolate backward from the mid-century by using a variety of indicators of output and exchange.

## I. *Farm-making*

Making a farm entailed numerous choices in the farm family's use of time and money. The issues can be seen from the perspective of an immigrant who intended to farm. Much depended on his means and his family. Information about the new world, typically acquired from kin and present or past neighbours at home, had much to do with where the family went, at least initially, and how it proceeded. Those with sufficient capital or credit for at least a down-payment could buy a farm that had already been started, or that was already well developed. Others might only be able to afford poorer or remoter land or land that had yet to be cleared. Still others might need or prefer to rent land or even to work initially for someone else before seeking land of their own.[2] None of these strategies was certain to succeed. Transiency indicates both failure and adaptability on the part of the pioneers and their descendants.

It has been common to assume that settlers were hindered or exploited by both government land policy and private speculation. But whatever the intent of speculators and the possibility that speculation made any specific piece of land unavailable (including the crown and clergy reserves, which were a form of government speculation), there was a flourishing land market in the province. Credit was generally available to assist in financing land purchases.[3] Nor did the initial alienation of crown land remove such land from availability to farmers and settlers. Sometimes speculators intended to store wealth for the long term, but as most expected to earn money by selling land, there must usually have been a price at which they would sell any specific holding. The price of land has been seen as a function of its scarcity, as measured in a land-man ratio, for example.[4] But because a farm was intended to be an income-earning asset, land's price must more fundamentally have been related to expectations of its earning power than to any particular local scarcity of it. On the larger continental scale, which is ultimately the relevant one for an economy that was competing for immigrants with other areas of new settlement, land was in a sense still unlimited in supply in 1851.

Farm-making was a protracted, multi-generational process. Intending farmers were often informed that they could clear four or more acres a year, but aggregate rates tended to be considerably lower than that.[5] Land-clearing involved numerous steps, including removing underbrush, tree-felling, cutting or burning trees to shorter lengths, hauling them together, piling, and burning.[6] And land-clearing was only one of the investments the family had to make. It had also to maintain and improve already cleared land, such as by stump removal and fencing; and to invest money and work in construction, extension, furnishing, and reconstruction of houses and farm buildings.[7] Later still, drainage and other improvements could further extend the farm's arable acreage. Investments were also needed in technology; though farming was still labour-intensive and relatively traditional, it involved appropriate saws, axes, harrows, harnesses, chains, shovels, rakes, and scythes. To the extent that these investments could be made by the labour of the farmer and family, the farm sustained them as they developed it and served as a launching point for children as they reached maturity. But the pioneer's labour alone was insufficient. Fundamental to the success of provincial agriculture was the local farm community, which extended the possibility for self-sustained, locally generated investment by providing labour at crucial moments, many supplies that the farm could not produce for itself, and a market for the farm's surpluses of various products.[8]

It is easy to depict such a household economy as traditional, but that downplays the implications of both transatlantic and shorter-distance migration, ignores the capital that had to be invested or created, neglects the multiplicity and complexity of choices that the farm household faced, and underestimates the knowledge that had to be acquired of successful farming in that region and even on that specific land. Migrants often felt pushed to move by the difficulty or impossibility of sustaining a family farm economy in the United Kingdom, under tenure and market conditions prevalent there. Re-establishing themselves on a family farm in the new world, however, made them anything but simple traditionalists carrying on in timeless peasant old-world ways.[9] Even if they succeeded in re-creating something resembling an older lifestyle, they did so only with much new knowledge and after what to them were large investments. The sophistication of the successful pioneer farmer deserves recognition; he required, as Norman Ball notes, a 'highly developed feeling for the balance between labour costs and the potential for return.'[10]

Provincial tax data record two principal elements of farm-making – land occupation, and land-clearing and cultivation. Under the assessment acts, 'arable, pasture or meadow' land (reported as land 'under culture') was appraised at £1 per acre, five times the value of 'uncultivated land' (land 'occupied').[11] Actual values generally exceeded the assessment standard for improved land by a considerable margin.

MAP 5.1
Upper Canadian Counties with 50 Per Cent or More of Occupied Land under Culture,
1851

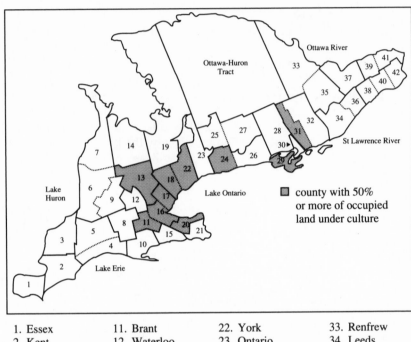

| 1. Essex | 11. Brant | 22. York | 33. Renfrew |
|---|---|---|---|
| 2. Kent | 12. Waterloo | 23. Ontario | 34. Leeds |
| 3. Lambton | 13. Wellington | 24. Durham | 35. Lanark |
| 4. Elgin | 14. Grey | 25. Victoria | 36. Grenville |
| 5. Middlesex | 15. Haldimand | 26. Northumberland | 37. Carleton |
| 6. Huron | 16. Wentworth | 27. Peterborough | 38. Dundas |
| 7. Bruce | 17. Halton | 28. Hastings | 39. Russell |
| 8. Oxford | 18. Peel | 29. Prince Edward | 40. Stormont |
| 9. Perth | 19. Simcoe | 30. Lennox | 41. Prescott |
| 10. Norfolk | 20. Lincoln | 31. Addington | 42. Glengarry |
| | 21. Welland | 32. Frontenac | |

SOURCE: Canada, *Census*, 1871, vol. 4, 194

For example, a study of land prices in Essex, at once one of the oldest
and also remotest of Upper Canadian counties, indicates that the average
price of farm land (improved and unimproved combined) between 1822
and 1851 was never as low as £1 per acre and in a third of the years
exceeded £2 per acre.[12] In 1826, 3.4 million acres were occupied in the
province, of which about one-sixth, some 620,000 acres, was under
culture. By 1851 almost 10 million acres had been occupied, and over
one-third, 3.7 million acres, was now under culture. This was extensive

growth: the ratio of land under culture to population was no higher in 1851 than it had been in 1805 and 1817 (table 1.1). In few areas was as much as half the land occupied actually under culture in 1851 (map 5.1).

The best analysis of actual farming patterns in Upper Canada is that of Marvin McInnis, who has studied a carefully drawn sample of farms from the 1861 census manuscripts.[13] Because there still were many new farms in the province in 1861, it is likely that McInnis's sample catches some of the essential features of the long period of extensive growth that was then coming to an end. He groups farms into four size categories, very small holdings (1–31 acres) that were not likely farms at all; small (32–69 acres); standard (70–169 acres); and large (170 acres or more). About 40 per cent of all farms were exactly 100 acres, and about 60 per cent were in the standard class. One-sixth of farms were large, though few exceeded 300 acres in extent.[14] Large marketable surpluses came disproportionately from the largest category of farms, but not all large farms had surpluses and in few products did surpluses increase proportionately with the occupied acreage of the farm. At the other extreme, even small farms typically produced enough to support their occupants and leave some surplus to market. Most farms in 1861 still contained much uncleared land and much that was used mainly as pasture.

Thus even in 1861, when the margins of farming settlement in southern Upper Canada were being reached and the province had some farms that were nearly three-quarters of a century old, Upper Canadian agriculture had enormous potential for expansion by further clearing and more intensive cropping. Only a small proportion of farmers was wholly committed to a commercial agriculture which entailed cultivation of more lands than a single family could manage. Even in 1861, one of the all-time peak years of the province's wheat economy, much more land had been cleared and improved than was required for wheat alone. Such investments were, we must assume, not irrational but economically motivated. To understand them, it is necessary to examine both wheat farming and the remainder of the province's farm economy.

## II. *The Role of Wheat*

Because wheat has been the focus of the standard story of the provincial economy, it is appropriate to begin with it. Wheat, John McCallum has argued, 'was the only significant *cash* crop' in the province. Even if 'a low price for [it] brought steadily mounting debt and the threat of financial ruin' to farmers, he says, they 'did not turn to livestock' because of American competition and because 'especially before 1850, markets for other crops were generally non-existent or unattractive.'[15] Yet we have seen that in the province's early years, and on assumptions

MAP 5.2
Variation, by District, in Wheat Output Per Capita, Upper Canada, 1848

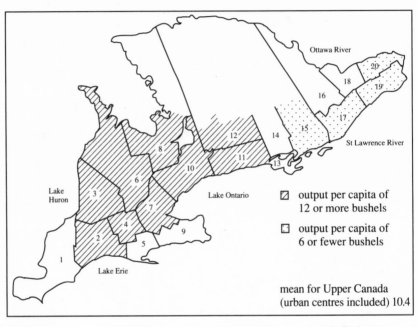

| 1. Western | 6. Wellington | 11. Newcastle | 16. Bathurst |
| 2. London | 7. Gore | 12. Colborne | 17. Johnstown |
| 3. Huron | 8. Simcoe | 13. Prince Edward | 18. Dalhousie |
| 4. Brock | 9. Niagara | 14. Victoria | 19. Eastern |
| 5. Talbot | 10. Home | 15. Midland | 20. Ottawa |

SOURCE: Canada, *Census*, 1871, vol. 4, 164, 170

designed not to underestimate wheat's importance, considerably less than half of the province's land under culture could have produced provincial wheat requirements, and only half of that land would have been needed in any one year; total annual wheat output would ordinarily have required around one-fifth of total land under culture.[16]

Such estimates of land use can be made for any year in which there are data on wheat exports, provincial population, and land under culture. After 1821, just as before, less than one-quarter of all land under culture was required for wheat production in any one year (see tables 3.3 and 5.1).[17] It is probable that land use was not quite as volatile from year to year as the tables show. Rather, they suggest the range within which actual land use in the province fell. Harvest variations and adjustments to net stocks held in the province also contributed to variance in export volumes.

MAP 5.3
Variation, by County, in Wheat Output Per Capita, Upper Canada, 1851

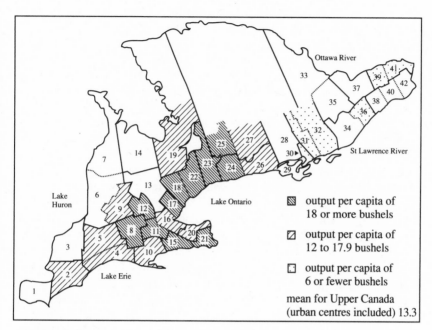

SOURCE: As map 5.1. For county names, see map 5.1.

Census data are not available on wheat output until 1842. The reported crop, presumably for 1841, was 3.2 million bushels; but that substantially understates total output, the figures for output in the Home District, a major centre of wheat production, being particularly suspect.[18] In most respects, however, the areas of greatest wheat output in 1842 are confirmed by subsequent censuses. From the Midland District eastward and in the Western District (areas where one-third of the province's population lived), per capita wheat output in 1842 was less than the approximately six bushels per person estimated as normal annual consumption.[19] In just six districts (Prince Edward and Victoria, east of Toronto; Talbot, Gore, and Wellington, west of Toronto; and, we must assume, the Home District), did wheat output exceed ten bushels per capita.

The 1848 census reports production equal to 10.4 bushels per capita for the province. The eastern areas still produced less than six bushels per capita, and the Western District only just exceeded that threshold. From 1842 to 1848 there was little if any increase in wheat output per capita in the Victoria, Prince Edward, and Talbot districts. In nearly all other districts, wheat output in 1848 was 12 or more bushels per capita (map 5.2). In 1851, data are available on a county basis. Per capita output for the province had risen to 13.3 bushels, as much as or more than in the peak previous years for which such a figure can be estimated (1803 and 1831). Only a handful of counties did not produce at least 6 bushels per capita, and some, ranging from Durham and Victoria in the east to Oxford in the west, produced 18 or more bushels per person per year (map 5.3). The latter were the mid-century heartland of provincial wheat production. Their climate and soil suggest that even earlier their settled areas were core areas of the wheat economy. On the other hand, Hastings and Prince Edward, among the leading producers in 1842, did not follow the trend to increased wheat output per capita over the subsequent decade.[20]

Because wheat was both a marketable crop and a major element in farmers' own diets, it was a high priority for farmers wherever it would grow.[21] Total output was, however, constrained by the labour that the farm family could supply for planting and harvesting. Except for families with a number of men of appropriate age, it was difficult to sow and harvest much more than ten acres of wheat without recourse to paid labour from beyond the household. Relatively few farms seem to have found it remunerative to hire such labour. In 1861 McInnis finds that, of the 16 per cent of all farms that he groups as large, less than one in six had resident non-family labour. Of course, more farms might occasionally have hired day labour, and the hiring of resident non-family labour could also have been a feature of more families over their life cycle than the data of a single census reveal. Nevertheless, as farms got larger, wheat acreage did not grow proportionately, or sometimes even absolutely. Where climate permitted, however, a second crop of wheat could be planted and harvested each year with the same labour, by growing both fall and spring wheat.[22]

In 1860, one of the peak years of wheat production in Upper Canada, somewhat over one-third of the province's farms of 70 or more acres grew fall wheat. In that year, 89 per cent of farms in the 70–169 acre category planted spring wheat (on average 8.2 acres of it) but only 36 per cent planted fall wheat (the average for those planting it being 8.7 acres per farm). Over 91 per cent of large farms (170 or more acres) planted spring wheat (on average 10.9 acres of it), while 47 per cent planted fall wheat (averaging 15.4 acres of it per farm growing it).[23] Spring wheat was planted on about one-sixth of the province's land under culture, or one-quarter of land actually cultivated.

The income generated for the province by wheat exports varied with the volume of wheat exported and the prevalent wheat price. In table 5.2 downriver exports from Upper Canada are related to the population of the province in the area from Kingston west (1817–23) and from Hastings County west after 1824, on the assumption that all of the province's wheat surplus came from this area.[24] Even with eastern districts omitted, prior to 1850 there was just one year (1831) when the volume of wheat shipped downriver approximated the volume required for domestic consumption. Otherwise, volumes were moderately or substantially below wheat needed locally. Indeed, of the twenty-five years recorded in the table, in sixteen (from 1817 to 1825, 1829, from 1835 to 1839, and 1848) exports from the province were half or less than half of what was required for seed and local consumption in the region of production. With the exception of 1817, the last year of wartime price levels, the per capita value of wheat exports from the region in those years ranged downward from £1. By no measure can that level of income be made into a large sum.

When such data are considered at the level of the household, the basic decision-making unit of the economy, even the highest per capita values scarcely seem large. The exceptionally high 1831 figure of 35s per capita equalled £10 5s ($42) for a six-person household. For the entire decade 1830–9, exports averaged less than £1 per person a year (less than £6 per household) in the producing region, and in the 1820s the figure was just half of that. These are crude measurements, but they allow us to ask whether emigrants sold their assets at home, risked the Atlantic crossing, and undertook all the labour of farm-making primarily in order to participate in an export trade whose annual earnings prior to the 1840s rarely exceeded a figure equivalent to $25 per household in the region of production.

As the 1851 and 1861 data reveal (table 5.2), the mid-century brought increases from earlier per capita levels of wheat output and income. The ascent to higher levels began in the 1840s and resulted in part from continuing expansion of settlement in the prime wheat-growing areas and the changing legal context of the trade, which at last opened the British market reliably to colonial producers and increasingly facilitated cross-border trade in both directions between Canada and the United States. Although we lack data for Upper Canada alone in these years, it is reasonable to assume its output and exports generally paralleled the combined totals for Canada and the United States. Shipments down the St Lawrence from the United States and Upper Canada, which had seldom exceeded one million bushels before 1840, leaped to three times that level in 1841, 1844, and 1845, exceeded four million bushels in most years after that, and approached seven million in 1847, the peak year of Irish famine-induced wheat shipments from North America. Counting exports to the United States, in 1850 Upper Canada exported the equivalent of about 4.6 million bushels of wheat, in 1851, 4.4 million, and in 1852, 5.4 million bushels.[25] On a per capita basis, the 1851 figure was similar to that of 1831. In 1850 and 1852, and probably at times in the 1840s, per capita exports from the region of production in Upper Canada somewhat exceeded the levels of 1831 and 1851.

It is, however, inappropriate to assess the entire half-century of development before the 1840s as mere prelude to the mid-century wheat boom. Those who emigrated and settled earlier could scarcely know that eventually such a boom would take place. Moreover, even at the height of the boom, whether measured by land use or income generated, much more was going on in the province's agriculture than wheat production. The other aspects of the agricultural system, both at mid-century and earlier, require analysis in their own terms and not as minor adjuncts to wheat.

### III. *Farm Marketing and the Local Economy*

Thus far we have seen that farmers in Upper Canada cleared far more land than wheat-growing required and that per capita incomes generated by wheat exports were typically modest. Nor was the momentum of provincial expansion, as measured by overall rates of population growth and land-clearing, checked by years of low prices or bad harvests. It would have been risky for the farmer to depend exclusively on one crop, less because of the dangers of soil exhaustion through wheat monoculture that exercised critics of provincial farming[26] than because seasonal requirements of wheat-growing left much time available for other farm activities and labour constraints limited the possibility of quick expansion of wheat output. Farmers could recognize the threat to crops, income, indeed economic survival, of bad weather, insect infestation, a bumper crop in Britain, or a change in imperial duties.

In the implicit model of the provincial economy that many have used, in which wheat alone drove the agricultural economy forward, the farmer could have responded to such vicissitudes by abandoning the market to wait out hard times in self-sufficiency. But this was a commercial frontier, whose development required capital and credit. As we shall see below, the credit system, operating in part through the province's general country merchants, was an essential part of the farm household's system of support and supply. Because debts to stores and to others had to be met, or at least carried, there could be no retreat into absolute self-sufficiency. To sustain operations, the family had to have other sources of income.[27]

The tendency to explain colonial development in terms of exports rests on contemporary perceptions. To many in Upper Canada, and particularly the articulate elite, the key problems were carrying external debt, increasing the inflow of immigrants and capital, and increasing exports to increase both imports and public revenues. The internal economy of the province was, in essence, known intuitively, and discussions of it focused on its problems, not its performance. In the census era there is direct evidence that Upper Canadian farms produced many other outputs. With the exception of barley, rye, and corn, all the items included in table 5.3 were widely produced. Thus in 1861 most farms, of whatever size, owned assorted livestock and produced fodder crops and other outputs (table 5.4). Nor do the commodities and stocks recorded in tables 5.3 and 5.4 exhaust the list of Upper Canadian farm production. Though not recorded in the census, garden vegetables, fruits, and poultry were clearly important; so were more localized outputs such as tobacco. There is also reason to suspect that some products, notably dairy products, were greatly under-represented in census data, perhaps in part because they represented the semi-visible outputs of women's work.[28]

Such products were grown, but were they marketed? Were they also part of earlier agriculture in the province? Fortunately, other kinds of documentation give some dimensions of rural output and marketing prior to the census era. The ledgers and daybooks of country merchants often recorded transactions in kind, and some farmers kept records that permit us to analyse their market activities. A review of the local trades revealed in such documentation shows that, from its earliest days, the provincial economy produced and exchanged many other commodities besides wheat.

Table 5.5 is based on the form of credits listed in the accounts of some thirteen merchants whose records permit analysis in these terms. Chronologically, the data range from 1791 to 1842; geographically, they range across the province. The Robert Hamilton and Richard Cartwright Jr stores (rows 1 and 9) were among the principal firms in the province and several others were prominent in their own areas (for example, rows 4 and 5).[29] But in key respects their payments structures seem representative of wider patterns. The table records the method of payment by ordinary customers for as long a period as the original source permits consistent recording. It includes four standard categories, payments in cash, in the form of promissory notes, in wheat, and by 'third parties' (in which a credit on one person's account derived from a transaction involving another person). A fifth category, payment in the most prominent commodity other than wheat, varies according to the individual store. Among them, the five categories cover anywhere from 39 to 86 per cent of credits at the thirteen stores. The records do not show how promissory notes were ultimately paid, that being a separate dimension of a firm's accounting and collections process. The underlying basis for third-party credits is also not usually clear, except that such payments must often have been part of a market relationship between the paying party and the person to whom the payment was credited. For example, a farmer who owed a carpenter money might deliver produce to the store and have it credited to the carpenter's account. Other data make up the residual percentages. Most important of those not reported in the table were varieties of work and local artisan products. In particular years lumber, livestock, or other animal products or field crops were also important.

At five of the stores (rows 5 to 9), all in the area around Lake Ontario, and all but one with records focused on the 1830s, wheat accounted directly for more than one-sixth (and up to almost one-third) of total payments. Farther east (rows 1 to 4) and west (rows 10 to 13), wheat accounted for a smaller proportion of payments and at all but the Kyle store (row 3) was exceeded in importance by some other commodity. There was considerable annual variation, although even the highest one-year percentages at the less wheat-oriented stores were lower than the averages in the stores around Lake Ontario. The highest one-year proportion recorded was in 1836, at Barker and Stevenson's store in Prince Edward County (row 5), where 45 per cent by value of customer payments were made in wheat. On the other hand, in 1829 just 10 per cent came in that form. Thus even in strongly wheat-oriented areas, firms had to allow for market and crop variations that produced wide swings in their receipts of wheat.

In only four cases was there no other commodity accounting for at least 10 per cent of payments. In the east, ashes and lumber were prominent. Around Lake Ontario, pork shows up consistently. To the west, rye, tobacco, and barley were, for the stores recorded, more important than wheat as sources of payment. It is impossible to know if similar patterns would show up in other years or in records of other stores. But the data do show clearly that rural Upper Canada produced and marketed other commodities besides wheat. Rye could be distilled and barley brewed, and both could be fed to animals. Tobacco was shipped in substantial quantities from the west to Montreal from early in the 1820s.[30] Trade across Lake Erie was locally important.[31]

It is not clear from these records if or how notes were eventually settled. Nevertheless, payments recorded in cash, notes, and by third party all indicate the existence of other local exchange transactions and/ or sources of income. Cash payments often rivalled or exceeded payments in wheat; even if they and third-party payments all derived from sales of wheat by the farmer to others, they would still indicate more complex patterns in the settling of accounts than a story focused simply on wheat would suggest. Given wheat's utility as a means of paying debts further up the credit chain, merchants had an incentive to prefer payment in wheat to other modes apart from cash. Thus, there is no reason to believe these commercial records understate the significance of wheat to the storekeeper or the local economy.

For one of the largest firms, Barker and Stevenson (row 5), selected data on produce receipts and shipments for 1826 to 1837 are presented in table 5.6. For this firm, which was very active in the wheat market, payments received in pork exceeded those in wheat in three years (1829–31) and over the seven years from 1829 to 1835 inclusive totalled over 90 per cent of wheat receipts. Thus for much of the period, pork was as significant a source of payment as wheat. In addition to major produce items, Barker and Stevenson also credited many other local commodities in smaller amounts. At least thirty local products, of which butter and cheese were most prominent, can be found in an 1836 'barter book.'[32] These purchases by the firm reflected its needs and those of the Stevenson family and the possibility of reselling some farm produce locally.

Surviving records for individual farms also show something of local exchange patterns. Table 5.7 records sales from twelve farms for which data on off-farm sales permit such analysis. Because more than half the records are mainly or exclusively for the 1840s, when the wheat economy was expanding rapidly, and none are from eastern areas (map 5.4), the data should not underrepresent wheat's importance. It is possible that the sort of farmer who kept such records was, by definition, atypical, but the records are not especially sophisticated in form and all but two of the farms (rows j and m) record incomes in the normal range for provincial farms in the era (column E). Moreover, given the seasonal imperatives of agriculture, even very large farms worked within constraints that could make them representative of wider patterns (see columns G and J).[33]

The table shows sales of farm-produced commodities as recorded by the farmer. Sales were recorded in money terms or in volumes with sufficient internal reference to prices to permit valuation of transactions. No attempt has been made to distinguish sales of quasi-capital farm outputs, such as teams of oxen, from other sales, though dispositions of tools and equipment are omitted. Credits earned by the farmer and family from off-farm work, credits earned by farm help on their own account, payments in kind to help, and transactions of an explicitly barter nature are all omitted. By barter is meant exchange of one item for another, without reference to prices; often such trades involved more or less simultaneous exchanges. Thus, the table is a record, for the

MAP 5.4
Location of Stores and Farms Included in Tables 5.5 and 5.7

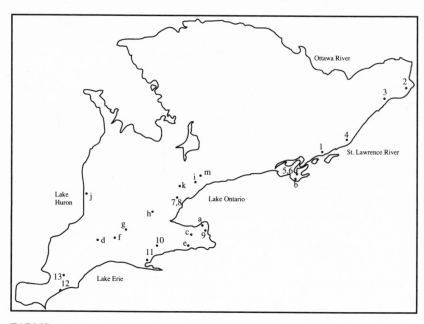

FARMS

a   Willson, Niagara
b   Spencer, Hallowell
c   Comfort, Gainsborough
d   Stiles, London
e   Anon, Dunnville
f   Crawford, Beachville
g   Thompson, South Easthope
h   Case, Galt
i   Cambers, Etobicoke
j   Brown, Bayfield
k   Forster, Norval
m   Parsons, Thornhill

STORES

1   Richard Cartwright Jr, Kingston
2   McLean store, Charlottenburg
3   Kyle store, Williamsburg
4   Jones businesses, Yonge Mills
5   Barker & Stevenson store } Hallowell
6   S. Washburn store
7   Patterson store } Streetsville
8   Hammond & Goble store
9   Hamilton store, Queenston
10  Foster store, Townsend
11  Cross & Fisher store, Newport (Fisher's Glen)
12  Coyne store, Erieus (later known as Dealtown)
13  Thames Steam Navigation store (Chatham)

period of availability of data, of the farm family's 'earnings' through the sale of produce in the marketplace. The roles of wheat and one other product on each farm are highlighted, but other products of some significance are also indicated.

Although at best impressionistic on the commercial world of the Upper Canadian farmer, these data reinforce those from retail stores.

For only one farm, the earliest, was wheat not a major source of income (column G); for three farms, two of whose records are from the 1840s, wheat represented two-thirds or more of income. For the remaining eight farms, wheat provided from 20 to 50 per cent of income, and in all but three cases it was the largest single source.[34] Wheat's importance to these farms is clear. But even these levels of wheat-generated income are well below levels that have often been assumed. For example, John McCallum argued that 'wheat made up about three-quarters of the cash sales of Ontario farmers.'[35] For this to be true, however, *every* farm in the most wheat-oriented areas would have had to earn well over 80 per cent of its income from wheat, which *none* of these farms did, given that wheat was a less significant source of income for farmers along the St Lawrence and Ottawa Rivers; 24 per cent of Upper Canadians lived east of Hastings County in 1851 and that percentage was higher in earlier years – 37 per cent in 1830, for example.

For only one farm was there no second product (column H) yielding more than 10 per cent of income (column J), and for half the farms there was a product responsible for over 20 per cent of income. In most cases the second product consisted of an animal product, though rye and barley appear on this list, as they do in table 5.4. Twelve of the fifteen products listed in table 5.3 appear in column H as being one of the two principal income earners for one or more farms. Even the exceptions in table 5.3 (peas, potatoes, and horses) are known to have been regularly marketed, as the extended series of prices of peas and potatoes, dating from the 1780s, demonstrates (see table C.1). The near complete absence of ashes on the list (column K) tends to confirm other evidence on the more easterly location of most ash production. The Hallowell farm (row b) confirms evidence from Barker and Stevenson and other retail stores that local pork was sold extensively around Lake Ontario. Because every farm earned at least some income from the sale of animals and their products, it is evident that those who have stressed American dominance of Upper Canadian markets in animal products greatly exaggerated the situation.[36] Combined, all animal products frequently came close to rivalling wheat as a source of farm income. It is clear that most of the meat consumed on and off farms in Upper Canada was produced there.

For two farms, the one at Dunnville and the Crawford farm near Beachville (rows e and f), more extended runs of evidence help to show how farm income was made up over a longer period (table 5.8). Neither farm was exceptional in scale, nor is there anything to suggest that they were not their owners' main sources of income. With sales between 1846 and 1850 of close to $200 (£50) per year, the Dunnville farm was quite close to the $210 per year surplus estimated by McInnis for all farms in his sample of a decade later. The Crawford farm, which reached this level in 1842, and in 1846 and 1847 had sales of $360 and $280 respectively, was in line with the average annual surplus of $280 that McInnis found for farms that had marketable surpluses.[37] For purposes of clarity, the table includes only commodities that generated 10 per cent of the farm's income in the particular year, though the final total for all years includes all sales of the commodity. Actual total sales and wheat's share of them are shown in figure 5.1. The data reveal a continuing reliance on wheat, which represented 43 per cent of the income of the Dunnville farm over fifteen years and 33 per cent of the Beachville farm over nine years. In one-third of the years for each farm (including 1839 and 1841 for both), wheat produced over half the farm's income. Total farm income tended, moreover, to fluctuate with the value of wheat sales. But despite wheat's prominence, other commodities combined to make up a substantial majority of each farm's income, hay and pork being particularly noteworthy in the case of the Beachville farm.

Two other examples of 1830s farm practice, based on land use on relatively substantial farms rather than on market activity, may also be cited. One is an established farm near Cobourg purchased by Charles Butler, newly arrived in Upper Canada in July 1833; 35 per cent of the value of its crops and livestock consisted of wheat, according to a valuation by local assessors, and 41 per cent of acreage cropped was in wheat. Remaining acreage was devoted to hay, peas, clover, oats, and buckwheat. Livestock constituted 29 per cent of the value of crops and stock. The other farm, Henry Ransford's, located near Goderich, was purchased in 1834. Ransford's cropped acreage expanded from 15 acres in 1835 to 20.5 in 1836, 24.5 in 1837, 38 in 1838, and 41.5 in 1839. Wheat and hay were his chief crops. The former took 23 per cent of acreage in 1835, 24 per cent in 1836, 45 per cent in 1837, 26 per cent in 1838, and just 14 per cent in 1839, when the spring wheat crop was destroyed by late frost. Hay took 27 per cent in 1835, 24 per cent in 1836 and 1837, 42 per cent in 1838, and 46 per cent in 1839. Barley, oats, peas, and potatoes were his other significant crops.[38]

Wheat is often seen as a cash crop, unlike others. But what cash actually means in the Upper Canadian context, especially in rural areas, is not so clear. It is difficult to see any difference to the farmer between credits earned (at the store or elsewhere in the local economy) from wheat and from any other product. Anything the farm produced with the household's own time, on its own land, that earned credits in the local economy, would help to sustain farm-making. Equally, the use of hard-won lands and scarce time for such production is clear evidence

FIGURE 5.1
Wheat Sales and Total Sales, Two Upper Canadian Farms, 1836–50

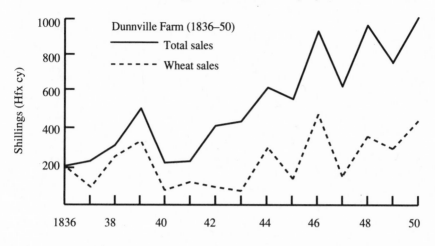

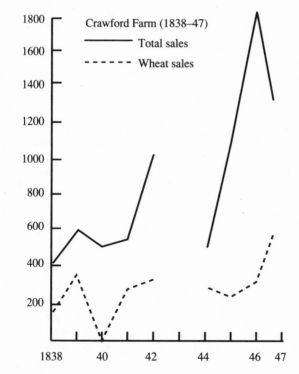

SOURCE: See Tables 5.7, 5.8.

that tangible returns were sought, frequently in the marketplace, from those other crops and commodities.

These findings are, in essence, compatible with McInnis's argument that in 1861 average marketable surpluses were, for most products and on most farms, modest. For his entire sample, marketable surpluses were equal to 55 per cent of net farm output; on farms in the largest category and in the earliest settled areas, that percentage was only slightly higher. On the other hand, our assorted data suggest that from its beginnings, provincial agriculture produced surpluses of numerous products sufficient to support newly established farms and non-farmers in the local economy. Because there was always some local market for other produce, farmers were never exclusively reliant on wheat production for their livelihood.

## IV. *Native Lands and Native Agriculture*

The spread of white settlement strained and then transformed the initial relationship between the settler economy and the economies of the native population, whether they were agricultural or woodland-based. By 1817 the province's European population was from seven to ten times as large as the native population, and the disproportion was rapidly widening. Although the Rebellion of 1837 reminded other Upper Canadians that Indians could still take an autonomous military role, the end of the War of 1812 proved to be the beginning of the end of the military significance of the native population. The Indian Department was an important part of British expenditure in the province until mid-century, but by 1830 imperial policy saw the native peoples not as important allies but as a problem.

As their power diminished, the Indians came under mounting pressure to cede even land they had retained or been granted as reserves. Many whites desired the removal of people seen as alien. Land speculators and settlers sought land for themselves or for resale. Government officials, often in a position of trusteeship for Indian funds and claiming a sincere interest in Indian well-being, sold reserved lands either to augment Indian communities' annual incomes or just to fund the government's existing financial obligations to the Indians.[39] Some Indian groups and individuals also sold or proposed to sell land to raise band (or personal) income. As a result of all these pressures, Indian landholdings in southern Upper Canada were sharply reduced. Over 350,000 acres of the Grand River reserve had been alienated by 1800, and another quarter-million were lost between 1830 and 1841.[40] At somewhat over 50,000 acres, this was still the largest and most populous southern reserve at mid-century. Next largest were the Oneida and

Muncey reserves, amounting together to 14,000 acres along the Thames River, and the reserve at Walpole Island at the mouth of the St Clair River. The Quinte Mohawks still had some thousands of acres, but much less than initially had been granted. Smaller reserves and populations were found at the trans-border St Regis Reserve, at Rice and Mud lakes, on Lake Simcoe, on several islands in Georgian Bay, at the Moravian mission on the Thames near Chatham, and at several points along Lake Huron. Fewer than 10,000 Indians lived in Upper Canada south of Manitoulin Island at mid-century, and some of them were members of communities that had arrived as recently as 1840.

Although their total numbers were relatively small and little changed from 1800, the Indians' economic adjustment to the changes in their own situation and in the settlement economy is an important part of the history of the province's rural economy. Unlike settlers of European background, the native population came increasingly under the surveillance of the state. Any chance most native groups had to build truly adequate land endowments for their future was undercut by the systematic reduction in their holdings, at prices that cannot be interpreted as anything but very low in even the most expensive transactions.[41] The underlying causes of this process were largely beyond their control, even if some groups or leaders consented or contributed to the land alienation. Indians' collective lives were in various ways constrained by the agenda of an unsympathetic government; even the Indian department, transferred to local control in 1860, had priorities that accorded only in part with those of most Indians. At the same time, it is important not to exaggerate the loss of autonomy. Most aspects of local government and allocation of land on the reserves were controlled by the communities themselves.[42]

The mid-century rural economy of the province's native population ranged from the established agriculture of the Six Nations and several other southern communities to the hunting, fishing, and trading of woodland groups on the northern fringe of the settlement economy. By then, public policy aimed to convert the latter to the former. Most Indian groups continued to receive government-paid annuities and presents. The latter were entirely terminated in 1858, and the former were being intensely scrutinized by an economy-minded government. The original purposes of these payments, as perpetual returns for lands surrendered and for participation in vital alliances, were increasingly forgotten by later generations of officials. It is, nevertheless, through such officials and missionaries that we obtain much of our information about the character and extent of native agriculture.[43]

In some areas, whites farmed Indian lands on shares, but there is little to suggest that Indians relied on these farmers, rather than on their own efforts, for food. They also had many other links to the wider settler economy. Men often worked off reserves, for example for nearby farmers during the harvest. Women sold crafts in local markets. Income was also earned by some resale of presents, the continuing sale of furs, sales of produce and timber, and rental of lands, mill sites, and other property. Assuming the whole reserve was not forced to move (which sometimes happened), the communal elements of the reserve system of land tenure evidently did not preclude families from having secure tenure on reserve farms. Efforts to restrict Indian indebtedness suggest also that Indians must have had access to at least some credit, both on and off the reserve.

Commenting on agriculture on the Six Nations reserves in the 1850s, the Indian Affairs commissioners wrote that 'there is not much difference observable in the system of farming pursued ... and that of the surrounding Whites. They use the same implements, and raise the same Crops. Some of the Indians have several hundreds of Bushels of Wheat to dispose of in a Season, after providing for their own wants.' Similarly, some Oneidas on the Thames were 'able annually to dispose of considerable quantities of grain after providing for the comfortable support of their families.'[44] Evidence is provided in table 5.9 on produce and livestock of the principal agriculturally oriented communities and on several reserves at the margin between farming and woodland economies. By comparison with contemporary province-wide data, the per capita figures for most of the farming communities were somewhat lower, but each had at least one product that exceeded provincial averages (pigs on the Six Nations reserve, wheat for the Mississauga group there, rye for the Mohawks at Tyendinaga, corn for the more westerly reserves, and potatoes for the Rice Lake and Saugeen communities). In townships adjacent to these reserves, farmers also tended to produce above-average amounts of the same crops. By such local standards, the surpluses from native farmers' operations seem more modest, but household census data suggest that the leading farmers on reserves with some good land produced at levels comparable to the average for the surrounding region.[45]

How the various native communities would have coped under other policy regimes is impossible to know. The most clear-cut evidence that things were not well with the province's native peoples was the failure of total reserve populations to grow. It is desirable, however, to know more about the complex migration patterns of the various native groups before assessing the exact nature and degree of demographic difficulty faced by Upper Canada's Indians during the era of white settlement in the province. In their numbers and as they were viewed by many settlers, natives were at the margin of society. But it is less clear that they were actually marginalized in terms of their level of material well-being, relative either to their earlier standards or to those of at least some people in adjacent settlements. Although there is evidence of some groups and individuals experiencing much hardship, as long as hunting and fishing could continue it is likely that most woodland communities could at least sustain traditional diets.[46] At mid-century, the principal agricultural communities were sustaining balanced local economies linked in various ways to the surrounding settler economy. Such reserves were thus part of the complex network of such local economies that constituted the larger provincial economy.

## V. *Conclusion*

In his analysis of Upper Canadian agriculture in 1860–1, Marvin McInnis notes that about one-sixth of farms in his sample had no marketable surplus, that only another one-sixth produced a surplus equal to the consumption needs of more than three other households, and that the median surplus was enough to feed just one other household, about $150. The apparent modesty of the latter figure and the overall distribution of marketable surpluses prompt him to comment that the frequent 'distinction between self-sufficiency and commercialization is not very important. The great majority of farms in a wide range of circumstances was producing an excess over household consumption needs. Conversely, substantial surpluses were much less common. Only a small fraction of farms was producing a marketable surplus great enough to provide for more than just the local non-agricultural population.'[47]

Such evidence makes it possible to see the farm household as striving essentially for autonomy, producing primarily for itself and in only a limited way for the marketplace. In its demographic behaviour, its use of technology, its evident reliance on wheat, and its generally limited recourse to hired non-family labour, the household hardly seems to have been engaged in the kind of profit-maximizing activities that we associate with full reliance on markets. But the intensifying market involvement and integration that lay ahead are not, as it is so easy to assume, evidence that markets were not significant earlier. In fact, the evidence is no less consistent with an essential integration of the provincial farm economy into the wider world of prices and markets. It is less likely that farmers' values were fundamentally antithetical to more intense engagement in market-oriented activities than that opportunities for local marketing were constrained by the simultaneous and continuing expansion of many similar production units, all selling into a non-farm sector that was expanding only at the same rate as agriculture. In Donald Akenson's apt phrase, it is reasonable to see Upper Canadian farmers as 'economically alert.'[48]

In this economy, some farms were not their owners' or occupiers' main source of livelihood. At the other extreme were some, such as the largest farms in McInnis's sample, the Parsons farm at Thornhill (table 5.7, row m), and those of gentleman farmer-settlers, whose patterns of investment, cropping, and marketing reflected their owners' relative affluence, a greater use of hired labour, and a diversification into other rural pursuits such as stock-breeding and milling.[49] Both extremes were undoubtedly important in the local exchange economy of rural Upper Canada; for example, the former might supply labour and buy farm produce, and the latter hired labour and participated actively in other markets too. It will help to understand the economy's growth, however, if we set the extremes to one side and focus here on the large majority of farms between. It is then possible to develop a stylized, semi-abstract model of the provincial farm system focused on the successful 'ordinary' farmer.

As McInnis suggests, the ordinary farm family appears to have had an integrated strategy, in which each activity played a part in building the farm as a long-term enterprise. Thus, production of wheat, ashes, pork, or other commodities (such as barrel staves) that could be marketed at greater distances from the immediate community, production of commodities for marketing to the local non-farm population and some-times to neighbouring farmers, production for household consumption, and work on maintaining, improving, and creating the farm itself were essentially complementary, not competing, aspects of the farm strategy. Indeed, the distinction among outputs by destination is somewhat artifi-cial, for the price system linked them, and many outputs were produced simultaneously for more than one objective (wheat, for example, was grown for on-farm consumption and for sale into both local and extraprovincial markets).

It is typical to see the province as moving from an initial extreme phase of dependence on wheat through a complex mid-century transi-tion into a later nineteenth-century era of mixed farming focusing on dairying. In terms of what farmers actually did, however, Upper Canadian agriculture was always a mixed farming system, with wheat as a sub-stantial element in much of the province. Around mid-century, wheat's importance in the system actually increased, though it was by no means the only factor in the 1850s boom. From the 1860s, dairying became much more visible, and the growth of urban centres continued to expand markets for other produce.[50] But wheat remained a principal crop long after the 'cheese' economy began, and we have seen that much farm produce other than wheat was grown, some of which was marketed, even in the earliest years of the 'wheat staple.'

This is not mere quibbling over terminology. The issues are essential to understanding the process of development, and particularly whether it involved unbalanced growth, as staples theory implies, or balanced growth, as is argued here.[51] Most significant to the latter view is that the economy sustained a relatively constant rate of expansion, as measured in its population growth and growth in land under culture, through about seventy years; in only a few of those years was wheat proportionately as large a generator of export income as it was at the mid-century, the era with which we are most familiar. Moreover, expansion of agriculture went forward simultaneously from the several initial points of settlement in Upper Canada, including the Western District, which was never especially focused on wheat, and eastern areas where climate and soil were not very favourable to wheat production. Finally, as we shall argue below, cycles and crises more closely followed patterns of general trade fluctuations than those of the wheat market, with expansion and considerable diversification and institutional development being sustained through protracted periods when the wheat market seemed scarcely favourable, such as most of the 1820s and the period from 1832 to 1835.

The place of wheat in the Upper Canadian economy can be modelled on a stylized basis, using evidence from around the mid-century. For simplicity, we can imagine farm output as consisting of three elements: production for household consumption, production for local markets, and production of wheat for local and export markets. The assorted evidence of this chapter suggests dividing income from the market equally betweeh wheat and all other income sources. We need to discount for the fact that some areas of the province did not rely on wheat exports, however, by excluding the Ottawa valley and everywhere east of Kingston along the St Lawrence, where almost 25 per cent of the population lived in 1851. In the area west of Kingston, we need to allow for non-farm population: about 7 per cent of the population in 1851 lived in Toronto, Hamilton, and London alone; and even in rural areas, only about 60 per cent of households were farmers.[52]

We can estimate the direct contribution of wheat to provincial income as the product of these percentages; thus, wheat would have provided 50 per cent of the income from marketing of produce for 60 per cent of 93 per cent of households in an area representing 75 per cent of the province. When these are multiplied, the resulting estimate is that about 21 per cent of provincial income came from wheat. To assess the real impact on farmers' welfare of the wheat economy, however, household production should be included in the calculation of total 'income.' Here we may use McInnis's calculation that in 1860 the average marketable surplus for a standard farm of 100 acres was 55 per cent of net farm output. Including household production, the share of total provincial 'income' attributable to the wheat staple could be as low as about 12 per cent (55 per cent x 21 per cent).

The meaning of the figures of 12 or 21 per cent can be debated. For a single output they are quite large, but they are more modest from the perspective of the argument of this chapter. Their modesty can be illustrated if we introduce a hypothetical fall in wheat-produced income into this system. In this model, a 50 per cent fall in wheat-generated income[53] would result in a drop of 10.5 per cent of market-generated, or 6 per cent of 'real,' provincial income. In a province where many economic indicators grew at something like 7 per cent per year, such a loss could be offset in a variety of ways. These essentially notional calculations are intended only to illustrate wheat's role in a simplified way, but some further complexities can be added. First, a fall in wheat prices, if wheat was the independent variable in the process, could affect prices of other commodities, thereby tending to make the loss of income to the farmer larger than in this calculation (table C.1). Second, if farmers reduced their expenditures, others in the economy who sold to them, worked for them, or were owed money by them could lose income; but because the latter groups were also buyers of farm produce, such losses could in turn be offset by lower prices for some of the products they had to buy.

Because of its presumed dependence on income from a single staple, wheat, this economy has been described as 'highly vulnerable to changes in international markets' and subject to 'a high variance in income.'[54] But our schematic view of the impact of a very large drop in wheat income shows that the economy was by no means as exposed as such a conceptualization portrays it. In subsequent chapters we shall examine further institutional and economic factors in the economy's ability to absorb this sort of cut without its momentum of growth being checked. Here it is enough to say that through credit and investment, the adjustment of stocks, and the production and marketing of much besides wheat, the rural economy limited its vulnerability to the sort of decline that a presumed dependence on one commodity might imply. In the work it actually did and in its marketing, the successful farm household had much to sustain it even when its presumed staple was not working.

On the other hand, as we noted above, the economy may have needed the idea of wheat as a staple to justify farmers' and others' faith in the system. Their work and choices were guided by expectations about levels and predictability of income. The occasional years of real wheat boom, such as 1817 and 1830–1, may thus have validated expectations. In that farmers could not, in planting, know what results would be, such years delivered almost windfall returns to established farmers. In another sense, that there would be occasional outstanding years may have been part of farmers' expectations as they pursued their investment in farming. There is a world of difference, however, between a rural economy that thought in terms of a single crop and one whose survival truly rested on it. Farmers from the beginning produced at levels well beyond subsistence and, as we have seen, had numerous choices in what they did. Upper Canada never depended on wheat in the way, say, that a one-industry town or a mining community depends on markets in a single output or commodity.

# 6 Artisans, Manufacturing, and the Provincial Economy to 1851

The variety of most households' economic activities make it artificial to insist on sharp distinctions among sectors, such as forests and agriculture, farming and manufacturing, or subsistence and market activity. It is clear, however, that a substantial minority of rural households were not primarily engaged in agriculture. And by the 1830s there was a growing urban sector. Manufacturers and artisans, in the country and in town, supplied essential services and products to agriculture (and to one another), consumed and/or processed locally marketed farm and forest products, and shared labour with other elements in the rural economy. Although Upper Canada's economy has often been seen as profoundly dependent on imports, especially manufactures, and lacking the capital needed for industry, a considerable range of manufacturing went on in the province and the local economy was able to create much capital. Indeed, artisans and local industry provided a substantial indigenous foundation for subsequent provincial industrialization.

Upper Canadian manufacturing included primary processing of raw materials for export: grist- and sawmilling, potash boiling, and the cooperage that supplied containers for that flour and potash. It also included necessarily local industry, making things that were immobile, such as buildings, or that were in wide demand and for which continuing direct contact of maker and customer was required. In this group were carpenters, masons, and blacksmiths; mills oriented to the local market (saw, grist, carding and fulling); and shoemakers, tailors, and others linked to final making of clothing (where fit, for example, was involved). Finally, some manufacturing was oriented to urban, regional, or provincial, not export, markets. Foundries, breweries, printing, papermaking, soap and candle-making, gasworks, shipbuilding, distilleries, and producers of building materials such as bricks, lime, and plaster served both markets that were wider than the radius of convenient daily travel for the ordinary farmer and also the concentrated markets of towns and cities.

A few craftsmen with valuable and specialized skills, such as mill-wrights, travelled widely to jobs in the province's early years; a few others developed more specialized trades in towns and cities. But in rural Upper Canada, crafts were likely to be relatively unspecialized. Carpenters were also glaziers and cabinet-makers; shoemakers both made and repaired shoes; blacksmiths shoed horses and made carriages and farm implements; and many men combined farming with a craft.

Upper Canada imported textiles, except for some of its wool cloth, much iron and hardware, and foodstuffs that could not be indigenously produced. These constituted close to 70 per cent of the value of imports to the Province of Canada in the early 1850s.[1] Local production of to-bacco and alcohol competed with more expensive imports.[2] So did some woollens, tools, and hardware. Successful exporting, increased capital imports, and transportation developments that cheapened the movement of goods over longer distances all enhanced the economy's ability to consume imports and intensified competition for some local manufac-turers. The position of such Upper Canadian producers was in this respect analogous to that in the adjacent American 'old northwest,' exposed to competition from Britain and eastern manufacturers.[3]

Published documentation on 'industry' does not indicate how multi-purpose establishments were counted and categorized, nor can one always be sure how establishments were defined. Over 1,000 potash works were listed in the 1842 census;[4] judging by location, such operations prob-ably were most of the almost 1,300 'other factories' in 1848; they do not seem to have been counted as industries at all in 1851. 'Country' saw and grist mills that served a purely local market are not distinguished from 'regular manufacturing' enterprises oriented to wider markets.[5] Most saw mills prior to the 1840s were local, but a larger number of grist mills produced for export. The latter required extra runs of stones to produce commercial grades of flour (table 6.1), but as the largest mills had four, five, or even six runs of stones, it is not possible to obtain exact numbers of merchant mills. Moreover, there are sometimes substantial discrep-ancies between census and assessment data.[6] Steam power, increasingly an indication of commercial mills, was not systematically reported until 1861.[7] Not until 1851 did the census report data on occupations that permit a comprehensive view of the artisan sector of manufacturing.[8] And there are puzzling inconsistencies in several series derived from mid-century censuses (tables 6.1, 6.3).

In fact, only saw and grist mills were routinely recorded in Upper Canada's assessments. Principally rural, they were distributed quite closely in accordance with population. Clusters of mills developed where water-power was abundant, such as along the Niagara Escarpment; where trade routes focused, such as at the eastern end of the lake system; and where the local flour market was large, such as in the Home District. Saw mills were always more numerous than grist mills. In the Home District in 1805, there was a grist mill for every 631 inhabitants and a saw mill for every 378. Rates were similar for the entire province in the mid-1820s, when comprehensive data first become available (see tables 6.1, 6.2). The ratio of population to grist mills rose gradually until by 1851 there were 1,376 Upper Canadians for every grist mill; in York County, including Toronto, there were 1,423 people per mill. The ratio of population to saw mills increased less: even in 1851 there was a mill for every 608 Upper Canadians. This lower rate did not reflect sawmilling for export; as chapter 4 showed, there were too few export mills to affect this simple ratio.

Some other industries were reported in the published 1842 census, in considerably smaller numbers than the two principal ones (table 6.3). Thus, in 1842 there was a saw mill for every 542 Upper Canadians, a grist mill for every 1,176, a tannery for every 1,866, a carding mill for every 2,618, and a distillery for every 3,313. It is reasonable to assume that the 1842 geographic dispersion of the last three, like that of the first two, resembled earlier years, since 1825 at least. Table 6.4 shows the leading six districts, by number of establishments, for the three next largest industrial categories – tanning, carding, and distilling. Population per establishment is indicated to recognize the variation in population among districts. The three districts that appear for all three industries (Home, Gore, and Niagara) were the most populous and the most central. They also had the highest concentration of commercial grist mills.[9] The Wellington and Newcastle districts, west and east respectively of the Home District, appear on two lists each. The nine districts not on any list were, with the exception of the Midland and Western districts, less populous than these. Every district had at least one tannery, only the Eastern District had no distillery, and just two districts, the Huron and the Dalhousie, recorded no carding mills at all. The wide diffusion of such industries is noteworthy; equally striking is that, as in other respects, the heartland of the provincial economy was already evident in the pattern of industrial location in 1842.

I. *Case Studies of Manufacturing: Gristmilling and the Rural Milling Complex*

The characteristic rural manufacturing establishment resembled the well-located Albion Mills in Barton Township, at the head of Lake Ontario, which was described in 1825 by Andrew Bell, a young teacher there.

It is not above ten years since a clearing of any consequence was made when Mr. Secord came here. He has now between one and two hundred acres cleared, and keeps a farmer, who farms it on shares. He has a grist mill, a saw mill, a potash manufacturer, a distillery, and a store, in all of which he keeps men, and looks over the whole himself. Besides these, he has a blacksmith, carpenter's and cooper's shops on his farm, for his own convenience and provides them with tools. All of these, with the people's houses, a tavern, a public school house, and my school house, all on the farm, and his own dwelling house, storehouses, and offices, make something of a village.[10]

John Secord's enterprises lacked only a carding and fulling mill and a tannery to be fully representative of rural industry in the province.[11] Here one man controlled an entire complex. Doing so could increase his income, make fuller use of available water-power, make better use of labour by sustaining work in seasons when specific industries were inactive, spread risks over more ventures, and increase his ability to meet all the locality's needs. Often, as at Albion Mills, the craftsmen who operated each element in the complex worked on shares and/or for wages. Or they might build, rent, or buy (on credit or for cash) particular elements of a complex, such as a blacksmith's shop or a tannery. However owned, and even if not all were located on one site, the mills, shops, and crafts in an area were linked in a variety of ways, including the credit system (see chapter 8).

A large commercial flour mill, such as the new one opened in 1826 by C. and J. McDonald, at Gananoque, with its four runs of stones, could produce 110 barrels of flour per day, when worked on a 24 hours-per-day basis.[12] In 1845 a new mill at Port Hope produced 100 barrels in a 24-hour workday, 600 barrels a week, during the peak flouring season.[13] Charles Jones's Yonge Mills, near Brockville, could produce 200 barrels every 24 hours.[14] Had the mill routinely worked at that rate, even its 1836 output, a record 18,000 barrels (see table 6.5) could have been produced in just ninety days. Such intense working was not an everyday, or even an every year, occurrence, given seasonal and year-to-year fluctuations in demand, power, and wheat supply. Like much else in the rural economy, even the largest mills were seasonal operations. In the Upper Canadian context, they were major businesses, yet even at their largest, mill workforces were scarcely large. At Yonge Mills, ten to fifteen men worked relatively full-time in peak months, but occasionally as many as twenty-five men were at work at the same time, and as few as five or six were employed at others.[15]

Only particularly well-located mills were as large as Yonge Mills, the McDonald mill, or others such as W.H. Merritt's Welland Canal Mill.[16] Output in the range of 1,000 to 5,000 barrels was more usual for commercial mills at least into the 1840s. Alexander McNeilledge's Dover Mills on Lake Erie, for example, took in almost 20,000 bushels of wheat between September 1834 and August 1835, which would have produced about 4,000 barrels of flour.[17] To function at the level of the mid-1830s, Yonge Mills had to incur the cost of bringing wheat by ship from farther west in Upper Canada and at times from the United States. Deliveries at the mill (that is, from within the region) ranged between 4,000 and 10,000 bushels per year in the 1830s, and the wheat received as the standard toll for custom milling (one-twelfth) shows wheat ground on farmers' accounts to have ranged between 4,300 and 11,200 bushels in years for which tolls are recorded (table 6.5). Thus, the mill produced from 800 to over 2,000 barrels per year from local wheat. Similar outputs are indicated for a mill in Prince Edward County in 1840, for George Ball's Louth Mills west of St Catharines, until the early 1840s, for the newly built Goldie mill, near Galt, in 1851, and for the Tench mill in the Newmarket area, in 1852–3.[18]

Below these mills in the provincial system were country mills that ground local grain on commission for local consumption. For example, Hamnett Pinhey's mill, in the Ottawa valley, apparently ground just 834 bushels of wheat (and 700 of other grains) in 1829. Similarly, the mill at Martintown, in Glengarry, appears to have ground only 660 bushels of wheat (and 300 of other grains) in 1845.[19] The standard toll of one-twelfth on such volumes of wheat, respectively 70 bushels (worth £21 in 1829) and 55 bushels (worth £11 in 1845), had to be shared between the mill-owner and the miller; it is evident that gristmilling was not a full-time job for either miller.

Although flour mills processed one of the province's principal exports, they were also part of the internal economy. Indeed, consumption within the province far exceeded exports until the 1840s, even in a year of exceptional exports like 1836. If we estimate local demand at 35 bushels of wheat (equal to 7 barrels of flour) per household a year, the 374,000 people in 1836 would have required up to 435,000 barrels of flour, or 2.5 times the volume exported.[20] Just ten mills with the output of Yonge Mills could have supplied all of the province's flour exports in 1836, the peak year in flour exports before the 1840s (tables 4.2 and 6.5), and thirty-three such mills could have supplied all of the province's requirements. By 1836, however, the province had over 350 grist mills.

Ordinary country mills spread with settlement. As settlement intensified, local grain production rose, as did demand for a higher quality of flour. To satisfy such changes in demand and even to maintain the province's stock of establishments as mills passed from production through fire, obsolescence, and shifts in water flows, continued milling investment was required.[21] If the initial construction of a country mill represented an investment in extensive growth, subsequent investments contributed to the improvement of productivity and thus were in part investments in intensive development. The number of people per grist mill in the province doubled between 1826 and 1851, and average output per mill more than doubled, from about 1,200 barrels a year in 1827 to about 2,900 in 1851.[22]

Grist mills required some imported components, but the provincial economy supplied an increasing share of the machinery for them. When Hamnett Pinhey set out to build a grist mill in his new settlement in 1822–3, he was advised to get 'some person whose abilities have been satisfactorily proven in this country.' He eventually contracted with two men for a new mill. Before coming to his site, where they spent an entire summer, they ordered castings in Montreal. Pinhey was meanwhile to supply a building 'as high as the ground floor,' plus the millstones.[23] Here the costs of iron work and castings and of the millstones were paid beyond the immediate locality, but still within the larger Canadian economy. For this and another contemporary mill in the Ottawa region, inputs from beyond the immediate locality constituted just over half of the total costs itemized, amounting to around £240 in each case (table 6.6).[24]

Even such country mills were major building projects in their localities. A major mill was one of the largest private building projects to be executed in Upper Canada. To build or buy a large mill was likely to cost about £3,000, and smaller commercial mills evidently cost from £500 to £1,000 or more.[25] Such projects might require two years to design and carry out, as was the case in two Niagara region mills (one seven storeys high) built in the 1820s by John Abbott, a Lockport, New York, millwright who worked on both sides of the river. He also assisted in the design of some other mills in the region, principally by specifying castings for the machinery. Those he ordered came often from Rochester, beyond the provincial economy, but by the mid-1820s, mill castings were also available within Upper Canada. In the west, for example, the Normandale ironworks supplied mill irons to specifications worked out between its moulder and the customer's millwright.[26]

The Ottawa valley country mills documented in table 6.6 were erected for men with outside sources of income, and for whom payment was quite straightforward. It was more common to finance construction, upgrading, or purchase of a mill on credit, and let the mill pay for itself as it worked. Especially for manufacturing mills, oriented to extra-regional exports, merchants would advance capital as part of developing sources of supply. The value of such mills' annual output was likely substantially to exceed their capital cost, though mills also had supply, labour, and other costs. A Port Hope mill built in 1844–5 with funds provided by the Gilmour interests in Montreal required at least £750 to equip the mill, but a vastly larger sum, £8,500, was employed to buy wheat for milling. In another case, the Goldie mill built near Galt in 1848–50, the millwright was paid in instalments extending up to eighteen months after completion of the contract, and £125 worth of castings and millstones were purchased on credit from the suppliers, located in nearby Hamilton and Dundas.[27] Similarly, costs could be spread over several years by upgrading existing dams and structures in stages.

Many grist mills were owned by or were linked to distilleries, which converted local grains into 'high wines' (unaged spirits at the end of the distillation process) and whisky. Distilling began early. Richard Cartwright Jr, for example, took delivery of a still, ordered through Schenectady, in 1793.[28] The logic of adding distilling to milling was explained by John Askin in 1803.

As I find I can errect [sic] my Distillery with next to no cost having Bricks, Lime the Stills, Plank Boards and round Timber, of which I mean to make it I purpose to put it up before June next. Whisky sells for 10/– per Gallon [York cy assumed] rye from 3/6 to 6/– per Bushell and as 1 Bushell makes from 3 to 3¹/₂ Galls. the profit is considerable and what increases it much is the Grain fattening Hoggs much and the Swill of great use to milch Cows. I can get Rye & Wheat in exchange for Whisky & there is a tolerable Distiller who is in my debt.[29]

Not everyone could count on every element that Askin could, but the links he saw among the aspects of his business were evident enough that, as wheat prices fell after 1801, distilling expanded swiftly. Between 1798 and 1802, the number of still licences and the distilling capacity in the province more than doubled. An estimate in Richard Cartwright's papers speaks in terms of output of twelve gallons of liquor for every gallon of still capacity; at this rate, the 6,000 gallons of capacity licensed in 1801–2 would have produced about six gallons per adult male in Upper Canada that year.[30] The same estimate said still capacity in the province was 13,000 gallons in 1804, a figure reached several years later by official records (see table 6.7). This was almost the all-time pre-1840 peak for licensed capacity in Upper Canada.

Nor was this all the drink available in the colony. Brewing was established early, and much rum was imported, for the military and the fur trade as much as or more than for local consumption. Some 9,400 gallons of rum (equivalent to one gallon per adult male) were imported to Upper Canada in the first six months of 1802, for example.[31] Clearly there was no shortage of distilling capacity in the province even by 1803. Prices for whisky in bulk fell sharply, from about 5s a gallon at the head of Lake Ontario in 1801–2 to as low as 2s 10d by 1804. Richard Cartwright Jr put his two stills, having a combined capacity of 220 gallons, up for sale in 1802, for about £260.[32]

During the War of 1812 the rum supply was interrupted, causing the commissariat to buy local spirits for the forces, and inflation also drove prices upward. From 5s 6d a gallon at York in 1812, whisky rose to 17s 6d by 1814.[33] For a time, as we noted in chapter 3, distilling was actually prohibited. But following the war, prices fell steeply to between 1s 2d and 1s 8d a gallon throughout the 1820s and 1830s.[34] Such prices did not eliminate the industry, because of its close links to other aspects of the milling business, which could make its marginal costs in a rural industrial complex low. One distillery calculated that it was feeding over fifty hogs on its swill, and computed their weight at slaughter at over 10,000 pounds. Yonge Mills supplied some of its 'whisky stuff' (i.e., rye and mill by-products) to a nearby distillery and received a stipulated share of the whisky in return.[35] At Alexander McNeilledge's rural milling complex in the late 1820s, employment records show the distillery working in tandem with the grist mill. The difficulty of controlling fermentation in summer's heat was a further cause of seasonality. At McNeilledge's distillery, the peak of work was from October to January, and much less work went on during the late spring and summer.[36] Following Richard Cartwright Jr, we estimated that up to 16 per cent of provincial wheat was distilled in 1803 (table 2.4). That was surely the highest rate ever. By the 1830s Thomas McIlwraith calculates that less than 1 per cent of provincial wheat was distilled. By then, 'Rye & Corn & *inferior* wheat' plus mill by-products were the main produce distilled.[37]

Licensed capacity reached almost 14,000 gallons in 1820, and rebounded to over 12,000 gallons in 1827 (table 6.7). Meanwhile, Upper Canada continued to import spirits. Though not all were for local consumption, some 179,000 gallons of rum and other drink went upriver in 1824, and 1825 imports totalled 139,000 gallons. Even the latter figure equalled more than three gallons a year per man in Upper Canada over sixteen years of age. During the 1830s, while population doubled, licensed capacity stayed below 10,000 gallons.[38] Some distilled spirits were exported to Lower Canada, the peak year being 1836, when about 2,400 barrels (assumed to be of 40 gallons and worth from £7,000 to £10,000) were shipped downriver. Exports were a small part of total output, however.

By the 1840s a less universal and extensive pattern of development began to be evident. Although there are gaps and discrepancies in the data series (which derive from tax and census records that variously reported numbers of stills, establishments, and licences, and volumes of stills and output), the trends are clear. The 147 establishments (not licences) counted in the 1842 census (equal to one for every 2.8 grist mills) do not suggest an expansion commensurate with population growth when they are compared to the 157 licences issued in 1827 (equal to one for every 1.7 grist mills).[39] If all 147 had output equal to the 10,000 gallons produced by one distillery near Peterborough a few years before, they would have produced enough liquor to provide for twice the exports of 1836 and for ten gallons for every Upper Canadian male aged eighteen or over.[40] By 1851 population doubled again, but the number of establishments declined to 102. The 1861 census counted 53 establishments, though licensing data showed over 80 licensed stills;[41] by 1866, only 32 distilleries were licensed in Upper Canada, and in 1871 the census reported just 18 distilleries remaining (table 6.7). By then, most of the grain distilled in Upper Canada was Indian corn, much of it evidently imported, not mill by-products.

Despite the rise of the temperance movement, provincial output held steady in the 1850s and rose substantially in the 1860s. The 2.9 million gallons of spirits distilled in Upper Canada in 1861 were equivalent to almost 7 gallons for every male of sixteen years or older, a figure comparable to our estimates for earlier in the century. Imports, though much lower than earlier on a per capita basis, remained considerable,[42] and indicate that distillers faced competition from outside the province as well as from one another in terms of taste, quality, and price. Distilling's transition from a widely diffused industry to a localized, concentrated, specialized business producing brand-name products was almost completed by 1871, and it represented the eventual course of many pioneer industries. But no other had gone very far by that date.[43]

Homespun woollens were produced by many rural households. Two aspects of their production were mechanized: carding, in which wool was combed by drawing it over cards to align the strands preparatory to spinning, and fulling, in which cloth was cleansed, thickened, and felted by a process of washing and beating. Carding was summer work, following the seasonal sheep-shearing, and fulling, which followed weaving, took place in the fall and winter. Because a site suited for one process was equally convenient for the other, many establishments performed both processes. The homespun industry supplied only a portion of the province's textiles; cottons and woollens were usually the two leading categories by value of provincial imports, and silks and linens were lesser ones.[44]

There were at least as many sheep as people in Upper Canada in 1842 and 1848, and in both years the wool produced averaged three pounds per person. That figure fell slightly by 1861, but even then about two-thirds of small and three-quarters of large farms kept sheep (tables 5.3, 5.4). Trade data record rising Canadian wool exports during the 1850s, and especially under the Reciprocity Treaty, but the majority of Upper Canadian wool was still destined for consumption within the province (tables 12.2, 12.3, 12.4).[45] The census reported 186 carding mills in 1842 and 144 fulling mills, and 239 of the latter in 1848 (but none of the former). Increasingly the census began to record establishments as woollen factories (table 6.3). Although ambiguities of classification and the sharp rebound from 1861 to 1871 in numbers of establishments complicate the analysis of industrial change, it is clear that absolute levels of household production of woollen cloth levelled off around mid-century; and on a per capita basis, output declined in Upper Canada from 2.4 yards of cloth per person in 1842 to 1.1 yard by 1870–1. By then a large proportion of the woollen cloth made in the province was produced in factories.[46]

The basic machinery for carding, usually two carding machines and an initial supply of cards, by the early 1820s could be acquired for about £125. A similar amount was needed to set up and begin to operate the machinery, assuming that a mill already existed on a site.[47] One or two men could operate a mill. From the 1820s to the 1840s the most common rate for carding in the province was 4d per pound of wool.[48] At an output per capita of about three pounds of wool, the value of wool carding in the province would thus have been just one shilling per person. For the provincial population of 487,000 in 1842, the maximum value of carding was thus about £24,000, equal to £130 for each of the 186 establishments in the province. To earn that much would have entailed carding almost 8,000 pounds of wool.

Fulling apparently cost as little as 4d per yard, but higher quality fulling cost considerably more.[49] According to the 1842 census, some 434,000 yards of 'home-made cloth' and 727,000 yards of unfulled 'home-made flannel' were produced in the province. If we assume that all wool cloth except flannel was fulled, at a cost of one shilling per yard, we can estimate the value of fulling at about £22,000, equal to £150 per establishment. Mills also earned income from oiling at the carding stage and washing, dying, and pressing after weaving.

Aspects of the pioneer wool industry at its peak are illustrated by the Owen and Stark mill in Norfolk County in the early 1840s.[50] Between mid-May and the end of June of 1841 it took in 9,000 pounds of wool for carding, and by season's end in October over 13,000 pounds had been received, which would have earned at least £220. Fulling began in mid-September and extended into mid-March of 1842. There is a two-month gap in the records which, order numbers suggest, means that one-quarter of the season's work is omitted; the remaining 334 orders totalled about 5,800 yards of cloth, for which the mill charged a total of £374. This establishment thus generated well over £600 in carding and fulling revenue in a single year, much above the provincial average. This was more than the volumes indicated for the McMartin establishment in Glengarry, though the businesses were in other respects similar. For a period of unknown duration ending in 1823, the latter earned £165 by carding, which suggests a total volume of 10,000 pounds. By contrast, in 1825 the mill carded only 1,131 pounds of wool, for eighty different customers; and in 1827 it must have carded about 3,000 pounds, because its gross earnings were £48. The carder received one-third of that as his share, McMartin getting the remainder in return for supplying the facilities. In a year like 1827 the carder's share, £16, was apparently an acceptable return for several months.[51] McMartin's 1827 share, £32, was likely a satisfactory return on his investment, at least if his capital in the mill was in the order of £300. Clearly it paid well enough that the business survived. In 1850 it was one of four carding and fulling mills in Glengarry and served 240 fulling customers, or almost 10 per cent of the families in the county.[52]

The total of between two and four shillings per capita that passed through carding and fulling mills before the 1850s represented only a small part of the value that was added in the transformation of both local wool and imported fabrics into clothing and other textile products such as bedding. Spinning, weaving, tailoring, and sewing were in part done by skilled craftspeople who worked in their own establishments or in customers' homes, and in part by women and daughters in a household setting.[53] As one drygoods merchant opening a store in the new village of Elora explained, it would not pay to stock clothing, 'as the women make all the clothes required and the Emigrants bring out enough to last them some time.'[54]

There was always some demand from merchants and carding mills to buy wool.[55] In the 1840s more complex woollen manufacturing began to appear. Carding and fulling were by no means eliminated, and indeed some of the census's 'factories' were continuations of the older carding and fulling establishments, perhaps operating less on consignment than on their own account. The new establishments seem still to have handled some spinning and weaving on a putting-out or subcontract basis, but the trend after 1840 was increasingly from home to factory production.[56]

Even more than sheep, cattle were a part of the stock of most provincial farms. Although some tanned leather was imported, local hides, sold to tanneries or tanned on shares, were the basis of a widespread rural leather industry and the primary source of the province's leather.[57] All farms needed harnesses, bridles, whips, and saddles, and everyone needed boots and shoes. In the 1840s Upper Canada had more tanneries than woollen mills (see table 6.3). Because of its demand for hemlock bark as a tanning agent, tanning was frequently combined with ownership of a farm; it also tended to be seasonal work, with a peak during the main slaughtering season in the autumn.[58]

An early tanner was Seneca Ketchum, who practised his trade near York before and after the War of 1812.[59] He bought and sold hides and leather, tanned for his own account and on commission, and bought and sold shoes, apparently on something akin to a putting-out basis; he also sold leather to others who may have been shoemakers themselves. In 1808 he purchased around £90 (Hfx cy) in hides over and above those he tanned on consignment and those he received in payment on ordinary accounts. The capital value of a country tannery is suggested by a contract to build a new tannery on an existing mill site on the Kingston Road east of Toronto in 1844. Here a new building of about 5,000 square feet was contemplated 'with the necessary vats viz 24 vats 4 Leaches 3 lime vats. heater house, back room ...'; the water-power already there was to be harnessed to bark grinding machinery that the tanner was to supply.[60] For the tannery so equipped, before the installation of grinding machinery, an annual rental of £50 was contemplated. That rent (if it represented, say, a 10 per cent rate of return) implies that the maximum value of the establishment was £500.[61]

Something very much larger than this was involved in the Thornhill tannery of B. Thorne & Company, which the bankrupt Thorne valued at £5,000 in late 1847 and described as the 'finest in the Province Superior to the Chippawa One.'[62] Growing commercialization of the leather business is indicated also by the records of an 1850s firm, with a tannery at Holland Landing and a hides, leather, and wool business in Toronto. The Toronto branch handled not only leather tanned at its country establishment, but leathers from Port Hope, Kingston, and Markham tanneries as well as imported leathers. Among those supplied with leather in 1855 were the shoe manufacturers Brown and Childs.[63] At mid-century tanning was beginning to be able to sustain larger and more complex operations, something to which the growth of an urban and mechanized boots and shoes industry undoubtedly would contribute. The fluctuations in numbers of establishments as reported in the census make mid-century patterns in the industry unclear, but its wide diffusion in 1871 and its persistence suggest that we should not exaggerate the extent and comprehensiveness of any transition and consolidation in the industry.[64]

Thus the processing of leather, wool, and grains was widely dispersed through the rural economy. Most rural industries were markedly seasonal, and it is clear that capital was not so scarce in the province as to warrant a bias towards intensive use of capital equipment. Except for major grist mills and one or two deal mills, prior to the 1840s most establishments were valued in the hundreds, not thousands, of pounds. Although in total they represented a considerable capital investment, their scale was such that they could be financed locally and on credit. As their development shows, the province's capital stock, except when it entailed very lumpy investments, was developed on an essentially self-financed, up-by-the-bootstraps basis. There is evidence of a trend to larger-scale establishments, notably in gristmilling, but also in distilling, tanning, and woollens. On the other hand, despite the tendency of industrialization from mid-century onward to involve increasing concentration and localization of production, even in 1871 there remained a place for smaller country tanneries, grist mills, saw mills, and woollen mills that catered principally to local business. Their persistence reflected their integration with other aspects of the rural economy in processing, use of labour, and marketing. Persistence should not be equated with a static and traditional economy, however, for investment and change were essential even within industries whose overall pattern looks to be simple additions of new establishments as population grew.

II. *Artisans and Manufacturing: Blacksmiths, Carpenters, and Shoemakers*

In addition to the artisans who operated the establishments we have so far considered, a much larger number of craftsmen participated in the provincial economy. In 1851, the first year in which the census provides data on the province's workforce by occupation, almost 40,000 Upper Canadians, representing from one-eighth to one-sixth of the male workforce, reported an occupation that we might classify as a skilled trade (see table 6.8).[65] Only about 10 per cent of these men were likely to have worked in establishments such as we have considered above. Over half of the total was accounted for by just four crafts: carpenters, boot- and shoemakers, blacksmiths, and tailors. By comparison, the census reported 86,000 farmers and 79,000 labourers. The latter, who appear at the lower end of most scales of wealth and social rank, supplied physical labour to farmers, artisans, merchants, and others who required occasional, seasonal, or longer-term help.

Because many men worked at a variety of jobs during a year, many were migrants, all moved through a life cycle, and many jobs could be described and classified in more than one way, occupational classification, even for those claiming a skilled trade, is a difficult and ambiguous task.[66] But there is no reason to believe that the census misrepresents the principal crafts in the provincial economy both in and before 1851. Of the seven leading occupations in 1851, six were well represented in a small sample of immigrants who received passes to enter Canada from the British consul in New York in 1817 (see table 6.9). Three of the five leading crafts at mid-century were represented at Albion Mills in 1825. Carpenters, shoemakers, tailors, masons, plasterers, bricklayers, and printers were among the crafts whose members went on strike in Toronto at least once in the 1830s.[67]

The most numerous crafts tended to be the most uniformly distributed in the economy. Eight, including six of the twelve most numerous ones, were actually under-represented in the five largest urban centres in 1851. Of the twelve crafts numbering 900 or more in 1851, only tailors and cabinet-makers had as many as one-fifth of their numbers in the five principal urban centres. By contrast, of the fifteen numbering 300 to 600, just four (tanners, millwrights, wheelwrights, and machinists) had as few as one-fifth of their numbers in the leading towns and cities.[68] It is impossible to discuss all the provincial trades, but a review of aspects of the three leading crafts involved in the rural economy – blacksmiths, carpenters, and shoemakers – indicates the scale and characteristics of such work.

In the fall of 1827 James Reid, a progressive farmer by then well established near Hamilton, wrote his relatives in Scotland that 'A Blacksmith and a shoemaker are most excellent trades here the wages of Labourers have been on the rise.' His views were shared, two decades later, by John Bowman, who wrote to his wheelwright father (and to his blacksmith brother) in Nottinghamshire that 'Blacksmith is the best Bisiness in Canada.' An 1854 letter-writer took a similar view: 'Mechanics of all kinds get along here wonderfully, and no wonder when we know their unreasonable charges ... Blacksmiths work is perhaps the most unreasonable.'[69] The blacksmith's main task was the maintenance of important parts of the community's capital. He shoed the horses (and sometimes oxen) that supplied much of Upper Canada's motive power and heavy farm and lumbering work, and he not only repaired but built ploughs, tools, sleighs, wagons, and harnesses. Smiths also made nails and other iron products used in building, but such manufactured products seem more commonly to have been imported. Reading any rural smith's accounts makes clear that an extensive variety of metal tools was used in the community and reminds us that in the long term, maintenance of such equipment often cost much more than the initial purchase price.[70]

Because horses were counted, we can use information on them to estimate a minimum value for blacksmiths' work in the economy at various times. Almost universally in Upper Canada, it cost either 6d or 7½d per horseshoe for 'setting.' The cost of making a shoe ranged between 1s 3d and 2s, evidently depending on the cost of iron. Thus, making and setting four horseshoes cost from 8s to 10s. William Wylie estimates that the Upper Canadian horse typically was reshod just once a year and had shoes reset once or twice between, although that was less often than experts recommended. At a minimum, horseshoeing thus cost 10s per horse a year. Early assessment records indicate that Upper Canada had about one horse aged three years or more for every seven people. In the late 1830s the ratio rose to about one horse per six Upper Canadians. There were over 30,000 horses in 1830 and over 72,000 in 1840; over 200,000 were counted in 1851, and by 1861 there were 378,000, equal to one horse for every 3.7 Upper Canadians.[71] The census counted all horses, unlike the assessment rolls, but this explains only part of the increase in the ratio of horses to people. The number of horses, and hence demand for blacksmithing services, thus rose faster than population. Using a minimum figure of 10s per horse a year, we can estimate that smiths earned at least £15,000 from shoeing in 1830, £36,000 a decade later, and £100,000 in 1851. On Wylie's estimate, shoeing represented 40 per cent of smiths' work and incomes. If so, total incomes for blacksmiths in 1830 would have exceeded £35,000; in 1840 about £90,000; and in 1851 about £250,000.

If divided equally among 4,200 blacksmiths (see table 6.8), the 1851 estimate equalled a gross revenue of at least £60 per smith. Capital costs to set up a smithy – principally tools, iron, coal, and a building in which to work – were not a large barrier to entry.[72] But in this immigrant economy there must have been many apprentices and journeymen only starting their careers, whose incomes were lower than average. Smiths engaged in making more expensive products such as sleighs, large items selling for as many pounds as horseshoeing cost in pence,[73] would have had larger incomes but also a need to buy more inputs, including hired help. Also, the continued immigration of blacksmiths suggests that the income earned by successful blacksmiths in the province was attractive.[74]

While the pioneer's first house was typically built of logs, there were by 1831 almost 10,000 houses in Upper Canada of non-log construction. By 1841 that figure had grown to about 30,000 and by 1851 to over 63,000. About 85 per cent of the latter total was of frame construction. The rate of growth in the number of houses for which carpentry, masonry, and other craft work was required thus exceeded 12 per cent a year over the two decades. This was much faster than the rate of population growth and reflected both additions to and upgrading of provincial housing stock. By 1851, in one-quarter of all townships in the province, principally those around Lake Ontario from Kingston west and in some areas of the western peninsula, half or more of houses consisted of non-log buildings.[75] In addition to housing, this economy built, improved, added to, rebuilt, and repaired mills, barns, churches, schools, offices, warehouses, and bridges. How these were built, at what total cost, and by whom they were built and financed are just beginning to be known.[76] But it is not surprising that the 7,600 carpenters represented the leading craft in Upper Canada in terms of numbers in 1851, and probably long before.

By comparison with blacksmiths, the work of carpenters was less defined and even more universal. At one extreme were developers, building houses and other property for rental or on a speculative basis for later sale, and contractors, who built or supervised the building of major urban structures, with the complexities that such projects entailed. At the other extreme were men who were essentially labourers or handymen with recognized ability to work with wood. The craft of carpenter also had links to such wholly or partially distinct trades as mill construction, masonry, cabinet-making, and wagon-making.[77]

The extent and variety of work involved in building can be seen in the work done by John Bird for Alexander Caterwood, in the Sarnia region, in 1841. During some fifty-one days, he was engaged in making two 'slays,' some window sashes, some doors, some steps, some harrows, a 'cubard,' a 'chist'; raising and working on a barn; working on chimneys; doing repair work on a mill, a house, a wheelbarrow, and a harrow; and hauling some lumber and a millstone. Here was a country woodworker, a generalist, doing a broad range of work. Parts of either a new or an existing building were involved along with the new barn that Bird notes, but none of this work represented what we would understand by building a house. Bird was paid about 4s a day, a rate lower than the 5s ($1) a day that is frequently indicated as a carpenter's wage.[78]

Barns and houses came at virtually every price, from a few pounds to many hundreds or even thousands, depending on scale, furnishing, finishing, and the degree to which the owner supplied his own labour.[79] Completion of a basic structure only began a long-term process of investment and improvement, moreover. As Robert Wade wrote to relatives at home in explanation of the progress being made on his new house, 'We have to get along a little at a time in this country as we have no landlords to build us houses and barns.'[80] One farmer's diary, for example, shows housing expenditures totalling around £40 over a span of four years from 1839 to 1843.[81] The investment represented by the province's stock of buildings thus was incremental and cumulative, built and paid for in stages. With the exception of glass and some iron and hardware, its inputs were supplied from within the provincial economy, and the economic stimulus accompanying expenditure on them stayed there.

Boot- and shoemakers, the second most numerous craft according to the 1851 census, were also universally met with and formed part of the local leather industry. Some worked in establishments employing apprentices and journeymen to produce shoes of standard types for retail sale, while others worked in smaller shops that both made and repaired boots and shoes, using mainly local and some imported leathers.[82] The accounts of one successful craftsman in Kingston from 1848 to 1854 show the wide range of footwear produced and that a significant share of the work was devoted to repairs.[83] Without knowing more about the variety, durability, and quality of the footwear of ordinary Upper Canadians, it is difficult to estimate the total value of work done by shoemakers. But if we assume that the average price of a pair of shoes was 5s,[84] that one pair was sold per person a year, and that making new boots and shoes represented only two-thirds of this craft's work and income, the average gross income per shoemaker in Upper Canada in 1851 would have been over £60.[85] The craft was at its peak in 1851; during the next twenty years it would be reorganized on a factory basis, as the sewing machine and later the McKay machine made centralized production increasingly economical. By 1871, except for repair and high-value custom work, the craft was transformed into an essentially industrial occupation.[86] A similar fate awaited some other crafts, including coopers; by 1851, however, few had faced such a challenge in Upper Canada.

III. *Case Studies in Urban Industry: Foundries, Newspapers, Brewing*

Before the War of 1812, many cast-iron products were supplied to Upper Canada by the Forges St Maurice and from American sources. Gradually, more of the province's growing requirements were supplied from within Upper Canada, in part by its many blacksmiths. The line between a large smith's establishment and a foundry may not have been easily drawn; still, according to the census, no industry expanded more rapidly than iron founding at the mid-century (table 6.3).

One long-lived foundry, the most successful of those smelting local iron, used bog iron found near Long Point on Lake Erie. Established in

1818, it began to be operated in 1822-3 by Joseph Van Norman, in partnership initially with Hiram Capron and subsequently with several others. The Van Norman family had been in the foundry business in New York State, and Capron evidently supplied capital. When the 'stockholders' began in the summer of 1825 to pay themselves 'dividends,' in the form of 'ware,' to be marketed by the holder, Capron received 51 per cent of the ware divided. Some smelted iron was sold to founders and blacksmiths, and the remainder was manufactured into stoves (for which the establishment was widely known), cauldrons, plough castings, barrow wheels, wagon boxes, kettles, potash kettles, and other products, shipped by team and schooner throughout the western peninsula.[87]

One author says that four hundred people 'directly and indirectly' worked for this business at its peak,[88] but much of that figure consisted of independent workers and suppliers who provided wood for charcoal, produce for its workers, teaming services, and so on. Even so, the furnace, with its associated works, was among the largest individual manufacturing enterprises in the province. Capron's record of dividends from 1825 to 1828 indicates output of at least £5,000 in the year ending 12 August 1826 and over £10,000 in total from spring 1825 to May 1828. If, as seems possible, the 'dividends' were net after some or all direct costs of operating had been covered, actual output would have been higher. Although the value of its output was likely equivalent to that of a major commercial grist mill, the value added by the ironworks greatly exceeded that added to wheat in the milling process.

The firm did not have a monopoly in the west. American products competed with it,[89] and several of those involved at Normandale later established their own foundries in the west, which might use Normandale iron but competed in selling finished products. Among these were George Tillson, son-in-law of Van Norman, and Elijah Leonard, who set up his business at St Thomas.[90] The price of British pig iron tended to decline, albeit with considerable fluctuations, and it could be shipped relatively cheaply as ballast on westbound shipping; competitive pressures on iron smelting in Upper Canada thus tended to mount. The Normandale furnace remained in production until the early 1850s, in part by using American iron ore, but then gave way entirely to imported iron.[91]

In 1830 or 1831, iron deposits in Gosfield Township, Essex County, were brought into production, to produce stoves, kettles, ploughs, millgears, and other cast products. The works were operated by a 15-horsepower steam engine and said to be able to produce five tons of pig iron in a twenty-four-hour working day. Employment in the winter of 1832 was said to be seventy men on a daily basis.[92] But such works were very vulnerable to competition, in terms of price and of the quality of iron produced. By 1837 the Gosfield works had closed. The same story held for the Marmora Iron Works, which were only occasionally in production after the 1830s. Here the works lacked a large agricultural community in the immediate environs, and the cost of overland transport to Lake Ontario was burdensome. Nevertheless, at their peak the works could produce four tons of cast and five of bar iron a day from two smelters, and claimed to be able to supply a wide range of products, including shot and shells and gun carriages for the military, stoves, pots, kettles, wagon and mill castings, and 'Bar Iron of a quality equal to Swedes.'[93] Not far from these were the Madoc Iron Works, which opened in 1836 with a furnace that in 1841 was said to be producing as much as two tons of iron a day.[94]

Apart from those linked to iron deposits, there were few provincial foundries in the 1820s. There were two at York in 1828, Dutcher's and Shepard's, both using old iron and iron from Long Point to produce ploughs, axes, and other products.[95] By 1842 the census reported twenty-two iron foundries, fourteen of which were located in the western half of the province, from Niagara and Hamilton westward. It was becoming clear then that the future of the iron business in the province lay in finished goods. In 1851, there were ninety-seven foundries, of which sixty were in the area west of York County and another eight in Toronto and York.[96] Still, only a handful of counties, principally outside Bytown along the Ottawa River, lacked foundries altogether.

There is exceptionally good documentation for one new foundry in the 1830s, that of John Fisher and Calvin McQuesten in Hamilton.[97] Fisher opened the foundry in early spring 1836, using $2,200 advanced by his cousin, McQuesten, a doctor in Brockport, New York. Fisher and a workforce of at least six began to make ploughs, of which he sold thirty-six in the first spring. Much more expensive, and probably the principal product in the first year, was threshing machinery; a single machine was priced at $150 cash or (as was more usual) $160 on credit.[98] There was considerable competition in this line from a maker in nearby Paris. The firm used American patterns, but quickly adapted as experience showed problems. Other castings and products were added, notably stoves, wheels, and scales. Iron for the foundry came from Scotland, the United States, and Van Norman's furnaces ('some of it very good'),[99] all at similar prices; coal from Pennsylvania was imported through Oswego or Rochester. By February 1838 Fisher calculated the business to be worth almost $5,000; sales for 1838 amounted to about the same figure.[100]

This story shows how even what might become a heavy industry could be fitted into the provincial economy without enormous investments in fixed capital. A summary of the business's position after one year indicated that working capital was the principal form of finance required (table 6.10). Of the over $7,000 in assets, less than $2,000 represented land, buildings, patterns, and equipment. Manufacturing of this type, while having a variety of specifically production-related problems, was equally a commercial operation. The new foundry was also able to draw in a small way on credit from Hamilton's new Gore Bank. If the firm could meet demand at appropriate costs, it could build itself up from its earnings. On the other hand, like any commercial house, it soon found itself with a substantial body of outstanding debts due to it. This was a factor in Dr McQuesten's eventual decision to follow his funds to Upper Canada.

The foundry required several skilled workers, notably an iron turner, a pattern-maker, and at times a moulder (Fisher himself sometimes did this work). Such men were evidently available in Hamilton, but finding new workers and dealing with existing ones were frequent subjects of correspondence. Like Van Norman's, this was an offshoot of a New York enterprise, which provided connections in launching the business. As its manufacture of farm implements reveals, the foundry's growth was part of the development of agriculture in the western peninsula. The rapid rise in the number of foundries recorded in the 1840s indicates that others likewise responded to the opportunities of the period.[101]

A principal industry later in the nineteenth century in Toronto was printing and publishing, which was important not only in itself but as part of the power of the city in the provincial and national communications systems.[102] This sector of the provincial economy, which began to take shape in the 1820s and 1830s, was already focused at Toronto. John Macaulay listed thirty-six newspapers published in Upper Canada in 1841, eight of which had survived for ten years or more; no fewer than twelve newspapers were published at Toronto (table 6.11). The industry expanded rapidly in the 1830s and 1840s, six papers being established in 1836 alone. By 1845 W.H. Smith counted forty-seven newspapers, ten in Toronto (at least five of them new since 1840). Except for those at Berlin and Sandwich, all the 1845 newspapers were located in communities with a population of 1,000 or more, and just six such towns – Amherstburg, Paris, Dundas, Oshawa, Port Hope, and Prescott – did not have a newspaper.[103]

Entry into the business was not prohibitively costly. Printing equipment might be acquired on credit; partnerships could ease ownership transitions or the capital required of a single owner; and presses and type could be rented or shared, as in two of the Toronto papers, *The Banner* and *The*

*Globe*.[104] William Lyon Mackenzie won £625 in damages following the 1826 destruction of his press and type, and that likely overstates the value of the equipment required to enter the industry.[105] With our eyes on the modern urban daily, we may not think of the typical colonial four-page weekly as an industry, but the principal newspapers were as substantial as most manufacturing establishments of their time, employing apprentices and journeymen to set type and operate the presses. W.L. Mackenzie's *Constitution* at the time of an 1836 strike employed four apprentices and up to eight journeymen. The first meeting of the York Typographical Society, established by and for journeyman printers in October 1832, was attended by twenty-four men, and there were thirty-five members in 1835.[106] By 1851, the census reported 436 printers in the province, 133 in Toronto alone, and another 99 in the other four principal urban centres.

Newspapers, like other industries, were general establishments which usually did job printing and often sold books, paper, and stationery. Unlike many industries, successful newspapers could provide relatively regular work at what were evidently good wages for a craftsman. The standard rate for a journeyman in Toronto in the mid-1830s was 35s a week (over $1 a working day), with overtime after 60 hours. While they relied heavily on imported news and some may have used imported paper, the newspapers were otherwise part of the provincial and local exchange economy. Almost all of the expenses of the province's largest newspaper at the end of the 1820s, Hugh C. Thomson's *Upper Canada Herald*, published in Kingston, were local.[107] He bought about £200 worth of newsprint in a year, from Crooks's mill at the Head of the Lake, and his other payments, which in total were several times this amount per year, were almost entirely made in Kingston.[108]

Brewing was one of the province's earliest industries. By 1802 the owners of a brewery at York had invested at least £1,000 in it, and a similar value was placed on a brewery at Niagara in 1823.[109] By then, deflation had reduced the value of a typical brewery to about £500.[110] As with other such establishments, a skilled craftsman was necessary; a brewer might be hired as an employee, work the brewery on shares, rent the property, or acquire a share of ownership by his work. Brewing was seasonal, for it required cool temperatures, or much ice, to stop the fermentation process at the appropriate time. It was principally an urban industry: fifty-three of the eighty-five breweries recorded by W.H. Smith in 1845 were in communities of 1,000 or more, and all such towns and cities except Cornwall had at least one brewery.[111] If we ignore the 1851 Census, which appears anomalous by comparison with those before and after (table 6.3),[112] from 1842 to 1871 there was little substantial growth in the number of brewing establishments. Nor do census employment data or published data on total output suggest increases in the average scale of establishments.[113]

## IV. Conclusion

The processing and fabricating activities discussed here show much about the structure of and changes within the Upper Canadian economy before 1850. It is evident that we have only seen limited aspects of the production of two necessities, food and clothing. Gristmilling, carding and fulling, tanning, distilling, and brewing, and the crafts of shoemaking, tailoring, dressmaking, baking, and butchery represent these areas. The remainder of the province's food and clothing either was produced at home and did not pass through the marketplace, or if market relationships were involved, was not captured by standard statistics.[114] In either case, much of the work was done by women.

We have depicted provincial growth as a balanced process, in which the local economy provided many of its own needs and grew with a momentum not closely tied to a particular export. If women's work was fully quantified and included, our sense of the scale of local production and consumption would be further enlarged. Many elements of the local economy were undramatic and individually modest, and have been little studied or 'invisible.' Yet cumulatively they represented a great deal of the province's productive activity, capital, and exchange.[115] There is a temptation to depict pioneers and their economy as simple, but in fact Upper Canadians were adaptable and resilient and had numerous choices to make as they sought to balance risks and returns in pursuit of personal and family security and success.[116]

The typical 'industry' of the pioneer era was rural, with establishments diffused widely, almost uniformly across the province, and closely integrated into the rural economy. With sustained urban development from the 1830s onward, industry grew that needed concentrated local markets, catered to a population that did not farm, and/or needed wider markets than the country mill required. In rural and even in urban areas, most producers did quite general businesses that suited the seasonal, cyclical, competitive, and communication constraints of the time and place. Few craftsmen did narrowly specialized tasks; few manufacturing establishments routinely employed as many as ten men on a full-time, year-round basis, and almost none had as many as one hundred workers; many rural artisans also owned land to which they devoted part of their efforts.[117]

The pre-eminent form of growth in the economy to 1850 was extensive. As we have seen, grist, saw, and carding and fulling mills, distilleries, tanneries, and craftsmen such as blacksmiths, carpenters, and shoemakers were universal parts of the process of settlement. Yet even in some of these sectors, growth involved more than just simple replication of identical units of production. The developments were partly quantitative and partly qualitative. The best-located, best-run grist mills were expanding their productive capacity and ability to produce higher grades of flour; the quality of housing, barns, and presumably furnishings was being steadily improved; larger and more sophisticated tanneries were being built in the 1840s; distilling was by then beginning its consolidation; woollen factories were beginning to join carding and fulling mills; and more specialized occupations such as wagon- and cabinet-making were beginning to be sustainable. As for sawmilling, to which we return in chapter 12, export markets were the driving force in the appearance of more-sophisticated, larger-volume mills at about the mid-century. We should not exaggerate the speed, scale, or comprehensiveness of most of these transitions, however, and many establishments of traditional style remained viable both in 1851 and in 1871.

After 1830, as the rapid growth of foundries and of the provincial newspaper business revealed, provincial manufacturing was adding new dimensions. The former competed in part with manufactured imports; the latter was necessarily quite local. The rise of founding contrasted with the absolute decline of the local smelting industry as imported pig and bar iron became much cheaper in the 1840s. Another development, the use of steam power, will be considered in the next chapter. As we shall see, there was no lag in the province's adoption of that technology.

It is not possible to calculate with great precision what proportion these productive activities were of total provincial output and income. But wage and income data and our analysis here of the structure of crafts and manufacturing permit at least a crude estimate of the significance of the manufacturing sector. Wage rates varied, as did intensity and terms of employment, by season, employer, place, and year; wages might be expressed as time or piece rates or a combination of the two; inclusion in wages of full or partial board and room was common; so was working on shares and full or partial worker self-employment. Nor were all the details of these arrangements typically committed to paper. Still, we can extend the argument made in chapter 5 on the scale and significance of the local economy by estimating a minimum total value of the artisan sector's earnings.

Virtually the lowest daily wage publicly reported for a craft through the 1830s and 1840s was 5s per day. For example, one extensive survey around 1840, intended for the information of immigrants, reported wage rates for seventeen of the twenty-seven occupations included in table 6.8.[118] These ranged from 5s per day for bakers to 9s for millwrights (both without room and board), and from £35 per year for bakers to over £90 for millwrights and bricklayers (with board and lodging). Only butchers, bakers, and tanners were said to earn less than £50 per year; blacksmiths, carpenters, shoemakers, tailors, millers, wheel-makers, and sawyers were all said to earn £54 to £62 per year plus room and board. As our evidence on the earnings of blacksmiths, shoemakers, carpenters, printers, and millers confirms, we are unlikely to overestimate annual artisan incomes by a large amount if we assume they averaged £40 per year (which could be earned in 160 working days at 5s). At that rate, the 40,000 who gave a craft as their occupation in Upper Canada in 1851 would in total have earned and spent at least £1.6 million, which almost exactly matches John McCallum's estimate for total Upper Canadian farm income from wheat in the same year ($6.5 million).[119] If labourers' incomes and artisans' earnings in kind were factored into the analysis, our sense of the extent of artisan and labourer incomes, and hence of local demand, would of course be further enlarged.

The argument we have developed thus far is that it has been analytically convenient but inaccurate in terms of actual historical development to treat wheat-generated income as the prime mover in the economy. As we have seen, that misrepresents the simultaneous and interdependent character of investment in farming and other sectors of the economy.[120] In fact, all the industry and crafts considered here (with the exception of export-oriented flour mills, themselves only a part of the gristmilling sector) were focused on the internal economy of the province. To a degree, the subsequent industrial transition of Ontario has been seen as a function of the mid-century, when a massive wheat boom, reciprocity with the United States, and railway investment all emphasized the economy's international links. It is important to emphasize, however, that the roots of most of the industrial sectors that would be important later in the century can be seen in the household, craft, and manufacturing production that was established before 1850.[121]

# 7 Transportation and Communications, 1800–1850

Like many other aspects of the provincial economy, Upper Canada's transportation and communication system has often been seen in terms of public policies that focused on the system's problems and on promoters' visions, and it has therefore been known more for what it lacked than for what it had.[1] Of the system under which Upper Canada developed until after 1830, during nearly fifty years of expansion, the usual accounts say little, and nothing positive; because it 'was slow, expensive, and goods frequently arrived in a damaged condition,' it placed 'an almost unbearable burden on trade.'[2] Many Canadians wanted public investment in canals, harbours, and roads, but their desires need to be understood in the context of the actual demand for transportation services in the Upper Canadian economy rather than being seen as the whole story. There were two components to the provincial system: one was long-haul transport, mainly provided by waterways, which in Upper Canada were relatively accessible from much of the potentially arable land; the other was local transport, largely provided by roads but sometimes by water. Although a common carrier system of stages, teaming, and carters existed, people often provided their own local modes of conveyance. Of course the system moved information as it moved visible cargoes – that is, exports, imports, products in local exchange, passengers, and mail.

## I. The System to 1820

As with much else in the economy of early Upper Canada, the British military and the fur trade provided the initial water transportation system. On the lakes, the government supplied all shipping until privately owned ships appeared about 1789. By 1812 the commercial fleet on Lake Ontario was probably larger than the government's. Along the St

Lawrence, a system of government and private boats, organized from Lachine, connected Montreal and Kingston. Each boat dispatched upriver was numbered in sequence, and merchants' bills of lading specified boat numbers as part of the documentation. Between 1779 and 1783 modest locks had been built at Coteau-du-Lac and Les Cedres to assist in upstream movement. The Royal Engineers improved these and added a canal at the Cascades between 1802 and 1806. An idea of the scale of the system is given by the traffic recorded in 1800 passing the customs house at Coteau-du-Lac.[3] About five hundred boats passed upwards, almost 80 per cent of them privately owned, and over four hundred carriages were recorded, mainly in the winter months. The capacity of boats increased over time as batteaux, with a capacity of about 3 tons, gave way to Durham boats, which carried from 8 to as much as 30 tons of cargo.[4] At the Niagara end of Lake Ontario, goods to and from the upper lakes were carried on a portage around the falls.[5] Above, a further, smaller fleet was required.

Among the best documented of the vessels sailing the lakes in this era are those connected with the enterprises of Richard Cartwright Jr of Kingston and his associates. By 1789 they were operating the *Lady Dorchester*, a schooner of perhaps 90 tons and costing about £1,600 to build. Following a very profitable 1793 season, in 1794 it was joined by and after 1795 replaced by their *Governor Simcoe*, apparently of similar size (sources give it a tonnage of anywhere from 87 to 136, the variance presumably depending on measurement system), and built at a cost of between £1,800 and £1,900.[6] By 1794 competition had arrived on the lake, as the *Dorchester*'s captain, James Richardson, left to command his own vessel.[7] The sharp rise in wheat prices in 1800–1 brought an immediate increase in demand for downriver shipping. But the bottleneck in the spring of 1801, which prompted shippers to try expedients including the construction of scows and rafts to convey flour downriver,[8] revealed not a structural flaw but a temporary problem. By 1802 new boats were available, and the downriver freight rate fell to more typical levels (table 7.5).

As local exports began to grow after 1800, they came to require more shipping capacity than did imports. Shipowners recorded each round trip as a voyage. Seasonal and other considerations meant that vessels seldom achieved a balance in loads each way on a single voyage even if, during the season, they carried freight in both directions. Kingston and Niagara were focal points of the shipping system, for both construction and operation of vessels, but other ports with demand for shipping were served and might occasionally be sites for construction of vessels.

The records of Richard Cartwright's sloop *Elizabeth* for 1807–8 depict the system on Lake Ontario well.[9] At 48 tons, it was almost exactly on the mean for vessel tonnage at the time (table 7.1). During 1808 it made one voyage to York and ten voyages between Kingston and Niagara or 40-Mile Creek, at the head of the lake. Once, in May, it completed the return trip in eight days. Presumably for lack of traffic, it made the trip only three times after mid-August. In total, 70 per cent of its revenue came from downward freight. On only three upward voyages did it earn much revenue; one of these, the trip to York in October, earned its largest freight, £74. Only on the single September voyage was there anything like a balanced cargo: it carried upward freight worth £33 and downward freight worth £54, largely fur packs. The single largest cargo, 4 barrels of potash and 437 of flour, would have weighed (net of barrels) around 39 tons (see table 7.3). In 1807 the *Elizabeth* also earned £55 carrying passengers; passenger revenue is not recorded for 1808. Of 1808's revenue of £523, about half came from carrying flour, a total of 2,800 barrels at 2s each.

Just two *Elizabeths* could easily have carried all the flour exports from the Niagara region in the period 1800–3 (see chapter 2). The growth in demand for shipping in the next decade is shown by the growth of the fleet. By 1812 commercial vessels totalling over 1,000 tons were active on Lake Ontario. Of these, between half and three-quarters were Upper Canadian (table 7.1).[10] The owners of the *Lord Nelson*, built in 1811, said it was worth £1,250.[11] That was considerably less than the *Dorchester* and the *Simcoe* had cost twenty years earlier. Even so, its value exceeded that of most of the province's manufacturing establishments. The investment was justified by the revenues a vessel could generate in a good year and by shipping's utility to many owners' other commercial activities.[12]

Although the provincial government's yacht *Toronto* required a crew of eight men and four boys,[13] private commercial vessels had crews of no more than five. Labour was also needed to load, transship, and unload cargoes and to move boats along the St Lawrence, but the latter segment of the system tended to employ Lower Canadian labour.[14] Richard Cartwright's correspondence indicates a periodic need to recruit labour outside the province, but this was increasingly a matter of routine, not a difficulty.[15] Clearly the provincial economy was amply responsive to rising demand for shipping.

## II. *Steamships*

Steam power was first successfully applied to river navigation, both in the United States and on the lower St Lawrence, in 1807–9, and in the postwar era it became widely used for inland navigation. When Upper Canadian interests, organized from Kingston but including investors elsewhere, launched the *Frontenac* in 1816, they were in the vanguard of the new technology. The *Frontenac* was one of the first two or three steamboats on the Great Lakes.[16] Built at a cost of over £15,000, and containing imported machinery (including a 50-horsepower Boulton and Watt engine) worth close to £4,000,[17] its cost was equivalent to twelve *Lord Nelsons*. The sharp rise in wartime prices complicates intertemporal comparison but in nominal terms the *Frontenac*'s cost was equivalent to the value of the entire provincial fleet in 1812. Because prices soon fell dramatically, the *Frontenac* was one of the most expensive vessels built in the province before 1854.[18] It was put into service in 1817 on a run made three times monthly from Kingston to York, the head of the lake, Niagara, and return.

Other vessels soon followed, as the technology was quickly and enthusiastically adopted in Upper Canada. By 1830 at least ten steamers had been built for service on Lake Ontario, although some, such as the *Frontenac*, laid up or burned in 1827, had already completed their working lives. Several steamers were at work on the Ottawa River too. By now local capitalists and builders were discussing in an informed fashion such technological issues as the choices between high- and low-pressure engines.[19] Most lake vessels were built in or near Kingston until the mid-1830s, when the Niagara Harbour and Dock Company became a substantial new participant in the business. Some vessels were built in other ports, including York.[20]

The steamship partly superseded sail, as its speed, growing reliability, and relative comfort made it almost at once the main carrier of passengers, mail, and higher-value imported goods. It was not just a substitute, however, because its convenience undoubtedly intensified passenger and mail movement. Steamboats carried some wheat, flour, pork, and ashes,[21] and also participated in commodity trades by towing rafts, barges, and sailing vessels. In June 1841, for example, the best use the proprietors could find for the *Cobourg*, one of the province's largest general-purpose steamers, was to charter it at £1,100 a month to tow masts.[22] Although steamers extended the lake transportation system as far down the St Lawrence as Prescott, Kingston remained the principal port of transshipment for sailing vessels and a hub in the steamshipping system.

Given their cost, steamers needed runs with substantial and consistent traffic. In the 1830s rapid immigration, population growth, and the completion of the Rideau Canal swiftly raised demand. The supply of vessels grew at least as rapidly. In 1831 four steamers were serving the

Prescott-Kingston-York-Niagara run. In 1833 alone, five new vessels were under construction.[23] By the mid-1830s daily scheduled service came to the principal ports, which were Prescott, Kingston, Cobourg, Port Hope, Toronto, Hamilton, Niagara, Lewiston, Rochester, Oswego, and several on the narrow, almost riverlike, Bay of Quinte.[24]

The accounts for 1836 of a steamer on the Prescott (or Kingston) to Toronto run suggest why the business was so attractive. Its revenues that year, the peak of the 1830s boom, totalled £6,600, of which £2,000 came from deck passengers and £1,800 from those travelling in the cabin. Freight generated £2,400, and some small accounts, including towing, provided the remainder.[25] As deck passage between Toronto and Kingston in 1836 cost 10s, some four thousand deck passengers would have been needed during a seven-month season to generate revenues of £2,000; if cabin passage cost 30s, as it did a few years later, another twelve hundred would have travelled inside. Similarly, most of the £2,600 revenue of the *Queenston*, which made daily round trips between Toronto and Hamilton in 1834, was from passengers.[26] There was also a substantial Rideau and Ottawa fleet, in part built and based in Lower Canada. By 1840 almost twenty steamships served routes within Upper Canada, and up to twenty more linked the province to Lower Canada via the Ottawa-Rideau system (table 7.1).[27]

By comparison with almost all the contemporary manufacturing establishments considered in chapter 6, steamers were expensive. Moreover, they depreciated rapidly. Vessels for towing cost up to £4,000 in the 1830s, and the larger and more luxurious passenger vessels cost £7,000 to £8,000 and sometimes more.[28] But as demand rose, enterprise and credit quickly augmented the fleet. Ownership was often divided into shares, which could be paid in instalments. When shares were widely held, vessels were managed by a committee elected by the shareholders, or, later, as limited partnerships.[29]

More than one vessel was required to provide a full schedule on a longer trunk route, such as Prescott-Toronto, or to provide regular freight service on the Ottawa-Rideau system. During the 1830s several major owner-operators appeared, including Macpherson and Crane on the Ottawa-Rideau-St Lawrence triangle and Donald Bethune, John Hamilton, Hugh Richardson, and Henry Gildersleeve, who focused mainly on Lake Ontario routes. In terms of the capital of ordinary Upper Canadians, they commanded very substantial assets. To finance the construction, purchase, and operation of their fleets, they secured credit from builders, banks, and commercial allies; sold shares in vessels to investors; and at times chartered vessels from others. They often combined with competitors to serve a route and to sustain rates.[30] Such agreements, typically for a season, were evidently fragile, and competition was strong. Many of the principal owners, indeed, passed through or ended in bankruptcy.[31]

By the 1830s several locations in the province routinely built and maintained steam engines for marine and land use. Although components of the boilers and/or machinery were imported, their assembly, installation, and maintenance were necessarily done locally. The 25 per cent of the cost of the *Frontenac* represented by imported machinery was probably high by the standards of later years. Most vessels fell into a range of between 16 and 50 horsepower, though several of the leading Lake Ontario vessels had up to 100 horsepower.[32] In total, the 1840 fleet of thirty-seven vessels represented 1,200 to 1,500 horsepower; such use of steam power suggests that if steam was not more widely used in provincial manufacturing in these years, it was for lack of need not lack of capital or knowledge.[33]

As an employer, steamshipping used much more labour per vessel than did sail, even for towing. An informed 1840 estimate suggested that an average crew on the Rideau-Ottawa steamers was eighteen, while crews of twenty to twenty-five were required on Lake Ontario and the St Lawrence.[34] Surviving accounts suggest those figures are high, but even if crews were only half as large, the total labour required for the steam fleet still exceeded that for the much larger number of sailing vessels. One leading lake steamer spent £1,200 on 'hands' account in 1836, or four times what a sailing vessel of equivalent tonnage paid to its crew even in the higher-wage 1850s. If that was a typical figure, the direct annual crew costs of almost forty steam vessels would have been more than £40,000.[35]

## III. *The Development of a Canal System*

The history of the Upper Canadian canal system, most dramatically told by Donald Creighton, has typically been presented in essentially tragic terms: in it, the St Lawrence lost a western empire, notably because capital scarcity and Canada's political division kept the two provinces from responding to New York State's brilliantly successful Erie Canal, completed in 1825, until virtually a generation later, in 1848.[36] But it is vital to recall that the Erie linked the American east to the American west; by far the largest portion of the traffic it carried was domestic American trade, initially generated within New York itself, and little of its growing volumes would have used the St Lawrence River no matter when it was improved.

There are other ways to see the Upper Canadian canal system than as a late and futile response to American enterprise and leadership. Here it will be seen primarily in terms of how it served Upper Canadian demands. In that context, canal projects were efforts to improve an established lake, river, and land transport system rather than to create something where absolutely nothing had been before. Important groups of Upper Canadians expected benefits from improving transportation, but by comparison with any other investment, a canal was a 'lumpy' project, in which substantial investment was needed before there could be any return. Moreover, although the Welland Canal raised about £100,000 from private investors, mainly in the United States and Britain, it soon showed that prospects of a private return on an investment in canals were very low. In Upper Canada, as in the United States, canal projects required government involvement and overseas investment.[37]

In light of their experience during the War of 1812, British military strategists intended to improve their ability to move men and supplies into Upper Canada, and they decided that the Ottawa-Rideau route best met their needs. It took fifteen years to complete this project, but routes and vessel sizes were essentially determined within four years of the war's end. Much the same chronology applied at the other end of Lake Ontario, where William Hamilton Merritt had concluded by 1818 that a canal based on the Twelve Mile Creek was a solution not merely to problems the war's end posed for him but to larger economic problems of the peninsula.[38]

Work began on the Ottawa River at its outlet to the St Lawrence. Immediately following the war, the St. Andrews' Steam Forwarding Company constructed a lock at Vaudreuil, intending this as a profit-making venture. The lock passed through several hands thereafter, and was enlarged to be compatible with the Grenville locks in 1832–3. Control of it gave considerable power to its operators, the leading forwarders on the system, especially as traffic grew in the 1830s. Complaints at this power led to the lock's being bypassed by the government-financed St Anne's lock in 1840–3.

Other segments of the Ottawa system were built by the British army's Ordnance Department, which was authorized to spend £8,000 stg a year from 1819 onwards to create a system to move boats to Upper Canada. The first three locks of the Grenville section, begun in 1819–20, dictated the maximum dimensions of vessels on the system. They were only slightly larger than the dimensions of the Lachine Canal, built by Lower Canada in 1817–18 (95 x 18½ x 5 feet). Planning for the Rideau system then led to a decision to build the remaining four Grenville locks on the scale of the Rideau (134 x 33 x 5 feet). The seven locks were finally finished in 1829. That year saw the beginning of the Chute à

Blondeau canal, and in 1830 work began on the Carillon canal. Their locks matched those on the Rideau in breadth and depth, but were shorter, at 110 and 128 feet respectively. Both were opened in 1834, and the Ottawa canals by then had absorbed £312,000 stg.[39]

The Rideau Canal, linking the Ottawa River to Lake Ontario, was built under the direction of Colonel John By. Recognizing the new steam technology, he set out to build not the boat canal his instructions called for but a canal able to handle the current side-wheel steamers. Authorized to spend £169,000 stg on the project, he drove it through to completion between 1826 and 1832 on an expenditure of almost five times that amount, £822,000.[40] Although he saw the Rideau as a commercial as well as a military project, he clearly gave little attention to probable levels of traffic. By 1834, when the Ottawa canals were finished, a complete line of canals totalling about sixty locks permitted steamers to operate all the way from Montreal to Kingston.[41]

The Welland Canal was initially a project of the private Welland Canal Company, chartered early in 1824 with an authorized capital of £25,000, raised a year later to £200,000. A substantial investment, eventually totalling £69,000, was made by Americans, led by New York lottery organizer J.B. Yates. In 1826 the first government funding was obtained, in the form of a loan of £25,000 from the Upper Canadian government. Much larger sums followed, until by 1833 about £230,000 in subscriptions and loans by governments had been invested, two-thirds by the Upper Canadian government, the remainder by Britain and Lower Canada. The canal was planned to carry sailing vessels between Lakes Erie and Ontario, minimum lock dimensions being 100 x 22 x 7½ feet. An attempt in 1826 to increase these to permit passage of steamships proved too costly. Initially the canal's upper terminus was the Welland River, but sailing vessels had difficulty working their way up the Niagara River from the mouth of the Welland, and it was decided to extend the canal all the way to Lake Erie. Thus, although two vessels were locked through late in 1829, and although traffic moved through the canal in subsequent years, the canal was not fully opened until 1833. Because it had been built with wooden locks, for economy's sake, it needed continual rebuilding; it was, for example, closed for repair for virtually half of the 1836 navigation season.[42]

Further government aid was promised in 1837, although only about a quarter of the £245,000 pledged then was actually raised and paid. In 1841 it was agreed that the province should take the company over entirely. By then, government funds in the company exceeded £300,000 (not counting the interest forgone on government 'loans' on which no interest was paid after 1828), and it was decided to issue £118,000 in debentures to pay out all private shareholdings at par, then to invest further funds to deepen the Welland and enlarge its locks. At no time was the canal physically taxed by the volume of ships seeking passage. The decision to expand evidently resulted from a desire to accommodate larger sailing vessels such as now served the American side of the upper lakes and some steam-powered vessels. The majority of the traffic on the Welland in most years was internal American trade – that is, ships bound from one American port to another – and it thus served as an adjunct to the Erie Canal. Other than helping to pay operating costs of the canal, such traffic had no developmental impact within the province. The Welland was not even remotely successful in commercial terms, but it did provide an all-water link between western Upper Canada and the rest of the province.[43]

Upper Canada took a strong interest also in improving the St Lawrence River. As it learned to use the London capital market in the mid-1830s, it began work on the Cornwall Canal, the chief Upper Canadian component in a system of St Lawrence canals. Work on the St Lawrence was far from complete at the time of the Union. But already total public expenditures there exceeded those on account of the Welland (table 9.5).

In addition to these major projects, the 1820s saw other private companies chartered to pursue projects such as the Desjardins Canal from Dundas to Burlington Bay and the Burlington Bay Canal to link the bay to Lake Ontario, and several harbour companies, which undertook to improve port facilities in return for the right to levy tolls. More of the latter followed in the 1830s. The province supported a number of these, and by 1840 £39,000 in public funds had been lent to private companies or otherwise expended to improve various harbours and navigation. Some of these projects were locally vital, including the Burlington Bay Canal, which opened Hamilton harbour, making it the main gateway to the western peninsula.[44]

By 1834 the major canal projects linked Montreal and Kingston by steamer and barge, and permitted sailing vessels that met the Welland's dimensions to pass between Lake Ontario and the upper lakes. Pork, flour, and perhaps potash could sustain the costs of portaging at Niagara, but oak almost certainly could not. Thus, the two systems combined to sustain the rapid expansion in the 1830s of the St Lawrence–Great Lakes hardwood timber trade, described in chapter 4. On the other hand, even after the St Lawrence canals were completed in the 1840s, the wood trade continued to use rafts for transport on the St Lawrence.[45]

Apart from their direct impact on the transport system, the canals had an impact on the provincial economy as importers of capital and employers of labour. The three principal sets of projects represented a total investment of over £2 million (cy), of which about three-quarters was spent between 1827 and 1833. In those years, capital imported for canal construction was equivalent to increasing the value of provincial exports by 50 per ceht – that is, by more than the value of Upper Canadian wheat exports in those years (see table 4.3). Until 1834, other than about £150,000 raised within Upper Canada for the Welland Canal, most of the money was paid by the British government and did not even entail payment of interest.

Canal work was labour-intensive. Many of the ordinary workers were immigrants, though how many of the adult men among the 200,000 migrants who arrived at Quebec between 1829 and 1834 worked directly in canal construction needs fuller investigation.[46] Few imports were required specifically for the projects, and those merchants already in position to sell provisions and other supplies in construction areas could benefit from the temporary but substantial expansion of the local market. Most of the capital invested in the canals was paid to contractors and subcontractors, who paid and provisioned workers and bought necessary stone, wood, and other inputs within the provincial economy. For the Rideau and the Ottawa, the developmental impact of such expenditures was partially felt in Montreal, a principal supply centre and the home of several contractors.[47]

Both in the comparatively well-settled Niagara region and in the rocky Rideau country, opportunities for canal workers to settle permanently as farmers near the works were more limited than in newer areas of settlement. But canal work, for shorter or longer sojourns, could sustain a longer-term process of migration towards more promising points of settlement.[48] Such may have been the case in Upper Canada, where the peak construction years coincided with the 1829–31 peak in the wheat market. Emigrant departures from Britain and arrivals at Quebec approximately doubled from 1829 to 1830 and again from 1830 to 1831. The peak came in 1832, which was almost the end of the first phase of canal construction. It is significant that completion of the Rideau and Welland projects in 1832–3 did not stop the province's rapid expansion. Levels of British emigration and arrivals at Quebec in fact remained at or near the levels of 1830 until the Rebellion of 1837 (figure 4.1). Construction began on the Cornwall Canal in 1834, which would have provided work for some experienced canal labourers and some of the new arrivals from Britain.

Following the Union of the Canadas, it was decided to use a British-guaranteed loan for construction of the Cornwall, Beauharnois, and Williamsburg canals and for rebuilding the Lachine Canal, all components of the St Lawrence canal system, and for expansion of the Welland.

A total of about £2 million more was expended on these projects by 1848, as a system capable of handling vessels drawing up to 9 feet of water was put into place. In the peak years of construction, 1843–5, more than five thousand workers at a time must have been directly employed.[49] By the ordinary standards of the economy, these were huge projects; but even at their peak of construction, the canals employed only a small fraction of immigrant arrivals or of total male population. Completion of the St Lawrence canals reduced the Rideau Canal to a local work. Traffic continued to grow on the Ottawa River, but the Ottawa-Rideau's effective life as part of the province-wide transport network was only fourteen years.

In hindsight, and even in the light of what was known in 1841, the decisions made in the early 1840s seem questionable, for the existing system had supported substantial increases in volumes in the 1830s and had ample capacity in hand. The Rideau obviously was not designed for the speedy movement of people, although it carried many passengers. By 1841, however, the superiority of rail technology in moving people was widely evident; indeed, as soon as the expanded canal system was completed, Canada's politicians quickly moved to support railway construction (see chapter 11).[50] For movement of imports and exports, in fact, the triangular system of barge movement between Montreal and Kingston worked well. Moreover, as the optimal size of sailing vessels in some trades tended to increase, the St Lawrence system was constantly exposed to the danger of obsolescence.

From the perspective of transportation alone, the new facilities, built principally in two phases, 1826–33 and 1842–8, at once became part of the physical and the economic landscape. But as Thomas McIlwraith notes, 'the rebuilt Welland Canal rarely functioned at more than ten or fifteen per cent of its capacity.'[51] Such overbuilding occurred because Canadians built canals to carry ships rather than, as on the Erie, boats; thus the minimum scale for physical reasons was massively excessive in terms of the volume of Upper Canada's interregional and international trades. The essence of the Canadian strategy was to eliminate points of transshipment, first at the Niagara portage and later on the St Lawrence. It does not seem to have been considered practical to plan the latter waterway to move boats only, yet for freight movement, that was surely what the St Lawrence required. The cheapness of capital, which was free to Canadians for the Rideau and, thanks to a British guarantee, exceptionally inexpensive for the St Lawrence in the 1840s, must also have contributed to the inappropriate strategy.[52] Although transport costs on the St Lawrence did decline in the 1840s, falling direct transport costs were not a measure of their net benefit, for Canadians paid in taxes for the capital and operating costs that traffic did not meet.[53]

## IV. The Water Transportation System, 1840–50

It is possible to obtain an overview of the provincial system on the eve of the Union and again almost a decade later (tables 7.1 and 7.2). John Macaulay listed ships that paid the provincial lighthouse duty in 1840; to his list it is necessary to add vessels serving the Ottawa-Rideau system. A decade later, the Tables of Trade and Navigation provide a brief but apparently comprehensive summary of provincial shipping. In addition to ships, at least 130 barges were used in the river segment of the system in 1840. Depending on the exact capacity of the provincial fleet in 1812, the total tonnage of Upper Canadian sailing vessels on the lakes increased by seven to ten times between 1812 and 1840, then grew approximately threefold in the next decade. Over the period, the average capacity of a sailing vessel increased from 50 to about 70 and then 80 tons. In addition, the sailing fleet had been joined by a steamer fleet that in 1840 totalled as many tons as the sailing vessels.[54] There were two quite distinct steamer fleets, one serving the Ottawa and Rideau, the other Lake Ontario.

By 1840 the sailing fleet included at least a dozen schooners of 100 tons or more. After the mid-1840s, many new vessels in the 230 to 270 ton range were added to the fleet, and by the end of the decade, the mean size of registered vessels was as much as 110 tons (tables 7.1, 7.2). It is evident that owners saw economies of scale in shipping on runs with sufficient and reliable volumes of cargo. On the other hand, such economies seem not to have lowered freight rates, at least for flour on Lake Ontario (table 7.5). For some larger current vessels, selected evidence of ordinary cargoes is provided in table 7.3. There are many examples of equivalent cargoes for contemporary vessels whose tonnage is not known.[55]

Ordinarily, the shipping season was about 210 days long, from mid-April to mid-November, though sometimes shipping continued into December.[56] When circumstances of weather and cargo were right, a sailing vessel could make the return voyage between Kingston and the head of the lake or the Welland in as little as seven days. This was an exceptional rate, however, especially as demand tended to diminish as the flour and timber accumulated each winter were moved in spring and summer. It was more usual to average one return voyage every ten to fourteen days, or from fifteen to eighteen voyages in a season.[57] From the western end of Lake Erie, about one voyage per month, seven per season, was usual.

Once the Welland Canal was reliably open, half or more of the provincial sailing fleet was needed to move export products from Lake Erie to the St Lawrence. Although it is difficult precisely to translate data on ships, cargoes, and volumes into evidence on the size of fleet required, this proportion is confirmed by estimates based on principal export commodities moving through the Welland downward from one 'British' port to another in 1840 and 1850 (table 7.4). In 1840 shipments of timber, staves, boards, flour, and wheat totalled about 40,000 tons. If it is assumed that a schooner made eight voyages per year (a reasonable figure given that many voyages originated at the eastern end of Lake Erie), this volume would have required 5,000 tons of shipping. As the total fleet was just 5,800 tons, it is clear that the estimate is too high. The most likely error is in timber shipments, some of which were probably made in rafts. If only half of 1840 timber shipments moved on vessels, then the demand for shipping would have been 29,000 tons, or about 3,600 tons of shipping capacity. An equivalent calculation for 1850 shows principal Welland traffic between 'British' ports requiring about 7,400 tons of shipping, or just under half of the estimated 16,300 tons of capacity in sailing vessels at the time. By then, further shipping capacity was required to move growing volumes of wheat, flour, and boards downward between 'British' and American ports. It is thus clear that more than half of the much-expanded provincial sailing fleet was still needed for cargoes originating above Niagara Falls.[58]

In 1845 the province inaugurated a registry for inland shipping. Unfortunately, it was far from comprehensive.[59] Just two of the twelve steamers whose owners agreed to organize a line serving Lake Ontario and Montreal in 1852 appear on the printed registry; it did not include a number of sailing vessels for which extensive documentation happens to survive, and it is unlikely that most barges were included.[60] The main purpose of the registry was to improve security on and legal title to vessels, for purposes of mortgaging and transfer, but many owners and even creditors evidently did not think they gained by registering their ships. Despite its limitations, the register permits us to look more closely at Upper Canadian shipping on the eve of the railway era (table 7.2). Between a list printed in 1854 and surviving registry volumes for specific ports, some 44 steamers, 123 sailing vessels, and 41 barges can be identified as having existed at some time between 1845 and 1854.

Over forty ports had been involved in constructing these vessels; for the 103 vessels of over 100 tons, twenty different locations appear. For steamships, ten locations are listed, several being outports of Kingston. What was meant by construction in the case of steam vessels is also not clear – making the engine(s), building the hull, and installing the motive power might each occur in a different location. The impression of a widely diffused system is, however, belied by the preponderance of a very few ports in the registry. Of the total registered tonnage, over half was registered in just two ports, Kingston and Toronto, though they accounted for only 44 per cent of the number of vessels. For steam alone, they accounted for 70 per cent of vessels and almost 90 per cent of tonnage.

The mean tonnage for registered vessels was over 110 tons (see tables 7.1, 7.2), and Kingston-registered vessels averaged 170 tons. Among the 123 sailing vessels were two giants of over 300 tons (both Kingston-registered) and sixteen vessels of 200 to 299 tons (seven registered at Kingston, four at Hamilton, two each at Sarnia and Toronto, and one at Port Hope). Except for the 431-ton *Eleonore*, built as the steamer *Great Britain* in 1830, none of the larger vessels for which construction dates are known was built before 1845, and this indicates the impact of the enlarged Welland Canal on size of sailing ships. At the other extreme, small vessels were still needed to serve ports that did not generate sufficient cargo volumes for larger ships and to cater to demands other than the main bulk export trades.[61] Between 1846 and 1854, at least seventeen new ships under 70 tons were built and registered, all but three of them on Lakes Erie and Huron. The mean tonnage of Goderich-registered vessels was just 44 tons, and only the 91-ton *Annexation*, built in 1849, greatly exceeded this mean. Small vessels also were prominent in the Toronto fleet; ten of the eighteen sailing ships registered there measured 55 tons or less. By contrast, at Kingston, only three small vessels (about 30 tons) were registered, and the remaining twenty-one were all 100 tons or more.

The registered steam fleet included river and canal steamers, which averaged not much more than 100 tons; lake steamers, most of which exceeded 200 tons; and several small local steamers, such as an 18-ton vessel registered at Dunnville, on the Grand River. At Kingston, seven of sixteen vessels were under 100 tons, and just one over 300, whereas the Toronto registry listed just one under 100 tons and five of over 300. All are net tons, after deducting space for the engine room. Kingston's pre-eminence was a function of its role as port of transshipment and of building; Toronto's represented its role as focus for imports, communications, and any water-borne internal trade. Both were banking centres, but data on ownership do not suggest that the registry misrepresents the focal points of actual ship ownership and operation.

The registry also included forty-one barges, with a mean tonnage of 90. Most belonged to Macpherson and Crane and came on the registry in 1853 when the company sold its business to Holcomb and Henderson and registered its fleet to help secure the latter's payments.[62] Of these barges, eleven had been built in or after 1850 – that is, after completion of the St Lawrence canals. Like the Calvin Company's continuing use of timber rafts, the barges and river steamers indicate that older patterns of river transportation persisted in the new decade. The deeper Welland Canal permitted larger vessels, up to 300 tons, to pass, but because sailing vessels had difficulty working their way upriver, or even down, through islands, locks, and currents, they did not often go below Kingston or Ogdensburgh. Barges towed by steamers were a more effective way to use the new system for bulky cargoes.[63]

As in the 1830s, only a few routes had the volume of passenger and high-value merchandise trade to support steamer service. Although passenger and import volumes continued to grow in the 1840s, few if any new steamer routes were added, and there was only limited scope to increase the frequency of service on the established routes.[64] At the end of the decade the St Lawrence canals greatly reduced the time needed for a steamer to move between Montreal and Kingston. Because of fires, wrecks, the relatively rapid physical deterioration of wooden-hulled vessels, and technological developments, however, there was continuing demand for new vessels. The Niagara Harbour and Dock Company alone built eighteen new steamships between 1839 and 1845, including three 90-ton propeller-driven vessels.[65] In 1846–7 the province's first iron-hulled steamer, the *Magnet*, was built, with a partial subsidy from the British government, which desired such a vessel for its potential military value at a time when war threatened with the United States.[66] Even after the mid-1840s, the Canadian side of Lake Erie could sustain only weekly scheduled steamer service from Buffalo and Port Colborne to Port Stanley, Amherstburg, and Detroit. Smaller vessels linked the latter to Lake St Clair and Chatham, and to Sarnia and Goderich.[67] Smaller vessels, not recorded in the 1840 data, served Lake Simcoe and the Grand River. Hence, though new vessels continued to be added, and we may assume that the quality and performance of the overall fleet was thereby enhanced, the total steam fleet grew little in the 1840s.

The growth of the sailing fleet was, clearly, a direct function of the growth of staple export trades, above all the trade in forest products. As we noted in chapter 4, timber exports had a high freight factor. In 1845, a year of peak prices and volumes, it cost £20 or more per thousand cubic feet (up to 5d per foot) to ship oak from the western end of Lake Erie to Kingston; for standard staves, the rate was £8 15s per thousand (not *mille*) from the eastern end of Lake Erie, £10 from the western end, and £12 10s from Chatham, inland from Lake St Clair. The freight cost from the west end of Lake Erie to Kingston thus represented about 30 per cent of the total price at Quebec, 18d per foot of oak and £40 per *mille*

(1,200) of standard staves in 1845 (see table 4.1). By comparison, Lake Ontario freights were £10 per thousand cubic feet and £4 per thousand standard staves, or from 10 to 20 per cent of Quebec prices.[68]

Given the importance of Lake Erie timber to the overall demand for schooners, it is evident that the builders, owners, crews, and port labourers associated with moving timber received a substantial share of the total revenues generated by timber exports. The crew of a sailing vessel numbered between three and six, plus the master, and total crew size and costs rose less than tonnage as vessels grew larger. The entire 210 sailing ships in 1849 cannot have numbered much more than one thousand crew members, a modest number in terms of the total workforce. Surviving crew accounts suggest, however, that it was unusual for a crew to remain together for a season. More commonly, only the master and at most one or two men served all season, while others served for briefer periods.[69] Both shipboard service and shore labour, and the income earned in either, were thus part of the local labour market, and were a point at which export-generated earnings diffused more widely.

In 1838 the new 125-ton schooner *Sir Robert Peel* cost £1,279 fully rigged, or about £10 per ton.[70] The Calvin Company's new 319-ton brigantine *London*, built in 1852, included timber and work totalling £2,021; if, as on the *Peel*, rigging and sails represented one-third of the ship's cost, then the total value of the *London* would have been almost £10 per ton.[71] A similar cost is suggested by the £2,000 valuation placed on the new *St. Andrews* by Norris and Neelon in 1853. In effect, the entire sailing fleet in 1849 could have been replaced for an investment of £160,000. Of course, the sailing fleet consisted of vessels of varying ages and thus was not worth this much. But as the rapid expansion of shipping capacity in the 1840s showed, it was possible to augment this kind of capital quickly. Such expansion could be financed on credit, or on the basis of cash flow. In fact, like many of the industrial establishments considered in chapter 6, a successful sailing vessel could gross its entire construction cost in a single year of freights.

At the end of the 1840s the steamer fleet was only marginally larger than a decade earlier (table 7.1). Of the steam vessels appearing on the registry at some point in the period 1846–54, at least three-fifths existed in or before 1847, and at least ten dated from 1840 or earlier. Some of the latter must have been refitted during the decade, and because of wrecks and other factors, some vessels built in the decade had already disappeared by 1850. In effect, the fleet is likely to have turned over almost completely in the decade. New vessels were still being built, but because of severe competition in the mid-1840s and a subsequent levelling off or fall in demand, there was a marked slowing of construction after 1847. Just five registered vessels, totalling almost 1,100 tons, were built between 1848 and 1850.

In 1845–6 Macpherson and Crane's twelve steamships were valued at about £28,000, while at the end of 1849 Donald Bethune's fleet of seven vessels was worth £22,000.[72] If these nineteen ships were worth £50,000, then the entire forty-four-vessel 1849 fleet was likely worth somewhat more than £100,000. We can also value the fleet in terms of replacement cost; if we assume that it consisted equally of river and lake vessels, at an average replacement cost of £3,500 for the former and £7,000 for the latter, then £230,000 would have been needed to replace the 1849 fleet entirely. As in the sailing fleet, this apparently substantial total cost was incurred over a number of years.

It is thus clear that the extent of demand, not capital scarcity, explains the slow growth of the steam fleet in the 1840s. The shipbuilding industry was very much concentrated at Kingston and Niagara, and it is also significant that neither became a major industrial centre despite their participation in the creation of these largest of privately owned fixed capital assets.

## V. Land Transport and Communications

Upper Canada's roads, both main and secondary, have generally been described as 'in appalling condition' with improvements 'almost non-existent.'[73] The merchants, officials, itinerant clergy, and other middle-class travellers who made these criticisms all sought reliable, year-round land communication. They complained that ruts, mud, washouts, inadequate maintenance, and the deterioration caused by freezing and thawing made even the best-built roads rough and all roads entirely impassable at times. Unpleasant though travel might be, however, such people were generally able to make the journeys that were necessary to their work. And, as Thomas McIlwraith demonstrated in a pioneering study of York County, it is clear that rural roads were adequate for the marketing and other local travel of Upper Canadian farmers and other rural workers.[74] Their essential needs could be met initially by a track cleared sufficiently to permit wagon axles to pass over remaining stumps. As settlement intensified, rural communities improved their most important roads and opened further concessions, using local statute labour and payments made in lieu of such labour by an increasing number of people.

'Old winter is once more upon us,' runs T.C. Keefer's well-known quotation. 'The animation of business is suspended, the life blood of commerce is curdled and stagnant in the St Lawrence ... On land, the heavy stage labours through mingled frost and mud in the West ... [F]rom Canada there is no escape: blockaded and imprisoned by Ice and Apathy, we have at least time for reflection.'[75] But even if all importing, exporting, and wholesaling and much retailing occurred mainly in spring and fall, commerce was by no means as idle in the winter as Keefer claimed. Much produce (including timber) moved to waterways, and winter was also a season for settling accounts. Farmers were less pressed by the insistent demands of the summer growing season. When snow and ice conditions were right, sleighing permitted ready movement of farm products to mills, visits to towns, attendance at township meetings, and other travel. Thus, one farmer's contract for 50 cords of wood for a Cobourg hotel specified delivery in 'sleighing season.'[76] The 1848 travels of another farmer, in well-established Yonge Township, indicate something of the journeys a farmer might take during a year. More than half of Walter Beatty's eighty-eight off-farm trips occurred in the four winter months, January, February, March, and December; by contrast in the peak harvest month, August, he made just three trips, all to church (table 7.6).

Like other records of marketing and work in the rural economy, Beatty's diary confirms McIlwraith's point that farmers could market crops in all seasons, notably the fall. As we saw in chapter 6, carding mills and other seasonal sectors of the artisan economy also necessitated summer travel. Stores and mills being widely diffused, in part because of the transportation system, only a small proportion of all journeys required more than a day to complete. Winter must still have been preferable for longer journeys; for example, members of the Crawford family took a load of wheat about thirty miles to Brantford in late February 1846, and a load of pork and butter over fifty miles to Hamilton in December.[77]

Travel by stage was generally seen as relatively expensive, and stage rates were usually higher than equivalent steamship rates. For example, in 1845 the Hamilton-Toronto rate by steamship was 7s 6d and by stage 10s, and the Chatham-Detroit rate was 10s by steamer and 12s 6d by stage. In 1845 stagecoach rates for a variety of provincial routes averaged over 5 cents a mile, apparently a high rate by the standards at least of the northeastern United States.[78] But farmers, most of whom had draught animals and some form of wagon or sleigh, used their own time and labour rather than hiring it. Travellers who did not have their own horses might negotiate with a teamster or farmer going in the right direction instead of paying to ride on the stage. If necessary, a young man going home, or to a party, could always walk.[79]

All off-farm travel by any family member, even if only to church, school, or a neighbour's farm, permitted rural households to hear the news and gossip from nearby and from the wider world. Equally, as almost every surviving emigrant letter attests, a letter to one member of a community could link much wider groups, by providing news of friends and acquaintances and by conveying a sense of events and ideas elsewhere. Slow and imperfect by later standards, such communications nevertheless permitted ordinary people to sustain links to a wider network of kin, as well as knowledge of conditions and opportunities throughout a fairly wide world.

In commercial and government circles, more frequent and reliable communications were a higher priority. Besides the official system, merchants ran their own networks; every ship carried messages and information as well as cargo. Indeed, while there were advantages to all in having a common system, the strongest private firms had a competitive advantage if, like Hamilton and Cartwright in the province's early years, they had preferential access to information via their own communications.

Like commerce and the newspapers, both of which were major users of the mails, the postal system focused on the province's principal urban centres. The British North American postal system was intended to be self-sustaining. Organized from London and with its colonial headquarters at Quebec, it was relatively remote from local political control. The spread of the system thus indicates something of growing demand for postal service. By 1810 Montreal and Kingston were joined by a fortnightly service. By 1824 York and Montreal were linked by twice-weekly posts, and by 1833 volumes were sufficient to sustain six trips a week on the Montreal to York and Niagara segment of the system. Increased frequency of service was associated with only modest increases in speed; for example, the usual time required to move mail on land from York to Montreal evidently dropped from eight days to six between 1817 and 1831. Although postal contracts specified that mail was to move at six miles an hour, a rate of three to four miles an hour was apparently the maximum speed that could be achieved by mail-carrying stages and sleighs over an extended distance; at least twice that speed was possible by steamboat during the navigation season.[80]

In addition to mail moving along the St Lawrence, a great deal of correspondence went, via the post office and private travellers, to the United States. Much of this was actually overseas mail, because in winter and usually in summer it was faster to send mail via New York or Boston, the advantage coming primarily because these ports had more regular and reliable packet service to Britain. Peter Goheen notes that over a quarter of postal revenue at a sample of offices north and west of Toronto and Hamilton in 1839–40 was derived from correspondence with the United States. The percentage was lower at offices nearer the border but that was because they had readier access to private travellers. In terms of postal communications and newspaper contents, Goheen argues that 'Quebec had closer contacts with Great Britain than with Toronto and ... Toronto relied more on its ties with the United States than with Quebec.'[81]

In 1812 there were about twelve post offices in Upper Canada. After the war, service began to increase at a more rapid rate than population. Most new post offices were on the province's main trunk, which ran along the St Lawrence, split west of Kingston to pass through either Napanee or Bath and Picton en route to Carrying Place, then ran west to York and Dundas; there it forked, one branch running east via Niagara to Fort Erie and the other west via Brantford to Sandwich and Amherstburg. Of the forty-three post offices in the province in 1824, just eight were not on this route.[82] The deputy postmaster general for Canada from 1827 to 1851, T.A. Stayner, responded rapidly to new levels of demand. By the summer of 1836 there were 185 post offices in Upper Canada, and by 1845 there were at least 280.[83] From Toronto in 1836, daily mail and/or passenger stages and sleighs ran eastward to Carrying Place and beyond, northward to Lake Simcoe, and westward to Hamilton and Niagara. Beyond Brantford in the west, the frequency of postal service from Toronto increased from twice weekly in 1833 to four or more times weekly by 1836 and daily in the 1840s.[84]

From the province's earliest days, when Lieutenant-Governor Simcoe used soldiers to begin work on trunk roads north, east, and west of York, the province sought to improve its main highways. As revenues rose and the province learned to borrow, it began to spend more extensively on roads. Disbursed through commissions of local notables, acting as trustees, such funds were open to political attack and to misuse, yet much was actually spent on clearing, grading, bridging, construction of plank roads, and, in a few cases, gravelling or macadamization.[85]

For political reasons at least £80,000 of road expenditures in the 1830s were distributed evenly across all districts. Increasingly, however, the province supported segments of the system that it was hoped would generate toll revenues to carry the debts. At least £400,000 were spent on such designated roads in the 1830s and 1840s (table 7.7). The favoured roads focused on three leading urban centres – Toronto, Hamilton, and London. The York roads ran from Toronto east to Rouge Hill, west to Springfield on the Credit River, and north to Holland Landing. From Hamilton and Dundas, roads ran northwest to Waterloo, west to Brantford, and south to Port Dover. From London, one ran east to Brantford and another south to Port Stanley. Two other principal roads

ran from Queenston to Grimsby and from Kingston to Napanee. Together these roads covered about 340 miles, of which some 170 were part
of the province's main trunk route.

That left over 400 miles of the main trunk, as described above (in
fact over 500 miles, when the alternate route from Kingston to Bath and
across Prince Edward County is included), and many other relatively
major roads, including some on which tolls were levied, amounting in
total to as many miles again. Such roads, by the late 1840s, included those
from Perth to Brockville and Bytown, Holland Landing to Penetanguishene, Dundas to Woodstock (Dundas Street), Preston to Stratford
and Goderich, Brantford to Simcoe, London to Sarnia, and Fort Erie to
Amherstburg.[86] Some of these had benefited from provincial or imperial
government funding not recorded in summary data in the 1840s;[87] they
were maintained, however, primarily by local efforts. It is not possible
to value the capital cost of even such main roads or the annual costs of
improvement and maintenance, but it is essential to recognize that the
totals in table 7.7 greatly understate the true scale of the investment
made by Upper Canadians in their roads.

Not even the most-travelled, best-located toll-roads proved able to
pay their operating costs, let alone contribute to repayment of capital.[88]
Maintenance costs were generally underestimated, and paying traffic
was always more limited than promoters envisaged. Local travellers,
the majority of users, could find alternate routes if tolls seemed too
high, and long-distance traffic was always modest. Even in the unlikely
event that the daily stages from Toronto to Kingston were always full to
their probable capacity of nine passengers, that added up to only about
fifty passengers each way per week, a total of no more than five thousand
a year. By comparison, as we have seen, just one of the steamboats on
the route could carry more passengers in a six-month navigation season.
London, the province's most important town not on a navigable waterway, relied on roads to move all its imports and exports. In 1844, on its
two main roads, a maximum of three thousand wagons made the return
trip between London and Brantford, and at most five thousand made the
return trip to the nearest port, Port Stanley. Over the year, traffic thus
averaged less than ten wagons per day to and from the east (tolls were
not charged on Sundays) and sixteen per day to the south.[89] In 1849 just
two of the province's 'productive' toll-roads, the Hamilton-Brantford
and the combination of three York County roads, generated over £100
per mile in tolls (table 7.7), and only the Hamilton-Brantford-London
and Kingston-Napanee roads covered costs of operation and repair (but
not interest) in the year.

At least £500,000 was invested by the province in road-building between 1831 and 1849. The York roads and the Hamilton-Brantford road
absorbed over £2,000 per mile. It would have required an enormous
sum to build another thousand miles of main roads and many times that
length of secondary rural roads in the province to these standards. Did
bad roads constrain growth, as is sometimes argued? Certainly there is
no evidence that demand warranted such outlays. Yet the entire period
of extensive growth from 1784 to the 1850s, with its sustained high rate
of increase in population, occurred during the period when such road
conditions prevailed – that is, when land travel ordinarily could move
little faster than a person could walk. By mid-century the province
actually possessed a road network that, like the rest of the rural economy,
had been opened, developed, and maintained in an undramatic but cumulatively very substantial way. A careful, comprehensive map of provincial roads prepared in about 1850 showed roads on many township
concessions that once had been just lines on paper. Many were labelled
'bad' by the map-maker, Baron de Rottenburg, but it is more striking
that he found a number of roads that were 'tolerably good.' Some, such
as Dundas Street between Dundas and Paris, were even 'very good.'[90]

VI. *Conclusion*

In 1847 the newest communications technology, the telegraph, came to
Upper Canada. Within three years of the first successful intercity trans-
mission of an electronic message in the United States, the Toronto,
Hamilton and Niagara Electro-Magnetic Telegraph Company connected
Toronto to the fast-developing American system; and just months later
the Montreal Telegraph Company established a link to the east.[91] Later it
would be clear that the telegraph and the other powerful new communications technology of the era, the railroad, had powerful centralizing
effects. But there had not yet been time in 1851 for the province's urban
system to be affected by either.

Even so, by 1851 the essential long-term spatial arrangements of output and exchange had taken shape in Upper Canada (see map 7.1). Four
of its five largest towns and cities – Toronto, Hamilton, Bytown, and
London – would remain the largest metropolitan areas in Ontario in
1986, Bytown (Ottawa) and Hamilton having changed places in the
ranking by population in the intervening period.[92] Only Kingston, the
largest urban place until about 1830 and still the third-largest in 1851,
would continue its relative decline. Its early pre-eminence, its strategic
location relative to many of the province's external commercial relations,

MAP 7.1
Urban Centres of 1,000 or More, 1851

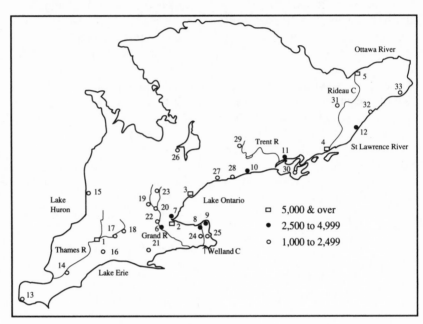

5,000 & over   2,500 to 4,999      1,000 to 2,499

| 5,000 & over | 2,500 to 4,999 | 1,000 to 2,499 | | |
|---|---|---|---|---|
| 1. London | 6. Brantford | 13. Amherstburg | 20. Galt | 27. Oshawa |
| 2. Hamilton | 7. Dundas | 14. Chatham | 21. Simcoe | 28. Port Hope |
| 3. Toronto | 8. St Catharines | 15. Goderich | 22. Paris | 29. Peterborough |
| 4. Kingston | 9. Niagara | 16. St Thomas | 23. Guelph | 30. Picton |
| 5. Bytown | 10. Cobourg | 17. Ingersoll | 24. Thorold | 31. Perth |
| | 11. Belleville | 18. Woodstock | 25. Chippawa | 32. Prescott |
| | 12. Brockville | 19. Preston | 26. Barrie | 33. Cornwall |

SOURCE: Province of Canada, *Census*, 1851–2, xvii

and any technological advantage it gained from its role in the province's steamshipping economy proved an insufficient basis for long-term urban leadership.[93] In the western peninsula, London was already the leading town, but the urban pattern was not yet fully defined. Indeed, two cities not even on the 1851 map of communities with over 1,000 people, Kitchener and Windsor, would later emerge to rank fifth and sixth in population in modern times.

Although Peter Goheen stresses the gulf between western Upper

Canada and Quebec, towns and cities in Upper Canada were part of a system that included Montreal, Quebec, and urban centres in the adjoining states. Bytown in fact was still linked more to Montreal and Quebec in 1851 than to anywhere in Upper Canada. The leading centres were complementary as well as competitive. Further study, along the lines pursued by Goheen, is needed to show more clearly how these centres interacted in and before the 1840s. It is evident, for example, that towns seeking their own improvement could not avoid assisting others too. Thus, the roads promoted by and focused on Hamilton also extended Toronto's hinterland and facilitated direct and autonomous access by Londoners to both.

In urban pattern, Upper Canada resembled the adjoining states, where, notwithstanding all the changes in technology, industry, and commodity flows over the intervening period, the leading cities in the northeast in 1790 remained the leaders, in the same order, almost two centuries later. In the Ohio valley and upper Mississippi and around Lake Erie, the leading cities in 1840 remained the leaders in 1960, though their order had changed.[94] The early establishment of what Allan Pred terms 'large-city rank stability' was caused by the mutual and interdependent nature of urban growth. In the process of urbanization, communications were central, Pred argues, and 'trade was as much the outcome of information flows as it was the generator of them.'[95]

The urban network of the province in 1851 (map 7.1) was both shaped by and in turn shaped the land and water communications systems we have discussed here. The main trunk, envisaged in Simcoe's years, was very evident on the map, twenty-one of thirty-three communities of over 1,000 being directly on it. With slight variations in the lines west of Toronto, indeed, the main trunk shows in all subsequent transport and communications maps of the region.[96] East of Toronto, all but three of the leading places were on Lake Ontario or the St Lawrence, and Bytown was on its own navigable waterway. West of Lake Ontario, and despite the evidence of port activity in the rising volume of shipping required to move exports from Lake Erie, the urban map in 1851 showed little orientation to the upper lakes. There the Grand and Thames rivers were more prominent than either Lake Erie or Lake Huron; five of the leading urban centres were located on the Grand (and a tributary) and four on the Thames. Both rivers were navigable on their lower stretches and were also sources of water-power. For all the imperfections of land transport, the main trunk from Hamilton to Brantford, London, and Chatham was the most prominent line in the peninsula. In the next decade the railway would confirm most and modify some of the main lines of the province. But the more striking feature of communications as they had developed to 1851 is how much of the subsequent spatial pattern of the provincial economy was established by 1851. By then the technology of sail and steamboat, of horses, oxen, wagons, and sleighs, and of water-powered mills, had combined with elements in the landscape to lay the basic pattern of communications and hence of urban development.

# 8 The Provincial Business System: Trade and Financial Institutions, 1821–51

As the transportation system suggests, the Upper Canadian econc.ny can be seen as a network built around a main trunk that extended beyond the province. At the same time, much of the province's actual economic life was conducted at a very local level. Local economies should not be visualized as if they were islands, for they overlapped with their neighbours and were connected also by communications and by government. But the principal connections in the province's economic network were provided by commerce, particularly by the leading import merchants. Although the names of the leading men changed, the pre-eminence of the principal merchants did not, until well after the mid-century. Banks were added to the institutional structure of the economy of Upper Canada in the 1820s.[1] They complemented rather than eliminated merchants' financial roles. It is not possible to offer a full history of banking policy, either public or institutional. Our interest here is in the basic structures of commerce and finance and their development.

## I. The Role of Merchants

The careers of Richard Cartwright Jr and Robert Hamilton demonstrate the full range of merchants' roles: they were at once partners and inde-

The first part of this chapter is particularly based on my 'Rural Credit and Rural Development in Upper Canada, 1790–1850,' in R. Ommer, ed., *Merchant Credit and Labour Strategies in Historical Perspective* (Fredericton 1990), 255–72; also in R. Hall, William Westfall, and Laurel Sefton MacDowell, eds., *Patterns of the Past: Interpreting Ontario's History* (Toronto 1988), 37–55. I am grateful to both publishers for permission to reprint material from this paper. See also my 'An Introduction to the Nineteenth-Century Business World,' in T. Traves, ed., *Essays in Canadian Business History* (Toronto 1984), 13–23; and *The Upper Canada Trade, 1834–1872: A Study of the Buchanans' Business* (Toronto 1979).

pendent businessmen; importers and exporters, the latter on others' account as well as their own; wholesalers and retailers; transshippers at points of break-in-bulk; owners of mills and ships; dealers in land; creditors and financial intermediaries; and central figures in the province's external and internal communications and, for a time, in its politics. Essential to their strength within the province was their participation in a network of trade and credit based in London and Montreal and reaching beyond them into fur trade country. However impressive their success in the years before 1812, their leadership in trade did not permit them to institutionalize their position in business. Descendants of both men played leading roles in the province and the country, but neither trading business long survived the death of its founder.

As the provincial market grew, the distinction between wholesaling and retailing became more sharply drawn. Men such as Quetton St George and his successors, J.S. Baldwin and Jules Quesnel, did considerable wholesaling but still retained their retail trades.[2] Beginning in the early 1830s some found it possible to concentrate entirely on wholesaling and, like St George earlier, to escape subordination to a Montreal firm. Wholesalers, of course, needed an extensive connection of retail stores to buy from them, and retailers, while independent businessmen, depended on wholesalers for credit.

In each town and principal village, one or more prominent merchants emerged at the head of the business world. By mid-century specialized retailing was common in larger towns and cities, and some functional differentiation was possible, for example between merchants emphasizing exports and those concentrating on importing. But the province's leading importers and smaller communities' leading retailers still engaged in general, not specialized, trades. Such merchants dealt in everything the province imported, including drygoods, hardware, and groceries. Except in the largest communities, they also handled all kinds of exports and much that was traded locally. The nature of local communications and the provincial credit and payments system both encouraged merchants to specialize in a territory rather than in particular lines of goods.

It is customary to think of a merchant's basic role as being the selling of goods, and merchants themselves evidently hoped that their assets could be kept secure and liquid. Thus, William Gilkison, launching the town of Elora, warned his storekeeper there: 'This country is bad to collect debts ... I would rather keep the goods than trust foolish persons.'[3] But merchants quickly found they could not sell unless they extended credit. As Benjamin Tett, newly launched in a store at a favourable location on the Rideau Canal, reported to his principal supplier, 'For the short time I have commenced business here my Sales have been considerable, nearly all however upon credit.'[4] Actually, extending credit and getting paid were as central to the merchant as buying and selling. 'It is easy enough to make large sales but the difficulty is to get paid,' one wholesaler remarked.[5]

Models of colonial economies that focus on staples tend to assign priority to the export trades. But to secure a niche in the export trades, a merchant needed a reliable connection of suppliers and had to grant them credit so they could buy. Importers acquired such connections as part of their ordinary businesses. Importing preceded exporting, moreover, and the business system had to ensure that the income generated by exports reached those who had extended credit – the local retailer, the importer, and ultimately the firms in Britain that traded with Canada. Physically, exports moved out of Upper Canada through many small lake ports and down the St Lawrence through, or past, Kingston. By contrast, wholesale importing was much more localized. It focused particularly on Toronto, although Hamilton, which was a relative latecomer to the urban world, founded twenty years or more after Kingston, York, and Niagara, began to close the gap on Toronto in the 1840s and 1850s. Thereafter, it fell back.[6] Importing was thus an integral element in the selective growth of principal towns that constituted urbanization.

Upper Canada's leading urban centre until after 1850 was actually Montreal. As we have seen, Upper Canada's external communications often used American channels, and there were always trade links across the border. Provincial merchants' use of New York as well as the St Lawrence indicates that Montreal firms faced competition from outside the city in the Upper Canadian trade. Toronto's rapid rise began around 1830 and Hamilton's by 1840, before American Drawback Acts, Britain's adoption of free trade, and the Reciprocity Treaty liberalized cross-border trade in the 1840s and 1850s. Until the 1850s at least, most of the province's imports and exports continued to move via the St Lawrence. And many of Upper Canada's 'local' wholesale firms actually were, or began as, extensions of Montreal firms, which established upriver branches to control their growing volumes of Upper Canadian business more effectively and to respond to competitors from Montreal, Britain, and Upper Canada. The commercial hinterland of Toronto was to its north and west and Hamilton's was very much in the west; despite its initial leadership, Kingston was at the wrong end of Lake Ontario for access to this region. What particularly fostered local wholesaling and growing commercial autonomy was the rapid growth of the western peninsula, a market large and dynamic enough to support both an expanding trade by Montreal merchants and a rapidly expanding local trade.

In some analyses of Canadian economic history,[7] the commercial system is seen as having had a bias to short-term investment that inhibited industrial development. But we have seen already that there is little evidence that the province required or could have sustained capital-intensive industry prior to 1850. Moreover, because wholesale and retail credit in Upper Canada typically provided twelve months for payment, with many debts running longer than that, commercial investments could not in fact be easily liquidated. They were every bit as long term as any other economic activity, with the possible exception of farm-making itself.

The leading merchants were among the richest men in the province, and their wealth far exceeded that of ordinary farmers, retailers, millers, and craftsmen. Their main assets were debts due to them, and they were themselves among the province's largest debtors. Thus, when Richard Cartwright Jr reviewed his position in 1800, his debts totalled about £10,000. His main assets were properties worth about £6,000 and debts due to him of about £18,000, and his net worth once some other assets were included was £16,000.[8] Robert Hamilton, by the time he died in 1809, had accumulated a vast amount of land, totalling 130,000 acres or more, acquired hopefully as a long-term endowment for his family; debts due to him exceeded £43,000.[9] As his heirs discovered, land could be liquidated only very slowly, and many of the debts could not be collected at all. Almost half a century later, the Buchanan family business, based on wholesaling in the west, had total assets in 1845 of £320,000, of which £208,000 consisted of debts due to it; in turn it owed £178,000. By 1857 its total assets exceeded £800,000, of which over £600,000 consisted of debts due; and the firm now owed £424,000 to its creditors.[10]

This pervasiveness of debt has led some to depict provincial commerce as exploitative. Usually, the issue is defined as one of unequal exchange, in which the merchants used credit to trap ordinary farmers and craftsmen into inescapable indebtedness that allowed the merchants to pay below-market prices for farm produce and charge above-market prices for imported goods that were essential to the pioneer's survival. As is now widely recognized, this vision of the credit system ignores competition among merchants at every level, from the British market to the village, the ability of farmers and craftsmen to communicate and travel to avoid periodic efforts by local merchants to fix prices, commercial credit's importance in sustaining the investment process by which Upper Canada was made, and above all, the merchants' interest in their customers' success, which alone would ensure that the merchant eventually received payment of debts due. Many credit relationships did not cross class lines, nor were regional boundaries necessarily involved, as the growth of local wholesaling suggests. Yet credit, class, and region were at least partially associated, and tensions were especially liable to rise during or following commercial crises. At such times, all in the credit chain could find it hard to get new credit to replace old credits as they expired, although the merchant could more easily do without a single customer than the customer could do without a source of credit. What commercial crises highlighted most, however, was not exploitation but rather the long-term nature of credit, even in ordinary wholesale and retail trades.[11]

The credit system is well illustrated by the firm of Barker and Stevenson in what would become the town of Picton (see table 8.1). Opened during 1825, this firm doubled its yearly sales in five years, and by the early 1830s it had 250 to 300 customers on its books and annual sales of over £2,000. Such sales made it a substantial country retail firm.[12] After just one year of trade, the value of debts due to it was its principal asset, greatly exceeding the value of inventory. In relation to sales of the previous year, customer debts mounted rapidly, and by 1832, after two excellent years in the province's wheat economy (in which customers might have been expected to reduce their obligations), the debts exceeded the annual sales. A growing balance of overdue debts is indicated by the rising value of promissory notes, which represented a later stage in a merchant's collection process, as he formalized his book debts in a way to permit lawsuits or the securing of bank credit. During 1832 no payments of any kind (even in the form of a promissory note) were made on over 20 per cent of Barker and Stevenson accounts.[13]

When the merchant sought payment of the sums due him, he encountered Upper Canada's chronic liquidity problem. A number of causes, including the province's relative capital scarcity, its ill-conceived currency laws,[14] and the limited development of financial institutions in the province before the 1830s, combined to make cash – that is, specie or bank notes – scarce in Upper Canada. Of the thirteen retail firms in the province whose records were used in table 5.5, only two recorded as much as 20 per cent of all credits on customer accounts in cash. For Barker and Stevenson, from 1829 to 1837, just 10 per cent of all credits were in the form of cash.

For the merchant, handling local exports was not just to seek further profit, as theories of unequal exchange might assert, but also to find ways for both him and his customers to make payments. He had every incentive to look for markets for the full range of products that the local economy might produce. Thus, Benjamin Tett entered the steamboat wood business: 'Several of my Customers being desirous of getting in Steam Boat wood, I would engage to supply during the present winter four hundred Cords.'[15] The process is also illustrated by Barker and

Stevenson's produce shipments (see table 5.6). Wheat, pork, staves, and timber were shipped to Montreal for sale.

Like Tett, the merchant could obtain some payments through the local exchange economy. At Barker and Stevenson at least thirty local products were purchased for the firm, the family, and local resale. As we have seen, not everyone in the rural economy farmed, nor could most farmers be wholly self-sufficient even in locally producible commodities. Because middlemen were often not needed in such local buying and selling, the Stevenson books offer only a glimpse of this activity. Records of artisans, merchants, farmers, and others such as innkeepers all confirm that locally traded goods and services, some of which were marketed only in modest amounts, added up to a significant source of income for those who produced them and of payment on commercial accounts.

Local exchange is often depicted essentially as a form of barter. But bargains were usually expressed in terms of prices that appear to have been quite standard (see table C.1), and because transactions were not usually simultaneous or equal in value, time was an essential element. Like the merchants, many ordinary Upper Canadians were at once debtors and creditors, as they extended credit to their neighbours and received credit from them. Each kept whatever record of transactions was thought necessary, and periodically people 'set off' their respective claims. Even wage records and payments took this form. In one vital respect, local exchange did not resemble extra-regional trade: to the extent that transactions were local and reciprocal, promises to pay in the future could be essentially equivalent to actual payment, for the promises were cancelled out in the periodic settlements of accounts. The process is illustrated by a settlement between Alexander McMartin, a merchant and miller at Martintown, in the Eastern District, and Donald McNaught, a carpenter. In March 1852 they reckoned their mutual dealings for the past seven years. During that period McNaught had earned £53 by his craft and run up £47 in charges at McMartin's enterprises. Here an exchange of £6 could settle £100 worth of transactions.[16]

Even where the country merchant was not a party to the bargain, he might have a part to play. When, as usually happened, such settlements left one party with a net obligation to the other, the account might simply be continued from the new base. If the net creditor required payment, however, both parties encountered the economy's liquidity problem. It was often in the accounts of the merchant, with whom all had dealings, that balances were most easily reconciled (see, for example, table 5.5, col. D).

When the farm or artisan household went into debt, as all but the small minority with substantial capital probably did, they surely did so with a view to what they expected to be able to pay, or at least carry, in the future. Buying imports on credit was convenient in terms of payment arrangements and permitted the use of scarce capital for other purposes, such as buying tools, stock, or land. Those to whom the farmer and his family became indebted had to share the family's view of its future for it thus to accumulate debts, though a creditor might not know how large other debts were. In the extent of its borrowing, a family might be proved over-optimistic in many ways, for example about crop yields, prices for produce or land, or the rate at which it could expand its output. Its ability to pay could also be affected by personal misfortunes, such as accident, illness, and death. It is thus understandable that farmers and artisans had cause to worry about their debts at times, and that some, through over-optimism, misfortune, bad judgment, incompetence, or bad timing (for example, buying land at the height of the market), became entrapped by debt. In a society where credit was fundamental, someone who could no longer obtain credit had little choice but to give up and move on. But this happened only to some, whereas others, working in the same system, established themselves as successful commercial farmers.[17]

Far from being the main cause of excessive farmer indebtedness, the credit system actually had an essential part in the farm economy. Not only did it help the farm family to create capital, it also assisted the family to cope with risks. Rather than having to guard entirely on its own against a bad harvest, livestock diseases, or lower prices than expected, the family could generally rely on retail credit to help sustain it. If a crop failure proved to be the beginning of a longer-term crisis of production, or if a turn in prices inaugurated a long downward slide, to rely on extra credit could be a recipe for deepening one's indebtedness rather than smoothing the fluctuations. All of this happened in prairie Canada in the twentieth century and, through the writings of scholars such as Harold Innis, S.D. Clark, W.T. Easterbrook, and W.A. Mackintosh, contributed to our ideas of 'staple' agriculture both then and earlier.[18] But in Upper Canada, institutional patterns were not those of the modern plains, nor, after 1821, did general and sustained crop failures and falling prices occur (table C.3).

## II. *The Development of Chartered Banking*

The origin of chartered banking in Upper Canada can be traced to the wartime experience with army bills and the perceived consequences of their subsequent withdrawal, and to the simultaneous development of banking in Lower Canada and the adjacent American states. The experiment in Upper Canada verged on being premature. Even before the Bank of Montreal opened in 1817 as an unincorporated association, a group of leading Kingstonians obtained a charter for a Bank of Upper Canada. A delay in imperial approval gave time for a York-based group of merchants and officials to capture their charter. As a result, York interests controlled the province's only chartered bank, the Bank of Upper Canada, when at last it opened in the summer of 1822.[19]

At Kingston what came to be called the 'Pretended' Bank of Upper Canada, a name applied by its incorporated rival of the same name, was opened in 1818. After serious breaches of trust by its officers, it failed by 1822. Surviving lists of debts due it and of shareholders indicate that it had been lending extensively to those who had invested in it. Of the 125 shareholders (who had paid a total of £11,100 on their shares), seventy-two owed the bank money in turn, to a total at the beginning of 1825 of £10,600.[20] Another nine were liable as endorsers of paper. Thus, fully two-thirds of shareholders were involved in borrowing from the bank. Of all those still owing money to the bank by then, only thirty-three were not shareholders, and on the debts of half of these one or more shareholders were endorsers. Because the power of those liquidating the bank to enforce the payment of debts at law was in doubt, non-payment may have represented less the inability of remaining debtors to pay than their efforts to set off at least some of what they would lose on their invested capital. Even so, commercial banking as practised by this bank had a circular element; investors and borrowers, if not quite identical, overlapped very substantially.

Such a formula for banking worked elsewhere as a way to generate credit and longer-term wealth. In the first part of the nineteenth century, deposits were a small part of most banks' operations;[21] and banks were not typically intermediaries, as theory might put it, between savers, who were few, and borrowers, who were numerous. A bank charter was literally a licence to print money, and investors were often themselves among the principal borrowers. Because a bank's capital was the basis for the credit it extended, however, it helped if its circle of investors was wider than those who invested principally in order to borrow. For the bank to succeed, the money it created still had to be used profitably. Borrower-investors had to be able to repay loans eventually, or at least continue to pay interest.[22]

What is not clear is whether Kingston was large and prosperous enough, and the 'Pretended' Bank's officers independent enough, to ensure some prudence in lending standards; and the bank's uncertain legal position would also have made it difficult to compete with chartered banks. This bank cannot have helped Kingston's second attempt at a chartered bank. A leading local group obtained a charter in 1819 for the 'Bank of Kingston,' but could not raise the £20,000 required as start-up capital. Kingston's early banking experience thus represented false starts. Still, the 'Pretended' Bank of Upper Canada suggests something of how banking might work in the province, and especially in a small community. Later, for example, the directors and officers of Hamilton's Gore Bank were among the largest borrowers.[23]

Chartered with an authorized capital of £200,000, the York-based Bank of Upper Canada was equally unable to raise the 10 per cent in specie that had to be paid in before opening. It succeeded only after that figure had been reduced to £10,000 and its total authorized capital to £100,000. It then took the 1820s to raise this sum (see table 8.2), even with the support of the provincial government, which, as provided for in the charter, subscribed for two thousand of the eight thousand shares (and named four of fifteen directors). The government also aided the bank by other means, such as by banning for some years in the 1820s the local operations of extraprovincial banks which did not redeem notes in specie within the province. This step assisted the bank to compete with the Bank of Montreal until the two banks eventually worked out ways of coexisting.

Cautious British officials, fearful of colonial monetary experimentation, and local authorities sought in this and later bank charters to guard against abuses. Although there were no explicit limits on note issue, the bank had to redeem its notes in specie, and if it could not do so, all operations were to cease until such payment resumed. Moreover, if debts except deposits (in practice this meant notes issued) exceeded three times capital, the directors who authorized the excessive issue were personally liable for it. No shareholder could have more than fifteen votes, however many shares he or she owned. The bank was expected to do a 'real' bills business, that is to lend against commercial paper deriving from actual transactions. It could not lend directly on the security of land and mortgages, but it could take these as collateral securities, and it was not prohibited from lending on the security of its own shares. Shareholders had limited liability.[24]

There were costs as well as benefits in having links with the government. For example, the bank was assumed, usually wrongly, to possess large reserves of government funds, and it was frequently denounced as part of more general reform attacks on the provincial administration. The bank often had difficulty in persuading the Legislative Assembly of the merits of its views, though here its own policies, which usually concentrated power and credit tightly at York, may have been the main issue. It did not even get all the government's business. The province's receiver general, J.H. Dunn, did most of his banking with a Montreal mercantile house, Forsyth, Richardson and Company. As Peter Baskerville has demonstrated, rather than being essentially political and governmental, the bank was pre-eminently a business, managed largely in accordance with the views of its founding president, the merchant William Allan. Its paper commanded sufficient respect that it needed a relatively small specie reserve (never more than 25 per cent in the 1826–31 period), while its 8 per cent dividend and periodic bonuses provided a return that attracted a growing shareholder group.[25]

Although the Bank of Upper Canada in particular, and chartered banks in general, were frequently depicted as monopolistic, the banks did not enjoy absolute power. In particular, their charters limited the rate of interest they could charge to 6 per cent. They also faced competition; at Kingston, for example, there were at times offices of Montreal banks, and as Dunn's system indicates, merchant firms with bases outside the province (and access to outside banks) could compete effectively with local banks for aspects of their business, including exchange operations, credit granting, and the holding of balances.[26] Save for the important power to issue notes that were legal tender, the early banks did not supply services that were otherwise unavailable within the province, but services that they were better equipped to provide. Because merchants continued to deal in exchange and to extend credit, the banks' services were, in effect, additional to those the merchants themselves provided rather than substitutes for them. Indeed, the chartered banking system helped merchants, especially leading ones, to manage the credit and exchange that were so integral to their activities.

The banks offered three related services: managing inter-city, interprovincial, and foreign exchange, through buying and selling of government and private bills, and through the operations of their branches and agencies; providing credit, chiefly by discounting commercial paper on a nominally short-term basis; and providing a circulating medium within the province, in the form of bank notes. To stress one of these more than others would be misleading, for all were essential and mutually reinforcing. Thus, it was through discounts that notes were most readily put into circulation. Nor were credit and exchange distinguishable in practice: merchants often used credit to buy bills with which to meet overseas payments, and even domestic exchange usually included credit, in that bills were drawn at terms as long as six months.[27] In addition, the Bank of Upper Canada had a variety of roles in public finance, such as handling government debentures.[28]

As in their criticism of merchants, some students of Canadian political economy have made much of the presumed national consequences of the banks' proclaimed dedication to short-term financing through the discounting of real bills. But even such discounts could provide long-term real credit, whenever a borrower could renew paper at its term or discount new paper as old expired. The new paper was sometimes 'accommodation' paper, which reflected not new transactions but an exchange of paper between two individuals or firms for the purpose of creating paper in the form required by banks; more often, the paper was acquired by a firm in the course of its ordinary business, and the merchant (and the bank) could reasonably expect the customer to pay at the due date.[29] In addition, merchants who regularly bought and sold foreign exchange could draw paper on overseas merchants or bankers, or even on their own overseas branches, then use the proceeds not to buy produce, but to meet paper falling due. This process was known to merchants as having bills 'on the circle.'[30] In such ways, banks did supply long-term credit. And of course banks could find they had lent at long-term when debtors could not pay. In fact, the distinction between long-term and short-term is analytic, not real, and has little applicability to the actual Upper Canadian economy. There, as we have seen, such fixed capital investments as farms, houses, steamships, and mills were rapidly built up through the ordinary channels of commerce and finance.

III. *The Rise of the Banks, 1830–7*

As we have already seen, there was a sharp upsurge in provincial wheat exports in 1830–1, following which there was a major investment boom, marked by substantial immigration and rising imports. The Bank of Upper Canada now wished to restore its authorized capitalization to £200,000. The politics of obtaining this power required meeting Kingston's continuing desire for a bank of its own. Both developments were agreed to in 1832. In the next four years, the Kingston bank, the Commercial Bank of the Midland District, quickly established itself, and it was soon pushing to double its authorized capital. Meanwhile a group in the well-situated, but still small, community of Hamilton sought a bank there. They secured a charter for the Gore Bank in 1835, and it opened for business midway through 1836. Reflecting the politics of its origin, it began with links to the Bank of Upper Canada, which vacated the field in Hamilton and for a time held some shares in the new institution.[31]

Given how slowly the Bank of Upper Canada had brought in its first £100,000, it is remarkable how readily the three banks raised the capital they now sought. Shares in the Bank of Upper Canada were at such a premium that there was massive excess demand for the new issue of 1832. Clearly, the province's growth was attracting or creating a larger group of potential investors.[32] Although shareholders' lists available from the later 1830s do not give the number of shares held by each investor, they are an indication of the sources of this capital. By 1838 the Bank of Upper Canada, which had begun with only about forty shareholders, had over three hundred, the Commercial had almost five hundred, and the new Gore Bank had 167 shareholders (table 8.4). There was some overlap among the banks' lists, and larger investors, to maximize their voting power under charters that limited the number of votes of any one shareholder, could place their shares in the hands of family.[33] Even so, the mean capital per shareholder was substantial by the standards of ordinary Upper Canadians: over £400 in the Commercial, over £500 in the Gore, and well over £600 in the Bank of Upper Canada. Among each bank's investors were some widows, estates, insurance companies, and savings banks, which indicates a demand in the province for forms of relatively secure investment that would be more certain in value and more liquid than land.[34] Each bank had many shareholders in and around its head-quarters city, and some of the non-residents undoubtedly had links with the community, for example through family or prior residence. But there was no narrow localization of the banks' investors. The many non-local and extraprovincial stockholders and the presence of many names that were not involved in provincial commerce also suggest that investors and borrowers were now less likely to be identical groups than was the case with Kingston's earlier bank.

Invested capital in the province's chartered banks increased over six-fold in the period from the beginning of 1830 to 1837. Other indicators of demand for banking services also rose sharply: in 1837, on the eve of the financial crisis, discounts were over four times higher, note circulation three times higher, and deposits, now a significant form of bank liability, at least for the Bank of Upper Canada, as much as eight times higher than the levels of 1830 (tables 8.2, 8.3). In 1830–1, the Bank of Upper Canada's discounts averaged £238,000, while the average annual value of provincial exports was just over £500,000 (table 4.3). That indeed was the amount that the Bank of Upper Canada, declaring its adherence to the real bills doctrine, said it currently lent in a year, 'principally ... at 90 days, to aid in the purchases of Wheat, Flour and Lumber, the chief exports of the Province.'[35] Across the middle years of the decade, from 1835 to 1838, provincial exports again averaged just over £500,000 a year; but now the average total discounts by the chartered banks had increased to £730,000 (table 8.2). If, as they often said, the banks' main role was lending at short term, say three to six months, on bills generated by the movement of exports, the 1835–8 level of discounts could have moved at least three times the actual value of exports. It is clear that bank credit was being put to many other uses then, and later.[36] In effect, the *additional* credit supplied by banks in 1836 as compared to 1831 was equivalent to a year's exports from the province.

On a per capita basis, bank discounts in 1836–7 were about £2 per Upper Canadian, a figure about double that of 1830; in the same period, note circulation per Upper Canadian rose by about 60 per cent, to almost £1.2 ($5) per Upper Canadian. Deposits in 1836–7 amounted to as much as £0.5 per Upper Canadian. If the two figures can be combined to serve as a measure of provincial money supply, then at its peak in the 1830s it was £1.7 ($7) per capita.[37] By comparison, total American money supply in 1836, including specie in circulation, was over $16 per capita, and the notes issued at the time by banks in Massachusetts amounted to around $13 per capita.[38] By these American standards, despite their swift growth, the Upper Canadian banks had not been guilty of overissuing notes, and this is confirmed by the ease with which they survived the 1837 crisis.

Far from satisfying all demands for banking services, the rapid expansion of 1832–6 was accompanied by calls for even more banks. Before the Assembly passed laws blocking the organization of new unincorporated banks, the mid-1830s brought five more banks to the province, the British-based Bank of British North America and four unincorporated local banks of varying solidity and permanence. Together, at their peak in the spring of 1837, the last four claimed to represent a capital of almost £100,000, note issue of over £80,000, and loans and discounts of close to £150,000.[39] The Agricultural Bank did not survive the 1837 panic for long.[40] The Farmers Bank, which claimed subscribed capital of £500,000, though operating on as little as £11,000 in paid up capital, came close to collapse then and limped through the 1840s on a very modest basis. The Bank of the People, small and closely linked to reform politicians in Toronto, survived and was taken over by the Bank of Montreal in 1840.[41] The Suspension Bridge Bank, which was very small, may have operated mainly on the American side of the Niagara River, and all but three of its stockholders were Americans.

Data on these four seem less likely to be reliable than those for the chartered banks, and the brevity of their flourishing, essentially from 1834–5 to 1837, also suggests omitting them from data intended to focus on larger trends in the provincial system. Nevertheless, their creation is suggestive of the climate of banking in the period, and if their reports were accurate, they added in total about the equivalent of another Gore Bank to the province's banking facilities for a year or two in the mid-

1830s. The Bank of British North America, with a London headquarters and branches in Lower Canada and the Maritimes, was unincorporated, though the Upper Canadian Assembly authorized it to sue and be sued like a corporation and it later secured a charter. It was just beginning local operations when the 1837 crisis intervened, and it became a substantial participant in the Upper Canadian economy only after 1840.

The banking enthusiasm of the mid-1830s indicates the perceived profitability of banks and that banks, as generators of credit, seemed to hold the key to local expansion. Leaders in every community dreamed that greater access to credit would permit the town to progress at the rate its citizens thought it capable of. Thus, despite the expansion of banking capital just witnessed, the Tory-dominated 1836–7 Assembly, joined by the usually conservative Legislative Council, passed bills that authorized a ninefold increase in bank capital in the province, to £4.5 million.[42] Such bills had to be referred to London, where the Treasury remained alert to the monetary and banking errors of credit-hungry colonists. The British government did not disallow the bills, but sent them back for reconsideration. By then, the world of banking had been transformed by the 1837 crisis, and the wave of enthusiasm for local banking passed, never to return in quite the same way. Although charters were again passed for some of the banks projected in 1836–7, none could establish themselves in the next decade.

## IV. The Crisis of 1837

The provincial banking system was still expanding in the spring of 1837. But pressure was mounting on British banks as early as March, and on 12 May many American banks suspended specie payments. Lower Canadian banks quickly followed, but Upper Canadian banks lacked the power to operate while payments of specie were suspended. Adding to their problems were rumours and then confirmation from Britain of the failure of Thomas Wilson and Company, London agents for the Bank of Upper Canada, the Commercial Bank, and the provincial government, and holder of considerable balances on their accounts.[43] By the middle of June, Upper Canadian banks' note issue had fallen by £100,000 (a figure equal to 25 per cent of the May peak), while the banks' stocks of specie, despite the import of £40,000 by the Bank of Upper Canada, had fallen by £30,000 (equal to almost 25 per cent of mid-May stocks).

When borrowers, hard-pressed by the banks and unable to realize funds quickly to meet the crisis of liquidity, anxiously sought an end to the credit crunch that maintaining payments entailed, the bankers wished to follow suit.[44] In July the legislature passed a law permitting them to suspend, subject to the lieutenant-governor's consent. But Sir Francis Bond Head regarded suspension as 'irreconcilable with British commercial integrity.'[45] He was convinced that a sharp contraction of credit would endanger only speculators. In fact, the situation of many in Upper Canada was better indicated by the Assembly's Select Committee on Banking, chaired by a staunch Conservative, G.S. Boulton, which wrote in February 1838: 'Your Committee cannot quit the subject without remarking, that had the Banks, during the last few months, rigidly enforced the payment of their debts, they would have spread distress and ruin through the whole community.'[46]

Putting enormous pressure on their customers, the banks sharply curtailed discounting and note circulation through the summer to guard against losses of specie. By September their note issues stood at less than half of spring peaks (table 8.5). The discounts of the Bank of Upper Canada fell as far and almost as fast, from £412,000 in April to £211,000 by January 1838. In late September the Commercial received permission to suspend.[47] Almost at once, its note issue and discounts began to recover, and it began to attract good customers who were unable to secure the accommodation they desired at the other provincial banks. The other two chartered banks suspended early in March 1838, following the enactment of new legislation governing suspension. That was not long before specie payment resumed elsewhere in North America, where suspension had taken place the previous May. It was intended that Upper Canada's banks would resume payment in May 1839, but resumption was postponed until November 1839, when the banks again began to redeem their notes in specie.

Because it was feared that the banks might drastically inflate their note issue, the maximum allowed by the law was double their paid-up capital.[48] Total notes in circulation more than doubled in the year after the second act was passed and reached almost £750,000 in the spring of 1839, but they never approached the nearly £1,000,000 that the law allowed. As Angela Redish has shown, the banks acted to seek maximum profits under the constraint of usury laws that limited interest charges to 6 per cent, and in expectation that they would have to resume payment at par.[49] What actually prompted much of the rise in note circulation was massive British military outlay in late 1838 and early 1839, which pumped £2.5 million stg into the economy, most of it in a few months. When payments resumed, the level of note issue in 1840 was not far removed from that of early 1837. This offers further indication that, even if there were individual cases of what was known as excessive speculation, the overall level of bank activity in the mid-1830s was not out of line with the needs of the community, as measured by the credit it carried in more normal times.

## V. Banking in Upper Canada in the Union Era to 1850

Following the Union, the governor general, Lord Sydenham, tried to reform the Canadian banking and monetary system. In 1841 he proposed that a provincial bank of issue be established, with sole power of note issue. This would, he argued, ensure a sounder currency than the banks could guarantee, and bring substantial revenue to the government as well. The banks resisted fiercely. Peter McGill, president of the Bank of Montreal and a member of the Legislative Council, warned the governor that the latter's 'War would not be with the Banks, *but with the Debtors of the Banks*, a very large, and influential Class.'[50] The proposal was soundly defeated in the Assembly. Clearly, the bankers and politicians did not see the provincial system as flawed in the way imperial officials, armed with the latest banking theories, did. Nor did Sydenham grasp the banks' importance (whether real or symbolic) in regional terms, and the importance banks attached to their credit creation being visible in the form of notes. Much other banking legislation was, however, passed at this time, including a requirement that a bank's notes could not exceed its paid-up capital.[51] The Bank of Upper Canada had substantially exceeded this level when it had not faced competitors, but overruns by the standard of the new rules had typically not been large thereafter (table 8.2). In addition, the Commercial and the Bank of Upper Canada were granted power to increase their capital to £500,000 each, though it took them more than a decade to reach that level.

A clear locational pattern of banking had emerged by the 1840s. Toronto, with branches or agencies of six banks in 1846, was the leading centre, while Kingston, Hamilton, and London had four each. The Commercial, although it still had offices in three western centres (London, Port Stanley, and Windsor) in 1846, focused most heavily in the area east of Toronto. The Gore concentrated entirely on the west. The best-represented bank in the province was in fact the Bank of Montreal, whose sixteen offices topped the Commercial's fourteen.[52] West of Hamilton, only Brantford, London, and Amherstburg had been served in 1837. Nine more communities there acquired services by 1846, while only Amherstburg lost out in the meantime.

The City Bank of Montreal was also active in the province in the 1840s, and the Bank of British North America grew rapidly, especially after 1844. By 1846 its note circulation in the two Canadas was second only to the Bank of Montreal. In the 1840s the increased competition from such banks means that data for the three chartered Upper Canadian banks offer a less comprehensive view of Upper Canadian banking. Their growth continued but less rapidly than Upper Canada's population. On a per capita basis, the peak levels of discounts, capital, and main liabilities (notes plus deposits) achieved early in 1837 were not surpassed before 1851. And only in 1847 did the circulation of Upper Canadian bank notes exceed the peaks reached in 1837 and 1841 (tables 8.2, 8.5, 8.6). At no time did the reported total of notes issued by the Upper Canadian banks approach the limit set by their capital.[53] Deposits were an increasingly important form of bank liability; at least on a per capita basis, however, the combined total of deposits and notes issued did not exceed the peaks reached early in 1837 and in 1841.

To estimate total and per capita provincial note circulation in the 1840s, it is necessary to allow for the activities of out-of-province banks. Thus, we may arbitrarily assign half the circulation of the Bank of Montreal and one-third of each of the other two out-of-province banks to Upper Canada.[54] On this basis, the per capita note circulation in the province remained at but not generally higher than levels of 1840–1. As judged by circulation, the level of economic activity in the province slid sharply from 1841 to 1843, then rebounded to 1847. The economy was depressed once more in 1848. Because the per capita estimates for 1842 and 1848 in table 8.2 come from points when the economy was declining, it is desirable also to estimate circulation for 1847, the peak year of the cycle. Such a calculation, including estimated note issue in the province of the three out-of-province banks, yields a total figure of £870,000, a total 80 per cent higher than for the three Upper Canadian banks alone; on a per capita basis, the total was equal to £1.33 per Upper Canadian, marginally beyond the peak early in 1837 for the province's three chartered banks alone, and very close to the 1837 peak if the four unchartered banks of the time are included. Like other data on the period, this estimate of note circulation suggests a pattern of bank expansion in Upper Canada in the 1840s that resembled extensive more than intensive growth. Certainly the spread of bank offices does not seem to have produced an intensification in the use of banks.[55]

After the peak in 1847, the economy entered a sharp cyclical downturn. Upper Canadian banks' note issue declined by 24 per cent, measured in annual averages, from 1847 to 1849;[56] discounts fell by a small amount; and deposits, both at interest and otherwise, fell sharply, the former by 37 per cent from June 1847 to March 1848, and the latter by 28 per cent. The data on discounts conceal substantial overdue and eventually bad debts. The Gore Bank had to write off 20 per cent of its £100,000 in capital, the City Bank wrote off even more, and all banks cut dividends below usual rates and drew heavily on reserve funds. By 1851, however, the various indicators of banking activity were moving sharply upward again.

## VI. *Other Financial Institutions*

In the 1830s and 1840s provincial entrepreneurs also began to develop other financial institutions.[57] The largest were fire and marine insurance companies. The first building societies appeared in the mid-1840s, and they proliferated rapidly in the subsequent decade, laying the basis ultimately for a much larger mortgage sector in the late-nineteenth-century Canadian economy.[58] Several savings banks were also founded. They were linked to the banks by deposits, share investments, and in some cases directors, but were much smaller and less-independent institutions. Still, they offer evidence that their depositors, who included ordinary men and women, had savings; the existence of such capital is an important theme elsewhere in this study.[59] In the late 1840s the Canada Life Assurance Company, later a major company in a field where Canadian business became internationally successful, was founded at Hamilton.

The St Lawrence Inland Marine Insurance Company, based in Prescott, and the British America Fire and Life Assurance Company, based in Toronto, were both chartered in 1833. Nominally capitalized at £100,000 each, they completed the 1830s with less than £25,000 in paid-up capital between them and the 1840s with just £50,000 in capital, an amount well below that of leading commercial firms of the period (table 8.7). On this capital, and annual premium incomes by the mid-1840s of up to £20,000, they took on growing risks; in 1847, a peak year, these totalled £1.75 million.[60] American and British companies were also active in the province's insurance market. They were widely represented by local agents and, because metropolitan merchants could effect insurance for country clients, even reached areas where they were not directly represented. Local companies complained that outside companies quoted unrealistically low premiums then did not honour policies when losses occurred, but no long-term business could be built on such a basis. In fact, the stronger outside companies were formidable competitors because they had sound reputations and knowledgeable and effective local agents.[61] Nevertheless, local companies secured niches in the market. At the margin, perhaps, they were better able to judge risks in their local market than were companies with much wider business interests; or perhaps there were savings from less-complex management than an international company required. It also helped that the overall market grew because of economic expansion and probably a widening of the market for insurance in the community.

Mutual insurance companies, organized on a district basis under 1836 legislation, institutionalized a community's management of the ever present risks of fire. By 1851 at least seven, and probably more, had been organized. Instead of paying an actual premium, mutual policy holders were assessed a premium for their type of risk, value of property, and term of insurance and gave the company a promissory note in this amount.[62] A deposit of 5 per cent was paid on the note to cover operating costs. When losses occurred, members were assessed at a percentage of their note to defray the costs. The Home District Mutual Fire Insurance Company, for example, made two assessments, totalling 5 per cent, in the first half of 1845. Such arrangements minimized immediate outlay for a clientele that had many uses for its capital.[63] In 1845 the Home District Company had over £300,000 in insurance effected within its district (the province's largest, and likely its most competitive, insurance market).[64] That bore comparison with the £400,000 in fire policies on the books of the British America Company at the end of 1844 (table 8.7).

Building societies began to develop in Upper Canada in the mid-1840s, at almost the same time as their use was growing rapidly in Britain.[65] Subscribers pledged to pay small monthly instalments on their shares. From the monthly income thus secured, funds were available for a new mortgage each month. Members especially anxious for a mortgage bid for the right to an early mortgage, and their premiums and interest payments could yield a growing surplus in the society. This, it was intended, would ultimately be paid out to the members when the society was wound up at the end of its cycle, after everyone had had a mortgage. All being well, members would then receive back their capital plus a bonus, and would have had a mortgage in the process. These proved very popular, and by 1851 at least twenty were organized, most of them by merchants, in Upper Canada.[66] In the 1850s, as the first reached the point of termination, the idea of organizing them on a permanent basis took hold. Out of this development came such long-lived companies as the Canada Permanent and the Huron and Erie.[67] Like the chartered and the mutual insurance companies, building societies and mortgage companies grew incrementally from relatively small beginnings. Because they were small, moreover, errors of judgment in a single institution had little effect on the health of the entire sector as it grew.

VII. *Conclusion*

Of the new institutions, the chartered banks were very much the main ones. Strongly competitive, the banks were nevertheless able to act collectively, as in their resistance to Sydenham in 1841 and during commercial crises.[68] By 1851 Upper Canada's three chartered banks represented over £800,000 in capital and their loans (discounts) exceeded £2 million, or more than £2 per person in Upper Canada. Together, their notes and deposits equalled £1.5 per person. In addition, provincial banking demands were served by the out-of-province banks, led by the Bank of Montreal. In capitalization, the Bank of Upper Canada and the Commercial Bank were among the largest of all businesses in Upper Canada. In organizational terms, banks were more modest and bore comparison to leading mercantile firms rather than later corporations. The largest, the Bank of Montreal, employed fifty-six people in 1847, including fourteen at head office, and seven each at Quebec and Toronto.[69] The other financial institutions were smaller still, and none had more than a handful of paid, full-time employees.

As institutions for the creation of capital and for the management of risk, debt, and payments, banks could facilitate capital formation and the expansion of trade and also, through the payments process, specialization and diversification. But the diffusion of banking and the growing quantity of money that the banks put into circulation did not fundamentally change the business system, which at mid-century was still focused on general merchants. Principal retailers in towns with bank offices were perhaps increasingly able to obtain bank credit in their own names, and that might enhance their autonomy relative to wholesalers, but the banks still sought the security of having the names of both the wholesaler and the retailer or the exporter and the forwarder on commercial paper that they discounted.[70] Although we know very little about who had bank notes and how money was used, there is nothing to suggest that banks ordinarily dealt directly with most of the producers in the economy.

The growing use of money, the growth of banking, and the development of a more sophisticated capitalism were closely associated. The process of institutional change in the financial system did not represent the creation of a 'money' economy where none had been before, however. There had always been some money in the province, principally specie; and from earliest times produce, services, and of course imports were usually valued in terms of money. Started late in the postwar deflationary era, the Bank of Upper Canada required government aid to begin operations, but by the mid-1820s, its capital, discounts, and note issue were growing very rapidly. Upper Canadian banking grew more swiftly still in the 1830s. The strength of out-of-province banks and the Bank of Upper Canada's accession to the role of government bank in 1850 make it more difficult to assess the total scale of specifically Upper Canadian banking after 1840; at least on a per capita basis, however, Upper Canadians may not have been using significantly more bank services in the mid-1840s than a decade earlier.

Evidence of this pattern is provided in table 8.6, which presents several indicators of banking activity at intervals of five years from 1826 to 1851. The years selected avoid two of the three peaks in the period, 1837 and 1847, and the principal troughs, 1842–3 and 1848–9; one peak year, 1841, is included, however. On a per capita basis, note circulation and discounts reached levels by 1836 that were at or near the high levels for the entire twenty-five years. Despite the banks' continuing belief in the necessity of note issue for their success, the ratio of deposits to notes rose quite steadily. Too little is yet known about those deposits and their use. In that most did not earn interest, it seems likely that deposits were part of commercial operations, not long-term savings (see table 8.3 for the 1840s).[71] Deposits notwithstanding, commerce continued to rely extensively on the bill of exchange as a means of settling accounts.

In the 1830s and 1840s a number of chartered and mutual insurance companies, building societies, and savings banks were created. In total volume of business, they constituted a sector of some significance, but they are probably more important for what they say about the character of development in Upper Canada. They grew from modest beginnings in an undramatic but cumulatively important process of institutional creation and diversification. Even more than the banks, these institutions had near-equivalents in the market, including foreign insurance companies; community mutual action, such as the pioneer bee, as a response to fire (which to a degree the mutual company extended); and private arrangement of mortgages. As in the case of merchants, market forces acted as a constraint on the power of any one company.[72]

Banks and other financial institutions, although linked to the wider network of credit and exchange, were largely owned by Canadians. Nevertheless, because it extended beyond provincial boundaries, the credit structure represented an aspect of metropolitan influence; and it is evident that outsiders' expectations about provincial prosperity, including prospective exports, affected the credit available to Upper Canadians. But, as the expansion of banking in the 1830s suggests, the supply of credit was not simply or uniquely related to actual exports. Moreover, the capital imported in a growing business was modest in comparison to the capital it built up within Upper Canada. Whatever its origins, the capital used in Upper Canada had to be paid for by Upper Canadians, either explicitly as interest charges or in the prices of goods. Those who paid their debts in effect paid also for those who did not pay. That so many felt they were getting ahead suggests that the benefits of participation in this economy seemed worth those costs.

# 9 Government and the Development of Upper Canada, 1820–41

Canadians have tended to think the state has been particularly important in Canadian development, in comparison with contemporary American and British experience. Although the Welland Canal is often seen as a starting-point for this distinctive tradition,[1] there has never been a full analysis of the developmental role of the state in Upper Canada, and such a study is beyond the scope of this book. It would need to consider fiscal dimensions – that is, taxes and expenditures – which form the core of this chapter; policies on financial institutions and on the development of transportation and communications, which are addressed elsewhere in this volume; commercial policy and resource policy, notably regarding land settlement and forest exploitation, issues only touched on in this study; the roles of courts and the legal system in defining and defending property rights, as agents of economic change, and as part of the processes of social control; municipal institutions; and social policies of economic relevance, such as education.[2] It would also need to assess consequences, because policy did not necessarily have the anticipated impact on provincial development. In Upper Canada it is important to recognize that governments, while undoubtedly elitist, were not simply creatures of a single, united interest, the 'family compact,' with coherent objectives that governments systematically pursued.[3] But if the state was not entirely the tool of a narrow group, neither was it purely autonomous.

The state in Upper Canada was plural and offered multiple sources of initiative and control. It embraced the imperial government, acting through officials of the Colonial Office and the Treasury in Whitehall and in the colony, and through centrally defined policies of relevance to the colonies (such as the Navigation Acts), the various branches of the military forces, and the post office; the provincial government; municipal authorities (both magistrates in quarter-sessions and, later, incorporated municipalities); semi-autonomous and quasi-official individuals and authorities, such as Thomas Talbot or the Canada Company; and the Lower Canadian state. In the early years, as we have seen, much of the Upper Canadian government's revenue was supplied by Britain, and during the War of 1812 such links were greatly enhanced. Thereafter, as the British government sought to reduce its costs and a more complex local politics grew up, the provincial state gradually emerged as a more distinguishable factor in the economy, one requiring consideration in an account that has placed emphasis on local roots of economic change.

Although only a small fraction of Upper Canada's production and exchange flowed through state channels, the provincial government's taxes, expenditures, and borrowing made it one of the more pervasive and substantial economic institutions in the province. As in the private sector, it was principally through credit that the government pursued longer-term developmental objectives. These focused on public works, especially the two main canal projects, the Welland and the St Lawrence. Throughout the period, British government expenditures remained a highly valued source of external capital, which helped sustain the economy's international and local liquidity and, unlike commercial credit, did not entail the obligation of repayment. Despite its efforts to economize, the British government's expenditures in Upper Canada actually exceeded those by the Upper Canadian government itself throughout the colony's history (tables 9.3, 9.6).

The role of the Upper Canadian government paralleled in essential respects that of nearby states such as New York, Ohio, and Indiana, all of which actively promoted development by public investment in canals and other works.[4] Upper Canada differed from its southern neighbours, however, in the tory ideology of some of its principal leaders, its colonial status, and its dependence on another colony, Lower Canada, for its prime source of tax revenue. And when the distinction between Upper Canada and its neighbours was most emphasized by extreme trans-border tension, such as in 1812–15 or 1838–9, British expenditure in the province increased dramatically.

I. *The Fiscal Development of the Upper Canadian Government*

Colonists everywhere were reluctant to tax themselves, and the difficulty of collecting most taxes also deterred higher taxation. But Upper Canada, the only British colony of its time without a seaport, lacked control even of most colonies' principal revenue source, customs duties. Because import duties collected by Lower Canada at Quebec applied to all goods imported to the St Lawrence, Upper Canada was able to claim a share of Lower Canada's revenues under imperial and Lower Canadian acts.[5] For much of the period until 1817, Upper Canada's share was calculated from records of dutiable goods passing Lower Canada's customs station at Coteau-du-Lac. Upper Canadians argued that this system understated provincial imports because, while no duty had to be paid there, stopping at Coteau took time, and the official there had no incentive to pursue information that was not brought to him. In terms of relative population levels, the province's share of Lower Canada's revenue appears equitable until 1800 (table 9.1). From then until 1813 it was not, for on average it was less than 10 per cent, although the province's population represented about one-sixth of total St Lawrence valley population by 1812.[6] During and just after the War of 1812 the substantial flow of goods into the province as a result of the British government's expenditures rapidly increased Upper Canada's share and its absolute revenues. The two provinces then agreed to divide revenues for 1817–19 on the basis of Upper Canada's having one-fifth of the total collected. Thus encouraged, Upper Canada began an ambitious program of government expenditures, notably on militia pensions.

When the agreement expired in the summer of 1819, Upper Canada was unable to negotiate a new agreement or obtain any of the sums it claimed it had earlier been deprived of by the workings of the Coteau-based system. Lieutenant-Governor Maitland was forced to borrow from the Military Chest to keep his administration functioning, and his interest in government participation in the new Bank of Upper Canada stemmed directly from this crisis.[7] This was the background to the British-imposed solution, the Canada Trade Act of 1822, which provided for arbitration to decide on claims for sums not paid earlier, and for quadrennial arbitrations to decide how to divide the duties henceforth. Upper Canadians argued that the province was a larger consumer of British goods on a per capita basis than Lower Canada, but the duties would now be allocated essentially on the basis of the two colonies' populations. In addition, Upper Canada received over £12,000 for its claims for lost revenues earlier (table 9.2). After the early 1820s the province could anticipate its receipts on this account, its largest single source of revenue, with more confidence than before. But the province did not share in all categories of Lower Canadian duties; it still had no say in the level of duties set at Quebec, and thus it could not, without setting up its own customs establishment between the two colonies, opt for higher or different taxes to support a different level of services.

Until the War of 1812 the imperial government's grant in support of the province's civil administration was the leading source of funds for the local government. After the war, the British government sought to eliminate this grant. Before doing so, it wished to give the colonial administration some security by providing for permanent local payment of the salaries that made up the civil list. This objective was essentially achieved with the establishment of the Canada Company, as its annual payments, beginning in 1827, would more than cover the amounts hitherto paid by the British government.[8] Collectively, the casual and territorial revenues, which derived from sales and leases of crown lands and resources, yielded a growing net revenue to the provincial administration (table 9.2), though the province now had to pay costs formerly paid by the British government. Payments by the Canada Company were much the largest part of the total, and they were due to end in 1843. Timber duties, mainly from the Ottawa valley, yielded the next largest share. They fluctuated considerably, and valley timber interests increasingly sought to have them used not for general revenue but for public investment in improvements to facilitate timber movements.[9]

Customs duties on imports from the United States yielded mounting net sums as trans-border trade grew.[10] After 1826 American goods were the basis of an annual revenue equivalent to between one-sixth and one-quarter of what the province derived from Quebec duties. Collecting duties along the extended frontier with the United States was more costly and complex to administer than where duties could be collected at a single port of entry. There were thirty-five ports of entry in Upper Canada by 1840, although over half of all duties were collected at just three points – Toronto, Kingston, and Burlington Bay (Hamilton). In addition to dutiable goods, and against the British laws of trade, Upper Canada illegally imported well over half of its tea, a low-volume, high-value commodity, from the United States.[11] The growth of revenues from duties on American goods suggests, however, that such evasion was an exception. Provided duties were fairly administered and policy did not offer inducement to risky evasive measures, as in the case of tea, major importers actually had little reason to try to escape payment.

The province imposed only two significant locally collected, internally generated taxes. The first, on the liquor trade, at the distilling, wholesaling, and retailing stages, was additional to imperial duties. Such taxes produced as much as 15 per cent of provincial revenue (in 1825), though in the 1830s, as other revenues grew, the proportion of revenue attributable to this item fell to less than half this share. The other, the municipally collected and expended property tax, produced revenues which, across the province, added up to the second largest of all Upper Canadian taxes (table 9.2, row K). Other provincial levies, such as auctioneers' duties, lighthouse taxes, and pedlars' licences, netted little for the provincial treasury. The province derived less revenue from all of them than from the annual 8 per cent dividend and periodic bonuses on its £25,000 investment in the stock of the Bank of Upper Canada.[12] Income from provincially assisted works appears in the province's revenue accounts, but it is unlikely that any projects yielded actual profits that could be used by the state for other purposes.[13]

A number of colonial government services were supplied without the intermediation of the tax system. Fees paid directly to the official supplying the service were central to the land title and transfer system, the legal system, and education. Land surveys were often paid for by a share of the land.[14] Other services that we might now think of as governmental were supplied directly by citizens. For example, road upkeep and some other local services were organized through township meetings. The obligation on adult men to serve in the militia was at times significant. In addition, much of the work of local government and administration of justice was performed on a largely unpaid basis by local notables appointed as magistrates by the provincial government.[15]

These factors make it impossible to calculate the 'real' costs of government to Upper Canadians. As indicated in table 9.2, however, it was usual for the Upper Canadian government's revenues from provincial sources in the period 1829–36 to have been between 7 and 8s per capita, or £2 to £2¹/₂ per average household. What a household actually paid was a function of the household's consumption of imports and alcohol and of whether it was buying land from the Canada Company or in some other way contributing to the casual and territorial revenues.

On the expenditure side, apart from public works and a growing outlay on interest, to be discussed below, the Upper Canadian government's annual expenditures amounted to about £25,000 to £30,000 in the mid-1820s, around £50,000 by 1830, and almost £100,000 by 1836–7 (table 9.3). On a per capita basis, these amounted to between 5s and 6s per Upper Canadian in the 1830s. When the revenues recorded in table 9.2 are compared to the expenditures in table 9.3, the revenues appear to have exceeded expenses by around £10,000 a year in the mid-1820s and by £20,000 to £30,000 in the 1828–34 period. The gap does not, in fact, reflect a surplus, but rather outlay on capital account and perhaps some peculiarities of the province's accounting. Capital items included repayment of provincial debt principal (over £40,000 by 1831), purchase of shares in the Bank of Upper Canada (£25,000 between 1821 and 1830), and outlay on public works. The data on public works do not permit easy separation of relatively routine annual outlay on construction and maintenance from larger expenditures, often made with borrowed funds. Other than items on capital account, the principal object of provincial expenditure was the basic administrative, political, and judicial apparatus of the province (table 9.3, row A), which required about half of the annual outlay. The other major expenses included education, the churches (Church of England, Church of Scotland, and Roman Catholic Church), and the province's new penitentiary, built in the 1830s. As the figures on religious expenditure indicate, not all of the rising provincial outlay reflected genuinely new spending; part of the increase in this category derived from a shift in the manner of payment, from direct support of the Church of England by the London-based Society for the Propagation of the Gospel to support through the Upper Canadian government's own accounts. Similarly, expenditures on account of Indian lands in part reflected the beginning of a shift in responsibility from Britain to Upper Canada. Other than interest, however, nothing in the expenditure data in table 9.3 suggests a rapid rise in the level of government activity over the period.

Because the centre of provincial administration was in Toronto, the funds for administration were to a significant degree spent there. Expenditures on education, the churches, and public works were more widely spread across the province, being allocated more or less in line with population. However they are viewed, the province's routine expenditures were scarcely sufficient to make the provincial state a dominant participant in the provincial economy, or its ordinary costs a burden to most participants in the economy.

## II. *Public Credit and Public Works*

Despite the modesty of the state's ordinary fiscal operations, Upper Canada found itself in a fiscal crisis in 1837. The problem was not routine expenditures but the province's debts, now owed and payable largely outside the province. Over one-third of the province's ordinary income was needed to meet interest payments by 1837, and annual interest payments by 1838 exceeded £60,000, or almost as much as all other current expense items combined.

Upper Canada's first experiment with public borrowing through the issuing of debentures occurred in 1821–2, when it borrowed £25,000 at 6 per cent, through the Bank of Upper Canada and the firm of Clark and Street, to fund the arrears that had accumulated under the province's militia pensions scheme (table 9.4). Another £24,000 was borrowed in 1824, two-thirds for 'public service' and the remainder for the Burlington Canal.[16] Thereafter, except for £57,000 in debentures issued in 1833 to those with War of 1812 losses claims and a few thousand pounds in rebellion losses debentures, all of Upper Canada's public debt was incurred for public works. Between 1825 and 1837 the province increased its debt thirty-four-fold, and its per capita debt more than tenfold. There was support for such public investment across the political spectrum. The largest single increase in provincial debt, 1835's £400,000 stg, occurred when reformers held a majority in the Assembly.[17]

The completion of the Rideau and Welland canals in the early 1830s in no way satisfied the demand for public investment in new projects. Assembly members had a strong incentive to seek provincial funding for local projects, and an administration that needed wider support had its own imperatives to try to respond to the clamour for development from the different regions. In light of the limitations on receipts from ordinary revenue sources and in view of the rapid expansion – and the desire for more – that marked the 1830s in Upper Canada, borrowing was the only way to achieve the large works that seemed most urgent and to reconcile the local calls for funds.[18]

At the end of 1833, Upper Canada's public debt totalled less than £300,000 cy, or less than £1 per capita. Over half of that debt had been incurred in support of the Welland Canal Company (tables 9.4, 9.5) which, far from becoming a source of revenue to the government or its stockholders,[19] could not meet its interest payments and continued to seek government aid for reconstruction and improvements. Most of the remainder was incurred in support of three principal roads in the Home District (about £30,000) and of the Burlington Canal (about £17,000), or had been paid, in the form of debentures, to war loss claimants (£57,000). In 1834 the province's receiver general, J.H. Dunn, effected a consolidation of much of the provincial debt by issuing £200,000 stg of 5 per cent securities payable in London, England. The advantages of this shift, Dunn argued, included the saving of 1 per cent in interest costs, some simplification and clarification of interest payments procedures; an infusion of external capital that would free local capital to seek other, higher, returns, and the creation of a London reputation for the province's securities.[20] In making this change, Upper Canada joined a number of American states which moved into the London market as the 1830s boom there moved towards its peak.[21]

Four years later, after the 1837 financial crisis, Upper Canada's debt, now largely owed in London, exceeded £1.25 million cy, almost all of which had been borrowed on account of public works. The Welland Canal represented £275,000 of this debt, and the St Lawrence canals even more, £352,000; together they accounted for almost 60 per cent of the public works expenditures that credit had permitted the Upper Canadian government to make down to 1840 (table 9.5). But the St Lawrence canals were far from complete, indeed never could be wholly finished without Lower Canadian cooperation; and we have seen that because of the Rideau Canal, they were of questionable value as a transport system, except possibly for passenger movements. Only politics, easy credit, and the largely unquestioned strategic assumption of the future value of an improved St Lawrence to the inland province could explain this project. Similarly, politics as much as economics explain most of the remainder of the 1830s debt. Roads and bridges took up over one-quarter of the public works debt. Assorted lesser canals, harbours, and lighthouses, the penitentiary, a new legislative building, and a railway accounted for the remaining sums.

When it incurred these debts, Upper Canada acted much like the adjacent states. While Upper Canada was borrowing £150,000 between 1826 and 1831 to support the Welland Canal, Ohio, with almost five times the population, was investing over eight times this amount in a 400-mile state-owned barge canal system. In 1836–7 Ohio took on millions more dollars in debt to expand this system and to support a broad array of other projects. By 1842 Ohio's annual interest costs were $800,000, roughly three times what Upper Canada had to pay.[22] Indiana in 1836 authorized borrowing $10.5 million for its public works program, and Illinois in 1837 sought to raise a similar sum, most of it for projects that would be 'an almost wholly unrelieved failure.'[23] Michigan, which only became a state in 1835, promptly set out to borrow $5 million in support of three railroad projects. Such comparisons suggest that Upper Canada's debt-supported works need not be explained with reference to a distinctive local economic culture of 'defensive expansion';[24] the province's behaviour looks much like a typical North American response to the developmental possibilities and external credit that the mid-1830s offered. By the standards of some of these states, Upper Canada's external debt, less than $5 million, was quite prudent. Even so, paying the interest on this amount challenged the existing fiscal system. In part the problem was that Upper Canada's public works investments, like many of the mid-1830s projects of its southern neighbours, proved fundamentally unprofitable. Some earned their operating costs, as these were then calculated, but few (and none of the major projects) would return the capital invested in them – or even the interest on that capital – to the province.

For many of the projects, optimistic predictions had been made as to returns, but it is hard to know if these were genuinely believed either by those making them or those voting to support the projects. The capital of J.B. Yates played a vital role in the early years of the Welland. Thereafter, it is evident that, though they embodied a general strategic design of wide appeal, not least to imperial statesmen who prided themselves on having a larger vision than did ordinary colonists, the two main canal projects, which needed large sums invested before they could yield any return, gave little prospect of a competitive private rate of return. Some smaller-scale developments, such as the Desjardins Canal or Oakville Harbour, began as private initiatives, but public support was soon called for, either in the wake of escalating costs or in recognition that private returns from holding stocks or bonds would not justify investment in them.[25] Similarly, local pressures brought about provincial legislation and borrowing that sustained public projects such as the Burlington Canal and the several harbours that received public aid. One significant exception was the Niagara Harbour and Dock Company, whose promoters clearly anticipated a private return, especially through shipbuilding.[26]

It is usual to say that the province's problem was a shortage of capital. But the province had annual access to hundreds of thousands of pounds in commercial credit and in the 1830s readily financed an increase in banking capital of over £350,000 and a fast-growing steamship fleet whose combined value was well over £100,000. None of the public works projects required much in the way of costly imported inputs; and even labour, which often did come from outside the province, not only paid its own way to the province but spent most of its earnings within the province once there.[27] Except for the two principal works, there is good reason to think that the other works, had there been realistic prospects of private return from them, could have been financed from within the colony or by outsiders like Yates. In effect, all of the projects for which Upper Canada borrowed, despite their different degrees of commercial plausibility, were essentially political and social investments, and those closest to them must have known or strongly suspected that they could not be made to pay an adequate return measured by ordinary private calculations. That factor as much as capital shortage explains the state's role in financing them. And it is vital to assessing the state's apparently poor performance as an investor.

It has been common to see Upper Canada's 1837–8 debt as huge, and Upper Canada as near bankruptcy from it.[28] The scale of the burden needs further consideration, however. In total, the £1,250,000 owed by 1838 bore an annual interest cost of about £65,000, which was equivalent to slightly over 3s per Upper Canadian, or about £1 per household, at a time when 5s was a not uncommon daily wage.[29] Unlike the pre-1834 debt, more than 80 per cent of this sum was owed and payable outside the country and thus did not represent an amount that Upper Canadians owed themselves. Interest at 5 per cent on the £870,000 stg of debt payable in London was about £44,000 stg, an amount equal to about 12 per cent of the average annual value of Upper Canada's exports down the St Lawrence (f.o.b. Quebec) in 1835–8 (table 4.3). Even if the projects funded by the debt did not directly carry their costs, it could in various indirect ways have encouraged enough development in total to enable the economy to meet these costs of servicing it.

## III. British Government Spending and Upper Canadian Development

As we have seen above, the British government's annual parliamentary grant to Upper Canada of around £10,000 in support of the civil administration was ended in 1826, but this was only a small component of British government expenditures in Upper Canada. Given the scale of British payments in Upper Canada or on Upper Canadian account, it is important to explore their dimensions and impact.[30] It has not been possible to survey exhaustively all the pertinent accounts and records, but an approximate, minimum estimate of relevant figures can be arrived at (table 9.6). While most of the British expenditures were on military account, some civilian costs continued.

Thus, in 1828 Britain lent £50,000 stg to the Welland Canal Company, and this effectively became a grant when the company failed to pay interest on it. Most of the costs of Indian Department operations, over £20,000 stg per year, continued to be borne by the British taxpayer, as, until the clergy reserves began to yield substantial funds in the 1830s, did an important part of the costs of the Church of England. Britain made several substantial grants directly in support of emigration projects, and in 1831–3, to help meet costs imposed on the province by emigration and the cholera epidemic, Britain paid out some £23,000 stg on account of Upper Canadian emigration costs (see table 9.6).[31]

A larger lump sum was entailed in Britain's payment in 1824 of £57,000 towards meeting the approved claims of Upper Canadians for losses suffered during the War of 1812. Augmented modestly by the proceeds of properties confiscated from wartime traitors, this sum was sufficient to pay an instalment of 35 per cent on such losses. In 1837 a further payment of £17,000 was made on the British government's account to bring this issue to an end, but it is not clear whether that sum derived from revenues generated within the province.[32] The 1824 payment, made to about 1,500 claimants, represented a substantial infusion of external capital for the time; for example, it considerably exceeded the £41,000 in provincial wheat exports in that year. Those opposing the manner of transfer of these funds through Montreal argued that so many Upper Canadians had long-overdue debts outside the province, stemming from the postwar deflation, that the British payment would quickly end up in the hands of outside creditors. In a credit-driven economy, such an external payment might affect the net external balance owed by that economy without having an impact, through leverage or the multiplier effect, on the economy into which it was nominally paid.[33] It is thus possible that, despite its size, this payment was essentially a further episode in the reorganization and revaluation of the provincial economy after the postwar deflation, not a stimulant to development.

The largest British government payments in Upper Canada continued to be on military account (table 9.6). By late 1821 the British garrison in Upper Canada had been reduced to about 1,200 to 1,300 men.[34] Detailed figures on the costs to maintain such an establishment, in wages, provisioning, and the purchase of other goods and services, are not readily available; the figures here are only estimates. They are confirmed, however, by other data. For example, the total cost of the garrisons in both Canadas in 1836, the last year before rebellion-influenced increases, was about £112,000 stg.[35] If Upper Canada accounted for one-third of this sum, then routine British expenditures there would have been about £35,000, which compares quite closely with the £33,000 estimated for earlier years in table 9.6. Such expenditures were not simply additions to the province's external resources, for the garrison affected what was imported, but they were valued parts of the local economies of the garrison towns.

In addition to payments on ordinary garrison account, the army made substantial expenditures on military works, of which the Rideau Canal was much the largest, at a cost of £830,000 stg, paid into the economy between 1826 and 1832. The Ordnance was involved in a number of other projects. In 1836 these totalled £54,000 stg in the two Canadas; between 1825 and 1837, in addition to the Rideau and Ottawa Canals, Ordnance expenditures in the two Canadas exceeded £500,000 stg.[36] Such expenditures went largely on goods and services that could be produced in the province, so they could sustain and extend local exchange in their vicinity. If 40 per cent of such payments were made in Upper Canada, where about 40 per cent of the garrison was stationed, they would have averaged £17,000 stg per year. When combined with routine garrison costs, British military expenditure in Upper Canada after 1825 would thus have been at least £50,000 stg per year. Somewhat higher outlay is suggested by Angela Redish, who provides data on total military expenditures in the two Canadas between 1832 and 1840; somewhat arbitrarily, table 9.6 assigns one-third of them to Upper Canada. On military account alone, Britain spent at least £1.6 million stg between 1825 and 1837; this would have equalled £1.8 million cy at official exchange rates, or an average of almost £140,000 per year.[37] That figure exceeded annual outlay by the Upper Canadian government in all but the last year of the period (table 9.3, row K). In addition, many officers, particularly from the Revolutionary and Napoleonic wars, had settled in the province and drew half pay.[38]

Following the rebellions, Britain sharply expanded the garrisons and Ordnance expenditures in the Canadas. In the three years 1838–40, such outlays totalled almost £3.5 million stg, of which at least one-third must have been spent within Upper Canada. At this level, military expenditures within the province came close to equalling the £600,000 cy a year value of Upper Canada's exports (f.o.b. Quebec) in the same period. Such expenditures contributed to the inflationary pressures felt in 1839, but as businessmen at the time delightedly discovered, they greatly enhanced provincial liquidity. Coming soon after the 1837 crisis, before debts accumulated to impossible-to-pay sums through the workings of compound interest, they undoubtedly helped many who had borrowed extensively in the 1830s boom to clear their accounts and make a fresh start.

Over the entire period from 1821 to 1840, British government expenditures in Upper Canada in various forms amounted to no less than £3.8 million stg (£4.2 million cy at the official exchange rate). If, to avoid double counting, we remove from the calculations the Upper Canadian government's expenditure of its British parliamentary grant in the early and mid-1820s, we may estimate the province's annual expenditures at about £20,000 in the early 1820s; by the peak years of the 1830s, that figure had grown to £140,000. Over the whole era the Upper Canadian government probably spent no more than £1.5 million cy, plus an additional £1.25 million cy (net) in borrowed funds. Although these figures are crude, they reveal clearly that state expenditure in Upper Canada through the entire period was considerably more British than Upper Canadian. If British expenditures are combined with the British capital borrowed by Upper Canada, it is clear that the two governments were directly responsible for bringing at least £4.5 million stg into the province during this twenty-year period. By comparison, in the fourteen years prior to 1839 recorded in table 4.3, the value (at Brockville) of Upper Canada's wheat exports down the St Lawrence totalled less than £2 million stg (about £2.2 million cy), and the value (at Quebec) of Upper Canadian timber exports would, with allowance for gaps in data, have totalled no more than £3.5 million stg (about £4 million cy). At any reasonable estimate of the value of Upper Canadian exports in years for which data are missing, it is clear that British government expenditures in Upper Canada were approximately equivalent in value to the earnings of the province's wood product exports and greatly exceeded earnings from wheat.

## IV. *Conclusion*

Taxes, expenditure, borrowing, and investment offer just one perspective on the role of the state in Upper Canadian development. Indeed, they largely omit the state's main contributions: disposition of the public lands; provision of law, notably in relation to the character and implications of property rights in the colony; and defence. Because of all three, but especially the last, while the province developed an economy resembling those across the lakes, it was not identical to them, nor was it fully a part of the wider American economy.

The development of routine government revenues and expenditures looks very much as might be expected in a process of extensive growth, growth in aggregate figures being quite closely correlated with growth in population (tables 9.2, 9.3). On a per capita basis, provincial revenues showed a significant increase with the phasing in of the Canada Company's payments in 1827–8, but thereafter fluctuated in a range of 7s to 8s per capita. Expenditures, excluding interest costs, showed an essentially similar pattern, with per capita outlay of between 4s and 5s in all but two years from 1829 to 1837. Some scope might be found for expanding responsibilities by spreading the overheads of the central administration over a larger population, but the principal way for the provincial state to expand its role was by borrowing. As well, the province began to discover in the 1830s, for example in its expansion of funding for education, that quite small provincial grants could have larger impacts by requiring or stimulating expenditures at the local level.[39] In this way, just as in the experiments in public debt and public works, the government of Upper Canada was increasing its capacity to achieve desired ends. Although colonists continued to desire British action and expenditure, in the long run, especially after the early 1840s, it was the local state that would increasingly serve their purposes. Even so, and despite the province's construction of an impressive new penitentiary,[40] the ordinary revenues and expenses of the Upper Canadian government of the 1830s are not self-evidently those of an active, intrusive state.

Given the modesty of the provincial state, it may seem paradoxical that patronage bulked so importantly in provincial politics, for it almost seems that the state had too little to give away to justify all the efforts. But the churches' anxious quest for state support and the assiduousness with which many Upper Canadians sought government posts and contracts, even small-community postmasterships and customs collectorships, reveal not the scale of government so much as the insecurities of everyday economic life and the limited range of occupations and offices that a decentralized rural economy had to offer. Even an apparently small but certain income was attractive, and a modest post might be combined with others or linked with private pursuits to yield a more substantial income than any one position would afford. Government salaries were relatively secure, and the probability of payment on government contracts was higher than in the private credit system. In addition, a salary could enhance its recipient's credit-worthiness, permitting him, in effect, to gain leverage from it by borrowing against his predicted future income. Such dimensions helped give both vitality and some security to demand within the local market economy.

As we have noted, the state's role as an investor in public works cannot be judged primarily in terms of profit and loss, for had there been much chance of profit, the state was unlikely to have been called upon to invest. Because tolls did not cover the entire real cost to the provincial taxpayer and because it is not possible to know what freight rates would have been in the absence of these investments, we cannot use changes in shipping costs as a reliable indicator of the success of the works either. The appropriate measure of the state's investment in new works would be the wider social return, but it is difficult to distinguish development fostered by these investments from that which would have occurred in any case. Such a rigorous measurement of the state's economic role is not possible here, but some chronological and locational implications of state investments can help us assess the significance of the state in Upper Canada's development.

Public works investments must have played some part in the province's attractiveness to emigrants. Still, the immigrants who made up the 1831–2 peak of the decade's immigration boom arrived very late in the first period of canal construction, and before the main Upper Canadian public works investments of the mid-1830s. Government expenditures on works could still have been important in the migration process, by playing a part in immigrants' longer-term progress, perhaps especially in their decision and ability to remain in the colony. Whether they worked directly on the projects or benefited indirectly from the demand such works fostered, they needed an income if they were to remain. The Upper Canadian government's projects of the mid-1830s may have heightened the province's expansion beyond what would otherwise have occurred, and expenditures in 1837–8 of funds raised in 1837 may also have helped maintain employment after the boom had peaked.

The two main canals built by Upper Canada were located in the Eastern and Niagara districts. Two of the longest-settled areas, they had the lowest rates of population growth of any in the province in the 1825–37 period of canal construction.[41] Some of the fastest-growing areas were in the west, where fewer public works expenditures were made. Because works were political, they tended to be allocated more in accord with existing than with future patterns of settlement and power. Of course, the return on investments in the two main canals was not intended to be felt exclusively or even primarily in the areas where they were situated, and the predictability of transportation improvements must have helped to draw settlers west, by holding out the possibility of profitable exporting from and more economical importing to remoter areas.

After the short-term local economic stimulus while actual construction was in process, many public works had only limited long-term local developmental consequences, despite the intensity with which politicians pursued them. Indeed, areas lost as well as gained from the new developments; teamsters were still required for towing sailing vessels, but canals eliminated some of the work that had hitherto existed in transshipment in the Niagara peninsula and in running or bypassing the St Lawrence rapids. Nevertheless, even if the total scale of a district's economy did not expand more than otherwise would have happened, many in the locality, including ordinary workers, farmers, and artisans as well as merchants and contractors, might use income from the projects to make long-term increments to their wealth.

Putting the issues in these terms may use the wrong standards. Contemporaries evidently saw government investment in canals, roads, and harbours as important to local development, although it is less clear what price, in tolls and taxation, they were prepared to pay for the predicted benefits. Upper Canada had existed, however, for forty years or more before the first canals were opened, and in a variety of ways it grew as quickly before as during and shortly after their construction. Even if such credit-based public works investments were not an absolute precondition for growth, they were representative of larger investment processes, in which credit was used to make investments that, it was argued, would yield sufficient returns to carry the costs of them. It was assumed that public investments gave the entire economy a sufficient boost to cover the costs.

It is difficult to make a case for differentially favourable impacts on the regions where actual canal construction went forward. On the other hand, it is often contended that the state was especially vital in the emergence of Toronto as the province's principal urban centre.[42] In some respects this is self-evident, for York was founded to be a capital. Other than the costs of public works and the public debt, half to two-thirds of the provincial government's expenditures were probably made in York/ Toronto, the proportion declining in the 1830s as expenditures on the clergy, schools, and the penitentiary increased. Such outlay by the government had a part to play in creating a local market in the Home District before the 'natural' flow of settlement was likely to have brought this about and in giving greater diversity to local demand than an agricultural community alone had.

For the British government, too, York was a centre of expenditure on garrisons and administration. But the British government's greatest expenditures were military, and Kingston, the leading garrison centre, benefited also as southern terminus of the Rideau Canal. Nevertheless, Toronto grew more rapidly from the late 1820s onward and soon passed Kingston in population. Niagara, long a principal garrison site, lost ground to St Catharines, which benefited from state investment in the Welland Canal. Bytown owed its establishment to construction of the Rideau Canal. Its subsequent growth until it became Canada's capital depended on the Ottawa valley economy, whose expansion, as we have seen, was only in part a function of state policy, represented by the timber duties.

Most pertinent to assessing the ways in which state expenditure and investment shaped urban growth, however, was the emergence of Hamilton and London as two of the province's five leading centres. Each was a centre for district administration, and each benefited from further state expenditures, notably on roads and the Burlington Canal. London also became a garrison site after the Rebellion.[43] But neither was as large a recipient of government funds in the period as the other three principal towns. Yet by the mid-1840s Hamilton was the second-largest urban centre in the province. This suggests that a more fundamental factor in economic localization was the force of long-term income and wealth generation, arising in the years before 1850 from the fertile soil and favourable climate of the area around and to the west of the head of Lake Ontario. If Toronto gained in relation to Hamilton from its status as capital, it is perhaps legitimate to say that in this limited way its rise was caused by state expenditure and policy.

In one version of Canadian mythology, government has been forced to take on economic roles in Canada that the private sector managed elsewhere. But in timing, scale, and thrust, Upper Canada's borrowing and investment, notably in the aid given to the private Welland Canal Company from the mid-1820s onward and in the larger works program of the mid-1830s, look very much like those of adjacent American states. What appear to have been different were the results of those investments, at least if the main Upper Canadian ones are compared to successful American projects like the Erie and the main line of Ohio canals. But such different outcomes derived not so much from the culture or philosophy of state action as from the inherent character of the projects themselves and the wealth they could realistically hope to generate. When all the state projects are considered, moreover, Upper Canada looks to have been a better investor than some states. Upper Canada's most evident difference from the states was in its links to the British government, which spent sums in the province that were large by local standards. The American federal government could not make such expenditures in every state, though it did provide some of the same core services, such as defence. Indeed, the level of such local expenditures may not have been the relevant factor in the story on either side of the border. The parallel trajectories of Upper Canada's and nearby states' population growth (figure 1.1) in fact imply that, whatever the distinctiveness of its leading officials' tory ideology, there was in practice no simply specified and unique role for the Upper Canadian state in the timing and scale of the province's economic development. To argue this is not to argue the counterfactual that Upper Canada would have grown just as much without such state investment and expenditure, nor does it deny the state's importance to the character of the society and the economy on both sides of the border.[44]

# 10 The Chronology of Provincial Development: Trends and Fluctuations, 1821–51

During the thirty years from 1821 to 1851, the predominant trend was sustained extensive growth, but the expansion was marked by substantial fluctuations. Because of the approximate nature of many of the statistical series, it is not appropriate to attempt a full account of such fluctuations, with detailed analysis of leading and lagging elements, precise dating of turning-points, and fine measurement of amplitudes. By reviewing data on population, prices, finance, production, and trade, however, we can see that fluctuations in levels of economic activity in Upper Canada reflected more general processes in the North Atlantic economy. In broad outlines, there were three principal waves in Britain and the United States in the period, with peaks in economic activity in 1825, 1836, and 1845–7, major commercial crises in 1837 and 1847, and deepest troughs in 1819, 1842, and 1848.[1] These dates serve as reference points for Upper Canada, though not all series conformed exactly to them. The dates also suggest that cyclical factors contributed to two of the period's principal political crises, the 1837 rebellions and the events of the late 1840s that to Donald Creighton marked the 'final collapse' of the 'empire of the St. Lawrence' (which G.N. Tucker, more neutrally, called 'the Canadian commercial revolution').[2]

I. *Immigration*

Immigration to and emigration from Upper Canada cannot be known precisely, because movements across Upper Canada's borders were undocumented. Fortunately, data on emigration from Britain to British North America and on immigrant arrivals at Quebec indicate changing levels of migration to Upper Canada. The century-long transformation of the British economy that we sum up as industrialization gave many farmers, skilled and unskilled workers, and members of the middle class continuing impetus to move, but there were variations in their movement. The great wave of British emigration that transformed British North America after 1815 had four main peaks: in 1819, 1831-2, 1841-2, and 1847. These peaks can be seen as part of three distinct waves of emigration: one that followed the war and ended by the mid-1820s; a second that began after 1829 and ended in 1837; and a third, peaking in 1847, that actually extended from about 1840 to 1854. Or we can see the process as a single long wave, punctuated by relative lows in 1824-5 and 1838-9.

The last peak, with its tragic association with the great Irish famine, was the highest, and remains the most familiar. Measured in terms of the existing population in Upper Canada, however, it was lower than the 1819 and 1831-2 peaks.[3] Between 1848 and 1854, emigrant numbers to British North America fluctuated at levels attained frequently in the 1830s and 1840s, between 30,000 and 40,000 per year, whereas vastly larger numbers were now leaving Britain for the United States.[4] A decline began in 1855; the 7,000 emigrants who left for British North America in 1859 were the lowest numbers since 1816, except for the 5,000 in 1838. After 1860 Upper Canada, like the rest of eastern British North America, experienced net emigration for the remainder of the century.

Figure 4.1 charts these movements against volumes of timber imports from the colonies to Britain. It was argued in chapter 4 that there was no direct, simple relationship between timber volumes and population movements, such as would have been the case if the chief variable in emigration was the availability of cheap passage on timber vessels returning to British North America. It was suggested in chapter 5 that emigrant movements might have been a lagged response to the fortunes of the provincial wheat economy. Thus the decline in emigration after 1819 can be associated with the continuing downward slide in wheat prices, and the 1831-2 peak in emigration followed the peak in prices in 1829 and in earnings from wheat exports in 1830-1. After 1832, however, such a direct relationship between colonial wheat prices and British emigration seems less likely.

Emigration was a complex decision involving money, connections, information, skills, family and kin networks, and anticipation of short- and long-term economic change on both sides of the Atlantic. In fact, most people of all affected classes in the United Kingdom did not emigrate, nor did all who crossed the Atlantic remain there; moreover, fluctuations in emigrant numbers and variation in their destinations show that emigrants were making choices.[5] With the significant exception of 1847, the essential British emigrant was not a refugee, forced at the worst moments of the British trade cycle to flee enclosure, industrialization, and hunger. Emigration was an investment process, driven primarily by longer-term thinking, though influenced by short-term considerations. On the other hand, variations in the rate of migration do not appear all that clearly in province-wide rates of increase in population and land under culture, which were much steadier. Had all those who arrived at Quebec settled in Upper Canada, the province's population would have grown substantially faster than it did.[6]

## II. *Commodity Prices in Upper Canada*

Prices for eight widely produced and marketed commodities in Upper Canada are provided in Appendix C, which also discusses the complexities and limitations of the series. The data offer evidence that farmers could make decisions on crops, marketing, and other matters with at least some expectation of the prices they might receive. The data can be analysed in a variety of ways. Here the emphasis is on the extent and character of price movements in Upper Canada and on the most clearly indicated trends and turning-points. Until 1845 most series are presented for both the eastern area of the province, around Kingston, and the centre, around the western end of Lake Ontario. One series (wheat) is presented for the west, above the Niagara Escarpment, and one (peas) is presented specifically for Prince Edward County (see table C.1). For the central area from 1838, prices are from Toronto newspapers, and those series are extended to 1870 in table C.2.

British wheat prices fell from their all-time postwar peak in 1817 to less than half that level by 1822. Subsequent peaks in British wheat prices were recorded in 1825, 1839, and 1847, while troughs, each lower than the previous one, occurred in 1835 and 1851. After the mid-century, peaks occurred in 1854–5 and 1867, but at least from the 1840s, the long-term trend was clearly downward. For a product exported down the St Lawrence, prices in Upper Canada could be expected to diminish with increasing remoteness from Montreal. Although that pattern was at times evident between 1800 and 1812, only from the 1820s were wheat prices in the west consistently lower than those in the centre and east. After the postwar decline reached its low in 1821–3, wheat prices in the province remained generally low until 1829, then rose sharply (see figure 2.1). Subsequent peaks were in 1837, 1855, and 1867; the principal troughs were in 1834, 1843, 1851–2, and 1863. During the 1840s, when the British market was at last reliably open to colonial wheat, prices fluctuated within a quite narrow range, above what had been ordinary levels in the 1820s but well below the peaks of 1829–30 and 1836–9.[7] Between 1853 and 1870 even lows in the province were at or above the highest prices in the 1840s. After the 1820s, therefore, the overall trend was rising.

Were there equivalent patterns in prices of agricultural commodities such as hay, peas, oats, and beef that were not exported to Britain, and not, in consistently large quantities, even to Lower Canada and the United States? Upper Canadian and selected external prices are related to each other in tables C.3 and C.4 by setting 1831 prices as 100 and showing the prices for selected periods relative to that level. That base year was chosen because prices were available for most Upper Canadian produce items in 1831, and it falls roughly at the mid-point of our period. In fact, wheat prices in 1831 were also quite near the mid-point of their long-term range. For some commodities (for example, hay and butter), Upper Canadian prices in 1831 were near all-time lows. Others, such as beef and pork, were relatively high by the standards of the postwar period. As the variation suggests, prices did not all move simultaneously and equally.[8]

At the most extreme points of fluctuation, however, there is considerable consistency among the Upper Canadian series and between them and those from elsewhere in the province's economic universe (table C.4). All the series in tables C.3 and C.4 were at peaks in the war years, particularly 1813–16. If not in 1822–3, then somewhere in the 1820s, all the price series for Upper Canada reached their lowest points in the period. For several indexes from the eastern United States, that low actually came in 1829–31.[9] The next clear peak was in 1837–8, which were years of high prices everywhere. Thus, wheat in Upper Canada was at 128 and oats at 136; in Lower Canada, wheat was at 125 and oats at 130; butter in the former was at 132 and in the latter at 109. Five agriculturally based American indexes were all between 136 and 141, and the Rousseau agricultural price index in Britain was at 104. In every case, these were the highest levels between the immediate postwar years and the mid-1850s. Only British wheat (91) and oats (90), which did not peak until 1839, were exceptional. Another trough followed, often in 1842–3, sometimes slightly sooner. Between these points, more variation can be seen among the Upper Canadian series, and between them and some American indexes.

All five American agricultural indexes in 1834–5 were higher than in 1829–31, whereas a number of Canadian series for which we have 1834–5 data were lower. On the other hand, the 'east' series for potatoes, peas, hay, and pork (fourth quarter) in Upper Canada all show 1834–5 as higher than 1829–31. There is a similar apparent contrast in 1849–51, when four of the five American agricultural series are above 100, and most of the Toronto series were lower, though potatoes, hay, and butter all exceeded 100. If a more comprehensive Upper Canadian data set were constructed, then combined into an appropriately weighted overall index, it is quite possible that the lows in wheat and some other series in the mid-1830s and late 1840s would be offset. In any case, the simultaneous peaks in 1837–8 and 1854–6 show that, however local the markets for some of their produce, the prices received by Upper Canadian farmers were set in a wider economic universe and not directly and exclusively determined by local supply and demand.

Comparable indexes of Canadian forest product prices for 1825–49 are given in table 10.1. Though there are some limitations in the data, the 1837–8 peak appears in most series, except deals;[10] prices for oak, elm, and potash were above levels of 1834–5, but their 1837–8 peaks were at about the same level as in 1831. All prices, except deals, were lower in 1842–3 than in 1837–8. Most prices, other than potash, then rebounded to peaks in 1844–6; the indexes for red pine, elm, and deals all were at their highest point, and white pine was almost as high. Prices then fell, but even in 1849 only deals were at a lower point than in 1842–3.

## III. Financial Data

Not until the 1830s was provincial banking sufficiently established to yield reliable evidence on fluctuations. There was a strong upward trend in the supply of currency and coin into early 1837 (table 8.2), which was abruptly and swiftly reversed in the spring. In 1838–9 an even sharper upswing, the result of the suspension of specie payments and of the massive British military expenditures in the province, took note issues to new heights. By 1841, however, the note circulation of Upper Canadian banks had returned to the level attained shortly before the crisis of 1837.

During the 1840s the Union introduced more direct competition with the Upper Canadian banks. In considering fluctuations, therefore, it is preferable to use note circulation data for both Upper and Lower Canada.[11] These data, which are available on a monthly basis for most of the 1840s, show a decline in the early 1840s to a low in January 1843, when the banks' combined circulation of £623,000 was fully one-third lower than in the same month a year earlier. A rapid resurgence followed, to peaks in February 1846 and March 1847, when notes issued reached £1,681,000. On an annual basis (table 10.2), 1843 was the trough, while 1846 and 1847 were peak years. Circulation fell after October 1847 to a trough in 1849 that was almost one-third lower than the levels of 1847. Even so, the low point in 1849 was still higher than any year before 1844. By 1851, as circulation revived rapidly, total notes issued exceeded any previous year.

A similar pattern is evident when considering only the Upper Canadian banks, except that it was not until 1847 that their circulation regained the level of 1841; from 1850 onward, new and higher levels were reached. Similar patterns mark the data on loans, discounts, and deposits of the Upper Canadian banks (tables 8.2, 8.3), troughs coming in 1842 or 1843, new peaks in 1846 or 1847, then troughs again in 1848 or 1849. In all cases, the strong, essentially cyclical, swing dwarfed monthly and seasonal fluctuations.

Such patterns also appeared in foreign exchange rates. There are considerable complexities in discounting for shifts in interest rates, prices of gold and silver, and other variables, but the movement of quoted rates, at least if for bills of equal quality, indicates the pattern of fluctuations in the exchange market. Such rates would have been the most evident feature of the exchange market to participants in the economy. There is sufficient similarity in Canadian and American data series to remind us that the Canadian exchange market was part of an American market that was becoming quite integrated in the 1820s.[12] Thus, the factors determining the market rate of exchange in Canada were to a significant extent not within Canadian control and only at the margin reflected specifically Canadian conditions. Our main interest here is to identify not those marginal dimensions of the exchange rate but the years of greatest volatility and greatest extremes, because these would have been the most disruptive in terms of the ordinary and routine calculations of most economic actors.

The single most marked change in the Canadian rate of exchange on London occurred after the War of 1812 and, as we have seen, was fully established by 1821, when Britain returned to the gold standard (see also Appendix A). That was a shift in the ordinary rate of exchange at Montreal and Quebec from £1.111 Halifax currency equalling £1 stg ($4.444 equals £1, a rate that remained the nominal par in Canada until 1858) to a rate of about £1.22 cy to £1 stg (actually $4.8667 equals £1 stg, the nominal par in Canada after 1858 and in the United States after 1837). There were, however, substantial fluctuations around this rate through the 1820s, 1830s, and 1840s. Thus, the Canadian rate on London first reached £1.22 in December 1821; was at £1.26 by October 1822; and had fallen by June 1823 to £1.17. An essentially similar swing occurred in the United States in 1822–3, with slightly different turningpoints. These limits were exceeded on the low side only in 1834, when a rate of less than £1.15 was reached in late summer, and on the high side only in 1837 (when the rate reached £1.31 in July) and 1848 (when a rate of £1.29 was recorded in February). In the United States 1834 and 1837 were similarly extreme; in 1834 sterling was at its largest discount from par and in 1837 at its highest premium in the postwar era. Rates swung most widely in Canada during 1823, 1831, 1834, 1837, 1847, and 1848; of these, only 1848 does not show up on a list of years of greatest swings in data from American sources. The peaks in 1837 and 1847–8 are further confirmation that in those years Canada's economy was particularly disrupted.

IV. *Production and Trade*

By comparison with what we know of prices, population, and finance, we know little about fluctuations in total production of many commodities or about how production, marketing, and prices combined to generate fluctuations in total incomes. For wheat and some forest products, data on exports may indicate fluctuations in overall outputs. Thus, total volumes of wheat and flour shipped downriver peaked at the equivalent of 225,000 bushels in 1818, fell to 62,000 in 1819, and again exceeded 200,000 bushels in 1822–3 (table 5.2). After 1825 a much higher threshold was reached; in 1827, 606,000 bushels were exported, and even the next trough in 1829, at 230,000 bushels, was higher than pre-1825 peaks. In 1831, 959,000 bushels were shipped downriver, a peak not surpassed for the remainder of the decade, though volumes were almost as high in 1833, 1834, and 1836. The next deep trough occurred in 1837, at 266,000 bushels. Downriver shipments in 1838–9 rebounded to over 600,000 bushels, roughly equivalent to the level first attained in 1827. A much higher threshold was reached in 1840, when total downriver shipments of flour and wheat (American produce included) totalled 2.9 million bushels, almost three times the level of 1839. Shipments increased to 3.4 million in 1841, were slightly lower in 1844, then rose to a peak of 5.8 million bushels in 1847. A decline followed to a trough in 1850, but even at that low, downriver exports from Upper Canada alone were higher than total exports prior to 1845.[13] Thanks to relatively high prices, the per capita incomes generated in the producing region by such exports reached exceptionally high peaks in 1817 and 1831.

Forest products shipments down the St Lawrence fluctuated substantially. The one pattern common to all data was the mid-1840s boom, which took every series for forest products to record highs (table 4.2). Other peaks and troughs were not so closely synchronized. Cycles in building and shipbuilding in Britain appear in Upper Canadian data too,[14] though not all wood products were destined for such capital projects. Potash shipments in the 1830s were more or less level at higher volumes than in the 1820s. Oak timber volumes hit a peak in 1825, then fell to much lower levels before rebounding sharply at the end of the 1830s to a new high in 1839. White pine shipments peaked in 1824, 1830, and 1836, while lowest shipment levels occurred in 1828 and 1834. Deals reached peaks in 1825 and 1835. In contrast to oak, exports of both pine and deals were at very low levels in 1839. Ottawa valley exports showed a clearer upward trend (table 4.5), except for quite modest downward fluctuations in 1838 and 1842–3. In 1845–6, the peak years for exports of Ottawa valley pine, volumes were double what had been shipped just four years earlier. A sharp contraction followed, but the trough in 1848 was still higher than exports before 1844.

Downriver exports are at best an imperfect representation of total production within the provincial economy, because so much of what was produced there was consumed there, and because variations in the level of trade with the United States occasionally changed the normal patterns of trade. Moreover, if peaks in wheat and flour exports were followed by increased immigration, domestic consumption might initially rise faster than production; that would tend to reduce exports, even though production continued to rise. Then, as new land was brought into cultivation, both on new and existing farms, exports might be expected to rise again, especially in the wake of higher prices. Thus, the higher 1827 export threshold can be seen as an outcome of immigration earlier in the 1820s and the peaking of British wheat prices in 1825. The high exports of 1831 followed a peak in British and Canadian prices in 1829 and in turn were associated with a major wave of immigration. Similarly, the new threshold reached in 1840 can be associated with the high immigration earlier in the 1830s, with high prices in Upper Canada for several previous years, and with the peak in British prices in 1839.

Given all that a farm could produce, ranging from wheat through fodder crops, animals and products, to a wide array of forest products, a decline in shipments of one product was not necessarily an indicator of difficulties in actual production representing a potential crisis for producers. Such fluctuations were the net outcome of the actions of thousands of farmers as they changed their allocations of time and resources. Per capita figures are, of course, complicated by the continuing addition of new producers at the beginning point in the process of farm and household establishment. It seems best to assume a generally steady upward trend in total farm output. If this assumption is reasonable, then the fluctuations that most affected ordinary producers were driven not so much by direct variations in growing conditions and demand for actual produce as by the financial, institutional, and psychological factors that determined how much credit was available, to whom, and at what cost. The implications of this argument can be pursued by analysing the two principal economic crises of the period, 1837 and 1847–9.

## V. The Crisis of 1837

As 1837 began, prices for farm products in Upper Canada were at their highest since the immediate postwar period;[15] at Dundas, the price of a bushel of wheat was 7s 6d ($1.50) for the first half of the year, and at Yonge Mills, in the east, over 9s was paid for a time in the spring. The financial panic in the spring, a surge in the cost of sterling exchange to the highest level ever (£1.308 = £1 stg, in July), and an extraordinary contraction of 55 per cent in the provincial banks' note circulation between April and September (table 8.5) all show the severe disturbance of the financial system. At the same time, the province's financial agent in London failed. In November rebellion broke out in Lower Canada, and rebellions followed in Upper Canada at the beginning of December, led by William Lyon Mackenzie in York County and at Toronto, and by Dr Charles Duncombe in the west, between Brantford and London.

The rebellions were obviously associated with the economic disruption. In Lower Canada, though the argument is increasingly contested, Fernand Ouellet has depicted 1837 as the culmination of a profound crisis in the provincial economic order that had been in the making since early in the century.[16] At its most fundamental level, the Upper Canadian rebellion has also been seen as an economic crisis.[17] In his classic article on the subject, Donald Creighton accurately depicted the immediate context in Upper Canada as 'a winter [1836–7] of high prices and real scarcity ... followed by an abrupt financial panic and a commercial slump.'[18] To him, 1837 was a climax in Upper Canada as much as in Lower Canada: both rebellions were 'the final expression of the conflict between agrarianism and commercialism.' Moved by 'simple animosities,' the Upper Canadian rebels represented 'the tragic inexpertness of a farming population' caught up in the transition of an economy built on fur and timber to one based on wheat and flour.

Few since Creighton have been as critical of the farmers, but many subsequent accounts reflect elements of his argument. To H. Clare Pentland, for example, the rebellion arose as farmers in what he depicted as the hitherto isolated economy in Upper Canada west of the Ottawa valley resisted integration into the larger world of staple production. But he saw local supply outrunning local demand, with a consequent 'sharp lowering of the price structure.'[19] Others also speak of a 'collapse' of the local economy, which was marked, from 1836, by 'falling agricultural prices.' Gerald Craig's standard work describes 1836 as a year when farmers faced 'low prices and lack of good markets,' then, rather confusingly, says it was only at the end of 1836 that 'the bottom suddenly fell out of the boom,' for farmers as for others in the society.[20]

The province's financial situation in 1837 has been depicted as one of near bankruptcy, and its difficulty in sustaining the works featured prominently in Creighton's discussion of 1837.[21] But actual expenditures in 1837 were much higher than in preceding years, and, if anything, must have had a counter-cyclical effect (see table 9.5A).[22] If public works problems were a major factor, moreover, rebelliousness might have been more evident near the major projects, notably along the St Lawrence. But though there were rumblings in the Welland Canal area, these areas were not focal points for the rebellion.

In fact, the Upper Canadian rebellions were focused north of Toronto and west of Hamilton in areas that had been actively engaged in commercial agriculture for twenty years or longer. Participants in the western rising included long-established farmers and their sons, skilled tradesmen, innkeepers, millers, doctors, some local commercial figures, and labourers.[23] In occupation and in such other economic indicators as land ownership, the rebels in the west were a representative cross-section of rural Upper Canada. These were not the new and the marginal in this frontier society, nor was the rebellion based in the newest frontier areas. The story was much the same along Yonge Street.[24] It is unlikely that actual hunger was a motivating force for the rebels whose names are known, nor were they simple peasants or ignorant farmers. Those who rebelled had much besides their lives to risk, and we should assume that they had a conception of their own interests, economic and otherwise.[25]

Such farmers have been seen as having 'difficulty in expanding' and 'finding land for their sons,' and with being in debt to various interests against whom the rebellion was thus directed.[26] The farmers' anger has even been related to their indebtedness to the banks, and to their hostility to a government which favoured the banks over them. But the chartered banks were barred from lending directly on mortgages and seldom lent directly to farmers. Moreover, in 1837 the government, in rejecting the banks' desire to suspend specie payments, did precisely what William Lyon Mackenzie, on this point an unlikely ally of Sir Francis Bond Head, demanded. If, as Creighton claimed, farmers and artisans were 'frantic to exchange their bank notes for coin,'[27] they could have obtained specie from all three Upper Canadian chartered banks until September, and from the two with headquarters closest to the areas of actual rebellion until the spring of 1838. Parents then as always must have worried about their children's futures, but it is impossible to picture real land shortage, however we define that concept, in an Upper Canada which had a thriving land market and enormous areas of undeveloped land.[28] Nor does the land scarcity argument explain why it was only in some long-settled areas that such motivation prompted reform politics and even outright rebellion.

Thus, there has been much debate about the nature of the rural crisis in 1837, and of its relationship to the financial crisis. Clearly, high rather than low prices were a vital element of the 1836–7 conjuncture. But high prices pose their own interpretive problems. There would be a direct and immediate connection if the rebellion and its discontents were especially associated with the province's small urban centres and the wage-earning population in particular. But the rural locus of active rebellion did not fundamentally misrepresent the nature of the events. And it is not usual to associate farm discontent with high prices for farm produce.[29]

Farmers, high prices, and discontent have been linked by arguing that Upper Canada, like Lower Canada and many adjacent American areas though to a lesser degree, suffered a crop failure in 1836 and perhaps 1837.[30] Presumably this left farmers short of accustomed crops or even compelled to buy at high prices what they would usually have grown for themselves. But sharply rising prices outside Upper Canada, unusual demand for wheat from the United States, and the rapid increase of the local money supply all make it unwise to attribute the level of prices in 1836–7 to physical shortages experienced by Upper Canadian farmers. And wherever farmers had something to sell, high prices could compensate, in whole or in part, for any shortage in output, as Robert Wade, a farmer near Port Hope, explained in his highly positive account of 1836, sent to his brother in England early in 1837.

Crops rather below the average but prices very good ... our wheat has gone principally to the States, their crops having in great measure failed ...
... Times have been much better for farmers than they have ever been since we came here.[31]

Although threshing and travel to market were mainly winter work, farmers could have accelerated threshing and marketing of wheat in the fall of 1836 in response to higher prices and the presence of American buyers in Upper Canada. Cross-lake exports also complicate the story apparently told by the sharp fall in downriver exports in 1837.[32] And any farmers who still had stocks in the summer of 1837 would have had considerable incentive to market them as prices started downward. In short, the widely reported mid-summer shortages in 1837 could well have been the result of earlier high prices instead of, or as well as, the short

crops that a term like 'harvest failure' implies. The partial recovery in
flour exports down the St Lawrence in 1838 suggests that the 1837
harvest was a greater success and/or that American demand had fallen
off. Similarly, 1838 exports from the west down the Welland Canal
included six times as much wheat as in 1837, of which at least half,
shipped before the 1838 harvest, must have derived from the 1837
crop.[33] If a sense of crisis in the west was harvest-induced, it should
have begun to abate by late summer of 1837, months before the rebellions actually broke out.[34] Even limited exports suggest that the province had some surplus wheat even in years that are often described as
ones of short crops.

Nor was the forest products sector, from which many in rural Upper
Canada earned income, vulnerable to crop failures. Operators at a commercial scale complained rather that in 1837 high wages and high prices
for their produce inputs undercut profitability;[35] in terms of volumes and
values of exports, as we have seen, the industry did not lag very notice-
ably in 1837 or 1838. Exports of wood products came largely from the
region east of Toronto, however.

Data on harvests and sales by two farmers in this period offer a
further perspective (table 10.3). Output from the two Parsons farms at
Thornhill (in the heart of the area of the Mackenzie rebellion) was
surely among the largest in the province, but even a large farm using
much hired labour would not have been immune to a general crop
failure caused by disease or bad weather. Parsons's 1836 output was
prodigious, and almost the entire decline in the farms' total revenue
shown for 1837 and 1838 is attributable to falling wheat production. As
we have seen, the Dunnville farm (not far from the area of the western
rising) conforms more closely in output to ordinary Upper Canadian
farms in the era. There, 60 bushels were sold from the farm's first crop,
harvested in 1835. Unlike Parsons, who harvested a bumper crop in
1836, the Dunnville farm had a marked drop in the net 1836 harvest
(after allowance for family food and for seed) from preceding, or subsequent, years. Equally, its records show how a farm could compensate
for problems with one crop, for farm income rose slightly from 1835–6
to 1836–7 despite the drop in wheat sales. Such evidence, while anecdotal, draws us away from an abstraction, 'the harvest,' into the specific
and complex world of actual rural production and exchange. In that
world, farmers' expectations surely included the possibility of short-
term fluctuations in harvests and prices. Even apart from the higher
prices that must have helped in 1837, farmers were protected against
economic disaster in the event of a single bad year because most produced more than just wheat and because they could usually buy inputs

on credit. Not all products had identical problems of weather, disease, and markets, and it was rare for crops to fail so absolutely that farmers could not even feed themselves.

Thus, nothing suggests an accumulating longer-term crisis in production. At most, the circumstances of 1836–7 constituted a bad year, not a total failure, in production of some crops. Lower output might have reduced employment in harvesting and transporting wheat, though in an economy in which so large a proportion of the workforce was in part or wholly self-employed, it is far from clear how to assess this dimension of the situation. Because there are indications that revival was under way by late summer 1837, there is further reason to question how deep, and how troubling, were any 1836 harvest difficulties. Nor was a one-year setback without precedent; from 1828 to 1829 and 1834 to 1835 the volume and value of provincial wheat exports dropped sharply, only to be followed by quick recovery in the next year. On the basis of such evidence as we have on physical output, therefore, it seems preferable to speak of recession rather than depression in Upper Canada in 1837.

It is in its financial dimensions that 1837 differed most dramatically from previous years.[36] There would have been a financial crisis of some kind in Upper Canada, whatever was done locally, given the panic that struck Britain and the United States in the spring of 1837. It is possible that the necessity to redeem notes for specie, something American and Lower Canadian banks did not have to do, intensified the contraction in Upper Canada. But local banks were not the only component of the provincial credit structure, and merchants were under equally heavy pressure for payments from their commercial backers in Montreal, New York, Glasgow, Liverpool, or London. As we have seen, ordinary Upper Canadians were linked to the credit system through local merchants and through the credit they routinely extended to one another in daily dealings and in capital transactions such as land sales and construction. In the 1830s many Upper Canadians, including farmers and artisans, had been building up permanent assets, but their wealth was in illiquid forms, notably land, buildings, and accounts receivable (from others whose wealth was likewise illiquid). When everyone simultaneously sought payment, few could meet obligations without their normal recourse to further credit, whether to cover new transactions or debts they could not pay immediately. There can have been few debtors, of any class, who did not feel the pinch, and few creditors (a group which overlapped substantially the previous group) who can have felt sure of receiving sums due them.

Financial pressures undoubtedly fostered tension between classes and among interests. But the stringency was not a deliberate device by one class to impose its will on another. Many debtor-creditor relationships were intra- rather than inter-class in character, and those most vulnerable to a stoppage of credit included many businessmen and land speculators. Among them were some of the rebellion's strongest opponents, such as that leading Tory and active speculator, Allan MacNab. Indeed, the interest of the commercial class was not to see credit cut off. It would also be reasonable to see the farmers who were caught not as the simple and misguided souls that Creighton described, but as entrepreneurs in their own right, undertaking risks in pursuit of gains. Though much of the basis for the rapid return of liquidity in 1838 was British military expenditure in Upper Canada, the quick revival and the post-1839 growth of the economy offer further strong evidence that what happened in 1837 in Upper Canada was a liquidity crisis more than a sign of deep structural flaws in the provincial economy.

None of the economic characteristics appears to have applied so specifically to a region or class that we can readily associate them particularly or exclusively with the areas or groups that actually rebelled. The state of the forest economy and the counter-cyclical effect of canal construction may suggest that eastern areas felt a recession in production less than those farther west. But even in the west there were substantial divergences of view on the rebellions among people and entire rural communities that, so far as we can currently see, faced similar economic circumstances. If there were stronger and more precise links between economic events in 1837 and the specific groups that rebelled, however, they are most likely to be found in exploring how those similar circumstances actually affected what were, in part, different local sub-economies.[37]

Looking so closely at 1837 may obscure the larger socio-economic causes of the rebellion, which it has been argued were to be found in a particular structure of classes and a particular kind of economic organization. But those who have argued such a case have not demonstrated the economics underlying why only a few areas and some groups from the much larger population of artisans, farmers, labourers, and others who were not part of the governing élite felt it necessary to go as far as outright rebellion. Those who have looked most closely at the evidence have shown, rather, that in economic terms the rebels were representative in many ways of rural Upper Canada as a whole. It is when one considers politics, religion, years in the country, and ethnic origin that it is possible more precisely to differentiate rebels and, to a degree, their sympathizers, from those who were actively loyal.[38]

There was still room for economic variables to contribute to the 1837 situation, above all by creating a general climate of insecurity, arising from the credit crunch, and the severe disruption of established patterns of growth and exchange that climaxed in the summer of 1837. Moreover, the crisis and Head's stubborn refusal to understand the local economy stirred members of the provincial establishment to criticism, which Mackenzie relayed to the people north of Toronto as evidence that the lieutenant-governor lacked authority and was opposed even by some of those who seemed most loyal.[39] In addition, if the Lower Canadian rebellion was caused by economic factors, then that represents economic causation for the Upper Canadian rebellion too, for the former directly sparked the latter.

The economic setback of 1837 was thus a substantial fluctuation more than a turning-point in larger growth trends in the Upper Canadian economy. To argue this is not to downplay the significance of the 1837 rebellion or the seriousness of purpose of those who rebelled. Rather, it is to argue for the autonomy of politics from reductionist views on the role played by economics, such as many interpretations assert or imply. In what seem to have been similar economic circumstances, rural Upper Canadians could, and often did in 1837, arrive at very different conclusions about where their economic and their overall interests lay. In deciding to rebel, one's own identity, and that of one's neighbours, mattered most, and economics provided only one dimension of identity.

VI. *The Crisis of 1846–9*

The Upper Canadian economy quickly resumed its expansion in 1838, and many statistical indicators reached new heights in 1840–1. Throughout the western economy 1842–3 was a deep trough, but it was followed by an intense round of expansion. In Britain a massive boom in railways and construction drew in record volumes and values of Canadian forest products. The increasingly speculative railway promotion boom climaxed in the fall of 1845, although construction resulting from the new promotions continued strongly into 1847 and even longer. At the same time, the failure of the Irish potato crop in 1845 produced deepening and disastrous famine in the early months of 1846. When the potato crop again failed in 1846, it had paradoxical impacts in grain-growing areas overseas. Wheat prices rose quickly, and large amounts of bullion were sent to the United States to buy grain. World supplies proved surprisingly elastic; the result was a massive increase in British grain imports, a sharp drop in the price of wheat, and in August 1847, a commercial crisis in Britain. Numerous business failures and growing panic followed, easing only in October, when permission was granted to suspend some provisions of the 1844 Bank Act.[40]

Annual price data do not capture the full extent of the volatility of commodity prices during 1846–8. Wheat prices in Britain doubled between August 1846 and June 1847, as did prices in Toronto; there wheat was around 3s a bushel in late summer 1846, but reached 6s for some weeks in June and July 1847. By September it had fallen to around 4s. The price of potatoes in Toronto rose rapidly in the summer of 1846 to 4s a bushel, a level seldom if ever seen since the War of 1812. The price then fell to as low as 2s in October, before rebounding to over 4s in the spring of 1847. After declining later in the summer, it again surged to as high as 5s a bushel in spring and early summer of 1848. Not until the fall of 1849 did potatoes return to traditional levels of 2s a bushel or less. On the other hand, except for potatoes, prices were never as high as in 1837. A similar chronology, though with price movements that were not quite as extreme, characterized Montreal prices; there, wheat, oats, and pork in July 1847 were at least half again as high as in the preceding August.[41]

As in 1837, the credit squeeze in Britain had an immediate impact on Canadian merchants and banks. Surprisingly, no banks had to suspend payments. Both the Gore Bank and the City Bank of Montreal subsequently wrote off capital, however, and profits vanished for most of the other banks, including the Bank of Upper Canada and the Bank of Montreal.[42] Two major British merchant houses trading in Toronto, Ross, Mitchell and Company, and Thorne, Parsons and Company, failed; and many other commercial houses experienced severe liquidity problems during 1847.[43] Governments were likewise pressed, and in 1848 and 1849 the Province of Canada had to have recourse to issuing low-denomination, short-term promissory notes to pay its bills.[44] Writing in April 1849, Lord Elgin, the governor general, offered a dark view of the state of the Canadian economy: 'The downward progress of events! these are ominous words! but look at the facts. Property in most of the Canadian towns has fallen 50 p ct in value within the last three Years ... Three fourths of the commercial men are bankrupt.'[45]

The crisis and depression were part of what has generally been understood as a watershed in Canadian economic and political history. Between 1846 and 1849, the repeal of the Corn Laws, the beginning of the phasing out of the protective timber duties, the repeal of the Navigation Acts, and Britain's acceptance of the principle of colonial responsible government marked the formal end of Britain's mercantile system and an acceptance of devolution of power to the colonies. At the same time the St Lawrence system, whose enlarged canals were only now completed, seemed threatened by American adoption of bonding legislation designed to foster Canadian through trade via American channels. Virtually overwhelming the province's rudimentary relief system, as many as 100,000 immigrants arrived at Quebec in 1847. Thousands died at Grosse Ile and thousands more in ports along the St Lawrence system, and death also claimed many citizens who came to the aid of the immigrants. On the other hand, though it was hardly clear at the time, the net increase in Upper Canadian population between the censuses of 1848 and 1851–2 suggests that many of the new arrivals survived and found niches in the economy.[46]

Credit stringency and other cyclical pressures combined with the changing political environment to produce a profound sense of crisis among leading Canadian businessmen, especially in Montreal. The introduction and passage of the Rebellion Losses Bill in 1849 fully confirmed the establishment of responsible government, but to tories it was an outrageous measure to compensate rebels. Their anger produced a major riot in Toronto on 21–22 March (and smaller ones later in the year).[47] On 25 April 1849, when Elgin signed the bill into law, a Montreal crowd burned the provincial parliament buildings and city streets were in an uproar for a week. Bytown's turn came on 17–19 September, when the 'Stony Monday' riots pitted warring political factions against each other. Many merchants and tory politicians, long in the forefront of colonial protestations of loyalty to Britain, were among the hundreds of signers of the Annexation Manifesto, published in October 1849, which called for speedy integration of the Canadas into the United States.

The riots of 1849 were urban in focus, unlike the rebellions in 1837. This time it was tories who fostered the violence, both by actual incitement and by the deliberate failure of authorities to respond when crowds gathered. The unrest actually occurred long after most prices had peaked and the worst of the immigrant crisis had eased. That working-class supporters of the tories were prepared to march and to fight suggests that the dislocations of illiquidity and unemployment lingered in the towns and cities, but also that, as in 1837, non-economic factors were vital determinants of which side a worker took.

In hindsight, it has become clearer that Elgin's Montreal-centred perspective exaggerated the incidence of business disaster. Nor did the period constitute the collapse of the 'empire of the St Lawrence.' What died in 1847–9 was a specific and particular view that had never been attainable; nor had it been the key to prosperity in the Canadas.[48] The trend to free trade in the 1840s did not destroy Canadian trade with Britain. Even timber exports to Britain reached new heights as early as 1852. Knowledge that the British wheat market was now consistently and reliably open to colonial grain was in fact a major gain to all overseas producers. Bonding legislation was not harmful to Upper Canadians, and indeed was not relevant to Canadian exports to the United States for consumption there; the latter resulted from the continuing development of the northeastern American economy, which now began to draw in more produce from remoter areas, both the old northwest and Canada. This was significant to American interest in freeing trade with the British North American colonies in primary products and underlay the Reciprocity Agreement of 1854. But it added new markets for Upper Canada's exports, rather than requiring any abandonment of the British market. As for the Canadian capital market and public finance, public policy continued to seek British immigrants and British capital to develop the Canadian economy, by fostering continuing frontier expansion and staple exports.[49] None of the troughs in statistics in Upper Canada in 1848–9 were below the levels of 1844. To Upper Canadians at least, in economic terms the late 1840s were another cyclical low. By 1850 the crisis had passed, and growth, by now in the form of both urbanization and extensive frontier development, was once more under way.

*Part Three:*
*The Province at Mid-Century*

# 11 Railways and Provincial Development, 1850–70

## I. Upper Canada Enters the Railway Age

Although Upper Canadians quickly adopted steam technology for ships and some industrial uses, building railways was a more complex matter. Like canals, railways entailed substantial indivisible capital investments and could not be built on as incremental a basis as the stock of roads, wagons, and ships. In the mid-1830s Upper Canada's two most likely candidates as centres of railway promotion were Toronto and Hamilton. For there to be any chance at all of quick provincial action on railways, they would have had to cooperate. But they were small and well-connected by steamers for much of the year, and their local élites were pursuing rival hinterland development visions. And there were more attractive uses for the limited resources commanded by local entrepreneurs than direct investment in social overhead capital.

Thus, major investments in railways depended on public funding or on outside investors and, in either case, on the trade cycle. Only in its expansionary, investment phase could promising new projects, even in established markets, secure funding. The timing of a quest for funds in Britain for unbuilt, unknown projects on the other side of the Atlantic was a more delicate matter still, as the history of American railway promotion in the period also made clear.[1] Once in existence, companies could sustain investment through retained earnings, the reputation given by current earnings, and established connections with suppliers, investors, politicians, and financiers.

The short Champlain and St Lawrence was built in Lower Canada in

Much of this chapter was first published as 'Railways and the Development of Canada West, 1850–1870,' in Allan Greer and Ian Radforth, eds., *Colonial Leviathan: State Formation in Mid-Nineteenth-Century Canada* (Toronto 1992). I am grateful to the University of Toronto Press for permission to reprint such material here.

the 1830s. In Upper Canada, a number of companies were chartered then, including the London and Gore (1834), to link London and Hamilton; the City of Toronto and Lake Huron (1836); and the Erie and Ontario (1835), to join the two lakes.[2] Meeting early in 1837, the provincial Assembly passed dozens of public works bills that would collectively have added enormously to the provincial debt, to support a wide range of canals, roads, bridges, and harbours.[3] Quite small sums were provided for the Erie and Ontario and the Cobourg railroads, while up to £200,000 was voted to aid the London and Gore (now renamed the Great Western) and up to £100,000 for the City of Toronto and Lake Huron. Such sums had hitherto been expended only on the province's two main canals. But a company first had to raise capital from shareholders; only then would the province issue, to the company or directly on the market, debentures to three times the sums raised privately. Of course, all prospects of obtaining funds from either public or private sources quickly vanished in the 1837 crash.

In the extended depression of 1839–43, virtually no North American railway securities could be sold in Britain. Then the English railway boom reawakened interest in more distant projects. In 1845 the Great Western charter was revived, and the St Lawrence and Atlantic was chartered as part of a project to link Portland, Maine, and Montreal, via Sherbrooke. Each sent representatives to London, where they succeeded in obtaining subscriptions.[4] Unfortunately, far more shares were subscribed for in Britain than could ever have been paid for, the stock boom collapsed, and the Canadians were unable to collect the funds that had been pledged. The Great Western was left essentially unbegun, though still alive in organizational terms. At the end of the 1840s about sixty miles of track were in operation in the Canadas, none in Upper Canada.

By comparison with the United States, where 9,000 miles of track were then in operation, Canada had lagged in the development of railways. This lag owed something to the preoccupation of Canadian politicians with completing the St Lawrence canal system in the 1840s. But there were non-official circles in Canada, and urban centres such as Sherbrooke and Hamilton, from which the principal promotions of the 1840s emerged, that were not obliged to wait for canals before promoting railways. Even in Montreal, the focal point of the navigation system, there were strong reasons to proceed at once with railways that seemed to complement canal development.[5] The will to adopt the new technology was present in Canada, but not the ability to finance the projects. That inability resulted from the nature of the technology, the availability of more attractive investments on the London market, American states' insolvency and repudiation between 1839 and 1843, and the collapse of the speculative English railway boom.

In assessing the early Canadian railway record, it is pertinent that, though most American states had begun to explore railways, a number continued in the 1840s to develop canals as well. The extent of the Canadian lag looks somewhat different too when Upper Canada is seen not as an eastern but as a western region, analogous to Ohio, Michigan, and Indiana more than to New York and Massachusetts. Only in 1851, when the Erie Railroad reached Lake Erie, were the Great Lakes and a major eastern port joined under one company. By then, the three nearby western states had the beginnings of railway systems, totalling almost 1,000 miles of track. Their lead over Upper Canada came from having been a few months earlier into the financial markets in 1836–7, which permitted work to begin, and from the growing interest of eastern American financiers from the mid-1840s onward. The states' early ventures into railways were hardly unalloyed successes, however, and Michigan sold off its state-owned lines at a loss in the mid-1840s. As for the impact of such projects on economic development, it is not clear how much ground these states gained on Upper Canada by their earlier start in railway construction; it was only in the 1850s that the main interregional trunk lines in the states south and west of Upper Canada were built and state networks filled out around them.

Upper Canada finally entered the railway age in the 1850s. By then, the government of the Province of Canada had joined the promotional efforts, through the 1849 Guarantee Act, the 1851 Main Trunk Act, and the 1852 Municipal Loan Fund legislation.[6] The first two put the provincial government's credit behind approved main line projects that succeeded in completing half of their mileage from private funding; under the Municipal Loan Fund, the province was the ultimate support for any project that could secure enough municipal backing and private credit to commence work. If the projects generated sufficient earnings, of course, no government money at all would be required.[7] Necessary though they may have been, the 1849 and 1851 provincial guarantees were not sufficient to get construction under way. Conditions in the capital markets and the overall chronology and geographical pattern of North American railway development were at least as important as public policy in the timing of Canada's first railway age.

For the Great Western, Upper Canada's most successful railway, a key cyclical factor was the widening premium available in London to investors in bonds of colonial railways by comparison with safe British securities, on which interest rates touched all-time lows in 1851. Late in 1851 the Great Western became one of the first overseas railway companies to use bonds convertible into equity stock on favourable terms to attract British investors. In its approach to them, it was advised and supported by an influential group of London railway brokers and financiers. Almost simultaneously, it was able to raise funds from the powerful Forbes-Corning alliance, which controlled the railways from Albany to Buffalo that were about to become the New York Central and the Michigan Central from Detroit westward towards Chicago.[8] The Great Western would link the two, especially for passengers, who were only moderately inconvenienced by having to change trains twice at the border, and who in the 1850s would save time by taking the shortest route between Buffalo and Detroit.

No other Canadian railway was in so favourable a position, but other lines that would benefit under the 1849 Guarantee Act, the St Lawrence and Atlantic and the Toronto-based Ontario, Simcoe and Huron (after 1858, the Northern), were well under way in 1852 and would open in 1853. Already chartered, but not yet under construction, were the links from Toronto to Hamilton, for which the Great Western's British backers were already raising funds; Toronto to Montreal; and a second line west from Toronto into the fertile western peninsula. As T.C. Keefer later argued, all would likely have been built because they 'closed the gap' in a system connecting the major trading centres of the province.[9] Instead, in 1852–3 British promoters, in alliance with or led by Francis Hincks and the Canadian government, launched an enormous project, one of the largest in the world at the time – the Grand Trunk Railway of Canada. It became at once the central focus of and a major influence on the provincial government's railway and financial policies. A project of this scale was, however, neither the only nor even the best possibility for completing the core central Canadian railway system. By the end of the decade, the Grand Trunk supplied over half of the railway mileage in Canada and was also the largest single company, in terms of mileage, in Upper Canada.

The decade's other lines were almost all built in Upper Canada. The choice to build was made by municipalities whose local boosters could secure municipal approval for funding companies thought essential to local development, either under the Municipal Loan Fund or independently, as Hamilton did. The process was shaped by inter-city competition and by the workings of contractors and promoters who quickly learned to use the new rules of funding and of local and provincial responsible government to promote their favourite schemes.[10] These factors, combined with rosy official expectations of the gains to be derived from railways, created a brief and spectacular railway boom, especially in Upper Canada, where over two-thirds of the track laid in

Canada in the 1850s was located and to which the Municipal Loan Fund initially applied exclusively.

It is generally thought that Canada lagged behind the United States and thus required unusually close relations between government and business. But it is useful to note that much of the expansion of railways in states to the south occurred at the same time as in Upper Canada, as the main elements of the trunk line system from the east coast to Chicago and beyond were put into place by 1856. Further, the United States too built at least its early transportation facilities as mixed enterprises. As Harry Scheiber notes, 'local governments contributed nearly half of an estimated 12.8 million dollars invested in Ohio's railroads up to 1850.' Michigan actually built and owned its railways for a time. In Indiana, government and business were linked at the municipal level, albeit on a more modest scale than in Ohio or Upper Canada.[11] Defensive arguments about faster American progress were important in the rhetoric of Canadian politics, but at times, as in the 1850s, actual developments in Upper Canada were not so much behind as simultaneous with and quite similar in institutional character to the southern developments to which they responded.

## II. *The Economic Impact of Railway Construction*

From 1852 to 1859, over 1,400 miles of railway were built in Upper Canada, almost three-quarters of which were opened between 1853 and 1856 (table 11.1 and map 11.1). All the major urban centres in the province were linked by the end of 1856.[12] By 1860 the railway system of Canada was capitalized at about $100 million, over half of it represented by the Grand Trunk and almost all the remainder by lines in Upper Canada, which together reported a capital cost of about $44 million (table 11.3). Railway capital accounts could be over- or understated by large amounts, depending on the valuations at which companies were taken over, the degree to which securities had been issued at discounts from par value, and the company's practice in distinguishing between capital and operating accounts after a line had opened. In Canada, because there was evident overvaluation in a number of companies, including the Grand Trunk and the Northern, these figures indicate the maximum investment made to open the railways.[13] Of these sums, up to $20 million were furnished under terms of the Guarantee and Main Trunk acts (plus other aid to the Grand Trunk) and up to $6 million from borrowings by municipalities in Upper Canada under terms of the Municipal Loan Fund.[14] Most of the money raised under these laws and of the remaining capital was provided by British investors,

MAP 11.1
Railways and Urban Centres, 1861

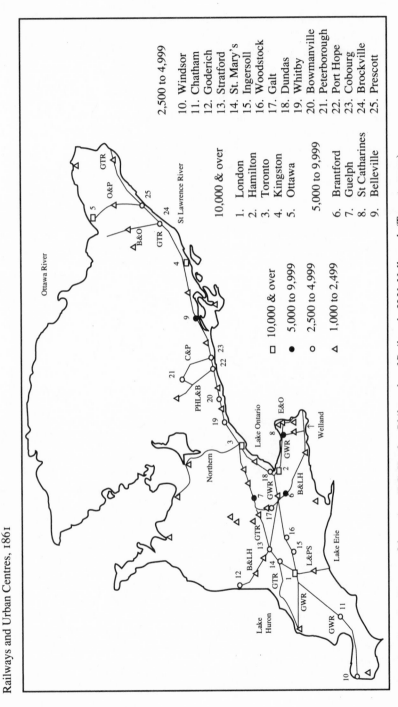

2,500 to 4,999

10. Windsor
11. Chatham
12. Goderich
13. Stratford
14. St Mary's
15. Ingersoll
16. Woodstock
17. Galt
18. Dundas
19. Whitby
20. Bowmanville
21. Peterborough
22. Port Hope
23. Cobourg
24. Brockville
25. Prescott

10,000 & over

1. London
2. Hamilton
3. Toronto
4. Kingston
5. Ottawa

5,000 to 9,999

6. Brantford
7. Guelph
8. St Catharines
9. Belleville

□  10,000 & over
●  5,000 to 9,999
○  2,500 to 4,999
△  1,000 to 2,499

SOURCE: Canada, *Census, 1861*, vol. I; T.C. Keefer, *Philosophy of Railroads*, H.V. Nelles, ed. (Toronto 1972)
Note: See table 11.3 (p. 311) for a key to the abbreviated names of railways.

their willingness to take bonds and stocks depending in varying degrees on state finance. As Scheiber argued regarding Ohio, 'the increased availability of private investment capital, during the recovery of the late 1840's, impelled railroad promoters to redouble their efforts for public aid: all recognized that a tangible expression of support by governmental authorities, in the form of stock subscriptions, loans, or guarantees, would be the most effective lure for foreign or eastern capital.'[15]

The economic impact of these railways was felt initially in their construction. Of the external investment of up to $100 million, at least $70 million was invested in Upper Canada. In the peak years from 1852 to 1856, over $10 million a year were being spent on railways there. This was an enormous sum by provincial standards. In relation to the province's 1851 population of almost one million, railway investment amounted to about $10 per person a year, a sum that far exceeded per capita annual investments from outside the province via formal, recorded channels in any previous year.[16] At a nominal 6 per cent rate of interest, the total capital of $70 million represented an annual cost of $4.2 million to the provincial economy, equal to $4 per person in 1851 or $3 in terms of the 1861 population of 1.4 million. Expressed in terms of an average household (six persons), the interest charge in 1861 would thus have been $18. As output increased, the relative weight on the economy of such a charge declined. For example, these costs can be related to off-farm sales by farmers in Upper Canada, which in 1851 averaged $125 per farm and in 1861 $210 (for all farms) or $280 (for farms with marketable surpluses).[17]

These investments were large compared to other measures of the scale of the provincial economy on the eve of the railway era. All exports from the Province of Canada combined averaged about $13 million a year in 1850–2, while the only estimate we have for Canadian Gross National Product in the period, by Firestone, gives a figure of $169 million for Canadian GNP in 1851. Thus, at $12.5 million a year in the two Canadas (for the eight years 1852 to 1859), the investment was equivalent to yearly exports in the early 1850s and to over 7 per cent of 1851 GNP. Firestone's GNP figures are probably too high and embrace the Maritime provinces too, so it is evident that the investment in Upper Canada expressed as a percentage of its output alone would have been considerably higher. External investments at or above 8 per cent of GNP also characterized later eras of major railway construction in Canada.[18] From 1851 to 1860 three adjacent American states – Ohio, Michigan, and Indiana – saw gross investment in their railway systems of $171 million, equal to $35,000 per mile of track and $39 per capita in terms of their 1860 populations. Upper Canada's figures were closer to $51,000 per mile and over $50 per head (table 11.6). Any lag as of 1850 had been made up by decade's end.

Of the British capital invested in Canadian railways, some never left England, being used to pay costs of raising capital, such as commissions and, for later issues, interest on the company's earlier ones. Other capital crossed the ocean as manufactured iron and hardware, steel, machinery, 'railroad iron,' pig iron, and bars and sheets. Such imports totalled about $3 million a year in 1851–2, surged to $9 million in 1854, then quickly fell back to $5 million from 1855 to 1857 and to 1851–2 levels thereafter. Over the entire construction period from 1851 to 1859, the Province of Canada imported iron and products worth over $40 million, of which about half is likely to have been directly attributable to railways.[19]

Exchange rates held relatively steady during the boom, as the capital movements generated a surge in the value of imports of all kinds into Canada. By 1854 the value of imports stood at 2.4 times the level of 1850, while exports had gone up 1.8 times, from a lower base. The total value of imports to the Canadas per year established at the 1854–6 peak was, after the crash of 1857, again attained by 1861–2; and by then the value of exports had caught up. It requires more evidence and analysis than is possible here to estimate how much those later exports were directly or indirectly the consequence of investments spurred by railway construction in the 1850s. But while some of the railway investment flowed immediately out in the purchase of goods for consumption, including some goods formerly supplied domestically, the higher levels of demand in the mid-1850s for many commodities, locally produced as well as imported, should have encouraged investment in farmsteads and other productive facilities beyond what would have occurred in the absence of railways. Additionally, though much of Upper Canada's productive land was near navigable waterways, some forest and farm products might not have been marketable without railways.

One of the most direct impacts of outside capital was in employment on construction. The provincial workforce has been estimated at about 250,000 in 1851,[20] which provides a scale against which to measure construction demands for labour. Some aspects of railway construction called for skill and experience, but other parts of the work entailed relatively unskilled tasks that local residents could certainly have done. Nevertheless, although detailed evidence on railway construction labour in Canada is not readily available, it is likely that much of the construction workforce consisted of recent immigrants or transient workers drawn by the construction boom. Albert Fishlow suggests that thirty to sixty men were needed per mile of track, the former on some successful American lines, the latter on English lines, where construction was to a higher standard.[21] If, as Fishlow argues, the stock of railways under construction at any time was equivalent to lines opened in that and the next year, 300 to 600 miles a year were under way from 1852 to 1858.

Despite the Grand Trunk's declared intention to build to British standards, contractors in Canada seem at least as likely to have followed North American patterns. In the summer of 1854 the Grand Trunk was said to have 8,000 men at work on the 333 miles of the Montreal-Toronto line. The company's overall peak demand for construction labour is said to have been 15,000 men; with over 400 miles being built in 1855–6, this number works out to less than forty workers per mile.[22] Even so, the high, British-based figures are also included in the estimates made here (table 11.2). Thus, the 300 miles under way in Upper Canada in 1852 and 1854 would have required between 9,000 and 18,000 workers, and the 600 miles in 1855 would have required 18,000 to 36,000 workers. The highest of these figures was equivalent to almost 15 per cent of the estimated workforce in Upper Canada in 1851 or 10 per cent of Pentland's estimate of the 1861 workforce. Even the lowest figure represents a demand for labour on a specific project or set of projects that was almost unprecedented in the province. On the other hand, even at the highest level estimated, more than enough immigrants arrived during the period at Quebec to yield the number required.

These calculations are not meant to suggest that most construction workers were immigrants who came, worked for five or six years as navvies, then departed. Rather it is likely that a much larger number of migrants and residents had some experience of the process as labourers or as suppliers of work and services on a contract or subcontract basis. By permanent and transient immigration and by reallocation of labour already within the province, the railways' demand for construction labour was met. The fall in the rate of net immigration for the decade by comparison with all previous decades (to which the evidently considerable emigration of the later 1850s contributed) shows that the economy could not absorb all those drawn to the province by the boom. It seems likely that railway construction had a quite modest impact on the process of permanent settlement. On the other hand, the railways did recruit for their operations and maintenance many skilled British workers who entered the workforce at the high end of the working-class wage scale.[23] And by 1860 the railways of Upper Canada employed between 4,000 and 5,000 workers, a very large number for a single sector of the non-farm labour market (table 11.3).

The expenditure of so much imported capital in so short a time had an immediate impact on prices.[24] The inflation was not unique to

Canada, nor was it all the result of the capital imports for railway construction. Similar forces were at work throughout the western economy from the beginning of the 1850s, prompted in part by the addition of gold from California to world supplies: British prices increased by about one-third in five years from their 1849–51 levels (the lowest in the entire century to that point), and American prices likewise rose rapidly. Still, on the limited basis of produce prices, it seems that price increases in Upper Canada were at the high end of the inflationary scale in the North Atlantic economy. The standard price index, Michell's, shows a sharp rise in commodity prices at Toronto after 1852. For virtually all produce, prices in Toronto in 1854–6 were at their highest levels since the War of 1812 (see tables C.2, C.3, C.4). The problem for the recipient of such higher prices was to use the money to augment long-term earning power. Those who paid off debts in the period were ahead of where they would otherwise have been, as were those who expanded output and sales without incurring new debt. On the other hand, as the numerous bankruptcies and widespread liquidity problems that followed the 1857 crisis showed, many who bought land in this period paid prices and incurred debts that would be burdensome when prices later fell, while those who lent on the basis of higher prices had much difficulty in securing repayment.[25]

Thus, it is important not to assume long-term growth was a consequence of a short period of inflation. We can best see the construction boom as an essentially short-term phenomenon, whose impact was limited by the involvement of transient workers, the use of imported inputs, the inflationary effects of capital imports, and the leakage of funds back to metropolitan centres in the form of sharply rising levels of all imports. Had the railways not been important in the long term as transportation systems, the construction boom would in retrospect seem almost entirely ephemeral.

III. *The Economic Impact of Railway Operations*

In Upper Canada there were eleven independent railway companies at the end of the 1850s and nine operating companies in 1870. For purposes of seeing the entire system, data on all companies are summarized in tables 11.3 and 11.4. The former focuses on 1860, at the end of the construction era, when traffic had begun to revive after the sharp business contraction of 1857. The latter is for 1870, just on the eve of additions that would almost double railway mileage in the province. To permit a focus on Upper Canada, half the Grand Trunk's revenues are arbitrarily assigned to the company's sections in Upper Canada. Because traffic on the line east of Lévis did not even cover operating costs, and the entire 214-mile eastern division showed the lowest earnings of the four divisions,[26] this allocation of Grand Trunk revenue and traffic to its western divisions is unlikely to be high.

The main components of the system were the Grand Trunk and the Great Western. In 1860 they accounted for over 80 per cent of railway revenues in Upper Canada, and in 1870 even more. When the Northern is added, about 88 per cent of 1860 revenues and 92 per cent of 1870 revenues are accounted for (see annual data on the three main companies in tables 11.7, 11.8, and 11.9). In 1860 only the Great Western, with revenues of $6,400 per mile of track, exceeded the provincial average of $3,600 a mile. In 1870 only the Great Western, by now close to $11,000 a mile, and the Northern exceeded the average of $6,400 a mile. By then, the Grand Trunk had surpassed $5,000, while the others remained at or below $3,000 a mile of track.[27]

All three companies, like their smaller counterparts, aimed to serve the American market, either for Canadian exports, as in the lines running north from Lake Ontario, or for through traffic from one point in the United States to another, as in the three main companies and the Buffalo and Lake Huron. In the 1860s, however, the Northern largely abandoned its money-losing quest for through traffic between Georgian Bay and Lake Ontario.[28] For the Grand Trunk, through traffic generated about one-fifth of revenues by the mid-1860s. The quest for such traffic was integral to the Grand Trunk's long-term strategy, but this business involved intense competition with American routes for a share of the western trade with the eastern seaboard. Its impact on revenues was thus constrained by typically very low rates per ton-mile.[29] The Great Western's figures as given in table 11.7 do not permit consideration of the role of through traffic; its importance to the company's strategy and swift success is nevertheless clear. For example, through traffic in the first half of 1855 produced 56 per cent of company revenue.[30] But as local traffic developed and new American alternatives appeared, that figure was as likely to decline as to increase. When the three main railways are considered together, there is nothing to suggest that traffic over their lines between American points grew more rapidly than Upper Canadian traffic, in either volumes or revenues. Changes in total volumes and revenues should therefore indicate at least minimum rates of change in the traffic of greatest concern to us – that generated by the Upper Canadian economy.

Between 1860 and 1870 revenues for railways in Ontario and Quebec increased at an average rate of 7.1 per cent a year (table 11.5). Only a few significant segments of the system, of which Great Western passengers are the most important, did not show growth at or above that level. During the 1860s the physical dimensions of the system grew more slowly than did revenues and traffic, as the system was improved and it became more productive. It is unlikely that increased revenues resulted from rising rates and fares, because freight and passenger volumes generally increased at least as fast as revenues.[31] Unfortunately, the data here do not show changes, if any, in average length of passenger journeys and freight hauls.

Some traffic growth reflected shifts in mode of travel and freight handling, from road and/or water. Rail almost at once became the major carrier of more valuable imported merchandise. As for exports, in the first half of 1855 alone the Great Western hauled about as much flour and almost half as much wheat from stations within Upper Canada west of Hamilton as passed downward through the Welland Canal from an Upper Canadian port during the entire navigation season. Three-quarters of the flour on the railway originated at the Paris and Galt stations and would otherwise have travelled by road to Lake Ontario; but over half of the wheat originated at or west of London and would likely have travelled by water but for the railway.[32]

Water transport did not disappear on the lower Great Lakes in these years; in fact, the volume of lake shipping serving Upper Canada increased almost fivefold between 1849 and 1874.[33] In 1859 the Grand Trunk claimed that it faced competition from twenty-two steamers on the Toronto or Hamilton to Montreal run and equally formidable competition between Montreal and Quebec. In setting rates, the railways had to recognize shippers' ability to use the waterway. For much of Upper Canada, the combination of lake access and competition by both local and nearby American railways gave highly competitive rates and ensured that the benefits of increased efficiency were passed to shippers and/or consumers. As the expansion of lake shipping suggests, the growth in railway traffic resulted primarily from the continuing expansion and integration of the provincial economy.

Except for mail and express shipments, it is unlikely that speed was the main reason for railways to attract growing volumes of freight. Rather, railways reduced transshipment costs, risks of navigation, seasonal constraints on the long-distance movement of goods, and lengths of wagon and sleigh haulage.[34] Thus, they provided greater reliability of movement. Although all generalizations on freight rates are problematic, railways evidently lowered unit costs of transport from levels that prevailed before the 1850s. During the 1840s it cost between 30d and 40d (50 to 67 cents) to ship a barrel of flour from a port at the western end of Lake Ontario to Montreal. By the mid-1860s the standard Grand Trunk rate from Brampton and Malton, northwest of Toronto, to Montreal was 41 or 42 cents a barrel, and some shippers had negotiated rates of 35 cents (equal to 1 cent per ton-mile) and even 30 cents, the lowest rates coming during the navigation season. From St Mary's, deep in the western peninsula, the rate was 60 cents a barrel (about 1.4 cents per ton-mile).[35]

In addition to its standard rates, the Grand Trunk quoted a variety of special rates for specific shippers of such products as oil, wool, wheat, ashes, hogs, sugar, butter, furniture, farm implements, apples, lumber, whisky, and clover seed. In most such cases in the mid-1860s, if a carload is assumed to be equivalent to 9 tons, the rates between principal stations for shipments of over 150 miles amounted to no more than 2 cents per ton-mile.[36] Subject to various qualifications, rates were higher for general first- and second-class freight, for smaller shipments, for shorter distances, for less-important customers, and between less-important stations.

Early timetables suggest that express trains were intended to average 20 to 25 miles an hour, including stops, while mixed and local trains averaged between 10 and 15 miles an hour. Running speeds ranged as high as 30 miles an hour.[37] Such speeds, much faster than any earlier mode of transport, were especially important to people. By the mid-1860s there were three or four scheduled passenger (or mail and mixed) trains a day (except Sunday) along the entire main trunk of the province and two a day on most of the feeder lines from the north, including the Northern Railway. The fastest express between Toronto and Montreal took about fifteen hours to make the journey. Guelph and Toronto were slightly over two hours apart, and London could be reached from Toronto in five or six hours. Hamilton and Toronto, with four conveniently timed trains a day, were as little as ninety minutes apart, and closely enough linked that it was possible to travel both ways in a day with a full working day in the other centre.[38]

Railways must usually have been more comfortable than stagecoaches or even steamships, although their early safety was called into question by several major disasters on the Great Western. Railways were also cheaper: an early Great Western schedule shows that fares were about 3 cents a mile, a substantial saving from the 5 cents that had earlier been common for stages and steamships.[39] On the Great Western, passengers provided over half of all revenues in the 1850s and between 36 and 47 per cent in the 1860s (table 11.7). After 1865 passenger revenues for the Grand Trunk were just over one-third of its total revenues each year (table 11.8). On the Northern, passengers accounted for about one-quarter of revenue during the 1860s (table 11.9).

Although we do not know enough about who travelled and why, such passenger volumes were vastly larger than those on previous commercial modes of travel. In the year from August 1854 to July 1855 the Great Western carried over a half-million people: 391,000 local passengers, who generated $536,000 in revenue ($1.37 per passenger), and 167,000 through passengers, who generated $720,000 in revenue ($4.20 per passenger).[40] If an average fare was 3 cents a mile, the revenue data suggest an average 'local' journey was forty-five miles and a 'through' journey averaged 140 miles.[41] On the Northern Railway, which was not on the main American westward migration route, revenues from the 100,000 or more passengers a year were generated by Upper Canadians; its passenger revenues averaged around $1.00 per passenger for most years in the 1860s.

Evidence of the extent of provincial utilization of the new technology can be found in the doubling of Canadian railways' revenues in the 1860s (see also table 12.5). In 1870 the revenues of the railways in Ontario and Quebec totalled almost $13 million (table 11.4). When revenues of the railways in Atlantic Canada are included, the total was about $13.7 million, of which, if the attribution of half the Grand Trunk's revenues to its Ontario lines is accurate, Ontario's share was two-thirds. The Canadian total equalled 3.6 per cent of Canadian GNP that year – a large figure for a single industry and technological development.[42] It bears comparison with Fishlow's estimate that the income flow of American railways was equivalent to about 3 per cent of American GNP in 1859.

As systems of transportation and communication, railways had a continuing impact on the location of economic activities, and they fostered the selective growth of some of the leading urban centres.[43] But in this pattern, causation was not one-way, for the railway map reflected the economic and political power of existing urban centres. In most areas, railways tended to reinforce and extend patterns already taking shape (compare maps 7.1 and 11.1). Even the Grand Trunk line west of Toronto, which penetrated territory that had, with the exception of Guelph, scarcely begun to urbanize, favoured the development not of entirely new towns but of villages that had local prominence in 1846, such as Brampton, Berlin, Stratford, and Sarnia, none of which had yet attained a population of 1,000 in 1851.[44] As Kitchener, Berlin eventually became one of Ontario's largest cities, surpassing its neighbours, Preston and Galt, both of which were served by a branch of the Great Western but bypassed by the Grand Trunk.

As the biggest businesses in Canada, the leading railways represented an important institutional development in the provincial economy. No other companies had such large fixed capital to maintain and account for; none had such large staffs and complex hierarchies of tasks and skills to organize; none had such large revenues. Railways faced much competition, but were unlike most producers in the oligopolistic characteristics of their markets; hence their frequent efforts to control competition by inter-company rate agreements.[45] Almost no other incorporated companies involved foreign ownership. Additionally, the Grand Trunk and Great Western railways became almost immediately the largest manufacturing enterprises in Canada, as they discovered the economies of internalizing not only the repair and maintenance of their costly plants but the manufacture of their new equipment. In this way they could most effectively use the skilled workforce that they had built up.[46]

## IV. *Conclusion*

The railway network created in Upper Canada by 1860 bears comparison with that in adjoining states (table 11.6). Revenues suggest that Ohio and Michigan railways were somewhat more successful than those in Upper Canada, while Indiana's were much less so. Compared to an average of the three, which we might somewhat arbitrarily take as a standard, Upper Canada built fewer miles of track in proportion to its population, and the track generated more revenue per mile. Indeed, the $3,600 in revenues per mile of track in Upper Canada in 1860 fell only slightly below the average for the entire United States in 1859, $3,900 per mile.[47] The capitalization of Upper Canadian railways was much higher than to the south and west. In part, that was because 20 per cent of the American mileage had been completed by 1851, at much lower costs per mile than the 1850s cost structure allowed. It is also possible that the broader Canadian gauge imposed significantly higher costs for roadbed and bridges.[48] The higher Canadian capitalization derives from the Great Western, whose relatively heavy traffic may have justified its capital cost of almost $67,000 per mile, and from the Grand Trunk, whose $54,500 per mile represented an overcapitalization that would continue to grow (table 11.3).[49]

In the next decade the three leading provincial railways all increased revenue and traffic at rates that doubled total amounts in about a decade. Revenue and expenditure data for these years are complicated because of the inflationary impact of the Civil War, which generated what the companies reported as a 'discount' or a 'loss' on American currency.[50] As a proportion of revenues, such discounts peaked in the mid-1860s and were diminishing in the late 1860s. Thus annual data on finances, like evidence on volumes of traffic, show that growth was not particularly or exclusively a phenomenon of the Civil War years (tables 11.7, 11.8, 11.9). If their calculations were accurate, each company did much better for most or all of the 1860s than it had in the later 1850s by a key measure of performance – the ratio of ordinary working expenses to revenues.

The Great Western reduced fixed charges on its capital by using convertible bonds, which investors converted to common shares in 1855 and 1856. During the 1860s it replaced most of its original rails and wooden bridges, added a third rail on much of its line to permit movement of standard- as well as broad-gauge cars, and negotiated favourable terms for completion of its payment of sums owed on Canadian government account. Its outlay on account of interest actually declined, and between 1865 and 1870 it paid dividends of 3½ to 5 per cent per year.[51] Such dividends were not large by the standards that railway promoters had offered in their initial projections of profitability, but the returns on that part of a railway's capital represented by its common stock were the concern principally of those British common stockholders who had bought their shares at too high a price. When shares turned over, as a great many must have by the 1860s, new shareholders bought in at rates of discount on the par value of shares that reflected current and predicted earnings levels, not those of the original promotional literature. The company would have been in better financial health if it had not, at the height of its initial success in the 1850s, made an unfortunate investment in an American extension, the Detroit and Milwaukee. Although competitive pressures were building that would squeeze it between increasingly powerful Canadian and American railway systems in the 1870s, the Great Western remained the most successful Canadian railway by most measures.

The Grand Trunk was another matter, but it is unlikely that its Upper Canadian sections were the main cause of its problems. Its basic strategy to seek American through trade helped dictate its excessive scale. And its overcapitalization and the politically imposed necessity to build unremunerative lines reflected Lower Canadian circumstances: it acquired existing companies there at excessive valuations, and it had to build an unpromising line of over two hundred miles from Richmond to Rivière-du-Loup. Going into bankruptcy or seeking reorganization through a private bill would have been very risky both for its political allies and for its owners.[52] But in avoiding those perils, it also avoided the necessity-cum-opportunity to restructure capital on a more realistic basis. The considerable success in the 1860s of the Northern owed a good deal to its forced reorganization in the late 1850s. In the 1860s the Brockville and Ottawa underwent a similar restructuring of capital, and the turn of the Midland came in the 1870s.

During the 1850s the essential elements of the central Canadian trunk railway system were put in place, linking all major Canadian urban centres and connecting at a number of points with the United States. To this day the first main lines are major components in the Canadian railway network. At the same time Upper Canada fully entered the transition from mainly extensive to mainly intensive growth, as declining rates of population growth, rising output per farm, and other indicators demonstrate (see chapter 12). Producers quickly adapted to new circumstances, as David Gagan has shown for the farmers of Peel County. By 1870 there was substantially more evidence of industrial development in the leading cities. Railways were not universally or uniformly associated with the growth of other industries, however. Nor should all of the shift in the character of Upper Canada's development at the mid-century be attributed to railways, although the transition occurred during the first provincial railway era and was undoubtedly influenced by the new technology. The demographic pressure that Gagan discusses, for example, coincided with the boom but was not a result of it.[53]

Railway technology was a critical element in the transformation of Canadian society in the mid-nineteenth century. But it is best to see railways less as the cause of than as a part of a larger development process, extending for decades. As a major new technological system, railways were far from fully developed anywhere in 1850 or 1860.[54] As the railways were increasingly integrated into an international network with standards set by the system as a whole, managers would continue to discover that there was enormous scope for further investment and the expansion of traffic. Developments within companies and at the system-wide level improved productivity, reduced unit costs, and lowered real costs of transport, especially between major centres well served by competing modes of transport.[55] Hence railways tended to reinforce the power of the most favourably located cities and to foster more internal exchange, wider and more complex markets, and increasing rural integration into markets, all of these being factors in the post-Confederation development of southern Ontario as the economic heartland of Canada.

Railways had no immediate imitators as big businesses. Until late in the century their overall size and complexity and the scale and sophistication of their manufacturing operations made them exceptions in the business world. The state played a major part in the railway story, both by facilitating their initial funding and by direct and indirect involvement in a myriad other ways, through the legislature, the law, the actions of politicians and officials, and the efforts of municipalities. In the process, the state itself was much changed, notably in the context of public finance. Of course, there was ample evidence of scandal, inefficiency, and failure. One of the principal vehicles of state activity was the Grand Trunk Railway; as a 'chosen instrument' of public policy,[56] it was weakened by its excessive scale and its inappropriate capitalization. Yet even it generated substantial increases of traffic and revenue in the 1860s. Through a complex mix of state and private activity, the province acquired and in many ways domesticated a major imported technology at virtually the same time as did adjacent states, and in apparently similar quantities. Growth in traffic during the 1860s suggests the demand for and something of the value of that technology in a progressive economy.[57]

# 12 The Economy at Mid-Century, 1851–70

Beginning approximately at mid-century, Canadians collectively began to be more interested in and adept at counting.* As a result, there are much better contemporary statistics to support research on the province's economic history after the mid-century;[1] indeed, it is possible to survey them only very selectively in one chapter. By most measures of output and productivity, the Ontario economy was pre-eminent in the new Canadian dominion, as Ian Drummond's subsequent volume in this series, *Progress without Planning*, also makes clear in its evidence on the province in and after 1870–1.[2] The scale and complexity of the provincial economy look different from the perspective of a book that ends in 1870, however, than they do from the perspective of a book that begins then. The principal themes considered in this chapter are population change, developments in the rural economies of farm and forest, and the growing industrial and tertiary sectors of the economy, with their more strongly urban orientation. A major commercial crisis in 1857–8 and a second cyclical downturn in 1866–7 both appear, sometimes with the lag of a year, in major time series. Although the 1857–8 crisis was exceptionally severe in Upper Canada, neither crisis interrupted for long the basic expansionary trend in Upper Canadian output.[3]

## I. Population Growth and Change

Elements of extensive growth continued in Ontario (for example in northern Ontario) long after Confederation, and we have seen elements

* Although Canada West eventually became common usage during the Union era, for simplicity Upper Canada is used to refer to the province, unless the reference is uniquely to the period after 1867. Because the province switched to dollars in 1858, that more familiar currency is used in this chapter, as in chapter 11. As always, £1 Hfx cy was equal to $4. See also Appendix A.

of intensive growth even before mid-century. But in some respects the end of the long era of extensive growth can be dated quite precisely, to between 1854 and 1856, when net immigration to Upper Canada ended. There was substantial emigration during and after the crisis of 1857. For the whole decade from 1851 to 1861, provincial population grew more slowly than in any previous decade, at an average rate of about 4 per cent a year. From 1861 to 1871 the rate was just 1.5 per cent, well below natural rates of increase. Like the other provinces that formed the Dominion of Canada in 1867, Ontario had net emigration in every decade from 1861 to 1901. Immigration did not cease, but because more people left Ontario than arrived, at the end of each decade the population was lower than it would have been on the basis of births and deaths alone.

Although the manuscript census makes it possible to probe the demographic structure and behaviour of the province's population much more systematically in this period, it is possible here to note only some quite general changes at aggregate levels. In particular, the passing of the era of extensive growth is reflected in changes in the ratio of men to women and in the age structure of the population. For every 100 'adult' females in the province (adult defined as aged fifteen or sixteen and over), there had typically been about 120 men, but that proportion fell steadily after the 1840s. By 1871 it was 103 (table 12.1). Until the 1840s about half the province's population had fallen into the assessors' category 'under 16'; in the 1840s, 45 per cent were in the age categories 'to 14' or 'to 15.' By 1881, however, just 40 per cent were aged 'to 16.'

In an earlier book in this series, David Gagan's *Hopeful Travellers,* these and related population changes have been seen as part of, or a response to, a 'crisis' marked by land scarcity and population pressure.[4] Whether that terminology is needed can be debated, but in key respects the main demographic changes Gagan discusses for his sample region characterized Upper Canada as a whole, as the province entered the 'fertility transition,' which extended over the next eighty years.[5] That transition, in which birth and death rates fell sharply from historical levels, represented a cultural, economic, and biological transformation under way widely in western society in the latter half of the nineteenth century. The motivations behind and mechanisms of effecting that demographic transition are still the subject of much research, and it took a considerable time to reveal itself unambiguously in the sophisticated calculations that demographers make to allow for relevant variables, particularly variations in age, sex, and marriage structures. In Peel County, the average age at first marriage was tending to rise for both men and women between 1840 and 1870, and fertility began to fall; for example, there were 1,762 children under ten per 1,000 married women aged twenty to twenty-four in 1851 and 1,302 in 1871, and the decline was even steeper in the rate for married women aged 15 to 19.[6]

Wherever there has been detailed research based on record linkage of census manuscripts and documents such as land records and assessment rolls, it has been clear that there was much transiency (that is, the movement of people into and out of the region of study). In Gagan's Peel County, just 39 per cent of householders in 1851 remained in 1861, and just 31 per cent of the 1861 householders remained in 1871; of all the 10,000 households captured on one of the three census manuscripts, only a tenth were present on all three.[7] A similar pattern prevailed in Hamilton; after correction for mortality, only about 35 per cent of men recorded in the 1851 census persisted in Hamilton to be enumerated in 1861 and 30 per cent from 1861 to 1871.[8] Even in very short periods, and after allowing for errors and omissions in the records, there is evidence of rapid population turnover. Hamilton in the 1850s was very much an immigrant city, a stopping-point for many in the course of a longer migration. But Peel, with no major urban centres as late as 1851, evidently had some similar characteristics. In a detailed study of one small township in Peel County, Toronto Gore, Herbert Mays has shown that, although the recorded population peaked in 1851 at 1,820 people in 318 households, at least 826 different households, counting more than 4,000 people, lived there between 1851 and 1890.[9]

As Gagan noted, persistence and property ownership were closely correlated. To this can be added early establishment, in rural areas especially. Thus, Mays notes that all of the 132 Toronto Gore households that persisted for twenty or more years between 1851 and 1890 'came from the ranks of early settlers and their children' (that is, from 102 families settled in the township before 1846). A number of other recent studies of rural communities also emphasize persistence.[10] Not all who came early persisted, but first-comers had a better chance to acquire the best farmland (in soil quality and location), and in the local exchange economy, they could hope to sell their produce to new arrivals. That population was levelling off by no means suggests stagnation, or that people were not continuing to make choices in terms of work and location. All areas, including apparently stable established rural economies, were affected by transiency and net emigration, and even marginal population movements and demographic changes could have a large cumulative effect. The resultant aggregate population numbers were, in Chad Gaffield's phrasing, actually 'the complex product of persistence and transience.'[11]

In 1871, 227,000 people, fully 49 per cent of those stating an occupation, were 'farmers.' The make-up of that group is clarified by Gordon

Darroch and Michael Ornstein's study of a sample area covering much of the Upper Canadian heartland; there in 1871 just over 51 per cent of men with occupations were farmers and farmers' sons working on the family farm.[12] No other group of occupations came close to rivalling these numbers. On the other hand, such numbers suggest that about half of the workers in the province were not farmers. Clearly there was a considerable local market for both farm and non-farm outputs. In 1851 the thirty-three towns and cities of 1,000 or more (map 7.1) accounted for 14 per cent of provincial population; by 1871 almost 21 per cent of the population lived in the eighty-four towns and cities that now numbered 1,000 or more.[13]

The transitions discussed in this section were common in northeastern North America. They did not, however, mark the end of extensive growth for Upper Canadians who were prepared to leave the province and move farther west in the United States or, later, to the Canadian west, where the process continued until the 1920s. Nor did all northeastern areas have exactly identical trajectories in population and urbanization.[14] And population was scarcely the only measure of economic change.

II. *The Rural Economy*

In the pioneer economy many individuals and households who were not primarily farmers lived in rural areas, or areas that were not yet clearly demarcated as urban. In part, early urbanization was a spatial rearrangement of the rural economy, as such people became increasingly likely to live in villages and smaller towns.[15] The growth of the latter made more visible, and probably more intense, the kinds of rural exchange that had long existed in the province, and the sustained growth of larger towns and cities also provided expanding, nearby markets for provincial farmers.[16] Despite urbanization, during the 1860s there was actually a substantial increase in the percentage of the provincial workforce who were farmers. In Darroch and Ornstein's sample area, farmers increased during the decade from 31.8 to 37.7 per cent of men with occupations, while 'farmer's sons' declined slightly from 14.7 to 13.5 per cent. In the entire province the number of occupiers of more than ten acres increased in the decade from 127,600 to 152,300.[17] Certainly farming remained primarily a matter of physical labour rather than of mechanization, a large majority of the population still lived and worked in rural areas, and virtually all the province's exports were produced in the rural economy of farm and forest (tables 12.2, 12.3).

The changes in provincial agriculture in the last third of the nineteenth century have been summarized as a 'shift from wheat to cheese.'[18] But we have already noted that growing wheat for export was in many areas not the principal activity of farmers, and even in strongly export-oriented wheat-growing districts, farmers produced and marketed much more than wheat, in particular animals and their produce (and fodder for animals, for farm use and for sale). During the 1860s animals and their produce also became important exports. In 1865–6 and 1870–1 their value rivalled that of forest products or wheat (table 12.2).[19] Beginning around 1870, a rapidly expanding, export-oriented cheese industry was added to the province's cattle economy, but cheese was never as significant a rural output as butter, milk, or beef.

The mid-century represented the high point of provincial wheat exports, which exceeded 8 million bushels in most years from 1852 to 1869. The peaks were in 1856 and 1861; in both years, for the only time in the province's history, net exports were 12 million bushels or more and total values exceeded $12 million (for 1861, see also table 5.2). By 1869, though the province still had a surplus, Canada as a whole had become a net importer of wheat. Throughout the mid-century, provincial wheat acreage remained at levels consistent with our earlier estimates of land use. From 17 to 24 per cent of land under culture in the province had evidently been required each year to produce the provincial wheat crop. In 1870 the 1.4 million acres seeded in wheat equalled 16 per cent of all 'improved' land in the province, or 22 per cent of land 'under crops.' The all-time peak of wheat acreage and output in Ontario still lay ahead, in 1880–2, when at least 23 per cent of acreage under crop was in wheat.[20]

Wheat was a pioneer's crop, of course, but also a part of well-established mixed farming in some of the province's most-developed regions.[21] In several census districts of relatively recent settlement in 1870 (Simcoe North, Wellington North, Grey North, and Bruce North and South) in which less than half of occupied land had yet been improved, over 25 per cent of cropped land was in wheat. But the same proportion of land was in wheat in Durham East and West and Northumberland West, areas east of Toronto where settlement dated from about 1800, and in Waterloo North and South, Perth North, and Wellington Centre, in all of which over two-thirds of occupied land was improved. If we assume that local consumption of wheat was 5.5 bushels per capita and allow 1.5 bushels per acre of wheat as seed, all but two of the above districts (Perth North and Wellington North) had net surpluses of 100,000 bushels or more in 1870, a year of deficient wheat yields, which across the province averaged only 10.4 bushels per acre.[22] A number of other census districts also had surpluses of 100,000 bushels or more; all were in the heartland of the provincial economy, from Oxford North, Brant and Haldimand through Waterloo, Halton, Peel, York North, and Ontario. The remaining areas in the west, from Niagara to Essex, had more modest surpluses. From Hastings east, no district had a wheat surplus except Carleton, which had a slight surplus. Still, almost all eastern areas continued to grow wheat, often in sufficient quantities to meet most of the consumption requirements of at least their rural population. With the addition of the more recently settled areas noted, a map of wheat production in the province in 1870 would show that the same areas were principal wheat producers then as in 1851 (see map 5.3).[23] Although in a few districts spring and winter wheat were both grown in substantial amounts, from Peel southwest to Essex, the wheat grown was primarily winter wheat; east of Toronto and in the new districts, spring wheat was similarly pre-eminent.

These are aggregate data, and we must be wary of assuming that all farmers in any area behaved identically. As W.H. Graham notes in his superb study of a small area inland from Oshawa, there was 'an astonishing diversity of experience within a single occupation, farming. The picture that emerges from the statistical evidence of the operations of the protagonists and their neighbours makes of "the average farmer" a chimera.'[24] Moreover, as the spatial distribution of wheat production shows, there were considerable variations in farm output across the province. If most elements of mixed farming were widely practised, they could be combined in differing ways depending on soil and climate and on farmers' knowledge, capital, and expectations regarding markets.[25] To understand such local and regional variations in detail, it is desirable to study selected farms over time. That, unfortunately, is beyond the scope of a single chapter. Data from the census and from the export trades can at least provide an overview of other aspects of provincial agriculture and farm marketing across the mid-century.

The quantities of some principal farm stocks and outputs in the period were noted in table 5.3. By comparison with 1848 or 1851, total outputs or stocks of all items in the table except oxen rose across the period. But when the data are presented on a per capita basis,[26] outputs of only butter, barley, and perhaps hay expanded throughout the period. For other commodities, trends depend on the base year selected. In relation to 1860 levels, only per capita output of wool was higher a decade later, while wheat, as we have seen, was very much lower. If 1851 is chosen as a base, outputs of potatoes and peas were also substantially higher in 1870. The per capita stock of horses rose somewhat during the two decades; stocks of swine and sheep declined slightly; and oxen almost disappeared from the records, their decline being offset by rising numbers of horned cattle and milch cows.

Because much wheat and flour were exported to or through Lower Canada, the data in tables 12.2 and 12.3 understate wheat's importance; however, the tables do make clear that provincial farmers were marketing a wide and growing range of produce. All of the farm-produced exports, with the exception of barley and rye, were quite universally grown in 1860, and many producing areas participated in export trade. Evidence is given in table 12.5 on selected points of export of commodities worth $200,000 or more in 1865–6; that was the last year in which such comprehensive port-by-port data are available and a peak year in the 1860s trade cycle. Some exports by rail are reported for an inland point such as Stratford, while others are reported for the point of rail connection with the United States (such as Clifton and Prescott). Because Prescott was a convenient point of transfer from the Grand Trunk to the American railway system via the Ogdensburgh Railway, its exports could have come from anywhere in the province; on the other hand, census data for adjoining areas suggest that cattle and butter exports reported from there could have been locally produced. For other points of potential transfer from the Grand Trunk, such as Port Hope, Cobourg, Kingston, and Brockville, it is also reasonable to assign most exports to their region. If so, the share of exports of a number of commodities from points east of Toronto was very much in line with that region's share of provincial population and with its output of the various products as shown in the 1871 census.

In terms of agricultural exports, there was some very limited evidence of localization. Exports of swine, horned cattle, sheep, wool, flour, wheat, barley, and peas left from almost the entire breadth of the province. There were no pork exports from east of Toronto, but that region was responsible for a disproportionately large share of exports of butter and horses. The most widespread export of all was barley, exports of which expanded rapidly during the two decades; it was reported by all but four of the twenty-eight selected ports. The principal railway centres in the western peninsula, from Chatham to Guelph, appear as exporters of virtually all commodities. When their shipments are added to those recorded at Clifton, where the Great Western met the New York Central, it is clear that the railways carried much of the western peninsula's farm produce shipments.[27]

In table 12.4 exports are related to outputs reported in the 1861 and 1871 census. Exports were highest in relation to output for barley and wheat. Some of the net wheat exports shown in the table must have come from stocks in 1870–1, however, if per capita consumption levels within the province were sustained.[28] Between one-quarter and one-third of total production of cattle, sheep, and wool was exported in 1870–1.

Given the prominence of animals and their products in the export data, the lack of upward trend in per capita stocks of animals is particularly striking (table 5.3). Of course, the data record only numbers, not size and quality, and the latter may well have changed across the mid-century. Or other marketing changes may have been involved, such as offsetting imports of animal products from the United States to Upper Canada, shifts in local consumption patterns, and shifts in patterns of supply for the Lower Canadian market.

All of the products exported were also consumed in the domestic economy, as were many others, including the fruits and vegetables needed for farm and non-farm consumption. The 'gross value' of agricultural production in Ontario in 1870 has been estimated by John McCallum at $94 million, of which wheat contributed 15 per cent, 'other crops' 53 per cent, and animals and products the remainder. By his reckoning, 'agricultural cash income' was $33 million, 25 per cent of which came from wheat. Approximately half of the wheat income is attributable to export sales of wheat. If the 1870–1 value of farm exports other than wheat in table 12.2 (some $9 million) is combined with McCallum's estimate that all wheat sales together generated $6.7 million in farm income in 1870, it is clear that all farm-grown exports plus domestic sales of wheat accounted for less than half of cash income as McCallum calculates it.

McCallum also seems to understate the role of animals and their products in farm income. M.C. Urquhart has calculated, for all of Canada, that in 1870 wheat represented 14 per cent of the value of farm output (including produce consumed by the farm household itself); by comparison, animals and products represented 55 per cent, beef and dairy products alone amounting to 35 per cent of 1870 farm output. In a companion study, also of all Canada, Marvin McInnis calculates a 'gross value of final agricultural product' series, net of the cost of inputs. Wheat accounted for 16 per cent of that total, animal products for 60 per cent, and other outputs (vegetables, fruits, maple syrup, honey, tobacco, etc.) for the remainder. And his is a 'lean' estimate of farm output and income, particularly in that it omits wood products. Ontario represents at least half the total output for Canada, and even if much the largest share of wheat is assigned to Ontario, it still seems likely that animals and products were a more significant part of farm incomes and output than McCallum's calculations suggest.[29] Even on McCallum's estimate, however, the essence of provincial agriculture in 1870 clearly was mixed farming, in which wheat was only one component in the allocation of land, work, and time on the farm, the generation of farm income from marketing, or its contribution to family well-being.[30]

The 1861 census placed the 'cash value' of farms in the province at $295 million; implements worth $11 million and livestock totalling $41 million were additional to, rather than included in, this capital. Two decades later, in 1882, farmland was valued at $632 million, implements at $37 million, livestock at $80 million, and farm buildings at $133 million, making a total value of $883 million.[31] Such figures make clear that much of the province's stock of capital was represented by its more than 100,000 farms, built up over many decades in a decentralized investment process. For example, the almost $350 million in farm capital in 1861 was almost five times the capital invested in railways in the province by then (table 11.3). The most evident dimension of continuing investment was the addition of new land under culture, both at the margin of settlement and in established farming areas. Between 1851 and 1871 total acreage in use rose more rapidly than provincial population, and for the first time in provincial history the ratio of improved land to population began to rise. Though drainage would be increasingly significant as the century went on,[32] at least through the 1860s clearing must have been the principal factor in the increase in this ratio.

It is clear that investments in housing, barns, fencing, and stock improvement all went on steadily as well.[33] During the 1860s Upper Canadian farmers began to buy the newly developed self-raking reaper in substantial numbers, to permit the cultivation of increased acreages, a reallocation of the farm household's time, and/or a diminished resort to hired labour. From 1861 to 1871 the value of Canadian farm implements production increased more than sixfold, and the number of reapers and mowers on Upper Canadian farms increased sevenfold. By 1871 provincial farmers reported a total of 37,000 reapers and mowers.[34]

In addition to farms, the province's forests continued to be a large contributor to exports and a significant part of the overall economy. After 1850 there were both continuities and changes in this sector. As before, published data permit only partial designation of Upper Canada's share; nor is it particularly useful to distinguish between the two sides of the upper Ottawa. Using data gathered initially by A.R.M. Lower, Marvin McInnis provides an overview of the Canadian export trade that serves as context for a more specific discussion of trends in Upper Canada.[35] The two principal trends were the relative expansion of the manufactured sector (boards and deals) and the growth of a substantial American demand alongside the traditional British market. From 1850 to 1870 the total value of 'Canadian' wood products exports (including those from New Brunswick and Nova Scotia) tripled, from $6.4 million to $20.4 million. Values doubled from 1850 to 1853-4, fluctuated between $10 and $15 million for a decade, then began to rise again; the next peak was in 1873, at $27.9 million, the highest level until 1897. The proportion of exports destined for Great Britain fell from around 80 per cent in 1850–4 to about 67 per cent in most years from 1858 to 1865, then to about 50 per cent from 1868 to 1871. The total value of exports to Britain reached a peak in 1854 ($10.8 million) that was not exceeded until 1871. In most subsequent years Britain purchased $10 million or more in Canadian wood products, the all-time peak for the century coming in 1877, at $16.6 million.

John Keyes, drawing on timber merchants' market letters as well as official sources, provides data on the volume of square timber exports from Quebec for the entire century. Total exports of all species reached peaks of about 25 million cubic feet in 1854, 1857, and 1861; the all-time peak came in 1863, at 32 million cubic feet. Although the figure for total exports was dominated by white pine, exports of red pine and elm timber also peaked in 1863. Thereafter volumes in most years remained at or above 20 million cubic feet (that is, still above levels during the years of the timber duties, except 1845–6) until 1877. Oak exports, which first passed 2 million cubic feet in 1863, actually peaked in 1877, at 3.6 million cubic feet.[36]

McInnis shows that manufactured lumber, which constituted half the value of exports in 1850, increased to almost three-quarters in 1870 and almost four-fifths in 1879. The value of squared pine exports exceeded $4 million in 1853 and 1854, and occasionally thereafter. The value of squared oak, around $250,000 in the early 1850s, exceeded $500,000 in 1854, 1857, and 1861–2, after which it expanded quickly to over $1 million in 1865. After falling back somewhat, this total reached a new high of $1.4 million in 1871, and this level was attained in a number of years from then until 1878. It is evident that the Ottawa valley mills provided most of the upper province's share of the expanding deal trade. Output of all kinds of planks and boards grew rapidly. From $1 million in 1850–1, total exports rose to over $3 million in 1858–60 and 1863–5, exceeded $5 million in 1866–7, then rose to an all-time peak for the century of $11.6 million in 1873.[37]

Selected data on specifically Upper Canadian forest product exports are provided in tables 4.2, 4.5, 12.2, and 12.3. The first two show much of the province's British-oriented export trade; those in this chapter are for exports, largely to the United States, direct from Upper Canadian ports. In addition, an unknown proportion of Upper Canada's exports of planks and boards travelled from the Ottawa valley via Lower Canada, in particular through St Jean.[38] In 1852 the volume of squared white pine produced on the Ottawa surpassed the peak of 1846, and it also attained that level in at least 1857 and 1861–3, all years of high export volumes from Quebec (table 4.5). Red pine volumes tended to decline, but recovered for several years in the early 1860s. Timber produced in remoter regions did not always reach Quebec in the same year, culling did not always occur immediately on the timber's arrival at Quebec, and not all timber was exported in the year it arrived at Quebec. Nevertheless, fluctuations and trends in total square timber exports given by Keyes accurately mirror the experience of the Ottawa portion of the larger Quebec hinterland. Indeed, the Ottawa evidently supplied virtually all red pine exports and a substantial majority of white pine.[39] Even in the 1840s most white and nearly all red pine came from above Ottawa; by the 1860s very little square pine of any kind came from the Gatineau, the Rideau, and areas below Ottawa.

Upper Canadian oak shipments in the 1860s were sufficient to account for most of the rising volume of oak exports from Quebec. As it had since the mid-1830s, that oak travelled to market by water, most of it on lake vessels from above Niagara Falls to Garden Island, then by raft to Quebec, before being shipped to Britain. In most years, nearly all the pine recorded in table 4.2 as shipped down the St Lawrence was white pine, which came largely from Lake Ontario and the upper St Lawrence. Volumes in the early 1860s, when squared white pine reached its peak as an export, exceeded all earlier years except 1846. Thus, the Quebec-focused timber trade of Upper Canada continued at volumes that matched or exceeded those from the years when the timber duties applied. After the trade peaked in 1861–3, its subsequent decline would be gradual rather than abrupt.

By 1850 a new sector of Upper Canada's forest exports had been established, the trade in planks and boards to the United States, which was oriented particularly to the Albany market (tables 12.2 and 12.3). From about $500,000 in 1850, such exports rose quickly past $2 million during the early and middle 1850s; by 1870–1 they totalled almost $5 million. And as we noted, exports also went to the United States from the Ottawa valley via Lower Canada. In that the export values shown in table 12.2 are between half (1854, 1868–9) and three-quarters (1853, 1858) of the total value of Canadian exports recorded by McInnis for the same years, it is clear that Upper Canada produced a substantial majority of total Canadian exports. At least thirty ports in the province participated in those exports in 1865–6. Most of the planks and boards were pine, produced in the region north of Lake Ontario from Simcoe County to the Ottawa River. In 1865–6, however, almost one-third of lumber exports came from west of Toronto (table 12.5). Similarly, 30 per cent of the value of sawmill output in the province in 1870 was produced in the region southwest of a line from Toronto to Bruce

County.[40] For the years included in table 12.2, exports of planks and boards represented from 13 to 29 per cent by value of all exports from Upper Canadian ports. Almost 200 million board feet were shipped in 1853, and shipments exceeded 300 million in 1858 and again after the mid-1860s; subsequently they surged to over 500 million feet by 1870–1 (table 12.3).

To assess the relative scale of the principal forest products, it is desirable to compare lumber to square timber. Because of the loss of wood in sawing, 12 board feet were not necessarily the equivalent of 1 cubic foot.[41] Timber-making also entailed a wastage of wood, and many more trees were appropriate for sawing than squaring. For simplicity, the conversion rate used by Grant Head, 10 board feet equals 1 cubic foot, will serve our purposes; at that rate, the lumber shipments recorded in table 12.3 would in 1858 have represented about 34 million cubic feet, in 1863 about 22 million, and in 1870–1 over 50 million. These figures suggest that in peak years for square timber, such as 1862–3, half or more of Upper Canada's forest exports in total volume may still have left as square timber for the British market. In the forest industry the mid-century is often seen as an era of transition from timber to lumber, but it is more accurate to see the two decades as a time when lumber was added to, but scarcely replaced, timber exports.

There were over 1,800 saw mills in the province in 1871, and the value of saw mill outputs exceeded $100,000 in over one-third of the province's census districts in 1870. If a higher threshold is set, say $400,000, just four districts appear as principal producers of sawn lumber, responsible for one-quarter of total provincial output: Simcoe North, Hastings West, Prescott County, and the City of Ottawa.[42] These were the sites of major saw mills with much larger capacity than had been usual prior to 1850. They were among the largest and most impressive industries in the province, and their conveyors for logs and boards and larger and more complex gangs of saws represented as sophisticated an approach to continuous processing as in any industry in the province.

The export value of Canadian planks and boards was $9.75 per thousand board feet in 1870, $10.07 in 1871, and averaged almost exactly $10 over the entire decade from 1863 to 1872.[43] That $10 figure is convenient for the conversion of census data on values to volumes. Thus the total 1870 output, valued at $12.7 million, would have equalled 1,270 million board feet. With output worth $2.2 million, the mills in Ottawa and at Hawkesbury, in Prescott County, accounted for about 220 million feet. That can be added to the 509 million feet of exports shown for 1870–1 in table 12.3 to yield a reasonable estimate of total provincial exports of sawn lumber in 1870–1. If so, the province's internal lumber market amounted to as much as 500 million feet, a volume equalling the direct exports.

There were four or five establishments at Ottawa capable of producing 30 million board feet or more a year, and several reported such outputs in the 1871 census. As early as the 1850s, at favourable locations, there were mills with annual capacities of 6 million feet or more. Just twenty-four mills like those at Ottawa and the Hamilton Brothers establishment at Hawkesbury could have produced all the 1870–1 exports; so could just 120 mills with 6 million feet of capacity. Clearly, although smaller mills participated in the export trade, most of the saw mills in Upper Canada existed primarily to serve the domestic market. If exports are assumed, arbitrarily, to have come from the leading 10 per cent of the mills, the average annual output of the remainder would have been in the order of 300,000 feet per mill, with much variation around that mean. Serving local markets evidently continued to seem remunerative to owners of these mills (see also tables 6.1 to 6.3).

Although Ottawa was an exception, export-oriented sawmilling was not generally an industry that fostered sustained local urban growth. Exports were important to the economies of areas such as Simcoe North, Renfrew, and the forested regions on the Trent watershed, but because the costs of getting logs to the mill tended to rise as the prime forest frontier gradually receded, the industry was ultimately impermanent. The leading saw mills were relatively significant capital investments, reported by their owners as worth $100,000 or more. As they aged or supply receded, however, they were quite readily moved or abandoned. Some of the leading mills were American-owned; some of their owners accompanied their capital to Canada and settled permanently, while others remained in the United States and could shift their main production farther westward as new regions opened in the United States.[44]

It is important, however, not to exaggerate the transitory nature of the trade or the speed of forest exhaustion. Employment in sawmilling actually grew in many counties in southern Ontario in the second half of the nineteenth century; except for the replacement of Prescott by Renfrew in the interval, the leading counties by employment in 1871 still ranked at the top in 1891.[45] Most mills, including many large ones, evidently were still seasonal operations, whose workers combined sawmilling work with other activities in the rural economy during the course of a year. In a number of areas, French Canadians continued to be an important element in the workforce. Indeed, the industry was one factor attracting francophones to settle in the province, particularly in the Ottawa valley, where agriculture and woods work could be combined to yield a living from what otherwise were unpromising soils. What has been termed the 'système agro-forestier' thus established itself more clearly in Upper Canada too.[46]

Three other exports – potash, staves, and firewood – linked forest and farm.[47] All could represent outputs from specialist woods operations, but also were produced by farmers and rural labourers as part of their annual round of activities. Downriver shipments on the St Lawrence canals in the 1850s suggest that the province's potash trade continued at traditional levels (table 4.2). The 1871 census reported pot and pearl ash output in the province valued at $392,000, and at least one establishment was reported in most districts. Essex, Kent, and Grey were by 1870 among the leading districts, but outputs of over $30,000 were reported in Hastings West and over $20,000 at Kingston.[48]

Like potash, downriver stave shipments persisted at traditional volumes, most such exports coming from above Niagara Falls (table 4.2). Staves were not simply a by-product of the timber industry. If 500,000 staves is taken as a threshold level, fourteen census districts met that standard of output. They included western districts that also produced much squared oak (Essex, Bothwell, Lambton, Norfolk South, and Middlesex West), relatively newly settled areas (Grey North and Simcoe North and South), and well-established, settled districts that produced little or no squared oak (Elgin West, Middlesex East, Wellington Centre, Halton, and Durham West). Total output of staves in the province was 21 million in 1870; after exports are deducted, it is clear that about three-quarters of these staves were for the domestic market. Of course, barrels containing flour and other exports represented further stave exports.

Although coal consumption was beginning to mount in the province,[49] wood was by far the principal source of fuel for heat and for steam engines. The census indicates that the principal regions of cordwood production were in the west and in newly settled areas such as Grey, Huron, and Simcoe. During the 1850s from 150,000 to 200,000 cords of wood were recorded annually as passing down the St Lawrence canals from Upper Canada. Similar quantities, mainly from places in the west, are recorded in trade data for the 1860s (tables 12.3, 12.5), and it is likely that some firewood was still shipped from eastern locations into the Montreal market. But about 4 million of the 4.5 million cords reported as provincial output in 1870 were consumed within the province. If we estimate the domestic market as just the 330,000 people who lived in towns of 1,000 or more, and allow per capita consumption of 3 cords, they would have constituted a market for at least 1 million cords per year. The lowest retail price in Toronto in the 1850s and 1860s was around $2.50 a cord, while exports were valued at $1.80 to $2.20 a cord in the trade statistics. If we value firewood at a minimal $2 a cord, it is evident that the total internal market was at least $2 million a year,[50] a figure equivalent to the value of some 200 million board feet of sawn lumber, or to much more than the value of provincial oak exports in any year. Such comparisons indicate that this was a substantial commercial product from the rural economy, which we might even call a staple if it were exported in such amounts.

## III. *The Urban Economy: Industry and Services*

Between 1851 and 1871 the number of people living in places of 1,000 or more almost tripled, a more rapid rate of growth of urban population than in any subsequent pair of decades before the Second World War. The percentage of total provincial population in urban centres later grew more rapidly, but that was because rural population stopped growing in the 1870s. Although urbanization was already proving to be a selective process, the widespread character of the urban development at mid-century is in many ways more striking. Ottawa's population almost tripled in the two decades, but the two leading cities, Toronto and Hamilton, did not even double; and Kingston, which grew only modestly, fell from the third to the fifth largest city. The share of population living in the five largest urban centres, which were the only ones with over 10,000 people in 1871, increased only from 7.5 per cent to 8.2 per cent in the twenty years. Toronto, Hamilton, Ottawa, and London accounted for 7.4 per cent of provincial population in 1871, up from 6.3 per cent in 1851. Toronto's share rose only from 3.2 to 3.5 per cent. In the 1850s Toronto and Hamilton grew no more rapidly than total provincial population, and their share of provincial population grew in the 1860s primarily because total population grew even more slowly; Toronto in fact grew at just 2.3 per cent a year for the decade. Nevertheless, because it was already larger, in numerical terms the gap between Toronto and the next largest city, Hamilton, continued to widen (from 17,000 to almost 30,000 in the two decades).

In the second rank of the province's urban hierarchy were seven places with between 5,000 and 10,000 people. Belleville and Brockville, in the east, increased by only about 60 per cent in two decades; in the west, Chatham almost tripled and Guelph more than tripled. Below these cities and towns in the hierarchy were twenty-four towns and villages (including several future industrial cities, such as Windsor, Berlin, and Oshawa) with between 2,500 and 4,999 people, and forty-eight communities with between 1,000 and 2,499. The last group included a number of towns that once had been relatively important in the province, such as Amherstburg, Niagara, Perth, Picton, and Cornwall.[51]

Why did some urban centres, and the entire system of such centres, continue to grow? The most convincing models, such as those of the geographer Allan Pred, suggest ways in which growth was self-sustaining for the most favourably endowed centres. In a cumulative process, their expansion tended continuously to bring at least some local sectors to thresholds that justified further investment in them. In a competitive economy, the leading centres differentiated themselves increasingly from smaller places by the external economies that their greater scale created for enterprises within them. Such a circular, or spiral, path was not open to all centres, however, and the process worked also in reverse. When industries failed, and as market areas for more efficient producers, often in the leading centres, widened, opportunities could shrink in less-well-endowed centres.[52]

We almost automatically associate urbanization with the growth of industry (secondary manufacturing and construction). No less important, however, was the sustained development of the tertiary sector. It has actually tended to grow more rapidly than manufacturing, as measured in terms of the share of the workforce engaged in each.[53] Services, which included transportation and communications, commerce, finance, religion, medicine, education, culture, personal services, and government, were even more likely than manufacturing to be located in urban centres. Urbanization depended in part on the intensification of exchange between town and country, as the latter became increasingly specialized. But because urban centres generated their own growth too, through expanding intra- and inter-urban exchange, they grew substantially faster than the rural economy around them, and continued to grow even at times of outright rural decline. As in the rural economy, the mid-century growth of provincial towns and cities was a process marked by both continuity and change. This can be seen in a necessarily selective overview of aspects of the secondary and tertiary sectors in the period.

Measured by the total value of their output, Ontario's leading industries in 1870 and as late as 1910 were still two of its oldest industries – 'flour and gristmill products' and 'log and lumber products.' They were 'primary' industries, processing natural resources, and were quite strongly rural. They accounted for almost two-thirds by value of 'manufacturing' output in 1870, but less than one-fifth forty years later. In many respects, a better measure of an industry's significance than value of output (a measure incorporating the cost of raw materials, which can be a large part of costs in some industries) is its share of total value-added by manufacturing (here the measure is on the added value given to raw material inputs by the manufacturer). By this measure, 'primary wood' ranked second in 1870 and 'primary food' third; the two accounted for just over one-quarter of industrial value-added in 1870. All but one of the other significant industry groups in the province in 1870 were already part of the industrial economy whose development before the 1850s was discussed in chapter 6. The leading industry in 1870, with almost one-fifth of industrial value-added, was 'secondary iron and steel products.' Following it in importance were leather products, secondary food, clothing, transportation equipment, textiles, secondary wood products, petroleum, and printing and publishing. Within each of these broad categories there could be great change in products, technologies, markets, and location of production, but of these, only petroleum, which grew rapidly during the 1860s, was a recent arrival on the provincial scene.[54]

Because much secondary production was not in what we would now think of as industrial establishments, in chapter 6 we considered the role of a variety of crafts in the provincial economy in and before 1851. Similar data from 1871 suggest something of the mix of continuity and change that marked the period (table 6.8). Despite some changes in the occupational titles, the lists derive from apparently similar economies. In total, the lists include 13 per cent of men over fifteen in 1851 and 14 per cent of those over sixteen in 1871. The disappearance of such 1851 occupations as wagon-makers, millwrights, and machinists helps to suggest the composition of comparatively large new groups in 1871, notably mechanics and foundrymen, and to explain the exceptional intervening growth in numbers of carriage-makers and millers.

Of the nine leading groups in 1851 (those with 1,000 or more workers), all were more numerous in 1871; the ninth-ranked in 1851, cabinet-maker, ranked fifteenth in 1871. Whether mariners should be included in a list of skilled crafts may be questioned; still, the great increase in their numbers during the railway age is striking. Overall, workers in wood, metal, cloth, leather, and stone are well represented on both lists. As before, food-processing, apart from primary milling, was in 1871 represented only by butchers and bakers; most food-processing continued to be done on the farm and in the home, largely by women. The crafts that were part especially of the largest centres' economies included bookbinders, printers, foundrymen, barbers, and more specialized building trades such as plasterers, painters, and bricklayers. At the other extreme, some crafts integral to the rural economy were not oriented to the largest cities. About 8 per cent of blacksmiths and tanners were located in the cities that represented 8 per cent of the population, and weavers, carders, and sawyers were seldom found in the larger centres. As before, the few explicitly women's crafts that were counted were markedly urban.[55]

Except for millers, between 1851 and 1871 the number of carpenters grew faster than any other leading craft. The expansion in their numbers suggests the extent of investment in building in the mid-century years. Much the slowest growing of the larger crafts were shoemakers and coopers, crafts under pressure from new machinery and new organizational developments. In shoemaking, larger establishments based on division of labour, use of machinery, such as sewing-machines and the McKay machine, and externally imposed discipline became a normal mode of production for much of the market. Barrel-making machinery and other attributes of factory organization were coming to coopering in the 1860s and would do so more strongly in the 1870s. On the other hand, numerous small cooper shops persisted in 1871, and many small-scale shoemaking establishments remained for custom work and repair work.

Some other industries also showed aspects of industrialization, as larger production units became more common in clothing,[56] metalworking, and printing and publishing especially. In Toronto in 1871 there were about forty establishments employing fifty or more workers, and almost half of all industrial workers worked in establishments of that size; seventeen of them reported one hundred or more employees each. Of the approximately 10,000 industrial workers, about one-third were women and children. Greg Kealey has gone so far as to argue that 'the major sectors of the Toronto economy in 1871 ... were highly industrialized with large concentrations of workers, extensive mechanization, and an elaborate division of labour.' There was similar evidence of industrial growth and change in Hamilton.[57] Elsewhere, occasional industries, notably the leading saw mills, also ranked as major industrial employers. There were thirty-seven establishments in the province with 150 or more workers in 1870; sixteen were in Toronto and Hamilton, eight were saw mills (four of them in Ottawa), and the remaining thirteen were found in eleven different towns.[58] About 8,400 workers (including 6,300 men) out of an 'industrial labour force' of over 50,000 in the province worked in these largest of establishments.

Industries grew in many towns and cities, not just the principal ones, in a complex and uneven process. In most industries, establishments varied widely in size, measured in terms of output, workforce, and mechanization. These points are illustrated by a comprehensive data base derived from the industrial schedules of the 1871 census manuscripts.[59] Thus, some ninety-two Ontario urban centres had an 'industrial labour force' of one hundred or more workers. Steam engines were now common, but water-power was virtually as widely used to drive machinery. Some 436 urban industrial establishments in 1870 reported using 25 or more horsepower; 49 per cent were steam-powered, 45 per cent water-powered, and 5 per cent used both water and steam. The leading Ottawa saw mills were water-powered; indeed in 1870, of the thirty 'largest industrial users of steam and water power in Ontario urban centres' (those using 120 horsepower or more) only seven used steam. They were four saw mills, the leading rolling mills in Toronto and Hamilton, and a salt works. Twelve of the largest water-powered establishments were along the Ottawa or along the Welland Canal in the St Catharines area; the other eleven, seven of which were flour mills, were in eleven different urban centres.

In total, the thirty-three urban flour mills in the province with output valued at $100,000 or more in 1870 were located in twenty-four different urban centres. The twenty-six breweries in the province with output worth more than $10,000 were located in just twelve centres (and associated suburbs), and five different places had more than one such brewery. No brewery or flour mill reported as many as fifty employees, and only four had more than twenty workers. Furniture and cabinet-making were more widely diffused; the leading thirty-four establishments, with output of $10,000 or more, were located in twenty-five different towns and cities. Only four employed more than fifty men, women, and children; only five had output valued at over $50,000; on the other hand, these accounted for two-thirds of the thirty-four firms' total output and about three-fifths of all workers. The thirty-four companies identifying themselves as agricultural implement makers and having output of $20,000 or more were located in twenty-five different towns and cities; the ten largest, with output valued at $60,000 or more, all employed fifty or more workers and accounted for almost two-thirds of the output and workforce. The leading firms were located in eight different towns and cities. In both flour-milling and implement-making, moreover, a significant minority of the largest establishments were located outside any defined urban area, albeit near one in most cases. Just in the selected industries reviewed here, almost sixty different villages, towns, and cities are represented.

Changes in work processes were likewise uneven, subtle, and modulated. Even in Toronto and Hamilton only a minority of the workforce was employed in industry, and not all of them worked in factory-like conditions. Though the issue is complex, it seems likely that only a minority secured relatively continuous year-round employment in a single establishment. If a few crafts were under pressure, none had been swept away. Indeed, in trades such as metalworking and printing, skilled workers gained or retained control of basic work processes (if not of the businesses themselves) even as these changed. And new crafts were being defined as industrialization and technological change continued. Except in a few large-scale establishments, most carpenters continued to work in small groups or alone in a quite decentralized manner.[60] Most industries continued to be owned by individuals and partnerships, and managed by their owners. Strikes, the nine-hour movement, and the subsequent growth of the Knights of Labor make it clear, however, that workers from many sectors sought greater control of their lives, were aware of collective interests, and felt threatened by economic changes around them.[61]

The mid-century transition was closely tied to technological developments elsewhere in the industrial world. We have already seen that new reaping technology was quickly adopted. Other examples include the sewing-machine, which was the basis of industrialization of both shoemaking and clothing manufacture. Moreover, enterprising Americans began to manufacture such machines in the province for local sale and exports, as a way of bypassing American patent pools. In 1870 R.M. Wanzer's factory in Hamilton, with 275 employees (193 men), was the seventh-largest industrial employer in the province.[62] Newspapers continued to acquire new equipment as it was developed and their markets allowed.[63] Like the adjoining states of the old Northwest, the province in most sectors was in step with wider technological change, not a lagging follower.[64]

To varying degrees, provincial industries faced competition from outside the province, but the character and extent of such competition has not been fully studied.[65] Calls for tariff protection, both during the depression of 1857–9 and in the 1870s, suggest where pressure was felt. While the rhetoric of campaigns for protection was aimed at outsiders, much of the competition actually putting pressure on businessmen must have been from within the provincial economy. That is one reason why the eventual imposition of a protective tariff could not save all Canadian producers and did not check ongoing processes of localization and concentration in many industries.[66]

In some respects, as we saw in chapter 11, communications changed more than any other sector of the provincial economy in the mid-century period. Of the eighty-four urban centres of more than 1,000 in 1871, only thirteen were not on a rail line by 1860 (and still awaited such connections in 1870). Eight of these were on the northern fringe of the province's settled area (Pembroke, Orillia, Owen Sound) or in the large tract of land between the Northern, the Grand Trunk, and the Buffalo and Lake Huron (Kincardine, Mount Forest, Fergus, Orangeville, Elora). In longer-settled regions, only Amherstburg, Simcoe, Picton, and Hawkesbury had yet to join the rail network. They and many smaller places were, however, closely connected to each other and the wider world by the telegraph, including the transatlantic cable. In 1870 the Montreal Telegraph Company, the leading company, listed more than three hundred communities in the province with one or more stations. The network included many of the small Lake Erie lumber ports, most of the growing towns in the region between the Northern and the Buffalo and Lake Huron railways, various communities inland from Lake Ontario, and most centres along the Ottawa.[67]

The newspaper was both an industry and a form of communication. The number of printers in the province quadrupled in the years from 1851 to 1871 (table 6.8). Almost half these men lived in the five leading cities, where seventeen of the twenty-four daily newspapers in the province in 1871 were published.[68] The *Globe* was the first to succeed as a daily, in 1853, and others soon followed. By 1871 only Brockville, Chatham, and Brantford of the towns of over 5,000 people lacked a daily; and by 1876 only Chatham did. About thirty-five newspapers had been published in 1841, in seventeen centres (table 6.11). In addition to ten dailies, there were about 130 weeklies in the province in 1857, published in seventy-five different places; by 1871, not counting extra editions of the dailies, published for their rural audience, there were about two hundred, in over 110 places. Not counting suburbs, like Yorkville, only about ten villages and towns of 1,000 to 2,499 people did not have even a weekly newspaper in 1871. Published lists of newspaper titles, editors, owners, and publishers suggest that there was much turnover in this sector. On the other hand, of 166 newspapers established by 1871 and still being published in 1876, ten had been founded before 1840, sixty before 1857, and about half before 1862.[69]

The 1857–8 crisis crippled all three principal Upper Canadian banks, the Gore Bank, Commercial Bank, and Bank of Upper Canada. They survived, but encumbered with uncollectable assets, and they could not meet their payments or sustain customer confidence when the next crisis arrived in 1866–7. Their passing cut a visible institutional link to earlier times, but helped to make the next few years exceptionally propitious for the establishment of new banks in Ontario and elsewhere in Canada. By 1874 the number of chartered banks in Canada would reach its all-time peak.[70] The principal surviving banks in 1871 were the Bank of Montreal, which had twenty-three branches and agencies in the province, and Montreal's Merchants' Bank, with twenty-four branches and agencies. Of the other four externally controlled banks, only the Bank of British North America (six branches and agencies) was widely established. They could not prevent the emergence of new banks controlled within Ontario, however. In 1871 the Canadian Bank of Commerce, the Bank of Toronto, and the Ontario Bank were the principal local banks, though the Dominion was about to join them, and others such as the Imperial, the Bank of Hamilton, and the Bank of Ottawa would soon follow. No local bank was all that widely established in the province in 1871. The Bank of Toronto, with two of its three branches outside Toronto in Cobourg and Port Hope, and the Ontario Bank, headquartered in Bowmanville and with five of its six branches and agencies in the same area, both focused in a small region east of Toronto. So far, the Commerce had eleven offices outside Toronto, of which only one was in the same region (in Peterborough).[71]

In 1851 some thirty-two communities had bank branches or agencies, and eighteen were served by more than one chartered bank. By 1857 the number of towns served had grown to forty-two, of which twenty-three (including sixteen of the eighteen from 1851) had two or more branches or agencies.[72] In the next ten years, four provincial banks disappeared (the Zimmerman Bank in 1857 and the others in 1866–7). Nevertheless, in 1871, at least forty-five towns were served, twenty-four of them with two or more establishments. In the intervening period, nine communities, including Niagara, Chippawa, Port Stanley, Paris, and Dundas, which had been more prominent earlier in the province's development, lost banks, while twelve acquired branches or agencies. The latter included towns in the newer area in the northwest of the province (Orangeville, Elora, Walkerton, Fergus), several on the Grand Trunk main line (Oshawa, Napanee, and Brampton), and two in the Ottawa valley (Pembroke and Almonte). The principal centres remained the same through the two decades; all of the twelve largest towns and cities in 1871 had had two or more banks even in 1851, and all but Brockville still did in 1871. Kingston had three, Ottawa, Hamilton, and London had five, and Toronto had nine. Further down the urban hierarchy, there was more volatility. Ten of the thirty-eight towns and cities with a bank branch or agency in 1851 did not have one in 1871; including Brockville, five places with two or more banks represented locally in 1851 had been reduced to a single bank by 1871. Still, only five of the thirty-six towns and cities larger than 2,500 people lacked a chartered bank of any kind in 1871, and fourteen smaller places had a branch or agency. Being or becoming 'bankless' did not cut a community off from credit and might even create scope for a local private bank to operate; nevertheless, it was a sign of a town's economic weakness and it might perpetuate such marginal status by reducing at least some people's access to the provincial financial system.[73]

By 1870 changes in transportation and communications, institutional developments in business structure and organization, and technological developments in production had only begun to make possible more substantial economies of scale in a growing number of industries; nevertheless, such changes were at least implicit in the provincial economy. The largest cities already diverged in the scale and complexity of their economies from smaller towns. The largest industrial establishments dwarfed smaller establishments. The principal daily newspapers were quite different enterprises from the weeklies. Railways, the most advanced contemporary form of capitalism, coexisted in the transport system with individually owned schooners of a scale familiar half a century before. Leading chartered banks were powerful, multi-branch, potentially long-lived institutions in a world where nearly all businesses were single-establishment and owner-operated enterprises. Other financial enterprises, such as insurance and mortgage companies, were beginning to grow into a major sector of the economy. The next two decades would make the implications of new communications and changing technology much clearer, and the dichotomies between the 'core' or 'centre' of the economy and its more marginal elements would be much wider.[74] Yet it would be inappropriate to overstress such contrasts in 1870. For example, Timothy Eaton had just moved from being a small country retailer to being a small city one; it would be the next quarter-century that turned his establishment into something unlike any merchant's operation in Canada in 1870.

# 13 Conclusion

Across the mid-century, the rural economy was affected by at least three 'political' developments: the Reciprocity Treaty with the United States, which was in effect for the twelve years from 1855 to 1866; the Crimean War, from 1854 to 1856; and the American Civil War, which ran its long course from 1861 to 1865. All three are sometimes used to explain the changes going on in mid-century Canada, but such phrasing is essentially misleading. As the entries for 1853 in tables 12.2 and 12.3 suggest, the principal trends in exports, including the development of Canadian exports to the United States of wheat and flour, planks and boards, and animals and their products, had their beginnings *before* reciprocity came into effect. The rise in wheat prices that is often associated with the Crimean War began earlier and had other causes as well (table C.2 and chapter 11). Similarly, by 1860, before the Civil War, the province's range of exports to the United States had broadened further. Even the peak in exports in 1865–6 relates not only to the war and to the imminent end of reciprocity, but also to more general economic fluctuations. After the Civil War and the end of reciprocity, volumes of many Canadian exports to the United States, including barley, butter, planks and boards, and wool, continued to grow. In 1870–1, for example, values of all were much higher than in 1863.

Moreover, some of the increased Canadian-American trade under reciprocity represented subtler kinds of exchange, what Officer and Smith term trades of 'convenience,' in which commodities passed both ways across the border, reflecting quite local supply arrangements and quite fine differentiations in quality within a single commodity.[1] Those sorts of trade, or the export of, say, horses, were important to those who participated in them – and to the arguments of this book on market responsiveness and the diversity of rural production; but they are likely to have had relatively marginal rather than large net effects on the overall scale of the provincial economy.

The swift establishment of new Ontario banks after 1867 filled the gap left by the demise of three major banks, but it also reflected the sustained expansion of the provincial economy. Provincial railway traffic and revenues, an indicator of larger trends in the economy, grew quite steadily through the 1860s, rather than being concentrated in the Civil War years. In short, the financial and even the industrial development of the province was under way prior to the Civil War, on lines that would continue afterwards.[2] As for Confederation in 1867, it clearly had economic causes and consequences, but patterns of actual interprovincial exchange in 1870 had not yet been much altered.

This is not to argue that none of the large political events that often frame discussion of the period had economic significance. Rather, their impact was subtle, not determining, and they were just a part of the environment in which the investment, production, and consumption decisions of Upper Canadians were made. When we single out political events that were beyond Canadian control as a way of naming an economic era, we convey an image of profound vulnerability and dependence, and we risk concealing from ourselves that the process of economic growth was deeply rooted and quite pervasive within the provincial economy.

There were, of course, major external influences on the economy. Between 1851 and 1871 the most significant of these was probably the impact of railway technology and capital. The wider trade cycle was also critical; in this regard, it should be noted that among the years included in tables 12.2 and 12.3 are 1858, a year of depression, and 1868–9, which came just after the next of the major cyclical crises of the century.

By comparison with 1851, the provincial economy was quite different and much more complex twenty years later. A larger minority of the population relied for its living primarily on wages, though still within the context of a household economy that, even in urban areas, retained markedly informal elements. Demographic adjustments reflecting fundamental changes in family lives and strategies were under way. Net emigration had become a fundamental element in the economy, as more left than arrived, mainly headed to the United States. Although the economy retained a substantial orientation towards Britain, the United States in a host of ways was now the more prominent external factor in the frame of reference that defined what kind of economy Ontario would have.

But if the economy of 1851 is compared to that of 1831, a strong case for profound change could also be made. In fact, we misrepresent the character of provincial growth if we single out ten or twenty years in a more-or-less continuous development process extending over more than eighty years (and still in process in 1871). The Ontario of 1871 was not suddenly produced. In the language and technique of film, we can better capture the essence of its development not in cuts – sudden and dramatic transitions – but in fades. Or we can think in terms of layers, new ones being added to, more than driving out, the old. Change was modulated, balanced, and cumulative. It is appropriate here to reiterate for the mid-century decades the argument that has run throughout this book. Technological change, developments in the forest economy, the increase in exports of farm produce other than wheat, the end of extensive growth, and the growth of towns and cities were simultaneous, mutually interconnected, reciprocal processes. The clarity that comes of having a unique prime mover, 'the staple,' in the model of growth that we employ is achieved only at an unreasonable level of abstraction. There is actually no reason to see any one of these forces as the unique, fundamental cause for developments in all others. Thus, the province would have secured railways and the telegraph, daily newspapers, and machine-made shoes, to name some examples from the mid-century, even if volumes of wheat or sawn lumber exported had been, say, just half what they actually were.

Although continuity was only part of the story, the rural economy of 1870 bore some resemblance to the economy of twenty, forty, and even more years before. In 1871 there were farms that had been in existence for the entire period; elsewhere, notably in Grey and Bruce counties, new farms were still being established. In wheat-growing areas a share of the land that was roughly equivalent to that in 1800 was still dedicated to wheat, and farmers everywhere continued to grow at least some wheat. All of that economy's traditional exports continued to be produced and exported, including pork, potash, barrel staves, and square pine, oak, and elm timber. And all of the province's exports, including its newest ones of petroleum and minerals, were produced primarily within the rural economy.

Throughout the rural economy saw and grist mills manufactured local produce for local markets. Many other products of the rural economy, such as animals, dairy products, and firewood, now appeared more clearly in the official statistics of external trade and in the census, but we have seen that they had always been produced and marketed in substantial quantities.

The prosperous farmsteads that appeared in the handsome county atlases of the 1870s were far removed from pioneers' log cabins and clearings. They represented the outcome of a process of exchange and investment that over the previous three-quarters of a century had turned what was, to Europeans, a frontier into a prosperous, settled, increasingly sophisticated agricultural economy. The partial regional specialization that began to appear even early in the province's economic history was clearly visible; wheat was of particular importance in the core of the province, but established farms there grew and marketed much more. In the west, which included one of the very first settlement nodes in the province, Essex County, forest products continued to be important local outputs, as was also true along much of the Lake Erie shore.[3] From Cobourg eastward, the forest economy and a growing commercial dairy economy were more evident. Along the Ottawa, pine remained the principal export, increasingly in sawn form as well as in square timber. Yet everywhere the rural economy involved wheat, cattle, and forest products; specialization was nuanced, not absolute. The essence of the rural economy was its balance, not its specialization.[4] Constrained by climate and soil, and influenced by family values and expectations about markets, farm households had many choices to make in allocating time and resources. Although we tend to think of the province as re-source-rich, much the largest part of provincial output relied on the efforts and skills of farmers, workers, entrepreneurs, and others – and their families – rather than simple extraction of resources. The farms and the growing urban economy of the province reflected the human capital of institutions and expertise at least as much as the basic environment of soils, climate, forest, and water. If the provincial economy must be summarized in terms of a single, pre-eminent product, the farms themselves were its chief accomplishment.

# Appendix A: A Note on Values, Currency, and Rates of Exchange

The colonial monetary system expressed values in a number of ways.[1] Except during the War of 1812, when the Lower Canadian Assembly authorized the issuing of army bills, no government issued notes or coins in Upper Canada until late 1858, when official Canadian coins were first issued. Earlier, a wide variety of coins, initially mainly French and Spanish and later British and American, circulated. Notes of local chartered banks became an important part of Upper Canada's money in the 1820s.

By the time settlement began in Upper Canada, the established monetary system in British North America was based on the Halifax standard (abbreviated Hfx cy, or sometimes just cy), which rated the Spanish dollar at 5 shillings. This was a money of account – that is, a standard in which accounts were kept, and a measure by which the various coins in circulation were valued and related to one another. Confusingly, many Upper Canadians, even including some officials in earlier years, ignored this rate in favour of the New York standard (abbreviated NY cy, or sometimes York cy), which rated the Spanish dollar at 8 shillings. In the 1850s the Province of Canada officially adopted the decimal system, based on the dollar; it was increasingly accepted after 1858, when public accounts began to be kept and published in this form.

Accounts in New France had used *livres françaises 'ancien cours,'* which in turn were related to the system in Paris, *livres tournois*, nine of the latter being equivalent to ten of the former. Long after the Conquest, many Lower Canadians continued to express their accounts in *livres*. Published data from Lower Canada sometimes did so too. In Halifax currency, 24 *livres ancien cours* (or *livres courantes françaises*) were equal to £1.[2] Occasionally in this volume, where indicated, it has been necessary to relate Lower and Upper Canadian prices directly. But the persistence of the older system, which reflected the customary as well as statutory elements in colonial monetary practice, is significant in itself.[3]

The relationship between colonial money and the British system, based on sterling (abbreviated stg), fluctuated around a par value in accordance with supply and demand. Until 1858 the nominal par was £9 stg = £10 Hfx cy (i.e., in sterling the Spanish dollar was rated at 4s 6d). In 1858 a new par was recognized; but the rate, in which the dollar was about 4s 2d stg, had actually been near the real par since 1821 (see chapters 3 and 10). During and after the American Civil War, American paper money ('greenbacks') depreciated in terms of sterling and Canadian currency.[4]

The elements in the various currencies and their principal relationships and rates of exchange were as follows:

*Fixed relationships*
£1 (in all currencies) = 20 shillings (s) = 240 pence (d)
1 *livre* = 20 *sols* (*sous*) = 240 *deniers* (d)
$1.00 = 100 cents
£1 Halifax Currency = $4.00
£1 New York (or York) currency = $2.50
£1 Halifax Currency = 24 *livres françaises ancien cours*
⠀⠀⠀⠀⠀⠀⠀⠀⠀⠀⠀⠀(or *livres courantes françaises*)

*Fluctuating relationships*
£1 sterling = *c*. £1.111 Halifax currency (to 1820)
£1 sterling = *c*. £1.217 Halifax currency (from 1820)
£1 sterling = *c*. $4.8667 (from 1858)

Knowing these relationships is helpful, but does not always permit unambiguous conversion of values. For example, it may not be clear if a recorded value already represented a conversion from another system, and, if so, what rate was employed. Which was the original currency may not be known at all. Official documents may not make clear whether conversions between sterling and colonial values, especially in the period between 1820 and 1857, were made at the official par rate (9:10) or at the actual rate. *Blue Books,* for example, appear to have used the official rate, not the one that actually prevailed in the market.[5] Private records often mixed systems; fortunately, it is usually possible to establish whether New York, Halifax, or sterling was meant by noting references to dollars.[6]

In the tables that follow and in the text, Halifax currency is usually employed. Conversions and exchange rates when originals used other standards are indicated in notes to individual tables. Sterling or New

York currency is indicated by appending stg or NY cy to the value. Some data are presented in dollars after 1850. As the discussion in chapter 12 notes, it would be tedious and inappropriate to convert all such material to Halifax currency, especially as many primary and most secondary sources for the era express values in dollars.

The actual money in circulation in the province, what merchants and others evidently meant by 'cash,' consisted of bank notes and a wide variety of coins, mainly silver.[7] Notes were denominated in dollars and often in Halifax cy too. Values of common coins were fixed by statutes, which, as Angela Redish has shown, tended to undervalue coins of the highest quality.[8] Hence the circulating medium tended to be old, worn, or clipped coins. Upper Canadians complained, but evidently misunderstood why coins of higher quality disappeared when they were put in circulation. In 1866, under authority of that year's Provincial Notes Act, the government of Canada began to issue its own notes, but by comparison with the notes of chartered banks, these were a modest part of the provincial (and later dominion) money supply.[9]

# Appendix B: Statistical Tables

TABLE 1.1
Population and Land under Culture,* Upper Canada, 1785–1871 (selected years)

| Year | Population (000s) | Acres under culture (000s) | Acres per person |
|------|-------------------|----------------------------|------------------|
| 1785 | 6     |       |     |
| 1791 | 14    |       |     |
| 1796 | 25    |       |     |
| 1805 | 46    | 179   | 3.9 |
| 1811 | 60    |       |     |
| 1817 | 83    | 325   | 3.9 |
| 1821 | 118   | 422   | 3.7 |
| 1826 | 166   | 620   | 3.7 |
| 1831 | 237   | 818   | 3.5 |
| 1836 | 374   | 1,284 | 3.4 |
| 1842 | 487   | 1,752 | 3.6 |
| 1848 | 726   | 2,547 | 3.5 |
| 1851 | 952   | 3,706 | 3.9 |
| 1861 | 1,396 | 6,052 | 4.3 |
| 1871 | 1,621 | 8,834 | 5.4 |

SOURCES: From 1826, Canada, *Census*, 1871, vol. 4. Earlier data involve estimation; see my 'The "Loyalist" Economy of Upper Canada, 1784–1806,' *HS/SH* 16 (1983), 279–304; and J.D. Wood, 'Population Growth on an Agricultural Frontier: Upper Canada 1796 to 1841,' in Roger Hall, William Westfall, and Laurel Sefton MacDowell, eds., *Patterns of the Past* (Toronto 1988), 55–77.

* Until at least 1817, and possibly until the 1840s, this is population of European ancestry only; from 7,000 to 10,000 Indians should be added.

TABLE 2.1
Population of Upper Canada, by District, 1805–6

| District | Approximate population | Percentage of the total |
|---|---|---|
| Eastern | 7,500[1] | 16 |
| Johnstown | 4,900 | 11 |
| Midland | 8,200 | 18 |
| Newcastle | 2,000 | 4 |
| Home | 3,800 | 8 |
| Niagara | 11,000[2] | 24 |
| London | 5,300 | 12 |
| Western | 3,200 | 7 |
| Total | 45,900 | 100 |

[1] Average of estimated population of 6,500 to 8,500 based on 1816 population discounted by assumed annual growth rates of 3.5 to 6.5 per cent.
[2] Average of population range estimated from 10,000 to 12,000. Population of the district was estimated at 6,000 in the mid-1790s and this estimate for 1805–6 represents an annual growth rate of 7 per cent over 8 to 10 years; see Bruce Wilson, *The Enterprises of Robert Hamilton* (Ottawa 1983), 6.

SOURCES: NA, Upper Canada Population and Assessment Returns, RG5, B26, 1, 6, 10, 771, 774, 776, 779–80, 784; MG11, CO42, vol. 347, 189–90 (Midland District); AO, F.P. Smith Papers, MU 2831, pkg 23 (Johnstown District)

TABLE 2.2
Annual Expenditures by British Government in Upper Canada, *c.* 1795 to *c.* 1805

| Item | Estimated expense | |
|---|---|---|
| | Minimum | Maximum |
| Half–pay | £ 6,000[1] | £ 10,000 |
| Army provisions (mainly pork and flour) | 5,000 | 8,000 |
| Salaries, Indian Department | 3,000 | 3,000 |
| British parliamentary grant, for civil administration | 7,000 | 8,000 |
| Estimated overrun[2] beyond parliamentary grant | 3,000 | 5,000 |
| Garrison-related expenditures[3] within Upper Canada | 25,000 | 35,000 |
| Total, in £ stg | 49,000 | 69,000 |
| Approximate total in £ cy[4] | 54,000 | 77,000 |

[1] Higher figure applies to earlier, lower to later years.
[2] The existence of this category of expenditure is easier to demonstrate than the total amount.
[3] Based on average garrison of 1,000 in this period and estimated expenditure of £25 to £35 per man
[4] Conversion at official rate of £1.111 cy = £1 stg

SOURCES: See text, especially ch. 2, notes 26 to 33.

TABLE 2.3
Exports of Upper Canadian Produce to Lower Canada, Selected Data, 1794–1803

| | Exporting area | | | | | | |
|---|---|---|---|---|---|---|---|
| | Midland District[1] | UC from Midland District west | | | | All UC, est. vol. | All UC, est. value[2] |
| Item | 1794 | 1800 | 1801 | 1802 | 1803[3] | 1797 | 1801 |
| Wheat & flour | | | | | | | |
| Value[2] | 3,100 | 8,400 | 24,400 | | 18,000 | | |
| Volume | 3,500 | 4,700 | 14,000 | 11,400[4] | 16,200 | | |
| Pork | | | | | | | |
| Value[2] | 0 | | | | 6,200 | | |
| Volume | 0 | | | 200 | 1,500 | | |
| Potash | | | | | | | |
| Value[2] | 300 | 2,100 | 2,200 | | 2,000 | | |
| Volume | 68 | 430 | 500 | 800 | 530 | 670[5] | |
| Staves & timber | | | | | | | |
| Value[2] | | 1,000 | | | | | 15,600 |
| Quantity | | | | | | 400,000 | |
| Total value | £3,400 | £12,100 | £27,900 | | £26,200 | | £46,700[6] |

NOTES: Exports are exclusive of furs. Volumes are in barrels (wheat converted to flour at 5 bu = 1 bbl). Rows may not add because of omission of some minor export items. Where no value or volume is given, data are not available.

[1] The only district for which data are available for 1794; it included the province's leading town, Kingston.

[2] Values are in Hfx cy. 1801 UC estimate converted from £ stg, at official rate of £1 stg = £1.111 cy

[3] Values estimated on basis of volumes, at current prices; for price levels in 1803 see MTL, John McGill papers, vol. B-40, receipts, 25, 27 Jan. 1804.

[4] Cartwright estimated that a further 4,000 barrels were exported from the Eastern and Johnstown districts.

[5] Volume was 150 tons; converted to barrels at rate of 4.5 bbl = 1 ton.

[6] Furs from east of Detroit represented an additional export value of £40,000 in 1801.

SOURCES: For 1794 from E.A. Cruikshank, ed., *The Correspondence of Lieut. Governor John Graves Simcoe*, vol. 3 (Toronto 1925), 223, Richard Cartwright Jr to Simcoe, 15 Dec. 1794; 1797 from C.E. Cartwright, ed., *The Life and Letters of the Late Hon. Richard Cartwright* (Toronto 1876), 76, Cartwright to Davison & Co., 4 Nov. 1797; for 1800–3 from AO, Cartwright letterbooks, 1787-1808, MU 500 (transcripts), 137–8, 150–1, 181–2, 206–8, 229–30

TABLE 2.4
Wheat Output in Upper Canada, 1803 (estimated)

| Item | Number of bushels | Percentage of total output[1] |
|---|---|---|
| Seed requirements[2] | 102,000 | 20 |
| Civilian consumption[3] | 234,000 | 46 |
| Army purchases[4] | 14,000 | 3 |
| Wheat distilled[4] | 80,000 | 16 |
| Wheat exported[4] | 81,000 | 16 |
| Total | 511,000 | |

[1]   Column adds to 101 because of rounding.
[2]   Yield ratio of seed estimated at 1:5; see T.J.A. LeGoff, 'The Agricultural Crisis in Lower Canada, 1802–12: A Review of a Controversy,' CHR 55 (1974), 17–26, which suggests a ratio between 1:5 and 1:6.
[3]   Calculated on basis of 35 bushels per household. Population in 1803 assumed to be 40,000 and household size assumed to be 6. Standard army civilian rations were $2/3$ lb of flour per person per day (= $6^{1}/4$ bushels of wheat per person per year); at this ration, civilian consumption would have been 250,000 bushels, and seed requirements would have been slightly higher. For rations, see AO, Miscellaneous Collection, 1783, item 3, Haldimand Papers photostats, estimates of Loyalist provisions in 1783–4.
[4]   AO, Cartwright letterbooks, 1787–1808, MU 500 (transcripts), 206–8, 213

TABLE 3.1
Distribution of Upper Canadian Population, by District, 1805–21 (000s)

| District | 1805–6 | 1811 | 1817 | 1821 |
|---|---|---|---|---|
| Eastern | 7.5 | | 12.7 | 13.6 |
| Ottawa* | – | | 1.5 | 1.7 |
| Johnstown | 4.9 | | 9.2 | 17.9 |
| Midland | 8.2 | | 14.9 | 20.3 |
| Newcastle | 2.0 | | 5.0 | 7.0 |
| Home | 3.8 | | 7.7 | 12.8 |
| Niagara | 11.0 | | 12.5 | 13.8 |
| Gore* | – | | 6.7 | 10.3 |
| London | 5.3 | | 8.9 | 14.6 |
| Western | 3.2 | | 4.2 | 6.2 |
| Total | 45.9 | 60.0 ± | 83.3 | 118.2 |

*Implied Annual Percentage Rates of Population Growth*
1805–11   4.5
1805–17   5.0      1811–17   5.6
1805–21   6.1      1811–21   7.0      1817–21   9.2

* Ottawa District created in 1816 from territory formerly in Eastern; Gore District created in 1816 from territory formerly in Niagara and Home Districts

SOURCES
1805–6: from table 2.1
1811: based on estimate of 9,600 households in the province, with average of 6 persons per household
1817: from Robert Gourlay, *Statistical Account of Upper Canada*, S.R. Mealing, ed. (Toronto 1974), 286–93
1821: from NA, Population and Assessment Returns, RG5, B26, vol. 1, 92, 111

TABLE 3.2
Acres of Land under Culture in Upper Canada, 1805–21 (000s)

| District | 1805–6 | 1817 | 1821 |
|---|---|---|---|
| Eastern | [25] | 37 | [44] |
| Ottawa | – | 4 | 5 |
| Johnstown | 22 | 33 | 46 |
| Midland | 43 | [69] | 85 |
| Newcastle | 5 | 17 | 28 |
| Home | 9 | 28 | 40 |
| Niagara | 47 | [52] | [63] |
| Gore | – | 37 | 43 |
| London | [15] | [33] | 47 |
| Western | 13 | 16 | 22 |
| Total | 179 | 326 | 423 |
| Acres/person | 3.9 | 3.9 | 3.7 |

NOTES
Square brackets indicate estimated figures.
1805–6: data from chapter 2
1817: from NA, Population Returns, RG5, B26, vol. 4, 799, 808, 812, 814, 817, 818, 822, 829, 853, 854, 862, 867, 877. Estimates are derived as follows: Eastern interpolated from 1816 and 1819 data; London extrapolated backward from 1821 and 1822 on assumed rate of growth of 9 per cent per year; Midland extrapolated backward from 1821 and 1822 data on assumed rate of growth of 5 per cent per year; Niagara extrapolated backward from 1824 on assumed rate of growth of 5 per cent per year.
1821: from ibid., vol. 1, 106, 113, 118; vol. 4, 829, 843, 848, 851, 853, 854, 869. Eastern District extrapolated from 1819 at rate of 4 per cent per year; Niagara extrapolated from 1824 at rate of 5 per cent per year

TABLE 3.3

The Upper Canadian Wheat Economy, 1803 and 1817 (estimated)

|  | 1803 | 1817 |
|---|---|---|
| A. *Volume* (000 bushels) | | |
| Exports | 81 | 194 |
| Distilled | 80 | 78 |
| Army purchases | 14 | na |
| Civilian consumption | 234 | 483 |
| Seed required | 102 | 189 |
| Total | 511 | 944 |
| B. *Land Required to Produce These Crops* (estimated; 000 acres) | | |
| Acres/year in crop | 34 | 63 |
| Acres in fallow | 34 | 63 |
| Total wheat acreage | 68 | 126 |
| Land under culture | 150 | 326 |
| Share required for wheat (%) | 45 | 39 |

NOTES: For assumptions, see table 2.4; other data from tables 3.1, 3.2, 3.4, 6.7. Distilling capacity in 1817 assumed to be 13,000 gallons, based on 1820 capacity of 13,648 gallons. Strictly speaking, seed figure should be based on amount needed to produce next year's crop; not doing this effectively assumes a slightly higher seed:yield ratio. See also table 5.1.

TABLE 3.4
Upper Canadian Exports to Lower Canada (recorded at Coteau-du-Lac), 1817–22
(all figures 000s)

| Year | Flour (bbl) | Wheat (bu) | Total wheat (bu) | Ashes (bbl) | Pork (bbl) |
|------|------|------|------|------|------|
| 1817 | 39 | – | 195 | 5 | 1 |
| 1818 | 45 | – | 225 | 7 | 1 |
| 1819 | 12 | 2 | 62 | 11 | 1 |
| 1820 | 33 | 1 | 166 | 5 | 2 |
| 1821 | 28 | 13 | 153 | 3 | 2 |
| 1822 | 40 | 10 | 210 | 6 | 2 |

SOURCE: *LCJ*, 1823–4, App. W


TABLE 3.5
Imports of Goods Paying Ad Valorem Duties
at Quebec, 1813–22 (£000 cy)

| | | | |
|------|------|------|------|
| 1813 | 182 | 1818 | 772 |
| 1814 | 1196 | 1819 | 969 |
| 1815 | n/a | 1820 | 675 |
| 1816 | 1556 | 1821 | 536 |
| 1817 | 673 | 1822 | 723 |

SOURCES: *LCJ*, 1823–4, App. W. (Source does not
indicate currency used; Halifax assumed.)


TABLE 3.6
British Emigrants to British North America,
1815–25 (000s)

| | | | |
|------|------|------|------|
| 1815 | 1 | 1821 | 13 |
| 1816 | 3 | 1822 | 16 |
| 1817 | 10 | 1823 | 11 |
| 1818 | 15 | 1824 | 9 |
| 1819 | 24 | 1825 | 9 |
| 1820 | 18 | | |

SOURCES: Helen I. Cowan, *British Emigration to
British North America: The First Hundred Years*,
rev. ed. (Toronto 1961), 288

TABLE 4.1
Canadian Timber Prices, 1825–49

| | Red pine (d/cu ft) | White pine (d/cu ft) | Oak (d/cu ft) | Elm (d/cu ft) | Pine deals (£/std 100) | Potash (s/cwt) | Staves (£/mille) WI | Staves (£/mille) Std. | Pipe | Source |
|---|---|---|---|---|---|---|---|---|---|---|
| 1825 | 8 | 4 | 19 | 7.5 | 8.5 | 30.5 | 14 | 47.75 | | a,g |
| 1826 | 7 | 3.5 | 12.5 | 4 | 7.75 | 26 | | 35.5 | | a,g |
| 1827 | 8* | 2.5* | 11* | 4 | | 24.75* | 12.5* | | 30* | b,g |
| 1828 | 9.25 | 4.25 | 13.5 | | | 28.25* | 11.5 | 30* | 35.75 | b,j |
| 1829 | 8.5* | 3.75* | 13.5 | 7.5 | 8.25 | 32.25* | 9* | 41.5 | 22.5* | b,c |
| 1830 | 7 | 4.75 | 17 | 7 | 8.25 | 30.25* | 11.5* | 35 | | b,c |
| 1831 | 8 | 4.25 | 17 | 7.5 | 11 | 32 | 10.5 | 30.5 | | a |
| 1832 | 7.5 | 4 | 15 | 7.5 | 8 | 28.75* | | 34 | 30* | b,c,d |
| 1833 | 8 | 4.5 | 16 | 7.5 | 9.5 | 24.75* | 12.5 | | | b |
| 1834 | 9 | 4.75 | 16 | 5.5 | 8 | 22.75* | | 47.5 | | b,c,d |
| 1835 | 8 | 4.5 | 14 | 6 | 8 | 32* | | 35 | | c,e |
| 1836 | | 4.75 | | 8* | | 35* | 11* | | | b,c,f |
| 1837 | | | 20* | 7.5* | 7.25* | | 11* | 41 | | c |
| 1838 | | 6 | 15 | 7* | 7.25* | 30* | | | | c,g |
| 1839 | | | 18* | | | | | 45 | | c,h |
| 1840 | | 4 | 18 | 6 | 9.25* | 24.75* | 12.5 | 44 | | b,c,h |
| 1841 | 9 | 5.5 | 16 | 4 | 12.25 | 28* | 13 | 42.5 | | b,i |
| 1842 | | 2.75 | 11 | 7 | 10* | 27.25* | 10.75 | 35 | 37.5 | b,h |
| 1843 | 7.5 | 4.75 | 9.5 | 6 | 12 | 25* | 10.5 | 31 | | a,b |
| 1844 | 9.5 | 5.75 | 15 | 7 | 10.5 | 24* | 12.5 | 37.5 | | a |
| 1845 | 12 | 6.75 | 18 | 12.75 | 11.75 | 23* | 12 | 40 | 42.5 | b |
| 1846 | 11 | 5.25 | 16 | 7.5 | 12 | 21.5* | 11.5 | 37.5 | 38.75 | a,b |
| 1847 | 9.25 | 4.25 | 15 | 8.5 | 12 | 27* | 12.5 | 35 | | a,k |
| 1848 | 8 | 4.25 | 14 | 8.25 | 9.75 | 26.75* | 12.75 | 30 | 33.75 | a,k |
| 1849 | 8 | 4.75 | 14.5 | 8.5 | 9.5 | 26* | 13.25 | 37.5 | 40 | b |

* Indicates price at Montreal; all other prices are at Quebec.  SOURCES: See next page.

SOURCES FOR TABLE 4.1: Prices are derived from summer (June–Aug.) newspaper quotations in Quebec *Mercury* (a) and Montreal *Gazette* (b). Because of gaps in newspaper reports, other sources have been drawn upon as indicated.

c  NA, MG11, CO47, vols. 129–140, *Lower Canada Blue Books*, 1829–40. Actual total export values for Quebec or Montreal divided by volume to yield a price; prices are converted to Halifax currency on the basis of £1.11 cy = £1 stg (the official rate used in the *Blue Books*). Conversion rates for volumes were deals, 100 3-inch pieces = 1 std 100; staves, 1,200 pieces = 1 mille; timber, 1 ton = 40 cu ft.

d  *British Parliamentary Papers*, 1835 (519), xix, Report of the Select Committee on Timber Duties, evidence of James Dowie, qq. 3736–43. Prices are said to be in sterling but those overlapping with other sources are so close to currency prices that I include them as given. Deals converted from St Petersburgh to Quebec standards.

e  Lower Canada, Legislative Council, *Journals*, 1835–6, App. C, evidence of William Price

f  AO, McLachlin Brothers Papers, MU 1957, Agreement between D. & W. McLachlin and Wm. Sharples Son & Co., 6 July 1836

g  NA, Wright Papers, MG24, D8, vol. 98, cashbook, 1825–27, vol. 120, p. 64548, Agreement between Atkinson, Usborne & Co. and P. Wright & Sons, 20 Aug. 1838

h  QUA, Calvin Company Records, vol. 56, Quebec 'Sales Book,' 1841–5; vol. 107, Calvin, Cook & Counter ledger

i  AO, Andrew Russell Papers, MU 2564, R. McIntyre to A. Russell, 4 and 20 July 1841

j  NA, James Hamilton Papers, MG24, D45, 362–3, market circular, Horatio Gates & Co., 1 Sept. 1828

k  *JLA*, 1849, App. Z


NOTES TO TABLE 4.2:

a  1823 figures are for 6 months ending 10 Oct. 1823 (i.e., most of the navigation season).

b  Assume 2.75 cu ft = 1 'piece' (pc).

c  'Timber' data for 1835 largely undifferentiated between oak and pine; data divided on basis of 90% pine (pieces of 70 cu ft), 10% oak (pieces of 34 cu ft).

d  Figures reported for WI staves after 1844 have been converted from milles to pieces by multiplying by 1,200.

e  In 1855 and 1858, ashes converted from tons to barrels at an estimated rate of 1 ton = 4 bbl.

SOURCES

1823: from *LCJ*, 1823–4, App. W

1824: (year ended 10 Oct. 1824) from *LCJ*, 1825, App. AA

1825: (year ended 10 Oct. 1825) from *LCJ*, 1826, App. U

1827–39: from NA, MG11, CO47, vols. 127–39, *Lower Canada Blue Books*, 1827–39 inclusive, data on imports at Coteau-du-Lac. The *Blue Books* provided total volumes, divided by value into Upper Canadian and American components; if average prices were the same for both, Upper Canadian volumes can be calculated. On the problem of valuations at Coteau, see note to table 4.3. Similar data, also said to be from the collector at Coteau, can be found for 1830–2 in *JUC*, 1832–3, App., 101; 1833–4, App., 98, 101; where data in the two differ, I have followed the latter source.

1844–63: from *JLA*, 1844–5, App. K; 1846, App. T; 1847, App. AA; 1856, App. 36 and App. 29, t. 2; 1858, App. 15; 1859, App. 17 and App. 6, t. 2; 1861, SP 15; 1862, SP 11; 1863, SP 6; 1864, SP 5

1866: from Canada, Parliament, *Sessional Papers*, 1867, #6

TABLE 4.2
Volume of Selected Upper Canadian Exports via the St Lawrence, 1823–66

| | Wood products | | | | | | | Leading farm products | | |
|---|---|---|---|---|---|---|---|---|---|---|
| Year | Ashes (000 bbl) | Pine (000 pc) | Deals (000 pc) | Oak (000 pc) | Staves std. (000) | Staves WI (000) | Elm (000 pc) | Flour (000 bbl) | Wheat (000 bu) | Pork (000 bbl) |
| A. 1823–39 | | | | | | | | | | |
| 1823[a] | 5 | 32 | 87 | 9 | 1,518 | 13 | 7 | 39 | 5 | 1 |
| 1824 | 8 | 42 | 137 | 20 | 1,101 | 350 | 1 | 26 | 1 | 1 |
| 1825 | 7 | 29 | 217 | 30 | 852 | 259 | 5 | 34 | 9 | — |
| 1827 | 8 | | | | | | | 94 | 136 | 9 |
| 1828 | 9 | 19 | 142 | 13 | 1,909 | 1,582 | 3 | 78 | 135 | 14 |
| 1829 | 9 | 25 | 134 | 8 | 1,643 | 1,583 | 5 | 42 | 20 | 12 |
| 1830 | 10 | 40 | 185[b] | 9 | 1,534 | 1,383 | 7 | 94 | 280 | 11 |
| 1831 | 11 | 25 | 117 | 6 | 849 | 1,473 | 6 | 99 | 464 | 13 |
| 1832 | 12 | 23 | 215 | 5 | 642 | 833 | 9 | 65 | 303 | 7 |
| 1833 | 10 | 23 | 217 | 6 | 754 | 1,450 | 4 | 113 | 367 | 2 |
| 1834 | 8 | 15 | 196 | 1 | 1,569 | 2,002 | — | 119 | 350 | 1 |
| 1835 | 11 | 28[c] | 304 | 6[c] | 2,457 | 3,580 | 9 | 102 | 39 | 13 |
| 1836 | 9 | 52 | 145 | 5 | 640 | 2,519 | 2 | 173 | 57 | 13 |
| 1837 | 13 | 31 | 120[b] | 16 | 1,107 | 2,495 | 11 | 52 | 6 | 8 |
| 1838 | 12 | 22 | 249[b] | 16 | 1,165 | 3,033 | 3 | 124 | 16 | 6 |
| 1839 | 12 | 20 | 72 | 36 | 995 | 2809 | 3 | 125 | 31 | 9 |
| B. 1844–66 (timber only) | | (000 cu ft) | | (000 cu ft) | | | (000 cu ft) | | | |
| 1844 | n/a | 2,585 | 134 | 671 | 1,064 | 2,711 | 213 | | | |
| 1845 | n/a | 4,612 | 98 | 1,597 | 2,488 | 3,702 | 732 | | | |
| 1846 | n/a | 8,098 | 86 | 2,315 | 1,826 | 1,704[d] | 2,087 | | | |
| 1855 | 12 | 1,846 | 62 | 1,981 | 1,963 | 3,511 | 1,261 | | | |
| 1857 | n/a | 1,844 | 1 | 1,040 | 2,178 | 2,449 | 928 | | | |
| 1858 | 15 | 1,670 | — | 1,553 | 1,860 | 2,231 | 491 | | | |
| 1860 | n/a | 4,780 | — | 979 | 1,404 | 2,510 | 920 | | | |
| 1861 | n/a | 4,759 | 119 | 1,408 | 1,002 | 2,369 | 867 | | | |
| 1862 | n/a | 5,057 | 173 | 2,096 | 1,451 | 2,838 | 1,392 | | | |
| 1863 | n/a | 4,917 | 17 | 1,618 | 1,878 | 5,604 | 2,220 | | | |
| 1866 | n/a | 5,023 | 115 | 1,831 | 1,282 | 1,868 | 936 | | | |

NOTES and SOURCES: See p. 258.

TABLE 4.3
Estimated Value of Principal Upper Canadian Exports, 1825–46 (all figures £000 cy)

| | Via Coteau-du-Lac | | | | | | | | | Upper |
| Year | Ashes | Pine | Deals | Oak | Std staves | WI staves | Elm | Total wood | Total wheat | Ottawa pine |
|------|-------|------|-------|-----|-----------|-----------|-----|-----------|------------|-------------|
| 1825 | 49 | 44 | 16 | 75 | 43 | 4 | 7 | 238 | 44 | n/a |
| 1827 | 45 | n/a | n/a | n/a | n/a | n/a | n/a | n/a | 131 | 28 |
| 1828 | 57 | 24 | [11] | 25 | 48 | 15 | [3] | 183 | 117 | 50 |
| 1829 | 65 | 27 | 11 | 15 | 57 | 12 | 6 | 193 | 69 | 56 |
| 1830 | 68 | 55 | 15 | 22 | 45 | 13 | 7 | 225 | 194 | 89 |
| 1831 | 79 | 31 | 13 | 14 | 22 | 13 | 7 | 179 | 256 | 63* |
| 1832 | 78 | 27 | 17 | 11 | 18 | 8 | 10 | 169 | 157 | 32* |
| 1833 | 56 | 30 | 21 | 14 | 30 | 15 | 3 | 169 | 221 | n/a |
| 1834 | 41 | 21 | 16 | 2 | 52 | 18 | - | 150 | 185 | n/a |
| 1835 | 79 | 37 | 24 | 12 | 72 | 33 | 8 | 265 | 110 | 104 |
| 1836 | 71 | 72 | 12 | 11 | 19 | 23 | 2 | 210 | 238 | 115 |
| 1837 | 97 | 45 | 10 | 45 | 38 | 23 | 12 | 270 | 102 | 133 |
| 1838 | 81 | 39 | 18 | 34 | 42 | 28 | 3 | 245 | 193 | 113 |
| 1839 | 73 | 29 | 5 | 92 | 37 | 26 | 3 | 265 | 191 | 123 |
| 1840 | | | | | | | | | | 152 |
| 1841 | | | | | | | | | | 193 |
| 1843 | | | | | | | | | | 140 |
| 1844 | n/a | 62 | 14 | 23 | 33 | 28 | 6 | 166 | n/a | 303 |
| 1845 | n/a | 134 | 12 | 77 | 83 | 37 | 36 | 379 | n/a | 447 |
| 1846 | n/a | 185 | 10 | 95 | 57 | 16 | 64 | 427 | n/a | 373 |

NOTES: Values for 1825 are from *LCJ*, 1826, App. U. Other values are estimated by multiplying prices (table 4.1 except wheat from table C.1) times quantities (tables 4.2, 4.5). Where prices are unavailable, the following estimates are used: (a) white pine, 1837, 1839, 5d/ft; (b) deals, 1828, 1836, 1837, £8/std 100; (c) red pine, 1836–40, 8d/ft; (d) oak, 1836, 16d/ft; (e) elm, 1828, 1839, 6d/ft; (f) ashes, 1837, 33s per cwt, 1839, 27s per cwt ($4^{1}/_{2}$ cwt assumed = 1 bbl); (g) std staves, 1834, £40, 1836, £35, 1838, £43; (h) WI staves, 1832, 1834–5, 1838–9, £11.

Data on volumes at Coteau-du-Lac also gave total values, but these almost invariably yield unit prices well above those known to have prevailed in Montreal and Quebec markets; evidently the *Lower Canada Blue Books* applied some notional value to the volume data.

* Indicates data for Upper Canadian side of the upper Ottawa only

TABLE 4.4
Western Upper Canada Produce Exports, 1831–50

| Year | Square timber (000 cu ft)[2] | Staves (000) | Boards (000 bd ft) | Ashes (bbl) | Pork & beef (bbl) | Wheat (000 bu) |
|------|------|------|------|------|------|------|
| A. | Traffic through Welland Canal (British port to British port only)[1] | | | | | |
| 1831 | 28 | | | | | |
| 1832 | 76 | | | | | |
| 1833 | 31 | | | | | |
| 1834 | 94 | | | | | |
| 1836 | 280 | | | | | |
| 1837 | 106 | 563 | 2,608 | 96 | 509[3] | 26 |
| 1838 | 232 | 447 | 992 | 172 | 435[3] | 200 |
| 1839 | 464 | 689 | 2,246 | 70 | 470 | 240 |
| 1840 | 900 | 514 | 1,665 | 100 | 1,700 | 600 |
| 1841 | 1,151 | 766 | 2,672 | 181 | 5,148 | 866 |
| 1844 | 462 | 682 | 3,355 | 1,035 | 2,109 | 749 |
| 1850 | 938 | 3,613 | 3,470 | 1,611 | 283 | 1,016 |
| B. | From Supervisor of Cullers' Accounts, Quebec (timber only)[4] | | | | | |
| 1844 | 565 | 3,071 | | | | |
| 1845 | 1,600 | 4,960 | | | | |
| 1846 | 2,353 | 3,092 | | | | |
| C. | Value of Welland Canal shipments (estimated; £000)[5] | | | | | |
| | Total | | | | | |
| 1837 | 38 | 8 | 12 | 5 | 1 | 2 | 10 |
| 1838 | 90 | 14 | 10 | 2 | 1 | 2 | 61 |
| 1839 | 125 | 32 | 16 | 5 | – | 2 | 70 |
| 1840 | 221 | 62 | 12 | 3 | – | 6 | 138 |
| 1841 | 321 | 72 | 18 | 6 | 1 | 18 | 206 |

[1]  'British' ports, as source puts it, assumed to be in Upper (and perhaps Lower) Canada.
[2]  Breakdown of traffic by origin and destination not available before 1837, but all square timber fell into this category.
[3]  1837–8, pork only
[4]  Close to 90% of square timber (by volume) was oak in 1844–6.
[5]  Prices used in C are from Quebec or Montreal except wheat prices used are for eastern Upper Canada (table C.1). Timber assumed to be 90% oak, 10% white pine; staves assumed 50% std, 50% WI. Boards estimated at 1/2d/bd ft; beef and pork at £3 10s per bbl; pine (1837 and 1839) 5d; WI staves (1837–9) £11; std staves (1838) £41.

SOURCES: *UCJ*, 1831–2, App., 119; 1832–3, App., 51; 1833–4, App., 193; 1835, App. 46, 13; 1837–8, App., 333-8; 1839, App., 150-4; 1839–40, App., 303–6; and *JLA*, 1841, App. D; 1842, App. F; 1844–5, Apps. AA (D-2) and K; 1846, App. T; 1847, App. AA; 1851, App. A, schedule 6

TABLE 4.5
Timber Exports, Ottawa Valley, 1823–66

| Year | Red pine pieces (000) | cu ft (000) | White pine pieces (000) | cu ft (000) | Total cu ft (000) |
|---|---|---|---|---|---|
| **A.  From Bytown up, UC only** | | | | | |
| 1823 | | 413 | | 1 | 414 |
| 1824 | | | | | 1,200 |
| 1828 | 28 | 985 | | 4 | 989 |
| 1829 | 29 | 1,068 | | 14 | 1,082 |
| 1831 | 49 | 1,839 | 2 | 95 | 1,934 |
| 1832 | 25 | 971 | 2 | 129 | 1,100 |
| 1835 | | | | | [2,000]* |
| 1836 | | | | | [2,300] |
| 1837 | | | | | [2,200] |
| 1838 | 55 | 2,090 | 2 | 140 | 2,230 |
| 1839 | 61 | 2,318 | 5 | 350 | 2,668 |
| 1840 | 66 | 2,508 | 14 | 980 | 3,488 |
| **B.  From Bytown up, UC and LC** | | | | | |
| 1826 | | 881 | | 173 | 1,054 |
| 1827 | | 843 | | 32 | 875 |
| 1828 | | 1,203 | | 211 | 1,414 |
| 1829 | | 1,334 | | 597 | 1,931 |
| 1830 | | 2,662 | | 573 | 3,235 |
| 1835 | | [2,800] | | [600] | [3,400] |
| 1836 | | [3,100] | | [600] | [3,700] |
| 1837 | | [3,600] | | [700] | [4,300] |
| 1838 | 78 | 2,964 | 8 | 560 | 3,524 |
| 1839 | 81 | 3,078 | 14 | 980 | 4,058 |
| 1840 | 94 | 3,572 | 28 | 1,960 | 5,532 |
| 1841 | 93 | 3,521 | 39 | 2,675 | 6,196 |
| 1843 | 96 | 3,636 | 19 | 1,322 | 4,958 |
| 1844 | 103 | 3,989 | 92 | 6,053 | 10,042† |
| 1845 | 110 | 4,259 | 128 | 8,319 | 12,578† |
| 1846 | 118 | 4,544 | 126 | 7,533 | 12,077† |

TABLE 4.5 (*continued*)

| Year | Red pine pieces (000) | cu ft (000) | White pine pieces (000) | cu ft (000) | Total cu ft (000) |
|---|---|---|---|---|---|
| **C. *Entire valley, UC and LC*** | | | | | |
| 1844 | 106 | 4,108 | 146 | 9,220 | 13,328 |
| 1845 | 112 | 4,358 | 226 | 13,918 | 18,276 |
| 1846 | 128 | 4,865 | 268 | 15,652 | 20,517 |
| 1847 | 167 | 6,252 | 119 | 7,659 | 13,911 |
| 1848 | 104 | 4,164 | 70 | 4,748 | 8,912 |
| 1849 | 86 | 3,728 | 131 | 9,002 | 12,730 |
| 1850 | 47 | 2,113 | 173 | 11,350 | 13,463 |
| 1851 | 74 | 3,156 | 198 | 12,557 | 15,713 |
| 1852 | | 2,497 | | 16,929 | 19,426 |
| 1855 | 55 | 2,209 | 168 | 10,694 | 12,903 |
| 1857 | 45 | 1,885 | 271 | 17,362 | 19,247 |
| 1858 | 28 | 1,191 | 191 | 12,354 | 13,545 |
| 1860 | 73 | 3,070 | 176 | 13,330 | 16,400 |
| 1861 | 61 | 2,535 | 258 | 16,272 | 18,807 |
| 1862 | 85 | 3,358 | 299 | 17,527 | 20,885 |
| 1863 | 106 | 4,179 | 297 | 17,941 | 22,120 |
| 1866 | 40 | 1,932 | 191 | 11,928 | 13,860 |

**D. *Other timber output, entire valley (minor items excluded)***

| Year | Elm (000 cu ft) | Oak (000 cu ft) | Pine deals (000 'pieces') |
|---|---|---|---|
| 1844 | 462 | 50 | 810 |
| 1845 | 832 | 236 | 972 |
| 1846 | 1,192 | 227 | 628 |
| 1855 | 523 | 42 | 729‡ |
| 1857 | 431 | 46 | 672 |
| 1858 | 206 | 51 | 771 |
| 1860 | 195 | 19 | 1,326 |
| 1861 | 180 | 38 | 963 |
| 1862 | 282 | 33 | 817 |
| 1863 | 719 | 71 | 1,110 |
| 1866 | 19 | 5 | 2,164 |

\* Figures in square brackets are estimates; see source notes (p. 264) for details.

† Gatineau and Rideau Rivers excluded

‡ From 1855, deals figure combines two categories in cullers' report, 'pine deals culled' and 'deals, pine and spruce, counted off only.' I have assumed that pine predominated in the latter category.

TABLE 4.6
Duties on Upper Canadian Timber
at Bytown (Gross), 1827–40

| 1827 | £57   | 1834 | £2,522 |
|------|-------|------|--------|
| 1828 | 4,177 | 1835 | 7,701  |
| 1829 | 3,718 | 1836 | 8,642  |
| 1830 | 6,948 | 1837 | 8,316  |
| 1831 | 7,929 | 1838 | 9,408  |
| 1832 | 4,380 | 1839 | 10,599 |
| 1833 | 596   | 1840 | 13,200 |

NOTES: There is a discrepancy between
the two sources for 1836 and 1837; the
later is more plausible. The first gives
1836 as £10,162 and 1837 as £4,025. On
the low receipts in 1833, see R. Peter
Gillis, 'Charles Shirreff,' *DCB* 7
(Toronto 1988), 796–7.
SOURCES: *UCJ*, 1839, App., 431–3;
*JLA*, 1841, App. G

SOURCES FOR TABLE 4.5
1823: from NA, Philemon Wright Papers, MG24, D8, vol. 120, 64402, statement of timber ... per
    return of sheriff of Bathurst district
1824: from NA, MG11, CO42, vol. 375, 115–19, Charles Shirreff to Major Hillier, 29 Jan. 1825
1826–30: from NA, Wright Papers, vol. 120, 64438, statement of timber passing the Chaudière
    Falls
1828–9: (UC only): from *UCJ*, 1831, App., 149–50
1831–2: from *UCJ*, 1833–4, App., 133, 139
1835: based on Upper Canadian revenue (table 4.6). I have assumed five times as much red as
    white pine. See also AO, RG1, F-I-8, vol. 11, collector at Bytown's letterbook, pp. 1–18.
1836–40: from *JLA*, 1841, App. G; estimates made as for 1835. Pieces converted to volume at rate
    of 70 ft = 1 piece for white pine and 38 ft = 1 piece for red.
1841–63: from *JLA*, 1842, App. T; 1844–5, Apps. K and P; 1846, App. T; 1847, App. AA; 1852–3,
    Apps. OO and QQQQ; 1856, App. 36; 1858, App.15; 1859, App. 17; 1861, SP 15; 1862, SP 11;
    1863, SP 6; 1864, SP 5
1866: from Canada, Parliament, *Sessional Papers*, 1867, #6

TABLE 5.1

Wheat and Land Use in Upper Canada, Hypothetical, Selected Years, 1821–51

|  | 1821 | 1825 | 1829 | 1831 | 1835 | 1836 | 1848 | 1851 |
|---|---|---|---|---|---|---|---|---|
| *(000 bushels)* |  |  |  |  |  |  |  |  |
| Wheat for UC consumption | 688 | 904 | 1,167 | 1,383 | 2,024 | 2,182 | 4,235 | 5,593 |
| Wheat exports | 153 | 111 | 230 | 959 | 549 | 922 | 1,706 | 4,376 |
| Seed for next crop | 225 | 272 | 373 | 626 | 688 | 830 | 1,618 | 2,714 |
| Total wheat | 1,066 | 1,287 | 1,770 | 2,968 | 3,261 | 3,934 | 7,559 | 12,683 |
| *(000 acres)* |  |  |  |  |  |  |  |  |
| Land required | 71 | 86 | 118 | 198 | 217 | 262 | 504 | 846 |
| Land (2 years) | 142 | 172 | 236 | 396 | 434 | 524 | 1,008 | 1,692 |
| Total land under culture | 423 | 561 | 718 | 818 | 1,310 | 1,284 | 2,547 | 3,750 |
| Percentage of land needed for wheat | 34 | 31 | 33 | 48 | 33 | 41 | 40 | 45 |

NOTES

Exports from table 4.2, except 1851 from I.D. Andrews, *Report on the Trade and Commerce of the British North American Colonies* ..., US Senate Document, 32nd Cong., 1st Sess., Ex. Doc. 112 (Washington 1853), 413. A slightly different 1851 figure (4.3 million bu) is given in the Canadian TTN.

Output in 1848 and 1851: from 1871 *Census*, vol. 4, 170, 195; 40,000 bu added to domestic consumption in 1851 to balance

Land under culture from table 1.1 and from 1871 *Census*, vol. 4. Actual land required for wheat in 1851 was 795,000 acres; see R.M. McInnis, 'Perspectives on Ontario Agriculture, 1815–1930,' ch 2, 'Ontario Agriculture at Mid-Century,' *CPRH 8* (1992), 70.

Other data estimated; see table 2.4 for assumptions. Seed assumes 7% increase in subsequent crop. Years include peak years.

TABLE 5.2
Estimated Per Capita Income from Wheat Exports, Upper Canada (West of Kingston), 1817–61

| Year | Population (000) | Wheat exports (000 bu) | Exports/ person (bu) | Price (s/bu) | Exports/ person (s) |
|---|---|---|---|---|---|
| *Midland District & West* | | | | | |
| 1817 | 60 | 195 | 3.3 | 10/– | 33 |
| 1818 | 65 | 225 | 3.5 | 5/– | 18 |
| 1819 | 71 | 62 | 0.9 | 3/9 * | 3 |
| 1820 | 78 | 166 | 2.1 | 3/9 * | 8 |
| 1821 | 85 | 153 | 1.8 | 3/– * | 5 |
| 1822 | 93 | 210 | 2.3 | 2/6 * | 6 |
| 1823 | 100 | 200 | 2.0 | 3/9 | 8 |
| *Hastings County & West* | | | | | |
| 1824 | 91 | 131 | 1.4 | 4/– | 6 |
| 1825 | 98 | 179 | 1.8 | 4/5 | 8 |
| 1827 | 109 | 606 | 5.6 | 4/4 | 24 |
| 1828 | 114 | 525 | 4.6 | 4/5 | 20 |
| 1829 | 124 | 230 | 1.9 | 6/– | 11 |
| 1830 | 132 | 750 | 5.7 | 5/2 | 29 |
| 1831 | 148 | 959 | 6.5 | 5/4 | 35 |
| 1832 | 171 | 628 | 3.7 | 5/– | 19 |
| 1833 | 195 | 932 | 4.8 | 4/9 | 23 |
| 1834 | 215 | 945 | 4.4 | 3/11 | 17 |
| 1835 | 236 | 549 | 2.3 | 4/– | 9 |
| 1836 | 258 | 922 | 3.6 | 5/2 | 19 |
| 1837 | 278 | 266 | 1.0 | 7/8 | 8 |
| 1838 | 280 | 636 | 2.3 | 6/1 | 14 |
| 1839 | 288 | 656 | 2.3 | 5/10 | 13 |
| 1848 | 530 | 1,812 | 3.4 | 4/2 * | 14 |
| 1851 | 721 | 4,376 | 6.1 | 3/7 * | 22 |
| 1861 | 1,052 | 11,553 | 11.0 | 5/6 * | 61 |

* Indicates price at the western end of Lake Ontario; all other prices are from east of Kingston.
All shipments downriver assumed to be from region west of Kingston
SOURCES: From tables 3.4, 4.2, 4.3, 5.1, C.1; and Canada, *Census*, 1871, vol. 4

TABLE 5.3
Output of Selected Farm Products in Upper Canada, 1848–70

|  | 1848 | | 1851 | | 1860 | | 1870 | |
|---|---|---|---|---|---|---|---|---|
|  | Total (000) | per cap. | Total (000) | per cap. | Total (000) | per cap. | Total (000) | per cap. |
| *Output* | | | | | | | | |
| Wheat (bu) | 7,559 | 10.4 | 12,683 | 13.3 | 24,620 | 17.6 | 14,033 | 8.7 |
| Oats (bu) | 7,058 | 9.7 | 11,395 | 12.0 | 21,221 | 15.2 | 22,139 | 13.7 |
| Barley (bu) | 516 | 0.7 | 625 | 0.7 | 2,822 | 2.0 | 9,461 | 5.8 |
| Rye (bu) | 446 | 0.6 | 472 | 0.5 | 973 | 0.7 | 548 | 0.3 |
| Peas (bu) | 1,753 | 2.4 | 3,028 | 3.2 | 9,601 | 6.9 | 7,654 | 4.7 |
| Corn (bu) | 1,138 | 1.6 | 1,689 | 1.8 | 2,256 | 1.6 | 3,148 | 1.9 |
| Potatoes (bu) | 4,751 | 6.5 | 4,973 | 5.2 | 15,326 | 11.0 | 17,139 | 10.6 |
| Hay (tons) | na | na | 694 | 0.7 | 862 | 0.6 | 1,805 | 1.1 |
| Butter (lb) | 3,380 | 4.7 | 16,062 | 16.9 | 25,822 | 18.5 | 37,624 | 23.2 |
| Wool (lb) | 2,340 | 3.2 | 2,710 | 2.8 | 3,660 | 2.6 | 6,411 | 4.0 |
| *Stock* | | | | | | | | |
| Horses | 151 | 0.2 | 202 | 0.2 | 378 | 0.3 | 489 | 0.3 |
| Oxen | na | na | 192 | 0.2 | 100 | 0.1 | 48 | 0.03 |
| Cattle | 566 | 0.8 | 552 | 0.6 | 916 | 0.7 | 1,355 | 0.8 |
| Sheep | 834 | 1.1 | 967 | 1.0 | 1,170 | 0.8 | 1,515 | 0.9 |
| Swine | 484 | 0.7 | 571 | 0.6 | 776 | 0.6 | 875 | 0.5 |

SOURCE: Canada, *Census*, 1871, vol. 3, tables 22, 23; vol. 4, 169–70, 195–7, 272–5

TABLE 5.4

Percentage of Farms Reporting Selected Produce, Upper Canada, 1861
(crops reported by 50% or more farms only)

| | Size of farm | | |
| --- | --- | --- | --- |
| | Small (32–69 acres) | Medium (70–169 acres) | Large (170 + acres) |
| Spring wheat | 79 | 89 | 91 |
| Oats | 77 | 86 | 84 |
| Peas | 66 | 77 | 82 |
| Potatoes | 88 | 91 | 91 |
| Hay | 82 | 84 | 86 |
| Butter | 85 | 88 | 89 |
| Pork | 77 | 80 | 82 |
| Wool | 59 | 71 | 72 |
| Cloth | 57 | 70 | 70 |
| Oxen | | | 53 |
| Horses | 68 | 72 | 79 |
| Steers/heifers | 77 | 86 | 89 |
| Milk cows | 92 | 94 | 96 |
| Swine | 86 | 91 | 91 |
| Sheep | 63 | 73 | 74 |

SOURCE: R.M. McInnis, 'The Size Structure of Farming, Canada West, 1861,' in 'Agrarian Organization in the Century of Industrialization: Europe, Russia and North America,' *Research in Economic History* suppl. 5 (1989), table 2

SOURCE NOTES FOR TABLE 5.5
 1  QUA, Cartwright Family Papers, Additions, vol. 1, Richard Cartwright Jr Account Book, 1791–8
 2  NA, MG23, H II 14, Donald and John McLean Accounts
 3  AO, William Kyle Papers, MU 615–16
 4  AO, Yonge Mills Day Books, MU 3168–81
 5  AO, D.B. Stevenson Papers, Ledger, MU 2888
 6  AO, Washburn Papers, MU 3107
 7  AO, W.H. Patterson Ledger, MU 690
 8  AO, Oliver Hammond Papers, Ms 623
 9  NA, MG24, I26, Hamilton Papers, vols. 17–18 (converted from NY cy)
10  UWO, Foster & Co. Papers, B5035 (converted from NY cy)
11  NA, MG9, D8 (24), 15572–16248, Norfolk Historical Society Collection, Cross & Fisher Accounts (converted from NY cy)
12  UWO, Coyne Papers, X1425 (Hfx cy assumed)
13  UWO, Thames Steam Navigation Co. Daybook, X1449 (despite its title, this is the record of a general store)

TABLE 5.5
The Structure of Retail Payments, Upper Canada to 1840

| Firm (see map 5.4 for location) | Years | Total credits (£ Hfx cy) | A % credits by wheat, flour | B % 2nd (or higher) ranked local product | | C % credits by cash | D % '3rd party' | E % notes | A to E as % of all credits | % wheat in highest, lowest years |
|---|---|---|---|---|---|---|---|---|---|---|
| 1. Richard Cartwright Jr | 1791–6 | 9,335 | 12 | ashes | 12 | 3 | 37 | 21 | 85 | 1792–17%; 1796–7% |
| 2. McLean Store | 1827–9* | 1,545 | 3 | ashes | 6 | 21 | 15 | 26 | 71 | |
| 3. William Kyle | 1823–30 | 9,125 | 8 | ashes | 4 | 8 | 10 | 36 | 66 | 1826–16%; 1829–1% |
| 4. C. Jones | 1824–38‡ | 20,528 | 6 | lumber<br>ashes | 13<br>11 | 10 | 10 | 11 | 61 | 1833–17%; 1829–1% |
| 5. Barker & Stevenson | 1829–37 | 21,140 | 24 | pork | 15 | 10 | 15 | 10 | 74 | 1836–45%; 1829–10% |
| 6. S. Washburn | 1834–40§ | 4,721 | 18 | pork | 18 | 6 | 8 | 36 | 86 | 1840–34%; 1837–9% |
| 7. W.H. Patterson | 1840–2§ | 2,691 | 29 | pork | 2 | 17 | 5 | 5 | 58 | |
| 8. Hammond & Goble | 1836–9* | 4,627 | 19 | pork | 3 | 16 | 12 | 4 | 54 | 1836–30%; 1838–13% |
| 9. Hamilton's Store | 1806–12† | 8,815 | 25 | pork | 12 | 10 | 21 | 11 | 71 | 1808–33%; 1811–14% |
| 10. E. Foster | 1819–20 | 593 | 9 | rye | 31 | 8 | 12 | 11 | 71 | |
| 11. Cross & Fisher | 1830–37† | 4,703 | 5 | rye | 19 | 18 | 4 | 18 | 63 | 1835–7%; 1836–3% |
| 12. J. Coyne Store | 1833–38† | 4,208 | 7 | tobacco | 11 | 8 | 13 | 0 | 39 | 1834–19%; 1837–1% |
| 13. Thames Steam Navigation | 1835 | 1,863 | 6 | barley | 19 | 30 | 28 | 2 | 85 | |

\* Last year incomplete     ‡ First, last year incomplete
† First year incomplete     § First, last year incomplete

First, last year incomplete; some data from Brockville store used for parts of 1828–30; no data for 1834 and part of 1835

SOURCES: See p. 268.

TABLE 5.6
Produce Transactions at Barker and Stevenson (Principal Items), 1826–37
(figures are values in £Halifax cy)

| | Wheat & flour | Pork | Staves | Total wood[a] | Potash | Total | Percentage wheat & flour |
|---|---|---|---|---|---|---|---|
| **A. Shipped to Lower Canada[b]** | | | | | | | |
| 1826 | 206 | – | 92 | 252 | – | 458 | 45 |
| 1827 | 254 | 160 | 102 | 102 | 6 | 522 | 49 |
| 1828 | 492 | 200 | 213 | 241 | 22 | 955 | 52 |
| 1829 | 191 | 473 | 175 | 200 | 13 | 877 | 22 |
| | | | | | | | |
| **B. Credited to Customer Accounts** | | | | | | | |
| 1829 | 121 | 347 | | 95 | – | 563 | 21 |
| 1830 | 229 | 384 | | 102 | 13 | 728 | 31 |
| 1831 | 237 | 566 | | 59 | 54 | 916 | 26 |
| 1832 | 386 | 282 | | 8 | 48 | 724 | 53 |
| 1833 | 559 | 250 | | 38 | 22 | 869 | 64 |
| 1834 | 421 | 250 | | 9 | 24 | 704 | 60 |
| 1835 | 682 | 345 | | 62 | 58 | 1,147 | 59 |
| 1836 | 1,813 | 420 | | 8 | 5 | 2,246 | 81 |
| 1837 | 663 | 385 | | 34 | 79 | 1,161 | 57 |

a  Total wood includes staves
b  In year ended May. Note that the basis of the two series is different, and this explains the discrepancies in 1829, the year in which there is an overlap.
SOURCES: A: UG, Goodwin-Haines Collection, William Grant Papers, XR1 Ms. A131002, Barker and Stevenson Inventory Book. B: AO, D.B. Stevenson Papers, MU 2887–8, ledgers, 1828–37

SOURCES FOR TABLE 5.7
a  NA, MG24, I5, Willson Papers (converted from NY cy)
b  NA, MG24, D49, Spencer Papers
c  UWO, Robert Comfort Papers, B4647, photocopies (converted from NY cy)
d  UWO, Edward Stiles Accounts, X1499 (converted from NY cy)
e  MTL, Account Books of a Farmer near Dunville [sic], 1834–58
f  AO, Crawford Family Papers, vol. 1, Diaries of B.B. Crawford, 1810–59, MU 754–6
g  UWO, William Thompson Diary, B4205
h  NA, MG24, I72, Jacob Case Transcripts, account book, 1837–47 (converted from NY cy)
i  UWO, William B. Cambers Papers, B4014, file 14–11, account of rental of R. Fields Farm
j  UWO, Diary and Account Book of Atchison Brown, M321
k  MTL, Thomas Forster Account Book
m  MTL, William Parsons Account Book

TABLE 5.7
Upper Canadian Farm Sales Records, 1798–1850

| | A | B | C | D | E | F | G | H | J | K |
|---|---|---|---|---|---|---|---|---|---|---|
| | Farmer | Location | Years | Gross sales (£ Hfx cy) | Mean sales per year | Gross wheat & flour sales | Wheat sales as % of D | Second (or first) commodity sold | Second (first) commodity sales as % of D | Other commodities ≥5% of gross sales |
| a. | Willson | Niagara | 1798–9 | 49 | 25 | 5 | 10% | Rye | 39 | Beef, pork, oats |
| b. | Spencer | Hallowell | 1805–9 | 121 | 24 | 80 | 66 | Pork | 21 | – |
| c. | Comfort | Gainsborough | 1818–9 } 1823–5 | 155 | 31 | 62 | 40 | Cattle & products* | 28 | Buckwheat, rye, pork, hay |
| d. | Stiles | London | 1831–6 | 64 | 11 | 13 | 20 | Corn | 24 | Beef, pork, wood |
| e. | Anon. | Dunnville (15 crop years) | 1836–50 | 409 | 27 | 175 | 43 | Sheep & products* | 12 | Beef, pork, butter, eggs, potatoes |
| f. | Crawford | Beachville | 1838–42 } 1844–7 | 391 | 43 | 129 | 33 | Hay | 17 | Butter, oats, pork, potash |
| g. | Thompson | South Easthope | 1842–7 | 280 | 56 | 207 | 74 | Pork & products* | 6 | Beef |
| h. | Case | Galt | 1843–5 | 50 | 17 | 10 | 20 | Beef & oxen | 35 | Hay, potatoes, buckwheat |
| i. | Cambers | Etobicoke | 1845–9 | 175 | 35 | 63 | 36 | Barley | 13 | Livestock, pasturage, lumber, hay, potatoes, rye, cabbages |
| j. | Brown | Bayfield | 1847 | 102 | 102 | 23 | 23 | Cattle | 22 | Oats, potatoes, peas, a pony |
| k. | Forster | Norval | 1847–8 (14 mo) | 37 | 37 | 25 | 68 | Butter | 18 | Beef & products* |
| m. | Parsons | Thornhill | 1836–43 | 3,981 | 498 | 1,826 | 46 | Oats | 16 | Cattle & products, hay, sheep & products* |

* 'Products' includes hides, wool, tallow, lard, etc. SOURCES: See p. 270.

TABLE 5.8
Percentage of Farm Revenue, by Commodity, Two Upper Canadian Farms, 1836–50*

| | 1836 | 1837 | 1838 | 1839 | 1840 | 1841 | 1842 | 1843 | 1844 | 1845 | 1846 | 1847 | 1848 | 1849 | 1850 | Total‡ |
|---|---|---|---|---|---|---|---|---|---|---|---|---|---|---|---|---|
| **A. Dunnville Farm** | | | | | | | | | | | | | | | | |
| Wheat ‡ | 100 | 39 | 79 | 66 | 35 | 52 | 22 | 17 | 49 | 25 | 52 | 24 | 38 | 38 | 44 | 43 |
| Hay | | 16 | 13 | 13 | 11 | 10 | | 11 | | | | | | | | 3 |
| Peas | | 32 | | | | | | | | | | | | | | 1 |
| Wool | | | | 12 | 29 | | 10 | | | | | | | | | 6 |
| Sheep/mutton | | | | | 25 | | 19 | 13 | | | | | | | | 6 |
| Butter | | | | | | 16 | | | | | | 12 | | | | 6 |
| Beef | | | | | | | 20 | | 19 | 29 | | 11 | | | | 7 |
| Clover | | | | | | | | 27 | | | | | | | | 1 |
| Pork | | | | | | | | | 11 | 10 | | 19 | 12 | | | 7 |
| Eggs | | | | | | | | | | 12 | | 11 | | | | 6 |
| Potatoes | | | | | | | | | | | | | 12 | 12 | 10 | 5 |
| Corn | | | | | | | | | | | | | | 16 | 13 | 4 |
| Total, these commodities | 100 | 87 | 92 | 91 | 100 | 78 | 71 | 68 | 79 | 76 | 52 | 77 | 62 | 66 | 67 | 95 |
| **B. Crawford Farm** | | | | | | | | | | | | | | | | |
| Wheat ‡ | | | 31 | 63 | – | 52 | 34 | | 54 | 24 | 18 | 45 | | | | 33 |
| Buckwheat | | | 12 | | | | | | | | | | | | | 2 |
| Potash | | | 43 | | 24 | | | | | | | | | | | 5 |
| Oats | | | | 11 | | | 12 | | | 12 | 15 | | | | | 9 |
| Hay | | | | | 60 | | 10 | | 13 | | 23 | | | | | 17 |
| Pork | | | | | | 19 | 18 | | 13 | 31 | 20 | 22 | | | | 14 |
| Maple sugar | | | | | | | | | | 11 | | | | | | 4 |
| Butter | | | | | | | | | | | 11 | 13 | | | | 8 |
| Total, these commodities | | | 86 | 74 | 84 | 71 | 84 | | 80 | 78 | 87 | 80 | | | | 92 |

\* Only percentages greater than 10 are included.     ‡ For actual wheat sales and total sales, see figure 5.1.

† Total includes all sales of the commodity, not just those over 10 per cent.     SOURCE: See notes to table 5.7.

TABLE 5.9
Indian Agriculture in Upper Canada at Mid-Century, Per Capita Stocks
and Outputs (selected)

| | Grand R (1) | Grand R (2) | Bay of Quinte | Thames R | Walpole Island | Sarnia | Rice Lake | Saugeen |
|---|---|---|---|---|---|---|---|---|
| Year | 1843 | 1856 | 1856 | 1856 | 1856 | 1856 | 1856 | 1856 |
| Population | 2,220 | 210 | 560 | 1,350 | 820 | 510 | 360 | 260 |
| Acres cleared | 3.1 | | 6.9 | 2.5 | 3.0 | 1.4 | 2.5 | 1.2 |
| Wheat (bu) | | 16.7 | 2.3 | 2.3 | 1.9 | 1.3 | 5.0 | 0.3 |
| Corn (bu) | | 1.2 | – | 6.0 | 7.8 | 4.7 | 0.4 | 0.4 |
| Potatoes (bu) | | 3.4 | 3.0 | 2.1 | 4.8 | 3.8 | 5.4 | 6.2 |
| Oats (bu) | | 2.8 | 2.2 | 1.8 | 0.7 | 1.3 | 1.2 | |
| Hay (tons) | | | 0.3 | 0.2 | 0.4 | 0.2 | 0.2 | |
| Rye (bu) | | | 4.5 | | | | | |
| Oxen | 0.3 | | | 0.2 | 0.1 | 0.1 | 0.1 | |
| Cattle* | | | | 0.3 | 0.3 | 0.2 | | |
| Cows* | 0.4 | | 0.2 | 0.2 | 0.1 | 0.1 | 0.1 | |
| All horses* | | | | 0.2 | 0.4 | 0.2 | | |
| Horses* | 0.2 | | 0.1 | 0.1 | 0.2 | 0.2 | 0.1 | |
| Pigs | 0.9 | | 0.3 | 0.4 | 0.6 | 0.2 | 0.3 | |

NOTES

Grand River (1) is Six Nations and associated groups.

Grand River (2) is the Credit River Mississauga, who had relocated to the Grand; together, the two
groups totalled 2,530 people in 1856, with an average of 3.3 acres per person in cultivation.

Bay of Quinte is the Mohawk community there.

Thames River embraces three reserves, the Delawares, the Oneidas, and the Munceys and
Chippewas.

Walpole Island included Chippewas, Pottawatamies, and Ottawas. The same three groups were
represented on the Sarnia area reserves.

Rice Lake included two Mississauga communities, at Alnwick and on the north shore.

From Mud Lake to Georgian Bay, there were another 1,300 Indians; their agricultural outputs
were akin to the Saugeen band.

* Some of the census data distinguish between cows and young cattle, horses and young horses;
some record all young animals as 'young stock.'

SOURCES: Report of the Special Commissioners ... on Indian Affairs, *JLA*, 1858, App. 21
(unpaginated); Six Nations are from C.M. Johnston, *The Valley of the Six Nations*, 306–7.

TABLE 6.1
Saw and Grist Mills in Upper Canada, 1826–71 (selected years)

|  | Grist mills | | Additional | Saw mills | |
|---|---|---|---|---|---|
|  |  | Pop. per | pairs of |  | Pop. per |
| Year | No. | mill | stones | No. | mill |
| 1826 | 250 | 666 | 80 | 422 | 394 |
| 1831 | 291 | 813 | 135 | 533 | 440 |
| 1836 | 356 | 1,051 | 227 | 902 | 415 |
| 1842 | 455 | 1,070 | 359 | 982 | 496 |
| 1848 | 553 | 1,313 | na | 1,584 | 458 |
| 1851 | 692 | 1,376 | na | 1,567 | 608 |
| 1861 | 502* | 2,781 | na | 1,164* | 1,199 |
| 1871 | 951 | 1,705 | na | 1,837 | 882 |

* Indicates an apparently anomalous figure in series; see also F. Leung, *Grist and Flour Mills in Ontario*, 73, 232 re 1861 data.

SOURCES: For 1826–42, *JLA*, 1849, App. N, 'enclosure in # 6;' for confirmation of 1842 data, see *JLA*, 1843, App. DD, record of Upper Canada municipal assessments for 1842, 1843. For 1848 to 1871, Canada, *Census*, 1871, vol. 4, 171, 198, 270; vol. 3, 321–3, 340–2. Figures reported in the latter source are different in varying degrees from those given here for 1826 to 1842, but variations do not affect trends indicated.

TABLE 6.2
Population per Mill, Selected Districts, 1805–51

|  | Home District. | | Johnstown | | London | | Prince Edward | |
|---|---|---|---|---|---|---|---|---|
| Year | Grist | Saw | Grist | Saw | Grist | Saw | Grist | Saw |
| 1805 | 631 | 378 | 167 | 246 |  |  |  |  |
| 1817 | 482 | 207 | 215 | 160 |  |  |  |  |
| 1821 | 676 | 214 | 448 | 281 | 635 | 337 |  |  |
| 1826 | 635 | 270 | 541 | 357 | 517 | 362 |  |  |
| 1831 | 717 | 287 | 814 | 502 | 639 | 340 |  |  |
| 1836 | 1,141 | 326 | 1,093 | 556 | 892 | 356 | 683 | 946 |
| 1842 | 1,141 | 434 | 1,409 | 926 | 1,045 | 514 | 784 | 481 |
| 1848 | 1,198 | 392 | 1,510 | 635 | 994 | 251 | 1,006 | 369 |
| 1851 | 1,423 | 492 | 1,378 | 850 | 716 | 555 | 945 | 556 |

SOURCES: Canada, *Census*, 1871, vol. 4, 92, 104, 120, 140, 171, 198, 270; and NA, population and assessment returns, RG5, B26, vol. 4, 771, 776, 814, 817, 848, 851, 853. District boundaries are those current at each date, except in 1851, when Home = York County and Toronto; Johnstown = Leeds and Grenville counties; London = London town, Middlesex, Oxford, and Norfolk counties.

TABLE 6.3
Upper Canadian Industry, from Printed Census, Number of Establishments,
Selected Industries, 1842–71

|  | 1842 | 1848 | 1851 | 1861 | 1871 |
|---|---|---|---|---|---|
| Grist mills | 455 | 553 | 692 | 502* | 951 |
| Saw mills | 982 | 1,584 | 1,567 | 1,164* | 1,837 |
| Carding mills | 186 |  |  |  |  |
| Fulling mills | 144 | 239 |  |  |  |
| Carding & fulling mills |  |  | 147 | 62* | 158 |
| Woollen mills |  | 65 | 74 | 85 | 233† |
| Distilleries | 147 | 138 | 102 | 53 | 18 |
| Breweries | 96 | 99 | 50* | 90 | 105 |
| Tanneries | 261 | 354 | 222* | 271 | 426 |
| Foundries | 22 | 105 | 97* | 124 | 258† |

\* Indicates a figure that is anomalous in terms of trends in series; see discussion in chapter 6.
† 1871 definitions: wool cloth making, foundries and machine-working

SOURCE: Canada, *Census*, 1871, vol. 3, 310–12, 330–2, 341–3, 351–3, 360–2, 420; and vol. 4, 140, 171, 198, 270; grist and saw mills from table 6.1

TABLE 6.4

Diffusion of Tanneries, Carding Mills, and Distilleries, Leading Districts, 1842

| District | Tanneries No. | Pop./ est. | District | Carding mills No. | Pop./ est. | District | Distilleries* No. | Pop./ est. |
|---|---|---|---|---|---|---|---|---|
| UC | 261 | 1,866 | UC | 186 | 2,619 | UC | 147 | 3,313 |
| Home | 43 | 1,937 | Home | 32 | 2,603 | Home | 38 | 2,192 |
| Niagara | 27 | 1,356 | Niagara | 29 | 1,262 | Newcastle | 19 | 1,632 |
| Eastern | 25 | 1,280 | Wellington | 16 | 906 | Gore | 17 | 2,651 |
| Gore | 23 | 1,957 | Gore | 15 | 3,000 | Niagara | 11 | 3,331 |
| Johnstown | 18 | 1,800 | Johnstown | 15 | 2,160 | Wellington | 9 | 1,608 |
| Newcastle | 16 | 1,938 | London | 11 | 2,755 | Bathurst | 7 | 3,094 |
|  |  |  |  |  |  | Brock | 7 | 2,469 |
| Subtotal | 152 | 1713 | Subtotal | 118 | 2,052 | Subtotal | 108 | 2,306 |
| 13 other dists | 109 | 2,080 | 13 other dists | 68 | 3,601 | 12 other dists | 39 | 6,103 |

*   There is great variation in data series for distilleries, based, for example, on establishments, licences, capacity, and output; and even these have discrepancies. I have followed the census for consistency with other data in the table. Establishments paying duty in 1842 numbered 116. See *JLA*, 1843, App. A, series A-2, statement of revenues from licences in 1842. Assessments (*JLA*, 1843, App. DD) also recorded distilleries in a few districts. See also table 6.7.

SOURCE: Canada, *Census*, 1871, vol. 4, 140

TABLE 6.5
Output of a Commercial Grist Mill, 1828–40

| Year* | | | Wheat received (bu) | | Flour output (bbl) |
|---|---|---|---|---|---|
| 1829 | | | 5,864 | | 1,259 |
| 1830 | | | 12,088 | | 2,768 |
| 1831 | | | 27,644 | | 6,010 |
| 1832 | | | 37,292 | | 8,378 |
| 1833 | | | 50,819 | | 11,795 |
| 1834 | At mill | 8,459 | | | |
| | By toll | 930 | | | |
| | Brockville | 19,488 | | | |
| | 'Lake Wheat' | 54,983 | | | |
| | Total | | 83,861 | | |
| 1835 | | | 48,573 | | |
| | Less stock on hand | | 4,822 | Total, | |
| | Net | | 43,751 | 1834–5 | 29,508 |
| 1836 | At mill | 8,633 | | | |
| | By toll | 557 | | | |
| | Brockville | 74,129 | | | |
| | Total | | 83,320 | | 18,481 |
| 1837 | At mill | 10,414 | | | |
| | By toll | 362 | | | |
| | Brockville | 37,806 | | | |
| | Total | | 48,518 [*sic*] | | 11,026 |
| 1838 | At mill | 8,152 | | | |
| | By toll | 375 | | | |
| | Brockville | 21,311 | | | |
| | Total | | 29,838 | | 6,602 |
| 1839 | At mill | 4,227 | | | |
| | By toll | 424 | | | |
| | Brockville | 6,396 | | | |
| | Total | | 11,047 | | 2,354 |
| 1840 | | | 70,520 | | 14,976 |

* Years end 9 Dec.; but 1829 data are for 17 months from July 1828 and 1840 are for 9 months ending 31 Aug. 1840.

SOURCE: AO, Yonge Mills Records, MU 3185, Flour Sales Book A, 1828–33; Flour Book B, 1833–38; Flour Book C, 1838–40; Wheat Book A, 1832–9

TABLE 6.6
Capital Cost of Two Ottawa Valley Mills, 1823–4

| Local costs | | Non-local costs | |
|---|---|---|---|
| *A.  March Mills* | | | |
| Sawmill frame | £50 | 1 pr. millstones | £35 |
| Gristmill frame | 75 | Bolting cloth | 15 |
| 2 dams | 25 | Running gear, sawmill | 50 |
| Sawmill floor | 10 | Running gear, grist mill | 75 |
| Boards, planks | 10 | Iron works, both mills | 50 |
| Laying floors, clap- | | Shingles, glass, nails | 10 |
| boarding, etc. | 25 | | |
| Canal | 10 | | |
| Total | £205 | Total | £235 |
| *B.  Pinhey's Mill* | | | |
| Framers | £11 | Paid at Montreal for | |
| Sawyer | 26 | hardware, gearing, etc. | £125 |
| Planks, timber | 8 | Travel, provisions, etc. | |
| Blacksmith | 1 | paid at Montreal | 50 |
| Carpenters' accounts | 66 | Carpenters' accounts | 10 |
| Board | 21 | Cash at Lachine | 3 |
| Other wages | 12 | Tin for roof | 4 |
| Local expenses of | | Other cash at Montreal | 52 |
| millwrights | 44 | | |
| Total | £189 | Total | £244 |

SOURCE: AO, Hamnett Pinhey Papers, MU 2324, Account of Pinhey's dealings with Riddle &
Watson (Millwrights), to 28 Apr. 1824 and jottings by Riddell [*sic*] & Watson of Montreal
purchases, n.d.; contract for Capt. Monks' mills, 11 Mar. 1823

TABLE 6.7
Licensed Distilling in Upper Canada
(selected data and years, 1797–8 to 1871)

| Year | Licences (no.) | Census establishments (no.) | Licensed capacity (gal) | Output (000 gal) |
|---|---|---|---|---|
| 1798 | 26 | | 2,500 | |
| 1801 | 53 | | 4,200 | |
| 1802 | | | 6,200 | |
| 1813 | 130 | | 13,100 | |
| 1820 | | | 13,600 | |
| 1825 | 101 | | 8,300 | |
| 1827 | 157 | | 12,300 | |
| 1830 | | | 9,700 | |
| 1834 | 79 | | 6,500 | |
| 1836 | | | 8,000 | |
| 1838 | | | 6,500 | |
| 1840 | 152 | | | |
| 1842 | 116 | 147 | | |
| 1848 | | 138 | | |
| 1851 | 138 | 102 | | 2,003 |
| 1856 | 107 | | | 2,346 |
| 1861 | 70 | 53 | | 2,912 |
| 1866 | 32 | | | 3,583 |
| 1871 | | 18 | | |

NOTES: data are for fiscal year ending during the year indicated (except for fiscal years ending 5 Jan.). Capacity was the volume that the body of the still was capable of holding; see 34 Geo. III cap. 11 (1794), 4 Geo. IV cap. 13 (1823).

SOURCES

1798, 1820–38: *UCJ*, 5 July 1798 (printed in OBA, *Sixth Report*, 1909, 89); 1821, Public Accounts, table 1 (in OBA, *Report*, 1913, 291); 1825–6, App., Public Accounts, schedule 9; 1828, App., Public Accounts for 1827; 1831, App., Public Accounts for 1830, 11; 1835, App. 1, Public Accounts for 1834, 20, 38; 1836–7, App. 2, Public Accounts for 1836, 11 and 1837–8, Public Accounts for 1837, 6–7; 1839, App., Public Accounts for 1838, 22

1801–2: NA, Civil Secretary's Subject Files, RG5, B9, vol. 53, list of still licences, Upper Canada, year ending 5 Apr. 1801; and Peter Russell to John McGill, 26 Jan. 1803

1813: NA, Inspector General's Records, RG5, B34, vol. 9, statement of licensed stills, 1813

1840, 1842: *JLA*, 1841, App. B, Upper Canada Public Accounts for 1840; 1843, App. A, Public Accounts for 1842, A-2

1842, 1848, 1851, 1861, 1871: Canada, *Census*, 1871, vol. 4, 140, 171, 198, 271; vol. 3, 420

1851-66: *JLA*, TTN: 1853, App. A, statement 28; 1858, App. 2, statement 20; 1864, SP 3, statements 36 and 37; Canada, Parliament, *Sessional Papers*, 1867, 1, statements 2 and 3

TABLE 6.8
Number of Craftsmen, Upper Canada, 1851 and 1871 (250 or more men* only)

| 1851 | Total | % in 5 cities† | 1871 | Total | % in 5 cities† |
|---|---|---|---|---|---|
| Carpenters | 7,600 | 15.6 | Carpenters | 15,000 | 16.9 |
| Boot & shoemakers | 5,900 | 14.2 | Blacksmiths | 7,900 | 8.6 |
| Blacksmiths | 4,200 | 6.8 | Shoemakers | 6,700 | 20.7 |
| Tailors | 2,700 | 20.3 | Tailors | 4,500 | 25.5 |
| Coopers | 1,900 | 5.2 | Millers | 3,500 | 4.1 |
| Weavers | 1,700 | 1.7 | Carriage makers | 3,000 | 9.6 |
| Masons | 1,500 | 17.1 | Mariners | 2,900 | 18.0 |
| Millers | 1,100 | 3.6 | 'Mechanics'‡ | 2,700 | 33.7 |
| Cabinet makers | 1,000 | 24.4 | Weavers | 2,600 | 1.6 |
| | | | Stonemasons | 2,600 | 15.7 |
| Sawyers | 900 | 5.4 | Coopers | 2,400 | 11.3 |
| Saddlers/harness | 900 | 15.9 | Painters/glaziers | 2,300 | 32.2 |
| Wagon makers ‡ | 900 | 7.0 | Saddlers | 2,000 | 13.2 |
| | | | Foundrymen ‡ | 2,000 | 40.0 |
| Painters | 600 | 31.0 | | | |
| Butchers | 600 | 25.5 | Cabinet makers | 1,900 | 22.3 |
| Mariners/sailors | 600 | 50.5 | Butchers | 1,900 | 21.2 |
| Tanners | 600 | 10.0 | Printers | 1,600 | 47.0 |
| | | | Engineers | 1,600 | 26.4 |
| Carriage makers | 500 | 21.7 | Sawyers | 1,300 | 3.3 |
| Millwrights ‡ | 500 | 6.6 | Bakers | 1,100 | 28.9 |
| Tinsmiths ‡ | 500 | 32.6 | Tanners | 1,000 | 8.2 |
| Bakers | 500 | 39.2 | | | |
| | | | Plasterers | 800 | 35.6 |
| Printers | 400 | 53.2 | Bricklayers | 800 | 31.9 |
| Wheelwrights | 400 | 5.1 | Shipbuilders ‡ | 600 | 15.5 |
| Engineers | 400 | 40.2 | Brickmakers ‡ | 600 | 8.2 |
| | | | Watchmakers ‡ | 500 | 22.5 |
| Moulders ‡ | 300 | 31.8 | Barbers ‡ | 400 | 36.2 |
| Machinists ‡ | 300 | 15.6 | Bookbinders‡ | 300 | 88.3 |
| Plasterers | 300 | 40.6 | Wheelwrights | 300 | 7.5 |
| Bricklayers | 300 | 44.0 | Carders ‡ | 300 | 2.0 |
| | | | Photographers ‡ | 300 | 25.2 |
| Totals | 37,100 | 15.2 | | 65,400 | 21.3 |

* Three women's groups were recorded:

| | | | | | |
|---|---|---|---|---|---|
| Dressmaker/milliners | 1,200 | 29.3 | Dressmakers | 3,900 | 33.1 |
| Seamstresses | 300 | 51.3 | Seamstresses | 2,600 | 37.6 |
| | | | Laundresses‡ | 300 | 67.8 |

† Five cities (towns) were the largest in the province in both years: Toronto, Hamilton, Kingston, Bytown (Ottawa), and London. Together they held 7.5% of provincial population in 1851, 8.2% in 1871.

‡ Indicates an occupation on only one of the two lists, either because not recorded at all or because numbers were below the threshold for inclusion here

SOURCE: Canada, *Census*, 1851–2, pp. 506–25; 1871, vol. 2, table 8

TABLE 6.9

Occupations Given by British Applicants to British Consul in New York, 1817

| | | | |
|---|---|---|---|
| Farmer | 57 | Sawyer | 5 |
| Labourer | 16 | Wheelwright | 4 |
| Smith | 12 | Millwright | 4 |
| Weaver | 11 | | |
| Tailor | 11 | Subtotal | 144 |
| Mason | 10 | All others | 48 * |
| Carpenter | 9 | | |
| Shoemaker | 5 | Total | 192 |

\* 33 other occupations or combinations (e.g., farmer and butcher) are represented here.

SOURCE: NA, Upper Canada Sundries, RG5, A1, vol. 37, 17227–578, passes signed by British Consul at New York for emigrants from Great Britain, 1817

TABLE 6.10

Capitalizing a New Foundry, 1836–7*

| Obligations | | Assets | |
|---|---|---|---|
| 1. Dr McQuesten's investment & 1 year interest | $2,400 | 1. Land at cost | $275 |
| 2. Due Backus & Co. | 1,350 | 2. Machine shop & furnace | 800 |
| 3. Due for iron | 800 | 3. Tools & equipment | 386 |
| 4. Due for coal | 133 | 4. Coal & iron | 561 |
| 5. Due Gore Bank | 340 | 5. Horses, wagon, hay, coal house | 245 |
| 6. Due 4 employees & a smith | 796 | 6. Castings & work in progress | 1,611 |
| 7. Misc. other obligations | 162 | 7. Accounts due | 1,326 |
| Total | $5,981 | 8. Due for machines | 1,124 |
| | | 9. Other notes | 531 |
| | | 10. Patterns | 250 |
| | | Total | $7,109 |

\* Table is in dollars, because they were used in original.

SOURCE: AO, McQuesten Family Papers, Ms 434, reel 4, 231, John Fisher to C. McQuesten, n.d. [Jan. 1837]

TABLE 6.11
Newspapers in Upper Canada, 1841

A.  *Location of Publication (1841)*

| | |
|---|---|
| Toronto | 12 |
| Kingston | 5 |
| Hamilton | 2 |
| London | 2 |
| Niagara | 2 |
| Brockville | 2 |

Communities with one newspaper:

| | |
|---|---|
| Sandwich | St Catharines |
| Cobourg | Peterborough |
| Belleville | Cornwall |
| Bytown | Woodstock |
| Perth | Berlin  (German language) |
| | Waterloo (German language) |

B.  *Year of Founding*

| | | | |
|---|---|---|---|
| 1819 | 2 | 1835 | 1 |
| 1820 | 1 | 1836 | 6 |
| 1826 | 2 | 1837 | 2 |
| 1829 | 2 | 1838 | 1 |
| 1831 | 1 | 1839 | 2 |
| 1832 | 1 | 1840 | 5 |
| 1833 | 2 | 1841 | 1 |
| 1834 | 1 | n/a | 5 |

SOURCES: NA, MG11, CO42, vol. 476, Macaulay's
Report on Upper Canada, 2 Mar. 1841, 355. With a
few exceptions (semi-weekly or bi-weekly or monthly)
these newspapers were weeklies. For 1840, see NA,
Upper Canada Sundries, RG5, A1, vol. 255, 138463–4,
Return of newspapers and proprietors for the year
ended 5 July 1840, which includes Brantford and
Preston.

TABLE 7.1
The Upper Canadian Fleet, Selected Data, 1812–49

| Year | Sail No. | Total tonnage | Mean | | Steam No. | Total tonnage | Mean |
|------|------|------|------|------|------|------|------|
| 1812 | 12–18 | 500–800 | c.50 | | – | – | – |
| 1840 | 81 | 5,600 | 69 | L.Ontario/St L. | 18 | c.3,900 | 216 |
| | | | | Ottawa/Rideau | 19 | c.1,900 | 100 |
| | | | | Total | 37 | 5,800 | 163 |
| 1849* | | | | | | | |
| Regist. | 65 | 7,496 | 115 | | 32 | 6,045 | 189 |
| Unregist. | 145 | 8,815 | 61 | | 12 | 1,105 | 92 |
| Total | 210 | 16,311 | 78 | | 44 | 7,150 | 163 |

* The registered vessels in 1849 were 'inland' from Montreal; it is likely that some Montreal-registered steamships also served the interior. Unregistered inland vessels are assumed to have been in Upper Canada.

SOURCES

1812: E.A. Cruikshank, 'Notes on the History of Shipbuilding and Navigation on Lake Ontario up to the Time of the Launching of the Steamship Frontenac, at Ernesttown, Ontario, 7th September 1816,' OHSPR 23 (1926), 37

1840: NA, MG11, CO42, vol. 476, 'Mr. Macaulay's General Report to Governor Sir George Arthur upon Canada,' 2 Mar. 1841, 139–40, 335–6; Normand Lafrenière, The Ottawa River Canal System (Ottawa 1984), 63; and JLA, 1841, App. EE. Average tonnage of vessels listed in the last assumed equal to the average of those individually listed by Macaulay. But see UCJ, 1839–40, App., 302, for a report that 61 British schooners, with an average tonnage of 81, used the Welland Canal in 1839.

1849: JLA, 1850, App. A, TTN, statement 17

TABLE 7.2
Aspects of the Registered Upper Canadian Fleet, 1845–54

| Port | Steam No. | Tonnage | Mean | Sail No. | Tonnage | Mean | Total tonnage | Cumulative % |
|------|------|------|------|------|------|------|------|------|
| Kingston | 16 | 2,321 | 145 | 24 | 4,071 | 170 | 6,392 | 30 |
| Toronto | 15 | 3,671 | 245 | 18 | 1,539 | 86 | 5,210 | 55 |
| Hamilton | 3 | 612 | 204 | 21 | 2,752 | 131 | 3,363 | 71 |
| Port Hope | 1 | 82 | 82 | 8 | 983 | 123 | 1,065 | 76 |
| Port Dover | 1 | 39 | 39 | 8 | 908 | 114 | 947 | 81 |
| Picton | – | – | – | 5 | 513 | 103 | 513 | 84 |
| Goderich | – | – | – | 11 | 486 | 44 | 486 | 87 |
| Subtotal (7 ports) | 36 | 6,725 | 187 | 95 | 11,252 | 118 | 17,977 | |
| Total (all ports) | 44 | 7,237 | 164 | 123 | 13,510 | 110 | 20,747 | 100 |

NOTE: Not all these vessels necessarily existed at the same time.

SOURCES: JLA, 1854–5, App. PPP, Schedule of Vessels Registered ... in the Province ... 1846–54; NA, Shipping Registers, RG42, I, vols. 205, 209, 221, 225, 362, 367, 368, 383

TABLE 7.3
The Growth of Sailing Ships, Selected Vessels and Cargoes, 1808–53

| Year | 1808 | 1841–3 | 1841–2 | 1853 |
|---|---|---|---|---|
| Ship | *Elizabeth* | *Amelia* | *Hannah Counter* | *St Andrews* |
| Tonnage | 48 | 97 | 136 | 232 |
| *Cargoes* | | | | |
| Wheat (bu) | | c.3,500 | | 13,500 |
| bushels/ton | | 36 | | 58 |
| Flour (bbl) | 440 | | | |
| barrels/ton | 9 | | | |
| Oak (cu ft) | | | 5,500 | 11,000 |
| cu ft/ton | | | 40 | 47 |
| Standard staves | | 11,000 | 13,000 | 25,000 |
| number/ton | | 113 | 96 | 108 |
| Boards (ft) | | | | 195,000 |
| bd ft/ton | | | | 841 |

NOTE: A bushel of wheat = 60 lb; a barrel of flour = 196 lb, plus containers.

SOURCES: QUA, Cartwright Family Papers, Additions, vol. 2, 'Packing Book 1810' [*sic*], accounts of the sloop *Elizabeth*, 1807–8. AO, Smith and Chisholm Papers, MU 2846, 'Receipt Book, 1840–47, Steamer [*sic*] Ladings,' receipt for 29 June 1841. QUA, Calvin Company Records, vol. 143, 'Record of Vessels,' 1840–51, 38, 95, 100; see also Box 119, file 1, 'Ready Reckoner for the Use of ... Measurers of Timber,' which notes that, while one mille of staves was 343 cu ft (equal to 6.8 loads of timber), 'owing to the variations in the breadth and thickness of the staves' it was standard to treat that quantity as equal to 650 cu ft (i.e., 74 standard staves equal 1 ton of capacity). AO, Norris and Neelon Records, Ms 490, series A-1-2, 'time books' [*sic*], accounts of the 'new vessel' (*St Andrews*), 1853; series A-1-3, 'account books,' accounts of the *St Andrews*, cargo books of the *St Andrews*

TABLE 7.4

Shipping Requirements for Principal Welland Canal Cargoes
(British Port to British Port only), 1840 and 1850 (all figures 000s)

| Commodity | 1840 | | 1850 | |
|---|---|---|---|---|
| (conversion factor) | Vol. | Tons | Vol. | Tons |
| Square timber | | | | |
| (40 cu ft/ton) | 900 | 22.5 | 348 | 8.7 |
| Staves | | | | |
| (100 std/ton) | 308 | 3.1 | 1866 | 18.7 |
| (333 West Indies/ton) | 206 | 0.6 | 1747 | 5.2 |
| Flour | | | | |
| (11 bbl/ton) | 111 | 10.1 | n.a. | 11.4 |
| Wheat | | | | |
| (37 bu/ton) | 45 | 1.2 | n.a. | 9.8 |
| Sawn lumber | 1,700 | 2.5 | 3,470 | 5.2 |
| Total tonnage | | 40.0 | | 59.0 |
| Shipping required | | 5.0 | | 7.4 |
| (8 voyages/ship) | | | | |
| Adjusted 1840 tonnage (assuming only | | 28.8 | | |
| $^{1}/_{2}$ timber – 11,300 tons – in vessels) | | | | |
| Adjusted shipping requirements | | 3.6 | | |
| Total UC fleet | | 5.8 | | 16.3 |

SOURCES: For conversion factors, see table 7.3 and E.F. Haites, James Mak, and G.M. Walton, *Western River Transportation: The Era of Early Internal Development, 1810–1860* (Baltimore 1975), 127. For volumes, see *JLA*, 1841, App. D., Report of the Welland Canal Company; 1851, App. A, TTN, schedule 1 (see also tonnage data in schedule 9).

TABLE 7.5
Freight Cost of One Barrel of Flour (selected years), 1802–52 (in d/bbl)

| Year | Head of Lake Ontario to Kingston | Kingston to Montreal |
|---|---|---|
| 1802 | | 48 |
| 1808 | 24 | |
| 1819 | 22 * | 48 |
| 1823–5 | 10 | 33 |
| 1840 | 9 | 24 |
| 1845 | 8 | 21 |
| 1846 | 9$^1$/$_2$ | |
| 1847 | 10$^1$/$_2$ | 18 |
| 1848 | 6$^1$/$_2$ – 9 | |
| 1852 | 12 † | |

\* To Prescott
† Rates this year range from 6d to 16d; this is most likely figure.

SOURCES
1802: AO, Cartwright Papers, Ms 44, copy of typescript, letterbooks, vol. 5, 105–7, R. Cartwright Jr to Robert Hamilton, 30 Jan. 1802
1808: QUA, Cartwright Family Papers, Additions, vol. 2, accounts of sloop *Elizabeth*
1819: NA, Upper Canada Sundries, RG5, A1, vol. 44, 21739–42, Pease to Gifford & Macmillan, 28 Aug. 1819; vol. 45, 21816, bill of lading, 7 Oct. 1819
1823–5: Archives Nationales du Québec, Québec, Fonds Jules Quesnel, b. 1, J.S. Baldwin to Quesnel, 17 Apr. 1823, 12 Jan. 1825; b. 2, J. McCutcheon to Quesnel, 23 May 1823
1840: NA, MG11, CO42, vol. 476, Macaulay's Report, p. 282
1845–8: AO, Norris and Neelon Records, Ms 490, series A-1-1, ledger of the *Merchant Miller*, 1845–9; E.F. Bush, *Commercial Navigation on the Rideau Canal, 1832–1961* (Ottawa 1981), 109, 113
1852: MTL, schooner *Almira* cargo book

TABLE 7.6
Off-farm Travels by W. Beatty, Yonge Township, 1848
(number of trips per month)

| Place | Jan | Feb | Mar | Apr | May | Jun | Jul | Aug | Sep | Oct | Nov | Dec | 1848 |
|---|---|---|---|---|---|---|---|---|---|---|---|---|---|
| Caintown (church) | 4 | 2 | 4 | 2 | 3 | 2 | 3 | 3 | 3 | 3 | 3 | 3 | 35 |
| Brockville Mills | 2 | 4 | 2 | 1 | 1 | 3 | 1 |  | 2 | 2 | 2 |  | 20 |
| Yonge |  | 4 | 5 |  |  |  |  |  |  |  |  |  | 9 |
| Temperance (cloth) | 2 |  |  |  |  |  |  |  |  |  |  | 1 | 3 |
| Mackintosh |  |  |  |  |  |  |  |  |  |  |  | 1 | 1 |
| Farmersville | 1 | 1 |  |  |  |  |  |  | 1 | 1 | 1 |  | 5 |
| Charleston |  |  |  |  |  |  |  |  |  | 1 |  | 3 | 4 |
| Coleman's Corner | 1 | 2 |  |  |  | 1 |  |  |  |  |  |  | 4 |
| Gananoque |  |  |  |  |  |  | 1 |  |  |  |  |  | 1 |
| Mallorytown |  |  |  |  |  |  |  |  |  |  |  | 1 | 1 |
| Other* | 3 |  |  |  | 1 |  |  |  |  | 1 |  |  | 5 |
| Total | 13 | 13 | 11 | 3 | 5 | 6 | 5 | 3 | 6 | 8 | 6 | 9 | 88 |

* Included a bee, town meeting, election, 'old chapel'

NOTE: Visits to neighbours and journeys by other family members are excluded here. Except for 'other' destinations, only Brockville (nearest large market town, about 12 miles away) and Gananoque (20 miles) were not in the Front or Rear townships of Yonge (an area of c. 100 sq mi).

SOURCE: QUA, Walter Beatty Papers, farm journal for 1848. See also W.H. Smith, *Canadian Gazetteer, 1846*, reprint ed. (Toronto 1970).

TABLE 7.7
Principal Provincial Road Expenditures, 1831–49

| Road | Miles | Year first funded | Total funding to 1849 (£000) | Funds per mile (£) | Toll revenues 1849 (£) | Tolls per mile 1849 (£) |
|---|---|---|---|---|---|---|
| York roads* | 71 | 1833 | 148 | 2,085 | 7,400 | 104 |
| Kingston–Napanee | 25 | 1837 | 36 | 1,440 | 1,700 | 68 |
| Hamilton–Brantford | 24 | 1837 | 50 | 2,080 | 2,600 | 108 |
| Dundas–Waterloo | c.35 | 1837 | 31 | 886 | 1,200 | 34 |
| Hamilton–Port Dover | c.36 | 1842 | 26 | 703 | na | na |
| Queenston–Grimsby | c.30 | 1838 | 20 | 667 | na | na |
| London–Brantford | 58 | 1841 | 49 | 845 | 2,900 | 50 |
| London–Port Stanley | 27 | 1841 | 25 | 926 | 1,900 | 70 |
| Port Hope–Rice Lake | 10 | 1841 | 7 | 700 | 400 | 40 |
| Other † | 22 | 1836 | 11 | 500 | 100 | 5 |
| Subtotal | 338 | | 403 | 1,192 | 18,200 | |
| District roads, bridges | na | 1831 | 81 | | na | |
| Bridges ‡ | na | 1833 | 17 | | 900 | |
| Total outlay | | | 501 | | | |

* York roads were Yonge Street, to the north (34 miles); Dundas Street, to the west (20 miles); and Kingston Road, to the east (17 miles).

† Other roads were in West Gwillimbury, at the end of Yonge Street (3 miles), given £1,000 in 1836; and from Windsor (i.e., Whitby) to Lake Scugog (19 miles), given £10,000 in 1841.

‡ Bridges were in Delaware Township, on the London-Chatham Road (n.d.); at Brantford (1833); at the Trent River (1833); at Chatham (1837); at Caledonia, on the Hamilton to Port Dover Road (1841); and at the Narrows, Lake Simcoe (n.d.).

SOURCES: *JLA*, 1850, App. YY, table F 3, Statement of Expenditure upon 'Productive Local Works'; and 1844–5, App. PP, Statement of Moneys Expended for Public Improvements

TABLE 8.1

Credit Extended by Barker and Stevenson, 1825–33

|  |  | A<br>Book<br>debts<br>due<br>(£) | B<br>Due on<br>promissory<br>notes<br>(£) | C<br>Total<br>customer<br>debts<br>(£) | D<br>Sales in<br>calendar<br>year<br>(£) | E<br>C/D<br>(prev. year)<br>x 100<br>(%) | F<br><br><br>Inventory<br>(£) |
|---|---|---|---|---|---|---|---|
|  | 1825 |  |  |  | 676 |  |  |
| 25 May | 1826 | 273 | 21 | 294 | 1,213 | 43 | 119 |
| 13 June | 1827 | 455 | 72 | 527 | 1,484 | 43 | 64 |
| June | 1828 | 658 | 113 | 771 | 1,642 | 52 | 120 |
| 1 May | 1829 | 1,196 | 177 | 1,373 | 1,801 | 84 | 228 |
| 5 June | 1830 | 1,300 | 457 | 1,757 | 1,999 | 98 | 123 |
| 7 June | 1831 | 1,558 | 522 | 2,080 | 2,448 | 104 | 239 |
| 1 June | 1832 | 1,723 | 845 | 2,568 | 2,320 | 105 | 338 |
| 1 June | 1833 | 1,684 | 968 | 2,652 | 2,326 | 114 | 358 |

SOURCE: UG, Goodwin-Haines Collection, William Grant Papers, XR1, Ms A131002, Barker and Stevenson Inventory Book, plus memo of sales, 1825–33. Inventory was taken at or near its annual low.

SOURCES FOR TABLE 8.2

a  *UCJ*, 1823–4, 543; Statement of the Affairs of the Bank of Upper Canada, 8 Dec. 1823

b  *JLA*, 1841, App. O, sections B3–4, B6, D1–3, F, G.

 – Discounts (b) for BUC, 1836–41 are averages of monthly totals of 'discounts' as given in B3 (mean of 12 monthly observations for 1836–40, first seven months of 1841).

 – Discounts for all three banks in 1841, including BUC (a) are 'discounts' recorded insection F as at 1 July 1841. There is an unexplained difference of £77,000 in the two July figures the BUC.

 – If note circulation and specie for all of 1837, 1838, and 1839 are calculated for 1836 and 1840, data are as follows:

|  | Note circulation (£000) | | | | Specie in Vaults (£000) | | | |
|---|---|---|---|---|---|---|---|---|
|  | BUC | CB | GB | All | BUC | CB | GB | All |
| 1837 | 165 | 143 | 34 | 342 | 63 | 27 | 21 | 111 |
| 1838 | 192 | 193 | 34 | 419 | 79 | 51 | 22 | 152 |
| 1839 | 281 | 261 | 69 | 611 | 86 | 82 | 24 | 192 |

 – Specie data are means of figures reported twice monthly except for 1841, which run to July only.

(Sources continue on p. 292.)

TABLE 8.2
Upper Canadian Chartered Banking, Selected Data, 1823–58

| Year | Source | Pop. (000) | Paid-up capital (£000) | | | | Loans & discounts (£000) | | | | | Discs per cap. |
|------|--------|------------|------|------|------|------|------|------|------|------|------|------|
| | | | BUC | CB | GB | All | (a) BUC | (b) BUC | CB | GB | All | |
| 1823 | a, b | | 13 | | | 13 | 32 | | | | 32 | c.021 |
| 1824 | b, c | 150 | 28 | | | 28 | | | | | | |
| 1825 | b, c, d | 158 | 38 | | | 38 | 80 | | | | 80 | |
| 1826 | b, e | 166 | 54 | | | 54 | 108 | | | | 108 | 0.65 |
| 1827 | b | 177 | 63 | | | 63 | | | | | | |
| 1828 | b, f | 186 | 72 | | | 72 | 172 | | | | 172 | 0.92 |
| 1829 | b, g | 198 | 77 | | | 77 | 181 | | | | 181 | 0.91 |
| 1830 | b, h | 213 | 100 | | | 100 | 214 | | | | 214 | 1.00 |
| 1831 | b, i | 237 | 100 | | | 100 | 261 | | | | 261 | 1.10 |
| 1832 | b | 264 | 100 | | | 100 | | | | | | |
| 1833 | b, j, k | 296 | 183 | 60 | | 243 | 310 | | | | | |
| 1834 | b, j, m, n | 321 | 200 | 100 | | 300 | 380 | | 169 | | 549 | 1.71 |
| 1835 | b, j, n, o | 347 | 200 | 100 | | 300 | 391 | | 208 | | 599 | 1.73 |
| 1836 | b, j, n | 374 | 200 | 120 | | 320 | 435 | | 343 | | 778 | 2.08 |
| | b | | | | | | | 360 | | | | |
| 1837* | b, j, n | 397 | 200 | 197 | 80 | 477 | 457 | | 344 | 106 | 907 | 2.28 |
| | b | | | | | | | 319 | | | | |
| 1838* | b, j | | 200 | 200 | 89 | 489 | | 219 | 328 | 89 | 636 | ≤1.60 |
| 1839* | b, p | 409 | 200 | 200 | 100 | 500 | | 246 | | 111 | | |
| 1840 | b | | 200 | 200 | 100 | 500 | | 321 | | | | |
| 1841 | b, q | 456 | 200 | 200 | 100 | 500 | | 335 | | | | |
| | b | | | | | | 407 | | 462 | 165 | 1,034 | 2.27 |
| 1842 | q, r | 487 | 200 | 200 | 100 | 500 | 385 | | 297 | 148 | 830 | 1.70 |
| 1843 | q, s | | 217 | 239 | 100 | 556 | 375 | | 449 | 157 | 981 | |
| 1844 | q | | | | | | | | | | | |
| 1845 | q, t | | 246 | 292 | 100 | 638 | 517 | | 599 | 171 | 1,287 | |
| 1846 | q, u | | 282 | 326 | 100 | 708 | 596 | | 683 | 196 | 1,475 | |
| 1847 | q, v | | 333 | 372 | 100 | 805 | 579 | | 651 | 194 | 1,424 | |
| 1848 | q, w | 726 | 379 | 397 | 100 | 876 | 614 | | 629 | 141 | 1,384 | 1.91 |
| 1849 | x | | 381 | | | | 564 | | | | | |
| 1850 | y | | 381 | 403 | 80 | 864 | 692 | | 653 | 194 | 1,539 | |
| 1851 | z | 952 | 381 | 411 | 80 | 872 | 1,015 | | 852 | 227 | 2,094 | 2.20 |
| 1852 | aa | | 381 | 419 | 80 | 880 | 1,102 | | 773 | 192 | 2,067 | |
| 1854 | bb | | 499 | 500 | 112 | 1,111 | 2,035 | | 1,185 | 380 | 3,600 | |
| 1858 | cc | | 778 | 945 | 200 | 1,923 | 1,846 | | 1,537 | 335 | 3,718 | |

BUC = Bank of Upper Canada; CB = Commercial Bank of the Midland District; GB = Gore Bank (it began to operate in the latter part of 1836, but data on it for part of the year are excluded from 1836 totals).

| Note circulation (£000) | | | | Notes per cap. | Specie in vaults (£000) | | | | Ratio, notes: specie | | | |
|---|---|---|---|---|---|---|---|---|---|---|---|---|
| BUC | CB | GB | All | | BUC | CB | GB | All | BUC | CB | GB | All |
| 27 | | | 27 | c0.18 | 11 | | | 11 | 2.5 | | | 2.5 |
| 45 | | | 45 | 0.30 | | | | | | | | |
| 64 | | | 64 | 0.41 | | | | | | | | |
| 87 | | | 87 | 0.52 | 19 | | | 19 | 4.6 | | | 4.6 |
| 123 | | | 123 | 0.66 | 21 | | | 21 | 5.9 | | | 5.9 |
| 140 | | | 140 | 0.71 | 23 | | | 23 | 6.1 | | | 6.1 |
| 156 | | | 156 | 0.73 | 33 | | | 33 | 4.7 | | | 4.7 |
| 187 | | | 187 | 0.79 | 43 | | | 43 | 4.3 | | | 4.3 |
| 190 | | | | | 62 | | | | 3.1 | | | |
| 198 | 76 | | 274 | 0.85 | 45 | 23 | | 68 | 4.4 | 3.3 | | 4.0 |
| 215 | 117 | | 332 | 0.92 | 88 | 29 | | 117 | 2.4 | 4.0 | | 2.8 |
| 198 | 129 | | 327 | 0.87 | 63 | 28 | | 91 | 3.1 | 4.6 | | 3.6 |
| 240 | 184 | 44 | 468 | 1.18 | 54 | 36 | 21 | 111 | 4.4 | 5.1 | 2.1 | 4.2 |
| 170 | 222 | 43 | 435 | 1.06 | 104 | 99 | 30 | 233 | 1.6 | 2.2 | 1.4 | 1.9 |
| 168 | 218 | 58 | 444 | | 78 | 76 | 30 | 187 | 2.2 | 2.9 | 1.9 | 2.4 |
| 152 | 213 | 89 | 454 | 1.00 | 67 | 65 | 29 | 161 | 2.3 | 3.3 | 3.1 | 2.8 |
| 133 | 138 | 80 | 351 | 0.72 | 25 | 58 | 22 | 105 | 5.3 | 2.4 | 3.6 | 3.3 |
| 108 | 113 | 56 | 277 | | 32 | 38 | 22 | 92 | 3.4 | 3.0 | 2.5 | 3.0 |
| 158 | 150 | 73 | 381 | | | | | | | | | |
| 180 | 163 | 82 | 425 | | 52 | 57 | 25 | 134 | 3.5 | 2.9 | 3.3 | 3.2 |
| 178 | 178 | 81 | 437 | | 45 | 56 | 20 | 121 | 4.0 | 3.2 | 4.1 | 3.6 |
| 194 | 207 | 81 | 482 | | 32 | 61 | 18 | 111 | 6.1 | 3.4 | 4.5 | 4.3 |
| 167 | 168 | 60 | 395 | 0.54 | 35 | 52 | 12 | 99 | 4.8 | 3.2 | 5.0 | 4.0 |
| 150 | 158 | 60 | 368 | | | | | | | | | |
| 194 | 188 | 108 | 490 | | 50 | 47 | 9 | 106 | 3.9 | 4.0 | 12.0 | 4.6 |
| 251 | 224 | 133 | 608 | 0.64 | 51 | 58 | 15 | 124 | 4.9 | 3.9 | 8.9 | 4.9 |
| 363 | 242 | 121 | 726 | | 106 | 49 | 10 | 165 | 3.4 | 4.9 | 12.1 | 4.4 |
| 655 | 444 | 266 | 1,365 | | 139 | 78 | 25 | 242 | 4.7 | 5.7 | 10.6 | 5.6 |
| 538 | 325 | 96 | 959 | | 95 | 116 | | | 5.7 | 2.8 | | |

\* Because of the 1837 financial crisis (which began in May) and the subsequent suspension of specie payments by the Upper Canadian banks no data are recorded on specie and circulation for 1838; 1837 data are for Jan. to Apr. only, and 1839 for Dec. only.

SOURCES FOR TABLE 8.2 (continued)

c   NA, Upper Canada Sundries, RG5, A1, vol. 73, T.G. Ridout to Major Hillier, 2 July 1825; printed in Baskerville, *The Bank of Upper Canada*, 28–9

d   NA, Adam Shortt Papers, MG30, D101, vol. 1, T.G. Ridout to Major Hillier, 22 Feb. 1825 (typed extract from Upper Canada Sundries)

e   *UCJ*, 1826–7, 13 (data as of Dec.)

f   *UCJ*, 1828, 61 (data as of Feb.)

g   *UCJ*, 1829, 67 (data as of March)

h   *UCJ*, 1830, 56 (data as of Feb.)

i   *UCJ*, 1831, 31 (data as of Jan.)

j   *UCJ*, 1837–8, App., 212–34, Report of the Select Committee on Banking. Data on discounts for 1838 are from 221, 228, 230, and are for the beginning of Jan. in the case of the GB and BUC; data are for 30 Nov. 1837 for the CB (and its 1836 data at 1 Jan. 1836).

k   *UCJ*, 1832–3, 118 (data as of Feb.)

m   *UCJ*, 1833–4, 65–6 (data are actually for mid-Dec. 1833)

n   *UCJ*, 1837, App., Report on the Monetary System, appendix, iv, 58
  – For the BUC, data on discounts are averages of figures reported for 'bills and notes discounted' and are reported in BUC (a) column. They are means of last seven months 1835, of twelve months in 1836, and of first six months of 1837. No explanation is available for the discrepancy between this source and that cited in (b) above.
  – circulation data for 1834 to 1836 for Commercial Bank are means of data for 1 Jan. and 1 June of each year; the same is true for the BUC in 1834.

o   *UCJ*, 1835, 78, Statement of the Commercial Bank as of 22 Jan. 1835

p   Gore Bank discount figures for 1839 are from two reports, 11 Mar. and 9 Dec., of 'all debts due ... excepting balances due from other Banks,' and also excluding provincial debentures held in London. NA, Upper Canada Sundries, RG5, A1, vol. 218, 119930; vol. 234, 128374

q   *JLA*, 1849, App. Z. This gives monthly data from the final two months of 1841 until the end of Oct. 1848. Data are means of monthly totals.

r   *JLA*, 1842, App. R (data are for Sept.)

s   *JLA*, 1843, App. Y (data as of Oct.)

t   *JLA*, 1845, App. Q (data as of Jan.)

u   *JLA*, 1846, App. U (data as of Apr.)

v   *JLA*, 1847, App. U (data as of June)

w   *JLA*, 1848, App. T (data as of Mar.)

x   *JLA*, 1850, App. C, statement 7; record of bank note duties paid in year ended 31 Oct. 1849 (i.e., two months of 1848 included in these figures in lieu of two last months of 1849)

y   *JLA*, 1850, App. H (data as of July)

z   *JLA*, 1851, App. I (data as of June)

aa  *JLA*, 1852–3, App. R (data as of Aug.)

bb  *JLA*, 1854–5, App. EE (BUC data are averages of Jan.–Feb. quotations, CB for Aug., GB for Sept. 1854)

cc  *JLA*, 1858, App. 8 (data as of Mar.)

*Appendix to Table 8.2: A Note on Banking Statistics*

Most of the statistics in chapter 8 are from public records. Financial institutions, because they were the subject of much debate, some regulation, and a requirement to report to the public, are among the best-documented components of the colonial economy, and data on banking are among the longest quantitative series for the Upper Canadian economy. There are possible biases in some of the data, however. Because those preparing material for publication, whether in the government or one of the banks, could make short-term adjustments to conceal underlying realities if that seemed desirable, published data cannot always be taken at face value. For example, the figures on the government account in the Bank of Upper Canada in the 1850s were fundamentally false. And the valuation of assets, particularly overdue debts, offered substantial interpretive scope.

Despite such problems, these data offer essential evidence on provincial development. For the most part, they survive as occasional, perhaps once or twice per year, reports, and not always at the same date for the different banks. For some years in the later 1830s, data on note circulation, specie holdings, and exchange dealings are available on a monthly or twice-monthly basis, and the first of these series continues to 1848. Discounts, the chief form of bank lending, were reported in two ways: some reports appear to focus just on paper discounted, while others, including data from the 1840s on, include all debts due the bank with the exception of inter-bank balances. Deposits, initially a relatively modest part of bank liabilities, are noted separately because of the various methods of reporting (see table 8.3). Inter-bank balances were internal to the banking system and are omitted from the tables, to focus on core bank operations in the wider economy. Data are presented on an annual basis, with the exception of adjustments made for 1837–9, when specie payments were suspended. Although some abstraction from short-term, especially seasonal, fluctuations is entailed, annual data are appropriate to consideration of trends and of the broader pattern of fluctuations in levels of economic activity.

Another series for the Bank of Upper Canada, diverging in some respects from these, can be found in Peter Baskerville, ed, *The Bank of Upper Canada* (Toronto 1987), tables 12A and 12B. The discrepancies, which are principally for the period 1835–41, may arise because his data are for a particular date, whereas mine include averages based on monthly and even twice-monthly data for these years.

As noted in the text, after 1840 the data on the Upper Canadian banks are not comprehensive records of banking within Upper Canada. On the other hand, even if their post-Union experience is not a full record of banking within Upper Canada, their experience should have reflected the changes in the region's economy. Hence tables 8.2 and 8.3 carry the data into the 1850s. During the 1850s, in the inflationary climate of the railway era, all three Upper Canadian banks lent increasingly substantial sums that would subsequently prove impossible to recover. As their failures in the 1860s revealed, their accounts, notably of assets, were misleading by no later than the 1857 crisis; their reported data must have begun even earlier to diverge from underlying long-term realities as measured by the test of being able to realize the amounts shown as assets.

TABLE 8.3
Upper Canadian Chartered Bank Deposits, 1823–58 (£000s)

| | Date | | Item | BUC | CB | GB | Total | Deps: notes | Source |
|---|---|---|---|---|---|---|---|---|---|
| 8 | Dec. | 1823 | 'Funds' | 8 | | | 8 | 0.30 | a |
| 2 | Feb. | 1830 | 'Funds' | 26 | | | 26 | 0.16 | h |
| 1 | Jan. | 1831 | 'Funds' | 16 | | | 16 | 0.09 | b |
| 2 | Feb. | 1833 | Deposits not at interest | 107 | | | | | i |
| 16 | Dec. | 1833 | Deposits not at interest | 118 | 19 | | 137 | 0.50 | j |
| 1 | June | 1836 | Deposits not at interest | | 21 | | | | c |
| | Nov. | 1836 | 'cash deposited' | 155 | 29 | 6 | 191 | 0.58 | b |
| | June | 1837 | 'Deposits' | 159 | 38 | 8 | 205 | 0.44 | d |
| | Jan. | 1838 | Deposits not at interest | 75 | 29 | 11 | 115 | 0.57 | c |
| 9 | Dec. | 1839 | 'Deposits' | | | 8 | | | e |
| 1 | July | 1841 | 'Deposits' | 144 | 99 | 14 | 257 | 0.57 | f |
| | Sept. | 1842 | Deposits not at interest | 116 | 33 | 21 | 170 | | g |
| | | | Total deposits | 122 | 40 | 21 | 183 | 0.52 | |
| | Oct. | 1843 | Deposits not at interest | 106 | 51 | 14 | 171 | | g |
| | | | Total deposits | 117 | 66 | 15 | 188 | 0.68 | |
| | Jan. | 1845 | Deposits not at interest | 135 | 73 | 14 | 222 | | g |
| | | | Total deposits | 166 | 96 | 24 | 286 | 0.67 | |
| | Apr. | 1846 | Deposits not at interest | 116 | 80 | 18 | 214 | | g |
| | | | Total deposits | 185 | 140 | 38 | 363 | 0.83 | |
| | June | 1847 | Deposits not at interest | 90 | 115 | 21 | 226 | | g |
| | | | Total deposits | 137 | 179 | 42 | 358 | 0.74 | |
| | Mar. | 1848 | Deposits not at interest | 87 | 62 | 13 | 162 | | g |
| | | | Total deposits | 112 | 95 | 19 | 226 | 0.57 | |
| | July | 1850* | Deposits not at interest | 269 | 69 | 27 | 365 | | g |
| | | | Total deposits | 430 | 157 | 38 | 625 | 1.28 | |
| | May | 1851 | Deposits not at interest | 397 | 90 | 19 | 506 | | g |
| | | | Total deposits | 546 | 226 | 35 | 807 | 1.33 | |
| | Aug. | 1852 | Deposits not at interest | 356 | 133 | 27 | 516 | | g |
| | | | Total deposits | 539 | 239 | 44 | 822 | 1.13 | |
| | | 1854† | Deposits not at interest | 814 | 168 | 72 | 1,054 | | g |
| | | | Total deposits | 990 | 425 | 118 | 1,533 | 1.12 | |
| | Mar. | 1858 | Deposits not at interest | 525 | 191 | 44 | 760 | | g |
| | | | Total deposits | 562 | 294 | 62 | 918 | 0.96 | |

* After 1850, BUC had government account, which inflates deposits.
† BUC data from Feb., CBMD from Aug., GB from Sept. 1854

SOURCES: (a) *UCJ*, 1823–4, 543; (b) Breckenridge, *The Canadian Banking System*, 52, 63; (c) *UCJ*, 1837–8, App., 221–30; (d) *UCJ*, 1837, App., iv; (e) NA, RG5, A1, vol. 234, 128374, Statement of Gore Bank; (f) *JLA*, 1841, App. O, section F; (g) *JLA*, see notes to table 8.2 for detailed citations; (h) *UCJ*, 1830, 56; (i) *UCJ*, 1832–3, 118; (j) *UCJ*, 1833–4, 65-6

TABLE 8.4
Locational Pattern of Chartered Bank Shareholders, 1837–8

|  | BUC | CB | GB |
|---|---|---|---|
| Toronto | 69 | 68 | 23 |
| Other Home District | 20 | | |
| Kingston | 24 | 68 | 8 |
| Midland & PE Districts | | 28 | |
| Hamilton | 8 | 12 | 35 |
| Other Gore District | | | 20 |
| All other UC | 112 | 176 | 42 |
| Outside UC | 41 | 122 | 39 |
| Other (no address) | 28 | 12 | – |
| Total | 302 | 486 | 167 |

Shareholders in common among the banks: BUC–CB–GB, 12; BUC–CB, 72; BUC–GB 25; CB–GB, 26

TABLE 8.5
Chartered Bank Note Issues, 1837–9, Selected Months
(all figures £000)

| Month | BUC | CB | GB | Total |
|---|---|---|---|---|
| 1836 mean | 198 | 129 | 36† | 363 |
| Apr. 1837 | 248 | 183 | 49 | 480 |
| July 1837 | 130 | 100 | 27 | 257 |
| Sept. 1837 | 109 | 82* | 25 | 216 |
| Dec. 1837 | 79 | 177 | 20 | 276 |
| Mar. 1838 | 117* | 203 | 13* | 333 |
| Sept. 1838 | 269 | 185 | 39 | 493 |
| Apr. 1839 | 334 | 310 | 96 | 740 |
| Oct. 1839 | 219 | 250 | 46 | 515 |
| 1840 mean | 168 | 218 | 58 | 444 |

*   Indicates that bank suspended specie payments during this month.
†   Figure is for 1 Jan. 1837, as bank operated only part of 1836.
SOURCE: *JLA*, 1841, App. O, section D

TABLE 8.6
Banking Ratios, Upper Canadian Banks Only, Selected Indicators, Selected Years, 1826–51

| Year | Notes per cap. | Notes/ specie | Discounts per cap. | Deposits/ notes | Notes + deps per cap. |
|------|------|------|------|------|------|
| 1826 | 0.52 | 4.6 | 0.65 | na | na |
| 1831 | 0.79 | 4.3 | 1.10 | 0.09 | 0.86 |
| 1836 | 0.87 | 3.6 | 2.08 | 0.58 | 1.39 |
| 1841 | 1.00 | 2.8 | 2.27 | 0.57 | 1.56 |
| 1846* | 0.73 | 3.6 | 2.46 | 0.83 | 1.33 |
| 1851 | 0.64 | 4.9 | 2.20 | 1.33 | 1.49 |

* Population in 1846 assumed to be 600,000.

SOURCES: See tables 8.2, 8.3.

TABLE 8.7
Upper Canadian Fire and Marine Insurance Companies, Selected Data, Selected Years (1836–51), (all figures £000)

| Year | Company | Paid-up capital | Value of investments | Premium Income Fire | Marine | Losses Paid Fire | Marine | Risks Fire | Marine |
|------|------|------|------|------|------|------|------|------|------|
| 1836 | StL | 10 | 11 | | 2.3 | | 1.3 | | 337 |
| 1838 | StL | 10 | 11 | | 1.6 | | 0.9 | | 212 |
| | BA | 11 | 10 | 2.1 | | | | 206 | |
| 1844 | StL | 15 | na | | 4.9 | | 3.3 | | 445 |
| | BA | 35 | 30 | 4.3 | 1.5 | 2.5 | 0.7 | 412 | 111 |
| 1847 | StL | 15 | 16 | | 8.7 | | 7.6 | | 860 |
| | BA | 35 | 37 | 7.2 | 2.0 | 3.5 | 0.4 | 770 | 129 |
| 1851 | StL | 15 | 14 | | 3.0 | | 1.6 | | 342 |
| | BA | 45 | 33 | 8.7 | 1.4 | 2.6 | 2.9 | 842 | 99 |

NOTE: StL = St Lawrence Inland Marine Insurance Co. (of Prescott); BA = British America Fire and Life Assurance Co. (Toronto).

SOURCES: *UCJ*, 1836–7, App. 63; *JLA*, 1844, App. S; 1847, App. U; 1851, App. I. See also UTL, British America Assurance Company, Cash Book, 1834–47; Day Books, 1837–41, 1845–7; Statement Book, 1850–3.

TABLE 9.1
Upper Canada's Share of Principal Customs Revenues Collected
by Lower Canada on Goods Entering the St Lawrence, 1795–1840
(percentages)

| 1795–1800 | *c.* 12.5 | 1817–24 | 20.0[†] |
|-----------|-----------|---------|---------|
| 1801–12   | *c.* 9.0 [*] | 1824–32 | 25.0 |
| 1813      | 8.3       | 1832–36 | 33.3 |
| 1814–16   | *c.* 25.0 | 1836–40 | 38.5 |

[*] The rate ranged in these years from as low as 4.3%, in 1805, to as high as
16.7%, in 1808.

[†] No duties were received in 1820 or 1821, though the 1822 payment and a
further payment on arrears in 1824 largely compensated for the earlier
non-payment; see table 9.2.

SOURCES: for 1795–1816, *UCJ*, 1823-4, printed in OBA, *Report* (1914),
506–8; Agreement between Upper and Lower Canada on division of duties,
31 May 1817, in *UCJ*, 16 Feb. 1818, printed in OBA, *Ninth Report* (1912),
447; *UCJ*, 1825, App. A, schedules 1–3 and p. 6; *UCJ*, 1829, App., Report
of Upper Canadian Arbitrator on ... duties levied at Quebec; *UCJ*, 1833–4,
App., 52–62, Report of arbitrators on ... duties; *UCJ*, 1836–7, App. 4,
arbitrator's report on duties ...

TABLE 9.2
Tax and Other Revenues of the Upper Canadian Government, 1819–40
(all figures except per capita in £000 cy)

| | | 1819 | 1820 | 1821 | 1822 | 1823 | 1824 | 1825 | 1826 | 1827 | 1828 | 1829 |
|---|---|---|---|---|---|---|---|---|---|---|---|---|
| A. | Customs duties* | | | | | | | | | | | |
| | 1. From Lower Canada | 21 | – | – | 47 | 16 | 29 | 22 | 27 | 24 | 25 | 29 |
| | 2. On US goods | 1 | 2 | 2 | [ ] | [ ] | 3 | 3 | 5 | 4 | 6 | 7 |
| B. | Licences: shop, still, tavern | 4 | 6 | 5 | [ ] | [ ] | 4 | 6 | 5 | 6 | 5 | 5 |
| C. | Casual & territorial | | | | | | | | | | | |
| | 1. Crown timber | | | | | – | 1 | 1 | 1 | – | 1 | 3 |
| | 2. Canada Company | | | | | – | – | – | – | 8 | 26 | 17 |
| | 3. Other | | | | | | 2 | 3 | 3 | 3 | 9 | 5 |
| D. | Bank dividends | | | | | – | – | 1 | 1 | 2 | 1 | 1 |
| E. | Other | | | | | | 2 | 2 | 1 | 2 | 6 | 2 |
| F. | Subtotal | 26 | 8 | 7 | | | 41 | 38 | 43 | 50 | 79 | 69 |
| G. | Public works | | | | | | | | | | – | 1 |
| H. | British parliament | 12 | [ ] | 12 | [ ] | 9 | [ ] | [ ] | [ ] | | | |
| I. | Total revenues | 38 | | | | | | | | | | |
| J. | Row F/population | 8s | | | | | | 6s | 5s | 5s | 6s | 9s | 7s |
| K. | Total municipal taxes | | | | | | | 10 | 10 | 12 | 13 | 13 |
| L. | Source notes | b,c, d,f | b,c, e | b,c, e | c | c,f | a,c | a,g | a,h | a,h | a,h | a,h |

* Customs revenues for 1816–18 were as follows:

| | 1816 | 1817 | 1818 |
|---|---|---|---|
| From Lower Canada | 27 | 22 | 17 |
| On US goods | 1 | 4 | 1 |
| (source note b) | | | |

TABLE 9.2 *(continued)*

|  | 1830 | 1831 | 1832 | 1833 | 1834 | 1835 | 1836 | 1837 | 1838 | 1839 | 1840 |
|---|---|---|---|---|---|---|---|---|---|---|---|
| A. Customs duties |  |  |  |  |  |  |  |  |  |  |  |
| 1. From Lower Canada | 30 | 38 | 43 | 55 | 65 | 46 | 56 | 42 | 44 | 63 | 59 |
| 2. On US goods | 9 | 9 | 9 | 11 | 11 | 14 | 11 | 11 | 14 | 18 | 18 |
| B. Licences: shop, still, tavern | 5 | 6 | 6 | 7 | 7 | 7 | 8 | 8 | 7 | 9 | 13 |
| C. Casual & territorial |  |  |  |  |  |  |  |  |  |  |  |
| 1. Crown timber | 4 | 6 | 3 | 6 | 2 | 5 | 9 | 8 | 9 | 11 | 13 |
| 2. Canada Company | 17 | 19 | 19 | 21 | 22 | 22 | 22 | 22 | 22 | 22 | 22 |
| 3. Other | 6 | 7 | 8 | 10 | 21 | 21 | 12 | 14 | [ ] | [ ] | [ ] |
| D. Bank dividends | 3 | 2 | 5 | 4 | 2 | 3 | 2 | 2 | 2 | 2 | [ ] |
| E. Other | 3 | 3 | 3 | 5 | 5 | 4 | 3 | 6 | 1 ? | 2 ? | 3 ? |
| F. Subtotal | 77 | 90 | 96 | 119 | 135 | 122 | 123 | 113 |  |  |  |
| G. Public works | 2 | 1 | 1 | 1 | 2 | 3 | 2 | 3 | 10 | 7 | 11 |
| H. British parliament |  |  |  |  |  |  |  |  |  |  |  |
| I. Total revenues |  |  |  |  |  |  |  |  |  |  |  |
| J. Row F/population | 7s | 8s | 7s | 8s | 8s | 7s | 7s | 6s |  |  |  |
| K. Total municipal taxes | 13 | 15 | 17 | 18 | 22 | 25 | 27 | 27 | 30 | 33 | 37 |
| L. Source notes | a,h | a,h | a,h | a,h | a,h | a,h | a,h | a,h | h,j | g,j, k | g,j, k |

SOURCES

a   NA, MG11, CO42, vol. 471, 117, statement of Upper Canadian revenues, 1824–37, enclosed in J. Macaulay to S.B. Harrison, 30 June 1840

a   *UCJ*, 1821, printed in OBA, *Report* (1913), 283–4, 291, 315

c   *UCJ*, 1825–6, App. A, and Report of Select Committee on Public Accounts

d   *UCJ*, 1819, printed in OBA, *Report* (1913), 105–7, 139–42

e   *UCJ*, 1821–2, printed in OBA, *Report* (1914), 78–9. Until 1831 liquor licence revenues were divided between crown and legislature-controlled shares, the former applicable directly to certain costs of civil administration. In 1821 the total for the former was £1,500 and for the latter £3,400. The latter was £4,200 in 1820, and I have assumed that the former fell into the range of £1,500 to £2,000.

f   NA, MG11, CO42, vol. 374, 411–18, John Strachan to R. Wilmot Horton, 25 May 1824

g   *JLA*, 1849, App. N, 'Enclosure in No. 6,' statement of rateable property in Upper Canada, 1825–47

h   *UCJ*, 1839, App., 465–8, Population and Assessment Returns, 1824–38

j   *JLA*, 1841, App. B

k   George C. Patterson, *Land Settlement in Upper Canada 1783–1840*, in AO, *Sixteenth Report* (1920), 200

See also appendix to table 9.2 on p. 300.

*Appendix to Table 9.2:* Chapter 9 is not meant as a disquisition on the subtleties of pre-1840 government finance and administration, but the meaning of the data depends in part on the system under which revenues were gathered and expended. As much as possible this table is based on the continuous table provided in CO42 (see note a); excluded are proceeds of debentures, treated as income in the original source. Revenues from public works are indicated separately, as it might be more appropriate to think of them in the framework of a capital account. It is not always possible to be sure whether some items were a component of revenue or not. The [ ] symbol indicates a probable gap.

In the regime of public finance prevailing under the Quebec Act and thereafter, some revenues, collected under imperial statutes, were directly for crown purposes and not subject to local Assembly control or accounting. The principal source used here for 1824–37 gives data for both such crown revenues and those collected under local statutes and subject to Assembly control. Before 1824 it is not always clear from public accounts whether both categories of revenue are included in reported figures (sometimes they undoubtedly were). The situation became clearer in 1831, when Upper Canada conceded a permanent civil list and its legislature was in turn accorded control of most of the hitherto crown duties. The 'Casual and Territorial' revenues, however, remained under the executive's control, or at least were not routinely reported in the public accounts.

'Other' (row C3) derives from series in the original for sale and rental of crown lands, including some clergy reserves and school lands and rental of mills and ferries. 'Other' (row E) includes duties on auctioneers and pedlars, some interest received on 'loans to public works,' legal fines and seizures, and 'incidental.'

Other sources also offer evidence on the revenues received by the provincial government, but they frequently do not agree with one another and are unclear on important aspects of the figures offered. Records of the Assembly Public Accounts Committee, for example, often refer to projected receipts for a specific period rather than to actual sums already paid in. Other types of problems include the following.

1. Some categories appear only inconsistently in the sources, and data were sometimes recorded inconsistently (e.g., collections might appear either net of costs of collection or gross; where possible, revenues are presented net of direct costs of collection).

2. Time periods are often unclear, or less than a full year. Also, collectors might not report at the same time or for the same period. Thus, omission of data from one district may or may not mean that there was no revenue collected there in a period, or a collector might send funds in for more than one year or period at a time, without this appearing in the record. Fiscal and calendar years might also disagree. And it is not always clear whether data are for the year the revenue was earned or actually received.

3. Occasionally there is ambiguity over either the currency of the figure (Hfx or stg) or over the appropriate exchange rate to apply, in that official and actual rates were not necessarily the same. Because public accounts often used the par rate, figures originally given in sterling are converted at the rate of £1.111 cy = £1.0 stg, rather than at actual rates of exchange. The largest potential area of underestimation is the payment on Canada Company account. If it was actually made in sterling, then another £2,000 cy would have been received in real terms on a payment of £20,000 stg.

4. There may be deliberate biases introduced by particular sources, both through politics (e.g., the desire of a government not to make full disclosure to a Reform committee) and through the varying viewpoints of different agencies.

5. Thus, where multiple sources exist for a specific item of data, it is far from uncommon to

find different figures given. Colonial government was a rather complex and in some respects unsystematic process: even responsible officials might be misled by their own information, or simply lack knowledge on particular points. This is very evident in the presentation of the public accounts, in which capital and current accounts are thoroughly intermingled, proceeds of bond issues being treated as revenue in the same manner as tax receipts, for example.

TABLE 9.3
Expenditures of the Upper Canadian Government, 1824–40
(all figures except per capita in £000 cy)

|  | 1824 | 1825 | 1826 | 1827 | 1828 | 1829 | 1830 | 1831 | 1832 |
|---|---|---|---|---|---|---|---|---|---|
| A. Civil administration & admin. of justice | 9 | 10 | 11 | 16 | 29 | 21 | 23 | 22 | 21 |
| B. Legislature | 3 | 5 | 4 | 4 | 5 | 5 | 6 | 6 | 7 |
| C. Churches, clergy | 1 | 1 | 2 | 2 | 3 | 3 | 3 | 5 | 4 |
| D. Education, schools | 5 | 5 | 4 | 5 | 5 | 5 | 6 | 6 | 6 |
| E. Militia (inc. pensions) | 6 | 2 | 3 | 3 | 3 | 3 | 2 | 2 | 2 |
| F. Other pensions | 1 | 1 | 1 | 3 | 4 | 3 | 4 | 5 | 5 |
| G. Other | | | | | | | | | |
| 1. Emigration | | | | | | | | 5* | 10* |
| 2. Indians | | | | | | | | 2 | |
| 3. Lighthouses | | | | | 1 | 2 | 1 | | 1 |
| 4. Penitentiary | | | | | | | | | |
| 5. Surveys | | | | 1 | 1 | | 2 | 1 | 1 |
| H. All other | 2 | 2 | 5 | 1 | 1 | 3 | 1 | 1 | 4 |
| I. Subtotal | 27 | 26 | 30 | 35 | 52 | 45 | 48 | 55 | 61 |
| J. Interest on debt | 2 | 3 | 2 | 4 | 7 | 7 | 7 | 6 | 9 |
| K. Total | 29 | 29 | 32 | 39 | 59 | 52 | 55 | 61 | 70 |
| L. Row I/population (shillings) | 3.6 | 3.3 | 3.6 | 4.0 | 5.6 | 4.5 | 4.5 | 4.6 | 4.6 |
| M. Row K/population (shillings) | 3.9 | 3.7 | 3.9 | 4.4 | 6.3 | 5.3 | 5.2 | 5.1 | 5.3 |

|  | 1833 | 1834 | 1835 | 1836 | 1837 | 1838† | 1839† | 1840† |
|---|---|---|---|---|---|---|---|---|
| A. Civil administration & admin. of justice‡ | 22 | 25 | 21 | 23 | 28 | 35 | 43 | 37 |
| B. Legislature | 7 | 10 | 11 | 12 | 16 | 13 | 10 | 9 |
| C. Churches, clergy | 15 | 17 | 14 | 13 | 13 | ? | ? | ? |
| D. Education, schools | 10 | 10 | 12 | 10 | 12 | 10 | 8 | 11 |
| E. Militia (inc. pensions) | 2 | 2 | 2 | 2 | 2 | ? | ? | ? |
| F. Other pensions | 5 | 5 | 2 | 2 | 2 | 4 | 2 | 4 |
| G. Other | | | | | | | | |
| 1. Emigration | 12* | 4 | 3 | 3 | 2 | ? | ? | ? |
| 2. Indians | | | 6 | 7 | 3 | ? | ? | ? |
| 3. Lighthouses | 2 | 1 | 4 | 2 | 4 | 3 | 2 | 2 |
| 4. Penitentiary‡ | | 8 | 3 | 5 | 5 | | | |
| 5. Surveys | 4 | 1 | 4 | 4 | 3 | ? | ? | ? |
| H. All other | 6 | 5 | 3 | 7 | 5 | 1 | 2 | 5 |
| I. Subtotal | 85 | 88 | 85 | 90 | 95 | 66 | 67 | 68 |
| J. Interest on debt | 10 | 14 | 17 | 19 | 43 | 48 | 71 | 58 |
| K. Total | 95 | 102 | 102 | 109 | 138 | 114 | 138 | 126 |
| L. Row I/population (shillings) | 5.7 | 5.5 | 4.9 | 4.8 | 4.8 | | | |
| M. Row K/population (shillings) | 6.4 | 6.4 | 5.9 | 5.8 | 7.0 | | | |

\*   These expenditures were reimbursed by the British government; see NA, MG11, CO42, vol. 418, 195, statement by A.B. Hawke, York, 22 Mar. 1834.

†   Data for these years are incomplete, as Public Accounts did not report on the categories of expenditure marked by '?'. Hence totals (rows I, K) are not comparable to earlier years and per capita figures are not offered.

‡   Penitentiary is included with administration (row A) in 1834–40.

NOTES TO TABLE 9.3: The sources for this table did not treat capital and current accounts as distinct, and included receipts on loans as current revenue and payments on the public debt as current expenses, whether these were of principal or interest. Some expenditure items related to capital accounts are omitted (e.g., public works, bank stock instalments, and principal repayments on the public debt; see tables 9.4 and 9.5). Some public works were routine annual outlays, but it is not possible to distinguish those paid for from current receipts from those funded by borrowing. To a degree, therefore, this statement underrepresents the routine expenditures of the provincial government, but not by more than a few thousand pounds.

Certain categories of outlay, such as for the Church of England, were accounted for differently as time went by, so that not all the rise in expenditure shown here represents a real increase; in this case, outlay formerly charged directly to the SPG later was brought into the provincial account. Despite the unusual rise in row A from 1827 to 1828, longer trends are clear. It is also possible that some accounts were not treated consistently from year to year. For example, public debt charges are presented in varying fashions, depending, for example, on whether the province's London agents had made payments on the province's account from principal balances still held there.

SOURCES FOR TABLE 9.3: Principal source is NA, MG11, CO42, vol. 471, 119, summary statement of Upper Canadian expenditures, 1824–37, enclosed in J. Macaulay to S. B. Harrison, 30 June 1840. See also *UCJ*, 1836, Apps. 26 and 102; and 1837, App., Third Report of Committee on Finance, 116–17. 1838–40 data are from *JLA*, 1841, App. B. Revenues from the Casual & Territorial account (including the Canada Company) and the expenditures made from those revenues are omitted.

TABLE 9.4
The Upper Canadian Public Debt, 1821–40 (£000 cy, except per capita debt)

| | New debts | Debentures redeemed | Net UC debt | Net Debt (shillings per cap.) | Total interest paid out | Purpose of new debt |
|---|---|---|---|---|---|---|
| 1821 | 25 | | 25 | 4 | | Pensions |
| 1822 | | | 25 | | | |
| 1823 | | | 25 | | | |
| 1824 | 24 | 7 | 42 | 6 | 2 | General |
| 1825 | | 7 | 35 | 5 | 3 | |
| 1826 | 25 | 6 | 54 | 7 | 2 | Welland |
| 1827 | 58 | | 112 | 13 | 4 | Welland |
| 1828 | | | 112 | 12 | 7 | |
| 1829 | | 9 | 103 | 10 | 7 | |
| 1830 | 29 | | 132 | 12 | 7 | Welland |
| 1831 | 74 | 13 | 193 | 16 | 8 | Welland |
| 1832 | 13 | 11 | 195 | 15 | 9 | |
| 1833 | 69 | | 264 | 18 | 10 | War loss |
| 1834* | 286 | 104 | 446 | 28 | 14 | Refund |
| 1835* | 498 | 21 | 923 | 53 | 18 | Works |
| 1836* | 2 | 1 | 924 | 49 | 20 | |
| 1837* | 252 | | 1,176 | 59 | 46 | Works |
| 1838* | 79 | | 1,255 | 63 | 48 | |
| 1839 | 8 | | 1,263 | 62 | 71 | |
| 1840 | 6 | | 1,269 | 58 | 58 | |

*Total Upper Canadian Public Debt at the Union*
Denominated in stg  £870,000 x 1.21 =   £1,054,000  cy
Denominated in cy                                    214,000

Total                                          £1,268,000

* See notes for fuller discussion of data for these years.
NOTES: These data derive from two principal sources: (1) *JLA*, 1841, App. B, schedule of government debentures redeemed and outstanding, issued under the authority of acts of the provincial legislature (see also return of Upper Canadian revenue and expenses for 1838–9 there), and (2) NA, MG11, CO42, vol. 471, 117, 119, statement of Upper Canadian revenue and expenditures, 1824–37, enclosed in J. Macaulay to S.B. Harrison, 30 June 1840; see also vol. 461, 177–185a, return of Upper Canadian public revenue and expenses, 1833–8.
    There are growing discrepancies between these two sources in the 1830s. I have largely followed the former, because data on public borrowing in the latter do not total to the actual public debt as given in the former. The former series reflects when debentures were dated, however, and there could be a gap of a year or more in the mid-1830s between debenture date and receipt of funds in the province. Because my focus is on the decision to borrow, and on the level and incidence of debts, I followed the *Journals* here. The figures given in the CO42 series for these years are as follows:
    1834  gross  £209,000  less redemptions of £ 104,000 =  £105,000
    1835  gross    79,000  less redemptions of    21,000 =    58,000
    1836  gross   104,000  less redemptions of     1,000 =   103,000
    1837  gross   312,000                                  312,000
    1838  gross   151,000                                  151,000
    totals        £855,000                                 £729,000

TABLE 9.5
Public Works Expenditures by the Upper Canadian Government
(all figures £000 cy.)

A.  *Chronology, 1826–43*

|  | Welland Canal | St Lawrence canals | All other projects | Total outlay |
|---|---|---|---|---|
| To end 1830 | 100 | | 48 | 148 |
| 1831 | 50 | | 25 | 75 |
| 1832 | | | 14 | 14 |
| 1833 | 7 | 3 | 10 | 20 |
| 1834 | 43 | 35 | 54 | 132 |
| 1835 | 8 | 105 | 11 | 124 |
| 1836 | | 90 | 36 | 126 |
| 1837 | 68 | 83 | 82 | 233 |
| 1838 | | 35 | 113 | 148 |
| 1839 | | 1 | 19 | 20 |
| 1840 | 2 | | 23 | 25 |
| Subtotal to end 1840 | 278 | 352 | 435 | 1,065 |
| 1841 | | | 4 | 4 |
| 1842 | 35 | 89 | 38 | 162 |
| 1843 | 149 | 142 | 187 | 478 |
| Subtotal | 184 | 231 | 229 | 644 |
| Total expenditures | 462 | 583 | 664 | 1,709 |

NOTES: A is based primarily on *JLA*, 1844-5, App PP. B is based primarily on *UCJ*, 1839, App., First Report on Finance, table H. See also *UCJ*, 1832–3, App., First Report of Select Committee on Finance, 103; and NA, MG11, CO42, vol. 471, 119.

(*Table continued on p. 306*)

TABLE 9.5 *(continued)*

B. *Expenditures by Project, 1826–38*

| | Canals | Harbours & lighthouses | Roads & bridges | All other |
|---|---|---|---|---|
| Welland | 275 | | | |
| St Lawrence | 352 | | | |
| Burlington | 35 | | | |
| Desjardins | 17 | | | |
| Trent R/Newcastle | 26 | | | |
| Other | 2 | | | |
| Cobourg harbour | | 4 | | |
| Port Hope     " | | 2 | | |
| Kettle Creek  " | | 7 | | |
| York          " | | 5 | | |
| Oakville      " | | 3 | | |
| Lighthouses | | 18 | | |
| Home District roads | | | 90 | |
| Midland     "    " | | | 29 | |
| Johnstown   "    " | | | 7 | |
| Gore        "    " | | | 51 | |
| Niagara     "    " | | | 15 | |
| Bridges | | | 12 | |
| 'Roads and bridges'* | | | 105 | |
| New parliament bldgs | | | | 11 |
| Penitentiary | | | | 31 |
| Steam dredge | | | | 3 |
| Erie & Ontario Rwy. | | | | 5 |
| Total | 707 | 39 | 309 | 50 |

\* Roads and bridges, funded under general authorizing statutes, were made available in roughly equivalent amounts to each district, including the five listed here. In theory, the special projects were intended to earn a return through tolls.

TABLE 9.6

British Government Expenditures in Upper Canada (estimated), 1821–40  (all figures £000 stg)

A.  *Items in the Account*

| | Year | £ |
|---|---|---|
| 1. Annual grant for civil administration estimate based on £10,000/year | 1821–6 | 60 |
| 2. Rideau Canal | 1826–32 | 830 |
| 3. War losses | 1824 | 50 |
| War losses | 1837 | 17 |
| 4. Indian Department estimate based on £20,000/year | 1821–40 | 400 |
| 5. Welland Canal 'loan' | 1828 | 50 |
| 6. Army Ordnance expenditures, Rideau excepted estimate based on £17,000/year | 1825–31 | 120 |
| 7. Ordinary garrison costs: pay, provisions estimate based on £30/man/year | 1821–31 | 360 |
| 8. Military costs in 1830s; estimate based on one-third of total for both Canadas | 1832–40 | 1,700 |
| 9. All other (emigration, half-pay, SPG, etc.) estimate based on £10,000/year | 1821–40 | 200 |
| Total | | 3,787 |

B.  *Outlay by Year*

| Year | Item (see A) | | | | | | | | | Total |
|---|---|---|---|---|---|---|---|---|---|---|
| | 1 | 2 | 3 | 4 | 5 | 6 | 7 | 8 | 9 | |
| 1821 | 10 | | | 20 | | | 33 | | 10 | 73 |
| 1822 | 10 | | | 20 | | | 33 | | 10 | 73 |
| 1823 | 10 | | | 20 | | | 33 | | 10 | 73 |
| 1824 | 10 | | 50 | 20 | | | 33 | | 10 | 123 |
| 1825 | 10 | | | 20 | | 17 | 33 | | 10 | 90 |
| 1826 | 10 | 30 | | 20 | | 17 | 33 | | 10 | 120 |
| 1827 | | 50 | | 20 | | 17 | 33 | | 10 | 130 |
| 1828 | | 100 | | 20 | 50 | 17 | 33 | | 10 | 230 |
| 1829 | | 150 | | 20 | | 17 | 33 | | 10 | 230 |
| 1830 | | 210 | | 20 | | 17 | 33 | | 10 | 290 |
| 1831 | | 210 | | 20 | | 17 | 33 | | 10 | 290 |
| 1832 | | 80 | | 20 | | | | 51 | 10 | 161 |
| 1833 | | | | 20 | | | | 80 | 10 | 110 |
| 1834 | | | | 20 | | | | 95 | 10 | 125 |
| 1835 | | | | 20 | | | | 69 | 10 | 99 |
| 1836 | | | | 20 | | | | 74 | 10 | 104 |
| 1837 | | | 17 | 20 | | | | 87 | 10 | 134 |
| 1838 | | | | 20 | | | | 388 | 10 | 418 |
| 1839 | | | | 20 | | | | 494 | 10 | 524 |
| 1840 | | | | 20 | | | | 280 | 10 | 310 |

NOTES AND SOURCES: See p. 308.

NOTES AND SOURCES FOR TABLE 9.6: This table summarizes the discussion in chapter 9 by presenting a hypothetical overview of British expenditures. Some elements are reasonably accurate (items 1, 2, 3, 5); others are *lower*-bounded estimates. The totals are compatible with H.C. Pentland's estimate that total British public and private outlay in both Canadas totalled £5 million stg between 1827 and 1837; see his 'Further Observations on Canadian Development,' *Canadian Journal of Economics and Political Science* 19 (1953), 406.

1  British parliamentary grant in aid of civil administration. See table 9.2.
2  Rideau Canal. Total outlay from George Raudzens, *The British Ordnance Department and Canada's Canals 1815–1855* (Waterloo, Ont. 1979), 56, 95. Distribution of expenditures between 1826 and 1832 is hypothetical.
3  War Losses. See NA, MG11, CO42, vol. 471, 119; and NA, RG5, A1, vol. 178, 98293–5, Routh to Head, 10 Oct. 1837.
4  Indian Department. John Leslie, 'The Bagot Commission: Developing a Corporate Memory for the Indian Department,' CHA, *HP* (1982), 34, 41; R.J. Surtees, 'The Development of an Indian Reserve Policy in Canada,' *OH* 61 (1969), 94–9, and 'Indian Land Cessions in Upper Canada, 1815-1830' in I.A.L. Getty and A.S. Lussier, eds., *As Long as the Sun Shines and Water Flows* (Vancouver 1983), 75. Estimate is based on annual British parliamentary grant after 1830 and on the fact that the majority of Indians receiving presents or other funds lived in Upper Canada. Most presents were actually purchased in Britain. The typical annuity provided under land cessions was 50s per person, and at least 7,000 Indians were resident or semi-resident in Upper Canada in the 1830s.
5  Welland Canal. H.G.J. Aitken, *The Welland Canal Company* (Cambridge, Mass. 1954), 88–9
6  Army Ordnance. Raudzens, *British Ordnance Department*, 23; see also *British Parliamentary Papers*, 1844, 34, 23, which show Ordnance expenditures of £106,000 in the two Canadas in 1836–7.
7  Garrison costs. The figure of £33,000 per year is based on an assumption that it cost on average £30 per man to sustain a force in Upper Canada (including salaries, rations, allowances, etc.), with an average garrison of 1,100 men in the province. Over the five years 1843–7, it cost on average £41 to £44 per man to sustain the forces in the two Canadas. In the last two pre-Rebellion years, 1836 and 1837, the forces in the Canadas cost £166,000 and £189,000 respectively. At any one time in the early and middle 1820s the military chests in Upper Canada ordinarily found it necessary to hold £20,000 to £30,000 (mostly coin, plus some bank notes). Sources include C.P. Stacey, *Canada and the British Army, 1846–1871* (Toronto 1963), 16; NA, RG8-I, vols. 339, 341, on the military chest, 1822–7; NA, Upper Canada Sundries, RG5, A1, vol. 40, 19042 (Statement of military force and rations in Upper Canada, 25 July–24 Sept. 1818), vol. 46, 22838 (return of Quartermaster General's department, Upper Canada, 24 Feb. 1820), vol. 54, 27639 (return of regiments in Upper Canada, 1821), vol. 63, 33406 (return of troops in Upper Canada, 1 Dec. 1823); BPP, 1844, 34, 23, and 1849, 34, 224.
8  Angela Redish, 'The Economic Crisis of 1837–39 in Upper Canada: Case Study of a Temporary Suspension of Specie Payments,' *Explorations in Economic History* 20 (1983), 408. For post-Rebellion costs, see BPP, 1844, 34, 23, and 1849, 34, 224, and Stacey, *Canada and the British Army*, 18.
9  Other costs. This is a conservative estimate. For example, there were many half-pay officers in the province. At a lieutenant's rate of £80 per year, £10,000 would have paid 125 officers (see NA, RG 8-I, vol. 193, 92, G. Harrison to Commissary-General Wood, 307, 30 Dec. 1820). British government grants through the Society for the Propagation of the Gospel persisted into the 1830s and totalled from £2,000 to almost £4,000 per year (see *UCJ*, 1835, App. 68, Despatch and correspondence on clergy in North America).

TABLE 10.1
Indexes of Price Changes, Forest Products, Selected Periods, 1825–49 (1831 = 100)

| Years | Red pine | White pine | Oak | Elm | Deals | Potash | Std. staves | WI staves |
|---|---|---|---|---|---|---|---|---|
| 1825–6 | 94 | 88 | 93 | 77 | 74 | 88* | 136 | *133* |
| 1827 | 100* | 59* | 65* | 53 | na | 77* | na | 119* |
| 1829–31 | 98* | 100* | 93 | 97 | 83 | 98* | 117 | 98* |
| 1834–5 | 106 | 109 | 88 | *80* | 73 | 86* | 135 | na |
| 1837–8 | na | *141* | 103* | 97* | *66* | *94* | *134* | *105* |
| 1842–3 | *94* | 88 | 60 | 87 | 100* | 82* | 108 | 101 |
| 1844–6 | 135 | 139 | 96 | 121 | 104 | 71* | 126 | 114 |
| 1849 | 100 | 112 | 85 | 113 | 86 | 81* | 123 | 126 |

\* Price includes data from Montreal.
  Italicized numbers are from one of the two years only.
SOURCE: table 4.1

TABLE 10.2
Bank Note Circulation, Province of Canada, 1841–51

| | Canada (8 banks) (£000) | Index (1841=100) | UC (3 banks) (£000) | Index (1841=100) |
|---|---|---|---|---|
| 1841 | 926 | 100 | 454 | 100 |
| 1842 | 850 | 92 | 351 | 77 |
| 1843 | 778 | 84 | 277 | 61 |
| 1844 | 1,097 | 118 | 381 | 84 |
| 1845 | 1,373 | 148 | 425 | 94 |
| 1846 | 1,575 | 170 | 437 | 96 |
| 1847 | 1,587 | 171 | 482 | 106 |
| 1848 | 1,209 | 131 | 395 | 87 |
| 1849 | 1,097 | 118 | 368 | 81 |
| 1850 | 1,310 | 141 | 490 | 108 |
| 1851 | 1,624 | 175 | 608 | 134 |

SOURCES: *JLA*, 1849, App. Z, Return of Monthly Issue of Bank Notes; 1849–51 from A.B.
McCullough, *Money and Exchange in Canada to 1900* (Toronto and Charlottetown 1984), 117.
UC data from table 8.2

TABLE 10.3
Output and Sales of Two Upper Canadian Farms, 1835–8

| | Volume produced for sale (bu) | | | | Value as sold* | | | |
|---|---|---|---|---|---|---|---|---|
| | 1835 | 1836 | 1837 | 1838 | 1835 | 1836 | 1837 | 1838 |
| *Parsons Farms, Thornhill* | | | | | | | | |
| Wheat | | 1,408 | 925 | 553 | | £563 | £278 | £207 |
| Oats | | 847 | 1,250 | 1,022 | | 106 | 125 | 96 |
| Barley | | 232 | 270 | | | 44 | 54 | |
| Peas | | 129 | 107 | | | 40 | 20 | |
| Animals & products | | | | | | 135 | 130 | 134 |
| Hay | | | | | | 25 | 25 | 25 |
| Total value of sales | | | | | | £913 | £632 | £462 |
| *Farm near Dunnville (anon)* | | | | | | | | |
| Wheat | 60 | 19 | 57 | 61.5 | £10 8 s | £4 14 s | £13 6 s | £17 5 s |
| Peas | | 19 | | | | 3 17 | | |
| Hay | | 1.5 T | ? | 1.6 | | 1 18 | 2 4 | 3 7 |
| Wool | | 16 lb | 25 | 40 | | 16 | 1 5 | 3 0 |
| Veal | | 50 lb | | | | 13 | | |
| Sheep | | | | 3 | | | | 2 8 |
| Total value of sales | | | | | £10 8 | £11 18 | £16 15 | £26 0 |

\* Sales records are essentially for crops produced in the year indicated, but actual sales occurred as late as early summer of the subsequent year.

SOURCES: MTL, William Parsons Account Book, 1832–47; Account Book of a Farmer near Dunnville, 1834–45

TABLE 11.1
Railway Construction in Upper Canada, 1852–60
(all figures are miles of track opened in year*)

| | 1853 | 1854 | 1855 | 1856 | 1857 | 1858 | 1859 | 1860 | Total |
|---|---|---|---|---|---|---|---|---|---|
| GWR | 229 | 12 | 38 | | 15 | 51 | | | 345 |
| GTR ‡ (UC only) | | | 125 | 297 | | 31 | 70 | 2 | 525 |
| B & LH | | | | 116 | | 45 | | 1 | 162 |
| Northern | 63 | 32 | | | | | | | 95 |
| O & P | | 54 | | | | | | | 54 |
| B & O | | | | | | | 63 | 1 | 64 |
| C & P | | 28† | | | | | | | 28 |
| PHL & B | | | | | | 43 | 14 | | 57 |
| E & O | | 17† | | | | | | | 17 |
| Welland | | | | | | | 25 | | 25 |
| L & PS | | | | 24 | | | | | 24 |
| Other | | | | | 11† | | 4† | | 15 |
| Total | 292 | 143 | 163 | 437 | 69 | 141 | 162 | 4 | 1,411 |

NOTE: GWR = Great Western; C & P = Cobourg & Peterborough; GTR = Grand Trunk; B & O = Brockville & Ottawa; O & P = Ottawa & Prescott (later St Lawrence & Ottawa); PHL & B = Port Hope, Lindsay & Beaverton (later Midland); E & O = Erie & Ontario (later leased by GWR); B & LH = Buffalo & Lake Huron (later leased by GTR); L & PS = London & Port Stanley.
* Lines opened in January credited to previous year.
† Indicates lines not in use in 1862.
‡ In addition, the GTR had about 500 miles of track in Lower Canada and the United States.
SOURCE: T.C. Keefer, *Philosophy of Railroads and Other Essays*, H.V. Nelles, ed. (Toronto 1972), 132–5


TABLE 11.2
Demand for Construction Labour, Railways in Upper Canada, 1852–9 (estimated)

| | Miles opened this year | Miles opened next year | Total miles under way | Labour required | |
|---|---|---|---|---|---|
| | | | | At 30/mile | At 60/mile |
| 1852 | – | 292 | 292 | 8,760 | 17,520 |
| 1853 | 292 | 143 | 435 | 13,050 | 26,100 |
| 1854 | 143 | 163 | 306 | 9,180 | 18,360 |
| 1855 | 163 | 437 | 600 | 18,000 | 36,000 |
| 1856 | 437 | 69 | 506 | 15,180 | 30,360 |
| 1857 | 69 | 141 | 210 | 6,300 | 12,600 |
| 1858 | 141 | 162 | 303 | 9,090 | 18,180 |
| 1859 | 162 | 4 | 166 | 4,980 | 9,960 |

SOURCE: Data from table 11.1; estimate based on Albert Fishlow, *American Railroads and the Transformation of the Ante-Bellum Economy* (Cambridge, Mass. 1965), 411

TABLE 11.3
The Railway System of Upper Canada in 1860

| Company | Miles of track | Capital cost to date ($000,000) | Revenue ($000) | Revenue per mile ($000) | Operating expenses ($000) | Expense as % of revenue | Number of employees | Number of locomotives | Number of Cars (passenger) | Cars (freight) | Capital cost per mile ($000) |
|---|---|---|---|---|---|---|---|---|---|---|---|
| GWR | 345 | 23.0 | 2,198 | 6.4 | 1,121* | 51* | 2,049 | 89 | 127 | 1,269 | 66.7 |
| B & LH | 162 | 6.4 | 316 | 2.0 | 264 | 83 | 458 | 28 | 24 | 255 | 39.5 |
| Northern | 95 | 3.9 | 333 | 3.5 | 260 | 78 | 370 | 17 | 20 | 301 | 41.0 |
| O & P | 54 | 1.4 | 75 | 1.4 | 51 | 68 | 92 | 5 | 8 | 79 | 26.5 |
| B & O | 64 | 1.9 | 54 | 0.8 | 34 | 64 | 74 | 3 | 8 | 79 | 29.7 |
| C & P | 28 | † | na | | | | na | 4 | 2 | 66 | † |
| PHL & B | 57 | 5.0† | 54 | 0.9 | 40 | 75 | 66 | 5 | 3 | 65 | 49.0† |
| E & O | 17 | † | na | | | | na | 1 | 4 | 10 | † |
| Welland | 25 | 1.3 | 65 | 2.6 | 51 | 79 | 104 | 4 | 4 | 87 | 52.4 |
| L & PS | 24 | 1.0 | 29 | 1.2 | 23 | 78 | 38 | 2 | 2 | 50 | 42.4 |
| Subtotal | 871 | 44.0 | 3,124 | 3.8 | 1,844* | 59* | 3,251 | 158 | 202 | 2,261 | 50.5 |
| GTR | 1,022 | 55.7 | 3,350 | 3.3 | 2,807 | 84 | 3,118 | 217 | 135 | 2,538 | 54.5 |
| Canada total | 1,893 | 99.6 | 6,474 | 3.5 | 4,651* | 72* | 6,369 | 375 | 337 | 4,799 | 52.6 |
| UC (incl ½ of GTR) | 1,396 | 72.0 | 4,800 | 3.6 | 3,227* | 67* | 4,800 | 267 | 270 | 3,530 | 51.5 |

NOTES: All $ figures are *current* $. Where conversion from sterling is required, rate used is par of $4.866 = £1 stg.

\* Source for all data is T.C. Keefer, *The Philosophy of Railroads and Other Essays*, H.V. Nelles, ed. (Toronto 1972), 132–7, 156; except where marked \* for GWR (and in totals) from J.M. and E. Trout, *The Railways of Canada for 1870–1*, reprint ed. (Toronto 1970), 100. Minor discrepan-cies from tables 11.7 and 11.8 derive from the different sources used.

† No data given in original source for capitalization of C & P, E & O, and PHL & B; $5 million is assumed to be their combined cost (see Keefer, 136). C & P and E & O not operating in 1860; non-operating mileage is excluded from revenue per mile totals.

TABLE 11.4
The Ontario Railway System in 1870

| Company | Miles of track | Revenue ($000) | Revenue per mile ($000) | Operating expenses ($000) | Expense as % of revenue | Number of locomotives | Cars (passenger) | Cars (freight) |
|---|---|---|---|---|---|---|---|---|
| GWR | 381* | 4,152 | 10.9 | 2,527 | 59 | 133 | 129 | 1,737 |
| Northern | 95 | 734 | 7.7 | 426 | 58 | 24 | 18 | 660 |
| St L & O (ex O & P) | 54 | 129 | 2.4 | 88 | 69 | 7 | 17 | 85 |
| B & O | 90 | 203 | 2.3 | 104 | 51 | 7 | 5 | 138 |
| C & P† | 26 | 21 | 0.8 | 10 | 48 | 4 | 2 | 150 |
| Midland (ex PHL & B) | 79 | 242 | 3.1 | 129 | 53 | 11 | 5 | 382 |
| Welland | 25 | 74 | 3.0 | 76 | 103 | 5 | 3 | 147 |
| L & PS | 24 | 49 | 2.0 | 30 | 61 | 2 | 6 | 44 |
| Subtotal | 774 | 5,604 | 7.2 | 3,390 | 60 | 193 | 185 | 3,343 |
| GTR‡ | 1,377 | 7,278 | 5.3 | 4,915 | 68 | 326 | 211 | 3,968 |
| Ontario & Quebec total | 2,151 | 12,882 | 6.0 | 8,305 | 64 | 519 | 396 | 7,311 |
| Ontario (inc ½ of GTR) | 1,443 | 9,243 | 6.4 | 5,847 | 63 | 356 | 290 | 5,327 |

\* GWR mileage includes leased branch lines (Erie & Niagara; Galt & Guelph; but not Wellington, Grey & Bruce, the first sections of which were only completed in 1870).

† C & P data are for 1869.

‡ GTR includes B & LH; half of all GTR data except mileage is arbitrarily assigned to Ontario. GTR mileage between Montreal and Sarnia was 669.

SOURCE: J.M. & E. Trout, *The Railways of Canada for 1870–1*, reprint ed. (Toronto 1970), 101, 109, 113, 116, 119–20, 141–3, 145–6, 168, 172

TABLE 11.5
Growth of Canadian Railway Revenues and Traffic Volumes, 1860–70
(1860 = 100)

| | Index | Rate of change per annum (%) |
|---|---|---|
| **A.   *Revenues*** | | |
| GWR passengers | 147 | 3.9 |
| Freight | 238 | 9.1 |
| Combined | 191 | 6.7 |
| GTR combined* | 199 | 7.1 |
| Northern passengers | 193 | 6.8 |
| Freight | 226 | 8.5 |
| Combined | 220 | 8.2 |
| O & P | 172 | 5.6 |
| B & O | 271 | 10.5† |
| PHL & B | 448 | 16.2† |
| Welland | 114 | 1.3 |
| L & PS | 169 | 5.4 |
| All railways | 199 | 7.1 |
| (Ontario & Quebec) | | |
| **B.   *Quantities*** | | |
| Ontario & Quebec | | |
| Miles of track | 114 | 1.3 |
| No. of locomotives | 138 | 3.3 |
| No. of freight cars | 152 | 4.3 |
| No. of passenger cars | 118 | 1.7 |
| GWR | | |
| No. of passengers | 148 | 3.8 |
| Tons of freight | 248 | 9.5 |
| Northern | | |
| No. of passengers | 177 | 5.9 |
| Tons of freight | 237 | 9.0 |

\* Base figure includes B & LH, leased by the GTR after 1860.
† These companies had relatively large extensions to their mileage in the decade.
SOURCE: tables 11.3, 11.4, 11.7, 11.8, 11.9

TABLE 11.6
Railways in Upper Canada in American Context, 1859–60

|  | Ohio | Michigan | Indiana | 3 states | UC |
|---|---|---|---|---|---|
| Total railway mileage built | 2,978 | 1,051 | 2,088 | 6,117 | 1,411 |
| Population per mile of track | 786 | 713 | 647 | 726 | 989 |
| Revenue per mile of track | $4,341 | $3,839 | $1,436 | $3,263 | $3,600 |
| Revenue per capita | $5.52 | $5.39 | $2.22 | $4.50 | $3.42 |
| Gross railway investment per mile of track |  |  |  | $31,682 | $51,500 |
| Gross railway investment per capita |  |  |  | $43.66 | $51.58 |

NOTE: UC data for 1860, US data (except population, from 1860) for 1859. Data in the text for the US are for railways built from 1851 to 1860 only, whereas data here are for all railways in the three states.

SOURCES: table 11.3; Albert Fishlow, *American Railroads and the Transformation of the Ante-Bellum Economy* (Cambridge, Mass. 1965), 172, 337, 397

TABLE 11.7
Great Western Railway Traffic and Revenue Data, 1854–70

| | 1854 | 1855 | 1856 | 1857 | 1858 | 1859 | 1860 | 1861 | 1862 | 1863 | 1864 | 1865 | 1866 | 1867 | 1868 | 1869 | 1870 |
|---|---|---|---|---|---|---|---|---|---|---|---|---|---|---|---|---|---|
| Passengers (000) | 481 | 664 | 861 | 792 | 569 | 495 | 526 | 527 | 573 | 637 | 688 | 714 | 756 | 716 | 745 | 748 | 781 |
| Passenger revenue ($000) | 987 | 1,452 | 1,742 | 1,562 | 1,238 | 1,072 | 1,009 | 899 | 976 | 1,098 | 1,272 | 1,548 | 1,525 | 1,525 | 1,517 | 1,547 | 1,485 |
| Freight (000 tons) | 83 | 176 | 221 | 193 | 177 | 213 | 374 | 442 | 547 | 528 | 476 | 455 | 489 | 582 | 626 | 775 | 926 |
| Freight revenue ($000) | 331 | 783 | 1,151 | 869 | 736 | 737 | 1,071 | 1,333 | 1,644 | 1,714 | 1,689 | 1,582 | 1,610 | 2,008 | 2,138 | 2,267 | 2,554 |
| Total revenue ($000)* | 1,383 | 2,326 | 2,999 | 2,544 | 2,067 | 1,897 | 2,177 | 2,313 | 2,704 | 2,894 | 3,055 | 3,269 | 3,283 | 3,730 | 3,796 | 3,938 | 4,153 |
| Track open (miles) | 241 | 245 | 283 | 290 | 290 | 330 | 345 | 345 | 345 | 345 | 345 | 345 | 345 | 350 | 350 | 350 | 350 |
| Revenue/mile ($000) | 5.74 | 9.49 | 10.60 | 8.77 | 7.13 | 5.74 | 6.31 | 6.70 | 7.84 | 8.39 | 8.86 | 9.48 | 9.52 | 10.66 | 10.85 | 11.25 | 11.87 |
| % revenue from passengers | 71 | 62 | 58 | 61 | 60 | 57 | 46 | 39 | 36 | 38 | 42 | 47 | 46 | 41 | 40 | 39 | 36 |
| Ordinary working expenses as % of total revenue | 49 | 54 | 55 | 57 | 59 | 63 | 51 | 51 | 44 | 43 | 42 | 40 | 45 | 47 | 52 | 57 | 59 |

* Total revenue includes express, mail, sundries in addition to freight and passengers.

NOTES: All financial data are converted from £ stg at par. The revenue series in Ann Carlos and Frank Lewis, 'The Profitability of Early Canadian Railroads: Evidence from the Grand Trunk and Great Western Railway Companies' (unpublished ms, 1991), table A.2 diverges from mine after 1861, evidently because of the depreciation of the American dollar against sterling. I have followed the Trout series because it sums passenger and freight revenues; 'discount on Am. cy.' appears later in their data as a deduction. Except for 1862–4, the trend is the same in both sources, and most of the divergence falls between the base years for table 11.5. I have benefited greatly from discussions on these issues with Ann Carlos and Frank Lewis, as well as from the opportunity to read their paper before its publication.

SOURCE: J.M. and E. Trout, *The Railways of Canada for 1870–1*, reprint ed. (Toronto 1970), 99–101

TABLE 11.8
Grand Trunk Railway Traffic and Revenue Data, 1857–8 to 1869–70 (data are for fiscal year ended 30 June)

| | 1857–8 | 1858–9 | 1859–60 | 1860–1 | 1861–2 | 1862–3 | 1863–4 | 1864–5 | 1865–6 | 1866–7 | 1867–8 | 1868–9 | 1869–70 |
|---|---|---|---|---|---|---|---|---|---|---|---|---|---|
| *Passengers* | | | | | | | | | | | | | |
| Through (000) | | | | | 95 | 114 | na | 264 | 230 | 251 | 231 | 238 | 265 |
| Total (000) | | | | | 768 | 748 | na | 1,434 | 1,423 | 1,416 | 1,413 | 1,461 | 1,593 |
| Revenue, through ($000) | | | | | | | | | 758 | 779 | 718 | 763 | 790 |
| Revenue, total ($000) | | | | | | | | | 2,448 | 2,394 | 2,326 | 2,409 | 2,448 |
| *Freight* | | | | | | | | | | | | | |
| Through (000 tons) | | | | | 87 | 110 | na | 118 | 131 | 141 | 123 | 135 | 183 |
| Local (000 tons) | | | | | 602 | 534 | na | 758 | 815 | 829 | 844 | 863 | 940 |
| Total* (000 tons) | | | c.600 | na | 695 | 665 | na | 939 | 1,021 | 1,014 | 1,033 | 1,078 | 1,225 |
| Revenue, through ($000) | | | | | | | | | 626 | 658 | 586 | 572 | 815 |
| Revenue, total ($000) | | | | | | | | | 3,946 | 3,854 | 4,068 | 4,365 | 4,657 |
| *Total revenue ($000)* | 2,332 | 2,281 | 2,909 | 3,518 | 3,975 | 4,248 | 4,798 | 5,445 | 6,579 | 6,462 | 6,574 | 6,963 | 7,280 |
| % revenue from passengers | | | | | | | | | 37 | 37 | 35 | 35 | 34 |
| % revenue from through freight & passengers | | | | | | | | | 21 | 22 | 20 | 19 | 22 |
| Ordinary working expenses as % of total revenue | | 91 | na | 86 | 73 | 62 | 58 | 60 | 59 | 64 | 65 | 64 | 66 |

\* Total freight includes some other categories, principally livestock.

NOTES: Financial data converted from £ stg at par. The revenue series in Ann Carlos and Frank Lewis, 'The Profitability of Early Canadian Railroads: Evidence from the Grand Trunk and Great Western Railway Companies' (unpublished ms, 1991), table A.1 diverges from mine after 1862–3 because of the depreciation of the American dollar against sterling. I have used Carlos and Lewis's revenue data for 1863–4 and 1864–5, to fill gaps in the series, but have followed the Trout series from 1865–6 to 1869–70, because it sums passenger and freight revenue series; 'loss on American currency' appears later in the Trout data as a deduction. The trend is the same in both sources, and most of the divergence falls between the base years of table 11.5.

SOURCES: J.M. and E. Trout, *The Railways of Canada for 1870–1*, reprint ed. (Toronto 1970), 83–5; T. Storrow Brown, *A History of the Grand Trunk Railway of Canada, compiled from Public Documents* (Quebec 1864), PAC Pamphlet 3170, 42–3; and Walter Shanly, *Notes and Corrections to the Report of the Government ... [on] the Grand Trunk Railway of Canada* (Toronto 1861), PAC Pamphlet 2925, 22

TABLE 11.9
Northern Railway Traffic and Revenue Data, 1854–70 (1854–6 for fiscal year ending 30 June)

| | 1853–4 | 1854–5 | 1855–6 | 1857 | 1858 | 1859 | 1860 | 1861 | 1862 | 1863 | 1864 | 1865 | 1866 | 1867 | 1868 | 1869 | 1870 |
|---|---|---|---|---|---|---|---|---|---|---|---|---|---|---|---|---|---|
| Passengers (000) | | | | | | | 92 | 101 | 102 | 108 | 104 | 105 | 137 | 129 | 139 | 145 | 163 |
| Passenger revenue ($000) | | | | | | | 89 | 94 | 97 | 102 | 102 | 107 | 124 | 137 | 147 | 151 | 172 |
| Freight (000 tons) | | | | | | | 125 | 146 | 174 | 156 | 189 | 119 | 175 | 201 | 195 | 271 | 296 |
| Timber* (000,000 bd ft) | | | | | | | | 424 | 243 | 280 | 70 | 70 | 69 | 77 | 74 | 116 | 137 |
| Freight revenue | | | | | | | | | | | | | | | | | |
| Local ($000) | | | | | | | 186 | 260 | 209 | 275 | 333 | 341 | 340 | 377 | 364 | 479 | 505 |
| Through ($000) | | | | | | | 50 | 48 | 93 | 18 | 15 | 26 | 24 | 22 | 13 | 9 | 28 |
| Total ($000) | | | | | | | 236 | 308 | 302 | 293 | 348 | 367 | 364 | 399 | 377 | 488 | 533 |
| Total revenue ($000) | 118 | 213 | 290 | 313 | 262 | 240 | 333 | 411 | 406 | 407 | 467 | 507 | 513 | 561 | 550 | 671 | 734 |
| % revenue from passengers | | | | | | | 27 | 23 | 24 | 25 | 22 | 21 | 24 | 24 | 27 | 23 | 23 |
| Revenue/mile ($000) | | 2.2 | 3.1 | 3.3 | 2.8 | 2.5 | 3.5 | 4.3 | 4.3 | 4.3 | 4.9 | 5.3 | 5.4 | 5.9 | 5.8 | 7.1 | 7.7 |
| Ordinary working expenses as % of total revenue | 75 | 79 | 102 | 80 | 100 | 82 | 78 | 68 | 74 | 54 | 52 | 56 | 60 | 59 | 61 | 50 | 58 |

* Square timber converted to bd ft by multiplying by 12.

SOURCE: J.M. and E. Trout, *The Railways of Canada for 1870–1*, reprint ed. (Toronto 1970), 111–13.
See also *JLA*, 1864, SP 15, for one correction.

TABLE 12.1
The Composition of Provincial Population, Selected Indicators and Years, 1825–81

|  | Males per 100 females | Males per 100 females (children excluded) | Children (%) |
|---|---|---|---|
|  |  |  | under 16 |
| 1825 | 113 | 121 | 50 |
| 1836 | 112 | 117 | 50 |
|  |  |  | 14 & under |
| 1842 | 114 | 122 | 46 |
| 1848 | 115 | 123 | 45 |
|  |  |  | 15 & under |
| 1851 | 110 | 115 | 45 |
| 1861 | 108 | 112 | 43 |
|  |  |  | up to 16 |
| 1871 | 103 | 103 | 44 |
| 1881 | 103 | 103 | 40 |

NOTE: It is unclear in the printed data how children at age-dividing categories (14, 15, or 16) were assigned (e.g., prior to 1841, the categories were 'under' 16 and 'over' 16).

SOURCES: *Census*, 1871, vol. 1, table 2, vol. 2, table 7, and vol. 4, 86, 120, 135–7, 165–7, 180–1, 184–190, 256–7, 260-66; and 1881, vol. 2, table 8

TABLE 12.2

Value of Upper Canadian Exports, Selected Principal Produce Items, Selected Years, 1850–71 (all figures $000)

| | 1850 | 1853 | 1856 | 1858 | 1860 | 1863 | 1865–6 | 1868–9 | 1870–1 |
|---|---|---|---|---|---|---|---|---|---|
| Planks, boards | 515 | 1,644 | 1,852* | 2,382 | 2,200* | 2,035 | 3,073 | 3,412 | 4,966 |
| Firewood | | | | | | 280 | 463 | 439 | 385 |
| Oak | | | | | | 132 | | | |
| White pine | | | | | | | 104 | | |
| Staves | | | | | | 118 | 113 | | |
| Shingles | | | | | | | 145 | 132 | 147 |
| 'Other woods' | | | | | | 102 | 153 | | |
| Wheat & flour | 2,164 | 4,220 | 8,604 | 3,195 | 5,387 | 3,464 | 5,862 | 1,881 | 816 |
| Barley & rye | | | 596* | 586 | 1,294 | 1,665 | 3,946 | 4,498 | 3,211 |
| Oats | | | | 159 | 214† | 230 | | | |
| Peas | | | | | 142 | 249 | 303 | 350 | 254 |
| Flax | | | | | | | | | 103 |
| Malt | | | | | | | | | 133 |
| 'Other seeds' | | | | | | | | | 109 |
| Cattle | | 148 | 360 | 352 | 424 | 323 | 3,599 | 917 | 1,923 |
| Horses | | 108 | | | 473* | 935 | 1,519 | 293 | 650 |
| Swine | | | 112 | | 196 | 143 | 287 | 104 | |
| Sheep | | | | | | 129 | 435 | 339 | 634 |
| Butter | | 128 | 128 | 156 | | | 614 | 418 | 487 |
| Pork, bacon, & ham | | | | | 247 | 116 | 439 | 374 | 547 |
| Wool | | 152 | 274* | 166 | 240 | 841 | 637 | 454 | 651 |
| Sheep pelts | | | | | | 175 | | 151 | |
| Hides | | | 176* | 111 | | | | | |
| Eggs | | | | | | | 108 | 127 | 260 |
| Cheese | | | | | | | | | 233 |
| Subtotal, animal products | | 536 | 1,050 | 785 | 1,583 | 2,662 | 7,638 | 3,177 | 5,385 |
| Total, all exports | 3,276 | 7,223 | 13,923 | 8,114 | 12,549 | 11,716 | 23,955 | 15,930 | 19,527 |
| % planks, boards | 16 | 23 | 13 | 29 | 18 | 17 | 13 | 21 | 25 |
| % wheat, flour | 66 | 58 | 62 | 39 | 43 | 30 | 24 | 12 | 4 |
| % animal products | – | 7 | 8 | 10 | 13 | 23 | 32 | 20 | 28 |
| % other items, this table | – | – | 4 | 9 | 13 | 24 | 22 | 34 | 22 |
| Total %, this table | 82 | 89 | 87 | 88 | 87 | 93 | 91 | 87 | 79 |

NOTES FOR TABLE 12.2

Only products valued at $100,000 or more in a year are included.

\* Indicates that other ports, not separately itemized, account for more than 10 per cent of total export values. Because the majority of exports that can be accounted for were from Upper Canadian ports, the 'other' total is included here.

† Indicates that other ports, not separately itemized, account for more than 10 per cent of total export values. Because the majority of exports that can be accounted for were from Lower Canadian ports, the 'other' total is excluded here.

After 1863, data are for years from 1 July to 30 June.

This table *underestimates* Upper Canada's total exports because (1) except after 1867, almost all exports to Britain are recorded under the Lower Canadian ports from which they were ultimately shipped; (2) Upper Canadian exports that went to the United States via Lower Canada are likewise recorded under Lower Canadian ports; (3) Upper Canada's 'surplus' produce included some consumed within Lower Canada which thus was not recorded as an export; and (4) published data routinely added 20 per cent to total value of exports from inland ports to compensate for presumed under-reporting.

Barley and rye were reported together, but census data suggest that barley was the principal export product.

From 1863 to 1870–1 exports of coin and bullion are excluded from provincial totals.

Cattle includes oxen in 1853 and 1856.

The TTN give essentially identical data for almost all commodities for 1865–6 and 1866–7; I have assumed that the data are for the earlier year.

Sault Ste Marie data are not included.

SOURCES: TTN, breakdowns of exports by port (to 1867) and province (after 1867): *JLA*, 1851, App. A; 1854–5, App. A; 1856, App. 29; 1857, App. 2; 1858, App. 2; 1859, App. 6; 1861, SP 2; 1864, SP 3; Canada, Parliament, House of Commons, 1867–8, SP 1; 1870, SP 1; 1872, SP 3

TABLE 12.3
Volumes of Upper Canadian Exports, Selected Principal Produce Items, Selected Years, 1850–71

| | 1850 | 1853 | 1856 | 1858 | 1860 | 1863 | 1865–6 | 1868–9 | 1870–1 |
|---|---|---|---|---|---|---|---|---|---|
| Planks, boards (000 M bd ft) | 79 | 188 | 167 | 336 | 235 | 217 | 320 | 340 | 509 |
| Firewood (000 cords) | | | | | | 156 | 240 | 210 | 182 |
| Wheat (000 bu) | 1,027 | 1,878 | 4,173 | 1,687 | 2,895 | 1,527 | 2,217 | 1,230 | 738 |
| Flour (000 bbl) | 314 | 488 | 435 | 310 | 377 | 448 | 459 | 84 | 16 |
| Wheat & flour (000 bu 1 bbl = 5 bu) | 2,597 | 4,318 | 6,348 | 3,237 | 4,780 | 3,767 | 4,512 | 1,650 | 818 |
| Barley & rye (000 bu) | | | 661 | 801 | 2,003 | 2,029 | 5,393 | 4,498 | 4,527 |
| Oats (000 bu) | | | | 453 | 697 | 538 | | | |
| Peas (000 bu) | | | | | 220 | 464 | 459 | 407 | 312 |
| Cattle (000) | | 7.8 | 14.8 | 16.4 | 15.6 | 13.8 | 123.5 | 37.8 | 66.4 |
| Horses (000) | | 1.0 | | | 5.4 | 11.8 | 16.4 | 3.5 | 6.7 |
| Swine (000) | | | 15.7 | | 32.3 | 16.9 | 33.0 | 30.4 | |
| Sheep (000) | | | | | | 46.2 | 119.3 | 147.2 | 239.1 |
| Butter (000 lb) | | 974 | 952 | 141 | | | 2,860 | 1,901 | 2,367 |
| Pork, bacon, & ham (000 lb) | | | | | 5,170 | 2,822 | 6,272 | 3,987 | 6,462 |
| Wool (000 lb) | | 363 | 805 | 873 | 877 | 2,149 | 1,477 | 1,628 | 2,111 |

For notes and sources, see table 12.2.

TABLE 12.4

Upper Canadian Exports as Percentage of Census Output/Stock, Selected Items,
1861 and 1871 Census Data

|  | Exports in 1860 | Exports in 1870–1 |
|---|---|---|
| *Outputs* | | |
| Wheat and flour | 44 | 41 |
| Barley and rye | 53 | 45 |
| Oats | 3 | – |
| Peas | 2 | 4 |
| Wool | 24 | 33 |
| Firewood | – | 4 |
| Cattle | 8 * | 24 |
| Swine & pork | 10 * | 6* |
| Sheep | – | 28 |
| *Stocks* | | |
| Oxen and cattle | 1.5 | 4.7 |
| Horses | 1.4 | 1.4 |
| Swine | 4.0 | – |
| Sheep | – | 15.8 |

\* Outputs are inferred from stocks in 1860 using ratios from 1871 *Census*, vol. 3, table 22, and pork is converted to live weight using estimates of slaughter weights from the appendix to John Isbister, 'Agriculture, Balanced Growth, and Social Change in Central Canada since 1850: An Interpretation,' *Economic Development and Cultural Change* 25 (1976–7), 673–97.

SOURCES: tables 12.3, 5.3; data on animals slaughtered or sold in 1870 from *Census*, 1871, vol. 3, table 22. Wheat exports are *net* provincial exports as estimated by John McCallum, *Unequal Beginnings* (Toronto 1980), 126. Exports recorded in table 12.3 were 19 per cent in 1860 and 6 per cent in 1870–1.

TABLE 12.5
Volume of Upper Canadian Exports, 1865–6, Selected Ports, Commodities

| | Sawn lumber (000 M bd ft) | Fire wood (000 cords) | Swine (000) | Pork (000 cwt) | Horses (000) | Cattle (000) | Butter (000 lb) | Sheep (000) | Wool (000 lb) | Flour (000 bbl) | Wheat (000 bu) | Barley (000 bu) | Peas (000 bu) |
|---|---|---|---|---|---|---|---|---|---|---|---|---|---|
| *Main cities* | | | | | | | | | | | | | |
| Toronto | 46 | | x | | 1 | 3 | 105 | x | 13 | 31 | 405 | 1,207 | 11 |
| Hamilton | 9 | | | | | | | | 128 | 15 | 289 | 783 | 72 |
| *Rail termini/E* | | | | | | | | | | | | | |
| Prescott | 4 | | 6 | x | 3 | 15 | 241 | 10 | 33 | 36 | 31 | 30 | |
| Clifton | 1 | | 5 | 8 | 2 | 22 | 352 | 29 | 366 | 88 | 65 | 10 | 13 |
| Fort Erie | 5 | 3 | 3 | 2 | 1 | 9 | 45 | 14 | 5 | 19 | 67 | 50 | 14 |
| *Rail termini/W* | | | | | | | | | | | | | |
| Sarnia | | 59 | | | 2 | 1 | 61 | 2 | | 1 | | | 7 |
| Windsor | | 5 | 1 | 6 | 1 | 5 | 75 | 2 | | 2 | | 17 | |
| *Rail centres/W* | | | | | | | | | | | | | |
| Chatham | 10 | 17 | | 6 | x | 4 | 109 | 3 | 37 | 2 | 107 | 197 | |
| London | | | 5 | 10 | 1 | 9 | 43 | 12 | 246 | 10 | 49 | 20 | |
| Woodstock | | | | 1 | | | 152 | | 35 | 9 | | 21 | 11 |
| Brantford | 1 | | x | 2 | x | 4 | | 9 | 7 | | | 79 | |
| Stratford | 1 | | 2 | 4 | x | 3 | 205 | 3 | 5 | 6 | 62 | 26 | 12 |
| Guelph | | | 2 | 9 | x | 10 | 168 | 2 | 101 | 25 | 16 | 25 | |
| *Rail centres/E* | | | | | | | | | | | | | |
| Whitby | 5 | | | | | | | | | | 103 | 366 | 32 |
| Port Hope | 51 | | x | | 1 | 4 | 88 | 3 | 83 | 10 | 203 | 144 | 22 |
| Cobourg | 12 | 2 | | | x | 1 | 16 | | 218 | 40 | 58 | 60 | 10 |
| Belleville | 21 | | | | | x | | x | | 12 | 30 | 362 | 7 |

| | | | | | | | | | | | | | |
|---|---|---|---|---|---|---|---|---|---|---|---|---|---|
| Kingston | 15 | 2 | 3 | x | 2 | 12 | 623 | 11 | 8 | | 33 | 258 | |
| Brockville | 11 | 3 | 1 | | 1 | | 326 | 5 | 42 | | | | |
| *Small ports* | | | | | | | | | | | | | |
| Goderich | 3 | 1 | 5 | | 3 | | 16 | | | 19 | 132 | | 5 |
| Wallaceburg* | 2 | 55 | | x | x | | | | | | 14 | | |
| Port Stanley | 1 | | | | | | | | | | 164 | 244 | 145 |
| Port Dover* | 6 | | | | | | | | 13 | | 81 | 114 | |
| Dunnville | 7 | 10 | 1 | | 2 | | 23 | 4 | | 9 | 62 | 123 | 6 |
| Oakville | 2 | | x | | 1 | x | | 1 | | 2 | 11 | 72 | |
| Darlington | | | x | | x | x | | | 38 | 26 | 43 | 112 | 28 |
| Picton* | | | | | | | | | | | | 235 | 4 |
| Napanee | 19 | 5 | | | | | | | | | | 191 | |
| Morrisburg | | 2 | x | | 2 | | 162 | 2 | | | | 50 | |
| Total/these ports | 229 | 166 | 30 | 54 | 15 | 111 | 2,810 | 112 | 1,378 | 362 | 2,025 | 4,796 | 399 |
| % ports not inc.† | 28 | 31 | 9 | 3 | 9 | 10 | 2 | 6 | 7 | 21 | 9 | 11 | 13 |
| % eastern ports‡ | 53 | 12 | 33 | 1 | 48 | 31 | 52 | 28 | 28 | 27 | 26 | 41 | 29 |

NOTES

* Town not on a railway.

x Exports of under 500 head or cwt are included in totals.

† Other ports for which exports were recorded but that are not included in table are: (1) rail centres/W: Dundas, Paris; (2) rail centres/E: Newcastle, Cornwall, Gananoque, Oshawa, Trenton, Brighton, Colborne, Bytown; (3) other ports: Amherstburg, Port Burwell, Port Rowan, Kingsville, Chippawa, Cramahe, Port Dalhousie, Penetanguishene, Saugeen.

‡ % from ports east of Toronto includes 'ports not inc.' in table.

SOURCE: Canada, Parliament, *Sessional Papers*, 1867–8, 1, TTN for 1865–6

TABLE 12.6
Per Capita Outputs and Stocks, Selected Counties, 1870

|  | Glengarry | Leeds South | Prince Edward | Halton | Haldimand | Essex | UC |
|---|---|---|---|---|---|---|---|
| Population (000s) | 20.5 | 20.7 | 20.3 | 22.6 | 20.1 | 32.7 | 1,821 |
| Improved land as % of occupied | 43 | 51 | 71 | 69 | 64 | 55 | 55 |
| *Outputs* | | | | | | | |
| (bu/person) | | | | | | | |
| Spring wheat | 4.2 | 5.0 | 5.3 | 2.5 | 1.7 | 0.9 | 4.7 |
| Fall wheat | 0.2 | 0.7 | 0.1 | 10.8 | 13.8 | 5.0 | 3.9 |
| All wheat | 4.4 | 5.7 | 5.5 | 13.3 | 15.6 | 5.9 | 8.7 |
| Oats | 20.1 | 11.9 | 5.2 | 12.1 | 13.8 | 14.9 | 13.7 |
| Barley | 1.0 | 2.6 | 13.1 | 6.9 | 14.8 | 1.7 | 5.8 |
| Rye | – | 1.5 | 2.9 | – | – | 0.1 | 0.3 |
| Peas | 2.6 | 2.4 | 7.8 | 7.6 | 5.2 | 0.4 | 4.7 |
| Corn | 0.4 | 1.5 | 4.6 | 1.2 | 0.7 | 20.5 | 1.9 |
| (lb/person) | | | | | | | |
| Butter | 32.9 | 32.7 | 31.1 | 26.3 | 28.1 | 19.4 | 23.2 |
| Wool | 4.1 | 5.2 | 5.1 | 4.9 | 6.5 | 3.3 | 4.0 |
| *Stocks* | | | | | | | |
| (stock/person) | | | | | | | |
| Milch cows | 0.6 | 0.8 | 0.5 | 0.4 | 0.4 | 0.3 | 0.4 |
| Horned cattle | 0.5 | 0.5 | 0.4 | 0.5 | 0.6 | 0.4 | 0.4 |
| Horses | 0.3 | 0.2 | 0.3 | 0.3 | 0.3 | 0.3 | 0.3 |
| Sheep | 1.2 | 1.2 | 1.1 | 1.0 | 1.7 | 0.9 | 0.9 |
| Swine | 0.5 | 0.3 | 0.3 | 0.6 | 0.8 | 1.0 | 0.5 |

SOURCE: Canada, *Census*, 1871.

# Appendix C: Produce Prices in Upper Canada

This appendix provides time series for prices of some principal items of Upper Canadian produce. Commodities selected were among the most universally produced and consumed in the province. They include food (wheat and potatoes), animal fodder (oats, peas, and hay), principal meats (pork and beef), and butter. Although all were regularly marketed, this analysis should not be taken to imply that all were equally important in farm incomes. It is hoped, rather, that this selection adequately represents larger trends in prices.[1] Prices of two wood products often marketed by farmers, potash and barrel staves, are provided in table 4.1.

The objective in collecting these prices was to clarify overall trends and levels of prices. For most items (wheat being the chief exception) data are not sufficiently abundant and unambiguous to permit very fine-grained analysis. Apparently undue variations in the data, such as unexpectedly large deviations in price between the two main regions discussed, are as likely to derive from the data as from any underlying economic reality. That is, while local price variations must at times have led to arbitraging, an unknown level of variation is introduced by the character of the data that have to be employed. Even so, main trends and fluctuations, the principal concern of this book, appear quite clearly.

The longest continuous series of Upper Canadian prices is to be found in market reports in the Toronto press.[2] Beginning in 1838, it is possible to find reports in a number of months (and eventually in virtually all months) in one or more of the newspapers. These are prices on the Toronto market, presumably for the benefit of merchants and farmers (and perhaps consumers). No indication is ever given of how they were determined, but we may presume that they represent a blend of wholesale and retail prices, that being a distinction that was only gradually emerging in local produce markets at mid-century. Increasingly, by the 1850s they were not merely prices for nearby produce, but also the local price of produce imported from farther afield by middlemen.[3]

Nevertheless, they are the most consistent and accessible series for the entire 1838–70 era. Even if actual prices received by most farmers were lower than those quoted by the press of the province's largest urban market, there is no reason to think they do not fairly represent trends.

Many of the remaining prices are from merchants' accounts and are for prices credited to farmers at stores and mills. Details are given below. A few other sources have been used to supplement these or in preference to them. Here the main ones are the war loss claims for the War of 1812,[4] which offer quite consistent figures, though not specifically dated, of prices prevalent during the war.[5] The *Upper Canada Gazette* provided a series for the Town of York from late 1817 to early 1822, analogous to the later newspaper series, though more clearly retail at this early time. For wheat in the 1830s, one major source is a well-known series in the Colonial Office records, based on information supplied by a merchant at Dundas.[6] Some other prices also come from official reports, but I have preferred commercial records to these in the event of disagreements.

Until 1845, series are offered for two (or, for wheat and peas, three) sub-regions. These depend on evidence from more than one source and for more than one location. The most valuable sources are used for as many years as they can be made to cover, to minimize the variation arising from locational shifts. There is a variety of evidence to suggest that no radical variations in trend are created by the necessity to draw from multiple locations, though it would be tedious to offer item-by-item discussion of every instance where such splicing of series has been necessary. A few prices have been drawn from the province's easternmost region, the Eastern District, but the majority of 'east' prices are from Yonge Mills (east of Kingston), Kingston and environs, Newboro (on the Rideau Canal northeast of Kingston), and (in a very few instances) Picton. At the west end of Lake Ontario, prior to 1817, prices derive chiefly from the Niagara peninsula; thereafter the focus is principally but not exclusively at York. For wheat in the 1830s and for a few other prices, the head of the lake (i.e., Hamilton, Dundas, Burlington) also furnished some prices. There is evidence that people at the time thought of these areas as having quite closely matching prices.[7] Details for the locational series are provided below.

For most commodities there were important variations in quality, embodied to a degree in grades employed at the time (notably for pork in the barrel and for flour). It is seldom possible from the available sources to know what quality of a commodity is involved in a particular transaction.[8] In recognition of the problem, the mid-point of any price range has been selected for any month where there was a range; this should help to avoid biasing the data strongly to exceptional 'grades,' good or bad, of the produce involved. Where prices have been encountered that were radically out of line with series that they might have gone into, I have had simply to omit them; this avoids extreme biases and also recognizes that entries in account books could be confusingly or ambiguously dated.

A related problem is the lack of homogeneity in certain commodity series. Pork might be fresh or salted, and so might butter; hay might be old and seasoned or fresh and green; ashes (which are not included here) might be house or field; firewood (also excluded here) might be hardwood or softwood. That is, a common name in some cases applied to products that were, to those at the time, quite distinct. All too seldom did the creator of a particular document record the distinction. It is frequently possible to infer which was meant, but some variation may have been introduced in some series by this factor.

There were significant swings over the year in prices of some commodities. Most had definite seasonal patterns of production and apparently of marketing, but consistent seasonal price variation is much less evident in some than in others.[9] With this in mind, two series, one annual and one for the quarter where prices were usually lowest, are offered for hay, fresh beef, fresh pork, and butter. For meat, late fall or early winter was the normal time of slaughter; for hay and butter, summer and early fall were the usual times of greatest availability and lowest prices. When set alongside the annual series, a series based on only one quarter can help to show such systematic seasonal variations, as well as indicating, by deviations from the usual patterns, periods when larger trends were strong enough to obscure the normal seasonal fluctuations. That is, ordinarily, the quarters chosen for these four commodities would have been those of lowest price during the seasonal cycle; where they are not lower than the annual price, a larger price swing was usually under way.

As much as possible, the data in table C.1 are prices that were actually credited to a producer's account. Merchants' selling prices (i.e. those debited to someone's account) have not been used. Some credits may have arisen from essentially inter-merchant rather than merchant-farmer transactions which is not always clear from the original record, but this should not affect the overall patterns that these data show. Similarly, for some commodities some merchants offered two prices, a 'cash' and a 'credit' or 'store' price; by the nature of the documentation used, most data from commercial records are the latter, slightly higher, prices.

The technique followed here, for the press, has been to choose the first occasion each month on which a price was quoted. Commercial records have been scanned for evidence on the range of prices prevailing in each month. Such month-by-month data are then averaged by quarters, then quarterly averages are combined to produce an annual average. This approach avoids biasing a year's figures unduly when some quarters have more data than others. For series derived from commercial records, there is often a necessity to make one or two observations serve for an entire year. This may make for some imprecision, but there was no alternative if the sources were to be used at all.[10] The main trends considered in the text are unlikely to be figments of such statistical variations. Only occasionally, as notes indicate, have entries from two sources been combined in a single year's price.[11] That is, what shows here is ordinarily the actual price, or average, paid somewhere (or quoted for a specific place in a newspaper), not a composite figure deriving from multiple locations.

On the basis of these data, several broad periods were defined that marked benchmarks or turning-points in some or even all of the series. Table C.3 offers index numbers (based on 1831 = 100 in each case) for all the series. Table C.4 offers selected evidence from some Lower Canadian, American, and British series as well. The periods used do not always have prices available for all years, but any years available for the period are used.

## Sources of Prices in Tables C.1 and C.2

### ABBREVIATIONS

AM  QUA, Archibald McLean Papers, loose accounts, 1802–55, records of a substantial farming operation in Yonge Township, Leeds County

AO  Archives of Ontario, Toronto

Ball  AO, Jacob Ball Account Book, MU 610, records of a Niagara area mill and business, 1786–1812; prices converted from NY cy

B&S  AO, D.B. Stevenson Papers, MU 2887–8, Barker and Stevenson Ledgers, 1828–c. 1839, records of a leading country business in Hallowell (later Picton), Prince Edward County. For some further early records of this firm, see UG, Goodwin-Haines Collection, William Grant Papers.

Bell  Lennox and Addington County Museum, Napanee, William Bell Papers, loose accounts, 1787 and after, 373–7

Brock  QUA, anonymous Brockville daybook, 1819–28

CO42  NA, MG 11, Colonial Office Records, CO42 series, vols. 377–89 include a variety of current prices at York and Kingston, 1826–9; vol. 394 includes prices of a number of commodities at various provincial locations in 1831; vol. 476, 281, gives a monthly price series for wheat at Dundas from 1831 to 1840.

Cooper  AO, Niagara Historical Society Records, Ms 193, reel 5, James Cooper accounts (converted from NY cy)

Fair  QUA, Fairfield Family Papers, Box 6, ledger, 1802–c. 1813; Box 4, accounts, records from Amherstview, west of Kingston along the lake

Gonder  AO, Niagara Historical Society Records, Ms 193, reel 18, Gander (Gonder) family papers; see also M.G. Sherk, ed., 'An Old Family Account Book,' *OHSPR* 7 (1906), 120–39, records of a farm in Willoughby Township, Niagara area (converted from NY cy where necessary)

IW  AO, Isaac Wilson letters, 1811–45, Ms 199, typescript, correspondence of a farmer a few miles north of York; prices often refer to those prevailing on the city market (converted to Halifax cy where necessary).

JMW  QUA, John M. Willard Papers, ledger, 1816–20, records of a business at Williamsburg, near the St Lawrence in Dundas County

McGill  MTL, John McGill Papers, records of the chief buyer of military provisions in Upper Canada

M&M  NA, Records of the Lennox and Addington Historical Society, MG9, D8 (18), 35897–36451, McNeil & McHenry Ledger, 1834–45, records of a Napanee business

MTL  Metropolitan Toronto Library, Baldwin Room

NA   National Archives of Canada, Ottawa

Parsons   MTL, William Parsons Account Book, 1832–47, the record of a large farming operation at Thornhill, north of Toronto

press   See text above for fuller discussion, and item by item discussions below for variations. Basically, 1838–50 Toronto prices are from *British Colonist*; 1851 from it and the *Globe*; 1852–4 and 1856–70 from the *Globe*; 1855 from the *Leader*. Many Toronto prices for 1817–22 are drawn from the *Upper Canada Gazette* from Dec. 1817 to May 1822.

QUA   Queen's University Archives, Kingston

RC   QUA, Richard Cartwright Jr Papers, Additions, vol. 1, ledger 1791–8; vol. 11, daybook 1809–11; vol. 9, memoranda, 1808–15; the records of Cartwright's business at Kingston, one of the largest in the province, but not so large that it did not deal directly with country-dwellers. A few prices are from AO, Richard Cartwright Jr letterbooks and typescripts, MU 500, Ms 43, Ms 44. All are cited by the one abbreviation; most prices are from the two account books.

Reid   AO, James Reid Papers, MU 2382, correspondence of a gentleman farmer in the Gore District, near the head of Lake Ontario (currency not always clear, but converted to Halifax cy if another is evident)

RG8   NA, RG8-I, vols. 119, 329, 546, 1076, 1090, 1127, 1913, various military provisioning, ration, and related data, for a variety of locations

RG19   NA, Record of War Losses Claims, RG19, E5 (a), vols. 4356–8. These are not dated, but offer abundant and generally consistent indications of prevalent prices for various items during the War of 1812 (where necessary, prices have been converted to Halifax cy).

RH   NA, Hamilton Papers, MG24, I26, vols. 17–18, 20, 22–3, 25, assorted daybooks and ledgers, 1806–31, records of the business of Robert Hamilton and several successors, mainly at Queenston, on the Niagara River (prices converted from NY cy where required)

Ridout   MTL, Thomas Ridout account book, 1797–1801, records kept at York (some prices converted from NY cy). *Note*: used for 1800 only; these are prices he paid for produce, and may be inconsistent in nature with others in the tables. But they are quite in line with those around them, and fill a gap in data for 1800.

Rousseau   AO, J.B. Rousseau Papers, MU 2555, records of a milling operation at the head of Lake Ontario (prices converted from NY cy)

SJ   QUA, Jones Family Papers, Box 15, account books, esp. of Solomon Jones; records from Gananoque area, east of Kingston

Seymour   QUA, B. Seymour Daybook, 1796–8, Fredericksburg, west of Kingston in Lennox and Addington

Silver   Alice Wetherall, ed., 'The Joseph Silverthorn Account Book,' *OH* 43 (1951), 97–104, records of an Oakville–Port Credit area tradesman

Tett   QUA, Tett Papers, vols. 57–8, ledgers 1833–46, the records of a country
       store and milling operation in Leeds County at Newboro, on the Rideau
       Canal northeast of Kingston. Despite the inland location of this operation,
       local prices compare quite closely with those for Yonge Mills, where data
       series overlap. One factor here was demand from the Ottawa valley, whose
       timber economy tended to set relatively high prices for a number of farm
       products.
UG    University of Guelph Library, Macdonald Stewart Room
Wood  MTL, Alexander Wood letterbooks, correspondence of one of the leading
       merchants of York
YM    AO, Yonge Mills Records, MU 3164–81, daybooks from Yonge Mills, near
       the St Lawrence River in Leeds County, 1803–12, 1824–38. A few prices
       are derived from this business's Brockville daybooks to fill gaps (these are
       in MU 3173, 3178, 3182). Further wheat prices have been derived from
       wheat and flour books in MU 3185. The daybooks evidently record local
       operations, though this was a business engaged in a large non-local wheat
       and flour trade. Correspondence of the business has been informative on
       context.

## WHEAT

*east*: YM: 1803–4, 1808–12, 1824–40; Tett, B&S (mean of two): 1841–4; RC: 1791–8,
   1800–1; SJ: 1786, 1788, 1790, 1792 (combined with RC), 1813, 1817; Fair: 1807,
   1817 (combined with SJ), 1818
*centre*: press: 1817–22; CO42: 1826–9, 1831–40; Ball: 1787–1800, 1803–4, 1806; RH:
   1807–12; Gonder: 1813–14, 1825; Cooper: 1805, 1816; IW: 1823, 1830; Rousseau:
   1801–2; RG8: confirms 1814
*west*: AO, Hiram Walker Museum Collection, Ms 594, reels 2–3, McCormick Family
   Papers, William McCormick accounts: 1794, 1796–7 (converted from NY cy).
   AO, M. Dolsen Papers, Ms 621, reel 1: 1797 (combined with McCormick – also
   converted from NY cy). NA, Records of the Norfolk Historical Society, MG9, D8
   (24), 14957–15324, Francis Leigh Walsh account book: 1798–1807, 1818–19
   (converted from NY cy); ibid., 15325–524, Noah Fairchild Accounts: 1807 (combined with Walsh) to 1812 (converted from NY cy); ibid., 15572–16021, Cross &
   Fisher Accounts (converted from NY cy): 1830–36. RG19: 1814. MTL, records of a
   farmer near Dunnville: 1837–45

## OATS

*east*: YM: 1804, 1808–12, 1824–38; RC: 1792–3; Tett: 1839–45; Seymour: 1797–8;
   JMW: 1817–19; Fair: 1803, 1806; RG19: 1814
*centre*: press: 1817–22; Ball: 1790–1806; RH: 1807, 1809, 1810–12, 1816–17 (1817
   combined with press); IW: 1813, 1832–3; RG19: 1814; CO42: 1826–9, 1831; Reid:
   1825; Silver: 1813 (combined with IW); Parsons: 1836–7

POTATOES

*east*: YM: 1809–10, 1824–37; Tett: 1834–44 (1834–7 combined with YM); RC: 1793, 1796–7; SJ: 1789; Seymour: 1798; RG 19: 1814; JMW: 1818-19
*centre*: press: 1817-22; Ball: 1787-1799, 1802-3; RH: 1806-10, 1815-16, 1828-9; RG 19: 1814; IW: 1813, 1828 (combined with RH), 1834; Ridout: 1800

PEAS

*east*: YM: 1804, 1808–12, 1824–31, 1835–8; Tett: 1834–6 (combined with YM in 1835–6); 1838 (combined with YM) to 1844; RC: 1793–7; Seymour: 1798; Fair: 1803, 1818; RG19: 1814; AM: 1823; M&M: 1837 (combined with YM); JMW: 1818 (combined with Fair)
*Prince Edward*: B&S: all years
*centre*: Ball: 1788–1810 (with gaps, as table indicates); RH: 1811–12; RG8: 1814 (confirmed in part by RG19, which gives a number of examples at this price, but some at less); press: 1817–22; IW: 1823; Reid: 1825

HAY

*east*: YM: 1808–12, 1824–38; Tett: 1834–45 (1835–8 combined with YM); RC: 1791–7; Seymour: 1796–7 (combined with RC); Fair: 1813 (confirmed by RG19)
*centre*: press: 1818–22; Ball: 1793, 1802–3; RH: 1807–12, 1816–17, 1827, 1830; IW: 1815, 1828; CO42: 1831; RG19: 1814

BUTTER

*east*: YM: 1804, 1808–12, 1824–38; Tett: 1834, 1838 (combined with YM) to 1845; RC: 1791–7; Bell: 1790–1 (combined with RC in latter year); Seymour: 1798; Fair: 1803; JMW: 1816–20; RG 19: 1814
*centre*: Ball: 1788–99, 1802–6; Ridout: 1800; RH: 1807–12, 1816; press: 1817–22; IW: 1823, 1827–8; CO 42: 1831; RG19: 1813

BEEF

*east*: YM: 1809–11, 1824–9; Tett: 1833–43; RC: 1791, 1795, 1797; SJ: 1789; Seymour: 1796; JMW: 1817–19; CO42: 1831
*centre*: press: 1818–22; Ball: 1797–8; RH: 1806–12, 1815–17, 1825, 1827–30; Ridout: 1800; RG 8: 1803; CO42: 1831; IW: 1832–3

PORK

*by pound/east*: YM: 1803–4, 1808–12, 1824–33, 1835–8; Tett: 1840–3; RC: 1792–5; Seymour: 1796–8; SJ: 1802; JMW: 1816–20
*by pound/centre*: Ball: 1789, 1794; Ridout: 1800; RH: 1806–11, 1813, 1816–22, 1825, 1827–8; CO42: 1831; McGill: 1812; RG8: 1814. AO, Niagara Historical Society Records, Adds., Ms 833, reel 1, Louth Mills day books, 123–5: 1818 (converted from NY cy)

*by barrel/east*: YM: 1804, 1825–8, 1830–1, 1835; Tett: 1834, 1836–45; RC: 1791–
1803, 1810; McGill: 1809; Fair: 1814; SJ: 1815; Brock: 1819

*by barrel/centre*: press: 1822; McGill: 1804–5, 1807, 1809, 1812; Ridout: 1800; Wood:
1806; RG8: 1814; RH: 1817; IW: 1821, 1823, 1834

TABLE C.1
Prices of Upper Canadian Produce, Selected Commodities and Areas, 1786–1845

| Year | Wheat (s/bu) East | Wheat Cent | Wheat West | Oats (s/bu) East | Oats Cent | Potatoes (s/bu) East | Potatoes Cent | Peas (s/bu) East | Peas PE | Peas Cent | Hay (s/ton) Annual East | Hay Annual Cent | Hay (s/ton) 3rd quarter East | Hay 3rd quarter Cent |
|---|---|---|---|---|---|---|---|---|---|---|---|---|---|---|
| 1786 | 5/– | | | | | | | | | | | | | |
| 1787 | | 6/3 | | | | | 1/11 | | | 6/3 | | | | |
| 1788 | 4/– | 5/10 | | | | | 2/2 | | | 6/3 | | | | |
| 1789 | | 6/3 | | | | 2/6 | | | | 6/3 | | | | |
| 1790 | 4/– | 6/3 | | | 3/9 | | 3/1 | | | 6/3 | 70 | | | |
| 1791 | 4/– | 5/11 | | | | | 2/6 | | | 6/3 | | | | |
| 1792 | 3/6 | 5/– | | 2/– | | | 2/6 | | | 5/– | | | | |
| 1793 | 3/– | 5/– | | 1/9 | 2/6 | | 2/6 | 3/5 | | 5/– | | 75 | | |
| 1794 | 2/9 | 5/– | 6/3 | | | 2/– | 3/5 | 3/1 | | 5/– | 50 | | | |
| 1795 | 3/– | 5/2 | | | | | 2/6 | 3/10 | | 5/1 | 40 | | | |
| 1796 | 5/6 | 7/2 | 8/4 | 2/3 | 3/1 | 2/6 | 3/1 | 4/– | | 7/– | 40 | | | |
| 1797 | 5/– | 8/4 | 7/2 | 2/2 | 2/6 | 2/6 | 3/9 | 3/– | | 5/5 | 47/6 | | | |
| 1798 | 5/– | 6/– | 6/2 | | | 2/– | 1/11 | 4/3 | | 5/8 | 52/6 | | | |
| 1799 | | | 6/7 | | | | | | | 5/– | | | | |
| 1800 | 5/– | 5/– | 5/6 | | | | 1/11 | | | 4/8 | | | | |
| 1801 | 5/– | 4/10 | 5/– | | | | 1/11 | | | | | | | |
| 1802 | | 4/5 | 3/9 | | | | 1/11 | | | | | 50 | | |
| 1803 | 3/– | 3/6 | 3/1 | 1/3 | | | | 2/6 | | | | 37/6 | | |
| 1804 | 3/– | 3/1 | 3/9 | 1/6 | | | | 2/6 | | | | | | |
| 1805 | | 5/– | 3/1 | | | | | | | | | | | |
| 1806 | | 5/7 | 5/6 | 1/6 | 2/6 | | 2/6 | | | | | | | |
| 1807 | 4/6 | 4/5 | 5/6 | | 3/1 | | 1/11 | | | 5/9 | | | | |
| 1808 | 5/– | 4/1 | 5/– | 1/9 | 1/7 | | 2/4 | 3/– | | | 30 | 50 | | |
| 1809 | 7/– | 4/8 | 5/– | 2/6 | 2/6 | 1/7 | 2/6 | 4/4 | | | 42/7 | 45 | | |
| 1810 | 7/8 | 5/11 | 5/– | 2/9 | 2/6 | 2/– | 2/6 | 4/10 | | 5/– | 50 | 50 | | |
| 1811 | 6/4 | 6/– | 6/3 | 2/1 | 2/– | | | 4/5 | | 4/5 | | 50 | | |
| 1812 | 5/1 | 5/– | 6/3 | 2/4 | 1/11 | | | 4/5 | | 4/– | 42/6 | 48/5 | | |

| Year | | | | | | | | | | | | | | |
|------|---|---|---|---|---|---|---|---|---|---|---|---|---|---|
| 1813 | 12/- | | | | 4/6 | | 3/- | | | | | | | |
| 1814 | | 10/- | 7/- | 5/- | 5/- | 3/7 | 5/- | 9/- | | 10/- | 60 | 70 | | |
| 1815 | | 12/6 | | | | | 3/3 | | | | | 67/6 | | |
| 1816 | 10/- | 10/- | | | | | 2/6 | | | | | | | |
| 1817 | 5/- | 5/- | 6/3 | 3/9 | 3/9 | 2/- | | | | 4/4 | 40 | 40 | | |
| 1818 | | 5/- | 5/- | 2/- | 2/7 | 2/- | 2/6 | 3/3 | | 3/2 | | 45 | | 45 |
| 1819 | | 3/9 | | 3/1 | 1/3 | | 2/9 | | | 3/9 | | 55 | | 60 |
| 1820 | | 3/9 | | | 2/5 | | 2/3 | | | 3/4 | | 67/8 | | 56/8 |
| 1821 | 3/9 | 3/- | | | 2/1 | | | 2/5 | | 2/6 | | 53/9 | | |
| 1822 | 4/- | 2/6 | | | 1/6 | | 1/10 | 2/6 | | 1/1 | | 50 | | |
| 1823 | 4/5 | 2/10 | | | 1/- | | 1/3 | 2/11 | | 2/3 | | 50 | | 50 |
| 1824 | | | | 1/3 | | 1/2 | | | | | 40 | | | |
| 1825 | | 3/5 | | 1/4 | 1/2 | 1/3 | | 3/1 | | 2/4 | 43 | 40 | 35 | |
| 1826 | 4/6 | 2/6 | | 1/6 | 1/5 | 1/6 | 1/7 | 2/9 | | | 37/6 | | | |
| 1827 | 4/4 | 2/7 | | 1/2 | 1/1 | 1/4 | 1/8 | 2/6 | 2/6 | | 29 | 42/2 | | |
| 1828 | 4/5 | 3/9 | | 1/2 | 1/3 | 1/1 | 1/8 | 3/6 | 3/- | | 26/11 | 45 | | |
| 1829 | 6/- | 6/5 | | 1/8 | 1/7 | 1/8 | | 2/6 | 2/4 | | 35 | | | |
| 1830 | 5/2 | 5/- | 3/9 | 1/8 | 1/11 | 1/4 | 1/7 | 3/- | | | 30 | 50 | | |
| 1831 | 5/4 | 4/9 | 4/4 | 1/7 | 1/5 | 1/2 | | 3/6 | 2/6 | | 30 | 46 | | 40 |
| 1832 | 5/- | 4/2 | 3/11 | 1/5 | 1/9 | 1/3 | | 3/- | 3/1 | | 30/4 | | 27/6 | |
| 1833 | 4/9 | 4/1 | 3/6 | 1/11 | 2/3 | 1/7 | | | 3/5 | | 29/10 | | | |
| 1834 | 3/11 | 3/4 | 3/1 | 1/6 | | 1/5 | 1/4 | | 2/7 | | 36/8 | | | |
| 1835 | 4/- | 3/8 | 3/1 | 1/3 | | 1/5 | | | 2/6 | | 37/6 | | 40 | |
| 1836 | 5/2 | 4/11 | 4/7 | 1/8 | 2/6 | 1/3 | 2/2 | 3/5 | 2/9 | 5/- | 36/7 | | | |
| 1837 | 7/8 | 6/7 | 5/- | 2/1 | 2/- | 2/1 | 1/2 | 4/7 | 3/10 | | 33/4 | | | |
| 1838 | 6/1 | 5/8 | 4/8 | 1/4 | 1/10 | 1/6 | 1/1 | 3/2 | 3/4 | 3/- | 33/9 | 52/6 | 35 | |
| 1839 | 5/10 | 5/11 | 5/7 | 1/10 | 1/4 | 1/7 | | 3/9 | 3/4 | 2/5 | 40 | | | |
| 1840 | 4/7 | 4/- | 3/1 | 1/5 | 1/- | 1/3 | | 2/6 | 2/10 | | 40 | 41/5 | | |
| 1841 | 4/9 | 4/5 | 3/- | 1/4 | 1/5 | 1/3 | 1/5 | 2/9 | 2/4 | 2/4 | 40 | 52/8 | | 56/8 |
| 1842 | 4/11 | 4/7 | 4/- | 1/2 | 1/4 | 1/4 | 1/2 | 2/8 | 2/4 | 2/- | 40 | 55/5 | | 45 |
| 1843 | 4/3 | 3/6 | 3/5 | 1/4 | 1/1 | 1/6 | 1/6 | 2/9 | 2/1 | 1/9 | 52/6 | 50/3 | | 30 |
| 1844 | 4/5 | 4/1 | 3/3 | 1/6 | 1/2 | | 1/6 | | 2/6 | 1/10 | 43/3 | 42 | | 38/4 |
| 1845 | | 3/11 | 3/11 | 1/3 | 1/6 | | 1/7 | | | 2/2 | 45 | 52/11 | | 47/6 |

TABLE C.1 (continued)
Prices of Upper Canadian Produce, Selected Commodities and Areas, 1786–1845

| Year | Butter (d/lb) Annual East | Annual Cent | 3rd quarter East | 3rd quarter Cent | Beef (d/lb) Annual East | Annual Cent | 4th quarter East | 4th quarter Cent | Pork (d/lb) Annual East | Annual Cent | 4th quarter East | 4th quarter Cent | Pork (s/bbl) East | Cent |
|---|---|---|---|---|---|---|---|---|---|---|---|---|---|---|
| 1786 | | | | | | | | | | | | | | |
| 1787 | | | | | | | | | | | | | | |
| 1788 | | 9.4 | | 9.4 | | | | | | | | | | |
| 1789 | | | | | | | | | | 7.5 | | | | |
| 1790 | 12 | 15 | | | | | | | | | | | | |
| 1791 | 11.5 | 14.1 | | | 3.5 | | 3 | | 4.5 | | 4.5 | | 100 | |
| 1792 | 11 | 15 | 12 | | | | | | 4 | | 4 | | | |
| 1793 | 10 | | | | | | | | 4 | 2.4 | 4 | | 85 | |
| 1794 | 8.3 | | 8 | | | | | | | | | | | |
| 1795 | 12 | 15 | | | 2.5 | | 2.5 | | 3.5 | | 3.5 | | 90 | |
| 1796 | | | | | 3 | | 3 | | 4.5 | | 4 | | 110 | |
| 1797 | 12 | 13.1 | | 11.3 | 3 | 4.2 | 3 | 4.2 | 4.3 | | 4.5 | | 130 | |
| 1798 | 11.7 | 17.5 | 12 | | | 3.8 | | 3.8 | 5.3 | | 4.5 | | 125 | |
| 1799 | | 15 | | 15 | | | | | | | | | | |
| 1800 | | 15 | | | | 3.8 | | 3.8 | | 3.8 | | | 100 | 100 |
| 1801 | | | | | | | | | | | | | | |
| 1802 | 10 | 10.6 | | | | | | | 3.5 | | | | | |
| 1803 | 10 | 7.5 | | 7.5 | | | | | 2.8 | | | | 80 | |
| 1804 | | 7.5 | | 7.5 | | 3 | | | | | | | 75 | 84 |
| 1805 | | 7.5 | | 7.5 | | | | | 4.9 | | | | | 83 |
| 1806 | | 7.5 | | 7.5 | | 2.7 | | 2.7 | | 3.8 | | 3.8 | | 100 |
| 1807 | | 7.5 | | 7.5 | | 3.4 | | 3.6 | | 3.8 | | 3.8 | | 95 |
| 1808 | 9 | 8.4 | 9 | | 3 | 3.5 | 3 | 3.2 | 4.8 | 3.6 | 4.8 | 3.4 | | 100 |
| 1809 | 10.2 | 9.4 | 9.2 | | 3.3 | 3.8 | 2.8 | 3.4 | 6.5 | 3.9 | 4.7 | 3.8 | 100 | 95 |
| 1810 | 10.3 | 7.5 | 9 | 7.5 | 3.6 | 3.6 | 3.3 | 3.5 | 6 | 4 | 6.4 | 3.8 | 100 | |
| 1811 | 9.9 | 9.4 | 8.4 | | | 3.3 | | | 7.2 | 3.8 | | | | |
| 1812 | 10.5 | 9.1 | | | 3.5 | 3.5 | | 3.3 | 7.5 | 3.1 | | 3.8 | | 90 |

| Year | | | | | | | | | | | | | |
|---|---|---|---|---|---|---|---|---|---|---|---|---|---|
| 1813 | | | | | | | 5.6 | 5.6 | | 3.4 | | 100 | 150 |
| 1814 | 16.5 | 15 | | | | | | | | 7.5 | | 125 | |
| 1815 | | | | | | | | | | | | | |
| 1816 | 15 | 18.8 | | | | | 4.4 | 3.8 | 6 | 4.7 | | | |
| 1817 | 13.5 | 14.3 | 15 | | 4 | 4 | 4.3 | 3.1 | 4.5 | 3.4 | | 90 | 80 |
| 1818 | 12 | 13 | 12 | 11 | 3.5 | 3 | 4.9 | 4.3 | 4.5 | 3.8 | 3.8 | | |
| 1819 | 13.5 | 14 | | 13 | | | 5.1 | 4.2 | 4.3 | 3.8 | 3.8 | | |
| 1820 | 10 | 10.9 | | 8.8 | | | 4.4 | 3.8 | 4.3 | 2.5 | | | |
| 1821 | | 10.8 | | | | | 4 | | 3 | | | | 60 |
| 1822 | | 7.5 | | | | | 3 | | | 3.1 | | | 50 |
| 1823 | | 6.8 | | | | | | | | | | | 42 |
| 1824 | 7.3 | | 6.5 | | 2.1 | 2.2 | 2.5 | 2.5 | 3 | 3.8 | | 75 | |
| 1825 | 7.7 | | 6.3 | | 1.9 | 1.9 | 3.1 | | 5.3 | | | 70 | |
| 1826 | 7.5 | | 6.8 | | 1.9 | 1.9 | 1.9 | | 4 | 2.5 | | 70 | |
| 1827 | 6.5 | | 5.8 | | 1.9 | 1.8 | 1.9 | | 3.5 | 3.8 | | 67 | |
| 1828 | 6 | 6.8 | 4.8 | | 2 | 1.9 | 3.1 | | 4.1 | | | | |
| 1829 | 7.1 | 6.8 | 6.8 | | 4 | | 2.3 | 1.9 | 5.9 | | | 80 | |
| 1830 | 6.7 | | 6 | | | | | | 5.4 | | | 80 | |
| 1831 | 6.7 | 6.5 | 5.7 | 6.3 | 3.2 | 3 | 3.4 | 3.1 | 5.4 | 3.5 | [3.5] | | |
| 1832 | 7 | | 7.5 | | | | 5 | 3.4 | 5.3 | | | | |
| 1833 | 7.3 | | 6.3 | | 3 | 3 | 3 | | 5.6 | | | | |
| 1834 | 6.8 | | 5.8 | | 2 | 2 | | | 5.4 | | | 80 | |
| 1835 | 6.3 | | 5.7 | | 1.8 | 1.8 | | | 5.3 | | | 69 | |
| 1836 | 7.9 | | 7.8 | | 3.1 | 3.1 | | | 5.4 | | | 76 | |
| 1837 | 8.2 | | 7.8 | | 3 | 3 | | | 5.3 | | | 71 | |
| 1838 | 7.5 | 8.6 | 6.5 | 8.4 | 2.4 | 2.4 | 3.8 | 3 | 6.5 | | | 67 | |
| 1839 | 7.6 | 8.8 | 7.3 | | 2.9 | 2.7 | 3 | 3 | 6 | | | 68 | |
| 1840 | 7.2 | 7.8 | 6.3 | | 1.8 | 1.8 | 3.1 | 2 | 3.9 | | | 59 | |
| 1841 | 7.1 | 7.1 | 6.2 | 7.3 | 2.2 | 2.6 | 1.9 | 1.7 | 2.4 | | | 55 | |
| 1842 | 7.2 | 6.7 | 6.5 | 5.9 | 1.8 | 1.8 | 2.3 | 3 | 2.6 | | | 48 | |
| 1843 | 6.3 | 7.7 | 6.5 | 6.8 | 1.7 | 1.7 | 3 | 2.7 | 3.1 | | | 50 | |
| 1844 | 6.6 | 5.9 | | 5.8 | | | 2.1 | 1.7 | | | | 59 | |
| 1845 | 6 | 7.1 | | 6.8 | | | 2.8 | 3.5 | | | | 55 | |

TABLE C.2
Produce Prices on the Toronto Markets, Selected Commodities, 1838–70

| Year | Wheat (s/bu) | Oats (s/bu) | Potatoes (s/bu) | Peas (s/bu) | Hay (s/Ton) Year | 3rd quarter |
|------|------|------|------|------|------|------|
| 1838 | 5/8 | 1/10 | 2/2 | 5/– | 52/6 | |
| 1839 | 5/11 | 1/4 | 1/2 | 3/– | | |
| 1840 | 4/– | 1/– | 1/1 | 2/5 | 41/5 | |
| 1841 | 4/5 | 1/5 | 1/5 | 2/4 | 52/8 | 56/8 |
| 1842 | 4/7 | 1/4 | 1/2 | 2/– | 55/5 | 45/– |
| 1843 | 3/6 | 1/1 | 1/6 | 1/9 | 50/3 | 30/– |
| 1844 | 4/1 | 1/2 | 1/6 | 1/10 | 42/– | 38/4 |
| 1845 | 3/11 | 1/6 | 1/7 | 2/2 | 52/11 | 47/6 |
| 1846 | 4/– | 1/9 | 2/7 | 3/2 | 57/– | 34/11 |
| 1847 | 4/6 | 1/7 | 3/3 | 2/6 | 41/11 | 40/9 |
| 1848 | 4/2 | 1/6 | 3/4 | 2/3 | 51/– | 45/– |
| 1849 | 4/– | 1/1 | 2/3 | 1/8 | 49/8 | 41/3 |
| 1850 | 4/1 | 1/3 | 1/10 | 2/- | 49/8 | 43/9 |
| 1851 | 3/7 | 1/5 | 2/4 | 2/7 | 52/9 | 52/11 |
| 1852 | 3/7 | 1/4 | 2/8 | 2/2 | 44/7 | 45/10 |
| 1853 | 4/9 | 2/1 | 2/8 | 3/2 | 58/8 | 51/6 |
| 1854 | 7/– | 2/9 | 3/11 | 4/– | 86/6 | 87/6 |
| 1855 | 9/3 | 3/1 | 3/7 | 5/2 | 117/4 | 106/8 |
| 1856 | 7/1 | 2/7 | 4/3 | 3/4 | 103/– | 71/8 |
| 1857 | 6/8 | 3/1 | 6/2 | 4/8 | 104/5 | 103/4 |
| 1858 | 4/11 | 1/10 | 3/5 | 2/10 | 65/7 | 63/4 |
| 1859 | 6/11 | 2/6 | 3/1 | 3/9 | 88/6 | 105/– |
| 1860 | 6/4 | 1/8 | 1/7 | 2/11 | 76/10 | 72/6 |
| 1861 | 5/6 | 1/5 | 1/9 | 2/5 | 65/6 | 60/– |
| 1862 | 4/9 | 2/– | 3/1 | 2/6 | 83/9 | 89/2 |
| 1863 | 4/6 | 2/1 | 2/4 | 2/8 | 75/11 | 51/4 |
| 1864 | 4/7 | 2/2 | 2/5 | 2/10 | 54/2 | 57/2 |
| 1865 | 5/7 | 1/11 | 2/2 | 3/6 | 63/11 | 45/10 |
| 1866 | 7/3 | 1/7 | 1/7 | 3/2 | 53/6 | |
| 1867 | 8/7 | 2/2 | 2/8 | 3/9 | 63/7 | 45/– |
| 1868 | 7/9 | 2/8 | 4/2 | 4/3 | 74/3 | 60/– |
| 1869 | 5/1 | 2/5 | 2/8 | 3/8 | 64/6 | 57/6 |
| 1870 | 5/– | 1/11 | 2/6 | 3/4 | 52/1 | 51/4 |

TABLE C.2 *(continued)*

| Year | Butter (d/lb) Year | 3rd quarter | Beef (d/lb) Year | 4th quarter | Pork (d/lb) Year | 4th quarter |
|------|------|------------|------|------------|------|------------|
| 1838 | 8.6  | 8.4  | 3.8  | 3    | 4.4  | 4.3  |
| 1839 | 8.8  |      | 3    | 3    | 3.3  | 2.5  |
| 1840 | 7.8  |      | 3.1  | 2    | 3.2  | 2    |
| 1841 | 7.1  | 7.3  | 1.9  | 1.7  | 1.9  | 1.5  |
| 1842 | 6.7  | 5.9  | 2.3  | 3    | 2.7  | 3    |
| 1843 | 7.7  | 6.8  | 3    | 2.7  | 3    | 2.7  |
| 1844 | 5.9  | 5.8  | 2.1  | 1.7  | 2.2  | 2    |
| 1845 | 7.1  | 6.8  | 2.8  | 3.5  | 2.3  | 3    |
| 1846 | 6.7  | 6.5  | 3.4  | 2.4  | 4    | 2.3  |
| 1847 | 6.3  | 6    | 2.9  | 2    | 2    | 2    |
| 1848 | 7.6  | 7.3  | 2.2  | 1.7  | 2.1  | 1.8  |
| 1849 | 7.1  | 7.7  | 1.8  | 1.5  | 2    | 2    |
| 1850 | 6.7  | 6.7  | 1.9  | 1.5  | 3    |      |
| 1851 | 7.7  | 7.8  | 3    | 3.5  | 2.7  | 2    |
| 1852 | 8.2  | 6.5  | 3.6  | 4.2  | 2.5  | 3    |
| 1853 | 8.8  | 6.8  | 4.1  | 3.8  | 4.3  | 5    |
| 1854 | 9    | 8.2  | 4.9  | 3.5  | 4    | 4    |
| 1855 | 11.8 | 9.9  | 5.3  | 4    | 4.5  | 4.5  |
| 1856 | 11.8 | 11.8 | 4.2  | 4    | 4.6  | 4.2  |
| 1857 | 12.6 | 11.8 | 4.7  |      | 5.4  |      |
| 1858 | 8.6  | 6.4  | 3.4  | 2.5  | 3.5  | 3.3  |
| 1859 | 8.9  | 7.3  | 3.6  | 2.3  | 4.6  | 4    |
| 1860 | 8.6  | 9.8  | 3.6  | 2.3  | 4    | 4    |
| 1861 | 8    | 7.5  | 2.9  | 2.3  | 3.2  | 2.3  |
| 1862 | 9.7  | 8.2  | 3    | 2.5  | 1.8  | 1.5  |
| 1863 | 8.6  | 7    | 2.4  | 3    | 2.5  | 2    |
| 1864 | 9.7  | 8.3  | 2.8  | 2.2  | 3.5  | 4    |
| 1865 | 10.2 | 8.5  | 3.9  | 4.5  | 5.4  | 6    |
| 1866 | 10.5 | 9.3  | 4.1  | 3.7  | 4.9  | 3.8  |
| 1867 | 8    | 7.5  | 4.1  | 3.8  | 5.2  | 5.3  |
| 1868 | 11.1 | 10.1 | 3.7  | 3    | 5.6  | 6    |
| 1869 | 11.8 | 9.5  | 3.7  | 3    | 7.4  | 7.5  |
| 1870 | 10.7 | 11   | 4.1  | 3.7  | 6.7  | 7    |

TABLE C.3

Indexes of Price Changes, Upper Canada, Selected Periods (1831 = 100)

| Years | Wheat (s/bu) East | Wheat (s/bu) Cent | Wheat (s/bu) West | Oats (s/bu) East | Oats (s/bu) Cent | Potatoes (s/bu) East | Potatoes (s/bu) Cent | Peas (s/bu) East | Peas (s/bu) PE | Peas (s/bu) Cent | Hay (s/Ton) Annual East | Hay (s/Ton) Annual Cent | Hay (s/Ton) 3rd quarter Cent |
|---|---|---|---|---|---|---|---|---|---|---|---|---|---|
| 1796–8 | 98 | 152 | 167 | 138 | 196 | 194 | 194 | 125 | | | 167 | | |
| 1802–3 | 56 | 69 | 79 | 84 | | | 119 | 83 | | | | 95 | |
| 1809–10 | 138 | 109 | 115 | 163 | 179 | 150 | 156 | 153 | | | 167 | 103 | |
| 1813–16 | 206 | 227 | 144 | 209 | 286 | 300 | 244 | 300 | | | 200 | 151 | |
| 1822–3 | 70 | 56 | | | 71 | | 78 | 80 | | | | 109 | 125 |
| 1824–6 | 83 | 59 | | 81 | 86 | 108 | | 93 | | | 134 | | |
| 1829–31 | 103 | 114 | 92 | 103 | 118 | 113 | 100 | 100 | 104 | n/a | 106 | 104 | 100 |
| 1834–5 | 75 | 70 | 72 | | | 117 | 83 | 108 | 100 | | 124 | | |
| 1837–8 | 128 | 128 | 113 | 104 | 136 | 150 | 138 | 128 | 144 | | 112 | 114 | 94 |
| 1842–3 | 80 | 84 | 83 | 78 | 79 | 104 | 83 | 90 | 88 | | 154 | 115 | 101 |
| 1844–6 | | 84 | 90 | 84 | 114 | | 119 | | | | 150 | 117 | 115 |
| 1849–51 | | 82 | | | 89 | | 135 | | | | | 110 | |
| 1854–6 | | 163 | | | 200 | | 244 | | | | | 222 | 222 |
| 1861 | | 116 | | | 100 | | 109 | | | | | 142 | 150 |
| 1863–4 | | 96 | | | 149 | | 151 | | | | | 141 | 136 |
| 1867–8 | | 173 | | | 171 | | 213 | | | | | 150 | 131 |

| | Butter (d/lb) | | | | Beef (d/lb) | | | | Pork (d/lb) | | | | Pork (s/bbl) |
| | Annual | | 3rd quarter | | Annual | | 4th quarter | | Annual | | 4th quarter | | |
| Years | East | Cent | East | Cent | East | Cent | East | Cent | East | Cent | East | Cent | East |
|---|---|---|---|---|---|---|---|---|---|---|---|---|---|
| 1796–8 | 177 | 235 | 211 | 179 | 94 | 124 | 100 | 124 | 87 | | 92 | | 152 |
| 1802–3 | 149 | 139 | | 119 | | 88 | | | 58 | | 67 | | 100 |
| 1809–10 | 153 | 130 | 160 | | 108 | 109 | 102 | 101 | 116 | 113 | 118 | | 125 |
| 1813–16 | 246 | 260 | | | 125 | 141 | 133 | 122 | 97 | 136 | 112 | | 141 |
| 1822–3 | | 110 | | | | 88 | | | | 89 | | | |
| 1824–6 | 112 | | 112 | | 63 | 82 | 67 | | 76 | 107 | 85 | | 83 |
| 1829–31 | 101 | 100 | 108 | 100 | 100 | 85 | 100 | 74 | 103 | 100 | 102 | 100 | 100 |
| 1834–5 | 98 | | 101 | | 59 | | 63 | 96 | 100 | | 117 | | 93 |
| 1837–8 | 118 | 132 | 125 | 133 | 84 | 112 | 90 | 88 | 116 | 126 | 160 | 121 | 86 |
| 1842–3 | 101 | 111 | 114 | 101 | 55 | 78 | 58 | 84 | 53 | 81 | 51 | 81 | 61 |
| 1844–6 | 94 | 102 | | 102 | | 91 | | 74 | | 80 | | 69 | 69 |
| 1849–51 | | 110 | | 117 | | 94 | | 64 | | 74 | | 57 | |
| 1854–6 | | 168 | | 159 | | 150 | | 112 | | 126 | | 120 | |
| 1861 | | 123 | | 119 | | 85 | | 68 | | 91 | | 66 | |
| 1863–4 | | 141 | | 121 | | 76 | | 76 | | 86 | | 86 | |
| 1867–8 | | 147 | | 140 | | 115 | | 100 | | 154 | | 161 | |

TABLE C.4
Some Other Price Indexes, 1796–8 to 1867–8, Selected Evidence (1831 = 100)

| Years | I Wheat Mtl | II Oats Quebec | III Beef Quebec | IV Butter Mtl | V Rosseaux Agric. | VI Wheat GB | VII Flour US | VIII Farm NY | IX Farm Phila. | X Farm Mass | XI Farm Md | XII Agric. S. Ohio |
|---|---|---|---|---|---|---|---|---|---|---|---|---|
| 1796–8 | 110 | 110 | 74 | 87 | | 93 | | 168 | 151 | 92 | 127 | 122 |
| 1802–3 | 86 | 112 | 88 | 85 | 126 | 97 | 120 | 137 | 128 | 91 | 140 | 83 |
| 1809–10 | 143 | 168 | 109 | 111 | 148 | 154 | 145 | 142 | 130 | 114 | 142 | 88 |
| 1813–16 | 214 | 240 | 155 | 161 | 148 | 123 | 155 | 185 | 164 | 122 | 158 | 132 |
| 1822–3 | 80 | 88 | 89 | 98 | 96 | 74 | 118 | 110 | 111 | 111 | 124 | 83 |
| 1824–6 | 89 | 96 | 93 | 101 | 104 | 95 | 91 | 104 | 105 | 113 | 94 | 84 |
| 1829–31 | 110 | 96 | 102 | 89 | 98 | 99 | 100 | 97 | 95 | 102 | 105 | 92 |
| 1834–5 | 79 | 93 | 90 | 91 | 94 | 64 | 95 | 114 | 121 | 122 | 118 | 109 |
| 1837–8 | 125 | 130 | 150 | 109 | 104 | 91 | 150 | 136 | 136 | 138 | 141 | 140 |
| 1842–3 | 99 | 72 | 84 | 77 | 93 | 81 | 91 | 83 | 98 | 103 | 100 | 72 |
| 1844–6 | 91 | 80 | 106 | 90 | 94 | 79 | 86 | 92 | 100 | 110 | 85 | 86 |
| 1849–51 | 75 | 96 | 110 | 87 | 78 | 62 | 85 | 111 | 113 | 133 | 115 | 97 |
| 1854–6 | 148 | 140 | | | 101 | 109 | 141 | 150 | 146 | 163 | | 141 |
| 1861 | | | | | 93 | 83 | 87 | 123 | 125 | | | 123 |
| 1863–4 | | | | | 90 | 64 | 120 | 225 | | | | |
| 1867–8 | | | | | 95 | 97 | 150 | 222 | | | | |

*Notes and Sources for Table C.4*

I–IV: F. Ouellet with J. Hamelin and R. Chabot, 'Les prix agricoles dans les villes et les campagnes du Québec d'avant 1850: aperçus quantitatifs,' *HS/SH* 15 (1982), 95–6, 99–101, 103–6

V and VI: B. Mitchell with P. Deane, *Abstract of British Historical Statistics* (Cambridge 1971), 471, 488

VII–IX and XII: *Historical Statistics of the United States: Colonial Times to 1970* (Washington 1975) vol. 1, 201–2, 205–6, 209. Series are Warren-Pearson, 'farm products,' basically for New York; Bezanson, 'farm crops' at Philadelphia; Berry, 'identified with northern agriculture' at Cincinnati; and 'superfine' flour. The flour price is used in place of wheat because there is a considerable break in the wheat series at 1825, when the series shifts from Philadelphia to New York, whereas flour prices run smoothly through the transition.

X: Winnifred Rothenberg, 'A Price Index for Rural Massachusetts, 1750–1855,' *JEH* 39 (1979), 93–5. Her index using 1855 weights has been selected; see discussion at pp. 986–7 of degrees of correlation between this index and the Warren-Pearson and Bezanson indexes.

XI: Donald R. Adams, 'Prices and Wages in Maryland, 1750–1850,' *JEH* 46 (1986), 630–1. Data here are his index of meat and grain prices. See also his 'Prices and Wages in Antebellum America: The West Virginia Experience,' *JEH* 52 (1992), 206–16.

Note that blank spaces indicate years not covered by a series; index numbers are given for periods partially covered (e.g., Rothenberg ends in 1855, not 1856, and Adams in 1850, not 1851).

# Notes

ABBREVIATIONS

AO    Archives of Ontario, Toronto
CHA   Canadian Historical Association
CHR   *Canadian Historical Review*
CPRH  *Canadian Papers in Rural History*
DCB   *Dictionary of Canadian Biography*
HP    *Historical Papers*
HS/SH *Histoire sociale/Social History*
JCS    *Journal of Canadian Studies*
JEH    *Journal of Economic History*
JLA    Province of Canada, Legislative Assembly, *Journals*
LCJ    Lower Canada, Legislative Assembly, *Journals*
MTL   Metropolitan Toronto Library, Baldwin Room
NA    National Archives of Canada, Ottawa
OBA   Ontario Bureau of Archives
OH  *(OHSPR) Ontario History*, formerly *Ontario Historical Society Papers and
      Records*
QUA   Queen's University Archives, Kingston
RHAF *Revue d'histoire de l'Amérique française*
SP     Sessional Papers
TTN   Tables of Trade and Navigation, published as appendices (later Sessional
      Papers) to *JLA*
UCJ   Upper Canada, Legislative Assembly, *Journals*
UG    University of Guelph Library, Macdonald-Stewart Room
UTL   University of Toronto Library, Thomas Fisher Rare Books Library
UWO  University of Western Ontario Library, Regional History Collection

CHAPTER 1: *Introduction*

1  For convenience, the designation Upper Canada will be used throughout. During the Union era, from 1841 to 1867, it became increasingly common to speak of Canada West, but even then, the name Upper Canada remained widely used.

2  On the concepts of 'extensive' and 'intensive' growth, see John Dales, *The Protective Tariff in Canada's Development* (Toronto 1966), 154–7.

3  For an overview of this literature (to 1979), see Kenneth Norrie, 'The National Policy and the Rate of Prairie Settlement,' *JCS* 14, 3 (fall 1979), 63–76.

4  With a very favourable age structure, natural rates of increase can run as high as 3 per cent per annum, though 2.5 per cent seems a more typical high rate. A provincial rate of 7 per cent per annum, sustained over a seventy-year period, indicates the continuing importance of immigration. For colonial America, see John J. McCusker and Russell R. Menard, *The Economy of British America, 1607–1789* (Chapel Hill 1985), 226–9. For contemporary Lower Canada, see Serge Courville, Jean-Claude Robert, and Normand Séguin, 'Population et espace rural au Bas-Canada: l'exemple de l'axe laurentien dans la première moitié du XIXᵉ siècle,' *RHAF* 44 (1990–1), 243–62.

5  On the problems, and the importance, of land improvement as a form of capital creation or accumulation, see, for example, R.M. McInnis, 'Output and Productivity in Canadian Agriculture, 1870–1 to 1926–7,' in Stanley L. Engerman and Robert E. Gallman, eds., *Long-Term Factors in American Economic Growth*, Studies in Income and Wealth, 51 (Chicago 1986), 751–3.

6  See M.C. Urquhart, 'New Estimates of Gross National Product, Canada, 1870–1926: Some Implications for Canadian Development,' in Engerman and Gallman, eds., *Long-Term Factors in American Economic Growth*, 9–94; and E.J. Chambers and G. Bertram, 'Urbanization and Manufacturing in Central Canada, 1870–1890,' in Canadian Political Science Association, *Conference on Statistics* (1964), 225–58.

7  Ian Drummond, *Progress without Planning: The Economic History of Ontario from Confederation to the Second World War* (Toronto 1987)

8  For material drawing extensively on census manuscripts, see Michael B. Katz, Michael J. Doucet, and Mark J. Stern, *The Social Organization of Early Industrial Capitalism* (Cambridge, Mass. 1982); David Gagan, *Hopeful Travellers: Families, Land and Social Change in Mid-Victorian Peel County, Canada West* (Toronto 1981); and Chad Gaffield, *Language, Schooling, and Cultural Conflict: The Origins of the French-Language Controversy in Ontario* (Kingston and Montreal 1987). The standard general account remains J.M.S. Careless, *The Union of the Canadas: The Growth of Canadian Institutions 1841–1857* (Toronto 1967).

9  Gary Teeple, 'Land, Labour and Capital in Pre-Confederation Canada,' in G. Teeple, ed., *Capitalism and the National Question in Canada* (Toronto 1972), 48; G.M. Craig, *Upper Canada: The Formative Years, 1784–1841* (Toronto 1963), 53

10  McCusker and Menard, *The Economy of British America.* See especially ch. 4, 'The Centrality of Trade.' The latest Canadian text is likewise set in staples terms; see Kenneth Norrie and Douglas Owram, *A History of the Canadian Economy* (Toronto 1991), esp. 197–8.

11  Charles Tiebout, 'Exports and Regional Economic Growth,' *Journal of Political Economy* 64 (1956), 161

12  Stanley Engerman, 'Douglass C. North's *The Economic Growth of the United States, 1790–1860* Revisited,' *Social Science History* 1 (1976–7), 253. See also Irving B. Kravis, 'The Role of Exports in Nineteenth-Century United States Growth,' *Economic Development and Cultural Change* 20 (1971–2), 405: 'The mainsprings of growth were internal; they must be sought in the land and the people and in the system of social and economic organizations.' Also highly relevant is Diane Lindstrom, *Economic Development in the Philadelphia Region, 1810–1850* (New York 1978), ch. 1 and passim.

13  Kenneth Buckley, 'The Role of Staple Industries in Canada's Economic Development,' *JEH* 18 (1958), 439–60; see esp. p. 450, which speaks of 'an organic view of internal economic development.' On the other hand, authors continue to argue for the modern relevance of staples theory. See, for example, C.B. Schedvin, 'Staples and Regions of Pax Britannica,' *Economic History Review* 2nd ser., 43 (1990), 533–59. But Schedvin admits that 'regional and staple characteristics are only part of the story' (p. 556); and he believes that 'Canada [was] without an effective staple for most of the nineteenth century' (p. 536).

14  See R.M. McInnis, 'Perspectives on Ontario Agriculture 1815–1930,' ch. 1, 'The Early Ontario Wheat Staple Reconsidered,' *CPRH* 8 (1992), 47–8.

15  I have discussed these matters further for one region in an unpublished paper, 'Above the Falls: The Economic Development of Western Upper Canada, 1784–1851,' presented to the Conference on the Rural Economy and the Beginnings of Industrialization, Université de Montréal, 28–29 Feb. 1992.

16  David Gagan, 'Geographical and Social Mobility in Nineteenth Century Ontario: A Microstudy,' *Canadian Review of Sociology and Anthropology* 13 (1976), 158

17  See R.M. McInnis, 'Marketable Surpluses in Ontario Farming, 1860,' and Richard Pomfret, 'The Mechanization of Reaping in Nineteenth-Century Ontario: A Case Study of the Pace and Causes of the Diffusion of Embodied Technical Change,' both reprinted in Douglas McCalla, ed., *Perspectives on Canadian Economic History* (Toronto 1987), 55–6, 81–2, 89–92.

18  See especially W.B. Rothenberg, 'The Market and Massachusetts Farmers, 1750–1855,' *JEH* 41 (1981), 283–314. See also McCusker and Menard, *The Economy of British America*, 295–308; Gloria L. and J.T. Main, 'Economic Growth and the Standard of Living in Southern New England, 1640–1774,' *JEH* 48 (1988), 27–46; and Christopher Clark, *The Roots of Rural Capitalism: Western Massachusetts, 1780–1860* (Ithaca 1990).

19  For example, J.F. Shepherd and G. Walton, *Shipping, Maritime Trade, and the Economic Development of Colonial North America* (Cambridge 1972), 25

CHAPTER 2: *The Loyalist Economy, 1784–1805*

1 Bruce Wilson, in *As She Began: An Illustrated Introduction to Loyalist Ontario* (Toronto 1981), 13, gives a total of 7,500, which includes Indians.

2 See Bruce Wilson, *The Enterprises of Robert Hamilton: A Study of Wealth and Influence in Early Upper Canada, 1776–1812* (Ottawa 1983) for a comprehensive analysis of this nexus.

3 See, for example, E.J. Lajeunesse, ed., *The Windsor Border Region: Canada's Southernmost Frontier: A Collection of Documents* (Toronto 1960).

4 J.R. Miller, *Skyscrapers Hide the Heavens: A History of Indian-White Relations in Canada* (Toronto 1989), 93

5 Peter Schmalz, *The Ojibwa of Southern Ontario* (Toronto 1991), 101–19; Donald B. Smith, 'The Dispossession of the Mississauga Indians: A Missing Chapter in the Early History of Upper Canada,' *OH* 73 (1981), 67–87; R.J. Surtees, 'Indian Land Cessions in Upper Canada, 1815–1830,' in I.A.L. Getty and A.S. Lussier, eds., *As Long as the Sun Shines and Water Flows: A Reader in Canadian Native Studies* (Vancouver 1983), 65–84. There is a convenient map of principal purchases in George C. Patterson, *Land Settlement in Upper Canada, 1783–1840,* 16th Report of Ontario Department of Archives (Toronto 1920), 220–1.

6 Two important books on land policy are Lillian F. Gates, *Land Policies of Upper Canada* (Toronto 1968), and Alan Wilson, *The Clergy Reserves of Upper Canada: A Canadian Mortmain* (Toronto 1968).

7 Louis Gentilcore and Kate Donkin, *Land Surveys of Southern Ontario,* Cartographica Monograph 8 (Toronto 1973), 1–24; also 'Plan of the North Side of Lake Ontario from Cataraque to Niagara ... [1784],' in L. Gentilcore and C.G. Head, eds., *Ontario's History in Maps* (Toronto 1984), 60 (and frontispiece to the limited Bicentennial Edition)

8 Leo Johnson, 'Land Policy, Population Growth and Social Structure in the Home District, 1793–1851,' *OH* 63 (1971), 60

9 See, for example, John Clarke, 'The Role of Political Position and Family and Economic Linkage in Land Speculation in the Western District of Upper Canada, 1788–1815,' *Canadian Geographer* 19 (1975), 28.

10 For a study emphasizing both opportunity for ordinary farmers and the length of time required to realize it, see Peter Russell, 'Upper Canada: A Poor Man's Country? Some Statistical Evidence,' *CPRH* 3 (1982), 134–44.

11 My understanding of Upper Canadian property law and the legal system has been enhanced by correspondence with John Weaver. See his 'While Equity Slumbered: Creditor Advantage, a Capitalist Land Market, and Upper Canada's Missing Court,' *Osgoode Hall Law Journal* 28 (1990), 871–914; and Peter George and Philip Sworden, 'The Courts and the Development of Trade in Upper Canada, 1830–1860,' *Business History Review* 60 (1986), 272–80.

12 R.C. Harris, ed., and G. Matthews, cartographer, *Historical Atlas of Canada,* 1,

*From the Beginning to 1800* (Toronto 1987), plate 68. See also Gentilcore and Head, *Ontario's History in Maps*, 74–5, and frontispiece to the Bicentennial Edition, and D.W. Smyth, *A Short Topographical Description of His Majesty's Province of Upper Canada* ... (London 1799, reprinted New York 1969), 34–5.

13  This view of the essential character of migration to Canada is sustained by numerous recent studies of immigration. See Bruce S. Elliott, *Irish Migrants in the Canadas: A New Approach* (Kingston and Montreal 1988), 6–7; Marianne McLean, *The People of Glengarry: Highlanders in Transition, 1745–1820* (Montreal and Kingston 1991), 205–17; Darrell A. Norris, 'Migration, Pioneer Settlement, and the Life Course: The First Families of an Ontario Township,' *CPRH* 4 (1984), 130–1.

14  Glenn J. Lockwood, *Montague: A Social History of an Irish Ontario Township: 1783–1980* (Kingston 1980), 40–2

15  Darrell A. Norris, 'Household and Transiency in a Loyalist Township: The People of Adolphustown, 1784–1822,' *HS/SH* 13 (1980), 399–415

16  E.g., D.B. Rutman, 'Assessing the Little Communities of Early America,' *William and Mary Quarterly* 3rd ser., 43 (1986), 72–8

17  But see Randy W. Widdis, 'Scale and Context: Approaches to the Study of Canadian Migration Patterns in the Nineteenth Century,' *Social Science History* 12 (1988), 269–303.

18  York's population was less than 500; see Edith Firth, ed., *The Town of York, 1793–1815: A Collection of Documents of Early Toronto* (Toronto 1962), lxxvii. Kingston was somewhat larger, and probably over 1,000 when the garrison is included; see Richard Preston, ed., *Kingston before the War of 1812: A Collection of Documents* (Toronto 1959), cxiv.

19  AO, Richard Cartwright Jr Letterbook, Ms 43, 1793–6, Cartwright to Robert Hamilton, 21 Nov. 1793, for seasonal migration of Canadian (i.e., French-Canadian) workers. See also NA, RG8-I, vol. 1090, 342, form signed by ship-builders, Kingston, 24 June 1790, which indicates that the workforce building two schooners consisted of Canadians.

20  The ratio for the province as a whole dropped below this figure during the 1830s, but areas of new settlement or heavy demand for seasonal labour continued to show a higher ratio even later.

21  Winnifred Rothenberg, 'The Market and Massachusetts Farmers, 1750–1855,' *JEH* 41 (1981), 289; Fernand Ouellet, *Lower Canada 1791–1840: Social Change and Nationalism* (Toronto 1980), 30–8

22  Wilson, *As She Began*, 107

23  Cartwright to Isaac Todd, 21 Oct. 1792; quoted in Wilson, *The Enterprises of Robert Hamilton*, 77

24  *UCJ*, 1812; printed in OBA, *Ninth Report* (1912), 4

25  Howard Temperley, 'Frontierism, Capital, and the American Loyalists in Canada,' *Journal of American Studies* 13 (1979), 15–18. The uncertainty

regarding the total is mainly because claims by Loyalists resident in both Upper and Lower Canada were heard at Quebec. See also Wilson, *As She Began*, 109.

26 Temperley, 'Frontierism, Capital, and the American Loyalist,' 18–22, shows payments in 1810 of £5,400. For a list of 110 officers in Upper Canada on half pay in 1807, see Canada, *Report on Archives for 1892*, 375–7.

27 In 1795 the grant was £7,175 stg; see E.A. Cruikshank, ed., *The Correspondence of Lieut. Governor John Graves Simcoe*, vol. 5 (Toronto 1931), 139, John King to Simcoe, 5 May 1795. By 1805 the grant was £8,379; see NA, MG11, CO42, vol. 337, 167, Peter Hunter to E. Cooke, 24 June 1805.

28 For 1798, salaries to those resident in Upper Canada were between £3,000 and £4,000; see E.A. Cruikshank and A.F. Hunter, eds., *The Correspondence of the Honourable Peter Russell*, vol. 2 (Toronto 1935), 53, 'Proposed Establishment of the Indian Department for 1798.' See also NA, MG11, CO42, vol. 350, 130–2, Establishment of Indian Department in Upper Canada for 1810, which shows salaries of *c.* £3,000. Indian presents amounted to more than four times this amount, but they were largely purchased outside the province.

For other expenses, see Cruikshank and Hunter, eds., *Peter Russell Correspondence*, vol. 1 (Toronto 1932), 152, 204, 269–70, 303, Russell to Robert Prescott, 28 Feb., 3 July, 3 Sept., 13 Oct. 1797, which in total suggest that Russell drew at least £10,000 for civil expenditure in the year, substantially more than the parliamentary grant would have covered. See ibid., vol. 3 (Toronto 1936), 39, Charles Long to Russell, 18 Dec. 1798 for a special grant of £1,000 for the construction of churches. See also *UCJ*, 1804, printed in OBA, *Sixth Report* (1909), 435.

29 MTL, John McGill Papers, 'Commissariat and Government Returns,' passim; also vols. B-38 to B-42. See also AO, Cartwright Letterbook (transcripts), MU 500, account of Upper Canadian exports in 1803; and Cruikshank, ed., *Simcoe Correspondence*, vol. 4 (Toronto 1926), 119, 263–4, 284, 336; J.G. Simcoe to Charles Long, 3 Nov. 1795; John McGill to Simcoe, 13 and 30 May and 18 July 1796.

30 MTL, John McGill Papers, 'Commissariat and Government Returns,' J. Craigie estimate of provisions required, 12 Apr. 1804 and 8 April 1805; NA, MG11, CO42, vol. 330, 78, and vol. 336, 32, Craigie's estimates of provisions, 28 Aug. 1802, 6 Aug. 1803; NA, RG8-I, vol. 546, 74, proposed distribution of new bedding, 12 Aug. 1797

31 NA, RG8-I, vol. 327, 188–90, Castlereagh to Sir James Craig, 8 Sept. 1809. See also C.P. Stacey, *Canada and the British Army 1846–1871*, rev. ed. (Toronto 1963), 11, which implies a somewhat higher figure for *c.* 1800 than that given here.

32 Note that 'bills drawn by public officers expended in this country' (i.e., the two Canadas) in 1802 totalled £120,000 stg; AO, Cartwright Letter Books (typescript), 1787–1808, MU 500, 188–9, list of exports from Quebec in 1802.

33 Cf. NA, RG8-I, vol. 326, 27, Memorial by John Taylor, acting paymaster of contingencies, to Sir James Craig, 14 Apr. 1809, which asserts that an ordinary

regimental paymaster distributed about £2,000 per month, which would have amounted to some £24 a year per man in a thousand-man regiment.

34 For Britain, see B. Mitchell and P. Deane, *Abstract of British Historical Statistics* (Cambridge 1971), 487–8.

35 G.M. Craig, *Upper Canada: The Formative Years* (Toronto 1963), 8

36 Cruikshank, ed., *Simcoe Correspondence*, I (Toronto 1923), 255, Richard Cartwright Jr to Simcoe, 12 Nov. 1792; AO, Cartwright Letterbook, Ms 43, Cartwright to Todd, McGill & Co., 16 and 28 Sept. 1793

37 AO, Richard Cartwright Jr Letterbooks (transcripts), Ms 44, vol. 5, 76, 82, 105–7, Cartwright to Hon. John McGill, 28 Feb. 1801; to Jas. & A. McGill & Co., 25 May 1801; to Robert Hamilton, 30 Jan. 1802. The peak in Britain, which was at or near the high for the entire century, came in March; prices then declined in response to rising imports and the conclusion of peace in Europe. See A.D. Gayer, W.W. Rostow, and Anna Jacobson Schwartz, *The Growth and Fluctuation of the British Economy 1790–1850*, new ed. (New York 1975), vol. I, 29–31, 502.

38 See, for example, Cruikshank and Hunter, eds., *Peter Russell Correspondence*, vol. 3 (Toronto 1936), 106–7, Extract from Minutes of the Executive Council on clerks' salaries vis-à-vis those of 'the most ordinary labour.'

39 For examples of the problems at Coteau-du-Lac, see *UCJ*, 14 Mar. 1814, 26 Mar. 1816, printed in OBA, *Ninth Report* (1912), 153, 286–7; an example of the data themselves can be found in NA, MG11, CO42, vol. 328, 143–70, accounts of articles passing Coteau-du-Lac upriver, I Jan. to 30 June, I July to 31 Dec. 1800.

40 See, for example, Theodore J. Kreps, 'Vicissitudes of the American Potash Industry,' *Journal of Economic and Business History* 3 (1930–1), 630–66, and MTL, Quetton St George Papers II, Hector MacKay to Q. St George, 9 May 1810. I owe the former reference to Kris Inwood.

41 See MTL, Alexander Wood Papers, Letterbooks, vol. I, 357–8, Wood to Leslie McNaught & Co., 6 Oct. 1804; Abner Miles Accounts, 'Ledger A, Yonge St. 1805.'

42 MTL, Alexander Wood Papers, Letterbooks, vol. 2, 88, Wood to Carl Hoffman, 19 Mar. 1806

43 Wilson, *The Enterprises of Robert Hamilton*, 28

44 AO, Baldwin Papers, Ms 88, D. David to St George, 25 Oct. 1808. See also Douglas McCalla, 'Laurent Quetton St George,' *DCB* 6 (Toronto 1987), 622–5.

45 Figure based on Table 2.1, discounted by 7 per cent a year to yield an 1803 estimate

46 Even doubled, on the assumption that only half the households in the region were primarily farmers, these figures do not seem high. One possible contemporary standard is supplied by E.V. Wilcox, 'Living High on $67.77 a Year,' *New York History* 7 (1926), 195–204; $68 was equivalent to £17.

47 Although large figures were sometimes claimed, Bruce Wilson's careful examination of fur trade provisioning leaves little doubt that the demand was limited by

comparison with the local economy (see *The Enterprises of Robert Hamilton*, 76). Richard Cartwright Jr recorded provision purchases in Kingston for up-country trade in 1803 of just £563 (see AO, Cartwright Letterbooks [transcripts], MU 500, 206–8). An example of larger claims is Simcoe's estimate of demand from the North-West of 80,000 barrels of flour per year (Cruikshank, ed., *Simcoe Correspondence*, vol. 3, 55, Simcoe to the Privy Council for Trade and Plantations, 1 Sept. 1794). At a ration of 1 lb of flour per man per day, such shipments would have fed 43,000 men for a year!

48 It was estimated that 159,000 gallons of liquor could be produced from this amount of wheat, or about 4 gallons per Upper Canadian (and nearly 20 gallons per adult male). It is unlikely that Table 2.4 underestimates wheat consumption by distillation! See also ch. 6.

49 But 1851 exports were 6.6 million bushels, or some 50 per cent of total output.

50 In Peel County during a period of extensive growth, around the middle of the nineteenth century, somewhere between 51 and 60 per cent of household heads were engaged in agriculture; see David Gagan, 'Geographical and Social Mobility in Nineteenth Century Ontario: A Microstudy,' *Canadian Review of Sociology and Anthropology* 13 (1976), 158–9; and his *Hopeful Travellers*, 109. For yield figures, see Thomas McIlwraith, 'The Logistical Geography of the Great Lakes Grain Trade, 1820–1850' (PH D thesis, University of Wisconsin 1973), 102. Higher figures (21 to 22 bushels per acre) are given in R.L. Jones, *A History of Agriculture in Ontario* (Toronto 1946), 97; and Robert Gourlay, *Statistical Account of Upper Canada*, S.R. Mealing, ed. (Toronto 1974), 291. If 60 per cent of households were actively farming, then output per farm was 127 bushels; if yields were 21 bushels per acre, that total could have been produced on about six acres per year. This argument is compatible with Graeme Wynn, *Timber Colony* (Toronto 1981), 21.

51 For a later period, see Peter Russell, 'Forest into Farmland: Upper Canadian Clearing Rates, 1822–1839,' *Agricultural History* 57 (1983), 326–39; Russell gives annual rates per township ranging from 0 to 6.9 acres per adult man, with long-term, province-wide rates ranging between 1.23 and 1.55 acres per year per adult male. These data are compatible with the sources from which the figure of 4 acres per farm per year derive in that (1) rates during intensive clearing were actually above the average figures, and (2) even at these rates, something like the 4 acres per year could be achieved by two adult men. See also McIlwraith, 'Logistical Geography,' 70, which suggests a farmer could be relatively self-sufficient in three years. Norris, 'Migration, Pioneer Settlement,' 146, notes that 'the average Euphrasia [Township] farm household managed to clear four or five acres annually up to 1851.'

52 For these valuations, see Upper Canada, *Statutes*, 43 Geo. III cap. 12 (1803), 'An Act particularizing the Property which shall be subject to Assessments and Rates ...' Some values, but not these, were revised downward by 47 Geo. III cap. 7

(1807). For prevalent prices of land in Essex County, the most remote of settlement areas in the province, see J. Clarke and D. Brown, 'The Upper Canadian Land Market: Insights from Essex County,' *CHR* 69 (1988), 226. Around 1805 land prices in Essex were about 10s per acre, but not all the land recorded by Clarke and Brown was improved; earlier land prices had been higher there, and within a year or two they rebounded to more than the assessment value.

53 K. Kelly, 'Wheat Farming in Simcoe County in the Mid-Nineteenth Century,' *Canadian Geographer* 15 (1971), 97

54 Note that assessments, if done during the winter, would primarily count draft animals and breeding stock, for late autumn saw the slaughtering of pigs intended for meat.

55 Cruikshank and Hunter, eds., *Peter Russell Correspondence*, vol. 3, 217–18, Robert Prescott to Russell, 3 June 1799: 'of Country cured Pork we have had sufficient experience, not to purchase any more of that Article for Military purposes.'

56 *UCJ*, 3 June 1802, printed in OBA, *Sixth Report* (1909), 257

57 Accounts of the Receiver-General for Upper Canada for 1801, printed in OBA, *Eleventh Report* (1914), 733, 748–53, 757–8

58 N. Ball, 'The Technology of Settlement and Land Clearing in Upper Canada Prior to 1840' (PH D thesis, University of Toronto 1979), 184–92

59 Norris, 'Household and Transiency in a Loyalist Township,' 408–10; Bruce Elliott, ' "The Famous Township of Hull": Image and Aspirations of a Pioneer Quebec Community,' *HS/SH* 12 (1979), 344–5

60 David Maldwyn Ellis, 'Rise of the Empire State, 1790–1820,' *New York History* 56 (1975), 14

61 See Report on the Affairs of the Indians of Canada, *JLA*, 1844–5, App. EEE, unpaginated. For a census of the Six Nations and their diverse allies, see C.M. Johnston, ed., *The Valley of the Six Nations: A Collection of Documents on the Indian Lands of the Grand River* (Toronto 1964), 52. See also Gentilcore and Head, *Ontario's History in Maps*, 84–5.

62 For population and acreage data, see Johnston, *Valley of the Six Nations*, 52, 127–9; and Report on the Affairs of the Indians in Canada [part 2], *JLA*, 1847, App. T. Crown and Clergy Reserves were to be deducted from the latter total.

63 For a slightly later period see the various travels by many individuals and groups referred to in Donald Smith, *Sacred Feathers: The Reverend Peter Jones (Kahkewaquonaby) and the Mississauga Indians* (Toronto 1987).

64 R.J. Surtees, 'The Development of an Indian Reserve Policy in Canada,' *OH* 61 (1969), 94

65 Fuller study would be needed of what Indians bought with furs they traded, but import data and evidence on local surpluses of various foods make it seem likely that most of the Indians' annual caloric requirements came from their own economy. For an approach along these lines, see Robert Jarvenpa and H.J.

Brumbach, 'The Microeconomics of Southern Chipewyan Fur Trade History,' in S. Krech, ed., *The Subarctic Fur Trade: Native Social and Economic Adaptations* (Vancouver 1984), 162–77; for this reference and much helpful advice on the native economy, I am indebted to John Milloy.

66 *JLA*, 1847, App. T, gives a full list of standard presents.

67 See, for example, R.L. Gentilcore, 'The Beginnings of Settlement in the Niagara Peninsula (1782–1792),' *Canadian Geographer* 7 (1963), 78–9.

68 See AO, Matthew Dolsen Journal, 1797–1799, for accounts of construction of the schooner *Thames*; and AO, Cartwright Letterbook, Ms 43, Cartwright to Robert Hamilton, 15 and 18 Apr. 1794, on cost of the new schooner *Simcoe*. Given the varying ages and rapid depreciation of sailing vessels, this figure is essentially an estimate of order-of-magnitude only. See also ch. 7, below.

69 For the values of early community builders, see Elliott, '"The Famous Township of Hull,"' 363.

CHAPTER 3: *The War Economy and After, 1806–22*

1 See, for example, AO, Isaac Wilson letters (typescripts), Ms 199, Isaac Wilson to Jonathan Wilson, 5 Mar. 1812, 20 Aug. 1815, 24 June 1817, and 13 July 1822.

2 Parts of the canal were open earlier; for example, Rochester was linked to Albany by the fall of 1823. See Blake McKelvey, *Rochester on the Genesee: The Growth of a City* (Syracuse 1973), 24.

3 See MTL, Alexander Wood letters, vol. 2, Wood to G. Dean, 21 Apr. 1808 and to Leslie McNaught & Co., 13 Sept. 1808. See also AO, Yonge Mills Records, MU 3167, Day Book, 12 Sept. 1810 to 19 Feb. 1812, for extensive winter ash transactions.

4 See AO, Baldwin Papers, J. Walton to Q. St George, 23 Jan. 1808; Robert Bach & Co. to Q. St George, 10 June 1808; G. Despard to Q. St George, 14 and 22 Sept. and 11 Oct. 1808.

5 Robert Gourlay, *Statistical Account of Upper Canada*, S.R. Mealing, ed. (Toronto 1974), 96, 287–9; see also NA, Upper Canada Sundries, RG5, A1, vol. 13, 5437–8, Annual Return of Militia of Upper Canada, 4 June 1811.

6 See, for example, AO, Isaac Wilson letters (typescript), Wilson to his parents, 19 Nov. 1811.

7 See map in M. Zaslow, ed., *The Defended Border, Upper Canada and the War of 1812* (Toronto 1964), 4–5.

8 AO, Isaac Wilson letters (typescript), Wilson to Jonathan Wilson, 5 Dec. 1813

9 Adam Shortt, 'The Economic Effect of the War of 1812 on Upper Canada,' reprinted in Zaslow, *The Defended Border*, 301–2. See also F.M. Quealey, 'The Administration of Sir Peregrine Maitland, Lieutenant-Governor of Upper Canada 1818–1828' (PH D thesis, University of Toronto 1968), vol. 1, 5–6, which sees the war 'as a catalyst in speeding up a transition to a commercial economy.'

10  A.B. McCullough, *Money and Exchange in Canada to 1900* (Toronto 1984), 268–9

11  In 1814 the British price was 74s 4d stg per imperial quarter, or 9s 4d per bushel. At the 1814 exchange rate (£0.951 cy = £1 stg), that was equivalent to less than 9s Hfx cy, at a time when prices in Upper Canada and Montreal were over 10s.

12  See MTL, Alexander Wood letters, vol. 3, Wood to John Stevens, 23 Dec. 1814; AO, Baldwin Papers, Ms 88, Inglis, Ellice & Co. to Q. St George, 10 Feb. 1815, and Hector MacKay to St George, 13 and 16 May 1815.

13  Prevost, Message to the Assembly of Lower Canada, 17 July 1812, reprinted in E.P. Neufeld, ed., *Money and Banking in Canada* (Toronto 1964), 42. This speaks of interest at 4 per cent, but the rate was 6 per cent from the start; see NA, Upper Canada Sundries, RG5, A1, vol. 15, 6334–41, Prevost to Isaac Brock, 28 July 1812.

14  For later totals see *LCJ*, 1817, App. D; 1818, App. B. See also McCullough, *Money and Exchange*, 83–5, 115.

15  MTL, Alexander Wood letters, vol. 3, Wood to James Irvine, 4 July 1814; AO, Baldwin Papers, Q. St George accounts with John Grant, 1812–16. See also NA, Alexander Hamilton Papers, MG24, I26, vol. 25, Daybook, Feb. 1812–Jan. 1817.

16  MTL, John McGill Papers, E. Couche to McGill, 4 Sept. 1812; NA, Upper Canada Sundries, RG5, A1, vol. 17, 7181–6, J. Green to E. Couche, 26 Mar. 1813

17  William Weekes, 'The War of 1812: Civil Authority and Martial Law in Upper Canada,' in *The Defended Border*, 198n; NA, Upper Canada Sundries, RG5, A1, vol. 18, 7651, J.B. Robinson to Maj.-Gen. de Rottenburg, 1 Nov. 1813; *UCJ*, 1814, printed in OBA *Ninth Report* (1912), 112, 118, 19 and 24 Feb. 1814; Upper Canada, *Statutes*, 53 Geo. III cap. 3 (1813), 'An Act to authorize the Governor ... to restrain the Distillation of Spirituous Liquors from Grain'

18  NA, Upper Canada Sundries, RG5, A1, vol. 19, 8143–9, W.H. Robinson to Sir George Prevost, 15 Mar. 1814; see also NA, RG8-I, vol. 118, 45–6, Gordon Drummond to Prevost, 10 Mar. 1814; and MG11, CO42, vol. 355, 49–51, 84, Drummond to Lord Bathurst, 5 Apr. 1814 and text of proclamation, 12 Apr. 1814.

19  NA, RG8-I, vol. 118, 97–8, E. Couche to Capt. Foster, 6 May 1814; Upper Canada Sundries, RG5, A1, vol. 20, 8616–19, Couche to Capt. Loring, 6 July 1814

20  MTL, Alexander Wood letters, vol. 3, Wood to Maitland, Garden & Co., 15 Dec. 1814, 15 Mar. 1815

21  MTL, W.W. Baldwin Papers, Baldwin to Q. St George, 15 Oct. 1814

22  George Raudzens, *The British Ordnance Department and Canada's Canals 1815–1855* (Waterloo 1979), 35

23  For war losses, see list of some 1,500 approved claims published in *Supplement to the Observer*, found in AO, Miscellaneous Collection, 1823 No. 8 (MU 2104). See also NA, MG11, CO42, vol. 371, 67–8, George Harrison to R. Wilmot Horton,

23 Sept. 1823. Note that there was some question of whether these payments, when made, would actually reach Upper Canadians, or would instead go directly to Montreal merchants in settlement of debts due to them. See CO42, 371, 227–31, J.B. Robinson to Wilmot Horton, 28 Jan. 1823.

24 MTL, W.W. Baldwin Papers, Baldwin to Q. St George, 16 July 1816; AO, Baldwin Papers, Hector MacKay to Q. St George, 13 and 16 May 1815. See also AO, Isaac Wilson letters, Wilson to his brother, 20 Aug. 1815, which speaks of the 'sudden fall' of retail prices of imports.

25 Helen I. Cowan, *British Emigration to British North America: The First Hundred Years*, rev. ed. (Toronto 1961), 27–39, 288; H.J.M. Johnston, *British Emigration Policy 1815–1830: 'Shovelling out Paupers'* (Oxford 1972), 24–5

26 Cowan, *British Emigration to British North America*, 40–64; and Richard Reid, ed., *The Upper Ottawa Valley to 1855: A Collection of Documents* (Toronto 1990), xxii–xxxi. For Peter Robinson's 1823 and 1825 emigration schemes, to Lanark and Peterborough respectively, and involving another 2,600 emigrants in total, see Wendy Cameron, 'Selecting Peter Robinson's Irish Emigrants,' *HS/SH* 9 (1976), 29–46.

27 Bruce Elliott, *Irish Migrants in the Canadas: A New Approach* (Kingston and Montreal 1988), 77

28 See, for example, Stanley C. Johnson, *A History of Emigration from the United Kingdom to North America, 1763–1912* (London 1913), 70.

29 G.M. Craig, *Upper Canada: The Formative Years* (Toronto 1963), 87–91, 114–22; see also Paul Romney, 'Reinventing Upper Canada: American Immigrants, Upper Canadian History, English Law, and the Alien Question,' in Roger Hall, William Westfall, and Laurel Sefton MacDowell, eds., *Patterns of the Past* (Toronto 1988), 78–107.

30 See, for example, Hartwell Bowsfield, 'Upper Canada in the 1820s: The Development of a Political Consciousness' (PH D thesis, University of Toronto 1976), 32–3, 118–20, 214, 353–6, 362.

31 AO, Alexander McMartin Papers, series F-3-6, MU 1973, Bill of Sale, McMartin to Boutheillier & Holt, 19 July 1816; Maitland, Garden & Auldjo, account of sale on account of McMartin, 4 Oct. 1820; see also AO, Samuel Street Papers, Ms 500, W.H. Merritt in account with D. Thompson, 1 Aug. 1835 [*sic*], which records potash transactions in 1820–3.

32 Such per capita and per household calculations of data on the wheat economy are somewhat notional but are provided to discount for population growth and to bring figures to the level relevant to individual decision-making, that of the individual and the household. Converting data on flour to equivalents in wheat may seem to deprive the provincial economy of the value added by milling, but it avoids the problem of flour quality (prices varied considerably by grade), and the conversion factor (5 bushels to 1 barrel) may tend to compensate for that problem. The appropriate valuation is likewise a matter for decision; if Montreal

prices are used, that gives Upper Canada credit for the costs of transportation
(which was often handled on Montreal account and using Lower Canadian
labour). Prices at the head of the river (in Kingston) or nearer the point of wheat
growth more closely represent the prices received by actual producers but may
understate the province's total income from the output. Of course, the provincial
economy included many non-farmers and there was substantial diversity in farm
scale and practice. When dividing by population, a choice must also be made
between using the whole of the province's population or that of areas that were
principal producers. Overall, the bias in calculations is to ensure that assumptions
do not tend to understate the significance of wheat.

33  Upper Canadian Arbitrator's Claim, A. No. 4, 31 July 1823, in *UCJ*, 1823–4;
printed in OBA, *Report*, 1914, 489

34  *LCJ*, 1825, App. T; 1826, App. U. Other items, recorded at Coteau by volume,
included:

| rum and other spirits | 180,000 gal in 1824; | 140,000 gal in 1825 |
| muscovado sugar | 478,000 lb in 1824; | 376,000 lb in 1825 |
| loaf sugar | 53,000 lb in 1824; | 35,000 lb in 1825 |
| tea | 15,000 lb in 1824; | 72,000 lb in 1825 |
| tobacco | 14,000 lb in 1824; | 13,000 lb in 1825 |

35  Potash was valued in Montreal in 1817 at 42s to 45s per hundredweight, but just
23s to 28s in 1820 and 1821.

36  For a sophisticated analysis of the situation, see T.W. Acheson, 'The Nature and
Structure of York Commerce in the 1820s,' *CHR* 50 (1969), 406–28.

37  H.G.J. Aitken, 'A New Way to Pay Old Debts: A Canadian Experience,' in W.
Miller, ed., *Men in Business: Essays on the Historical Role of the Entrepreneur*
(New York 1962 [first published Cambridge, Mass. 1952]), 71–90

38  Peter Baskerville, ed., *The Bank of Upper Canada: A Collection of Documents*
(Toronto 1987), xxxi–xxxiii, 6–8, 328, 332

39  For 1817, 5s was reported by 80 per cent of the townships responding to
Gourlay's survey: see Robert Gourlay, *Statistical Account of Upper Canada*,
176–7, 206–7, 238–9, 284–5, 291. For a similar wage in 1819, see for example,
AO, Wade Letters (typescript), MU 3074, Richard Wade to John Wade, 28 Sept.
1819, 44–5; 'Labor is very dear, a man in hay time and harvest has one dollar a
day ...' For examples from the Ottawa valley in 1822–3, see AO, Hamnett Pinhey
Papers, MU 2323–4, contract for building a mill for Capt. Monk, 11 Mar. 1823;
for an example from the Niagara area [Gainsborough Twp], UWO, Account book
of Robert Comfort (photocopy), account with James Miers, 11 Apr. to 5 Sept.
1823 (converted from NY cy); for the Gore District, AO, James Reid Papers, MU
2382, James Reid to Thomas Reid, 18 Dec. 1823 and 10 Feb. 1825.

40  See G.E. Hart, 'The Halifax Poor Man's Friend Society, 1820–27: An Early
Social Experiment,' *CHR* 34 (1953), 109–23; Judith Fingard, 'The Winter's Tale:
Contours of Pre-Industrial Poverty in British America, 1815–1860,' CHA, *HP*

(1974), 94 n109; Edith Firth, ed., *The Town of York, 1815–1834: A Further Collection of Documents of Old Toronto* (Toronto 1966), 224–9.

41  On the controversy, see Philip A. Buckner, *The Transition to Responsible Government: British Policy in British North America, 1815–1850* (Westport, Ct. 1985), 113–19; the Canada Trade Act was 3 Geo. IV cap. 119 (1823). On the Upper Canadian debate on these issues, see Robert Fraser, 'Like Eden in her Summer Dress: Gentry, Economy, and Society: Upper Canada, 1812–1840' (PH D thesis, University of Toronto 1979), 104–18.

42  Boyd Hilton, *Corn, Cash, Commerce: The Economic Policies of the Tory Governments 1815–1830* (Oxford 1977), 292–3; D.G. Barnes, *A History of the English Corn Laws from 1660–1846*, reprint ed. (New York 1961), 139, 174, 199, 201–2, 218 n88

43  See T.J.A. LeGoff, 'The Agricultural Crisis in Lower Canada, 1802–12: A Review of a Controversy,' *CHR* 55 (1974), 1–31; R.M. McInnis, 'Perspectives on Ontario Agriculture 1815–1930,' ch. 1, 'The Early Ontario Wheat Staple Reconsidered,' *CPRH* 8 (1992), 31.

44  A.R.M. Lower, *Great Britain's Woodyard: British America and the Timber Trade, 1763–1867* (Montreal 1973), 77–9; Graeme Wynn, *Timber Colony: A Historical Geography of Early Nineteenth Century New Brunswick* (Toronto 1981), 30–3

CHAPTER 4: *Forest Products and Upper Canadian Development, 1822–46*

1  See, for example, William Marr and Donald Paterson, *Canada: An Economic History* (Toronto 1980), 61–4, or Robert Armstrong, *Structure and Change: An Economic History of Quebec* (Toronto 1984), 115–22.

2  The story is now most conveniently available in A.R.M. Lower's *Great Britain's Woodyard: British America and the Timber Trade, 1763–1867* (Montreal 1973); the word 'artificial' is used on p. 67. See also his 'The Trade in Square Timber,' first published in 1933 and reprinted in W.T. Easterbrook and M.H. Watkins, eds., *Approaches to Canadian Economic History* (Toronto 1967), 28–48. For regional accounts of the Ottawa, see Richard Reid, ed., *The Upper Ottawa Valley to 1855* (Toronto 1990); Michael Cross, 'The Dark Druidical Groves: The Lumber Community and the Commercial Frontier in British North America, to 1854' (PH D thesis, University of Toronto 1968); Glenn Lockwood, *Montague: A Social History of an Irish Ontario Township: 1793–1980* (Kingston 1980); and Sandra Gillis, 'The Timber Trade in the Ottawa Valley, 1805–54,' Parks Canada Manuscript Report Series 153.

3  Graeme Wynn, 'Timber Trade History,' *The Canadian Encyclopedia* (Edmonton 1988), vol. 4, 2160–1

4  Lower, *Great Britain's Woodyard*, 92–5. Here, as at many other points, Lower's work offers leads that others have yet to pursue. But see John Keyes, 'The Dunn

Family Business, 1850–1914: The Trade in Square Timber at Quebec,
1850–1914' (PH D thesis, Université Laval 1988).

5 Lower, *Great Britain's Woodyard*, 250; Graeme Wynn, *Timber Colony: A
Historical Geography of Early Nineteenth Century New Brunswick* (Toronto
1981), ch. 2

6 See, for example, John McCallum, *Unequal Beginnings: Agriculture and
Economic Development in Quebec and Ontario until 1870* (Toronto 1980), 3.

7 Cf. Lower, *Great Britain's Woodyard*, 65, where the point is made that timber of
American origin often became 'Canadian' after it 'drifted into Canadian waters'
with the river current. In fact, the data underlying table 4.2 do distinguish Upper
Canadian from American timber, and because much timber was designated
American, there is no reason to assume that the timber designated Upper
Canadian was not produced in Upper Canada. Upper Canadians often contended
that data on trade passing Coteau were unreliable and underestimated the scale of
their economy. Nevertheless, they used them; I have taken a similar view. See
*UCJ*, 1836–7, App. 4, Report of John Macaulay, esp. exhibit G.

8 In addition, it is not always clear whether data offered for numbers of pieces
express actual numbers or are converted into the conventional dimensions of the
trade, around which sizes of pieces might vary considerably.

9 See QUA, Calvin Company Records, box 119, folder 1, 'Ready Reckoner for the
use of ... Measurers of Timber.' Moreover, Marvin McInnis reminds me, Quebec
merchants might, in contracts and correspondence, use the St Petersburg
standard.

10 NA, James Hamilton Papers, MG24, D45, J. Hamilton to James Hamilton, 14 May
1821

11 See Lower, *Great Britain's Woodyard*, 255–6; Fernand Ouellet, *Histoire
économique et sociale du Québec 1760–1850* (Montreal 1966), 607.

12 See Louise Dechêne, 'Les entreprises de William Price 1810–1850,' *HS/SH* 1
(1968), 25; and 'Forsyth & Bell's Price Current of Timber ....,' *Quebec Mercury*
25 June 1846, which reports five categories of white pine: inferior (3–3$^{1}$/₂d),
ordinary rafts (3$^{1}$/₂d), good rafts (4–5d), superior rafts (5$^{1}$/₂–6d), in shipping order
according to average quality and manufacture (4$^{1}$/₂–6d).

13 QUA, Calvin Papers, vol. 108, 'Stave Book, 1845'

14 Totals for 1844–6 do not include ashes, for which data are lacking. For the New
Brunswick pattern, see Wynn, *Timber Colony*, 34; here the all-time peak in
timber volume was in 1825, and the pattern of fluctuations, if not the actual
levels, appears roughly similar in the 1830s to the patterns indicated in table 4.2.

15 The *Blue Book* for that year shows immense haste in writing and the data for
Coteau omit reference to American-origin imports altogether, giving rise to a
suspicion that some American goods may have been counted with Upper
Canadian.

16 Data from Coteau-du-Lac on values are suspect, as the notes to the tables

indicate. But even if the timber values shown in table 4.3 are compared to the Coteau-furnished value for wheat and flour exports for these twelve years, the total values for forest products and wheat are almost identical.

17 For example, average annual shipments for Port Stanley (Kettle Creek) were 440 barrels in 1824–30 and under 60 in 1843–4; average annual shipments through the Desjardins Canal for 1837–44 were less than 100 barrels; and ash shipments through the Welland Canal (ports of origin and destination not specified) fell from 2,600 barrels in 1831 to 212 in 1836 (though a shutdown in the latter year may have been a factor). See *JLA*, 1844–5, App. A, sections Q and R; *UCJ*, 1826–7, App. N, 5, and 1831–2, App., 110.

18 See, for example, NA, Collections of the Lennox and Addington Historical Society, MG9, D8 (18), 35897–36451, McNeil and McHenry ledger, 1834–45.

19 For the Ottawa River ash trade, see NA, William Stewart Papers, MG24, D101, vol. 1, letterbook, 260, Stewart (per B. Gordon) to McKay & Russell, 21 Feb. 1838.

20 See, for example, Rosemary Ommer, 'The Truck System in Gaspé, 1822–77,' *Acadiensis* 19, 1 (autumn 1989), 113–14.

21 See QUA, Calvin Papers, vol. 143, 'Record of Vessels,' 1840–51, 211; and AO, Norris and Neelon Records, Ms 490, accounts of the *Sir Charles Napier*.

22 See QUA, Calvin Papers, vol. 134, Ledger, 1836–43, for freight accounts of forty-five different vessels in 1837.

23 *JLA*, 1844–5, App. HHH

24 QUA, Calvin Papers, vol. 139, statement of lumber received at Napanee, 1847–59; see also vol. 37, record of stave deliveries, n.d., for similar deliveries.

25 Ibid., vol. 171, 'Account Book, 1836–46,' for example, accounts of Henry Baldwin's and Edson Hastings's staves

26 See AO, Samuel Street Papers, Ms 500, W.H. Merritt in account with D. Thompson, 1 Aug. 1835, for kettle rentals at £2 each, Nov. 1820 to Apr. 1821. For evidence from four stores in the region from Kingston east at which ashes were an important mode of payment, see table 5.5.

27 See AO, Alexander McMartin Papers, MU 1973, 1810–12 ash book; 'Account of Ashes for the year 1822'; 'ash book,' Dec. 1823–Mar. 1824 for various delivery records to a Glengarry merchant. See also AO, Yonge Mills Records, MU 3169, Daybook, 1826–7; in February 1826, for example, some forty-four deliveries, totalling 1,227 bushels of ashes, were credited, at 4d to 6d per bushel, for a total of £26.

28 NA, Archibald Campbell Papers, MG24, D61, vol. 3, William & John Bell ledger, 1841–50. For the diary of a farmer near Lanark who was involved in potash-making, apparently as a summer activity, see NA, George Easton Diary, MG24, 1108 (photocopies), entries for 27 June, 8 Sept., 14 and 20 Oct. 1831; 10 Jan. 1832; 31 Oct. 1837; 12 July 1838; 25 June 1839. See also Larry Turner, 'The First Tay Canal in the Rideau Corridor, 1830–1850,' Parks Canada Microfiche Report Series, 142, 1984.

29  See the frequent journeys to nearby towns (Oshawa, Lindsay, Windsor Bay, and Toronto) from a stave shanty recorded in QUA, Calvin Papers, vol. 171, 'Account Book, 1836–46,' memo of 'Things got for shanty,' *c.* 1844–5.

30  See C. Grant Head, 'An Introduction to Forest Exploitation in Nineteenth Century Ontario,' in J. David Wood, ed., *Perspectives on Landscape and Settlement in Nineteenth Century Ontario* (Toronto 1975), 99.

31  For the economy of this area, see Chad Gaffield, *Language, Schooling, and Cultural Conflict: The Origins of the French-Language Controversy in Ontario* (Kingston and Montreal 1987), esp. ch. 3.

32  By 1851, these two districts (after boundary revisions when the Dalhousie District was created in 1842) were down to 10 per cent of provincial population.

33  The price differential also had to cover the Wrights' risk, interest costs, and profit, so it was not entirely attributable to transport costs per se. See NA, Philemon Wright Papers, MG24, D8, vol. 97, Ledger F; and vol. 120, 64418, receipt to Elijah Stanford, 4 Mar. 1824.

34  NA, MG11, CO42, vol. 427, 469–76, enclosure in Sir J. Colborne to Lord Glenelg, 26 Dec. 1835. The propensity of Colborne's informants to exaggerate may be indicated by their claim that exports from the Ottawa amounted to £800,000 per year, an improbable figure in light of the evidence in tables 4.3 and 4.5.

35  Sandra Gillis, 'The Timber Trade in the Ottawa Valley,' 131–2; Wynn, *Timber Colony*, 61; Head, 'An Introduction to Forest Exploitation'

36  NA, Wright Papers, vol. 120, 64566–7, 'List of Provisions and Sundries ...,' 1843 or 1844

37  This figure comes from a number of sources, including the records of the Hamilton Brothers operations; on another occasion, George Hamilton indicated that he thought in terms of 1½ pounds of meat per man a day, but this included meat that came from oxen. See AO, Hamilton Brothers Records, MU 1201, 'Meat Calculation for ... the Rouge,' 18 Mar. 1833. If the higher figure was typical, it implies a smaller total labour force than is estimated here.

38  See NA, Wright Papers, vol. 120, 64539–42, List of items taken on first 2 rafts, May 1837; vol. 111, 'Memorandum of ... Duties,' 1839, 1837. See also AO, Hamilton Brothers Records, MU 1201, 'List of Hands, up Rouge Fall of 1831 & 32,' data on 'Raft No. 1' for 1832, and 'Disposition of Hands on Rouge Spring 1833' for an indication that these orders of magnitude are appropriate. William Stewart estimated in 1848 that to produce a raft of 60,000 feet of red pine required the year-round labour of thirteen men and a half-year's work for seven more; by his calculations, labour costs were as much as one-third of total costs. See 'Estimate of the Cost of a Red Pine Raft,' printed in Reid, ed., *Upper Ottawa Valley*, 155–7. At twenty-five men per raft (apparently a large crew), seven thousand men could have manned almost three hundred rafts. Fewer than two hundred rafts descended the Ottawa from around Bytown in 1837, a year of equal or greater output than 1835, and hardly any of these were as large as 60,000 feet.

See AO, RGI, F-I-8, vol. 11, James Stevenson letterbook, 1–18.

39 The reasonableness of this figure is indicated by overall export figures from Quebec in the mid-1830s. For example, in 1835 total exports (to Britain and Ireland) were 17 million cubic feet of pine and deals. This would have required about seven thousand men to produce (at 2,500 feet per man), but it represented the combined output of the whole St Lawrence basin. See *LCJ*, 1835–6, Ap. GGG.

40 NA, Tucker & Laflamme Papers, MG2, D95, timber account book for 1856, 1859. As a percentage of timber sales, so far as the rather ambiguous phrasing of this source permits knowing them, wages were about 21 per cent. As the total value of Upper Canadian timber given in table 4.3 is for final selling price, it would perhaps be more appropriate to base an estimate of wages on this lower rate, but other biases in the source tend to offset this.

41 NA, Wright Papers, vol. 97, Ledger F, 1825–6: of 106 workers whose wages are readily noted, 61 per cent fell in this range; 16 per cent earned between £1 10s and £2, and 16 per cent earned between £3 and £4; vol. 104, ledger A, 1832–40: of 230 worker accounts here, 73 per cent fell in this range and 19 per cent in the £3 to £4 range. See also QUA, Calvin Papers, vol. 37, an employee record entitled 'ledger 1843–4,' where all but one of twenty-five men paid off on 19 Aug. 1843 had been earning a wage in this range.

42 Relative wage rates in different areas of recruitment, the structure of recruitment networks, workers' skills, and lack of local opportunity in some areas of Lower Canada were other pertinent factors here. For an analysis of these issues in the twentieth-century forest industry, see Ian Radforth, *Bushworkers and Bosses: Logging in Northern Ontario 1900–1980* (Toronto 1987), chs. 2 and 3.

43 NA, Wright Papers, vol. 104, Ledger, 1832–40; vol. 107, ledger, 1838–42. For a list of workers for the Hamilton operations on Lower Canada's Rouge River in the fall of 1835, see Reid, ed., *Upper Ottawa Valley*, 125–6; well over 80 per cent of the men had francophone names.

44 AO, McLachlin Brothers Records, MU 1959, 'Madawaska Accounts .... 1847 & 8.' See also Michael Cross, 'The Shiners' War: Social Violence in the Ottawa Valley in the 1830s,' *CHR* 54 (1973), 1–26; Allan Greer, 'Fur-Trade Labour and Lower Canadian Agrarian Structures,' CHA, *HP* (1981), 197–214; and Chad Gaffield, 'Boom or Bust: The Demography and Economy of the Lower Ottawa Valley in the Nineteenth Century,' CHA, *HP* (1982), 172–95. French-speaking settlement on the Upper Canadian side of the Ottawa had not yet begun at this time, though of course workers from the Lower Canadian side of the valley were important to the trade.

45 See NA, MG9, D8 (18), McNeil & McHenry ledger; see also NA, Mossom Boyd Papers, MG28, III-1, vols. 294–5, 875, general journals and time books, various years 1852–61; QUA, Calvin Papers, vol. 37, employee ledger, 1843–4. For river labour, see Lower, *Great Britain's Woodyard*, 186–7, and Calvin Papers, vol. 37,

summary of expenses of raft 5, 5 Sept. to 7 Oct. 1843; it cost almost £50 here for men at the Lachine rapids alone.

46 These comments are based on the 1832–40 employee ledger that is vol. 104 of the Wright Papers. For workers who finished the Hamilton Brothers' fiscal year (30 November) with credit balances in their accounts, the mean was typically in the same range, though a higher proportion (close to half, in most years) of Hamilton employees at that stage in the year, early in the new timber season, had debit balances on their accounts. See balance sheets and related statements in AO, Hamilton Brothers Records, MU 1217; these cover 1839–83.

47 NA, Tucker & Laflamme Papers, timber account book for 1856, 1859. William Stewart's 1848 calculation of red pine costs showed approximately one-quarter of total costs on account of provisions and their transportation; see Reid, ed., *Upper Ottawa Valley*, 155–7.

48 AO, Hamilton Brothers Records, MU 1201, 1202, memos dated 2 Nov. 1820, 1 Nov. 1848. See also the discussion in Gaffield, *Language, Schooling, and Cultural Conflict*, 78–82; the estimate of 1867 flour requirements for the Hamilton firm cited here seems quite excessive. The total, 9,000 barrels, at a high rate of consumption (2 barrels, or almost 400 pounds, per man per year), would have sustained a 4,500-man workforce.

49 McCallum, *Unequal Beginnings*, 11; Gillis, 'The Timber Trade in the Ottawa Valley,' 148; see also R.L. Jones, *History of Agriculture in Ontario, 1613–1880* (Toronto 1946), 126.

50 See NA, McNeil & McHenry ledger 1834–35; NA, William Stewart Papers, vol. 1, 207, Stewart to Wm Ritchie & Co., 7 Aug. 1837, which shows pork and flour coming to Bytown from Hamilton and Cleveland via the Rideau Canal and from Montreal as well; and AO, D.B. Stevenson Papers, MU 2884, R. Wilkins to D.B. Stevenson, 20 May 1841.

51 Industry spokesmen invariably claimed much higher figures than these for shanty provisioning. For example, the Bytown *Gazette* said that 1839–40 purchases would include 10,000 barrels of pork and 15,000 of flour. If the Wright calculations were accurate, this would have provisioned enough men to provide for 1840 production of at least 18 million cubic feet, when valley output was in fact nearer one-third of that total. See Gillis, 'The Timber Trade in the Ottawa Valley,' 143. To get a fuller picture of the pine timber industry's demand for wheat and flour, we may include the shanty-generated demand from the St Lawerence; 1835's exports from there of 31,000 pieces of white pine could have totalled as much as 2.2 million feet, which would have required another 1,100 barrels of pork and 1,800 barrels of flour.

52 NA, William Stewart Papers, 85, Stewart to William Ritchie & Co., 11 April 1836

53 NA, Upper Canada Sundries, RG5, A1, vol. 124, 68413–14, Abstract of Rideau Canal traffic in 1832; 243 barrels of pork and 284 of flour travelled only part of

the canal length in this, its first year; this was 75 per cent of the former and 30 per cent of the latter traffic.

54  This supports the argument of McIlwraith, 'The Logistical Geography of the Great Lakes Grain Trade,' 65.

55  NA, William Stewart Papers, 142, Stewart to W. Ritchie & Co., 9 Jan. 1837; and 161, Stewart to Wood & Gray, 13 Mar. 1837. See also tables C.1, C.3.

56  On the other hand, such provisions constituted a variable component in the cost structure of the timber economy, for prices of such supplies appear to have swung more widely than and not necessarily in the same direction as square timber prices. See NA, William Stewart Papers, 161, Stewart to Wood & Gray, 13 Mar. 1837: 'I understand from advices from home that contracts are made for timber as low as usual, rather a dark prospect for lumbermen as the article this year costs at least 50% more than any former years.'

57  AO, Hamilton Brothers Records, MU 1220, Hamilton & Low Instructions to John Donnally, Oct. 1835, 12

58  QUA, Calvin Papers, vol. 171, 'Things got for shanty.' See also NA, Stewart Papers, 15, Stewart to Alex Corbet, 17 Nov. 1834 re recruitment of men and teams from Glengarry for the Ottawa; and 141, Stewart to G. Campbell, 4 Jan. 1837, re hiring of horses at Massena (NY).

59  See NA, Wright Papers, 64619, 'Statement of Supposed Quantity of Deals ...' for an estimate of eight deals per log. If this was typical, then the Hamiltons' projected output would have exceeded 300,000 cubic feet and the total draught animal requirements would have been proportionately lower. I have assumed that the average log here was likely to yield the equivalent of five deals. In 1835 George Hamilton gave his annual output as over 12,000 loads (i.e., over 600,000 cubic feet); see Lower Canada, Legislative Council, Journals, 1835–6, App. C.

60  These totals are for both sides of the upper Ottawa and equal less than 10 per cent of horses and 15 per cent of oxen recorded in the 1836 Upper Canadian assessments for the Bathurst and Ottawa districts alone.

61  AO, Hamilton Brothers Records, MU 1201, 'Stock on the Rouge remg Spring 1834 for 1835'; QUA, Calvin Papers, vol. 171, 'Things got for shanty'; NA, Wright Papers, vol. 120, 64504–6, 'Preparations made on the Gatineau'; NA, Boyd Papers, vol. 305, 240–6; AO, McLachlin Papers, MU 1957, contract, Daniel McLachlin and Arthur Hughes, 27 Dec. 1853; NA, Tucker & Laflamme Papers, 1856, 1859. In every case, recorded purchases or stock of pork alone substantially exceeded the value of the fodder recorded. See table C.1 for fodder prices, which in eastern Upper Canada in the 1830s typically were less than £2 per ton for hay and less than 2s per bushel for oats.

62  This suggests a need for caution in accepting John Egan's 1851 claim that his enterprises alone consumed fodder worth £11,500. See JLA, 1852–3, App. MMMM, Egan & Co. to A.J. Russell, 14 Feb. 1851.

63  For an example of repair costs, see NA, Wright Papers, vol. 111, blacksmith's

book, 1830–1. Between February and October 1831 the Wrights' smith charged
them over £115, though given the diversity of the Wright operations, it is not
possible to relate this figure exclusively to their timber output.

64 For initial cost, see AO, Hamilton Brothers Records, MU 1201, 'Statement of the
Affairs of R. & J. Hamilton ...,' 1822; the later value is found in *British Parlia-
mentary Papers* 1835 (519), 19, Report ... on Timber Duties, 138–56, evidence of
John Neilson. George Hamilton himself claimed output of 280,000 deals in 1835;
Lower Canada, Legislative Council, *Journals*, 1835–6, App. C. For Lower
Canadian exports, see *LCJ*, 1835, App. Z; 1835–6, App. GGG; *JLA*, 1841,
App. QQ.

65 NA, Wright Papers, vol. 120, 64619, 'Statement of Supposed Quantity of Deals
sent to Quebec Market annually,' Oct. 1847; *JLA*, 1849, App. Z

66 Lower, *Great Britain's Woodyard*, 177–8; AO, Hamilton Brothers Records, MU
1217, balance sheet for 1854

67 Lower Canada, Legislative Council, *Journals*, 1835–6, App. C

68 Note that the valuation used for pork and flour was at Bytown prices at the peak
of 1836–7's high prices.

69 NA, Ward Papers, MG24, D19, John D. Ward to Silas Ward, 19 May 1827; $300
= £75 cy. See table 6.6; of the total cost of March's Mill (£440), over £200 was
specifically attributable to the grist mill. See also QUA, Wells Family Accounts,
Box 1, Augusta Twp. Mill records, for £105 as the initial cost of a sawmill in
connection with a grist and carding mill, with subsequent additional costs
between 1819 and 1823 of £150 on saw mill account. And see AO, McMartin
Papers, MU 1972, grist and saw mill accounts, 'Wm. Sylvester's Estimate of
Circular Saw Mill at Martintown,' 23 July 1863, for a mill costing *c*. £115. This
conforms to the lowest estimates given by those in the trade in *LCJ*, 1835–6,
App. C.

70 NA, Wright Papers, vol. 111, small saw mill account book 'Admeasurement of Boards
& Plank,' Mar.–July 1827; NA, Records of the Norfolk Historical Society, MG9, D8
(24), Alexander McNeilledge Papers, sawyer's book, 1829 [*sic*]–33, 8350–8405

71 For prices at the Wright saw mill, see NA, Wright Papers, vol. 102, daybook,
1828–31.

72 In addition, there was commercial-scale production of hemlock bark for leather
tanning and of charcoal.

73 AO, Smith & Chisholm Papers, MU 2840, Gunn & Browne to Smith & Chisholm,
24 Jan. 1843; AO, anon. Cargo Register 1838–42, MU 690; Hamilton Public
Library, Archives, James Sutherland Account Book. Fragmentary accounts of
another ship appear to say that it required over £1,000 in wood (about 3,000
cords) during the 1836 shipping season. See AO, Misc. Collection, 1837, 17,
MU 2107, Prescott Steam Ship Accounts, Feb.–June 1837.

74 A second example is that of a distillery that spent £10 per month on wood. There
were almost 150 licensed stills in the province in 1842. See AO, MU 610, Sir

James Kempt cash book, 1836–7 [sic]; the distillery wood purchase records are for 1848–51.

75 Robert E. Gallman, 'Gross National Product in the United States, 1834–1909,' in Conference on Research in Income and Wealth, *Studies in Income and Wealth,* 30, *Output, Employment and Productivity in the United States after 1800* (New York 1966), 32–3

76 See Brian Young and John Dickinson, *A Short History of Quebec: A Socio-Economic Perspective* (Toronto 1988), 131–2.

77 On transatlantic freight costs in this era, see C. Knick Harley, 'Ocean Freight Rates and Productivity, 1740–1913: The Primacy of Mechanical Invention Reaffirmed,' *JEH* 48 (1988), 851–76.

78 See Lower, *Great Britain's Woodyard,* 258; Cowan, *British Emigration,* 288.

79 New Brunswick grew from about 25,000 in 1800 to about 200,000 in 1851; Upper Canada grew from about 46,000 in 1805–6 to 950,000 in 1851.

80 It should be clear that this is not a comment on the significance of Lower Canada's own forest economy.

81 See Marvin McInnis, 'Marketable Surpluses in Ontario Farming, 1860,' *Social Science History* 8 (1984), 395–424.

82 This point reminds us that there was preferential treatment to colonial wood exports even before Napoleon.

83 Of course, full calculation of an Upper Canada without the timber duties would require estimation of impacts on Lower Canada and the Maritime colonies, in that some Upper Canadian produce was sold to each for domestic consumption.

CHAPTER 5: *The Structure of Agriculture, 1821–51*

1 Cf. Chad Gaffield, *Language, Schooling, and Cultural Conflict: The Origins of the French-Language Controversy in Ontario* (Kingston and Montreal 1987), 66–7.

2 Bruce Elliott, *Irish Migrants in the Canadas: A New Approach* (Kingston and Montreal 1988), 195–232; Peter Russell, 'Emily Township: Pioneer Persistence to Equality?' *HS/SH* 22 (1989), 317–32; and Donald H. Akenson, *The Irish in Ontario: A Study in Rural History* (Kingston and Montreal 1984), 258–62. On the advantages of tenancy, see the dissertation summary by Catharine Anne Wilson, 'Landlords, Tenants, and Immigrants: The Irish and the Canadian Experience,' *JEH* 51 (1991), 457–9.

3 On land speculation and the land market, see J. Clarke and D.L. Brown, 'The Upper Canadian Land Market: Insights from Essex County,' *CHR* 69 (1988), 222–34; John Clarke, 'Geographical Aspects of Land Speculation in Essex County to 1825: The Strategy of Particular Individuals' (1983), reprinted in Johnson and Wilson, eds., *Historical Essays on Upper Canada,* esp. 81–4; David Gagan, *Hopeful Travellers: Families, Land, and Social Change in Mid-Victorian Peel*

*County, Canada West* (Toronto 1981), 20–39; Akenson, *The Irish in Ontario*, 143–63; and Randy William Widdis, 'Speculation and the Surveyor: An Analysis of the Role Played by Surveyors in the Settlement of Upper Canada,' *HS/SH* 15 (1982), 443–58.

4 Gagan, *Hopeful Travellers*, 57–9, 150; elsewhere (e.g., p. 43), Gagan notes that 'land capability' or 'soil quality' was the relevant variable.

5 Peter Russell, 'Forest into Farmland: Upper Canadian Clearing Rates, 1822–1839,' *Agricultural History* 57 (1983), reprinted in Johnson and Wilson, eds., *Historical Essays on Upper Canada*, 131–50. Some of the most dynamic areas in Russell's sample did show annual rates of clearing over five or more years of two acres per adult male. At that rate, a man with help from sons or hired labour could easily add four or more acres a year.

6 Norman Ball, 'Technology of Settlement and Land Clearing in Upper Canada Prior to 1840' (PH D thesis, University of Toronto 1979), 193 and passim

7 See W.R. Wightman, 'Construction Materials in Colonial Ontario 1831–61,' in F.H. Armstrong et al., eds., *Aspects of Nineteenth-Century Ontario* (Toronto 1974), 115–21; J. I. Rempel, *Building with Wood, and Other Aspects of Nineteenth-Century Building in Central Canada*, rev. ed. (Toronto 1980), esp. 190–223 on barns; R. Cole Harris and John Warkentin, *Canada before Confederation* (New York 1974), 130–5.

8 Ball, 'The Technology of Settlement,' 209; Bruce Elliott, '"The Famous Township of Hull:" Image and Aspirations of a Pioneer Quebec Community,' *HS/SH* 12 (1979), 363

9 See Leo Johnson, 'Independent Commodity Production: Mode of Production or Capitalist Class Formation?' *Studies in Political Economy* 6 (autumn 1981), 106, which sees the province's farmers as 'typical peasants.' A thoughtful treatment of this and other issues is Béatrice Craig, 'Pour une approche comparative de l'étude des sociétés rurales nord-américaines,' *HS/SH* 23 (1990), 267.

10 Ball, 'The Technology of Settlement,' 244

11 These terms are from the 1819 Assessment Act: Upper Canada, *Statutes*, 59 Geo. III cap. 7 (1819), An act ... relative to ... rates and assessments ...; and from published summaries of tax data. Similar terms and rates are found also in earlier acts, such as 43 Geo. III cap. 12 (1803), 47 Geo. III cap. 7 (1807), and 51 Geo. III cap. 51 (1811).

12 Clarke and Brown 'The Upper Canadian Land Market,' 226–32. See also Gaffield, *Language, Schooling and Cultural Conflict*, 212 n27. Prices were evidently considerably higher in more favourably located Peel County; see Gagan, *Hopeful Travellers*, 46. For prices in two counties from 1842, see Edward C. Gray and Barry E. Prentice, 'Exploring the Price of Farmland in Two Ontario Localities since Letters Patenting,' *CPRH* 4 (1984), 227–39.

13 See his 'The Size Structure of Farming, Canada West, 1861,' in 'Agrarian Organization in the Century of Industrialization: Europe, Russia and North

America,' *Research in Economic History* suppl. 5 (1989), 313–29; and 'Marketable Surpluses in Ontario Farming, 1860,' *Social Science History* 8 (1984), 395–424, reprinted in D. McCalla, ed., *Perspectives on Canadian Economic History* (Toronto 1987), 37–57 (subsequent page references are to this reprinted version of the article). See also R.M. McInnis, 'Perspectives on Ontario Agriculture 1815–1930,' ch. 1, 'The Early Ontario Wheat Staple Reconsidered,' *CPRH* 8 (1992), 44–6.

14  The percentages would be higher if some of the farms in the smallest category were excluded.

15  McCallum, *Unequal Beginnings* 13, 14, 21 (emphasis his). See also Kenneth Kelly, 'Wheat Farming in Simcoe County in the Mid-Nineteenth Century,' *Canadian Geographer* 15 (1971), 109; and Harris and Warkentin, *Canada before Confederation*, 135–41. The classic account is R.L. Jones, *History of Agriculture in Ontario 1613–1880* (Toronto 1946), 85–108.

16  See also McInnis, 'Perspectives on Ontario Agriculture, ch. 2, 'Ontario Agriculture at Mid-Century,' 70–1. By comparison, in 1910, 34 per cent of land under culture on the Canadian prairies was in wheat. Canada, *Census*, 1911, vol. 4, 46–220.

17  The calculations were based on an assumed local rate of consumption of 35 bushels per six-person household, a seed-yield ratio of 1 to 5, and a wheat-fallow-wheat crop rotation. In this model, local consumption rose with population, at about 7 per cent per year, which was the approximate rate of land clearance as well; variations in export volumes are thus the source of variation in proportion of land used. See Gagan, *Hopeful Travellers*, 155, and T.F. McIlwraith 'The Logistical Geography of the Great Lakes Grain Trade, 1820–1850' (PH D thesis, University of Wisconsin 1973), 91–123.

18  Donald Akenson strongly defends the accuracy of the 1842 census in some areas at least; and in fact, per capita output or stocks for the Johnstown District in 1842 were very close to province-wide levels in 1848–61 in a wide range of produce, other than wheat and potatoes. Compare *The Irish in Ontario*, esp. Appendix C, 394–5, with table 5.3. One well-informed Upper Canadian, J.S. Cartwright, estimated the 1841 crop at 5 million bushels, which was equal to over 10 bushels per person in the province (the same rate as in 1848). See Kingston *Chronicle and Gazette*, 4 Sept. 1841, found in NA, Adam Shortt Papers, MG30, D101, vol. 4.

19  McInnis, 'Marketable Surpluses,' 40–1, deducts seed before estimating consumption. After allowing for seed, the threshold of self-sufficency was really 7.5 bushels per capita. By that standard, the Niagara District, at 6.7 bushels per person, also had a wheat deficit. Lower consumption figures would reduce the total land requirements in the table and slightly alter the threshold of self-sufficiency, but the variance from less to more wheat-oriented areas would not be affected.

20 By 1851 Prince Edward had 6.4 acres per person under culture, compared to a provincial average of 3.9. It was a long-established area, one of those shown on map 5.1 as having over 50 per cent of occupied land under culture by then, not much urbanized, but well located in terms of water transport; its agriculture was by no means backward. To illustrate some of the variations possible in provincial farming practice, per capita 1851 outputs of some products in Prince Edward County may be compared to provincial average outputs as shown in table 5.3.

| | Wheat (bu) | Oats (bu) | Barley (bu) | Rye (bu) | Peas (bu) | Corn (bu) | Butter (lb) | Wool (lb) |
|---|---|---|---|---|---|---|---|---|
| Prince Edward | 10.2 | 9.3 | 2.2 | 3.2 | 13.6 | 5.7 | 29.4 | 4.8 |
| Upper Canada | 13.3 | 12.0 | 0.7 | 0.5 | 3.2 | 1.8 | 16.9 | 2.8 |

21 The analysis in this paragraph depends heavily on Marvin McInnis's two previously cited papers on 1860–1.

22 See also James O'Mara, 'The Seasonal Round of Gentry Farmers in Early Ontario: A Preliminary Analysis,' *CPRH* 2 (1980), 105–7.

23 McInnis, 'The Size Structure of Farms ... 1861,' table 2; on the geography of wheat production in 1860, see also McIlwraith 'The Logistical Geography,' map, p. 27.

24 At least two of the major mills in the province, Yonge Mills and the McDonald milling complex at Gananoque, were located east of Kingston, however. Although they ground local grain, they relied heavily on wheat from farther west (see table 6.5).

25 McCallum, *Unequal Beginnings*, 124; *JLA*, 1852–3, App. A, TTN, schedule 24

26 For examples of such criticism, see Jones, *History of Agriculture*, 89–90.

27 For similar issues in the cotton south of the United States, see J.S. Otto, 'Slaveholding General Farmers in a "Cotton County",' *Agricultural History* 55 (1981), 167–78; Gavin Wright, *The Political Economy of the Cotton South* (New York 1978), 43–88; and Lacy K. Ford, 'Yeoman Farmers in the South Carolina Upcountry: Changing Production Patterns in the Late Antebellum Era,' *Agricultural History* 60, 4 (fall 1986), 17–37.

28 Marjorie Cohen, *Women's Work, Markets, and Economic Development in Nineteenth-Century Ontario* (Toronto 1988), 93–9; McInnis, 'Marketable Surpluses,' 41. On women's marketing activities, see the host of examples, many of them individually modest, in Catharine Parr Traill, *The Canadian Settler's Guide*, New Canadian Library ed. (Toronto, 1969); and Louis Tivy, ed., *Your Loving Anna: Letters from the Ontario Frontier* (Toronto 1972). See also Joan M. Jensen, '"You May Depend She Does Not Eat Much Idle Bread": Mid-Atlantic Farm Women and Their Historians,' *Agricultural History* 61, 1 (winter 1987), 29–46. On tobacco, the 1848 census shows just 2,000 lb of production in Upper

Canada; this evidently under-reported output because in 1851 a total of 777,000 lb was reported. See Canada, *Census*, 1871, vol. 4, 169, 196.

29 For Charles Jones, see Thomas McIlwraith's article in *DCB* 7 (Toronto 1988), 452–4. See also J.K. Johnson, *Becoming Prominent: Regional Leadership in Upper Canada 1791–1841* (Kingston and Montreal 1989).

30 *LCJ*, 1823–4, App. W shows exports in 1817–18. Modest downriver tobacco shipments in 1824 are shown in NA, Hamilton Papers, MG24, I26, vol. 34, Store & Portage Ledger 1823–4. See also my 'Above the Falls: The Economic Development of Western Upper Canada, 1784–1851,' unpublished paper presented to the Conference on the Rural Economy and the Beginnings of Industrialization, Université de Montréal, 28–29 Feb. 1992, esp. table 4.

31 One example, a large barley cargo from Port Stanley to Cleveland in 1845, is found in UTL, Western Assurance Company Records, British America Assurance Company Day Book, 25 Nov. 1845–25 May 1847. In 1851 Buffalo received 19,600 bushels of barley from Upper Canada; see I.D. Andrews, *Report on the Trade and Commerce of the British American Colonies* (Washington 1853), 97.

32 AO, D.B. Stevenson Papers, MU 2886, Barter Book, 5 July 1836–27 June 1837

33 O'Mara, 'The Seasonal Round of Gentry Farmers.' For an important argument, using farm account sources and making due allowances for their biases, see Clarence Danhof, 'The Farm Enterprise: The Northern United States, 1820–1860s,' *Research in Economic History* 4 (1979), 127–91.

34 For another strongly wheat-oriented farm (probably 50 per cent or more of marketed output), see the Benjamin Smith Diary, 1799–1849, in AO, Ms 199, reel 4. This records a farm in Ancaster Township, near Hamilton.

35 McCallum, *Unequal Beginnings*, 24; the quote refers to the 1850s, but McCallum means it to be more general, for he adds: 'in earlier years the proportion would have been no lower.'

36 R.L. Jones, *History of Agriculture*, 126–9; McCallum, *Unequal Beginnings*, 11. By contrast, Akenson, *The Irish in Ontario*, 251, offers evidence of shipments of cattle from the Johnstown District across the St Lawrence into American markets.

37 For net farm output data for 1851, see McInnis, 'Ontario Agriculture at Mid-Century,' 56. Net output per farm in 1851 averaged $198.

38 See AO, Charles Butler Diary, MU 838; UWO, Ransford Journal, M231. See also Mrs D.H. McInnes, 'The Diary of Henry Ransford,' *OH* 51 (1959), 251–8.

39 See John Leslie, 'The Bagot Commission: Developing a Corporate Memory for the Indian Department,' CHA, *HP* (1982), 41, 44–6; and Peter Schmalz, *The Ojibwa of Southern Ontario* (Toronto 1991), 165–71.

40 Report on the Affairs of the Indians of Canada, *JLA*, 1844–5, App. EEE, section I

41 See Report of the Special Commissioners ... on Indian Affairs, *JLA*, 1858, App. 35 to App. 21, list of Indian land surrenders in Upper Canada; on a per acre basis, the surrender of half the Moravian reserve in 1836 at 2s an acre was the most

costly transaction. By the calculations of this table, the overall price of the 16 million acres recorded was 1¹/₂d an acre!

42  See John S. Milloy, 'The Early Indian Acts: Developmental Strategy and Constitutional Change,' in Ian A.L. Getty and Antoine S. Lussier, eds., *As Long as the Sun Shines and Water Flows: A Reader in Canadian Native Studies* (Vancouver 1983), 57.

43  Unless otherwise specified, all evidence in this discussion derives from the three major published surveys and reports on Indian affairs in the 1840s and 1850s: Report on the Affairs of the Indians of Canada, in two parts (*JLA*, 1844–5, App. EEE; and 1847, App. T); and Report of the Special Commissioners ... on Indian Affairs (1858, App. 21). Because none of these is paginated, detailed citation is difficult. See also Leslie, 'The Bagot Commission,' and Schmalz, *The Ojibwa of Southern Ontario*, 176–9.

44  Both quotes from *JLA*, 1858, App. 21

45  See household census data in *JLA*, 1858, App. 21 for the Bay of Quinte Mohawks and the two bands on Rice Lake; and 1847, App. T for the Wyandotte community in Anderdon Township in 1840. Unfortunately, data for most of the leading farming reserves in the western peninsula are not provided on a household basis.

46  See the discussion in Schmalz, *The Ojibwa of Southern Ontario*, ch. 7.

47  McInnis, 'Marketable Surpluses,' 48

48  Akenson, *The Irish in Ontario*, 353

49  For some Ottawa valley examples, see Richard Reid, ed., *The Upper Ottawa Valley to 1855* (Toronto 1990), xxiv–xxx, and 29–32 (for a letter from Hamnett Pinhey). See also Michael Cross, 'The Age of Gentility: The Formation of an Aristocracy in the Ottawa Valley,' CHA, *HP* (1967), 105–17.

50  For contrasting views on this shift, see Marvin McInnis, 'The Changing Structure of Canadian Agriculture, 1867–1897,' *JEH* 42 (1982), 191–8; and Robert Ankli and Wendy Millar, 'Ontario Agriculture in Transition: The Switch from Wheat to Cheese,' *JEH* 42 (1982), 207–15. See also Ian Drummond, *Progress without Planning* (Toronto 1987), ch. 3.

51  A work that stresses balanced growth, for a later period, is John Isbister, 'Agriculture, Balanced Growth, and Social Change in Central Canada since 1850: An Interpretation,' *Economic Development and Cultural Change* 25 (1976–7), reprinted in McCalla, ed., *Perspectives on Canadian Economic History*, 58–80.

52  Gagan, *Hopeful Travellers*, 109

53  Declines of this magnitude may have occurred from 1818 to 1820 and 1831 to 1832. See tables 4.3 and 5.2 for income from downriver wheat sales in the 1820s and 1830s.

54  Cohen, *Women's Work, Markets*, 153; William Marr and Donald Paterson, *Canada, An Economic History* (Toronto 1980), 88

CHAPTER 6: *Artisans, Manufacturing, and the Provincial Economy to 1851*

1 Selected Imports, Province of Canada, 1850–2 (£100 Hfx cy)

|                        | 1850  | 1851  | 1852  |
|------------------------|-------|-------|-------|
| Cottons                | 907   | 976   | 774   |
| Linens                 | 69    | 114   | 84    |
| Silks                  | 139   | 195   | 201   |
| Woollens               | 548   | 733   | 767   |
| Subtotal               | 1,663 | 2,018 | 1,826 |
| Iron & hardware        | 330   | 464   | 466   |
| Tea                    | 234   | 275   | 314   |
| Sugar                  | 173   | 196   | 233   |
| Tobacco                | 99    | 111   | 93    |
| 'Spirits'              | 71    | 68    | 77    |
| Total                  | 2,570 | 3,132 | 3,009 |
| Total, all dutiable goods | 3,951 | 4,906 | 4,760 |

As the 1851 population of the two Canadas was just under two million, the principal textiles were valued at about £1 per person. Cottons and woollens were the two leading items in the import list.

2 See AO, Richard Cartwright Jr Letterbooks (typescript of originals held at Queen's University), Ms 44, vol. 5, 68–9, Cartwright to J. & A. McGill & Co., 18 Oct. 1800.

3 For an account of competition and complementarity in the textile industries, see David Jeremy, *Transatlantic Industrial Revolution: The Diffusion of Textile Technologies between Britain and America, 1790–1830s* (Cambridge, Mass. 1981).

4 If these were all as substantial as some that are documented, they collectively would have represented considerable capital. For two asheries valued at about £70, see QUA, B. Seymour Daybook, 1796–8, entries for 9 May and 18 July 1798; UG, Goodwin-Haines Collection, W. Grant Papers, Barker & Stevenson Records, 'Estimated Value of Ashery,' 2 Sept. 1833. By the 1840s, when farmers often produced their own potash, it seems unlikely that individual farmers' investments would have been as large as this.

5 For this essential distinction, see AO, Hamnett Pinhey Papers, MU 2324, R. Morris to Pinhey, 9 Feb. 1823.

6 The 1842 census says there were 414 grist mills and a total of 584 'pairs of stones used'; the municipal tax assessments for the same year record 455 such mills and 359 'additional pairs' of stones, for a total of 814 pairs. See *JLA*, 1843, Apps. DD and FF, for the 1842 assessments and the 1842 census returns. I have followed the assessment data until 1848, because they appear internally consistent.

7 See *Census*, 1871, vol. 4, 270, which shows 305 steam saw mills and 61 steam grist mills in 1861. For some early steam mills, two in Kingston and one in

Hallowell, see NA, Upper Canada Sundries, RG5, A1, vol. 115, 64345–7, Return of Industries in the Midland District, 2 Mar. 1832.

8  A partial overview for 1845 can be obtained from W.H. Smith, *Canadian Gazetteer ... [for] Canada West* (Toronto 1846, reprinted Toronto 1970). Its focus is establishments, not individuals, and it understates or excludes much activity that we have defined as manufacturing, such as carpenters and coopers. There is almost no reference to work done by women, such as seamstresses and milliners.

9  They had the largest number of runs of stone according to the 1842 census. They also had the most extra runs in 1824; see NA, RG5, B26, vol. 4.

10  AO, Miscellaneous Collection, 1825, 7, MU 2104, Andrew Bell to William Bell, 26 Sept. 1825 (typescript). See also T.M. Bailey et al., eds., *Dictionary of Hamilton Biography* I (Hamilton 1981), 180.

11  Many such complexes are documented. See, for example, W.P.J. Millar, 'George P.M. Ball: A Rural Businessman in Upper Canada,' *OH* 66 (1974), 65–78; S.T. Fisher, *The Merchant Millers of the Humber Valley* (Toronto 1985); David Ouellette, 'James Crooks,' *DCB* 8 (Toronto 1985), 186, 188; and P.C.T. White, ed., *Lord Selkirk's Diary 1803–1804* (Toronto 1958), 174–5, 179–80, 300–3.

12  NA, Upper Canada Sundries, RG5, A1, vol. 78, 42136–7, C. McDonald to Major Hillier, 5 July 1826. On this firm, see also Donald Akenson, *The Irish in Ontario: A Study in Rural History* (Montreal and Kingston 1984), 287–90. This was one of about 250 mills in the province in the mid-1820s. If it worked for only six months of the year and one shift a day, it could still have had an annual output of about 5,000 barrels of flour, an amount equal to one-seventh of provincial flour exports in 1825, one-twentieth in 1827 (table 4.2). C.J. Shepard, 'John McDonald,' *DCB* 8 (Toronto 1985), 534–5, says exports of this mill in 1831 were 20,000 barrels, an amount equal to one-fifth of all provincial flour exports that year. One of the principal early mills in the province, the Bridgewater Mill at Niagara, was also said to have produced 100 barrels a day in 1812; see NA, RG19, E5(a), vol. 4357, War Loss Claim 523. For an excellent account of technological and related dimensions of gristmilling, see Felicity Leung, *Grist and Flour Mills in Ontario: From Millstones to Rollers, 1780s–1880s*, Parks Canada History and Archaeology Series 53 (Ottawa 1981).

13  AO, F.H. Brown Account Book, July–December 1840, MU 598 [*sic* – actually the book was by R.A. Waddell and is in part an 1844–5 letterbook], Waddell to Gilmour & Co., 24 Mar. 1845, and to M. & C. Brown, 1 Apr. 1845

14  AO, Yonge Mills Records, MU 3187, J1, Charles Jones letterbook, 1834–8, Jones to W.H. Merritt, 14 Oct. 1836. On Jones and this mill, see also T.F. McIlwraith, 'Charles Jones,' *DCB* 7 (Toronto 1988), 452–4.

15  See AO, Yonge Mills records, MU 3184, series F, Work Books, vols. 1 and 2, for the mills, covering 1828 to 1836, and volume 3, covering another Jones establishment (at Brockville?) from 1833 to 1841.

16 On the latter, see NA, Merritt Papers, MG24, E1, 2136–7, Merritt to F. Harper, 17 Nov. 1839, which speaks of its transacting £20,000 a year in business through the Commercial Bank.

17 NA, Records of the Norfolk Historical Society, MG9, D8 (24), A. McNeilledge Papers, 8406–86, Miller's Wheat Book, 1834–5; see also 8311–49, saw and grist mill accounts, 1828–9. For outputs of similar scale in a slightly later period, see AO, Wadsworth Family Papers, MU 3076, series AII, Statement of Weston Mills flour shipped, amounting to 5,600 barrels from August 1854 to July 1855; or AO, Oxford Mills Letterbook, MU 1733, Waugh & Co. to N. Pennington, 23 Jan. 1861, which speaks of annual output at this eastern Ontario mill of 4,000 barrels.

18 The Prince Edward mill purchased 3,400 bushels of wheat (which would have produced 700 barrels of flour) and 800 of other grains in the year from Feb. 1840 to Feb. 1841; AO, John Twigg Papers, MU 3037, 'South Bay Grain Book,' 1840–1. During the four prime months of Nov. 1852 to Feb. 1853, the Tench mill bought almost 7,000 bushels of wheat (which would have yielded 1,400 barrels of flour); AO, Charles & William Tench accounts, MU 611, Charles Tench Account Book, 1852–80, 56 and after. For the Goldie Mill, see MTL, John Goldie Papers (typescript), John Goldie to James Goldie, 21 Apr. 1852. William Johnson's new mill in Georgina Township ground 70 to 100 bushels per day (which would yield 14 to 20 barrels); AO, William Johnson Diaries, Ms 18, 11 Feb. 1845. Similar outputs are indicated by AO, Gillies Brothers Records, MU 3238, 'Mill Book,' Sept.–Nov. 1856, 1866–7. With one exception, surviving data show flour exports from two small Lake Erie ports, Kettle Creek (Port Stanley) and Port Ryerse, ranging between 1,000 and 5,000 barrels a year; data for the former cover 1827–30 and 1844, and for the latter 1834–8. The exception is 1836, when almost 10,000 barrels left the latter. These volumes may primarily have represented the annual output of one or two mills. See *UCJ*, 1831, App., 110; 1839, App., 755–7; *JLA*, 1845, Apps. Q and AA; and Smith, *Canadian Gazetteer*, 152.

19 AO, Hamnett Pinhey Papers, Ms 199, reel 3, accounts of grist mill in 1829, appended to Pinhey's diary, 1829–40; AO, McMartin Papers, MU 1972, Grist & Saw Mill Accounts, statement of grain accounted for by Andrew McDonald [miller] for the year ending 22 May 1845. The value of tolls at Pinhey's mill was £27 8s, perhaps an acceptable return for part of a year for a miller, but it is unlikely that Pinhey could have earned a return on his invested capital.

A common salary for a commercial miller was £50 per year plus a house; see AO, Paris Historical Society Records, Ms 359, Hiram Capron ledger, 71, account of Freeman Campbell; and MTL, John Goldie Papers (typescript), John Goldie to James Goldie, 18 Mar. 1854 (which speaks of this as a 'high wage'). See also AO, William Johnson Diaries, Ms 18, 24 Nov. 1844, for the hiring of a miller at £5 per month plus a house 'and finds himself.'

20 Note that that figure was meant to ensure an upwardly bounded estimate (i.e., not to underestimate wheat's role). Here, where it is desirable not to underestimate

the export trade's share, a lower-bounded estimate might be preferred, but it would introduce an unnecessary complication to use different figures. It is also possible that 1836 exports included some that usually would have remained in the province for local consumption; certainly there was much talk of scarcity in 1837. For the assumption that home consumption of wheat in Upper Canada was 5$^1$/$_2$ bushels per capita (i.e., 33 bushels per household of six persons), see Canada, *Census*, 1851-2, xxxi.

21 For an early example of such rebuilding, see MTL, A. Wood Letter Books, vol. 2, 174, Wood to Joseph Forsyth, 21 Mar. 1808. One mill could also serve different purposes over time. For the conversion of a grist mill to a paper mill, see AO, Niagara Historical Society Records, Ms 193, reel 5, John Abbott Papers, James Crooks to Abbott, 1 Apr. 1826. On the character of these investments, see Leung, *Grist and Flour Mills*, 71-144.

22 Total Upper Canadian flour output is assumed to be 2 million barrels in 1851, a figure in accord with both census data and trade data. That output could, of course, have been produced by just 100 mills of the scale of Yonge Mills at its peak.

23 AO, Hamnett Pinhey Papers, MU 2324, R. Morris to H. Pinhey, 5 Feb. 1823; contract with Henry Riddle and Robert Watson, 18 Mar. 1823. Some local costs, such as the mill site itself, are not included in table 6.6.

24 A similar valuation is indicated by an undated paper (*c.* 1817-23) in QUA, Wells Family Papers, Box 1, Mill Accounts, which is a record of costs of a new grist mill in Augusta Township. Some £60 in repairs to an old mill, £44 for a mill dam, and £240 for a new mill are reported.

25 Mills valued at about £3,000 include the Crooks Mill near Hamilton (AO, Samuel Street Papers, Ms 500, schedule of property ... offered to ... Maitland, Garden & Auldjo [Sept. 1843]); a mill at Dunnville in the 1830s (NA, Merritt Papers, MG24, E1, 2536-8, S. Street to W.H. Merritt, 31 Jan. 1843); a mill at Paris in the early 1850s (AO, Paris Historical Society Records, Ms 359, reels 2 and 3, Norman Hamilton Papers, note of mortgage to T. Wright, 31 Aug. 1854). See also NA, RG19, E5(a), vol. 4357, war losses claims, for examples of claimed valuations of mills lost or damaged during the War of 1812: claim # 423, £2,500 (mill, 2 run of stones, double saw mill at Amherstburg); # 509, £2,500 (grist mill, 2 run of stones, saw mill in Woodhouse Township); # 523, £4,000 (Clark & Street's Bridgewater Mill at Niagara, 3 run of stones).

Mills in the £500 to £1,000 range include the McDonald Mill at Gananoque in 1819, £500 (AO, C. & J. McDonald Papers, MU 1760, 1819 account book, inventory of property, 24 Apr. 1819); a government mill at Peterborough in 1826, £1,000 for two run of stones plus a further £500 for a dam and canal (NA, Upper Canada Sundries, RG5, A1, vol. 79, 42834-46, H. Perry to Peter Robinson, 25 Sept. 1826); the Goldie Mill at Galt in 1850, £500 (MTL, John Goldie Papers [typescript], John Goldie to James Goldie, 13 Mar. 1850). See UTL, Western

Assurance Company Records, British America Assurance Company Accounts, Daybook, 1845–7, for some further examples.

26 AO, Niagara Historical Society Records, Ms 193, reel 5, John Abbott Papers; NA, James Hamilton Papers, MG24, D45, 156–7, J. & B. Van Norman to Hamilton & Warren, 24 Nov. 1829

27 AO, F.H. Brown Account Book, MU 598, R.A. Waddell to Gilmour & Co., 12 Apr. 1845; MTL, John Goldie Papers [typescript], John Goldie to James Goldie, 13 Mar., 18 July 1850

28 AO, Richard Cartwright Jr Letterbooks, 1799 [sic]–1812, Ms 43, Cartwright to J. Porteous [?], 27 Aug. 1793

29 NA, Askin Family Papers, MG19, A3, vol. 2, John Askin to Isaac Todd and James McGill, 7 Feb. 1803. For a similar analysis and discussion of the technology of distilling and brewing in upstate New York, see White, ed., *Lord Selkirk's Diary 1803–1804*, 111–14, 9 Nov. 1803.

30 AO, Richard Cartwright Jr letterbooks, 1787–1808 (typescript), MU 500, vol. 3, 213, Account of stills in Upper Canada for year ending 5 April 1804

31 NA, MG11, CO42, vol. 331, 133–40, account of imports at Coteau-du-Lac, 1 Jan. to 30 June 1802

32 Lennox & Addington County Museum, Napanee, Collections of the Lennox & Addington Historical Society, William Bell Papers, accounts, 441 (a 1794 price). MTL, Alexander Wood Letterbooks, vol. 1, Wood to William Bates, 29 Apr. 1801, and to Robert Hamilton, 22 June 1802; and AO, Robert Nelles Papers, Ms 503, W. & J. Crooks to Robert Nelles, 12 Nov. 1802, 7 Nov. 1804, and James Crooks to Henry Nelles, 4 Feb. 1806. Prices of 4s are indicated in QUA, Cartwright Family Papers, Richard Cartwright Jr Ledger 1791–8, 155 (a 1795 price at Kingston); and QUA, Stone Family Papers, Joel Stone Account with John Cumming, Mar.–July 1808. AO, Richard Cartwright Jr Letterbooks (typescript of originals held at Queen's University), Ms 44, vol. 5, 68–9, Cartwright to J. Goldsmith, 23 Aug. 1802. Quality factors were always of some significance; see, for example, MTL, Alexander Wood Letterbooks, vol. 1, Wood to Wm. Bates, 29 Apr. 1801, an order for 'tolerable wisky' with the injunction 'let it be good.' See also AO, Robert Nelles Papers, Ms 503, Robert Nelles to W. & J. Crooks, 8 Oct. 1804.

33 See MTL, John McGill Papers, vol. B42, E. Couche to McGill, 24 Aug. 1812; and Alexander Wood Letterbooks, vol. 3, Wood to James Crooks, 23 Dec. 1814.

34 For examples of prices in this range, see MTL, L. Heyden Papers, accounts for 1827, 1828; UWO, James Hamilton Papers, James Cummings to Hamilton & Warren, 25 Aug. 1827; MTL, Michie Family Papers, account book, May 1835–Mar. 1836; NA, Records of the Norfolk Historical Society, MG9, D8 (24), Cross & Fisher Accounts, ledger, 1830–43, 15574, 15582, 15589; NA, Jebb Papers, MG24, D78. It is possible that the strength of the local product changed over the period, but we might in that case wonder at the consistency of the prices quoted from a variety of distillers.

35  AO, Smith & Chisholm Papers, MU 2846, 'Inventory of Store Goods 1841.' AO,
    Yonge Mills Records, MU 3187, J1, Charles Jones letterbook, 1834–8, Jones to
    Samuel Warner, 2 Jan. 1837; a larger portion, totalling 26 tons in one case, was
    sold to an American distiller at Ogdensburgh (see Jones to W. Bacon, 2 Jan.
    1837).

36  NA, Records of the Norfolk Historical Society, MG9, D8 (24), Alexander
    McNeilledge Papers, 8311–49, Saw and grist mill account book, 1828–9. See also
    White, ed., *Lord Selkirk's Diary*, 302; and Merrill Denison, *The Barley and the
    Stream: The Molson Story* (Toronto 1955), 165.

37  T.F. McIlwraith, 'The Logistical Geography of the Great Lakes Grain Trade,
    1820–1850' (PH D thesis, University of Wisconsin 1973), 58. UG, Goodwin-
    Haines Collection, J.S. Cartwright correspondence, Allan Macpherson to
    Cartwright, 25 Dec. 1833. See also MTL, Quetton St George Papers, II, Hector
    MacKay to Q. St George, 17 Mar. 1810, arguing that the distillery would 'take
    every kind of produce amongst the rest, indifferent Wheat, Rye, & Buckwheat.'

38  *LCJ*, 1825, App. T; 1826, App. U. The steady level of licensed capacity was
    probably accompanied by technical improvements as new stills replaced old. For
    an example of a new still under construction, see NA, James Hamilton Papers,
    MG24, D45, Diofry [?] & Kircke to Hamilton & Warren, 8 Oct. 1828.

39  One establishment might in fact have more than one licence, however.

40  NA, William Jebb Papers, MG24, D78, Ledger, 1834–8, 246–8. For indications
    that these figures were not out of line, see MTL, James Macklem Papers, Joseph
    Cawthra to James Macklem, 6 May 1809, with the implication that 20 barrels
    were a considerable quantity for Macklem, a distiller at Chippewa, to supply; AO,
    'Sir James Kempt' cash book, 1836–7, MU 610 (*sic* – also includes accounts
    running into the 1850s of a subsequent retail business and a distillery) records
    daily receipts from a distiller of 30–40 gallons from February to August 1842
    (i.e., a rate of delivery of about 1 barrel a day); and NA, Records of the Norfolk
    Historical Society, MG9, D8, (24), A. Faure Records, 7127, account of delivery of
    1,200 gallons (i.e., about 30 barrels) from McNeilledge's distillery in Nov. 1829.
    Even the 116 licensed distilleries in 1842 (table 6.7) could at this rate have
    produced the same exports and over 7 gallons per adult male Upper Canadian.

41  Compare TTN, *JLA*, Sessional paper, 1861, 2; 1864, 36, which say respectively
    that in 1860 there were 85 and 71 licensed distilleries in Upper Canada.

42  Alcohol Imported to the Province of Canada
    (selected years, 000 gallons)

|  | 1851 | 1856 | 1861 | 1865–6 (to 30 June) |
|---|---|---|---|---|
| Brandy | 137 | 299 | 67 | 165 |
| Gin | 83 | 209 | 170 | 316 |
| Rum | 37 | 68 | 25 | 63 |
| Whisky | 41 | 736 | 37 | 44 |
| Cordials | 1 | 3 | 2 | 4 |
| Total spirits | 299 | 1,115 | 301 | 592 |

| Wines      | 237 | 471 | 249 | 639 |
| ---------- | --- | --- | --- | --- |
| Ale & beer | 91  | 451 | 48  | 100 |

43  Dianne Newell, 'William Gooderham,' *DCB* 11 (Toronto 1982), 358–61, discusses the development of Gooderham and Worts in Toronto, which in the mid-1870s was producing one-third of all the proof spirits in Canada. On this transition in general, see Drummond, *Progress without Planning*, chs. 7 and 10.

44  Valuing Upper Canada's homespun is somewhat arbitrary, in that most of it did not enter the market, but its value bore comparison with that of imported woollens. In 1851 the two Canadas imported woollens to a value of £733,000, of which over half surely went to Upper Canada. In the same year, some 1.7 million yards of homespun woollen cloth and flannels were produced in Upper Canada, which, if valued at between 2s 6d and 5s a yard, would have been worth from £212,500 to £425,000. Such valuations can be imputed from commonly met prices of raw wool (1s to 2s per pound), carding (4d per pound), fulling and other processes (4d to 1s per yard), and weaving (1s per yard).

45  The Province of Canada also imported wool, but in that export volumes exceeded imports, the province was a net exporter.

46  See Janine Roelens and Kris Inwood, '"Labouring at the Loom": A Case Study of Rural Manufacturing in Leeds County, Ontario, 1870,' *CPRH* 7 (1990), 218.

47  AO, McMartin Papers, MU 1972, Carding accounts, two untitled statements on the cost of a carding mill and of repairs made in 1823. See also NA, RG19, E5(a), vol. 4357, war loss claim 378, for £125 for a carding machine destroyed in Norfolk County (the commissioners allowed two-thirds of this claim); QUA, Wells Family Accounts, Box 1, Mill Accounts, untitled document on mill costs *c.* 1820, which indicates a cost for a building and carding machinery of £254, UTL, Western Assurance Company Records, British America Assurance Company Records, Daybook, 1845–7, 4 May 1846, policy 1857, insuring a carding machine and fulling mill for £100.

48  This rate appears for carding in Grimsby in 1829–32, in Glengarry from 1822–44 (with the exception of a few years when 5d was evidently charged), and in London in 1830, to cite just three cases. A mill in Norfolk County ordinarily charged 4d but sometimes up to 7d per pound in the early 1840s. Later, rates sometimes fell to as low as 2½d per pound for straight carding, or 3½d to 4d per pound for carding and oiling. AO, McMartin Papers, MU 1972, Carding accounts, numerous loose vouchers; AO, Miscellaneous Collection, 1821, 3, J. Beamer Papers (photocopies), 1830 account with William Crooks; NA, Thomas & Charles Jones Papers (typescript), MG24, D27, daybook 1828–36, entry for 21 July 1830; NA, Records of the Norfolk Historical Society, MG9, D8 (24), 16559–804, Owen and Stark ledger, 1840–3; AO, Gillies Brothers records, MU 3237, carding books and cloth books covering the mid-1850s to early 1860s

49 For the figure of 4d, see AO, Charles Butler Diary, MU 838, 27 Nov. 1834;
figures of up to 1s are indicated in the Owen and Stark records. It is possible that
the latter's fulling accounts were kept in York, not Halifax currency, but other
elements of the records seem to be in the latter currency.

50 NA, Records of the Norfolk Historical Society, MG9, D8 (24), 16559–17051,
Owen and Stark ledger and carding books and Joseph [*sic*] Holt fulling book,
1840–3

51 For an example of a carder being hired at £3 10s per month, in Georgina
Township, see AO, William Johnson Diaries, Ms 18, 7 May 1844. Housing may
also have been supplied.

52 The census recorded 2,561 families in 1851. AO, McMartin Papers, MU 1972,
Carding accounts, including 1823 capital accounting of carding operation,
account of wool carded in 1825, 1827 account 'of the cloathing work,' fulling
accounts 1850–1; MU 1971, General Accounts, account of Henry Vennor & Co.,
13 Mar. 1852; MU 3389, 1827 carding book. Gillies Brothers, one of three
woollen factories in Lanark County, dealt with a similar proportion of the local
populace. Its 370 to 460 customers for carding and/or fulling per year in the early
1860s equalled almost 10 per cent of the county's 4,800 households. See AO,
Gillies Brothers Records, MU 3237, Carding Books, 1859–61, 1862, 1863. For
the records of another carding mill, on the Thames River in Delaware Township,
see UWO, Comfort and Greer Papers, Account Books, 1846–9.

53 Marjorie Cohen, *Women's Work, Markets, and Economic Development in
Nineteenth-Century Ontario* (Toronto 1988), 3–82. For an example of custom
weaving in Lincoln County, see UWO, Robert Comfort Papers, accounts on
29 June 1818, 26 Mar. 1819.

54 UG, Gilkison-Fraser collection, Jasper Gilkison to William Gilkison, 31 Jan. 1833

55 NA, T. & C. Jones records (typescript), MG24, D27, daybook 1828–36, entries for
18 May and 21 Dec. 1830, which imply wool purchases at just under 2s per lb.
See also AO, Records of the Paris Historical Society, Ms 359, H. Capron records,
ledger, 145, record of 'wool account,' 20 June 1830, where wool is valued at 2s
6d cy per lb on the market; NA, Jacob Case transcripts, MG24, I72, entry for 6
June 1845, for wool at 1s 10d per lb; UWO, E. Stiles accounts, 1834, for sale of
wool at 1s 6d per lb. For the records of an active woollen business, see AO, Ball
Family Papers, Ms 840.

56 AO, William Gamble Diary [*sic* – is actually a daybook], 1847–8, MU 690
records of an Etobicoke mill that did carding and fulling on its own account and
on consignment and had weaving done on a putting-out basis. On Gamble and
this mill, see also Norah Story, 'William Gamble,' *DCB* 11 (Toronto 1982),
332–3; and Fisher, *Merchant Millers*. See also AO, Gillies Brothers Records, MU
3235, ledger, 1865–7, 134, account of William Dunn. For the transformation,
over about thirty years, of one carding establishment into a woollen industry, see
Richard Reid, 'The Rosamond Woollen Company of Almonte: Industrial Devel-

opment in a Rural Setting,' *OH* 75 (1983), 266–89. By 1871 home weaving plus carding and fulling mills produced only about one-fifth of the cloth made in Ontario; see Roelens and Inwood, ' "Labouring at the Loom".' See AO, Upper Canada Village Collection, Ms 551, reel 2, Account Book, Osnabruck Township, 1863–80 [*sic*] for the accounts of a Stormont County retail business linked closely to carding and weaving, plus some fulling and 'coloring.'

57 AO, [Anonymous] Merchants Ledger 1838–42 [*sic*], MU 596, records of a Toronto area tannery and leather merchant; e.g., folios 106, 110–13

58 For a discussion of basic country tanning processes and technology, see Ronald Labelle, 'La tannerie,' in Jean-Claude Dupont and Jacques Mathieu, eds., *Les métiers du cuir* (Quebec 1981), 129–49.

59 AO, Seneca Ketchum Account Book, 1807–32, MU 597. See also J.M.S. Careless, *Toronto to 1918: An Illustrated History* (Toronto 1984), 49, for a picture of Jesse Ketchum's Toronto tannery.

60 AO, Miscellaneous Collection, 1844, 2, MU 2109, draft agreement between C.C. Small and Samuel Hill, n.d. [1844]. See also AO, Hiram Walker Museum Collection, John O'Connor Jr Papers (20–173), contract between Thomas Woodbridge and Peter Penwell, 'Millwright & Engineer' for building a tannery at Sandwich, 8 Feb. 1857. Here a slightly smaller building was envisaged (about 3,300 square feet), at a cost of £210 ($850), but in this case the tanner, Woodbridge, was to supply all his own castings and machinery.

61 For a tannery renting at £40 per year in 1846 (in Hamilton Twp.), see AO, Wade Letters (typescript), MU 3074, book 2, 13–19, Ralph Wade to William Wade, 16 Mar. 1846. This tannery was operated in conjunction with a farm.

62 MTL, B. Thorne & Co. Papers, estimate of Thornhill Property, 22 Dec. 1847. For a tannery in London insured at £1,200 on the building and 'Engine & Engine house attached including other fixed machinery,' plus a further £650 in tanbark, tools, and unfinished leather, see UTL, Western Assurance Company Records, British America Assurance Company accounts, Daybook, 1845–7, 2 Nov. 1846, policy 2025.

63 AO, Parsons & Willcocks records, MU 689, daybooks 1 Jan. 1855; 2 Jan. 1855–Dec. 1855; inventory 1 Jan. 1857. I have discussed the career of one man who moved from shoemaking to the leather trade into the wider political and commercial world in 'James Beaty,' *DCB* 12 (Toronto 1990), 71–4.

64 See Bruce Davis and Carroll Davis, *The Davis Family and the Leather Industry 1834–1934* (Toronto 1934), esp. 57–95, which is an account of the gradual evolution from the 1830s to the 1880s (and beyond) of one country tannery near Toronto that would eventually be a very substantial Canadian firm; it was still very much a country establishment in the early 1870s.

65 The former represents share of males fifteen and over; the latter is share of total reporting an occupation.

66 For example, Michael Katz, 'Occupational Classification in History,' *Journal of*

*Interdisciplinary History* 3 (1972–3), 63–88; and his *The People of Hamilton, Canada West* (Cambridge, Mass. 1975), 74–5, 146–7

67 Bryan Palmer, *Working-Class Experience* (Toronto 1983), 300–1; Edith Firth, ed., *The Town of York*, vol. 2, *1815–1834: A Further Collection of Documents of Early Toronto* (Toronto 1966), 77–9, 85–7. See also the list of crafts derived from the 1833–4 *York Directory* in ibid., xxxii–xxxiii. Carpentry and shoemaking were the leading crafts in Toronto in 1834.

68 For a similar analysis, see McCallum, *Unequal Beginnings*, tables S–7, S–8.

69 AO, James Reid Papers, MU 2382, James Reid to John Reid, 22 Sept. 1827; AO, Misc. Collection, MU 2109, 1844, 20, John Bowman to John Bowman Sr, 11 Apr. 1844; and AO, Wade letters, 1819–67 (typescript), MU 3074, book 2, 54, Ralph Wade to William Wade, 3 Jan. 1854

70 On this craft and its context, see William Wylie's excellent paper, 'The Blacksmith in Upper Canada, 1784–1850: A Study of Technology, Culture and Power,' *CPRH* 7 (1990), 17–213. My analysis is also informed by the following records pertaining to blacksmiths: AO, Niagara Historical Society Records, Ms 193, reel 5, James Cooper Account Book, 1806–27; AO, Miscellaneous Collection, MU 2108, 1841, 17, H. Hall Accounts, 1841–2; AO, George Huntington Account Book, 1845–58, Ms 51, which records work in Canada after 1849; AO, Anonymous Prince Edward County Blacksmith's Daybook, MU 2334; AO, Upper Canada Village Collection, Ms 551, reel 2, Robert Cunningham ledger [*sic* – actually a daybook], 1865–78; Lennox and Addington Museum, Lennox and Addington Historical Society Collection, Benson family accounts, 5905–6, 6116; MTL, Anonymous Toronto blacksmith's ledger, 1835–6; NA, Records of the Norfolk Historical Society, MG 9, D8 (24), 15325–443, 16022–65, Noah Fairchild ledgers, 1800–16, 1832–8 [actually the record of Peter Price] and 15457–524, Noah Fairchild Daybook, 1805–11; NA, William Buck Papers, MG24, D107, vol. 1, account of a blacksmith in Leeds County, 1854–62.

71 *JLA*, 1849, App. N, 'enclosure in No. 6'; Canada, *Census*, 1871, vol. 4

72 £20 was apparently sufficient to buy a stock of coal, iron, and miscellaneous items, although this may omit some key tools. See UWO, Davidson papers, account of 'Money for the Smithy,' for an 1854–5 start-up. One Kingston area carriage-maker insured its 50 by 18 foot blacksmith shop, bellows, tools, benches, and stock for £65 in 1845; UTL, Western Assurance Company Records, British America Assurance Company accounts, Daybook, 1845–7, 1 Dec. 1845, policy 1683. Tools could also be rented; see AO, Rousseau Collection, MU 2555, Account Book 1799–1852, 71, for twelve months' rental at £5 in 1804–5 of 'Anvill, Bellows, vice & a number of Small Tools.'

73 MTL, Anon Toronto blacksmith's ledger, 1835–6, sale of a 'light carriage' for £30. AO, Joel Lewis Account Book, 1852–84, MU 595, records blacksmithing and considerable carriage- and sleigh-making.

74 In addition to income from their craft, blacksmiths and their households, like

other rural craftsmen, also farmed or engaged in other productive activity that contributed to their overall well-being. See, for example, AO, John Rose accounts, Ms 333, the records of a blacksmith who also farmed (and later was a marine insurance agent).

75 See W.R. Wightman, 'Construction Materials in Colonial Ontario 1831–1861,' in F.H. Armstrong et al., eds., *Aspects of Nineteenth-Century Ontario* (Toronto 1974), 114–34. Note that the census counted 'dwellings,' whereas assessments recorded 'houses of all kinds except shanties.' The former therefore outnumbered the latter substantially. Summary assessment data show that the number of houses in the province grew at a rate of 7.4 per cent a year from 1825 to 1847. *JLA*, 1849, App. N, 'enclosure in 6.'

76 See Michael Doucet and John Weaver, *Building the North American City* (Montreal and Kingston 1991); and John Rempel, *Building with Wood and Other Aspects of Nineteenth-Century Building in Central Canada*, rev. ed. (Toronto 1980), 107. On the scale and character of Upper Canadian barns, see Peter Ennals, 'Nineteenth-Century Barns in Southern Ontario,' *Canadian Geographer* 16 (1972), 256–70.

77 For the ledger of a cabinet-maker, and the wide range of his output, see AO, Thomas Kilkenny Daybook [*sic* – actually a ledger], 1847–50, Ms 113; principal products were tables, chairs, chests, and bedsteads. See also W.J. McIntyre, 'From Workshop to Factory: The Furnituremaker,' *Material History Bulletin* 19 (spring 1984), 25–31.

78 UWO, John Bird account book (photocopy), 1829–51. For a similar range of work, see AO, Daniel Boyde Time-book, 1854–5, MU 678; and AO Mott-Norwich Collection, Ms 280, item 207, Diary of William Francis Bain[e?]s, 1834–6. For records of another carpenter in the region, see UWO, W.B. Dixon Account Book, 1835–49, which indicates wages of 6s 3d to 7s 6d a day in the Woodstock area in 1836–7.

79 Rempel, *Building with Wood*, 170–2, provides an account of building a house for a teacher in the Windsor area in 1849–50; here the carpenter was evidently paid just over $90 for about the same number of days of work. A further $64 was expended on lumber and about $22 on hardware, glass, etc. Almost 90 per cent of the cost was for locally supplied inputs. By comparison, see Edith Firth, ed., *The Town of York*, 1793–1815 (Toronto 1962), lxxvi and 255, where a 'modest house' at York is estimated to have cost around $2,500 in 1803–4; see also p. 223, for the sale of a log house and lot in 1795 for $50. On the basis of his survey, *c*. 1817, Robert Gourlay estimated the cost of a 'good frame house' at £125 to £250 and a 'good frame barn' at £125; see his *Statistical Account*, abridged, S.R. Mealing, ed. (Toronto 1974), 292.

80 AO, Wade letters (typescript), MU 3074, book 1, 97–100, Robert Wade to Ralph Wade, 18 June 1826

81 MTL, Account books of a farmer near Dunnville, vol. 1, accounts for Dec. 1839–Dec. 1843

82 Some manufactured boots and shoes were imported, but only a small proportion of the province's footwear demands would have been satisfied by the volumes indicated in 1850s trade figures. Marvin McInnis informs me that a surprising number of those who reported themselves as shoemakers in 1851 were young single men, farmers' sons, living at home.

83 See Alain Laberge, 'Un cordonnier de Kingston au milieu du XIXème siècle,' unpublished research paper, York University, n.d. I owe this reference to J.L. Granatstein.

84 For that value (for men's shoes), see QUA, Joel Stone Papers, Account of Stone with A. Auchinvale, 3 May 1828; men's boots were 6s 3d per pair here. Values were evidently higher during and shortly after the War of 1812; see QUA, G. Purdy Papers, Daybook, 21 Aug. 1817, 28–29 Jan. 1822, which shows 'corse shoes' at 10s and fine at 12s / 6d and 13s a pair. For prices similar to or higher than the latter, see Trent University Archives, Fowlds Papers, Daybook, 1848. Children's shoes were, presumably, less expensive but would be offset in part by the higher price of boots.

85 In fact, the Kingston shoemaker billed up to three times this amount per year; but offsetting the income of established masters in any average was that of apprentices and journeymen.

86 On shoemaking and this transition, see Joanne Burgess, 'L'industrie de la chaussure à Montréal: 1840–1870 – Le passage de l'artisanat à la fabrique,' RHAF 31 (1977–8), 187–210; and G. Kealey, 'Artisans Respond to Industrialism: Shoemakers, Shoe Factories and the Knights of St. Crispin in Toronto,' CHA, HP (1973), 137–58.

87 AO, Paris Historical Society Records, Ms 359, reel 1, Hiram Capron Records Ledger, Long Point Furance, 1825–31. See also NA, Upper Canada Sundries, RG5, A1, vol. 60, 31609–11, note on the Norfolk Iron Works, 18 April 1823; and NA, James Hamilton Papers, MG24, D45, 145, J.B. Van Norman to Hamilton & Warren, 4 Nov. 1829.

88 UWO, R. Bythell, 'Report on the Normandale Iron Works, 1818–1853,' ms, n.d.

89 See, for example, UWO, James Hamilton Papers, H. Capron & Co. to Hamilton & Warren, 14 Nov. 1826; 'Estimate of Castings Iron & Brass for a mill of 3 Run of Stones for Messrs Hamilton and Warren Kettle Creek UC,' Black Rock Foundry, 24 May 1830.

90 See Norman Ball, 'Joseph Van Norman,' DCB 11 (Toronto), 897–8; C.A. Andreae, 'Elijah Leonard,' DCB 8 (Toronto 1985), 499; J.I. Cooper, 'George Tillson,' DCB 9 (Toronto 1976), 789–90. Elijah Leonard Jr began his career as a founder and general businessman at London a few years later. See C.A. Andreae, 'Elijah Leonard,' DCB 12 (Toronto 1990), 552–4; and F.H. Armstrong, 'From Family Compact to Canadian Establishment: Elite Evolution in London Canada,' paper presented to the CHA, Victoria, May 1990. For the subsequent history of Canadian charcoal iron smelting, see Kris Inwood, The Canadian Charcoal Iron Industry 1870–1914 (New York 1986).

91 For the use of imported ore, see QUA, Macpherson & Crane Papers, box 1,
letterbook, June 1845–June 1846, 368, Macpherson & Crane to Van Norman &
Company, 29 July 1845. Weekly ore shipments from Rochester were involved.
On the increase in the pig iron trade in Canada in the 1840s, see my *The Upper
Canada Trade, 1834–1872: A Study of the Buchanans' Business* (Toronto 1979),
53.

92 NA, Upper Canada Sundries, RG5, A1, vol. 114, 64195–8, Elliot to McMahon,
19 Feb. 1832. See also NA, MG11, CO42, vol. 476, 155–6, Macaulay's Report on
Canada, 2 Mar. 1841.

93 NA, Upper Canada Sundries, RG5, A1, vol. 217, 119001–73, Report on Marmora
Ironworks, 20 Feb. 1839; and vol. 259, 140918, 'Schedule of Castings which can
be made at the Marmora Iron works,' n.d. See also Dianne Newell, *Technology
on the Frontier: Mining in Old Ontario* (Vancouver 1986), 93–6. Joseph Van
Norman himself unsuccessfully attempted a revival here when the Normandale
works were in their late stages of decline.

94 NA, MG11, CO42, vol. 476, Macaulay's Report on Canada, 2 Mar. 1841, 155–6

95 Firth, ed., *The Town of York* vol. 2, *1815–1834*, 60–2

96 All data from Canada, *Census*, 1871, vol. 4. It should be noted, however, that
1848 census data showed 105 foundries, of which only 46 were in or west of
Toronto. The 1861 census showed just 4 foundries in Toronto and York County,
66 west of there, and over 50 to the east. Such variance suggests high turnover of
firms and/or the difficulty of distinguishing foundries from other heat-using,
metal-working establishments (such as axe factories).

97 AO, McQuesten Family Papers, Ms 434. I am grateful to John Weaver for
drawing my attention to the importance of this collection. See Weaver's article,
'The Location of Manufacturing Enterprises: The Case of Hamilton's Attraction
of Foundries, 1830–1890,' in R. Jarrell and A. Roos, eds., *Critical Issues in the
History of Canadian Science, Technology and Medicine* (Thornhill 1983),
197–217.

98 AO, McQuesten Family Papers, letter 169, J. Fisher to C. McQuesten, 24 Aug.
1836. See also NA, William Dow Papers, MG24, I195, 203, account book of
duties paid at Windsor [Whitby], 1840–3, for American-made threshing machines
being imported in 1842 at a declared value of $100.

99 AO, McQuesten Family Papers, letter 214, John Fisher to C. McQuesten, 20 May
[1837]

100 For a Toronto foundry of similar value in the 1840s, see George Mainer, 'James
Good,' *DCB* 11 (Toronto 1982), 357.

101 See AO, Thomas and William Smart Records, MU 618, Thomas Smart Daybook,
1857–9 for aspects of another foundry's trade. For an overview of the industry,
see the superbly illustrated book by Eric Arthur and Thomas Ritchie, *Iron: Cast
and Wrought Iron in Canada from the Seventeenth Century to the Present*
(Toronto 1982).

102 See E.J. Chambers and G. Bertram, 'Urbanization and Manufacturing in Central
    Canada, 1870–1890,' in Canadian Political Science Association, *Conference on
    Statistics* (1964), 236, 258; and Peter Goheen, 'Communications and Urban
    Systems in Mid-Nineteenth Century Canada,' *Urban History Review* 14 (1985–6),
    236–8.
103 W.H. Smith, *Canadian Gazetteer*, 1846; Port Hope's weekly had recently ceased
    publication.
104 J.M.S. Careless, *Brown of the Globe*, vol. 1 (Toronto 1959), 33–48. The marginal
    cost that the Browns had to raise from outsiders to start the *Globe* was evidently
    about £300.
105 Firth, ed., *The Town of York*, vol. 2, *1815–1834*, xxxviii, 99. An informed, if
    biased, observer termed the award 'large.' Of course, the cost of lost equipment
    alone was not a measure of the damages suffered in such a case. See also George
    C. Parker, *The Beginnings of the Book Trade in Canada* (Toronto 1985), 44–52.
106 F.H. Armstrong, 'The Reformer as Strike Breaker: William Lyon Mackenzie and
    the 1836 Printer's Strike,' in his *A City in the Making* (Toronto 1988), 128–9;
    Sally Zerker, *The Rise and Fall of the Toronto Typographical Union 1832–1972*
    (Toronto 1982), 17–29, 326
107 AO, Hugh C. Thomson account book, MU 631, ledger of the *Upper Canada
    Herald*, 1829–33. This shows wages ranging from £12 10s a year to £2 a week.
    On Thomson, see H.P. Gundy, 'Hugh C. Thomson,' *DCB* 6 (Toronto 1987), 772–4.
108 On the shaky history of the provincial paper industry after the War of 1812, see
    NA, Records of the Inspector General, RG5, B34, vol. 19, R.C. Horne to E.
    McMahon, 4 Nov. 1819; of the two papermakers then supplying the province,
    one had failed and the other had had a 'severe loss.' In 1826–7 two new mills
    were opened, at Dundas and York. See Firth, ed., *The Town of York*, vol. 2, 60n;
    and J.A. Blyth, 'The Development of the Paper Industry in Old Ontario,
    1824–1867,' *OH* 62 (1970), 119–33.
109 See MTL, Alexander Wood Letterbooks, vol. 1, 1801–4, 101–2, 146, Wood to
    James Richardson, 11 Jan. 1802; and to J. Forsyth, 11 Jan. and 21 Apr. 1802. See
    also Edith Firth, *The Town of York*, vol. 1, *1793–1815* (Toronto 1962), 136–41;
    and AO, Anonymous cash book, 1802–3, MU 596, which is some accounts from
    this brewery. For the Niagara example, see NA, Upper Canada Sundries, RG5,
    A1, vol. 59, 31302–4, T. Fitzgibbon to P. Maitland, 14 Mar. 1823. On the other
    hand, a few years later a brewery that was part of a milling complex at Port
    Dover sold for just £80; see UG, Goodwin-Haines Collection, Street Papers,
    agreement between Mark Gross and Colin McNeilledge, 28 Apr. 1834.
110 For the 1840s, see UTL, Western Assurance Company Records, British America
    Assurance Company Accounts, Daybook, 1845–7, for policies on five breweries,
    as follows: Toronto, £500 (23 Dec. 1845); Kingston, £500 (13 Jan. 1846); St
    Thomas, £400 (27 May 1846); Peterborough, £300 (13 June 1846); London, £600
    (15 Dec. 1846). There is a picture of Joseph Bloor's modest Yorkville brewery in

Careless, *Toronto to 1918*, 106. For the history of the much larger Molson brewing enterprises in Montreal, see Denison, *The Barley and the Stream*, 142–6; Thomas Molson evidently paid £245 for Thomas Dalton's Kingston brewery and distillery in 1824.

111 On subsequent locational trends, see James M. Gilmour, *Spatial Evolution of Manufacturing: Southern Ontario 1851–1891* (Toronto 1972), 153–68.

112 Thus, it lists one brewery in Kingston employing fifty hands, one in Toronto employing one, and five in York County employing five. Smith's *Gazetteer*, 195, reported thirteen breweries in Toronto and four in Kingston in 1845; the 1848 census reported six in Toronto and seventeen in the rest of the Home District, two in Kingston and six in the rest of the Midland District. The Kingston Brewery and Distillery was a substantial establishment, but it is most unlikely that it so entirely dwarfed its competition. On it, see M.L. Magill, 'James Morton,' and Alfred Dubuc, 'Thomas Molson,' both in *DCB* 9 (Toronto 1976), 577–8 and 557–9.

113 The 1861 census shows an average of twelve hands per establishment in London and nine in Hamilton, and shows one establishment each in Lincoln (fifteen hands) and Wentworth (fourteen hands); but no others approached double figures in employee numbers. Data in the TTN in the 1860s show annual provincial outputs of 'malt liquors' in the order of 2.9 million gallons. For an analysis of provincial brewing in 1871, see Elizabeth and Gerald Bloomfield, 'Research Note: Mills, Factories and Craftshops of Ontario, 1870: A Machine-Readable Source for Material Historians,' *Material History Bulletin* 25 (spring 1987), 39, 41.

114 Two such examples involving weaving can be cited: a woman hired to weave on the basis that she received half the output (AO, Charles Butler diary, MU 838, 27 Nov. 1834); and a commercial, custom weaver (AO, J.W. Lunau Collection, MU 1746, W. James Ledger, account of Edward Wiley). An example of what appears to be shirt- and dressmaking on a relatively substantial scale is the account of John Allen Jr with Sidney Jemima Creighton, Marysburgh, Prince Edward County, 20 Apr. 1837 (AO, Allen Family Papers, MU 2334, photocopies). On the subsequent clothing industry, see Gerald Tulchinsky, 'Hidden among the Smokestacks: Toronto's Clothing Industry, 1871–1901,' in D. Keane and C. Read, eds., *Old Ontario: Essays in Honour of J.M.S. Careless* (Toronto 1990), 257–84.

115 For an analysis in somewhat similar terms, see John J. McCusker and Russell R. Menard, *The Economy of British America 1607–1789* (Chapel Hill 1985), ch. 15.

116 Success could, of course, be defined in various ways; nor should this stress on the overall success of the economy be read as implying that all individuals found success there. For a recent work stressing success, see S.J.R. Noel, *Patrons, Clients, Brokers: Ontario Society and Politics 1791–1896* (Toronto 1990), 37–9 and passim.

117 See on this and related issues in the colonial American economy, Stephen Innes, 'Introduction: Fulfilling John Smith's Vision: Work and Labor in Early America' and Paul Clemens and Lucy Semler, 'Rural Labor and the Farm Household in

Chester County, Pennsylvania, 1750–1820,' in S. Innes, ed., *Work and Labor in Early America* (Chapel Hill 1988), 3–48, 106–43.

118 NA, Upper Canada Sundries, RG5, A1, vol. 260, 141925, undated survey of wages. For a thoughtful analysis of similar data from the same period (drawn from NA, RG5, B1), see Leo Johnson, 'Wages and Prices in Upper Canada, 1840,' unpublished paper, n.d.; I owe this reference to Greg Kealey.

119 McCallum, *Unequal Beginnings*, 127

120 See Joy Parr, *The Gender of Breadwinners: Women, Men, and Change in Two Industrial Towns 1880–1950* (Toronto 1990), 7–9.

121 See Drummond, *Progress without Planning*, 401, 407; and Greg Kealey, *Toronto Workers Respond to Industrial Capitalism 1867–1892* (Toronto 1980), ch. 2 and pp. 307–9.

CHAPTER 7: *Transportation and Communications, 1800–1850*

1 This chapter has benefited from the opportunity to present preliminary versions of parts of the argument to audiences at the University of Victoria and at Queen's University; I am grateful to both for criticism and advice.

2 G.M. Craig, *Upper Canada* (Toronto 1963), 149–50. Another standard account is G.P. deT. Glazebrook, *A History of Transportation in Canada*, Carleton Library ed. (Toronto 1964), vol. 1.

3 NA, MG11, CO42, vol. 327, 21–5, 'Report on the State of the Several Locks,' by Gother Mann, 24 Dec. 1800; and vol. 328, 143–70, 'General Accounts of Articles ... which have passed Coteau-du-Lac upwards,' 1 Jan. to 30 June and 1 July to 31 Dec. 1800. Because boats made a number of trips in a season, a vessel had several numbers per year.

4 See Edward Forbes Bush, *Commercial Navigation on the Rideau Canal, 1832–1961* (Ottawa 1981), 22.

5 Bruce Wilson, *The Enterprises of Robert Hamilton* (Ottawa 1983), ch. 6 and passim

6 AO, Richard Cartwright Jr letterbooks (typescript), Ms 43, letterbook for 1793–6, Richard Cartwright Jr to Todd, McGill & Co., 28 Sept. and 11 Dec. 1793, 1 Dec. 1794, 30 Oct. 1795, and to Robert Hamilton, 15 and 18 Apr. 1794; Ms 44, vol. 3, letterbook for 1786–99, 158–9, 161–2, Cartwright to Parker, Gerrard & Ogilvie, 13 and 30 Nov. 1797

7 Walter Lewis, 'James Richardson,' *DCB* 6 (Toronto 1987), 638–9. The new vessel, the *Kingston Packet*, was launched in 1795.

8 AO, Richard Cartwright Jr letterbooks, Ms 44, vol. 5, letterbook for 1799–1802, 80, 82, Cartwright to J. & J. McGregor, 14 May 1801, and to J. & A. McGill & Co., 25 May 1801

9 See QUA, Cartwright Family Papers, Additions, vol. 2, 'Packing Book 1810,' for these accounts.

10 See E.A. Cruikshank, 'Notes on the History of Shipbuilding and Navigation on

Lake Ontario up to the Time of the Launching of the Steamship *Frontenac* at Ernesttown, Ontario, 7th September 1816,' *OHSPR* 23 (1926), 33–44. Cruikshank's source was harbour registers, which did not record the nationality of vessels arriving.

11 NA, Upper Canada Sundries, RG5, A1, vol. 25, 11290–2, James Crooks to William Halton, 23 Dec. 1815. In the context, a claim for its loss, they were unlikely to understate its value.

12 The several hundred boats on the St Lawrence probably were worth at least as much in total as the lake fleet, but much of that investment was on Lower Canadian account. For an 1819 valuation of £40 to £53 per boat at Kingston, see NA, RG5, A1, vol. 44, 21594.

13 NA, RG5, A1, vol. 35, 16739–42, 16812–25, some accounts of the *Toronto,* 1816

14 Even in the late 1840s and early 1850s, for example, a majority of the raftsmen on Calvin Company rafts had French names. See QUA, Calvin Company Records, vol. 145, which is a raft book covering 1848–51 and 1855.

15 On the issue of labour supply, see AO, Richard Cartwright Jr letterbooks, Ms 43, letterbook for 1793–6, Cartwright to Todd, McGill & Co., 1 Nov. 1793, and to Robert Hamilton, 21 Nov. 1793; and Ms 44, vol. 5, letterbook for 1799–1802, 30–1, 120, Cartwright to Robert Hamilton, 4 Oct. 1799, and to J. & A. McGill, 19 Dec. 1799.

16 For the chronology of steam's development on American inland rivers, see E.F. Haites, J. Mak, and G.M. Walton, *Western River Transportation: The Era of Early Internal Development, 1810–1860* (Baltimore 1975), 18, 130–1; they note earlier experiments but accept 1817 as the basic beginning of regular steamboating. See also George Rogers Taylor, *The Transportation Revolution, 1815–1860* (New York 1968), 56–61. There has been debate on whether the *Frontenac* was the very first lake vessel, but as the argument hinges on a matter of months, it is immaterial for our purposes.

17 Cruikshank, 'Notes on the History of Shipbuilding,' 37–41; Bush, *Commercial Navigation on the Rideau Canal,* 20. On its value, see also *UCJ,* 1818, 2nd sess., printed in OBA, *Tenth Report* (1913), 47–8, petition of proprietors of the steamboat *Frontenac,* 23 Oct. 1818; MTL, W.W. Baldwin Papers, A90–91, Baldwin to Quetton St George, 2 Sept. 1818; and NA, RG5, A1, vol. 30, 14070–2, petition to Francis Gore, 12 Dec. 1816.

18 For a contract to build an engine for £4,500 in 1823, see NA, Ward Papers, MG24, D19, 78–83, contract between George Auldjo et al. and John D. Ward, 23 Feb. 1823; this engine was twice as powerful, at 100 horsepower. Two vessels that did cost as much as the *Frontenac* were the *Great Britain*, said in 1831 to have cost £20,000, and the iron-hulled *Magnet*, built with government subsidy for over £15,000 in 1846–7. On the former, see AO, Gilkison Papers, Ms 497, J.T. Gilkison to William Gilkison, 1 June 1831. On the latter, see QUA, James Sutherland Papers, bond of Sutherland et al., May 1846.

19  See, for example, NA, W.H. Merritt Papers, MG24, E1, 685–7, D. Thompson to Merritt, 4 Aug. 1831; Walter Lewis, 'James McKenzie,' *DCB* 6 (Toronto 1987), 470.

20  For the Niagara company, see Bruce Parker, 'The Niagara Harbour and Dock Company,' *OH* 72 (1980), 93–121. For York, see Archives Nationales du Québec – Québec, Fonds Jules Quesnel, b. 1, J.S. Baldwin to Quesnel, 28 Aug. 1824; b. 3, Samuel Washburn to Quesnel, 28 Aug. 1824, 6 Jan. 1825; and Edith Firth, ed., *The Town of York*, vol. 2, *1815–1834* (Toronto 1966), 81. For construction at Chatham, see F.C. Hamil, *The Valley of the Lower Thames 1640 to 1850* (Toronto 1951), 146, 262–8. The meaning of port of construction is not always clear; thus the *Thames*, built at Chatham in 1833, actually had its engine installed at Cleveland.

21  See AO, Samuel Street Papers, Ms 500, reel 1, W. Wynn to Street, 16 Apr.–15 Nov. 1828, for regular flour shipments by steamboats in 1828 totalling almost 5,000 barrels; UG, J.M. Duff Collection, Henry Nelles letterbook, 1831–2, Nelles to Gillespie, Moffatt & Co., 25 Apr. 1832, and to James Smith, 30 Apr. 1832, for use of both steamers and schooners; AO, Anonymous cargo register for ships 1838–42, MU 690, cargo records of steamer *Hamilton* on the Bay of Quinte, 1838.

22  AO, D.B. Stevenson Papers, MU 2884, J. Armstrong to D.B. Stevenson, 21 July 1841. The *Cobourg's* hourly charter rate in 1839 was £5; see NA, Upper Canada Sundries, RG5, A1, vol. 229, 125466–74, Berczy to Harrison, 23 Sept. 1839. For an hourly rate for towing of £7 to £8, on Long Point Bay, see QUA, Macpherson & Crane Papers, letterbook, vol. 1, 1845–6, 521–2, Macpherson & Crane to O.T. Shaver, 22 Aug. 1845.

23  Peter Baskerville, 'Donald Bethune's Steamboat Business: A Study of Upper Canadian Commercial and Financial Practice,' *OH* 67 (1975), 137

24  For the Bay of Quinte service, in which at least ten different vessels participated between 1838 and 1842, see AO, Anonymous Cargo Register, 1838–42, MU 690. See also Ruth McKenzie, 'Henry Gildersleeve,' *DCB*, 8 (Toronto 1985), 325–7. If traffic fell off, frequency of service on these routes might be reduced, but all these ports enjoyed daily service for much of the shipping season.

25  AO, Miscellaneous Collection, MU 2107, 1837, 17, Prescott steamship accounts, Feb.–June 1837, entry for 4 Mar. 1837

26  Hamilton Public Library, James Sutherland Papers, account book, said to be the *Queenston*, for 1834. If the standard Toronto-Hamilton fare was 10s, such revenues imply about five thousand travellers during the year. Passengers were also the principal revenue source for the *Sir James Kempt*; see AO, Sir James Kempt steamboat cash book, 1836–7, MU 610.

27  Some vessels were used in both main areas of service at various times, depending on demand.

28  Some examples include the *Kingston*, new in 1833 and built to the dimensions of

the Rideau, which cost £5,300 (NA, W.H. Merritt Papers, MG24, E1, 627, J.G. Parker to Merritt, 24 Sept. 1834); the *Queen Victoria*, a year–old lake vessel purchased by Hugh Richardson, backed by Samuel Street, in 1839 for £7,000 (AO, Samuel Street Papers, Ms 500, reel 2, receipt from James Lockhart to Street, 3 May 1839); the *Thames*, built for £3,500 and, after refitting, valued by its owners in 1838 at £4,500 (*UCJ*, 1839, App., claims arising from losses from the Rebellion, 676–7); the *Sir Robert Peel*, said to have cost £11,500 to build in 1836–7 (*UCJ*, 1839, 681–2); three new vessels acquired in 1843 by Donald Bethune for £25,000 (Baskerville, 'Donald Bethune's Steamboat Business,' 143); the *Chief Justice Robinson*, 315 tons, built for Hugh Richardson in 1843 and sold at the beginning of 1847 for £7,500 (NA, Donald Bethune Papers, MG24, D24, 263–72, mortgage documents, 11 Aug. 1848); a proposed new steamer to run on Lac des Chats, above Bytown, *c.* 1840 valued at £4,000 (NA, RG5, A1, vol. 260, 141929–32, prospectus of Chats steamboat); the *Raftsman*, a river vessel costing £3,350 in 1840 (QUA, Calvin Papers, vol. 107, Calvin, Cook & Counter ledger, 1839–44, Forsyth & Bell account for 1840).

29  See, for example, UWO, James Hamilton Papers, account current with Samuel Street, 16 June 1832, for Hamilton & Warren's purchase of four shares, £50 each, in the new Lake Erie steamer then being built; AO, D.B. Stevenson Papers, MU 2885, James Fraser to Stevenson, 16 Feb. 1843, enclosing circular to shareholders of the *Brockville*.

30  For a discussion of this point, see Peter Baskerville, 'John Hamilton,' *DCB* 11 (Toronto 1982), 377–9. See also QUA, Macpherson & Crane Papers, vol. 1, letterbook, 1845–6, 215, Macpherson & Crane (Kingston) to Macpherson & Crane (Bytown), 9 July 1845; and 503, 526–7, same to same 16 and 25 Aug. 1845.

31  See Peter Baskerville, 'Donald Bethune,' and F.H. Armstrong, 'Hugh Richardson,' *DCB* 9 (Toronto 1976), 48–50, 657; and H. Pietersma, 'Samuel Crane,' *DCB* 8 (Toronto 1985), 181–3.

32  Parker, 'The Niagara Harbour and Dock Company,' 108–10

33  For the extent of use of steam power in 1870, see also Elizabeth and Gerald Bloomfield, 'Research Note: Mills, Factories and Craftshops of Ontario, 1870: A Machine-Readable Source for Material Historians,' *Material History Bulletin* 25 (spring 1987), 35–47.

34  NA, MG11, CO42, vol. 476, Macaulay's General Report, 139–40. Smaller crews of twelve plus the master are indicated by payment records for the *Queenston* (Hamilton Public Library, Archives File, James Sutherland Cash Book, records of the *Queenston* for 1834): those paid included an engineer, carpenter, cook, cook's mate, steward, waiter, three sailors, and three firemen. Eleven men (captain, engineer, steward, cook, pilot, two firemen, and four deckhands) were required on the barge-towing *Mercury* (QUA, Macpherson & Crane Papers, vol. 2, letterbook, 1857, 81, Macpherson & Crane to James Craig, 23 Apr. 1857). Crew requirements (n.d.) for the *Passport* and the *New Era*

included a captain, purser, engineer, Coteau pilot, first mate, second mate, and steward who had to be paid, evidently, even if the vessels were laid up, their monthly wages totalling about £100 (QUA, James Sutherland Papers, 'steamship operations' file); firemen, sailors, cooks, and waiters were unlikely to take total crews to as high as twenty.

35 AO, Miscellaneous Collection, MU 2107, 1837, 17, Prescott Steamship Accounts. For examples of wage accounts on schooners, see AO, Smith & Chisholm Papers, MU 2846, account books of schooner *Widgeon* for 1839 and of schooner *Endeavour* for 1843–4; and trip record book of schooner *Phoenix* for 1849. For 1850s wages, see AO, Norris and Neelon Records, Ms 490, series A-1-3, summary account of the brig *Sir Charles Napier* for 1857, showing £279 in crew wages for the season, plus £113 paid to the master; accounts of the 230-ton *St Andrews* for 1853 showing wages paid of £393, and for 1856 showing wages of £368 plus £120 paid to the master; and series A-1-2, crew accounts of the *James Coleman* showing wages of £345 in 1853.

36 For that well-known story, see Creighton's *The Commercial Empire of the St. Lawrence* (Toronto 1937). A modern survey by economic historians that has many echoes of this approach is W. Marr and Donald Paterson, *Canada: An Economic History* (Toronto 1980), 312–16. On the uniqueness of the Erie, see L.E. Davis et al., *American Economic Growth: An Economist's History of the United States* (New York 1972), 476–84.

37 On the American experience, see Harry N. Scheiber, *Ohio Canal Era: A Study of Government and the Economy, 1820–61* (Athens, Ohio 1969), 355.

38 H.G.J. Aitken, *The Welland Canal Company: A Study in Canadian Enterprise* (Cambridge, Mass. 1954), 28–9

39 George Raudzens, *The British Ordnance Department and Canada's Canals 1815–1855* (Waterloo, Ont. 1979), 54. See also Normand Lafrenière, *The Ottawa River Canal System* (Ottawa 1984), 26–35; and Robert Legget, *Ottawa Waterway* (Toronto 1975), 137–44.

40 Raudzens, *The British Ordnance Department*, 54–99; for a more favourable view of By, see Robert Legget, *Rideau Waterway*, rev. ed. (Toronto 1972), 34–57 and passim.

41 See Bush, *Commercial Navigation on the Rideau Canal*, 68–115.

42 On the financing, see Aitken, *The Welland Canal Company*, ch. 4. See also L. Gentilcore and G. Head, eds., *Ontario's History in Maps* (Toronto 1984), 184–5.

43 The priority accorded the Welland by the provincial government is indicated by the fact that approximately one-quarter of the entire public debt of the province in 1841 had been accumulated on this one project. See Aitken, *The Welland Canal Company*, 147–8 and passim; and also T.F. McIlwraith, 'Freight Capacity and Utilization of the Erie and Great Lakes Canals before 1850,' *JEH* 36 (1976), 852–77.

44 John Weaver, *Hamilton: An Illustrated History* (Toronto 1982), 20–3. The best documented of the harbour companies is the Niagara Harbour and Dock Com-

pany, which received some government help in acquiring lands, but was not otherwise publicly subsidized; see Parker 'The Niagara Harbour and Dock Company,' 93–121. See also *JLA*, 1842, App. P, schedule of government debentures ... Upper Canada; and, for a list of all the companies chartered, F.H. Armstrong, *Handbook of Upper Canadian Chronology*, rev. ed. (Toronto 1985), 249–52.

45  Brian Osborne and Donald Swainson, *Kingston: Building on the Past* (Westport, Ont. 1988), 167, 195–6

46  The peak workforce on the Rideau was said to be 2,000 men. See Legget, *Rideau Waterway*, 48.

47  For lives of some of the main contractors, see E.F. Bush, 'Robert Drummond,' and John Witham, 'Andrew White,' *DCB* 6, (Toronto 1987), 220–1, 811–13; E.F. Bush, 'Thomas McKay,' *DCB* 8 (Toronto 1985), 551–3; and Gerald Tulchinsky, 'John Redpath,' *DCB* 9 (Toronto 1976), 654–5. On the other hand, government payment systems were so slow and contentious and estimating of contracts was so difficult that many of the contractors were actually bankrupted by their involvement in the project. See Legget, *Rideau Waterway*, 43, 53. For an example of a contentious subcontract, see AO, McMartin Papers, MU 1968, series C, 'Rideau Canal documents.'

48  Along the Rideau, the British had begun to encourage Irish settlement early in the development of the Rideau route, and this attracted further Irish settlement around the time of canal construction. See Glenn Lockwood, *Montague: A Social History of an Irish Ontario Township: 1783–1980* (Kingston 1980), 103, 108, 112; Bruce Elliott, *Irish Migrants in the Canadas: A New Approach* (Kingston and Montreal 1988), 117; C. Houston and W. Smyth, *Irish Emigration and Canadian Settlement* (Toronto 1990), 57–9, 207. In some sense, the wages and working conditions had to compete to attract workers with some alternative somewhere. It bears repeating that success in such migrations was not certain, and that the risks of injury and disease were considerable. That workers undertook them is an indication not that they literally had no choice, but that the other choices they perceived seemed no better.

49  On capital costs and dimensions, see John P. Heisler, *The Canals of Canada* (Ottawa 1973), 96. On workforces, see Ruth Bleasdale, 'Class Conflict on the Canals of Upper Canada in the 1840s,' *Labour/Le Travailleur* 7 (spring 1981), 11–12. She says the peak workforce was ten thousand, but, as she recognizes, not all the projects were in progress at once. Helen Cowan, *British Emigration to British North America* (Toronto 1961), 289, shows that 144,000 immigrants landed at Quebec between 1842 and 1846; of these, about 80,000 were from Ireland. If the Irish were a large part of the canal labour force, if only one-quarter of the latter were adult males, and if there was high turnover of workers, then a significant proportion might have spent some time in canal labour. Construction of the St Lawrence canals was almost complete when the huge wave of Irish migrants arrived in 1847.

50 For a similar persistence of emphasis on canals, see C.O. Smith Jr, 'The Longest Run: Public Engineers and Planning in France,' *American Historical Review* 95 (1990), 665.

51 McIlwraith, 'Freight Capacity,' 871

52 For explication of such a case in a later context, see Frank Lewis and Mary MacKinnon, 'Government Loan Guarantees and the Failure of the Canadian Northern Railway,' *JEH* 47 (1987), 175–96.

53 However, Canadians did not take responsibility for the operation of the Ottawa-Rideau system until 1856.

54 On the complexities of tonnage measurements, see Bush, *Commercial Navigation on the Rideau Canal*, 252 n.16. Because it is not usually clear how provincial figures were calculated in early years, and because there was considerable functional differentiation between steam and sailing fleets, I have reported tonnage data separately and without attempting a conversion. After 1845 registry requirements specified the British rules of measurement, spelled out in British statutes 5 & 6 William IV cap. 56 (1835–6) and 6 & 7 Vict. cap. 84 (1843–4). Tonnage was, in fact, a calculation of volume, net of the engine room in steam vessels. For the formula, see Province of Canada, *Statutes*, 8 Vict. cap. 5 (1845), para. 8.

55 For example, AO, Norris and Neelon Records, Ms 490, which include cargo records of ten vessels in the period 1845–57, none of them on the printed list of registered ships; QUA, Calvin Company Records, vol. 143, 'Record of Vessels,' 1840–51. For the 106-ton *Louise*, a cargo of 5,100 bushels of wheat (48 bushels per ton) was insured in 1846; see UTL, Western Assurance Company Records, British America Assurance Company Records, Daybook, 1845–7, 4 May 1846 (policies NP 392, 394, issued 14 Apr.), 12 June 1846 (NP 411, issued 8 May).

56 See McIlwraith, 'Freight Capacity,' 860, for discussion of shipping seasons on the various canals, and of the issue of Sunday operations.

57 QUA, Calvin Company Records, vol. 143, 'Record of Vessels,' 1840–51; AO, Smith and Chisholm Records, MU 2846, 'Receipt Book, 1840–47, Steamer Ladings' [*sic*; most are schooners]

58 In 1850 less than half of the square timber shipments through the Welland from one 'British' (i.e., Upper Canadian) port to another were in vessels (Table 7.4). In 1852 one-third were in rafts; see *JLA*, 1852–3, App. A, schedule 1. Total downward tonnage recorded through the canal in Upper Canadian vessels in 1850 was 122,000, of which 45,000 tons moved between a 'British' port and an American one. Many vessels must have made more than eight downward trips per year, or this volume would have required almost all the 16,300 tons of provincial sailing vessels. In addition, although almost all tolls were collected at the ports at the ends of the canal (including its feeder from the Grand River), it is not clear what proportion of cargoes (other than those between American ports, which used American vessels) actually went the whole length of the canal. In effect, there was likely to be double counting in cases such as cargoes of wheat from Cleve-

land to St Catharines and subsequent cargoes of flour from St Catharines to Oswego or an Upper Canadian port.

59 The statute governing the inland registry was 8 Vict. cap. 5; its purpose is evidenced by its title, 'An Act to secure the right of property in British Plantation Vessels navigating the Inland Waters of this Province, and not registered under the Act of the Imperial Parliament ... *An Act for the Registering of British Vessels* ...' For the published list of vessels, see *JLA*, 1854–5, App. PPP, Schedule of Vessels Registered ... 1 Jan. 1846–31 Dec. 1854. Some of the original registers are in NA, RG42.

60 The agreement, dated 24 Jan. 1852 and governing the 1852 season, is found in NA, Donald Bethune Papers, MG24, D24, 280–6. Only the *Princess Royal* and the *Champion* appear on the printed 1854 list. Unregistered sailing vessels include the *Phoenix*, the *Almira*, the *Merchant Miller*, the *Sir Charles Napier*, and the *St Andrews*. Although the Norris and Neelon vessels to which reference has been made were used as security for credit, their vessels do not appear on the printed 1854 list. Registry volumes for St Catharines do not survive for this period.

61 For an example, the 15-ton *Adelaide*, based at Point Pelee, see AO, Hiram Walker Museum Collection, 20–148, McCormick Family Papers, 443–62, cargo book of schooner *Adelaide* for 1835–6. Each year it took two or three cargoes of tobacco to the Welland or Buffalo, but it otherwise sailed among its home port and nearby Lake Erie and Detroit River ports.

62 In fact, payments were not maintained. Macpherson & Crane repossessed their fleet in 1857, but the business was bankrupt. Macpherson & Crane had forty barges in 1840; see *JLA*, 1841, App. EE.

63 For the Calvin Company, see QUA, Calvin Company records, vol. 145. See ibid., vols. 249, 250, for towing accounts of steamers *Chieftain* and *Charlevoix*, 1855–7. The former operated between Lachine and Beauharnois, the latter between Beauharnois and Cornwall. In 1852 about 100,000 tons of flour, pork, and ashes went down the St Lawrence, some undoubtedly on steamships; but that entire volume could be carried on seventy-four barges of 90 tons making fifteen return trips per season. For the tonnage data, see *JLA*, 1852–3, App. A, TTN, table 2.

64 One that could at times sustain twice-daily service was the Toronto-Hamilton run. See Smith, *Canadian Gazetteer*, 1846, 76. Competition at times put more than one boat or fleet on a run, but that was frequently a recipe for losses to all the operators involved.

65 Smith, *Canadian Gazetteer*, 129

66 QUA, James Sutherland Papers (photocopies), bond given by Sutherland, Sir Allan MacNab, and D. Gunn, May 1846; agreement with Robert Melville, 11 May 1846; Sutherland to MacNab, 14 July 1847

67 Smith, *Canadian Gazetteer*, 5. See also Hamil, *The Valley of the Lower Thames*, 146, 262–7. For the American side of Lake Erie, see Allan Pred, *Urban Growth and the Circulation of Information: The United States System of Cities, 1790–1840* (Cambridge, Mass. 1973), 137–8.

68 Freights from QUA, Calvin Papers, vol. 143, shipping ledger, 120–5; confirmed
by QUA, Macpherson & Crane Papers, vol. 1, letterbook, 1845–6, 442–3,
Macpherson & Crane to Mr. Hoadley, 8 Aug. 1845. Similar rates applied in 1856;
see AO, Norris and Neelon Papers, Ms 490, series A-1-3, cargo book for the *St
Andrews*, 1856: from near Chatham to Garden Island, standard staves were £11 5s
per thousand, and oak was £25 per 1,000 feet. For an example of slightly lower
charges for staves in 1851–2, a low point in the business cycle, see MTL, Cargo
Book of schooner *Almira*, 1851–8. River freights and any costs of transshipment
had also to be added to arrive at the total cost of shipping timber. In 1844
standard staves cost about £5 10s per thousand from Kingston to Quebec and oak
timber was 3d per foot. See Calvin Papers, vol. 107, Calvin, Cook, and Counter
Ledger, 1840–7. Earlier, standard staves had cost £7 10s in 1837, and £8 10s in
1819; see Calvin Company Records, vol. 257, for the former, and NA, Upper
Canada Sundries, RG5, A1, vol. 45, 21818, bill of lading, 10 Sept. 1819.
69 See AO, Norris and Neelon accounts, Ms 490, series A-1-2, crew accounts of the
*J.S. Ranney*, *James Coleman*, and *Northern Light*, various years, 1852–7; AO,
Smith and Chisholm Papers, MU 2846, Trip Record Book of the schooner
*Phoenix* for 1849. Here, the master excepted, the entire crew turned over three
times, in early July, mid-August, and (except for one man) again in early October;
in all, thirteen different men crewed on the *Phoenix* in one year.
70 AO, Smith and Chisholm Papers, MU 2841, Account of New Vessel, 18 Aug.
1838. Its tonnage is given in *UCJ*, 1839–40, App., 4, Public Accounts, Schedule
5. A second vessel of the same name but of 70-ton capacity sailed from Port
Stanley.
71 QUA, Calvin Company Records, vol. 144, shipyard daybook, 1846–55, 92–109.
The barque *Plymouth*, built in 1853–4, cost £2,493, vol. 144, 125–31.
72 QUA, Macpherson & Crane Papers, letterbook, 1845–6, 1220, Macpherson &
Crane to ?, 3 Jan. 184[6]; NA, Donald Bethune Papers, MG24, D24, 273–9,
agreement between Bethune and the Bank of Upper Canada, 11 Jan. 1850
73 Peter Goheen, 'Canadian Communications circa 1845,' *Geographical Review* 77
(1987), 45. See also Ian Drummond, *Progress without Planning* (Toronto 1987),
265: 'The [road] work was often badly done and badly supervised, but nobody
cared particularly.'
74 T.F. McIlwraith, 'The Adequacy of Rural Roads in the Era before Railways: An
Illustration from Upper Canada,' *Canadian Geographer* 14 (1970), 344–60. See
also his 'Transportation in the Landscape of Early Upper Canada,' in J.D. Wood,
ed., *Perspectives on Landscape and Settlement in Nineteenth-Century Ontario*
(Toronto 1975), 51–63.
75 T.C. Keefer, *Philosophy of Railroads* (Montreal 1850), reprinted in H.V. Nelles,
ed., *Philosophy of Railroads and Other Essays* (Toronto 1972), 3
76 AO, Butler Diary, MU 838, 27 Nov. 1834
77 AO, Crawford Diaries, MU 756, entries for 25 Feb. 1846 and 16 and 19 Dec.; the
diaries show a trip to one of the nearby mills in virtually every month through the

period 1837–50, usually with loads of grain or wool in amounts suggesting family consumption rather than milling for sale.

78 See Smith, *Canadian Gazetteer*, 31, 76, 101, etc. See also *York Commercial Directory ... 1833–4*, G. Walton comp. (York 1833), 146, 151. Here the steamship rate to Niagara was 10s for the main cabin, 5s for the forecabin and deck; to Hamilton, about the same distance from Toronto, a stage cost 12s 6d. In 1840–1 the steamboat fare from Kingston to Toronto or Hamilton was 30s (around 3 cents a mile) in the better cabin, including meals, and just 10s on the deck (without meals); see NA, MG11, CO42, vol. 476, Macaulay's General Report, 351. Given these rates and the faster speed of steamers, it seems unlikely that people used the stage at all for through trips between ports during the navigation season. For American rates, see Pred, *Urban Growth and the Circulation of Information*, 149.

79 See, for example, Nathaniel Carrothers to William Carrothers, 25 Dec. 1839, printed in C.J. Houston and W.J. Smyth, *Irish Emigration and Canadian Settlement: Patterns, Links, & Letters* (Toronto 1990), 256. See also the many trips of nineteen-year-old Larratt Smith between Toronto and his family's home in Richmond Hill in 1839–40; Mary Larratt Smith, ed., *Young Mr. Smith in Upper Canada* (Toronto 1980), 17–49.

80 William Smith, *The History of the Post Office in British North America 1639–1870* (Cambridge 1920), 121, 156. *York ... Directory ... 1833–4*, 146; A. Burghardt, 'Some Economic Constraints on Land Transportation in Upper Canada/Canada West,' *Urban History Review* 18 (1989–90), 235. See also M. Muntz, 'William Weller: Stage Coach Magnate,' in J. Petryshyn, ed., *Victorian Cobourg: A Nineteenth Century Profile* (Belleville 1976), 71–84.

81 Goheen, 'Canadian Communications circa 1845,' 41, 50; see also his 'Communications and Urban Systems in Mid-Nineteenth-Century Canada,' *Urban History Review* 14 (1985–6), 235–45.

82 The eight were Hawkesbury, Richmond, March, and Perth in the Ottawa-Rideau area; Marmora, where mining was being developed; Newmarket, north of York; and Vittoria and Port Talbot in the western peninsula.

83 For a convenient list of all post offices in Upper Canada, with date of opening, see F.H. Armstrong, *Handbook of Upper Canadian Chronology*, rev. ed. (Toronto 1985), 229–37. A list of offices for 1845 is given in Smith's *Canadian Gazetteer*, 257–66. Armstrong's data yield slightly larger totals than are given by William Smith's *The History of the Post Office in British North America*; see 102–4, 115–17, 132, 155–6, 195–6.

84 *York Commercial Directory ... 1833–4* (York 1833), 137–40, 146; *City of Toronto and Home District Directory ... 1837*, G. Walton comp. (Toronto n.d.), 25–33. See also the map of main routes in Goheen, 'Canadian Communications circa 1845,' 36.

85 For the surfacing of roads, see *JLA*, 1844–5, App. AA, Report on Public Works.

In fact, given the province's system of public works administration, payment, and accounting, more than the authorized sums were actually spent in some cases; see D. Owram, ' "Management by Enthusiasm": the First Board of Works of the Province of Canada, 1841–1846,' *OH* 70 (1978), 171–88. On the system of payments for public works, see also Peter Baskerville, ed., *The Bank of Upper Canada* (Toronto 1987), cx, 197.

86 For these roads, see L. Gentilcore and G. Head, eds., *Ontario's History in Maps* (Toronto 1984), 158, 188–90; see also C. Read and R. Stagg, eds., *The Rebellion of 1837 in Upper Canada* (Toronto 1985), 193, 332; and Burghardt, 'Some Economic Constraints on Land Transportation,' 232.

87 See NA, Upper Canada Sundries, RG5, A1, vol. 101, 57062–9, Contract for Napanee-Belleville Road, 12 July 1830, and further documentation on it at 57086–93, 57256–75, 57331–50. See also I. E. Pattison, *Historical Chronology of Highway Legislation in Ontario, 1774–1961* (Toronto 1964), 9–10, 239.

88 For the case of the York roads, see M.S. Cross, 'The Stormy History of the York Roads, 1833–1865,' *OH* 54 (1962), 1–24. One speculator was prepared to buy the York roads from the province in hopes of earning a profit, but the anticipated traffic did not materialize. See also D. McCalla, 'James Beaty,' *DCB* 12 (Toronto 1990), 71–4.

89 Burghardt, 'Some Economic Constraints on Land Transportation,' 233. Maximum estimates were based on total traffic volume at lowest point on the road; as some of that traffic was likely to be local, these are upwardly bounded data.

90 See Gentilcore and Head, eds., *Ontario's History in Maps*, 157–9; and 154–5, 160.

91 Goheen, 'Communications and Urban Systems in Mid-Nineteenth-Century Canada,' 242. The new device was put to early use in the 1847 financial crisis; see Canadian Imperial Bank of Commerce, Company Secretary's Office, Toronto, Gore Bank Records, 565, telegram, Thorne & Heward to A. Steven, 21 July 1847, re foreign exchange transactions. The cost for fifteen words between Toronto and Hamilton was 9d (1¢ per word); fifteen words to New York cost $1.

92 Rankings based on population of census metropolitan areas, not incorporated cities

93 See Osborne and Swainson, *Kingston.*

94 Buffalo, the largest in 1840 at 18,000 people, had fallen to third place behind Detroit and Cleveland by 1960. Note that Toronto, with 14,000 people in 1841, would have ranked second at the time. By 1961, the municipality of Metropolitan Toronto would have ranked third, ahead of Buffalo and just behind Cleveland (both metropolitan areas).

95 Pred, *Urban Growth and the Circulation of Information*, 1–19; quotes from 6, 19. On Toronto, see also Ann Carlos and Patricia Fulton, 'Chance or Destiny? The Dominance of Toronto over the Urban Landscape,' *Social Science History* 15 (1991), 35–66.

96  See Gentilcore and Head, eds., *Ontario's History in Maps*, 164, 206, for highway
    travel and railway passenger maps from the twentieth century. For an account
    stressing the 'enormous inertia' in urban systems' growth, see R.C. Harris and J.
    Warkentin, *Canada before Confederation: A Study in Historical Geography* (New
    York 1974), 148.

CHAPTER 8: *The Provincial Business System, 1821–1851*

1  Peter Baskerville's *The Bank of Upper Canada: A Collection of Documents*
   (Toronto 1987) is the essential starting-point now for any work on banking in
   Upper Canada. Among the other principal sources drawn on in this chapter are
   R.M. Breckenridge, *The Canadian Banking System 1817–1890* (Toronto 1894);
   R.C. McIvor, *Canadian Monetary, Banking and Fiscal Development* (Toronto
   1958); E.P. Neufeld, *The Financial System of Canada: Its Growth and Develop-*
   *ment* (Toronto 1972); Adam Shortt's numerous articles in the *Journal of the*
   *Canadian Bankers' Association*; and Bray Hammond, *Banks and Politics in*
   *America from the Revolution to the Civil War* (Princeton 1957). S.F. Wise's
   pioneering article 'Tory Factionalism: Kingston Elections and Upper Canadian
   Politics,' *OH* 57 (1965), remains valuable.
2  T.W. Acheson, 'John Baldwin: Portrait of a Colonial Entrepreneur,' *OH* 61
   (1969), 153–66. See also Douglas McCalla, 'Laurent Quetton St. George,' *DCB* 6
   (Toronto 1987), 622–5; and Peter Deslauriers, 'Jules-Maurice Quesnel,' *DCB* 7
   (Toronto 1988), 716–18.
3  UG, Gilkison-Fraser Collection, XR1 MS A116, William Gilkison to Simon
   Fraser, 13 Apr. 1833
4  QUA, Tett Papers, vol. 1, 1, Tett to Macintosh and Co., 11 Nov. 1833
5  NA, Buchanan Papers, MG24, D16, vol. 14, 12304–5, Peter Buchanan to R.W.
   Harris, 8 Dec. 1854
6  See T.W. Acheson, 'The Nature and Structure of York Commerce in the 1820s,'
   *CHR* 50 (1969), 406–28; John Weaver and Michael Doucet, 'Town Fathers and
   Urban Continuity: The Roots of Community Power and Physical Form in
   Hamilton, Upper Canada, in the 1830s,' *Urban History Review* 13 (1984–5), 75–
   90; and John Weaver, *Hamilton: An Illustrated History* (Toronto 1982), 18–55.
7  A recent example is W.T. Easterbrook, *North American Patterns of Growth and*
   *Development: The Continental Context* (Toronto 1990), 191, 204.
8  QUA, Cartwright Papers, vol. 9, statement of 'Property and Business, 1800–43'
9  Bruce Wilson, *The Enterprises of Robert Hamilton* (Ottawa 1983), 93–100,
   167–8 (data converted from NY cy)
10 McCalla, *The Upper Canada Trade*, 172–3
11 See the essays in Ommer, *Merchant Credit and Labour Strategies* on these
   points.
12 As measured by the standards employed by a leading wholesaler. See NA,

Buchanan Papers, MG24, D16, vol. 85, 60441, George Borthwick, 'Remarks upon Analysis of Outstandings at Hamilton, 30 June, 1856.'

13 AO, D.B. Stevenson Papers, MU 2887–8, ledgers

14 Angela Redish, 'Why Was Specie Scarce in Colonial Economies? An Analysis of the Canadian Currency, 1796–1830,' *JEH* 44 (1984), 713–28

15 QUA, Tett Papers, vol. 1, 27, Tett to McPherson and Crane, 28 Nov. 1839

16 AO, Alexander McMartin Papers, MU 1973, file F-3-7, A. McMartin in account with Donald McNaught. Here, in fact, no money changed hands, because McNaught agreed to rent a lot from McMartin for 30s a year for the next four years. See also Allan J. MacDonald, 'Alexander McMartin,' *DCB* 8 (Toronto 1985), 582–3.

17 D.A. Norris, 'Household and Transiency in a Loyalist Township: The People of Adolphustown, 1784–1822,' *HS/SH* 13 (1980), 399–415; early arrivals had some advantage here, but a far from absolute one. See also Norris's 'Migration, Pioneer Settlement, and the Life Course: The First Families of an Ontario Township,' *CPRH* 4 (1984), 130–52.

18 For the modern prairies, see John H. Thompson, *The Harvests of War* (Toronto 1978). A valuable analysis paying due attention to institutional structures is Jeremy Adelman, 'Prairie Farm Debt and the Financial Crisis of 1914,' *CHR* 71 (1990), 491–519.

19 Baskerville, ed., *The Bank of Upper Canada*, xxvii–xxxvi, 3–20

20 *UCJ*, 1825, Appendix B, Report on the Pretended Bank of Upper Canada, John Kirby & John Macaulay, as of Jan. 1825. This total excludes two large sums due from bank officers, because these were not commercial debts but represented a claim by the liquidators on bonds that the men had executed. Endorsing a note or bill made the endorser liable for payment if the maker of the note (or acceptor of the bill) did not pay when the paper fell due.

21 Deposits became more important in the 1830s and 1840s, particularly for the Bank of Upper Canada; the trend was similar for the Commercial and Gore banks, but they lagged behind the Bank of Upper Canada. The deposits indicated for each in table 8.3 may be compared to note circulation data for the same years in table 8.2 on this point.

Ratio of Deposits to Notes Issued

|  | 1836 | 1841 | 1846 |
|---|---|---|---|
| Bank of Upper Canada | 0.78 | 0.95 | 1.04 |
| Commercial Bank | 0.22 | 0.46 | 0.79 |
| Gore Bank | na | 0.16 | 0.47 |
| Three UC banks | 0.58 | 0.57 | 0.83 |

It is not clear whether rising levels of deposits were created through credit-granting or reflected the growth of medium- and longer-term surplus funds in the

hands of Upper Canadians. The former is implied by the generally high proportion of the deposits not at interest (in the years to 1845 at least); to the extent that
the latter was the cause, a form of intermediation between savers and borrowers
was taking shape.

22  Naomi R. Lamoreaux, 'Banks, Kinship, and Economic Development: The New
England Case,' *JEH* 46 (1986), 647–67; see also Richard Sylla, 'American
Banking and Growth in the Nineteenth Century: A Partial View of the Terrain,'
*Explorations in Economic History* 9 (1971–2), 197–227. Provided a borrower met
interest payments and appeared to have assets that warranted the advances against
them, credits could run for extended periods in normal times, particularly for
insiders. In a financial crisis, not all those with debts due could count on
continued support by the bank, and in the overall review of assets that normally
accompanied such crises, full repayment might be demanded.

23  Canadian Imperial Bank of Commerce, Corporate Secretary's Office, Toronto,
Gore Bank Records, files for company history [by V. Ross], extracts from
Toronto *Examiner* 2 and 9 Mar. 1842. See also Donald R. Beer, *Sir Allan Napier
MacNab* (Hamilton 1984), 152–5; and Douglas McCalla, 'John Young,' *DCB* 10
(Toronto 1972), 721.

24  For the charter's text, see Baskerville, ed., *The Bank of Upper Canada*, 328–32.
The charter of the Commercial Bank, which embodied similar terms, is 2 William
IV cap. 11 (1832).

25  Baskerville, ed., *The Bank of Upper Canada*, xxxvii–lxxiii. See also 'William
Allan,' *DCB* 8 (Toronto 1985), 7–8. On the implications of a low reserve ratio,
see Peter Temin, *The Jacksonian Economy* (New York 1969), 73, 75. T.W.
Acheson says there were forty shareholders in 1822–3, and ninety-seven by the
end of the 1820s; 'The Nature and Structure of York Commerce in the 1820s,'
422. By 1838, after capital had been doubled, there were about three hundred
holders (table 8.4). For bonuses, see *JLA*, 1841, App. O, section G; these were 6
per cent in 1827 and 1830, 18 per cent in 1832, paid to old shareholders before
capital was doubled, and 4 per cent in 1835.

26  The private agency and banking business of Samuel Street, conducted from
Niagara, is pertinent, though Street's role was complementary to the banks'. He
bought and sold shares and debentures and acted as agent for a number of British
investors in the province. See AO, Samuel Street Papers, Ms 500, cash book,
5 Oct. 1831–2 Nov. 1834; power of attorney, Robert Gillespie, 28 July 1836;
T.G. Ridout to Samuel Street, 12 Jan. 1841 and 29 July 1843. See also MTL,
Samuel Street Papers, for T.C. Street's role as agent for Gillespie. Such men
could, presumably, have supplied other dimensions of banking services had the
chartered banks not existed.

27  For an example of four- and five-month drafts, see QUA, John Solomon
Cartwright Papers, Box 2, F.A. Harper to J.S. Cartwright, 13 Dec. 1839.

28  See NA, MG11, CO42, vol. 415, 29–31, J.H. Dunn to Col. Rowan, 1 Aug. 1833;

the bank was middleman in the sale of debentures, and was the channel for paying interest on them.

29 For the ways in which such processes operated, see QUA, Tett Papers, vol. 1, letterbook, 1833–49, passim. For example, 15, 32, Benjamin Tett to William Macintosh, 7 Sept. 1838 and 13 Mar. 1840. See also McCalla, *The Upper Canada Trade*, 24. It is evident that the banks recognized that not all the bills they handled were 'real'; see, for example, NA, Bank of Montreal Papers, MG28, II2, Resolve Book 3, 272–3, 9 Aug. 1839: 'Resolved That it is expedient that no paper of an accommodation character be hereafter discounted ...'

30 MTL, John Fisken Papers, Ross, Mitchell & Co. Journal, 1847–9; see also McCalla, *The Upper Canada Trade*, 68, 96–8.

31 The bank's charter was 6 William IV cap. 34 (1836); its shareholders were subject to double liability, unlike those of the earlier banks. On inter-bank cooperation, see Canadian Imperial Bank of Commerce, Company Secretary's Office, Toronto, Gore Bank Records, Toronto Subscription Book, 28 Nov. 1835; typescripts of material for company history, item 18, T.G. Ridout to A. Steven, 3 Mar. 1836; and typed extract from Gore Bank minutes, 29 Apr. 1836. I am pleased to acknowledge the assistance of the CIBC in providing access to this material; it is unfortunate that a number of Gore Bank letterbooks and minute books, some of them seen by Peter Baskerville and referred to in these records, could no longer be located.

32 Baskerville, ed., *The Bank of Upper Canada*, 69–71. The shares of the Commercial Bank also went to a premium in 1833; see QUA, John Solomon Cartwright Papers, series of 1833 letters from David Thompson to Cartwright re share purchases.

33 See AO, Samuel Street Papers, Ms 500, Andrew Steven to Samuel Street, 22 Feb. and 15 Apr. 1841.

34 For example, the St Lawrence Inland Marine Insurance Company's investment portfolio (*c*. £15,000) was almost entirely in bank shares, as were the modest investments of the Hamilton and Gore Savings Bank (c. £2,000). See *JLA*, 1850, App. H. See also Lamoreaux, 'Banks, Kinship, and Economic Development,' 655.

35 Report of the Bank of Upper Canada to Lt. Governor Colborne, 6 June 1831, printed in Baskerville, ed., *The Bank of Upper Canada*, 57

36 For example, the value of Canadian wheat exports was £954,000 in 1850, all of which came, presumably, from Upper Canada. In 1851 it was £843,000. Yet the discounts of the three Upper Canadian banks alone rose by over £500,000 from 1850 to 1851. The total value of all Canadian exports rose by only about £150,000 from 1850 to 1851. Trade data from *JLA*, 1852–3, App. A, schedule 24.

37 Some Upper Canadian bank notes circulated in Lower Canada, and some Lower Canadian notes circulated in Upper Canada. The argument here is that the two may have offset one another, thereby allowing us to use the Upper Canadian banks as a measure of total money supply. For an example of Lower Canadian

bank notes in Upper Canada, see AO, Yonge Mills Records, MU 3187, J 1, C. Jones letterbook, 1834–8, Jones to Mr Thom, 8 May 1837.

38 Temin, *The Jacksonian Economy*, 71–2; Lamoreaux, 'Banks, Kinship, and Economic Development,' 654

39 *UCJ*, 1837 (2nd session), App., Statement A, iv

40 See 'George Truscott,' *DCB* 8 (Toronto 1985), 896–7.

41 For the strategy here, see NA, Bank of Montreal Papers, MG28, II2, Resolve Book No. 3, 325, 346, 358, 3 Apr., 24 June, 4 Sept. 1840.

42 See R.M. Breckenridge, *The Canadian Banking System*, 60–1; and Carol Lawrie Vaughan, 'The Bank of Upper Canada in Politics 1817–1840,' *OH* 60 (1968), 199. The banks concerned were the Brockville (Johnstown District), the Newcastle District (Cobourg), the Erie and Ontario (St Catharines), the Prescott, the Prince Edward District, the London District (London), the Western District, the Niagara District, and the Freeholders; and in addition, increases in capital were authorized for the three existing chartered banks. See NA, Adam Shortt Papers, MG30, D101, vol. 3, Glenelg to Head, 27 Nov. 1837 (typescript). It was also intended that the Bank of Upper Canada would become a provincial bank, i.e., a bank with public responsibilities and a larger government investment in it.
  The passage of all the bills did not indicate that anyone expected the province needed all such facilities; rather, the political logistics of passing any bill likely decreed the need to pass all. Each group of promoters presumably expected the next phase of the struggle to go on once this hurdle was passed. At three times capital, these bills authorized note issue totalling £13.5 million, which was equal to almost thirty times the current issues! On the role of the market, see, for example, QUA, John Solomon Cartwright Papers, Box 2, John Mowat to J.S. Cartwright, 17 Nov. 1836.

43 On this episode, see John Ireland, 'John H. Dunn and the Bankers,' *OH* 62 (1970), 83–100. See also QUA, John Solomon Cartwright Papers, Box 2, Thos. Wilson & Co. to J.S. Cartwright, 30 Mar. 1837.

44 NA, Upper Canada Sundries, RG5, A1, vol. 177, 97585, Hotham to John Joseph 28 July 1837; vol. 178, 97943–9, statement of affairs, Commercial Bank, 13 Sept. 1837. See also NA, Adam Shortt Papers, MG30, D101, vol. 3, items 614, 616, 625, 627, 628, 638, 640, 641, 652, 653, and 654, petitions from meetings held at Niagara, Kingston, Brantford, Hamilton, Dundas, Cobourg, Peterborough, Gananoque, Brockville, Toronto, and Bytown, dated between 19 May and 5 June 1837 (typescripts), all seeking suspension of specie payments.

45 Sir Francis Bond Head, *A Narrative*, S.F. Wise, ed. (Toronto 1969), 190; see also p. 91.

46 *UCJ*, 1837–8, App., 213, Report of the Select Committee on the Subject of Banking; H. Senior, 'George Strange Boulton,' *DCB* 9 (Toronto 1976), 68

47 NA, Adam Shortt Papers, MG30, D101, vol. 3, excerpts from Montreal *Gazette* 22, 25, and 29 July, 10 Oct. 1837 (typescripts)

48 The 1837 law (7 William IV and I Vict. cap. 2) specified a limit on circulation of no more than paid-up capital; the second law was 1 Vict. cap. 22 (1838).

49 Angela Redish, 'The Economic Crisis of 1837–39 in Upper Canada: Case Study of a Temporary Suspension of Specie Payments,' *Explorations in Economic History* 20 (1982–3), 402–17

50 NA, Adam Shortt Papers, MG30, D101, vol. 4, McGill to Sydenham, 2 Aug. 1841 (typescript). On McGill, see Robert Sweeny, 'Peter McGill,' *DCB* 8 (Toronto 1985), 540–4. On this episode, see also Ian Radforth, 'Sydenham and Utilitarian Reform,' in Allan Greer and Ian Radforth, eds., *Colonial Leviathan: State Formation in Mid-Nineteenth-Century Canada* (Toronto 1992), 93–4.

51 See clauses 25 and 26 of the new charter of the Bank of Upper Canada, 6 Vict. cap. 27 (1843), reprinted in Baskerville, ed., *The Bank of Upper Canada*, 336. In 1850–1 the Gore Bank was issuing notes well beyond its capital, but this is the only exception after 1841–2. The new rules gave banks an evident incentive to increase the amount and proportion of their liabilities that took the form of deposits.

52 For lists of bank branches, see *UCJ*, 1837–8, App., 221, 225, 229, 234; W.H. Smith, *Canadian Gazetteer* (Toronto 1846, reprinted Toronto 1970). Most of the locations were agencies, not branches. Only at some branches could notes be exchanged for specie, and branches, which had staff paid by the bank, might also have more independence in discounting. At the Bank of Montreal, for example, agents were empowered to do 'little else than the negotiation of Drafts on Lower Canada' to approved limits. See NA, Bank of Montreal Papers, MG28, II2, Resolve Book 3, 346, 24 June 1840.

53 For a not entirely convincing argument that, briefly, Lower Canadian banks suffered such constraints, see Tom Naylor, 'The Rise and Decline of the Trustee Savings Bank in British North America,' *CHR* 65 (1984), 530–3.

54 The proportion of Bank of British North America notes issued at Toronto and Kingston was about one-third in 1842–3; see *JLA*, 1843, 55; 1844, App. A, statement 7. The figures for the three banks (at one-half of Bank of Montreal and one-third of the others) are as follows:

|      | BM  | BBNA | City B | UC banks | Total | Per cap |
|------|-----|------|--------|----------|-------|---------|
| 1842 | 110 | 26   | 33     | 351      | 520   | £1.07   |
| 1847 | 205 | 98   | 85     | 482      | 870   | 1.33    |
| 1848 | 180 | 67   | 57     | 395      | 699   | 0.96    |

For purposes of estimate, 1847 population is assumed to be 650,000. This formulation assumes that all Upper Canadian bank notes circulated there, which is probably incorrect; but provided the proportion of Upper Canadian bank notes that circulated outside the province did not change, the data should be comparable to those from before 1841.

55 Indeed, to the extent that a bank's agencies attracted payments, in either its own

notes or those of other banks, instead of the paper's continuing to circulate, spread of agencies might actually contribute to a tendency for paper to return more quickly than before to the banks. A problem here is that there may have been agents in communities even before the banks formally designated offices as agencies; if so, formalization of the title of an office might follow actual establishment in the community, not initiate it.

56 Monthly note issue data indicate that the yearly averages are a quite accurate representation of the pace and extent of the decline.

|  | BUC | CB | GB |
|---|---|---|---|
| Feb. 1847 | 187 | 227* | 90* |
| June 1847 | 201 | 199 | 85 |
| Oct. 1847 | 203* | 221 | 77 |
| Feb. 1848 | 175 | 179 | 65 |
| June 1848 | 148† | 149† | 54† |
| Oct. 1848 | 163 | 190 | 68 |
| Low as % of peak | 73 | 66 | 60 |

* Peak month. † Lowest month.

57 For fuller discussion of the early fire and marine insurance companies, see my paper 'Fire and Marine Insurance in Upper Canada: The Establishment of a Service Industry, 1832–68,' in P. Baskerville, ed., *Canadian Papers in Business History* (Victoria 1989), 129–52. See also Ian Drummond, *Progress without Planning* (Toronto 1987), 316–22.

58 See John Whiteside, 'The Toronto Stock Exchange and the Development of the Share Market to 1885,' *JCS* 20, 3 (fall 1985), 70–5.

59 For the occupational background of over 150 depositors in one savings bank, see AO, Home District Savings Bank Records, MU 1383; ordinary soldiers, labourers, artisans, and women predominated, and only the few schoolteachers might not qualify as members of the working class. See also the report of the Hamilton and Gore District Savings Bank in *JLA*, 1847, App. U. By the 1850s these institutions were less clearly extensions of the banks; at least their investments typically were in municipal debentures rather than bank shares and deposits. In total they represented somewhat more substantial bodies of capital too, though scarcely a large sum in terms of the overall scale of the provincial economy.

Savings Banks, 1854 (from *JLA*, 1854–5, App. EE)

| Institution | Depositors | Deposits | Mean deposit |
|---|---|---|---|
| Hamilton & Gore District | 793 | £37,368 | £47 |
| London | 562 | 24,000 | 43 |
| Northumberland & Durham | 174 | 5,472 | 31 |
| Toronto | 203 | 8,415 | 41 |

60 Because marine insurance, particularly on cargoes, was shorter term than fire insurance, this figure, which in effect combines all marine policies of a season into a single total, tends to overstate the scale of risks.

61 See Gerald Tulchinsky, 'George Moffatt,' *DCB* 9 (Toronto 1976), 553–6; and Douglas McCalla, 'Lewis Moffatt,' *DCB* 12 (Toronto 1990), 744–5. On the problems posed by foreign competition for mutual insurers, see AO, W.H. Merritt Papers, Ms 74, pkg 33, R.J. Chapman to D.B. Stevenson, 15 July 1850.

62 Under the original legislation, 6 William IV cap. 18, policies could run for terms as long as seven years, and this helps to explain why apparent premium rates for such companies might appear higher than for the chartered companies.

63 It was also possible to pay regular insurance company premiums by note, but such notes did, of course, have to be paid when due, whereas, if losses did not require it, the mutual policy holder was not obligated to pay. In 1857 Holcomb & Henderson were able to pay their £600 in premiums to the Ætna company in a six-month note; see QUA, Macpherson & Crane Papers, Box 2, letterbook, 1857, 119, ? to S.F. Holcomb, May 1857.

64 See AO, Miscellaneous Collection, MU 1406, Report of the Directors of the Home District Mutual Fire Insurance Company, 2 June 1845.

65 See Allan Moscovitch, 'Les sociétés de construction au Canada avant 1867: préliminaires à une analyse,' *L'actualité économique* 59 (1983), 515–17; and D. Paterson and R. Shearer, 'Terminating Building Societies in Quebec City, 1850–1864,' *Business History Review* 63 (1989), 384–415.

66 See *The Canada Directory ... November 1851* (Montreal 1851), passim.

67 See, for example, AO, Letterbook of Canada Permanent Mortgage Co., 1857–9.

68 NA, Bank of Montreal Papers, MG28, II2, Resolve Books, vol. 3, 102–3, minutes of two special meetings, 13 May 1837

69 Ibid., Resolve Books, vol. 4, 362–3, 8 June 1847. The remaining twenty-eight were all in Upper Canada, at nine branches. Agents at seven other locations were paid solely by commissions on bills of exchange drawn. The highest-paid employee, the cashier, earned £1,000 per year.

70 Ibid., Resolve Books, vol. 4, 329–33, entries for 12 and 19 Jan., 2 and 5 Feb. 1847

71 Ibid., Resolve Books, vol. 4, 337, 26 Feb. 1847. Here a three-month term and fifteen days' notice of withdrawal were required in order to earn interest. To keep such deposits, the rate paid was increased to 4 per cent.

72 The usury laws, which set the legal interest rate at no more than 6 per cent, may also have been a constraint, but it is not yet clear what, if any, impact they had. In the 1850s businessmen campaigned vigorously against these laws.

CHAPTER 9: *Government and the Development of Upper Canada, 1820–41*

1 See K. Norrie and D. Owram, *A History of the Canadian Economy* (Toronto

1991), 190; and W.T. Easterbrook, *North American Patterns of Growth and Development* (Toronto 1990), 170–2. The classic statement is H.G.J. Aitken, 'Defensive Expansion: The State and Economic Growth in Canada,' reprinted in W.T. Easterbrook and M.H. Watkins, eds., *Approaches to Canadian Economic History* (Toronto 1967), 184. On the Canadian penchant for public enterprise, see Gad Horowitz, *Canadian Labour in Politics* (Toronto 1968), 10–11; and Herschel Hardin, *A Nation Unaware: The Canadian Economic Culture* (Vancouver 1974), 54–95.

2  On commercial and resource policies, see O.J. McDiarmid, *Commercial Policy in the Canadian Economy* (Cambridge, Mass. 1946); H.V. Nelles, *The Politics of Development: Forests, Mines and Hydro-Electric Power in Ontario, 1849–1941* (Toronto 1974), 1–23, 39–47; and Lillian F. Gates, *Land Policies of Upper Canada* (Toronto 1968).

On the role of the legal system, see John Weaver, 'While Equity Slumbered: Creditor Advantage, a Capitalist Land Market, and Upper Canada's Missing Court,' *Osgoode Hall Law Journal* 28 (1990), 871–914; Peter George and Philip Sworden, 'The Courts and the Development of Trade in Upper Canada, 1830–1860,' *Business History Review* 60 (1986), 258–80; and R.C.B. Risk, 'The Law and the Economy in Mid-Nineteenth-Century Ontario: A Perspective,' *University of Toronto Law Journal* 27 (1977), 403–38.

On municipal systems and social policies, see J.H. Aitchison, 'The Development of Local Government in Upper Canada, 1792–1850' (PH D thesis, University of Toronto 1953); Susan Houston and Alison Prentice, *Schooling and Scholars in Nineteenth-Century Ontario* (Toronto 1988); R.D. Gidney and W.P.J. Millar, 'From Voluntarism to State Schooling: The Creation of the Public School System in Ontario,' *CHR* 66 (1985), 443–73; and Bruce Curtis, *Building the Educational State: Canada West, 1836–1871* (London 1988).

3  See Peter Baskerville, ed., *The Bank of Upper Canada* (Toronto 1987), xxxviii–xl, lvi–lxx; Donald R. Beer, *Sir Allan Napier MacNab* (Hamilton 1984), 399–402; Alan Wilson, 'Sir John Colborne,' *DCB* 9 (Toronto 1976), 137–44; and Ken Cruikshank, 'John Henry Dunn,' *DCB* 8 (Toronto 1985), 251–7.

4  See, for example, Carter Goodrich, *Government Promotion of American Canals and Railroads 1800–1890* (New York 1960); and for the colonial period, John J. McCusker and Russell R. Menard, *The Economy of British America, 1607–1789* (Chapel Hill 1985), 331–44, 360–1.

5  For the acts from which Upper Canada's revenue derived in the later 1830s, see *JLA*, 1841, App. B. The statute defining the system of administration for Coteau-du-Lac was 39 Geo. III cap. 5 (1799).

6  Population data for Lower Canada were drawn from Canada, *Census*, 1871, vol. 4.

7  Baskerville, ed., *The Bank of Upper Canada*, xxx–xxxiii, 8

8  See Clarence Karr, *The Canada Land Company: The Early Years* (Ottawa 1974),

13–14, 24–8. The Canada Company appears here primarily as a public finance instrument rather than as a land settlement device, for it is impossible to imagine that the lands settled by the company would not have been brought into production more or less when they were, no matter how they were administered. Indeed, the company's initial focus was on settlement around Guelph, near existing settlements, rather than in the remoter Huron Tract. Control of imperial customs duties was transferred to the Assembly by 1 William IV cap. 14 (1831), which granted a permanent civil list.

9 Richard Reid, ed., *The Upper Ottawa Valley to 1855: A Collection of Documents* (Toronto 1990), 142–4, 189, 196, 200, 203

10 For the acts governing these duties, see 2 Geo. IV cap. 1 and 4 Geo. IV cap. 1.

11 'Report from Joint Committee on the Tea Trade of Canada,' *UCJ*, 1823–4, 15 Jan. 1824, printed in OBA, *Report* (1914), 652–61. See also Emily Cain, 'Customs Collection – and Dutiable Goods: Lake Ontario Ports, 1801–1812,' *Freshwater* 2, 2 (autumn 1987), 22–7. I am grateful to Emily Cain and the Hamilton-Scourge Project for sharing a substantial array of their data on shipping and trade with me, and for copies of this and other papers deriving from research for that project.

12 For example, receipts on these three taxes from 1838 to 1840 were as follows (figures from *JLA*, 1841, App. B, Return of Upper Canadian Revenue and Expenditure for 1838, 1839, and 1840):

|  | 1838 | 1839 | 1840 |
|---|---|---|---|
| Tonnage (lighthouses) | £225 | £289 | £431 |
| Hawkers and pedlars | 90 | 138 | 275 |
| Auctioneers | 382 | 566 | 1,328 |
| Total | 697 | 993 | 2,034 |

13 Much depended on accounting assumptions. For 1839 the revenues listed in the table were recorded. If these were net of all operating costs, including maintenance, a rate of return can be calculated on the initial amounts borrowed. In all probability the rate is upwardly biased. If actual total costs of borrowing averaged 6 per cent, then a modest net gain is implied by these percentages.

|  | Income to province (1839) | Amount borrowed re project | Return implied |
|---|---|---|---|
| Kettle Creek Harb. | £454 | £5,500 | 8.3% |
| Burlington Canal | 682 | 17,500 | 3.9 |
| Kingston-Napanee Rd | 561 | 5,500 | 10.2 |
| York roads (3) | 3,297 | 32,000 | 10.3 |
| Hamilton-Brantford Rd | 450 | 3,500 | 12.9 |
| Trent River Bridge | 125 | 2,000 | 6.3 |
| Total | 5,569 | 66,000 | 8.4 |

Data for the table come from *JLA*, 1841, App. B. See also table 7.7; by 1850 more capital had been expended on road projects, and returns were seldom as high as 6 per cent.

14 *UCJ*, 1836, App. 102, Upper Canada Blue Book for 1835, which shows land-granting fees and the income from fees of a wide array of legal officers, collectors, inspectors, and schoolmasters. Frequently, wages of clerks, etc. were also paid from fees received. See also Gates, *Land Policies of Upper Canada*, 158.

15 See J.K. Johnson, *Becoming Prominent: Regional Leadership in Upper Canada, 1791–1841* (Kingston and Montreal 1989), 61–8.

16 The pertinent statutes were 2 Geo. IV cap. 5 (1821) and 4 Geo. IV cap. 24 (1824). In part the 1824 credit helped tide the province over while it awaited sums due from Lower Canada under provisions of the Canada Trade Act and subsequent arbitration.

17 Statutory authority was needed for the borrowing; see 5 William IV cap. 31.

18 For public works expenditures, it was a common practice to name a commission, generally of local notables, to administer a project. The commission was to account for its expenditure of provincial grants; as borrowing for specific projects became usual, it might also be involved in arranging the actual credit needed to raise the funds. It was usually intended to charge users for the new work, but it often proved impossible to collect sufficient revenues to do more than pay operating costs.

19 H.G.J. Aitken, *The Welland Canal Company* (Cambridge, Mass. 1954), 102

20 John Ireland [Max Magill], 'John H. Dunn and the Bankers,' *OH* 62 (1970), 83–100; Baskerville, ed., *The Bank of Upper Canada*, lxviii–lxxi

21 Leland H. Jenks, *The Migration of British Capital to 1875* (New York 1927), 77–81

22 Upper Canada's population was about proportional, 30 per cent of Ohio's.

23 Carter Goodrich, *Government Promotion of American Canals and Railroads 1800–1890* (New York 1960), 134–47

24 It should be noted that H.G.J. Aitken, who first used the term, was fully aware of this point.

25 The incorporating statutes for these two projects were 7 Geo. IV cap. 18 (Desjardins Canal) and 9 Geo. IV cap. 19 (Oakville Harbour). In the latter case, William Chisholm individually was the incorporator.

26 Bruce Parker, 'The Niagara Harbour and Dock Company,' *OH* 72 (1980), 93–121; AO, Niagara Historical Society Records, Ms 193, reels 5 and 6, Records of the Niagara Harbour and Dock Company, 1836–67. While some other works were chartered and did not receive state aid, none were on the scale of this company.

27 Ruth Bleasdale, 'Unskilled Labourers on the Public Works of Canada, 1840–1880' (PH D thesis, University of Western Ontario 1984)

28 G.M. Craig, ed., *Lord Durham's Report* (Toronto 1963), 103–4; Donald

Creighton, *The Commercial Empire of the St. Lawrence* (Toronto 1937), 308–14.
A good modern account of the financial crisis is Michael Piva, 'Financing the
Union: the Upper Canadian Debt and Financial Administration in the Canadas,'
*JCS* 25, 4 (winter 1990–1), 82–98.

29 NA, Adam Shortt Papers, MG30, D101, vol. 10, 'Canada 1839 to 1840, P.F. 75,'
Enclosures in Sir G. Arthur's Despatch of 20 Nov. 1838, J.H. Dunn to ?, 8 Aug.
1838 (typescript copy)

30 For a thoughtful analysis of such issues, see Julian Gwyn, 'The Impact of War on
the Colonial Economy of Nova Scotia, 1755–1815,' paper presented to the CHA,
Kingston, June 1991.

31 The Peter Robinson emigrations of 1823 and 1825 were said to have cost over
£40,000, for example. See Gates, *Land Policies of Upper Canada*, 97. But
payments for recruitment and passage of such emigrants were not paid into the
Upper Canadian economy. The figure for emigration costs in 1831–3 is from NA,
Upper Canada Sundries, RG5, A1, vol. 143, 78151, Statement of Moneys Paid on
Account of Emigration, 1831–33, 18 July 1834. Essentially the same total, but
differently broken down, can be found in NA, MG11, CO42, vol. 418, 195,
statement by A.B. Hawke, 22 Mar. 1834.

32 In addition, Britain authorized the lieutenant-governor to pay out £20,000 from
the Casual and Territorial revenues on this account; those revenues were derived
from within the economy.

33 See Baskerville, ed., *The Bank of Upper Canada*, lxiii. For the use of the
multiplier concept here, see Allan Pred, *Urban Growth and the Circulation of
Information: The United States System of Cities 1790–1840* (Cambridge, Mass.
1973), 191–3, 211–15.

34 Charles H. Stewart, *The Service of British Regiments in Canada and North
America*, 2nd ed. (Ottawa 1964) shows that it was usual for elements of two
regiments to be stationed in Upper Canada at any one time, along with some
artillery, engineering, and navy personnel. See also Johnson, *Becoming Prominent*, 247.

35 *British Parliamentary Papers*, 1844, 34, 23, 'British Military Expenditures in
Canada, 1835–1843'

36 George Raudzens, *The British Ordnance Department and Canada's Canals,
1815–1855* (Waterloo, Ont. 1979), 23

37 On exchange rates, see Appendix A. Most official documents used the official
rate of £1.11 cy = £1.00 stg, whereas the actual rate was closer to £1.2 cy. If what
is recorded in Britain represents actual sterling expended, it is appropriate here to
use the higher rate; if, on the other hand, it represents an entry deriving from an
expenditure in Canada, the lower rate is more likely to show what was actually
spent in Upper Canada. I have used the official rate in most cases, unless the
other is clearly justified.

38 See Johnson, *Becoming Prominent*, 38–9 and biographical appendix; and M.S.

Cross, 'The Age of Gentility: The Formation of an Aristocracy in the Ottawa Valley,' reprinted in J.K. Johnson, ed., *Historical Essays on Upper Canada* (Toronto 1975), 226–40.

39 Curtis, *Building the Educational State*, 372

40 C.J. Taylor, 'The Kingston, Ontario Penitentiary and Moral Architecture,' *HS/SH* 12 (1979), 385–408

41 The Rideau's southern half was also in such districts, but it may have helped open rear areas of them. Upper Canada's population grew at an annual rate of 8 per cent from 1825 to 1837. Annual rates for counties in regions where canals were built were less than 4 per cent a year in Glengarry and Lincoln; less than 6 per cent in Dundas, Leeds, Lanark, and Frontenac; around 7 per cent in Stormont and Grenville; and almost 13 per cent in Carleton. By comparison, Hastings and Durham, east of Toronto, grew at 9 and 13 per cent respectively; York County grew at 10 per cent, Wentworth at over 8 per cent, and western counties at rates as high as Oxford's 10 per cent and Kent's 12.5 per cent. Some other longer-established areas also grew more slowly, including Norfolk and Essex, which both grew at 5.4 per cent.

42 See, for example, Jacob Spelt, *Urban Development in South-Central Ontario* (Toronto 1972), 54, 94, 100; J.M.S. Careless, *Toronto to 1918: An Illustrated History* (Toronto 1984), 19, 35, 43.

43 See F.H. Armstrong, 'From Family Compact to Canadian Establishment: Elite Evolution in London, Canada,' paper presented to the *CHA*, Victoria, May 1990.

44 See the essays in Allan Greer and Ian Radforth, eds., *Colonial Leviathan: State Formation in Mid-Nineteenth-Century Canada* (Toronto 1992).

CHAPTER 10: *Chronology of Provincial Development, 1821–51*

1 A.D. Gayer, W.W. Rostow, and Anna Jacobson Schwartz, *The Growth and Fluctuation of the British Economy 1790–1850*, rev. ed. (New York 1975), vol. 1, 342–57; W.B. Smith and A.H. Cole, *Fluctuations in American Business 1790–1860* (Cambridge, Mass. 1935)

2 G.N. Tucker, *The Canadian Commercial Revolution 1845–51*, H.G.J. Aitken, ed. (original edition New Haven 1936, rev. ed. Toronto 1964); D.G. Creighton, *The Commercial Empire of the St. Lawrence* (Toronto 1937)

3 The following table compares data on migration in peak years to the population of Upper Canada in the previous year, as an indication of the proportion the flow of migrants represented in the provincial population. These are crude measures of relative scale because emigration data include the Maritime colonies, data on immigrant arrivals at Quebec record people who would stay in Lower Canada and others who were destined for the United States, and it cannot be assumed that an identical proportion of the migrants were destined to settle in Upper Canada at

each time. The peak in 1842 was lower than these (e.g., the 44,000 emigrants who arrived at Quebec were about 10 per cent of the 1841 population of Upper Canada).

|  | 1819 | 1832 | 1847 |
|---|---|---|---|
| UC population, previous year (000) | c. 90 | 237 | c. 600 |
| British emigration to BNA (000) | 24 | 66 | 110 |
| Emigration/UC population (%) | 27 | 28 | 18 |
| Immigrant arrivals at Quebec (000) |  | 52 | 90 |
| Arrivals/UC population (%) |  | 22 | 15 |

4 Similar or greater numbers left Britain in every year from 1830 to 1854, except for 1835, 1838–9, and 1843–4. Until the mid-1830s, about equal numbers gave destinations in British North America and the United States; from then until 1847, up to twice as many named the United States. From 1848 it was normal for the number destined for the United States to be five or six times higher than for British North America. See Helen I. Cowan, *British Emigration to British North America: The First Hundred Years*, rev. ed. (Toronto 1961), 288.

5 A recent analysis stressing this point is Barbara Murison, 'The Search for the "Best Poor Man's Country": Shifting Emigration Patterns from Scotland in the 1830s and 1840s,' paper presented to the CHA, Kingston, June 1991.

6 For example, if we assume a net rate of natural increase in Upper Canada's population of 3 per cent annually, the population in 1830 (213,000) would have grown to about 262,000 by 1837. In fact, by 1837, it had reached 397,000 – that is, 135,000 more than natural increase would have produced. But 224,000 immigrants arrived at Quebec between 1830 and 1836. Similarly, from 1840 to 1848, natural increase would have carried Upper Canada from 430,000 to about 545,000; by 1848, there were 726,000 people in the province, about 180,000 more than natural increase would have produced. Between 1840 and 1847, over 280,000 immigrants had arrived at Quebec.

7 In fact, prices at Toronto reached 5s or a few pennies above that level in late 1841 and early 1842 and again in the second quarter of 1847, when for several weeks they were at 6s. Even so, whether on a quarterly or an annual basis, the highest price in the 1840s was lower than the peak in any other decade from the 1780s to 1870. On the nature of the relationship between British and Canadian wheat prices, see R.M. McInnis, 'Perspectives on Ontario Agriculture 1815–1930,' ch. 1, 'The Early Ontario Wheat Staple Reconsidered,' *CPRH* 8 (1992), 32.

8 Gaps and inconsistencies in data may be one explanatory factor in some of the series, but not in all.

9 See the graph in Donald R. Adams Jr, 'Prices and Wages in Antebellum America: The West Virginia Experience,' *JEH* 52 (1992), 207.

10  Their index reflects an 1838 price only, and that at Montreal rather than Quebec.
    Still, the trend in prices at Montreal after 1838 points to a divergent pattern from
    the other products.
11  My thinking here has benefited from discussions with, and the opportunity to read
    a number of working papers by, Donald Paterson and Ronald Shearer. Their 'The
    Supply of Canadian Money, 1842–1871: Estimates and Implications,' presented
    as work-in-progress to the 14th Conference on the Application of Quantitative
    Methods to Canadian Economic History, October 1985, is highly relevant to
    interpreting data on bank note circulation.
12  For data from Montreal and Quebec, see A.B. McCullough, *Money and Exchange
    in Canada to 1900* (Toronto and Charlottetown 1984), Appendix A, esp. graph at
    p. 265 and table at pp. 268–71. The American data, discounted for interest rate
    differentials and other variables to yield a net exchange rate, are from Lawrence
    Officer, 'Dollar-Sterling Mint Parity and Exchange Rates, 1791–1834,' *JEH* 43
    (1983), 579–616, and Edwin J. Perkins, 'Foreign Interest Rates in American
    Financial Markets: A Revised Series of Dollar-Sterling Exchange Rates, 1835–
    1900' *JEH* 38 (1978), 392–417. It is not intended here to test Canadian integra-
    tion into the continental exchange market, but just to use the data to indicate
    major points of volatility and uncertainty in Canada. For Canadian banks'
    connections with the American exchange system, see Peter Baskerville, ed., *The
    Bank of Upper Canada* (Toronto 1987).
13  See data in John McCallum, *Unequal Beginnings* (Toronto 1980), 124.
14  Thus, the cycles of brick production in England and Wales and of shipping built
    in the United Kingdom in the period were as given in the table below, which is
    from B. Mitchell and P. Deane, *Abstract of British Historical Statistics* (Cam-
    bridge 1971), 220–1, 235. See also Gayer, Rostow, and Schwartz, *The Growth
    and Fluctuation of the British Economy*, vol. 2, 690.

| Bricks | | | | | |
|---|---|---|---|---|---|
| Peaks | | 1825 | 1836 | 1840 | 1847 | |
| Troughs | 1821 | 1832 | 1838 | 1843 | 1848–9 |
| All ships | | | | | |
| Peaks | | 1825 | 1835 | 1840 | 1847 | |
| Troughs | 1822 | 1830 | 1836 | 1843 | 1849 |

15  This section draws extensively on my 'The Economic Context of the 1837
    Rebellion in Upper Canada,' unpublished paper presented to 'The 1837 Seminar,'
    University of Edinburgh, May 1987. I am grateful for that opportunity and for the
    comments and criticisms that I received there.
16  F. Ouellet, *Histoire économique et sociale du Québec 1760–1850* (Montreal
    1966), 416–25; and *Lower Canada 1791–1840: Social Change and Nationalism*
    (Toronto 1980), 276–82. A similar argument is made in Robert Armstrong,
    *Structure and Change: An Economic History of Quebec* (Toronto 1984), 79–84.

For contrasting views, see S. Courville, 'Le marché des "subsistances": l'exemple
de la plaine de Montréal au début des années 1830: une perspective géogra-
phique,' *RHAF* 42 (1988–9), 193–239; S. Courville and N. Séguin, *Rural Life in
Nineteenth-Century Quebec*, CHA Booklet 47 (Ottawa 1989), 8–12; and Alan
Greer, *Peasant, Lord, and Merchant: Rural Society in Three Quebec Parishes
1740–1840* (Toronto 1985), 214–17.

17 See, for example, Michael S. Cross, 'Afterword' to Benjamin Wait, *The Wait
Letters* (Erin, Ont. 1976), 151. This has been reprinted as '1837: The Necessary
Failure' in M.S. Cross and Greg Kealey, eds., *Pre-Industrial Canada 1760–1849*
(Toronto 1982), 141–58.

18 Donald Creighton, 'The Economic Background of the Rebellions of Eighteen
Thirty-Seven,' *Canadian Journal of Economics and Political Science* 3 (1937),
322–34. The same interpretation is to be found in his classic, *The Commercial
Empire of the St. Lawrence, 1760–1850*, ch. 11.

19 H. Clare Pentland, *Labour and Capital in Canada 1650–1860*, ed. Paul Phillips
(Toronto 1981), 144–5. By contrast, see Harold Innis, *Essays in Canadian
Economic History* (Toronto 1956), 68, 146, 179, where it is argued that it was
high costs of shipments of both imports and exports along the St Lawrence that
prompted the Upper Canadian Rebellion.

20 Leo Johnson, *History of the County of Ontario 1615–1875* (Whitby 1973),
116–17; W.T. Easterbrook and H.G.J. Aitken, *Canadian Economic History*
(Toronto 1956), 268; G.M. Craig, *Upper Canada: The Formative Years, 1784–
1841* (Toronto 1963), 241–2

21 Creighton, 'The Economic Background,' 326, 332; see also Easterbrook and
Aitken, *Canadian Economic History*, 268–9, and Innis, *Essays*, 160.

22 In addition to the sources for table 9.5, see NA, MGII, CO42, vol. 461, 177–
185A, Returns of Public Revenue ... in Upper Canada ... 1833 ... 1838; and vol.
476, Mr. Macaulay's Report ... upon Canada, 114; NA, Upper Canada Sundries,
RG5, A1, vol. 178, 98087–8, Jonas Jones to J.H. Dunn, 16 Sept. 1837.

23 Colin Read, *The Rising in Western Upper Canada, 1837–8* (Toronto 1982),
especially the appendices

24 Ronald J. Stagg, 'The Yonge Street Rebellion of 1837: An Examination of the
Social Background and a Reassessment of Events' (PH D thesis, University of
Toronto 1976), ch. 6 and appendices

25 On this point, see H.J. Mays, '"A Place to Stand": Families, Land and Permanence in Toronto Gore Township, 1820–1890,' CHA, *HP* (1980), 188–91.

26 Quotes are from Cross, 'Afterword,' 154. See also William Marr and Donald
Paterson, *Canada: An Economic History* (Toronto 1980), 96–7; and Johnson,
*History of the County of Ontario*, 116–17.

27 Creighton, 'The Economic Background of the Rebellions,' 329, 332–4

28 David Gagan, *Hopeful Travellers: Families, Land and Social Change in Mid-
Victorian Peel County, Canada West* (Toronto 1981), 30–7, notes that much of

the land in Peel had been alienated by 1837, but little of that as yet had been improved. Even if crown land was less available, that hardly meant no land was available. See also John Clarke, 'Aspects of Land Acquisition in Essex County, Ontario, 1790–1900,' *HS/SH* 9 (1978), 98–119. On the important, but essentially non-economic, role of the clergy reserves, see Alan Wilson, *The Clergy Reserves of Upper Canada: A Canadian Mortmain* (Toronto 1968), esp. 125–36.

29 It might be possible to argue a case that farm prices rose signficantly less than those of farmers' purchases, though no one has yet done this for Upper Canada. Cursory examination of series for non-agricultural as compared to agricultural prices elsewhere does not suggest that such a case would be easy to make, however. See, for example, Mitchell and Deane, *British Historical Statistics* 470–1; Smith and Cole, *Fluctuations in American Business*, 65.

30 See R.L. Jones, *History of Agriculture in Ontario 1613–1880* (Toronto 1946), 123–4.

31 AO, The Wade Letters (typescript), MU 3074, 140–5, Robert Wade to Ralph Wade, 10 Jan. 183[7]. The value of its sales for three years indicates the accuracy of this statement:

Wade Farm, Hamilton Township, Value of Sales (£ cy)

|      | Oats | Wheat | Pork | Peas | Barley | Cheese | Hay | Other | Total sales |
|------|------|-------|------|------|--------|--------|-----|-------|-------------|
| 1834 | 48   | 5     | 50   | 26   | 15     | 48     | 30  | 46    | 268         |
| 1835 | 35   | 10    | 55   | 5    | 2      | 67     | 67  | 88    | 329         |
| 1836 | 41   | 102   | 108  | 3    | 11     | 83     | 19  | 75    | 444         |

32 See also AO, Yonge Mills Records, MU 3187, Charles Jones letterbook, 1834–9, Jones to Tremaine and Moir, 18 Sept. 1836 and 22 Mar. 1837. At no time in this correspondence does Jones, a well-informed participant in the wheat trade, speak in terms of short Upper Canadian crops as a factor in the market in late 1836 and early 1837. For fluctuations in flour shipments from Port Ryerse, in Norfolk County, see *UCJ*, 1839, App., 755–7.

33 In 1838 over 40 per cent of the wheat and about 50 per cent of the flour shipped down the Welland Canal from western Upper Canada had passed through by the end of July – that is, before harvesting of the 1838 crop was done. On the other hand, Macaulay spoke of the 1837 provincial harvest as a partial failure. See NA, MG11, CO42, vol. 476, 286. See also Jones, *History of Agriculture*, 101.

34 Published summaries of assessment data show annual increases from 1825 to 1847, though with occasional pauses, of which the principal was from 1837 to 1838. But that pause was in part a consequence of under-reporting in the disturbed state of the province in the wake of the Rebellion. *JLA*, 1849, App. N; slightly different data appear in Canada, *Census*, 1871, vol. 4, 92–131.

35 NA, William Stewart Papers, MG24, D101, vol. 1, letterbook, #161, Stewart to Wood & Gray, 13 Mar. 1837

36 This point is made by most secondary accounts, although only the specialist
   literature explores the details of the story, which are vital to pinpoint the source
   and character of the economic disruptions of the time. Excellent analyses are
   found in Angela Redish, 'The Economic Crisis of 1837–39 in Upper Canada:
   Case Study of a Temporary Suspension of Specie Payments,' *Explorations in
   Economic History* 20 (1983), 402–17; R.M. Breckenridge, *The Canadian Banking
   System 1817–1890* (Toronto 1894), 57–84; Baskerville, ed., *The Bank of Upper
   Canada*, esp. section C.

37 Fred Landon pointed the way half a century ago, when he argued that 'not until
   we know more intimately the nature of the conditions and events in many
   communities of that era will we have a right understanding of the rebellion.' See
   his 'The Common Man in the Era of the Rebellion in Upper Canada,' in F.H.
   Armstrong et al., eds, *Aspects of Nineteenth Century Ontario* (Toronto, 1974),
   169. For a penetrating recent analysis focused on the west, see Graeme Paterson,
   *History and Communications: Harold Innis, Marshall McLuhan, the Interpreta-
   tion of History* (Toronto 1990), 185–96.

38 For an intriguing, somewhat speculative, linking of culture and craft in an urban
   setting, see the account of voting patterns in Toronto in 1836 in Paul Romney,
   'On the Eve of the Rebellion: Nationality, Religion and Class in the Toronto
   Election of 1836,' in D. Keane and C. Read, eds., *Old Ontario: Essays in Honour
   of J.M.S. Careless* (Toronto 1990), 192–216.

39 See the material in Colin Read and Ronald Stagg, eds., *The Rebellion of 1837 in
   Upper Canada: A Collection of Documents* (Toronto 1985), xl, 113–14, 119–21.
   See also Craig, *Upper Canada*, 242–3.

40 On the British crisis, see C.N. Ward-Perkins, 'The Commercial Crisis of 1847,'
   *Oxford Economic Papers* 2 (1950), 75–94; D. Morier Evans, *The Commercial
   Crisis, 1847–1848*, 2nd ed. (London 1849); and Gayer, Rostow, and Schwartz,
   *British Economy 1790–1850*, vol. 1, ch. 6. For the financial crisis in the United
   States, see Smith and Cole, *Fluctuations in American Business*, 118–19, 125–6.

41 *JLA*, 1849, App. Z. Wheat was 4s 6d a bushel in Aug. 1846, 8s 6d in June 1847,
   and 6s or less from July onwards; oats, 1s 10d through all of 1846, reached 3s 2d
   in June 1847; pork, 73s 9d per barrel late in 1846, exceeded £5 in late June 1847.
   See also table 5.8 for the emergence of potatoes as a source of income for the
   Dunnville farm.

42 Baskerville, ed., *The Bank of Upper Canada*, xcix–ciii, 356. The Gore Bank,
   squeezed by the failure of its London agent, Reid, Irving and Company, needed
   help from the Bank of Upper Canada late in 1847, though its problems were
   recognized by a write-off of capital only after the crisis had passed, in the
   summer of 1848. See Canadian Imperial Bank of Commerce, Company
   Secretary's Office, Toronto, Gore Bank Records, typed summary of a series
   of numbered documents, item 67, A. Steven to the President, Gore Bank,
   2 Nov. 1847; item 71, Resolution of thanks from Gore Bank, 25 Jan. 1848;

item 77, minutes of stockholders meeting, 7 Aug. 1848.

43  Evans, *The Commercial Crisis, 1847–1848*, xcvi, c; D. McCalla, *The Upper Canada Trade 1834–1872* (Toronto 1979), 64–73

44  Michael Piva, 'Continuity and Crisis: Francis Hincks and Canadian Economic Policy,' *CHR* 66 (1985), 196–8. The City of Toronto also issued such notes. See City of Toronto Archives, City Council Minutes (typescript), 15 May 1848, 3rd Report from Standing Committee on Finance and Assessment. The city had used this technique for years in paying for public works, however.

45  Elgin to Grey, 23 Apr. 1849, in Sir A. Doughty, ed., *The Elgin–Grey Papers, 1846–1852* (Ottawa 1937), vol. 1, 349

46  Thus, had population grown by 3 per cent per year, the 726,000 of 1848, which already included many of the 1847 immigrants, would have reached 817,000 in 1852. By then, however, there were 952,000 people in Upper Canada, a difference of 139,000. From 1848 to 1851 inclusive, almost exactly that number of immigrants were recorded as arriving at Quebec, though obviously not all the new arrivals settled in Upper Canada.

47  See Greg Kealey, 'Orangemen and the Corporation: The Politics of Class during the Union of the Canadas,' in Victor Russell, ed., *Forging a Consensus: Historical Essays on Toronto* (Toronto 1984), 44, 56–60; and Barrie D. Dyster, 'Toronto 1840–1860: Making It in a British Protestant Town' (PH D thesis, University of Toronto 1970), 219–25.

48  See also my 'The Canadian Grain Trade in the 1840s: The Buchanans' Case,' *CHA, HP* (1974), 95–114; and the account in the most recent survey, K. Norrie and D. Owram, *A History of the Canadian Economy* (Toronto 1991), 213.

49  M. Piva, 'Continuity and Crisis,' 210

CHAPTER 11: *Railways and Provincial Development, 1850–70*

1  See L.H. Jenks, *The Migration of British Capital to 1875* (New York 1927; reprinted London 1963), 75–108; Dorothy Adler, *British Investment in American Railways 1834–1898* (Charlottesville 1970), 9–15.

2  Others chartered included the Hamilton and Port Dover, the Cobourg, and the Niagara and Detroit Rivers.

3  For a list of the projects, see *UCJ*, 1839, App., First Report of the Finance Committee, 29–35; and Schedule of Government Debentures, 128–30.

4  A recent account for the Great Western Railway is D.R. Beer, *Sir Allan Napier MacNab* (Hamilton 1984), 210–25.

5  See Peter Baskerville, 'Entrepreneurship and the Family Compact: York-Toronto, 1822–1855,' *Urban History Review* 9, 3 (Feb. 1981), 21–3; Gerald Tulchinsky, *The River Barons* (Toronto 1977), 127–47.

6  See Peter Baskerville, 'Transportation, Social Change and State Formation, Upper Canada, 1841–1864,' in Greer and Radforth, eds., *Colonial Leviathan*, 234–7.

7 Hence the justification for treating such liabilities as 'indirect debts' in the provincial accounts. See Michael Piva, 'Government Finance and the Development of the Canadian State,' in Greer and Radforth, eds., *Colonial Leviathan*, 260–70.

8 See Douglas McCalla, 'Peter Buchanan, London Agent for the Great Western Railway of Canada,' in D.S. Macmillan, ed., *Canadian Business History: Selected Studies, 1497–1971* (Toronto 1972), 197–216; Peter Baskerville, 'Americans in Britain's Backyard: The Railway Era in Upper Canada, 1850–1880,' *Business History Review* 55 (1981), 315–24; A.M. Johnson and B. Supple, *Boston Capitalists and Western Railroads* (Cambridge, Mass. 1967).

9 T.C. Keefer, *Philosophy of Railroads and Other Essays*, H.V. Nelles, ed. (Toronto 1972), 145

10 See, for example, J.K. Johnson, '"One Bold Operator": Samuel Zimmerman, Niagara Entrepreneur, 1843–1857,' *OH* 74 (1982), 26–44. Although railways were the biggest and most dramatic examples here, there were other cases. For the York roads see Michael S. Cross, 'The Stormy History of the York Roads, 1833–1865,' *OH* 54 (1962), 1–24.

11 Harry N. Scheiber, *Ohio Canal Era: A Case Study of Government and the Economy, 1820–61* (Athens, Ohio 1969), 286; Carter Goodrich, *Government Promotion of American Canals and Railroads 1800–1890* (New York 1960), 138–41; see also Lance E. Davis et al., *American Economic Growth: An Economist's History of the United States* (New York 1972), 495.

12 For a generally accurate 1857 map of railways in Upper Canada, see Louis Gentilcore and Grant Head, eds., *Ontario's History in Maps* (Toronto 1984), 188.

13 Kenneth Buckley calculated net capital formation in railway transport and telegraphs in Canada between 1850 and 1860 at $90 million; see M.C. Urquhart and K.A.H. Buckley, eds., *Historical Statistics of Canada*, 1st ed. (Cambridge 1965), 512. From 1851 to 1859 Canadian imports exceeded exports by just over $100 million; see my 'Railways and the Development of Canada West,' 221–2. On the capitalization of the Grand Trunk, see Ann M. Carlos and Frank Lewis, 'The Profitability of Early Canadian Railroads: Evidence from the Grand Trunk and Great Western Railway Companies,' unpublished ms., 1991.

Overvaluation arose, for example, when a charter or line was taken over at a value beyond what its earning power justified; when securities were issued below par value (i.e., at an effective rate of interest higher than the nominal rate); and when values were deliberately overstated, as may have occurred in the Northern railway case, as part of getting more government backing under the Guarantee Act's provisions. See Keefer, *Philosophy of Railroads*, 147–8, 158; and G.R. Stevens, *Canadian National Railways*, vol. 1 (Toronto 1960), 245.

For the Grand Trunk, fully 20 per cent of total capitalization was said to represent interest during the construction period and discounts on the sale of securities. See A.W. Currie, *The Grand Trunk Railway of Canada* (Toronto

1957), 51. The average for American railways in the 1850s on this account was 14 to 15 per cent of total construction costs; see Albert Fishlow, *American Railroads and the Transformation of the Ante-Bellum Economy* (Cambridge, Mass. 1965), 351.

The practice of issuing par-value shares continued to produce nominal overcapitalization. For example, the Great Western in 1859 issued 5 per cent preferred shares for which it received 80 per cent; thus the capital raised was 20 per cent less than stated, and the actual interest rate was 6.25 per cent. See J.M. and E. Trout, *The Railways of Canada for 1870–1*, reprint ed. (Toronto 1970), 93.

14 Keefer, *Philosophy of Railroads*, 154–6. What the government actually had to pay depended on shortfalls in payments by the companies and municipalities. The Great Western, for example, repaid the sums obtained with the government's guarantee.

15 Scheiber, *Ohio Canal Era*, 284–5

16 The closest comparison was the mid-1830s; in 1835, the peak year of external borrowing by the province, the net external debt increased by 25s ($5) per person (see table 9.4).

17 See John McCallum, *Unequal Beginnings* (Toronto 1980), 127, and Marvin McInnis, 'Marketable Surpluses in Ontario Farming, 1860,' *Social Science History* 8 (1984), reprinted in D. McCalla, ed., *Perspectives on Canadian Economic History* (Toronto 1987), 45, 48. The value of average net output per farm in Upper Canada in 1851 was $198; see R.M. McInnis, 'Perspectives on Ontario Agriculture, 1815–1930,' ch. 2, 'Ontario Agriculture at Mid-Century,' *CPRH* 8 (1992), 72–3.

18 O.J. Firestone, 'Development of Canada's Economy, 1850–1900,' in Conference on Research in Income and Wealth, Studies in Income and Wealth, 24, *Trends in the American Economy in the Nineteenth Century* (Princeton 1960), 222. Firestone's figure for 1870 was $459 million; the recent work of Alan Green and M.C. Urquhart gives a figure of $383 million for 1870. See their 'New Estimates of Output Growth in Canada: Measurement and Interpretation,' in McCalla, ed., *Perspectives on Canadian Economic History*, 183, 187–8. The highest British figure for railway investment in this era was 6.7 per cent of GNP, in 1847; see François Crouzet, *The Victorian Economy* (London 1982), 299.

19 For detailed trade data, see 'Railways and the Development of Canada West, 1850–1870,' 221–2, table 7:11. On American railways in the 1850s, the superstructure represented about 28 per cent of total costs of construction, while iron costs represented 70 per cent of superstructure costs. In addition, equipment represented a further 9 per cent of total costs, and in Canada an unknown but important part of this was imported. On the basis of a total capitalization of some $100 million, these figures suggest that between $24 and $27 million would have been iron's share in the total. If discounts and related costs of capital are excluded, superstructure represented 31 per cent of construction costs and

equipment 10 per cent. In Canada, if capitalization minus financing and other costs was some $80 million, the total railway iron figure was likely in the range $20 to $24 million. See Fishlow, *American Railroads*, 350–1, 371.

20 H.C. Pentland, *Labour and Capital in Canada 1650–1860*, P. Phillips, ed. (Toronto 1981), 133; the 1851 census showed 280,000 men fifteen years of age and older in Upper Canada, of whom 184,000 were in the twenty to fifty age range.

21 See, for example, Stevens, *Canadian National Railways*, vol. 1, 260–4; Currie, *Grand Trunk Railway*, 28–9; and Fishlow, *American Railroads*, 409–13.

22 Stevens, *Canadian National Railways*, vol. 1, 260, 265. On Grand Trunk construction standards, see Currie, *Grand Trunk Railway*, 26–8, 53–6; and Keefer, *Philosophy of Railroads*, 149. The Grand Trunk's Victoria Bridge was, however, built to the higher, British standards. See Bruce Sinclair, 'Canadian Technology: British Traditions and American Influences,' *Technology and Culture* 20 (1979), 111. It is possible that the severity of the Canadian winter extended construction time beyond two years, but whether it did so as an average for the whole system is not known.

23 Paul Craven and Tom Traves, 'Dimensions of Paternalism: Discipline and Culture in Canadian Railway Operations in the 1850s,' in Craig Heron and Robert Storey, eds., *On the Job: Confronting the Labour Process in Canada* (Montreal and Kingston 1986), 47–74

24 The implication is that the 'large cost overruns' of the period were caused less by inexperienced management and scheming contractors than by macro-economic factors beyond any individual company's control. See Baskerville, 'Transportation, Social Change and State Formation,' 237.

25 For the sharp rise and subsequent fall in land prices, see David Gagan, *Hopeful Travellers* (Toronto 1981), 46; Edward C. Gray and Barry E. Prentice, 'Exploring the Price of Farmland in Two Ontario Localities since Letters Patenting,' *CPRH* 4 (1984), 232–5. On the 1857 crisis and its aftermath, see Douglas McCalla, *The Upper Canada Trade* (Toronto 1979), 95–116; and Peter Baskerville, ed., *The Bank of Upper Canada* (Toronto 1987), chs. D and E.

26 *Report of Mr. Thomas E. Blackwell ... [on] the Grand Trunk Railway ... 1859* (London 1860), PAC pamphlet 2872, 8, and App., 6. When this report was prepared, the line was not yet open to Sarnia, but already the lines west of Toronto had, on local traffic only, surpassed the eastern division as a generator of revenue. The situation had not changed a decade later; see Trout, *Railways of Canada*, 79.

27 By comparison, as we saw in chapter 7, on the eve of the railway era the leading toll-roads did well to average $400 a mile in tolls collected. Unlike the roads, of course, railways' charges covered both use of the roadbed and actual carriage of goods and people. The Nova Scotia Railroad, the leading Maritime line, took in $1,900 a mile in 1870; the European and North American and the New

Brunswick and Canada had revenues of around $1,600 a mile. In Upper Canada they would have ranked behind all but the almost moribund Cobourg and Peterborough. The figure for the New Brunswick and Canada would be only $1,200 if its branches were included. See Trout, *Railways of Canada*, 105, 121–2, 133.

28 Ibid., 110. On the Northern's strategy in this period, see F.H. Armstrong and Peter Baskerville, 'Frederick William Cumberland,' *DCB* 11 (Toronto 1982), 226–7.

29 *Report of Mr. Thomas E. Blackwell ... 1859* (App., 8–9) gives a through rate of *c.* 1¢ per ton-mile from west of Toronto to Boston in 1859. See Fishlow, *American Railroads*, 65, 339 for contemporary American rate levels. On the rate question in general and the particular competitiveness of the trade with the east coast, see Ken Cruikshank, 'The Transportation Revolution and its Consequences: The Railway Freight Rate Controversy of the Late Nineteenth Century,' CHA, *HP* (1987), 121.

30 Great Western Railway Company of Canada, *Report .... for the Half Year ending July 31, 1855* (Hamilton 1855), PAC pamphlets 2512, 10. For passengers, 61 per cent of revenue was from through travellers, and for freight the figure was 46 per cent. Contemporary American trunk lines earned 40 to 70 per cent of revenue from through traffic. See Fishlow, *American Railroads*, 64.

31 If anything, rate levels were steady or tending to decline in these years. See Cruikshank, 'The Transportation Revolution and Its Consequences.'

32 See Great Western Railway of Canada, *Report ... for the Half Year ending July 31, 1855*; and *JLA*, 1856, App. 29, TTN for 1855, schedule 1. The Welland carried a total of 9,000 tons of flour (equal to about 90,000 barrels) downward from a 'British' port to a 'British' or American port, and another 23,500 tons of wheat (equal to about 800,000 bushels). From west of Hamilton, the Great Western in six months carried about 90,000 barrels of flour and 300,000 bushels of wheat. Valuable imports, such as cottons, were not separately itemized in freight reports of either the canal or the railway, but it is safe to assume that they quickly came to move by rail.

33 For 1849, see Table 7.1. By 1874, there were 815 vessels on the Ontario register, totalling 113,000 tons; see Ian Drummond, *Progress without Planning* (Toronto 1987), 432.

34 The last factor has been particularly emphasized in American studies of the impact of railroads. On the complexity of arriving at an appropriate cost for road traffic, see Patrick O'Brien, *The New Economic History of the Railways* (London 1977), 46.

35 Keefer, *Philosophy of Railroads*, 147, argues that in fact the Grand Trunk had not (by 1862) become a major mover of grain to the Montreal market or beyond; if so, water rates must have been cheaper still than these.

36 NA, Canadian National Railways Records, RG30, vol. 2001, Grand Trunk

Railway Freight Rates, 1853–65, 239–41, 271–3, 300–4, 351–3; I owe this reference to Dr Richard G. Brown of the NA, whose assistance is greatly appreciated. For an early Northern Railway freight tariff, see Ontario, Simcoe & Huron Railroad, *Freight Tariff and Conditions ... from First September, 1854* (Toronto 1854), PAC pamphlet 2487, 9–11; here first-class freight was to be charged 8 cents per ton-mile and flour 5 cents per ton-mile. The Northern quickly became known for discounting its rates for preferred customers, however. Fishlow, *American Railroads*, 339, uses average rates of 2.3 cents per ton-mile for western, 2.7 cents for northern New England, and 2.5 cents for mid-Atlantic railways in 1859. Presumably, the Grand Trunk negotiated such rates to meet competition from the Great Western and from lake shipping, and in particular to foster longer hauls on its lines.

37 See F.N. Walker, ed., *Daylight through the Mountain: Letters and Labours of Civil Engineers Walter and Francis Shanly* (Engineering Institute of Canada 1957), illustration facing p. 338 for the Grand Trunk special; p. 276 for a Hamilton and Toronto timetable; and p. 310 for a Northern Railway timetable. The special train carrying the Prince of Wales from Toronto to London along the Grand Trunk in September 1860 was expected to average a running speed of 28 miles an hour west of Guelph (i.e., above the Niagara Escarpment).

38 See *Grand Trunk Railway Timetables and International Railway Guide*, 2nd ed. (Montreal, Sept. 1865); see also schedules in Toronto *Globe*, 4 Jan. 1870.

39 See MTL, Broadsides Collection, *Great Western Railway Timetable*, Dec. 1853. Fishlow (*American Railroads*, 325, 334, 339) uses a slightly lower fare for western American railways at the time, 2.54 cents per passenger mile. For a similar rate on a division of the Grand Trunk, see W. Shanly to J. Elliott, 18 Aug. 1860, in *Daylight through the Mountain*, 345–7.

40 Great Western Railway Company of Canada, *Report ... for the Half Year ending July 31, 1855*, 10

41 The meaning of 'through' is problematic in railway documentation, in that data on numbers of passengers and freight tonnage divided by reasonable rates per mile or ton-mile cannot be made to indicate traffic that travelled the entire length of the main line. The Great Western's main line from Niagara Falls to Windsor was 229 miles. At present I assume 'through' referred to traffic that went the entire length of a specific train's run or that was delivered to or received from another company.

42 The Ontario and Quebec figure may also be compared to the value of two of the principal categories of provincial exports in 1870: McCallum, in *Unequal Beginnings*, 128, gives the value of all forest products and ships at $17.6 million in that year and the value of wheat and flour exports at $6 million.

43 In all of Ontario south of a line from Collingwood to the Ottawa River around Renfrew, there is hardly an urban centre of even 10,000 people today that did not get on a rail line by 1860. Apart from township-sized modern municipalities

covering a number of smaller urban and suburban developments (e.g., Halton Hills) and suburbs of major centres (e.g., Markham, Kanata), the exceptions appear to be Dunnville, Leamington, Milton, Orangeville, Simcoe, Tillsonburg, Stouffville, and Wallaceburg. Of more northerly centres in this region, Midland, Owen Sound, and Orillia were beyond the end of tracks in 1860.

44 W.H. Smith, *Canadian Gazetteer ... 1846*, reprint ed. (Toronto 1970), 15, 18, 164, 183. On the impact of the Grand Trunk on Hamilton, see my 'The Decline of Hamilton as a Wholesale Centre,' *OH* 65 (1973), 247–54.

45 See Trout, *Railways of Canada*, 94, on an 1867 agreement between the Grand Trunk and Great Western. For government rejection of an agreement involving these two and the Buffalo and Lake Huron, see Baskerville, 'Transportation, Social Change and State Formation,' 247.

46 Paul Craven and Tom Traves, 'Canadian Railways as Manufacturers, 1850–1880,' CHA, *HP* (1983), 254–81. On the high pay of leading railway managers, see Keefer, *Philosophy of Railroads*, 151–2.

47 Fishlow, *American Railroads*, 337; and *Historical Statistics of the United States: Colonial Times to 1970* (Washington 1975), vol. 2, 731

48 I owe this point to Marvin McInnis. Canada required railways that were part of the main trunk to use the 5 foot 6 inch gauge adopted by the St Lawrence and Atlantic rather than the 4 foot 8$^{1}/_{2}$ inch gauge that became the standard.

49 See Carlos and Lewis, 'The Profitability of Early Canadian Railroads.'

50 Trout, *Railways of Canada*, 85, 99–101

51 Ibid., 92–5, 100–1. For its entire independent history, Ann Carlos and Frank Lewis have calculated its 'unaided private rate of return' at 4.1 per cent, a rate that actually exceeded the same rate for the CPR; see their 'The Profitability of Early Canadian Railroads.'

52 But see Province of Canada Statute 25 Vic. cap. 56 (1862) for a reorganization bill.

53 Gagan, *Hopeful Travellers*, 157, 160

54 See Albert Fishlow, 'Productivity and Technological Change in the Railroad Sector, 1840–1910,' in Conference on Research in Income and Wealth, Studies in Income and Wealth, 30, *Output, Employment and Productivity in the United States after 1800* (New York 1966), 583–646.

55 As Alan Green notes, however, 'for Canada at least, the simple exercise of examining the growth and efficiency of the railway system has not yet been undertaken.' Alan Green, 'Growth and Productivity Change in the Canadian Railway Sector, 1871–1926,' in Conference on Research in Income and Wealth, Studies in Income and Wealth, 51, *Long-Term Factors in American Economic Growth* (Chicago 1986), 798.

56 This is the terminology of H.G.J. Aitken; see his 'Government and Business in Canada: An Interpretation,' *Business History Review* 38 (1964), 5.

57 An overview that depicts the first railway era in the province in more negative

terms can be found in Drummond, *Progress without Planning*, 250. See also W. Marr and Donald Paterson, *Canada: An Economic History* (Toronto 1980), 320, which speaks of 'the sorry plight of Canada's first railways.'

CHAPTER 12: *The Economy at Mid-Century, 1851–70*

1 On the growth and implications of numeracy, see the companion volume in this series, Susan Houston and Alison Prentice, *Schooling and Scholars in Nineteenth-Century Ontario* (Toronto 1988), 189.

2 Kris Inwood and Jim Irwin, 'Inter-Regional Differences in Canadian Commodity Output in 1870: Preliminary Estimates,' paper presented to the 17th Conference on the Use of Quantitative Methods in Canadian Economic History, Kingston, November 1990; Kris Inwood, 'Maritime Industrialization from 1870 to 1910: A Review of the Evidence and Its Interpretation,' *Acadiensis* 21, 1 (autumn 1991), 132–55. See also Julian Gwyn, 'Golden Age or Bronze Moment? Wealth and Poverty in Nova Scotia: The 1850s and 1860s,' *CPRH* 8 (1992), 195–230. For other important research that begins in 1870, see M.C. Urquhart, 'New Estimates of Gross National Product, Canada, 1870–1926: Some Implications for Canadian Development,' in S.L. Engerman and Robert Gallman, eds., *Long-Term Factors in American Economic Growth*, Studies in Income and Wealth 51 (Chicago 1986), 9–94. When the work of Urquhart and his colleagues is regionally disaggregated, it will have much to say specifically on the Ontario economy.

3 For the delayed impact on land values, see David Gagan, *Hopeful Travellers* (Toronto 1981), 46. The impact of the 1857 crisis is a major theme in my *The Upper Canada Trade, 1834–1872: The Buchanans' Business* (Toronto 1979).

4 Gagan, *Hopeful Travellers*, 13–14, 40. An excellent overview of the period and issues is Chad Gaffield, 'Children, Schooling, and Family Reproduction in Nineteenth-Century Ontario,' *CHR* 72 (1991), 157–91.

5 See in particular R.M. McInnis, 'Women, Work and Childbearing: Ontario in the Second Half of the Nineteenth Century,' paper presented to the 16th Conference on Quantitative Methods in Canadian Economic History, Toronto, March 1989. McInnis's fertility and nuptiality indexes for Ontario's counties show Peel County as quite close to provincial averages. See also McInnis's 'The Demographic Transition,' in D. Kerr and D. Holdsworth, eds., *Historical Atlas of Canada*, 3 (Toronto 1990), plate 29.

6 See the data and discussion in Gagan, *Hopeful Travellers*, esp. 71–7, 86–7, and 176.

7 Ibid., 95–6, 115–16

8 See Michael Katz, Michael Doucet, and Mark Stern, *The Social Organization of Early Industrial Capitalism* (Cambridge, Mass. 1982), ch. 3, esp. 108–9. See also Michael Katz, *The People of Hamilton, Canada West: Family and Class in a Mid-Nineteenth-Century City* (Cambridge, Mass. 1975), 19–22, 122–34.

9 Herbert J. Mays, '"A Place to Stand": Families, Land and Permanence in Toronto Gore Township, 1820–1890,' CHA, *HP* (1980), 198–9. Families that came and went in the interval between two censuses are, of course, omitted from these calculations.

10 Ibid. The relationship of property and persistence is likewise stressed by Michael Katz. Other studies stressing persistence include R.S. Dilley, 'Migration and the Mennonites: Nineteenth-Century Waterloo County, Ontario'; Darrell A. Norris, 'Migration, Pioneer Settlement, and the Life Course: The First Families of an Ontario Township'; and Glenn J. Lockwood, 'Irish Immigrants and the "Critical Years" in Eastern Ontario: The Case of Montague Township 1821–1881'; all in *CPRH* (1984), 108–29, 130–52, 153–78.

11 Chad Gaffield, *Language, Schooling, and Cultural Conflict: The Origins of the French-Language Controversy in Ontario* (Kingston and Montreal 1987), 53

12 A.G. Darroch and Michael Ornstein, 'Ethnicity and Class, Transitions over a Decade: Ontario 1861–1871,' CHA, *HP* (1984), 122. See also Ian Drummond, *Progress without Planning* (Toronto 1987), tables 2.2, 2.3. Agriculture's contribution to *Canadian* GNP in 1870 was almost identical, 37.1 per cent; Urquhart, 'New Estimates of Gross National Product,' 42.

13 See Canada, *Census*, 1871, vol. 3, table 21.

14 See, for example, Patricia Thornton, 'The Problem of Out-Migration from Atlantic Canada: A New Look,' *Acadiensis* 15, 1 (autumn 1985), 3–34.

15 See, for example, Gagan, *Hopeful Travellers*, ch. 6, on the emergence and development of Brampton.

16 Of course, pigs, chickens, and milk cows were kept by many non-farmers, even in the largest cities.

17 Darroch and Ornstein, 'Ethnicity and Class,' 116, 121–4, 129, 132, 137; John McCallum, *Unequal Beginnings* (Toronto 1980), 127. Drummond gives the total number of farms in 1871 as 172,000 which apparently includes some farms of less than ten acres (*Progress without Planning*, table 3.9).

18 R. Ankli and W. Millar, 'Ontario Agriculture in Transition: The Switch from Wheat to Cheese,' *JEH* 42 (1982), 207–15

19 See notes to table 12.2 for a discussion of data limitations. Not unitl 1870–1 do these data include much of the province's exports to Britain, and wheat and forest products are evidently under-represented even then. According to John McCallum's figures on the value of wheat exports (*Unequal Beginnings*, 128), the animal products recorded in table 12.2 were marginally outranked by wheat exports in 1865–6.

20 Drummond, *Progress without Planning*, table 3.1; Ankli and Millar, 'Ontario Agriculture in Transition,' 208. In 1882 almost 1.8 million acres were sowed to wheat, two-thirds of this fall wheat; that was an increase of 30 per cent in acreage from 1870. See Ontario Bureau of Industries, *Annual Report for 1883* (Toronto 1884), 5.

21 See R.M. McInnis, 'Perspectives on Ontario Agriculture 1815–1930,' ch. 1, 'The Early Ontario Wheat Staple Reconsidered,' *CPRH* 8 (1992), 39–43.
22 R.M. McInnis, 'The Changing Structure of Canadian Agriculture, 1867–1897,' *JEH* 42 (1982), 195n
23 Only Welland of the counties producing over 18 bushels per capita in 1851 was not on the list of those with net surpluses of over 100,000 bushels in 1870–1.
24 W.H. Graham, *Greenbank: Country Matters in 19th Century Ontario* (Peterborough 1988), 16. Research on farming elsewhere in Canada is likewise revealing the complexity of rural patterns. See, for example, Rusty Bittermann, 'The Hierarchy of the Soil: Land and Labour in a 19th Century Cape Breton Community,' *Acadiensis* 18, 1 (autumn 1988), 33–55; Alan MacNeil, 'Cultural Stereotypes and Highland Farming in Eastern Nova Scotia, 1827–1861,' *HS/SH* 19 (1986), 39–56; and Catherine Desbarats, 'Agriculture within the Seigneurial Régime of Eighteenth-Century Canada: Some Thoughts on the Recent Literature,' *CHR* 73 (1992), 21–30.
25 The variation in outputs can be suggested, at least, as was done in ch. 5, n20; in 1870 per capita output and stocks by county varied quite widely in some commodities, less so in others. See table 12.6 for selected evidence from sample counties.
26 Output per farm might be preferable, but there are inconsistencies and complexities in determining what was a farm, and non-farmers might also keep some livestock.
27 In 1860 the Great Western ran an overnight cattle train from Windsor to Niagara Falls, with a number of stops along the way, presumably to load, not unload. See Great Western Railway of Canada, *Private Timetable No. 35* (1 Oct. 1860).
28 Wheat and flour data in Table 12.4 are from McCallum, *Unequal Beginnings*, 126. During the year ending 30 June 1871, net exports are given as 5.7 million bushels. If 1.5 bushels per acre are allowed for seed, about 2 million bushels would have been needed to plant the acreage reported in the 1871 census. That would have left less than 7 million bushels (about 4.4 bushels per person in Upper Canada) for local consumption, according to the total 1870 output reported in the 1871 census. Net wheat exports of 5.7 million bushels would have left only 1 million bushels for all off-farm consumption. (See *Unequal Beginnings*, tables S3, S5.)
29 On this point see McCallum's 'Agriculture and Economic Development in Quebec and Ontario to 1870' (PH D thesis, McGill University 1977), 227, where it is argued for 1850 at least that 'a very high proportion of the urban requirements for livestock and livestock products was met by imports.'
30 The argument in this paragraph is primarily based on Marvin McInnis, 'The Changing Structure of Canadian Agriculture, 1867–1897,' and his 'Output and Productivity in Canadian Agriculture, 1870–71 to 1926–27,' in Engerman and Gallman, eds., *Long-Term Factors in American Economic Growth*, 737–78. Both

articles have been reprinted in *CPRH* 8 (1992); page references are to the originals.

31 Ontario Bureau of Industries, *Annual Report for 1883*, 84–5

32 See Kenneth Kelly, 'The Artificial Drainage of Land in Nineteenth-Century Southern Ontario,' *Canadian Geographer* 19 (1975), 279–98.

33 Satisfactory data are lacking, however. See McInnis, 'Output and Productivity in Canadian Agriculture,' 752, 758.

34 That would have been enough to provide one for every farm of more than one hundred acres, though other factors than landholdings entered into the decision to buy such equipment. See the discussion in Richard Pomfret, 'The Mechanization of Reaping and Mowing in Nineteenth-Century Ontario: A Case Study of the Pace and Diffusion of Embodied Technical Change,' *JEH* 36 (1976), 399–415. See also Drummond, *Progress without Planning*, table 3.9, and W.G. Phillips, *The Agricultural Implement Industry in Canada: A Study of Competition* (Toronto 1956), 5–12.

35 Particularly good series are provided in R.M. McInnis, 'From Hewn Timber to Sawn Lumber: The Canadian Forest Industry in the Latter Half of the Nineteenth Century,' unpublished paper, Feb. 1988; these data also support his 'Canada in the World Market for Forest Products, 1850–1895,' paper presented to the Second Canadian Business History Conference, Victoria, Mar. 1988. See also the data in L. Officer and L. Smith, 'The Canadian-American Reciprocity Treaty of 1855 to 1866,' *JEH* 28 (1968). All the data derive ultimately from the TTN, which are likewise the basis of tables 12.2. to 12.5.

36 John Keyes, 'The Dunn Family Business, 1850–1914: The Trade in Square Timber at Quebec' (PH D thesis, Laval University 1987), 537. Keyes's data are for exports from Quebec; tables 4.2 and 4.5 are based on culling at Quebec.

37 R.M. McInnis, 'From Hewn Timber to Sawn Lumber,' tables 1 and 2. From 1865 on, his data are for fiscal years ending 30 June of the year specified (i.e., this peak came in 1872–3).

38 For example, exports of planks and boards through St Jean were 125.9 million board feet in 1865–6, with a value of $1.4 million; in 1868–9, St Jean's exports of planks and boards were valued at $1.7 million. Exports of planks and boards from there and other Quebec ports in 1870–1 totalled $2 million. Given the role of Upper Canada as a producer of deals and of Lower Canada as a producer of planks and boards, it is not possible to calculate an exact level of Upper Canadian exports of planks and boards from the St Jean data.

39 If data from tables 4.2 and 4.5 are combined and compared to Keyes's table 21 (p. 537), which gives annual exports by type of wood, Upper Canadian shipments in many years approximated or exceeded total recorded Quebec exports. It is possible that some Upper Canadian pine timber was sawn into deals after culling, and of course the ships that were built at Quebec used provincial timber.

40 In other words, York, Simcoe, Grey, and Bruce counties are *not* included in the

region as defined here. Grey and Bruce had only quite modest outputs in any case.

41 Grant Head uses 1,000 board feet equals 100 cubic feet; Ian Drummond uses 1,000 board feet equals 200 cubic feet, which seems to overstate the wastage in sawing. See Head, 'An Introduction to Forest Exploitation in Nineteenth Century Ontario,' in J.D. Wood, ed., *Perspectives on Landscape and Settlement in Nineteenth Century Ontario* (Toronto 1975), 111 n19; and Drummond, *Progress without Planning*, table 7.11. A.R.M. Lower suggests that slow cutting speeds and the thickness of circular saws in early water-powered saw mills resulted in a loss in cutting of up to one-third of the wood in a log; *The North American Assault on the Canadian Forest* (Toronto 1938), 48.

42 If Quebec's census district, Ottawa West, were included, it would have ranked with the City of Ottawa; each had sawmill outputs exceeding $1.5 million; the next highest in Ontario was Simcoe North, at just over $900,000.

43 McInnis, 'From Hewn Timber to Sawn Lumber,' table 3

44 On the locational geography of sawmilling, see J.M. Gilmour, *Spatial Evolution of Manufacturing: Southern Ontario 1851–1891* (Toronto 1972), 127; and E.J. Chambers and G. Bertram, 'Urbanization and Manufacturing in Central Canada, 1870–1890,' Canadian Political Science Association, *Conference on Statistics* (1964), 233. On the origins and development of the Ottawa sawmilling complex, see John Taylor, *Ottawa: An Illustrated History* (Toronto 1986), 51–60. On American entrepreneurship, see Anita S. Goodstein, *Biography of a Businessman: Henry W. Sage, 1814–1897* (Ithaca 1962), 49–65.

45 Cf. Canada, *Census*, 1871, vol. 3, table 33, pp. 340–3 with 1891 data in Gilmour, *Spatial Evolution of Manufacturing*, map 31.

46 See Gaffield, *Language, Schooling, and Cultural Conflict*, esp. ch. 3.

47 A fourth, tanbark, seems to have been relatively modest by comparison with these, though it was significant to the income of a number of rural dwellers.

48 *Census*, 1871, vol. 3, table 37

49 Coal imports, which in 1870 totalled 146,000 tons (Drummond, *Progress without Planning*, 399), were presumably intended particularly for foundries and other metal-working establishments. Had railways been coal-powered, such imports would have been sufficient to drive locomotives over something like 5 million miles. If we allow half of Grand Trunk mileage in Upper Canada, provincial railways actually recorded about 8 million locomotive miles in 1870. For coal requirements, see Alan Green, 'Growth and Productivity in the Canadian Railway Sector, 1871–1926' in Engerman and Gallman, eds., *Long-Term Factors in American Economic Growth*, 804. Railway data are from J.M and E. Trout, *The Railways of Canada* (Toronto 1871, reprinted 1970).

50 Census output was 2.8 cords per person, which seems low by the standards we employed in ch. 4 at least. See the discussion there as well. The text here aims at a lower-bounded estimate.

51 It also included three small urban centres whose environs and economy have been the subject of considerable modern study – Brampton, Hawkesbury, and Gananoque. See Gagan, *Hopeful Travellers*, ch. 6; Gaffield, *Language, Schooling, and Cultural Conflict*; and Donald Akenson, *The Irish in Ontario: A Study in Rural History* (Kingston and Montreal 1984), ch. 6. On Whitby and Oshawa, both in the 2,500 to 4,999 category, see Leo Johnson, *History of the County of Ontario 1615–1875* (Whitby 1973).

52 Allan Pred, *Urban Growth and City-Systems in the United States, 1840–1860* (Cambridge, Mass. 1980), 119–41

53 Drummond, *Progress without Planning*, table 2.3

54 Ibid., tables 7.9 and 7.2, and ch. 6

55 Some further context for the women's crafts can be found in Lorna McLean, 'Single Again: Widows' Work in the Urban Family Economy, 1871,' *OH* 83 (1991), 127–50.

56 But see also Gerald Tulchinsky, 'Hidden among the Smokestacks: Toronto's Clothing Industry, 1871–1901,' in David Keane and Colin Read, eds., *Old Ontario: Essays in Honour of J.M.S. Careless* (Toronto 1990), 257–84.

57 G. Kealey, *Toronto Workers Respond to Industrial Capitalism 1867–1892* (Toronto 1980), 29; data are from tables I.1 to I.12; John Weaver, *Hamilton: An Illustrated History* (Toronto 1982), ch. 2; and Bryan D. Palmer, *A Culture in Conflict: Skilled Workers and Industrial Capitalism in Hamilton, Ontario, 1860–1914* (Montreal 1979).

58 E. Bloomfield, 'Manuscript Industrial Schedules of the 1871 Census of Canada: A Source for Labour Historians,' *Labour/Le Travail* 19 (spring 1987), 128. I have included Garden Island, site of the Calvin timber enterprises, with Kingston in this count.

59 Elizabeth and Gerald Bloomfield, 'Mills, Factories and Craftshops of Ontario, 1870: A Machine-Readable Source for Material Historians,' *Material History Bulletin* 25 (spring 1987), 35–47; Elizabeth Bloomfield, 'Industry in Ontario Urban Centres, 1870,' *UHR* 15 (1986–7), 279–83; and her 'Manuscript Industrial Schedules of the 1871 Census of Canada: A Source for Labour Historians,' *Labour/Le Travail* 19 (spring 1987), 125–31. Although the data base on which these papers draw is now generally available, it has not been utilized in this chapter.

60 See Michael Doucet and John Weaver, *Housing the North American City* (Montreal and Kingston 1991).

61 Greg Kealey and Bryan D. Palmer, *Dreaming of What Might Be: The Knights of Labor in Ontario, 1880–1900* (Toronto 1987)

62 Elizabeth Bloomfield, 'Manuscript Industrial Schedules,' table 1

63 See Paul Rutherford, *A Victorian Authority: The Daily Press in Late Nineteenth-Century Canada* (Toronto 1982), 40–2, and elsewhere; and Greg Kealey, 'Work

Control, the Labour Process, and Nineteenth-Century Canadian Printers,' in Craig Heron and R. Storey, eds., *On the Job: Confronting the Labour Process in Canada* (Kingston and Montreal 1986), 75–101.

64 On the post-1850 development of this region, see Kris Inwood and Tim Sullivan, 'Comparative Perspectives on Nineteenth Century Growth: Ontario in the Great Lakes Region,' forthcoming in vol. 2 of *Canadian Papers in Business History*.

65 See, however, the excellent article by Ben Forster, 'Finding the Right Size: Markets and Competition in Mid- and Late Nineteenth-Century Ontario' in Roger Hall, William Westfall, and Laurel Sefton MacDowell, eds., *Patterns of the Past: Interpreting Ontario's History* (Toronto 1988), 150–73.

66 For these processes, see Chambers and Bertram, 'Urbanization and Manufacturing in Central Canada,' 225–9.

67 *Lovell's Canadian Dominion Directory for 1871* (Montreal 1871), notice of the Montreal Telegraph Company

68 According to Kealey, the three principal Toronto dailies in 1871 each employed a workforce of some seventy adult men, only a portion of which would have been skilled tradesmen. *Toronto Workers*, table I.5.

69 Data on newspapers come from the following directories: Lovell's *Canada Directory, 1857–58* (Montreal 1858), 1140–5; Lovell's *Canadian Dominion Directory for 1871* (Montreal 1871), 2375–8; Wood & Co.'s *Canadian Newspaper Directory* (Montreal 1876), 24–42. See also Rutherford, *A Victorian Authority*.

70 E.P. Neufeld, *The Financial System of Canada: Its Growth and Development* (Toronto 1972), 78, 97; R.M. Breckenridge, *The Canadian Banking System 1817–1890* (Toronto 1894), 205n

71 See Drummond, *Progress without Planning*, ch. 18; details of branches from *Lovell's Canadian Dominion Directory for 1871*.

72 *Lovell's Canada Directory* (Montreal 1851), and *Lovell's Canada Directory for 1857–58*, 1022–5

73 See Ronald Rudin, *Banking en français: The French Banks of Quebec 1835–1925* (Toronto 1985), 6–8. On private banking after 1870, see Drummond, *Progress without Planning*, 315–16.

74 The terminology here is borrowed from that of W.T. Easterbrook; see, for example, his *North American Patterns of Growth and Development* (Toronto 1990). For equivalent developments in adjoining states, see David R. Meyer, 'Midwestern Industrialization and the American Manufacturing Belt in the Nineteenth Century,' *JEH* 49 (1989), 921–37.

CHAPTER 13: *Conclusion*

1 L.H. Officer and L.B. Smith, 'The Canadian-American Reciprocity Treaty,' *JEH*

28 (1968), 619. For the correspondence of someone engaged in a trade involving quite subtle nuances of quality and price, see W.S. Fox, ed., *The Letters of William Davies, 1854–1861* (Toronto 1945).

2 Our discussion of railways in chapter 11 also showed that sharply rising Canadian imports and the gap between imports and exports were a direct consequence of the massive capital movements associated with railway construction; that gap would somehow have been closed after the capital imports ended, whether or not there was a civil war.

3 It should, however, be noted that Marvin McInnis (in a personal communication) has questioned the accuracy of the 1871 census data on volume of output of forest products in at least Essex County.

4 Contrast the view of W.A. Mackintosh, quoted in Paul Voisey, *Vulcan: The Making of a Prairie Community* (Toronto 1988), 86. As Voisey notes, Mackintosh's ostensibly historical analysis actually reflected the technological and institutional world of the twentieth century, in which prairie farming was established.

APPENDIX A

1 Further information on most of the issues discussed here can be found in A.B. McCullough, *Money and Exchange in Canada to 1900* (Toronto 1984), now the most authoritative source.

2 See Gilles Paquet and Jean-Pierre Wallot, 'Le système financier bas-canadien au tournant du XIXᵉ siècle,' *L'actualité économique* 59 (1983), 473; T.J.A. LeGoff, 'The Agricultural Crisis in Lower Canada, 1802–12: A Review of a Controversy,' *CHR* 55 (1974), 14; and Fernand Ouellet, Jean Hamelin, and Richard Chabot, 'Les prix agricoles dans les villes et les campagnes du Québec d'avant 1850: aperçus quantitatifs,' *HS/SH* 15 (1982), 89. For an example of such usage in a public document, see *JLA*, 1843, App. F, Report ... on Seigniorial Tenure, exhibit 126. The livre in Lower Canada was also known as the '*livre française de 20 sols.*' Allan Greer, *Peasant, Lord, and Merchant: Rural Society in Three Quebec Parishes 1740–1840* (Toronto 1985), 250, uses a 'rough' rate of 20 livres to £1 Hfx cy, but that seems to value the nineteenth-century livre too highly.

3 For a larger context on colonial exchange, see also John J. McCusker, *Money and Exchange in Europe and America, 1600–1775: A Handbook* (Chapel Hill 1978).

4 See McCullough, *Money and Exchange*, 111. The principal impact in terms of data in this volume was on railway accounts, which are discussed in the tables for chapter 11.

5 Somewhat analogously, British customs recorded values of imports and exports in 'official' values, initially laid down early in the eighteenth century, until the mid-nineteenth century; see A.H. Imlah, *Economic Elements in the Pax Britannica:*

*Studies in British Foreign Trade in the Nineteenth Century* (Cambridge, Mass. 1958), 21–3. A further complexity in foreign exchange was the divergence between the official par of $1 = 4s 6d stg and the British military standard, or 'Army Pay,' which rated $1 at 4s 8d stg. See McCullough, *Money and Exchange*, App. C.

6 Use of both dollars and Halifax or New York currency entries was common; for example, a quantity and a unit price given in cents might be extended to yield a total value in pounds, shillings, and pence. Sterling appeared at times in official records and in correspondence of merchants who dealt directly with Britain.

7 For illustrations of notes and coins, see McCullough, *Money and Exchange*, 62–6; and Peter Baskerville, ed., *The Bank of Upper Canada: A Collection of Documents* (Toronto 1987), pictures facing lxv and xcvi.

8 Angela Redish, 'Why Was Specie Scarce in Colonial Economies? An Analysis of the Canadian Currency, 1796–1830,' *JEH* 44 (1984), 713–28

9 E.P. Neufeld, *The Financial System of Canada* (Toronto 1972), 108, 419

APPENDIX C

1 Other items met frequently in account books (though less often than items included here) included corn, rye, barley, mutton, veal, cheese, tobacco, and eggs. It has not proved possible to get adequate series for non-food, non-forest farm outputs, such as hides, wool, and tallow; for livestock such as oxen, horses, and cattle; or for firewood.

2 These are the same sources used by Michell, from 1848 onward, in his familiar series of agricultural prices. For his data, see M.C. Urquhart and K.A. Buckley, eds., *Historical Statistics of Canada* (Cambridge 1965), 305.

3 W. Sherwood Fox, ed., *Letters of William Davies Toronto 1854–1861* (Toronto 1945) is highly pertinent here.

4 NA, RG19, E5 (a), vols. 4356–8

5 Strictly speaking, they are what were conventionally recalled as these prices by the time the claims were filed and documented – as these are in many cases based on 1820s affidavits. A surprising feature of war era documentation is that many fewer prices appear in accounts, presumably because, in the era of army bills, cash payments became usual. With few exceptions, the limited surviving evidence on actual transactions confirms the price levels indicated by claims data.

6 Also printed in F.W. Burton, 'Wheat in Canadian History,' *Canadian Journal of Economics and Political Science* 3 (1937), 215

7 See, for example, UG, John Macintosh Duff Collection, XR1 MS A210108, Henry Nelles letterbook, Nelles to Gillespie, Moffat & Co., 26 Dec. 1831.

8 Nor can we necessarily believe the grade a producer assigned to his own produce, in that he was likely to describe it as optimistically as possible. In fact, grades are

seldom specified in the data for this study. The principal exceptions are records of military purchases, for which consistent quality was significant and to which bureaucratic procedures applied.

9 Winnifred Rothenberg, 'A Price Index for Rural Massachusetts, 1750–1855,' *JEH* 39 (1979), 978, 981

10 For example, essentially seasonal fluctuations may, because of variations in the months for which price entries were found, cause annual data to look as if they were changing more than or differently from actuality.

11 The principal occasions are in the mid-1830s where some Yonge Mills and Tett prices are combined, on account of the scarcity of entries for some items in the former and as a way of splicing the two series together. In the case of wheat from 1841 to 1844, Tett and Barker and Stevenson data are combined because where these sources overlapped with Yonge Mills data in the 1830s, the former was consistently slightly higher and the latter slightly lower than the Yonge Mills price.

# Index